UNIVERSITY CASEBOOK SERIES®

# 2020 STATUTORY AND CASE SUPPLEMENT TO

# COPYRIGHT

## UNFAIR COMPETITION, AND RELATED TOPICS BEARING ON THE PROTECTION OF WORKS OF AUTHORSHIP

### TWELFTH EDITION

RALPH S. BROWN
Late Simeon E. Baldwin Professor of Law
Yale University

ROBERT C. DENICOLA
Margaret Larson Professor of Intellectual Property
University of Nebraska

FOUNDATION
PRESS

© 2017–2019 LEG, Inc. d/b/a West Academic
© 2020 LEG, Inc. d/b/a West Academic
    444 Cedar Street, Suite 700
    St. Paul, MN 55101
    1-877-888-1330

Printed in the United States of America

**ISBN:** 978-1-68467-950-8

# TABLE OF CONTENTS

UNIVERSITY CASEBOOK SERIES®

2020 STATUTORY AND CASE SUPPLEMENT TO

# COPYRIGHT

UNFAIR COMPETITION, AND RELATED
TOPICS BEARING ON THE PROTECTION
OF WORKS OF AUTHORSHIP

TWELFTH EDITION

# APPENDIX A

---

# THE COPYRIGHT ACT OF 1976

Public Law 94–553, 90 Stat. 2541, as amended through June 1, 2020

## Title 17—Copyrights

## CHAPTER 1.—SUBJECT MATTER AND SCOPE OF COPYRIGHT

## Sec. 101.    Definitions

Except as otherwise provided in this title, as used in this title, the following terms and their variant forms mean the following:

An "anonymous work" is a work on the copies or phonorecords of which no natural person is identified as author.

An "architectural work" is the design of a building as embodied in any tangible medium of expression, including a building, architectural plans, or drawings. The work includes the overall form as well as the arrangement and composition of spaces and elements in the design, but does not include individual standard features.

"Audiovisual works" are works that consist of a series of related images which are intrinsically intended to be shown by the use of machines or devices such as projectors, viewers, or electronic equipment, together with accompanying sounds, if any, regardless of the nature of the material objects, such as films or tapes, in which the works are embodied.

The "Berne Convention" is the Convention for the Protection of Literary and Artistic Works, signed at Berne, Switzerland, on September 9, 1886, and all acts, protocols, and revisions thereto.

The "best edition" of a work is the edition, published in the United States at any time before the date of deposit, that the Library of Congress determines to be most suitable for its purposes.

A person's "children" are that person's immediate offspring, whether legitimate or not, and any children legally adopted by that person.

A "collective work" is a work, such as a periodical issue, anthology, or encyclopedia, in which a number of contributions, constituting separate and independent works in themselves, are assembled into a collective whole.

A "compilation" is a work formed by the collection and assembling of preexisting materials or of data that are selected, coordinated, or arranged in such a way that the resulting work as a whole constitutes an original work of authorship. The term "compilation" includes collective works.

A "computer program" is a set of statements or instructions to be used directly or indirectly in a computer in order to bring about a certain result.

"Copies" are material objects, other than phonorecords, in which a work is fixed by any method now known or later developed, and from which the work can be perceived, reproduced, or otherwise communicated, either directly or with the aid of a machine or device. The term "copies" includes the material object, other than a phonorecord, in which the work is first fixed.

"Copyright owner", with respect to any one of the exclusive rights comprised in a copyright, refers to the owner of that particular right.

A "Copyright Royalty Judge" is a Copyright Royalty Judge appointed under section 802 of this title, and includes any individual serving as an interim Copyright Royalty Judge under such section.

A work is "created" when it is fixed in a copy or phonorecord for the first time; where a work is prepared over a period of time, the portion of it that has been fixed at any particular time constitutes the work as of that time, and where the work has been prepared in different versions, each version constitutes a separate work.

A "derivative work" is a work based upon one or more preexisting works, such as a translation, musical arrangement, dramatization, fictionalization, motion picture version, sound recording, art reproduction, abridgment, condensation, or any other form in which a work may be recast, transformed, or adapted. A work consisting of editorial revisions, annotations, elaborations, or other modifications which, as a whole, represent an original work of authorship, is a "derivative work".

A "device", "machine", or "process" is one now known or later developed.

A "digital transmission" is a transmission in whole or in part in a digital or other non-analog format.

To "display" a work means to show a copy of it, either directly or by means of a film, slide, television image, or any other device or process or, in the case of a motion picture or other audiovisual work, to show individual images nonsequentially.

An "establishment" is a store, shop, or any similar place of business open to the general public for the primary purpose of selling goods or services in which the majority of the gross square feet of space that is nonresidential is used for that purpose, and in which nondramatic musical works are performed publicly.

The term "financial gain" includes receipt, or expectation of receipt, of anything of value, including the receipt of other copyrighted works.

A work is "fixed" in a tangible medium of expression when its embodiment in a copy or phonorecord, by or under the authority of the author, is sufficiently permanent or stable to permit it to be perceived, reproduced, or otherwise communicated for a period of more than transitory duration. A work consisting of sounds, images, or both, that are being transmitted, is "fixed" for purposes of this title if a fixation of the work is being made simultaneously with its transmission.

A "food service or drinking establishment" is a restaurant, inn, bar, tavern, or any other similar place of business in which the public or patrons assemble for the primary purpose of being served food or drink, in which the majority of the gross square feet of space that is nonresidential is used for that purpose, and in which nondramatic musical works are performed publicly.

The "Geneva Phonograms Convention" is the Convention for the Protection of Producers of Phonograms Against Unauthorized Duplication of Their Phonograms, concluded at Geneva, Switzerland, on October 29, 1971.

The "gross square feet of space" of an establishment means the entire interior space of that establishment, and any adjoining outdoor space used to serve patrons, whether on a seasonal basis or otherwise.

The terms "including" and "such as" are illustrative and not limitative.

An "international agreement" is—

    (1)   the Universal Copyright Convention;

    (2)   the Geneva Phonograms Convention;

    (3)   the Berne Convention;

    (4)   the WTO Agreement;

    (5)   the WIPO Copyright Treaty;

    (6)   the WIPO Performances and Phonograms Treaty; and

    (7)   any other copyright treaty to which the United States is a party.

A "joint work" is a work prepared by two or more authors with the intention that their contributions be merged into inseparable or interdependent parts of a unitary whole.

"Literary works" are works, other than audiovisual works, expressed in words, numbers, or other verbal or numerical symbols or indicia, regardless of the nature of the material objects, such as books, periodicals, manuscripts, phonorecords, film, tapes, disks, or cards, in which they are embodied.

The term "motion picture exhibition facility" means a movie theater, screening room, or other venue that is being used primarily for the exhibition of a copyrighted motion picture, if such exhibition is open to the public or is made to an assembled group of viewers outside of a normal circle of a family and its social acquaintances.

"Motion pictures" are audiovisual works consisting of a series of related images which, when shown in succession, impart an impression of motion, together with accompanying sounds, if any.

To "perform" a work means to recite, render, play, dance, or act it, either directly or by means of any device or process or, in the case of a motion picture or other audiovisual work, to show its images in any sequence or to make the sounds accompanying it audible.

A "performing rights society" is an association, corporation, or other entity that licenses the public performance of nondramatic musical works on behalf of copyright owners of such works, such as the American Society of Composers, Authors and Publishers (ASCAP), Broadcast Music, Inc. (BMI), and SESAC, Inc.

"Phonorecords" are material objects in which sounds, other than those accompanying a motion picture or other audiovisual work, are fixed by any method now known or later developed, and from which the sounds can be perceived, reproduced, or otherwise communicated, either directly or with the aid of a machine or device. The term "phonorecords" includes the material object in which the sounds are first fixed.

"Pictorial, graphic, and sculptural works" include two-dimensional and three-dimensional works of fine, graphic, and applied art, photographs, prints and art reproductions, maps, globes, charts, diagrams, models, and technical drawings, including architectural plans. Such works shall include works of artistic craftsmanship insofar as their form but not their mechanical or utilitarian aspects are concerned; the design of a useful article, as defined in this section, shall be considered a pictorial, graphic, or sculptural work only if, and only to the extent that, such design incorporates pictorial, graphic, or sculptural features that can be identified separately from, and are capable of existing independently of, the utilitarian aspects of the article.

For purposes of section 513, a "proprietor" is an individual, corporation, partnership, or other entity, as the case may be, that owns an establishment or a food service or drinking establishment, except that no owner or operator of a radio or television station licensed by the Federal Communications Commission, cable system or satellite carrier, cable or satellite carrier service or programmer, provider of online services or network access or the operator of facilities therefor, telecommunications company, or any other such audio or audiovisual service or programmer now known or as may be developed in the future, commercial subscription music service, or owner or operator of any other transmission service, shall under any circumstances be deemed to be a proprietor.

A "pseudonymous work" is a work on the copies or phonorecords of which the author is identified under a fictitious name.

"Publication" is the distribution of copies or phonorecords of a work to the public by sale or other transfer of ownership, or by rental, lease, or lending. The offering to distribute copies or phonorecords to a group of persons for purposes of further distribution, public performance, or public display, constitutes publication. A public performance or display of a work does not of itself constitute publication.

To perform or display a work "publicly" means—

4

   (1)  to perform or display it at a place open to the public or at any place where a substantial number of persons outside of a normal circle of a family and its social acquaintances is gathered; or

   (2)  to transmit or otherwise communicate a performance or display of the work to a place specified by clause (1) or to the public, by means of any device or process, whether the members of the public capable of receiving the performance or display receive it in the same place or in separate places and at the same time or at different times.

"Registration," for purposes of sections 205(c)(2), 405, 406, 410(d), 411, 412, and 506(e), means a registration of a claim in the original or the renewed and extended term of copyright.

"Sound recordings" are works that result from the fixation of a series of musical, spoken, or other sounds, but not including the sounds accompanying a motion picture or other audiovisual work, regardless of the nature of the material objects, such as disks, tapes, or other phonorecords, in which they are embodied.

"State" includes the District of Columbia and the Commonwealth of Puerto Rico, and any territories to which this title is made applicable by an Act of Congress.

A "transfer of copyright ownership" is an assignment, mortgage, exclusive license, or any other conveyance, alienation, or hypothecation of a copyright or of any of the exclusive rights comprised in a copyright, whether or not it is limited in time or place of effect, but not including a nonexclusive license.

A "transmission program" is a body of material that, as an aggregate, has been produced for the sole purpose of transmission to the public in sequence and as a unit.

To "transmit" a performance or display is to communicate it by any device or process whereby images or sounds are received beyond the place from which they are sent.

A "treaty party" is a country or intergovernmental organization other than the United States that is a party to an international agreement.

The "United States", when used in a geographical sense, comprises the several States, the District of Columbia and the Commonwealth of Puerto Rico, and the organized territories under the jurisdiction of the United States Government.

For purposes of section 411, a work is a "United States work" only if—

   (1)  in the case of a published work, the work is first published—

   (A)  in the United States;

   (B)  simultaneously in the United States and another treaty party or parties, whose law grants a term of copyright protection that is the same as or longer than the term provided in the United States;

   (C)  simultaneously in the United States and a foreign nation that is not a treaty party; or

   (D)  in a foreign nation that is not a treaty party, and all of the authors of the work are nationals, domiciliaries, or habitual residents of, or in the case of an audiovisual work legal entities with headquarters in, the United States;

   (2)  in the case of an unpublished work, all the authors of the work are nationals, domiciliaries, or habitual residents of the United States, or, in the case of an unpublished audiovisual work, all the authors are legal entities with headquarters in the United States; or

   (3)  in the case of a pictorial, graphic, or sculptural work incorporated in a building or structure, the building or structure is located in the United States.

A "useful article" is an article having an intrinsic utilitarian function that is not merely to portray the appearance of the article or to convey information. An article that is normally a part of a useful article is considered a "useful article".

The author's "widow" or "widower" is the author's surviving spouse under the law of the author's domicile at the time of his or her death, whether or not the spouse has later remarried.

The "WIPO Copyright Treaty" is the WIPO Copyright Treaty concluded at Geneva, Switzerland, on December 20, 1996.

The "WIPO Performance and Phonograms Treaty" is the WIPO Performances and Phonograms Treaty concluded at Geneva, Switzerland, on December 20, 1996.

A "work of visual art" is—

(1)   a painting, drawing, print, or sculpture, existing in a single copy, in a limited edition of 200 copies or fewer that are signed and consecutively numbered by the author, or, in the case of a sculpture, in multiple cast, carved, or fabricated sculptures of 200 or fewer that are consecutively numbered by the author and bear the signature or other identifying mark of the author; or

(2)   a still photographic image produced for exhibition purposes only, existing in a single copy that is signed by the author, or in a limited edition of 200 copies or fewer that are signed and consecutively numbered by the author.

A work of visual art does not include—

(A)(i)  any poster, map, globe, chart, technical drawing, diagram, model, applied art, motion picture or other audiovisual work, book, magazine, newspaper, periodical, data base, electronic information service, electronic publication, or similar publication;

(ii)  any merchandising item or advertising, promotional, descriptive, covering, or packaging material or container;

(iii)  any portion or part of any item described in clause (i) or (ii);

(B)   any work made for hire; or

(C)   any work not subject to copyright protection under this title.

A "work of the United States Government" is a work prepared by an officer or employee of the United States Government as part of that person's official duties.

A "work made for hire" is—

(1)   a work prepared by an employee within the scope of his or her employment; or

(2)   a work specially ordered or commissioned for use as a contribution to a collective work, as a part of a motion picture or other audiovisual work, as a translation, as a supplementary work, as a compilation, as an instructional text, as a test, as answer material for a test, or as an atlas, if the parties expressly agree in a written instrument signed by them that the work shall be considered a work made for hire. For the purpose of the foregoing sentence, a "supplementary work" is a work prepared for publication as a secondary adjunct to a work by another author for the purpose of introducing, concluding, illustrating, explaining, revising, commenting upon, or assisting in the use of the other work, such as forewords, afterwords, pictorial illustrations, maps, charts, tables, editorial notes, musical arrangements, answer material for tests, bibliographies, appendixes, and indexes, and an "instructional text" is a literary, pictorial, or graphic work prepared for publication and with the purpose of use in systematic instructional activities.

In determining whether any work is eligible to be considered a work made for hire under paragraph (2), neither the amendment contained in section 1011(d) of the Intellectual Property and Communications Omnibus Reform Act of 1999, as enacted by section 1000(a)(9) of Public Law 106–113, nor the deletion of the words added by that amendment—

(A) shall be considered or otherwise given any legal significance, or

(B) shall be interpreted to indicate congressional approval or disapproval of, or acquiescence in, any judicial determination,

by the courts or the Copyright Office. Paragraph (2) shall be interpreted as if both section 2(a)(1) of the Work Made For Hire and Copyright Corrections Act of 2000 and section 1011(d) of the Intellectual Property and Communications Omnibus Reform Act of 1999, as enacted by section 1000(a)(9) of Public Law 106–113, were never enacted, and without regard to any inaction or awareness by the Congress at any time of any judicial determinations.

The terms "WTO Agreement" and "WTO member country" have the meanings given those terms in paragraphs (9) and (10), respectively, of section 2 of the Uruguay Round Agreements Act.

(As amended, Pub.L. 96–517, 94 Stat. 3028 (1980); Pub.L. 100–568, 102 Stat. 2853 (1988); Pub.L. 101–650, 104 Stat. 5089 (1990); Pub.L. 102–307, 106 Stat. 264 (1992); Pub.L. 102–563, 106 Stat. 4248 (1992); Pub.L. 104–39, 109 Stat. 336 (1995); Pub.L. 105–147, 111 Stat. 2678 (1997); Pub.L. 105–298, 112 Stat. 2827 (1998); Pub.L. 105–304, 112 Stat. 2860 (1998); Pub.L. 106–44, 113 Stat. 221 (1999); Pub.L. 106–113, 113 Stat. 1501A (1999); Pub.L. 106–379, 114 Stat. 1444 (2000); Pub.L. 108–419, 118 Stat. 2341 (2004); Pub.L. 109–9, 119 Stat. 218 (2005)).

## Sec. 102.    Subject Matter of Copyright: In General

(a) Copyright protection subsists, in accordance with this title, in original works of authorship fixed in any tangible medium of expression, now known or later developed, from which they can be perceived, reproduced, or otherwise communicated, either directly or with the aid of a machine or device. Works of authorship include the following categories:

(1) literary works;

(2) musical works, including any accompanying words;

(3) dramatic works, including any accompanying music;

(4) pantomimes and choreographic works;

(5) pictorial, graphic, and sculptural works;

(6) motion pictures and other audiovisual works;

(7) sound recordings; and

(8) architectural works.[a]

(b) In no case does copyright protection for an original work of authorship extend to any idea, procedure, process, system, method of operation, concept, principle, or discovery, regardless of the form in which it is described, explained, illustrated, or embodied in such work.

(As amended, Pub.L. 101–650, 104 Stat. 5089 (1990)).

---

[a] The Architectural Works Copyright Protection Act, Title VII of Pub.L. 101–650, 104 Stat. 5089 (1990), enacted Dec. 1, 1990, further provides:

**Sec. 706.    Effective Date.**

The amendments made by this title apply to—

(1) any architectural work created on or after the date of the enactment of this Act; and

(2) any architectural work that, on the date of the enactment of this Act, is unconstructed and embodied in unpublished plans or drawings, except that protection for such architectural work under title 17, United States Code, by virtue of the amendments made by this title, shall terminate on December 31, 2002, unless the work is constructed by that date.

### Sec. 103.    Subject Matter of Copyright: Compilations and Derivative Works

(a)  The subject matter of copyright as specified by section 102 includes compilations and derivative works, but protection for a work employing preexisting material in which copyright subsists does not extend to any part of the work in which such material has been used unlawfully.

(b)  The copyright in a compilation or derivative work extends only to the material contributed by the author of such work, as distinguished from the preexisting material employed in the work, and does not imply any exclusive right in the preexisting material. The copyright in such work is independent of, and does not affect or enlarge the scope, duration, ownership, or subsistence of, any copyright protection in the preexisting material.

### Sec. 104.    Subject Matter of Copyright: National Origin

(a)  **Unpublished Works.**—The works specified by sections 102 and 103, while unpublished, are subject to protection under this title without regard to the nationality or domicile of the author.

(b)  **Published Works.**—The works specified by sections 102 and 103, when published, are subject to protection under this title if—

(1)  on the date of first publication, one or more of the authors is a national or domiciliary of the United States, or is a national, domiciliary, or sovereign authority of a treaty party, or is a stateless person, wherever that person may be domiciled; or

(2)  the work is first published in the United States or in a foreign nation that, on the date of first publication, is a treaty party; or

(3)  the work is a sound recording that was first fixed in a treaty party; or

(4)  the work is a pictorial, graphic, or sculptural work that is incorporated in a building or other structure, or an architectural work that is embodied in a building and the building or structure is located in the United States or a treaty party; or

(5)  the work is first published by the United Nations or any of its specialized agencies, or by the Organization of American States; or

(6)  the work comes within the scope of a Presidential proclamation. Whenever the President finds that a particular foreign nation extends, to works by authors who are nationals or domiciliaries of the United States or to works that are first published in the United States, copyright protection on substantially the same basis as that on which the foreign nation extends protection to works of its own nationals and domiciliaries and works first published in that nation, the President may by proclamation extend protection under this title to works of which one or more of the authors is, on the date of first publication, a national, domiciliary, or sovereign authority of that nation, or which was first published in that nation. The President may revise, suspend, or revoke any such proclamation or impose any conditions or limitations on protection under a proclamation.

For purposes of paragraph (2), a work that is published in the United States or a treaty party within 30 days after publication in a foreign nation that is not a treaty party shall be considered to be first published in the United States or such treaty party, as the case may be.

(c)  **Effect of Berne Convention.**—No right or interest in a work eligible for protection under this title may be claimed by virtue of, or in reliance upon, the provisions of the Berne Convention, or the adherence of the United States thereto. Any rights in a work eligible for protection under this title that derive from this title, other Federal or State statutes, or the common law, shall not be expanded or reduced by virtue of, or in reliance upon, the provisions of the Berne Convention, or the adherence of the United States thereto.

(d)  **Effect of Phonograms Treaties.**—Notwithstanding the provisions of subsection (b), no works other than sound recordings shall be eligible for protection under this title solely by virtue of the adherence of the United States to the Geneva Phonograms Convention or the WIPO Performances and Phonograms Treaty.

(As amended, Pub.L. 100–568, 102 Stat. 2853 (1988); Pub.L. 105–304, 112 Stat. 2860 (1998)).

## Sec. 104A.   Subject Matter of Copyright: Copyright in Restored Works

**(a)  Automatic Protection and Term.—**

**(1)  Term.—**

(A)  Copyright subsists, in accordance with this section, in restored works, and vests automatically on the date of restoration.

(B)  Any work in which copyright is restored under this section shall subsist for the remainder of the term of copyright that the work would have otherwise been granted in the United States if the work never entered the public domain in the United States.

**(2)  Exception.—**Any work in which the copyright was ever owned or administered by the Alien Property Custodian and in which the restored copyright would be owned by a government or instrumentality thereof, is not a restored work.

**(b)  Ownership of Restored Copyright.—**A restored work vests initially in the author or initial rightholder of the work as determined by the law of the source country of the work.

**(c)  Filing of Notice of Intent to Enforce Restored Copyright Against Reliance Parties.—**On or after the date of restoration, any person who owns a copyright in a restored work or an exclusive right therein may file with the Copyright Office a notice of intent to enforce that person's copyright or exclusive right or may serve such a notice directly on a reliance party. Acceptance of a notice by the Copyright Office is effective as to any reliance parties but shall not create a presumption of the validity of any of the facts stated therein. Service on a reliance party is effective as to that reliance party and any other reliance parties with actual knowledge of such service and of the contents of that notice.

**(d)  Remedies for Infringement of Restored Copyrights.—**

**(1)  Enforcement of copyright in restored works in the absence of a reliance party.—**As against any party who is not a reliance party, the remedies provided in chapter 5 of this title shall be available on or after the date of restoration of a restored copyright with respect to an act of infringement of the restored copyright that is commenced on or after the date of restoration.

**(2)  Enforcement of copyright in restored works as against reliance parties.—**As against a reliance party, except to the extent provided in paragraphs (3) and (4), the remedies provided in chapter 5 of this title shall be available, with respect to an act of infringement of a restored copyright, on or after the date of restoration of the restored copyright if the requirements of either of the following subparagraphs are met:

(A)(i)  The owner of the restored copyright (or such owner's agent) or the owner of an exclusive right therein (or such owner's agent) files with the Copyright Office, during the 24-month period beginning on the date of restoration, a notice of intent to enforce the restored copyright; and

(ii)(I)  the act of infringement commenced after the end of the 12-month period beginning on the date of publication of the notice in the Federal Register;

(II)  the act of infringement commenced before the end of the 12-month period described in subclause (I) and continued after the end of that 12-month period, in which case remedies shall be available only for infringement occurring after the end of that 12-month period; or

(III) copies or phonorecords of a work in which copyright has been restored under this section are made after publication of the notice of intent in the Federal Register.

(B)(i) The owner of the restored copyright (or such owner's agent) or the owner of an exclusive right therein (or such owner's agent) serves upon a reliance party a notice of intent to enforce a restored copyright; and

(ii)(I) the act of infringement commenced after the end of the 12-month period beginning on the date the notice of intent is received;

(II) the act of infringement commenced before the end of the 12-month period described in subclause (I) and continued after the end of that 12-month period, in which case remedies shall be available only for the infringement occurring after the end of that 12-month period; or

(III) copies or phonorecords of a work in which copyright has been restored under this section are made after receipt of the notice of intent.

In the event that notice is provided under both subparagraphs (A) and (B), the 12-month period referred to in such subparagraphs shall run from the earlier of publication or service of notice.

(3) **Existing derivative works.**—(A) In the case of a derivative work that is based upon a restored work and is created—

(i) before the date of the enactment of the Uruguay Round Agreements Act, if the source country of the restored work is an eligible country on such date, or

(ii) before the date on which the source country of the restored work becomes an eligible country, if that country is not an eligible country on such date of enactment,

a reliance party may continue to exploit that derivative work for the duration of the restored copyright if the reliance party pays to the owner of the restored copyright reasonable compensation for conduct which would be subject to a remedy for infringement but for the provisions of this paragraph.

(B) In the absence of an agreement between the parties, the amount of such compensation shall be determined by an action in United States district court, and shall reflect any harm to the actual or potential market for or value of the restored work from the reliance party's continued exploitation of the work, as well as compensation for the relative contributions of expression of the author of the restored work and the reliance party to the derivative work.

(4) **Commencement of infringement for reliance parties.**—For purposes of section 412, in the case of reliance parties, infringement shall be deemed to have commenced before registration when acts which would have constituted infringement had the restored work been subject to copyright were commenced before the date of restoration.

(e) **Notices of Intent to Enforce a Restored Copyright.**—

(1) **Notices of intent filed with the Copyright Office.**—

(A)(i) A notice of intent filed with the Copyright Office to enforce a restored copyright shall be signed by the owner of the restored copyright or the owner of an exclusive right therein, who files the notice under subsection (d)(2)(A)(i) (hereafter in this paragraph referred to as the "owner"), or by the owner's agent, shall identify the title of the restored work, and shall include an English translation of the title and any other alternative titles known to the owner by which the restored work may be identified, and an address and telephone number at which the owner may be contacted. If the notice is signed by an agent, the agency relationship must have been constituted in a writing signed by the owner before the filing of the notice. The Copyright Office may specifically require in regulations other information to be included in the notice, but failure to provide such other information shall not invalidate the notice or be a basis for refusal to list the restored work in the Federal Register.

(ii)   If a work in which copyright is restored has no formal title, it shall be described in the notice of intent in detail sufficient to identify it.

(iii)   Minor errors or omissions may be corrected by further notice at any time after the notice of intent is filed. Notices of corrections for such minor errors or omissions shall be accepted after the period established in subsection (d)(2)(A)(i). Notices shall be published in the Federal Register pursuant to subparagraph (B).

(B)(i)   The Register of Copyrights shall publish in the Federal Register, commencing not later than 4 months after the date of restoration for a particular nation and every 4 months thereafter for a period of 2 years, lists identifying restored works and the ownership thereof if a notice of intent to enforce a restored copyright has been filed.

(ii)   Not less than 1 list containing all notices of intent to enforce shall be maintained in the Public Information Office of the Copyright Office and shall be available for public inspection and copying during regular business hours pursuant to sections 705 and 708.

(C)   The Register of Copyrights is authorized to fix reasonable fees based on the costs of receipt, processing, recording, and publication of notices of intent to enforce a restored copyright and corrections thereto.

(D)(i)   Not later than 90 days before the date the Agreement on Trade-Related Aspects of Intellectual Property referred to in section 101(d)(15) of the Uruguay Round Agreements Act enters into force with respect to the United States, the Copyright Office shall issue and publish in the Federal Register regulations governing the filing under this subsection of notices of intent to enforce a restored copyright.

(ii)   Such regulations shall permit owners of restored copyrights to file simultaneously for registration of the restored copyright.

**(2)   Notices of intent served on a reliance party.—**

(A) Notices of intent to enforce a restored copyright may be served on a reliance party at any time after the date of restoration of the restored copyright.

(B)   Notices of intent to enforce a restored copyright served on a reliance party shall be signed by the owner or the owner's agent, shall identify the restored work and the work in which the restored work is used, if any, in detail sufficient to identify them, and shall include an English translation of the title, any other alternative titles known to the owner by which the work may be identified, the use or uses to which the owner objects, and an address and telephone number at which the reliance party may contact the owner. If the notice is signed by an agent, the agency relationship must have been constituted in writing and signed by the owner before service of the notice.

**(3)   Effect of material false statements.**—Any material false statement knowingly made with respect to any restored copyright identified in any notice of intent shall make void all claims and assertions made with respect to such restored copyright.

**(f)   Immunity From Warranty and Related Liability.—**

**(1)   In general.**—Any person who warrants, promises, or guarantees that a work does not violate an exclusive right granted in section 106 shall not be liable for legal, equitable, arbitral, or administrative relief if the warranty, promise, or guarantee is breached by virtue of the restoration of copyright under this section, if such warranty, promise, or guarantee is made before January 1, 1995.

**(2) Performances.**—No person shall be required to perform any act if such performance is made infringing by virtue of the restoration of copyright under the provisions of this section, if the obligation to perform was undertaken before January 1, 1995.

**(g) Proclamation of Copyright Restoration.**—Whenever the President finds that a particular foreign nation extends, to works by authors who are nationals or domiciliaries of the United States, restored copyright protection on substantially the same basis as provided under this section, the President may by proclamation extend restored protection provided under this section to any work—

(1)  of which one or more of the authors is, on the date of first publication, a national, domiciliary, or sovereign authority of that nation; or

(2)  which was first published in that nation. The President may revise, suspend, or revoke any such proclamation or impose any conditions or limitations on protection under such a proclamation.

**(h) Definitions.**—For purposes of this section and section 109(a):

(1)  The term "date of adherence or proclamation" means the earlier of the date on which a foreign nation which, as of the date the WTO Agreement enters into force with respect to the United States, is not a nation adhering to the Berne Convention or a WTO member country, becomes—

(A)  a nation adhering to the Berne Convention;

(B)  a WTO member country;

(C)  a nation adhering to the WIPO Copyright Treaty;

(D)  a nation adhering to the WIPO Performance and Phonograms Treaty; or

(E)  subject to a Presidential proclamation under subsection (g).

(2)  The "date of restoration" of a restored copyright is—

(A)  January 1, 1996, if the source country of the restored work is a nation adhering to the Berne Convention or a WTO member country on such date, or

(B)  the date of adherence or proclamation, in the case of any other source country of the restored work.

(3)  The term "eligible country" means a nation, other than the United States, that—

(A)  becomes a WTO member country after the date of the enactment of the Uruguay Round Agreements Act;

(B)  on such date of enactment is, or after such date of enactment becomes, a nation adhering to the Berne Convention;

(C)  adheres to the WIPO Copyright Treaty;

(D)  adheres to the WIPO Performance and Phonograms Treaty; or

(E)  after such date of enactment becomes subject to a proclamation under subsection (g).

(4)  The term "reliance party" means any person who—

(A)  with respect to a particular work, engages in acts, before the source country of that work becomes an eligible country, which would have violated section 106 if the restored work had been subject to copyright protection, and who, after the source country becomes an eligible country, continues to engage in such acts;

(B)  before the source country of a particular work becomes an eligible country, makes or acquires 1 or more copies or phonorecords of that work; or

(C)  as the result of the sale or other disposition of a derivative work covered under subsection (d)(3), or significant assets of a person described in subparagraph (A) or (B), is a successor, assignee, or licensee of that person.

(5)  The term "restored copyright" means copyright in a restored work under this section.

(6)  The term "restored work" means an original work of authorship that—

(A)  is protected under subsection (a);

(B)  is not in the public domain in its source country through expiration of term of protection;

(C)  is in the public domain in the United States due to—

(i)  noncompliance with formalities imposed at any time by United States copyright law, including failure of renewal, lack of proper notice, or failure to comply with any manufacturing requirements;

(ii)  lack of subject matter protection in the case of sound recordings fixed before February 15, 1972; or

(iii)  lack of national eligibility;

(D)  has at least one author or rightholder who was, at the time the work was created, a national or domiciliary of an eligible country, and if published, was first published in an eligible country and not published in the United States during the 30-day period following publication in such eligible country; and

(E)  if the source country for the work is an eligible country solely by virtue of its adherence to the WIPO Performance and Phonograms Treaty, is a sound recording.

(7)  The term "rightholder" means the person—

(A)  who, with respect to a sound recording, first fixes a sound recording with authorization, or

(B)  who has acquired rights from the person described in subparagraph (A) by means of any conveyance or by operation of law.

(8)  The "source country" of a restored work is—

(A)  a nation other than the United States;

(B)  in the case of an unpublished work—

(i)  the eligible country in which the author or rightholder is a national or domiciliary, or, if a restored work has more than 1 author or rightholder, of which the majority of foreign authors or rightholders are nationals or domiciliaries; or

(ii)  if the majority of authors or rightholders are not foreign, the nation other than the United States which has the most significant contacts with the work; and

(C)  in the case of a published work—

(i)  the eligible country in which the work is first published, or

(ii)  if the restored work is published on the same day in 2 or more eligible countries, the eligible country which has the most significant contacts with the work.

(Added by Pub.L. 103–465, 108 Stat. 4976 (1994); as amended by Pub.L. 105–80, 111 Stat. 1529 (1997); Pub.L. 105–304, 112 Stat. 2860 (1998)).

**Sec. 105.    Subject Matter of Copyright: United States Government Works**

(a)  **In general.**—Copyright protection under this title is not available for any work of the United States Government, but the United States Government is not precluded from receiving and holding copyrights transferred to it by assignment, bequest, or otherwise.

(b)  **Copyright Protection of Certain Works.**—Subject to subsection (c), the covered author of a covered work owns the copyright to that covered work.

(c)  **Use by Federal Government.**—The Secretary of Defense may direct the covered author of a covered work to provide the Federal Government with an irrevocable, royalty-free, world-wide, nonexclusive license to reproduce, distribute, perform, or display such covered work for purposes of the United States Government.

(c)  **Definitions.**—In this section:

(1)  The term "covered author" means a civilian member of the faculty of a covered institution.

(2)  The term "covered institution" means the following:

(A)  National Defense University.

(B)  United States Military Academy.

(C)  Army War College.

(D)  United States Army Command and General Staff College.

(E)  United States Naval Academy.

(F)  Naval War College.

(G)  Naval Post Graduate School.

(H)  Marine Corps University.

(I)  United States Air Force Academy.

(J)  Air University.

(K)  Defense Language Institute.

(L)  United States Coast Guard Academy.

(3)  The term "covered work" means a literary work produced by a covered author in the course of employment at a covered institution for publication by a scholarly press or journal.

(As amended, Pub.L. 116–92, 133 Stat. 1198 (2019).

**Sec. 106.    Exclusive Rights in Copyrighted Works**

Subject to sections 107 through 122, the owner of copyright under this title has the exclusive rights to do and to authorize any of the following:

(1)  to reproduce the copyrighted work in copies or phonorecords;

(2)  to prepare derivative works based upon the copyrighted work;

(3)  to distribute copies or phonorecords of the copyrighted work to the public by sale or other transfer of ownership, or by rental, lease, or lending;

(4)  in the case of literary, musical, dramatic, and choreographic works, pantomimes, and motion pictures and other audiovisual works, to perform the copyrighted work publicly;

(5)   in the case of literary, musical, dramatic, and choreographic works, pantomimes, and pictorial, graphic, or sculptural works, including the individual images of a motion picture or other audiovisual work, to display the copyrighted work publicly; and

(6)   in the case of sound recordings, to perform the copyrighted work publicly by means of a digital audio transmission.

(As amended, Pub.L. 101–318, 104 Stat. 288 (1990); Pub.L. 101–650, 104 Stat. 5134 (1990); Pub.L. 104–39, 109 Stat. 336 (1995); Pub.L. 106–44, 113 Stat. 223 (1999); Pub.L. 107–273, 116 Stat. 1758 (2002)).

## Sec. 106A.    Rights of Certain Authors to Attribution and Integrity

(a)   **Rights of Attribution and Integrity.**—Subject to section 107 and independent of the exclusive rights provided in section 106, the author of a work of visual art—

(1)   shall have the right—

(A)   to claim authorship of that work, and

(B)   to prevent the use of his or her name as the author of any work of visual art which he or she did not create;

(2)   shall have the right to prevent the use of his or her name as the author of the work of visual art in the event of a distortion, mutilation, or other modification of the work which would be prejudicial to his or her honor or reputation; and

(3)   subject to the limitations set forth in section 113(d), shall have the right—

(A)   to prevent any intentional distortion, mutilation, or other modification of that work which would be prejudicial to his or her honor or reputation, and any intentional distortion, mutilation, or modification of that work is a violation of that right, and

(B)   to prevent any destruction of a work of recognized stature, and any intentional or grossly negligent destruction of that work is a violation of that right.

(b)   **Scope and Exercise of Rights.**—Only the author of a work of visual art has the rights conferred by subsection (a) in that work, whether or not the author is the copyright owner. The authors of a joint work of visual art are coowners of the rights conferred by subsection (a) in that work.

(c)   **Exceptions.**—

(1)   The modification of a work of visual art which is a result of the passage of time or the inherent nature of the materials is not distortion, mutilation, or other modification described in subsection (a)(3)(A).

(2)   The modification of a work of visual art which is the result of conservation, or of the public presentation, including lighting and placement, of the work is not a destruction, distortion, mutilation, or other modification described in subsection (a)(3) unless the modification is caused by gross negligence.

(3)   The rights described in paragraphs (1) and (2) of subsection (a) shall not apply to any reproduction, depiction, portrayal, or other use of a work in, upon, or in any connection with any item described in subparagraph (A) or (B) of the definition of "work of visual art" in section 101, and any such reproduction, depiction, portrayal, or other use of a work is not a destruction, distortion, mutilation, or other modification described in paragraph (3) of subsection (a).

(d)   **Duration of Rights.**—

(1)   With respect to works of visual art created on or after the effective date set forth in section 9(a) of the Visual Artists Rights Act of 1990, the rights conferred by subsection (a) shall endure for a term consisting of the life of the author.

(2)   With respect to works of visual art created before the effective date set forth in section 9(a) of the Visual Artists Rights Act of 1990, but title to which has not, as of such effective date, been transferred from the author, the rights conferred by subsection (a) shall be coextensive with, and shall expire at the same time as, the rights conferred by section 106.

(3)   In the case of a joint work prepared by two or more authors, the rights conferred by subsection (a) shall endure for a term consisting of the life of the last surviving author.

(4)   All terms of the right conferred by subsection (a) run to the end of the calendar year in which they would otherwise expire.

**(e)   Transfer and Waiver.—**

(1)   The rights conferred by subsection (a) may not be transferred, but those rights may be waived if the author expressly agrees to such waiver in a written instrument signed by the author. Such instrument shall specifically identify the work, and uses of that work, to which the waiver applies, and the waiver shall apply only to the work and uses so identified. In the case of a joint work prepared by two or more authors, a waiver of rights under this paragraph made by one such author waives such rights for all such authors.

(2)   Ownership of the rights conferred by subsection (a) with respect to a work of visual art is distinct from ownership of any copy of that work, or of a copyright or any exclusive right under a copyright in that work. Transfer of ownership of any copy of a work of visual art, or of a copyright or any exclusive right under a copyright, shall not constitute a waiver of the rights conferred by subsection (a). Except as may otherwise be agreed by the author in a written instrument signed by the author, a waiver of the rights conferred by subsection (a) with respect to a work of visual art shall not constitute a transfer of ownership of any copy of that work, or of ownership of a copyright or of any exclusive right under a copyright in that work.[a]

(Added by Pub.L. 101–650, 104 Stat. 5089 (1990)).

## Sec. 107.   Limitations on Exclusive Rights: Fair Use

Notwithstanding the provisions of sections 106 and 106A, the fair use of a copyrighted work, including such use by reproduction in copies or phonorecords or by any other means specified by that section, for purposes such as criticism, comment, news reporting, teaching (including multiple copies for classroom use), scholarship, or research, is not an infringement of copyright. In determining whether the use made of a work in any particular case is a fair use the factors to be considered shall include—

(1)   the purpose and character of the use, including whether such use is of a commercial nature or is for nonprofit educational purposes;

(2)   the nature of the copyrighted work;

(3)   the amount and substantiality of the portion used in relation to the copyrighted work as a whole; and

---

[a]   The Visual Artists Rights Act of 1990, Title VI of Pub.L. 101–650, 104 Stat. 5089 (1990), enacted Dec. 1, 1990, further provides:

**SEC. 610.   EFFECTIVE DATE.**

(a)   In General.—Subject to subsection (b) and except as provided in subsection (c), this title and the amendments made by this title take effect 6 months after the date of the enactment of this Act.

(b)   Applicability.—The rights created by section 106A of title 17, United States Code, shall apply to—

(1)   works created before the effective date set forth in subsection (a) but title to which has not, as of such effective date, been transferred from the author, and

(2)   works created on or after such effective date, but shall not apply to any destruction, distortion, mutilation, or other modification (as described in section 106A(a)(3) of such title) of any work which occurred before such effective date.

(4)   the effect of the use upon the potential market for or value of the copyrighted work.

The fact that a work is unpublished shall not itself bar a finding of fair use if such finding is made upon consideration of all the above factors.

(As amended, Pub.L. 101–650, 104 Stat. 5089 (1990); Pub.L. 102–492, 106 Stat. 3145 (1992)).

## Sec. 108.    Limitations on Exclusive Rights: Reproduction by Libraries and Archives

(a)   Except as otherwise provided in this title and notwithstanding the provisions of section 106, it is not an infringement of copyright for a library or archives, or any of its employees acting within the scope of their employment, to reproduce no more than one copy or phonorecord of a work, except as provided in subsections (b) and (c), or to distribute such copy or phonorecord, under the conditions specified by this section, if—

(1)   the reproduction or distribution is made without any purpose of direct or indirect commercial advantage;

(2)   the collections of the library or archives are (i) open to the public, or (ii) available not only to researchers affiliated with the library or archives or with the institution of which it is a part, but also to other persons doing research in a specialized field; and

(3)   the reproduction or distribution of the work includes a notice of copyright that appears on the copy or phonorecord that is reproduced under the provisions of this section, or includes a legend stating that the work may be protected by copyright if no such notice can be found on the copy or phonorecord that is reproduced under the provisions of this section.

(b)   The rights of reproduction and distribution under this section apply to three copies or phonorecords of an unpublished work duplicated solely for purposes of preservation and security or for deposit for research use in another library or archives of the type described by clause (2) of subsection (a), if—

(1)   the copy or phonorecord reproduced is currently in the collections of the library or archives; and

(2)   any such copy or phonorecord that is reproduced in digital format is not otherwise distributed in that format and is not made available to the public in that format outside the premises of the library or archives.

(c)   The right of reproduction under this section applies to three copies or phonorecords of a published work duplicated solely for the purpose of replacement of a copy or phonorecord that is damaged, deteriorating, lost, or stolen, or of the existing format in which the work is stored has become obsolete, if—

(1)   the library or archives has, after a reasonable effort, determined that an unused replacement cannot be obtained at a fair price; and

(2)   any such copy or phonorecord that is reproduced in digital format is not made available to the public in that format outside the premises of the library or archives in lawful possession of such copy.

For purposes of this subsection, a format shall be considered obsolete if the machine or device necessary to render perceptible a work stored in that format is no longer manufactured or is no longer reasonably available in the commercial marketplace.

(d)   The rights of reproduction and distribution under this section apply to a copy, made from the collection of a library or archives where the user makes his or her request or from that of another library or archives, of no more than one article or other contribution to a copyrighted collection or periodical issue, or to a copy or phonorecord of a small part of any other copyrighted work, if—

(1)   the copy or phonorecord becomes the property of the user, and the library or archives has had no notice that the copy or phonorecord would be used for any purpose other than private study, scholarship, or research; and

(2)   the library or archives displays prominently, at the place where orders are accepted, and includes on its order form, a warning of copyright in accordance with requirements that the Register of Copyrights shall prescribe by regulation.

(e)   The rights of reproduction and distribution under this section apply to the entire work, or to a substantial part of it, made from the collection of a library or archives where the user makes his or her request or from that of another library or archives, if the library or archives has first determined, on the basis of a reasonable investigation, that a copy, or phonorecord of the copyrighted work cannot be obtained at a fair price, if—

(1)   the copy or phonorecord becomes the property of the user, and the library or archives has had no notice that the copy or phonorecord would be used for any purpose other than private study, scholarship, or research; and

(2)   the library or archives displays prominently, at the place where orders are accepted, and includes on its order form, a warning of copyright in accordance with requirements that the Register of Copyrights shall prescribe by regulation.

(f)   Nothing in this section—

(1)   shall be construed to impose liability for copyright infringement upon a library or archives or its employees for the unsupervised use of reproducing equipment located on its premises: *Provided,* That such equipment displays a notice that the making of a copy may be subject to the copyright law;

(2)   excuses a person who uses such reproducing equipment or who requests a copy or phonorecord under subsection (d) from liability for copyright infringement for any such act, or for any later use of such copy or phonorecord, if it exceeds fair use as provided by section 107;

(3)   shall be construed to limit the reproduction and distribution by lending of a limited number of copies and excerpts by a library or archives of an audiovisual news program, subject to clauses (1), (2), and (3) of subsection (a); or

(4)   in any way affects the right of fair use as provided by section 107, or any contractual obligations assumed at any time by the library or archives when it obtained a copy or phonorecord of a work in its collections.

(g)   The rights of reproduction and distribution under this section extend to the isolated and unrelated reproduction or distribution of a single copy or phonorecord of the same material on separate occasions, but do not extend to cases where the library or archives, or its employee—

(1)   is aware or has substantial reason to believe that it is engaging in the related or concerted reproduction or distribution of multiple copies or phonorecords of the same material, whether made on one occasion or over a period of time, and whether intended for aggregate use by one or more individuals or for separate use by the individual members of a group; or

(2)   engages in the systematic reproduction or distribution of single or multiple copies or phonorecords of material described in subsection (d): *Provided,* That nothing in this clause prevents a library or archives from participating in interlibrary arrangements that do not have, as their purpose or effect, that the library or archives receiving such copies or phonorecords for distribution does so in such aggregate quantities as to substitute for a subscription to or purchase of such work.

(h)(1)   For purposes of this section, during the last 20 years of any term of copyright of a published work, a library or archives, including a nonprofit educational institution that functions as such, may reproduce, distribute, display, or perform in facsimile or digital form a copy or phonorecord of such work, or portions thereof, for purposes of preservation, scholarship, or research, if such library or archives has first determined, on the basis of a reasonable investigation, that none of the conditions set forth in subparagraphs (A), (B), and (C) of paragraph (2) apply.

(2)   No reproduction, distribution, display, or performance is authorized under this subsection if—

(A)   the work is subject to normal commercial exploitation;

(B)   a copy or phonorecord of the work can be obtained at a reasonable price; or

(C)   the copyright owner or its agent provides notice pursuant to regulations promulgated by the Register of Copyrights that either of the conditions set forth in subparagraphs (A) and (B) applies.

(3)   The exemption provided in this subsection does not apply to any subsequent uses by users other than such library or archives.

(i)   The rights of reproduction and distribution under this section do not apply to a musical work, a pictorial, graphic or sculptural work, or a motion picture or other audiovisual work other than an audiovisual work dealing with news, except that no such limitation shall apply with respect to rights granted by subsections (b), (c), and (h), or with respect to pictorial or graphic works published as illustrations, diagrams, or similar adjuncts to works of which copies are reproduced or distributed in accordance with subsections (d) and (e).

(As amended, Pub.L. 102–307, 106 Stat. 214 (1992); Pub.L. 105–298, 112 Stat. 2877 (1998); Pub.L. 105–304, 112 Stat. 2860 (1998); Pub.L. 109–9, 119 Stat. 218 (2005)).

## Sec. 109.   Limitations on Exclusive Rights: Effect of Transfer of Particular Copy or Phonorecord

(a)   Notwithstanding the provisions of section 106(3), the owner of a particular copy or phonorecord lawfully made under this title, or any person authorized by such owner, is entitled, without the authority of the copyright owner, to sell or otherwise dispose of the possession of that copy or phonorecord. Notwithstanding the preceding sentence, copies or phonorecords of works subject to restored copyright under section 104A that are manufactured before the date of restoration of copyright or, with respect to reliance parties, before publication or service of notice under section 104A(e), may be sold or otherwise disposed of without the authorization of the owner of the restored copyright for purposes of direct or indirect commercial advantage only during the 12-month period beginning on—

(1)   the date of the publication in the Federal Register of the notice of intent filed with the Copyright Office under section 104A(d)(2)(A), or

(2)   the date of the receipt of actual notice served under section 104A(d)(2)(B),

whichever occurs first.

(b)(1)(A) Notwithstanding the provisions of subsection (a), unless authorized by the owners of copyright in the sound recording or the owner of copyright in a computer program (including any tape, disk, or other medium embodying such program), and in the case of a sound recording in the musical works embodied therein, neither the owner of a particular phonorecord nor any person in possession of a particular copy of a computer program (including any tape, disk, or other medium embodying such program), may, for the purposes of direct or indirect commercial advantage, dispose of, or authorize the disposal of, the possession of that phonorecord or computer program (including any tape, disk, or other medium embodying such program) by rental, lease, or lending, or by any other act or practice in the nature of rental, lease, or lending. Nothing in the preceding sentence shall apply to the rental, lease, or lending of a phonorecord for nonprofit purposes by a nonprofit library or nonprofit educational institution. The transfer of possession of a lawfully made copy of a computer program by a nonprofit educational institution to another nonprofit educational institution or to faculty, staff, and students does not constitute rental, lease, or lending for direct or indirect commercial purposes under this subsection.

(B)   This subsection does not apply to—

(i)   a computer program which is embodied in a machine or product and which cannot be copied during the ordinary operation or use of the machine or product; or

(ii)   a computer program embodied in or used in conjunction with a limited purpose computer that is designed for playing video games and may be designed for other purposes.

(C)   Nothing in this subsection affects any provision of chapter 9 of this title.

(2)(A)   Nothing in this subsection shall apply to the lending of a computer program for nonprofit purposes by a nonprofit library, if each copy of a computer program which is lent by such library has affixed to the packaging containing the program a warning of copyright in accordance with requirements that the Register of Copyrights shall prescribe by regulation.

(B)   Not later than three years after the date of the enactment of the Computer Software Rental Amendments Act of 1990, and at such times thereafter as the Register of Copyrights considers appropriate, the Register of Copyrights, after consultation with representatives of copyright owners and librarians, shall submit to the Congress a report stating whether this paragraph has achieved its intended purpose of maintaining the integrity of the copyright system while providing nonprofit libraries the capability to fulfill their function. Such report shall advise the Congress as to any information or recommendations that the Register of Copyrights considers necessary to carry out the purposes of this subsection.

(3)   Nothing in this subsection shall affect any provision of the antitrust laws. For purposes of the preceding sentence, "antitrust laws" has the meaning given that term in the first section of the Clayton Act and includes section 5 of the Federal Trade Commission Act to the extent that section relates to unfair methods of competition.

(4)   Any person who distributes a phonorecord[a] or a copy of a computer program[b] (including any tape, disk, or other medium embodying such program) in violation of paragraph (1) is an infringer of copyright under section 501 of this title and is subject to the remedies set forth in sections 502, 503, 504, and 505. Such violation shall not be a criminal offense under section 506 or cause such person to be subject to the criminal penalties set forth in section 2319 of title 18.

(c)   Notwithstanding the provisions of section 106(5), the owner of a particular copy lawfully made under this title, or any person authorized by such owner, is entitled, without the authority of

---

[a]   The Record Rental Amendment, Pub.L. 98–450, 98 Stat. 1727 (1984), enacted Oct. 4, 1984, concludes as follows: Sec. 4. (a) The amendments made by this Act shall take effect on the date of the enactment of this Act.

(b)   The provisions of section 109(b) of title 17, United States Code, as added by section 2 of this Act, shall not affect the right of an owner of a particular phonorecord of a sound recording, who acquired such ownership before the date of the enactment of this Act, to dispose of the possession of that particular phonorecord on or after such date of enactment in any manner permitted by section 109 of title 17, United States Code, as in effect on the day before the date of the enactment of this Act.

[b]   The Computer Software Rental Amendments Act of 1990, Title VIII of Pub.L. 101–650, 104 Stat. 5089 (1990), enacted Dec. 1, 1990, further provides:

(a)   In General.—Subject to subsection (b), this title and the amendments made in section 802 shall take effect on the date of the enactment of this Act. The amendment made by section 803 [adding § 109(e)] shall take effect one year after such date of enactment.

(b)   Prospective Application.—Section 109(b) of title 17, United States Code, as amended by section 802 of this Act, shall not affect the right of a person in possession of a particular copy of a computer program, who acquired such copy before the date of the enactment of this Act, to dispose of the possession of that copy on or after such date of enactment in any manner permitted by section 109 of title 17, United States Code, as in effect on the day before such date of enactment.

(c)   Termination.—The amendments made by section 803 [adding § 109(e)] shall not apply to public performances or displays that occur on or after October 1, 1995.

the copyright owner, to display that copy publicly, either directly or by the projection of no more than one image at a time, to viewers present at the place where the copy is located.

(d)   The privileges prescribed by subsections (a) and (c) do not, unless authorized by the copyright owner, extend to any person who has acquired possession of the copy or phonorecord from the copyright owner, by rental, lease, loan, or otherwise, without acquiring ownership of it.

(e)   Notwithstanding the provisions of sections 106(4) and 106(5), in the case of an electronic audiovisual game intended for use in coin-operated equipment, the owner of a particular copy of such a game lawfully made under this title, is entitled, without the authority of the copyright owner of the game, to publicly perform or display that game in coin-operated equipment, except that this subsection shall not apply to any work of authorship embodied in the audiovisual game if the copyright owner of the electronic audiovisual game is not also the copyright owner of the work of authorship.

(As amended, Pub.L. 98–450, 98 Stat. 1727 (1984); Pub.L. 100–617, 102 Stat. 3194 (1988); Pub.L. 101–650, 104 Stat. 5089 (1990); Pub.L. 103–465, 108 Stat. 4981 (1994); Pub.L. 110–403, 122 Stat. 4256 (2008)).

## Sec. 110.    Limitations on Exclusive Rights: Exemption of Certain Performances and Displays

Notwithstanding the provisions of section 106, the following are not infringements of copyright:

(1)   performance or display of a work by instructors or pupils in the course of face-to-face teaching activities of a nonprofit educational institution, in a classroom or similar place devoted to instruction, unless, in the case of a motion picture or other audiovisual work, the performance, or the display of individual images, is given by means of a copy that was not lawfully made under this title, and that the person responsible for the performance knew or had reason to believe was not lawfully made;

(2)   except with respect to a work produced or marketed primarily for performance or display as part of mediated instructional activities transmitted via digital networks, or a performance or display that is given by means of a copy or phonorecord that is not lawfully made and acquired under this title, and the transmitting government body or accredited nonprofit educational institution knew or had reason to believe was not lawfully made and acquired, the performance of a nondramatic literary or musical work or reasonable and limited portions of any other work, or display of a work in an amount comparable to that which is typically displayed in the course of a live classroom session, by or in the course of a transmission, if—

(A)   the performance or display is made by, at the direction of, or under the actual supervision of an instructor as an integral part of a class session offered as a regular part of the systematic mediated instructional activities of a governmental body or an accredited nonprofit educational institution;

(B)   the performance or display is directly related and of material assistance to the teaching content of the transmission;

(C)   the transmission is made solely for, and, to the extent technologically feasible, the reception of such transmission is limited to—

(i)   students officially enrolled in the course for which the transmission is made; or

(ii)   officers or employees of governmental bodies as a part of their official duties or employment; and

(D)   the transmitting body or institution—

(i)   institutes policies regarding copyright, provides informational materials to faculty, students, and relevant staff members that accurately describe, and promote compliance with, the laws of the United States relating to copyright, and provides notice to students that materials used in connection with the course may be subject to copyright protection; and

 (ii) in the case of digital transmissions—

  (I) applies technological measures that reasonably prevent—

   (aa) retention of the work in accessible form by recipients of the transmission from the transmitting body or institution for longer than the class session; and

   (bb) unauthorized further dissemination of the work in accessible form by such recipients to others; and

  (II) does not engage in conduct that could reasonably be expected to interfere with technological measures used by copyright owners to prevent such retention or unauthorized further dissemination;

(3) performance of a nondramatic literary or musical work or of a dramatico-musical work of a religious nature, or display of a work, in the course of services at a place of worship or other religious assembly;

(4) performance of a nondramatic literary or musical work otherwise than in a transmission to the public, without any purpose of direct or indirect commercial advantage and without payment of any fee or other compensation for the performance to any of its performers, promoters, or organizers, if—

 (A) there is no direct or indirect admission charge; or

 (B) the proceeds, after deducting the reasonable costs of producing the performance, are used exclusively for educational, religious, or charitable purposes and not for private financial gain, except where the copyright owner has served notice of objection to the performance under the following conditions:

  (i) the notice shall be in writing and signed by the copyright owner or such owner's duly authorized agent; and

  (ii) the notice shall be served on the person responsible for the performance at least seven days before the date of the performance, and shall state the reasons for the objection; and

  (iii) the notice shall comply, in form, content, and manner of service, with requirements that the Register of Copyrights shall prescribe by regulation;

(5)(A) except as provided in subparagraph (B), communication of a transmission embodying a performance or display of a work by the public reception of the transmission on a single receiving apparatus of a kind commonly used in private homes, unless—

 (i) a direct charge is made to see or hear the transmission; or

 (ii) the transmission thus received is further transmitted to the public;

 (B) communication by an establishment of a transmission or retransmission embodying a performance or display of a nondramatic musical work intended to be received by the general public, originated by a radio or television broadcast station licensed as such by the Federal Communications Commission, or, if an audiovisual transmission, by a cable system or satellite carrier, if—

  (i) in the case of an establishment other than a food service or drinking establishment, either the establishment in which the communication occurs has less than 2,000 gross square feet of space (excluding space used for customer parking and for no other purpose), or the establishment in which the communication occurs has 2,000 or more gross square feet of space (excluding space used for customer parking and for no other purpose) and—

(I)   if the performance is by audio means only, the performance is communicated by means of a total of not more than 6 loudspeakers, of which not more than 4 loudspeakers are located in any 1 room or adjoining outdoor space; or

(II)   if the performance or display is by audiovisual means, any visual portion of the performance or display is communicated by means of a total of not more than 4 audiovisual devices, of which not more than 1 audiovisual device is located in any 1 room, and no such audiovisual device has a diagonal screen size greater than 55 inches, and any audio portion of the performance or display is communicated by means of a total of not more than 6 loudspeakers, of which not more than 4 loudspeakers are located in any 1 room or adjoining outdoor space;

(ii)   in the case of a food service or drinking establishment, either the establishment in which the communication occurs has less than 3,750 gross square feet of space (excluding space used for customer parking and for no other purpose), or the establishment in which the communication occurs has 3,750 gross square feet of space or more (excluding space used for customer parking and for no other purpose) and—

(I)   if the performance is by audio means only, the performance is communicated by means of a total of not more than 6 loudspeakers, of which not more than 4 loudspeakers are located in any 1 room or adjoining outdoor space; or

(II)   if the performance or display is by audiovisual means, any visual portion of the performance or display is communicated by means of a total of not more than 4 audiovisual devices, of which not more than one audiovisual device is located in any 1 room, and no such audiovisual device has a diagonal screen size greater than 55 inches, and any audio portion of the performance or display is communicated by means of a total of not more than 6 loudspeakers, of which not more than 4 loudspeakers are located in any 1 room or adjoining outdoor space;

(iii)   no direct charge is made to see or hear the transmission or retransmission;

(iv)   the transmission or retransmission is not further transmitted beyond the establishment where it is received; and

(v)   the transmission or retransmission is licensed by the copyright owner of the work so publicly performed or displayed;

(6)   performance of a nondramatic musical work by a governmental body or a nonprofit agricultural or horticultural organization, in the course of an annual agricultural or horticultural fair or exhibition conducted by such body or organization; the exemption provided by this clause shall extend to any liability for copyright infringement that would otherwise be imposed on such body or organization, under doctrines of vicarious liability or related infringement, for a performance by a concessionaire, business establishment, or other person at such fair or exhibition, but shall not excuse any such person from liability for the performance;

(7)   performance of a nondramatic musical work by a vending establishment open to the public at large without any direct or indirect admission charge, where the sole purpose of the performance is to promote the retail sale of copies or phonorecords of the work, or of the audiovisual or other devices utilized in such performance, and the performance is not transmitted beyond the place where the establishment is located and is within the immediate area where the sale is occurring;

(8)   performance of a nondramatic literary work, by or in the course of a transmission specifically designed for and primarily directed to blind or other handicapped persons who are unable to read normal printed material as a result of their handicap, or deaf or other handicapped

persons who are unable to hear the aural signals accompanying a transmission of visual signals, if the performance is made without any purpose of direct or indirect commercial advantage and its transmission is made through the facilities of: (i) a governmental body; or (ii) a noncommercial educational broadcast station (as defined in section 397 of title 47); or (iii) a radio subcarrier authorization (as defined in 47 CFR 73.293–73.295 and 73.593–73.595); or (iv) a cable system (as defined in section 111(f));

(9)  performance on a single occasion of a dramatic literary work published at least ten years before the date of the performance, by or in the course of a transmission specifically designed for and primarily directed to blind or other handicapped persons who are unable to read normal printed material as a result of their handicap, if the performance is made without any purpose of direct or indirect commercial advantage and its transmission is made through the facilities of a radio subcarrier authorization referred to in clause (8)(iii), *Provided,* That the provisions of this clause shall not be applicable to more than one performance of the same work by the same performers or under the auspices of the same organization;

(10) notwithstanding paragraph (4), the following is not an infringement of copyright: performance of a nondramatic literary or musical work in the course of a social function which is organized and promoted by a nonprofit veterans' organization or a nonprofit fraternal organization to which the general public is not invited, but not including the invitees of the organizations, if the proceeds from the performance, after deducting the reasonable costs of producing the performance, are used exclusively for charitable purposes and not for financial gain. For purposes of this section the social functions of any college or university fraternity or sorority shall not be included unless the social function is held solely to raise funds for a specific charitable purpose; and

(11) the making imperceptible, by or at the direction of a member of a private household, of limited portions of audio or video content of a motion picture, during a performance in or transmitted to that household for private home viewing, from an authorized copy of the motion picture, or the creation or provision of a computer program or other technology that enables such making imperceptible and that is designed and marketed to be used, at the direction of a member of a private household, for such making imperceptible, if no fixed copy of the altered version of the motion picture is created by such computer program or other technology.

The exemptions provided under paragraph (5) shall not be taken into account in any administrative, judicial, or other governmental proceeding to set or adjust the royalties payable to copyright owners for the public performance or display of their works. Royalties payable to copyright owners for any public performance or display of their works other than such performances or displays as are exempted under paragraph (5) shall not be diminished in any respect as a result of such exemption

In paragraph (2), the term "mediated instructional activities" with respect to the performance or display of a work by digital transmission under this section refers to activities that use such work as an integral part of the class experience, controlled by or under the actual supervision of the instructor and analogous to the type of performance or display that would take place in a live classroom setting. The term does not refer to activities that use, in one or more class sessions of a single course, such works as textbooks, course packs, or other material in any media, copies or phonorecords of which are typically purchased or acquired by the students in higher education for their independent use and retention or are typically purchased or acquired for elementary and secondary students for their possession and independent use.

For purposes of paragraph (2), accreditation—

(A) with respect to an institution providing post-secondary education, shall be as determined by a regional or national accrediting agency recognized by the Council on Higher Education Accreditation or the United States Department of Education; and

(B) with respect to an institution providing elementary or secondary education, shall be as recognized by the applicable state certification or licensing procedures.

For purposes of paragraph (2), no governmental body or accredited nonprofit educational institution shall be liable for infringement by reason of the transient or temporary storage of material carried out through the automatic technical process of a digital transmission of the performance or display of that material as authorized under paragraph (2). No such material stored on the system or network controlled or operated by the transmitting body or institution under this paragraph shall be maintained on such system or network in a manner ordinarily accessible to anyone other than anticipated recipients. No such copy shall be maintained on the system or network in a manner ordinarily accessible to such anticipated recipients for a longer period than is reasonably necessary to facilitate the transmissions for which it was made.

For purposes of paragraph (11), the term "making imperceptible" does not include the addition of audio or video content that is performed or displayed over or in place of existing content in a motion picture.

Nothing in paragraph (11) shall be construed to imply further rights under section 106 of this title, or to have any effect on defenses or limitations on rights granted under any other section of this title or under any other paragraph of this section.

(As amended, Pub.L. 97–366, 96 Stat. 1759 (1982); Pub.L. 105–298, 112 Stat. 2827 (1998); Pub.L. 106–44, 113 Stat. 221 (1999); Pub.L. 107–273, 116 Stat. 1758 (2002); Pub.L. 109–9, 119 Stat. 218 (2005)).

## Sec. 111. Limitations on Exclusive Rights: Secondary Transmissions of Broadcast Programming by Cable

**(a) Certain Secondary Transmissions Exempted.**—The secondary transmission of a performance or display of a work embodied in a primary transmission is not an infringement of copyright if—

(1) the secondary transmission is not made by a cable system, and consists entirely of the relaying, by the management of a hotel, apartment house, or similar establishment, of signals transmitted by a broadcast station licensed by the Federal Communications Commission, within the local service area of such station, to the private lodgings of guests or residents of such establishment, and no direct charge is made to see or hear the secondary transmission; or

(2) the secondary transmission is made solely for the purpose and under the conditions specified by paragraph (2) of section 110; or

(3) The secondary transmission is made by any carrier who has no direct or indirect control over the content or selection of the primary transmission or over the particular recipients of the secondary transmission, and whose activities with respect to the secondary transmission consist solely of providing wires, cables, or other communications channels for the use of others: *Provided,* That the provisions of this clause extend only to the activities of said carrier with respect to secondary transmissions and do not exempt from liability the activities of others with respect to their own primary or secondary transmissions;

(4) the secondary transmission is made by a satellite carrier pursuant to a statutory license under section 119 or section 122; or

(5) the secondary transmission is not made by a cable system but is made by a governmental body, or other nonprofit organization, without any purpose of direct or indirect commercial advantage, and without charge to the recipients of the secondary transmission other than assessments necessary to defray the actual and reasonable costs of maintaining and operating the secondary transmission service.

**(b) Secondary Transmission of Primary Transmission to Controlled Group.**— Notwithstanding the provisions of subsections (a) and (c), the secondary transmission to the public of a performance or display of a work embodied in a primary transmission is actionable as an act of infringement under section 501, and is fully subject to the remedies provided by sections 502 through 506, if the primary transmission is not made for reception by the public at large but is controlled and limited to reception by particular members of the public: *Provided,* however, That such secondary transmission is not actionable as an act of infringement if—

(1)   the primary transmission is made by a broadcast station licensed by the Federal Communications Commission; and

(2)   the carriage of the signals comprising the secondary transmission is required under the rules, regulations, or authorizations of the Federal Communications Commission; and

(3)   the signal of the primary transmitter is not altered or changed in any way by the secondary transmitter.

**(c)   Secondary Transmissions by Cable Systems.—**

(1)   Subject to the provisions of paragraphs (2), (3), and (4) of this subsection and section 114(d), secondary transmissions to the public by a cable system of a performance or display of a work embodied in a primary transmission made by a broadcast station licensed by the Federal Communications Commission or by an appropriate governmental authority of Canada or Mexico shall be subject to statutory licensing upon compliance with the requirements of subsection (d) where the carriage of the signals comprising the secondary transmission is permissible under the rules, regulations, or authorizations of the Federal Communications Commission.

(2)   Notwithstanding the provisions of paragraph (1) of this subsection, the willful or repeated secondary transmission to the public by a cable system of a primary transmission made by a broadcast station licensed by the Federal Communications Commission or by an appropriate governmental authority of Canada or Mexico and embodying a performance or display of a work is actionable as an act of infringement under section 501, and is fully subject to the remedies provided by sections 502 through 506, in the following cases:

(A)   where the carriage of the signals comprising the secondary transmission is not permissible under the rules, regulations, or authorizations of the Federal Communications Commission; or

(B)   where the cable system has not deposited the statement of account and royalty fee required by subsection (d).

(3)   Notwithstanding the provisions of paragraph (1) of this subsection and subject to the provisions of subsection (e) of this section, the secondary transmission to the public by a cable system of a performance or display of a work embodied in a primary transmission made by a broadcast station licensed by the Federal Communications Commission or by an appropriate governmental authority of Canada or Mexico is actionable as an act of infringement under section 501, and is fully subject to the remedies provided by sections 502 through 506 and section 510, if the content of the particular program in which the performance or display is embodied, or any commercial advertising or station announcements transmitted by the primary transmitter during, or immediately before or after, the transmission of such program, is in any way willfully altered by the cable system through changes, deletions, or additions, except for the alteration, deletion, or substitution of commercial advertisements performed by those engaged in television commercial advertising market research: *Provided,* That the research company has obtained the prior consent of the advertiser who has purchased the original commercial advertisement, the television station broadcasting that commercial advertisement, and the cable system performing the secondary transmission: *And provided further,* That such commercial alteration, deletion, or substitution is not performed for the purpose of deriving income from the sale of that commercial time.

(4)   Notwithstanding the provisions of paragraph (1) of this subsection, the secondary transmission to the public by a cable system of a performance or display of a work embodied in a

primary transmission made by a broadcast station licensed by an appropriate governmental authority of Canada or Mexico is actionable as an act of infringement under section 501, and is fully subject to the remedies provided by sections 502 through 506, if (A) with respect to Canadian signals, the community of the cable system is located more than 150 miles from the United States-Canadian border and is also located south of the forty-second parallel of latitude, or (B) with respect to Mexican signals, the secondary transmission is made by a cable system which received the primary transmission by means other than direct interception of a free space radio wave emitted by such broadcast television station, unless prior to April 15, 1976, such cable system was actually carrying, or was specifically authorized to carry, the signal of such foreign station on the system pursuant to the rules, regulations, or authorizations of the Federal Communications Commission.

**(d)  Statutory License for Secondary Transmissions by Cable Systems.—**

   **(1)  Statement of account and royalty fees.**—Subject to paragraph (5), a cable system whose secondary transmissions have been subject to statutory licensing under subsection (c) shall, on a semiannual basis, deposit with the Register of Copyrights, in accordance with requirements that the Register shall prescribe by regulation the following—

   (A)  A statement of account, covering the six months next preceding, specifying the number of channels on which the cable system made secondary transmissions to its subscribers, the names and locations of all primary transmitters whose transmissions were further transmitted by the cable system, the total number of subscribers, the gross amounts paid to the cable system for the basic service of providing secondary transmissions of primary broadcast transmitters, and such other data as the Register of Copyrights may from time to time prescribe by regulation. In determining the total number of subscribers and the gross amounts paid to the cable system for the basic service of providing secondary transmissions of primary broadcast transmitters, the system shall not include subscribers and amounts collected from subscribers receiving secondary transmissions pursuant to section 119. Such statement shall also include a special statement of account covering any nonnetwork television programming that was carried by the cable system in whole or in part beyond the local service area of the primary transmitter, under rules, regulations, or authorizations of the Federal Communications Commission permitting the substitution or addition of signals under certain circumstances, together with logs showing the times, dates, stations, and programs involved in such substituted or added carriage.

   (B)  Except in the case of a cable system whose royalty fee is specified in subparagraph (E) or (F), a total royalty fee payable to copyright owners pursuant to paragraph (3) for the period covered by the statement, computed on the basis of specified percentages of the gross receipts from subscribers to the cable service during such period for the basic service of providing secondary transmissions of primary broadcast transmitters, as follows:

      (i)   1.064 percent of such gross receipts for the privilege of further transmitting, beyond the local service area of such primary transmitter, any non-network programming of a primary transmitter in whole or in part, such amount to be applied against the fee, if any, payable pursuant to clauses (ii) through (iv);

      (ii)  1.064 percent of such gross receipts for the first distant signal equivalent;

      (iii) 0.701 percent of such gross receipts for each of the second, third, and fourth distant signal equivalents; and

      (iv)  0.330 percent of such gross receipts for the fifth distant signal equivalent and each distant signal equivalent thereafter.

   (C)  In computing amounts under clauses (ii) through (iv) of subparagraph (B)—

      (i)   any fraction of a distant signal equivalent shall be computed at its fractional value;

(ii)  in the case of any cable system located partly within and partly outside of the local service area of a primary transmitter, gross receipts shall be limited to those gross receipts derived from subscribers located outside of the local service area of such primary transmitter; and

(iii)  if a cable system provides a secondary transmission of a primary transmitter to some but not all communities served by that cable system—

(I)  the gross receipts and the distant signal equivalent values for such secondary transmission shall be derived solely on the basis of the subscribers in those communities where the cable system provides such secondary transmission; and

(II)  the total royalty fee for the period paid by such system shall not be less than the royalty fee calculated under subparagraph (B)(i) multiplied by the gross receipts from all subscribers to the system.

(D)  A cable system that, on a statement submitted before the date of the enactment of the Satellite Television Extension and Localism Act of 2010, computed its royalty fee consistent with the methodology under subparagraph (C)(iii), or that amends a statement filed before such date of enactment to compute the royalty fee due using such methodology, shall not be subject to an action for infringement, or eligible for any royalty refund or offset, arising out of its use of such methodology on such statement.

(E)  If the actual gross receipts paid by subscribers to a cable system for the period covered by the statement for the basic service of providing secondary transmissions of primary broadcast transmitters are $263,800 or less—

(i)  gross receipts of the cable system for the purpose of this paragraph shall be computed by subtracting from such actual gross receipts the amount by which $263,800 exceeds such actual gross receipts, except that in no case shall a cable system's gross receipts be reduced to less than $10,400; and

(ii)  the royalty fee payable under this paragraph to copyright owners pursuant to paragraph (3) shall be 0.5 percent, regardless of the number of distant signal equivalents, if any.

(F)  If the actual gross receipts paid by subscribers to a cable system for the period covered by the statement for the basic service of providing secondary transmissions of primary broadcast transmitters are more than $263,800 but less than $527,600, the royalty fee payable under this paragraph to copyright owners pursuant to paragraph (3) shall be—

(i)  0.5 percent of any gross receipts up to $263,800, regardless of the number of distant signal equivalents, if any; and

(ii)  1 percent of any gross receipts in excess of $263,800, but less than $527,600, regardless of the number of distant signal equivalents, if any.

(G)  A filing fee, as determined by the Register of Copyrights pursuant to section 708(a).

(2)  **Handling of fees.**—The Register of Copyrights shall receive all fees (including the filing fee specified in paragraph (1)(G)) deposited under this section and, after deducting the reasonable costs incurred by the Copyright Office under this section, shall deposit the balance in the Treasury of the United States, in such manner as the Secretary of the Treasury directs. All funds held by the Secretary of the Treasury shall be invested in interest-bearing United States securities for later distribution with interest by the Librarian of Congress upon authorization by the Copyright Royalty Judges.

(3)  **Distribution of royalty fees to copyright owners.**—The royalty fees thus deposited shall, in accordance with the procedures provided by paragraph (4), be distributed to those among

the following copyright owners who claim that their works were the subject of secondary transmissions by cable systems during the relevant semiannual period:

(A)  Any such owner whose work was included in a secondary transmission made by a cable system of a non-network television program in whole or in part beyond the local service area of the primary transmitter.

(B)  Any such owner whose work was included in a secondary transmission identified in a special statement of account deposited under paragraph (1)(A). and

(C)  Any such owner whose work was included in non-network programming consisting exclusively of aural signals carried by a cable system in whole or in part beyond the local service area of the primary transmitter of such programs.

(4)  **Procedures for royalty fee distribution.**—The royalty fees thus deposited shall be distributed in accordance with the following procedures:

(A)  During the month of July in each year, every person claiming to be entitled to statutory license fees for secondary transmissions shall file a claim with the Copyright Royalty Judges, in accordance with requirements that the Copyright Royalty Judges shall prescribe by regulation. Notwithstanding any provisions of the antitrust laws, for purposes of this clause any claimants may agree among themselves as to the proportionate division of statutory licensing fees among them, may lump their claims together and file them jointly or as a single claim, or may designate a common agent to receive payment on their behalf.

(B)  After the first day of August of each year, the Copyright Royalty Judges shall determine whether there exists a controversy concerning the distribution of royalty fees. If the Copyright Royalty Judges determine that no such controversy exists, the Copyright Royalty Judges shall authorize the Librarian of Congress to proceed to distribute such fees to the copyright owners entitled to receive them, or to their designated agents, subject to the deduction of reasonable administrative costs under this section. If the Copyright Royalty Judges find the existence of a controversy, the Copyright Royalty Judges shall, pursuant to chapter 8 of this title, conduct a proceeding to determine the distribution of royalty fees.

(C)  During the pendency of any proceeding under this subsection, the Copyright Royalty Judges shall have the discretion to authorize the Librarian of Congress to proceed to distribute any amounts that are not in controversy.

(5)  **3.75 percent rate and syndicated exclusivity surcharge not applicable to multicast streams.**—The royalty rates specified in sections 256.2(c) and 256.2(d) of title 37, Code of Federal Regulations (commonly referred to as the "3.75 percent rate" and the "syndicated exclusivity surcharge", respectively), as in effect on the date of the enactment of the Satellite Television Extension and Localism Act of 2010, as such rates may be adjusted, or such sections redesignated, thereafter by the Copyright Royalty Judges, shall not apply to the secondary transmission of a multicast stream.

(6)  **Verification of accounts and fee payments.**—The Register of Copyrights shall issue regulations to provide for the confidential verification by copyright owners whose works were embodied in the secondary transmissions of primary transmissions pursuant to this section of the information reported on the semiannual statements of account filed under this subsection for accounting periods beginning on or after January 1, 2010, in order that the auditor designated under subparagraph (A) is able to confirm the correctness of the calculations and royalty payments reported therein. The regulations shall—

(A)  establish procedures for the designation of a qualified independent auditor—

(i)  with exclusive authority to request verification of such a statement of account on behalf of all copyright owners whose works were the subject of secondary transmissions of primary transmissions by the cable system (that deposited the statement) during the accounting period covered by the statement; and

(ii)  who is not an officer, employee, or agent of any such copyright owner for any purpose other than such audit;

(B)  establish procedures for safeguarding all non-public financial and business information provided under this paragraph;

(C)(i)  require a consultation period for the independent auditor to review its conclusions with a designee of the cable system;

(ii)  establish a mechanism for the cable system to remedy any errors identified in the auditor's report and to cure any underpayment identified; and

(iii)  provide an opportunity to remedy any disputed facts or conclusions;

(D)  limit the frequency of requests for verification for a particular cable system and the number of audits that a multiple system operator can be required to undergo in a single year; and

(E)  permit requests for verification of a statement of account to be made only within 3 years after the last day of the year in which the statement of account is filed.

(7)  **Acceptance of additional deposits.**—Any royalty fee payments received by the Copyright Office from cable systems for the secondary transmission of primary transmissions that are in addition to the payments calculated and deposited in accordance with this subsection shall be deemed to have been deposited for the particular accounting period for which they are received and shall be distributed as specified under this subsection.

(e)  **Nonsimultaneous Secondary Transmissions by Cable Systems.**—

(1)  Notwithstanding those provisions of subsection (f)(2) relating to nonsimultaneous secondary transmissions by a cable system, any such transmissions are actionable as an act of infringement under section 501, and are fully subject to the remedies provided by sections 502 through 506 and section 510, unless—

(A)  the program on the videotape is transmitted no more than one time to the cable system's subscribers;

(B)  the copyrighted program, episode, or motion picture videotape, including the commercials contained within such program, episode, or picture, is transmitted without deletion or editing;

(C)  an owner or officer of the cable system (i) prevents the duplication of the videotape while in the possession of the system, (ii) prevents unauthorized duplication while in the possession of the facility making the videotape for the system if the system owns or controls the facility, or takes reasonable precautions to prevent such duplication if it does not own or control the facility, (iii) takes adequate precautions to prevent duplication while the tape is being transported, and (iv) subject to paragraph (2), erases or destroys, or causes the erasure or destruction of, the videotape;

(D)  within forty-five days after the end of each calendar quarter, an owner or officer of the cable system executes an affidavit attesting (i) to the steps and precautions taken to prevent duplication of the videotape, and (ii) subject to paragraph (2), to the erasure or destruction of all videotapes made or used during such quarter;

(E)  such owner or officer places or causes each such affidavit, and affidavits received pursuant to paragraph (2)(C), to be placed in a file, open to public inspection, at such system's main office in the community where the transmission is made or in the nearest community where such system maintains an office;

(F) the nonsimultaneous transmission is one that the cable system would be authorized to transmit under the rules, regulations, and authorizations of the Federal Communications Commission in effect at the time of the nonsimultaneous transmission if the transmission had been made simultaneously, except that this subparagraph shall not apply to inadvertent or accidental transmissions.

(2) If a cable system transfers to any person a videotape of a program nonsimultaneously transmitted by it, such transfer is actionable as an act of infringement under section 501, and is fully subject to the remedies provided by sections 502 through 506, except that, pursuant to a written, nonprofit contract providing for the equitable sharing of the costs of such videotape and its transfer, a videotape nonsimultaneously transmitted by it, in accordance with paragraph (1), may be transferred by one cable system in Alaska to another system in Alaska, by one cable system in Hawaii permitted to make such nonsimultaneous transmissions to another such cable system in Hawaii, or by one cable system in Guam, the Northern Mariana Islands, the Federated States of Micronesia, the Republic of Palau, or the Republic of the Marshall Islands, to another cable system in any of those five entities, if—

(A) each such contract is available for public inspection in the offices of the cable systems involved, and a copy of such contract is filed, within thirty days after such contract is entered into, with the Copyright Office (which Office shall make each such contract available for public inspection);

(B) the cable system to which the videotape is transferred complies with paragraph (1)(A), (B), (C)(i), (iii), and (iv), and (D) through (F); and

(C) such system provides a copy of the affidavit required to be made in accordance with paragraph (1)(D) to each cable system making a previous nonsimultaneous transmission of the same videotape.

(3) This subsection shall not be construed to supersede the exclusivity protection provisions of any existing agreement, or any such agreement hereafter entered into, between a cable system and a television broadcast station in the area in which the cable system is located, or a network with which such station is affiliated.

(4) As used in this subsection, the term "videotape" means the reproduction of the images and sounds of a program or programs broadcast by a television broadcast station licensed by the Federal Communications Commission, regardless of the nature of the material objects, such as tapes or films, in which the reproduction is embodied.

(f) **Definitions.**—As used in this section, the following terms mean the following:

(1) **Primary transmission.** A "primary transmission" is a transmission made to the public by a transmitting facility whose signals are being received and further transmitted by a secondary transmission service, regardless of where or when the performance or display was first transmitted. In the case of a television broadcast station, the primary stream and any multicast streams transmitted by the station constitute primary transmissions.

(2) **Secondary transmission.** A "secondary transmission" is the further transmitting of a primary transmission simultaneously with the primary transmission, or nonsimultaneously with the primary transmission if by a cable system not located in whole or in part within the boundary of the forty-eight contiguous States, Hawaii, or Puerto Rico: *Provided, however,* That a nonsimultaneous further transmission by a cable system located in Hawaii of a primary transmission shall be deemed to be a secondary transmission if the carriage of the television broadcast signal comprising such further transmission is permissible under the rules, regulations, or authorizations of the Federal Communications Commission.

(3) **Cable system.** A "cable system" is a facility, located in any State, territory, trust territory, or possession of the United States, that in whole or in part receives signals transmitted or programs broadcast by one or more television broadcast stations licensed by the Federal Communications

Commission, and makes secondary transmissions of such signals or programs by wires, cables, microwave, or other communications channels to subscribing members of the public who pay for such service. For purposes of determining the royalty fee under subsection (d)(1), two or more cable systems in contiguous communities under common ownership or control or operating from one headend shall be considered as one system.

**(4) Local service area of a primary transmitter.** The "local service area of a primary transmitter", in the case of both the primary stream and any multicast streams transmitted by a primary transmitter that is a television broadcast station, comprises the area where such primary transmitter could have insisted upon its signal being retransmitted by a cable system pursuant to the rules, regulations, and authorizations of the Federal Communications Commission in effect on April 15, 1976, or such station's television market as defined in section 76.55(e) of title 47, Code of Federal Regulations (as in effect on September 18, 1993), or any modifications to such television market made, on or after September 18, 1993, pursuant to section 76.55(e) or 76.59 of title 47, Code of Federal Regulations, or within the noise-limited contour as defined in 73.622(e)(1) of title 47, Code of Federal Regulations, or in the case of a television broadcast station licensed by an appropriate governmental authority of Canada or Mexico, the area in which it would be entitled to insist upon its signal being retransmitted if it were a television broadcast station subject to such rules, regulations, and authorizations. In the case of a low power television station, as defined by the rules and regulations of the Federal Communications Commission, the "local service area of a primary transmitter" comprises the designated market area, as defined in section 122(j)(2)(C), that encompasses the community of license of such station and any community that is located outside such designated market area that is either wholly or partially within 35 miles of the transmitter site or, in the case of such a station located in a standard metropolitan statistical area which has one of the 50 largest populations of all standard metropolitan statistical areas (based on the 1980 decennial census of population taken by the Secretary of Commerce), wholly or partially within 20 miles of such transmitter site. The "local service area of a primary transmitter", in the case of a radio broadcast station, comprises the primary service area of such station, pursuant to the rules and regulations of the Federal Communications Commission.

**(5) Distant signal equivalent.—**

**(A) In general.** Except as provided under subparagraph (B), a "distant signal equivalent"—

(i)   is the value assigned to the secondary transmission of any non-network television programming carried by a cable system in whole or in part beyond the local service area of the primary transmitter of such programming; and

(ii)   is computed by assigning a value of one to each primary stream and to each multicast stream (other than a simulcast) that is an independent station, and by assigning a value of one-quarter to each primary stream and to each multicast stream (other than a simulcast) that is a network station or a noncommercial educational station.

**(B) Exceptions.** The values for independent, network, and noncommercial educational stations specified in subparagraph (A) are subject to the following:

(i)   Where the rules and regulations of the Federal Communications Commission require a cable system to omit the further transmission of a particular program and such rules and regulations also permit the substitution of another program embodying a performance or display of a work in place of the omitted transmission, or where such rules and regulations in effect on the date of the enactment of the Copyright Act of 1976 permit a cable system, at its election, to effect such omission and substitution of a nonlive program or to carry additional programs not transmitted by primary transmitters within whose local service area the cable system is located, no value shall be assigned for the substituted or additional program.

(ii)  Where the rules, regulations, or authorizations of the Federal Communications Commission in effect on the date of the enactment of the Copyright Act of 1976 permit a cable system, at its election, to omit the further transmission of a particular program and such rules, regulations, or authorizations also permit the substitution of another program embodying a performance or display of a work in place of the omitted transmission, the value assigned for the substituted or additional program shall be, in the case of a live program, the value of one full distant signal equivalent multiplied by a fraction that has as its numerator the number of days in the year in which such substitution occurs and as its denominator the number of days in the year.

(iii)  In the case of the secondary transmission of a primary transmitter that is a television broadcast station pursuant to the late-night or specialty programming rules of the Federal Communications Commission, or the secondary transmission of a primary transmitter that is a television broadcast station on a part-time basis where full-time carriage is not possible because the cable system lacks the activated channel capacity to retransmit on a full-time basis all signals that it is authorized to carry, the values for independent, network, and noncommercial educational stations set forth in subparagraph (A), as the case may be, shall be multiplied by a fraction that is equal to the ratio of the broadcast hours of such primary transmitter retransmitted by the cable system to the total broadcast hours of the primary transmitter.

(iv)  No value shall be assigned for the secondary transmission of the primary stream or any multicast streams of a primary transmitter that is a television broadcast station in any community that is within the local service area of the primary transmitter.

**(6)  Network station.—**

**(A)  Treatment of primary stream.** The term "network station" shall be applied to a primary stream of a television broadcast station that is owned or operated by, or affiliated with, one or more of the television networks in the United States providing nationwide transmissions, and that transmits a substantial part of the programming supplied by such networks for a substantial part of the primary stream's typical broadcast day.

**(B)  Treatment of multicast streams.** The term "network station" shall be applied to a multicast stream on which a television broadcast station transmits all or substantially all of the programming of an interconnected program service that—

(i)   is owned or operated by, or affiliated with, one or more of the television networks described in subparagraph (A); and

(ii)  offers programming on a regular basis for 15 or more hours per week to at least 25 of the affiliated television licensees of the interconnected program service in 10 or more States.

**(7)  Independent station.**—The term "independent station" shall be applied to the primary stream or a multicast stream of a television broadcast station that is not a network station or a noncommercial educational station.

**(8)  Noncommercial educational station.**—The term "noncommercial educational station" shall be applied to the primary stream or a multicast stream of a television broadcast station that is a noncommercial educational broadcast station as defined in section 397 of the Communications Act of 1934, as in effect on the date of the enactment of the Satellite Television Extension and Localism Act of 2010.

**(9)  Primary stream.**—A "primary stream" is—

(A)  the single digital stream of programming that, before June 12, 2009, was substantially duplicating the programming transmitted by the television broadcast station as an analog signal; or

(B) if there is no stream described in subparagraph (A), then the single digital stream of programming transmitted by the television broadcast station for the longest period of time.

**(10) Primary transmitter.**—A "primary transmitter" is a television or radio broadcast station licensed by the Federal Communications Commission, or by an appropriate governmental authority of Canada or Mexico, that makes primary transmissions to the public.

**(11) Multicast stream.**—A "multicast stream" is a digital stream of programming that is transmitted by a television broadcast station and is not the station's primary stream.

**(12) Simulcast.**—A "simulcast" is a multicast stream of a television broadcast station that duplicates the programming transmitted by the primary stream or another multicast stream of such station.

**(13) Subscriber; Subscribe.—**

    **(A) Subscriber.** The term "subscriber" means a person or entity that receives a secondary transmission service from a cable system and pays a fee for the service, directly or indirectly, to the cable system.

    **(B) Subscribe.** The term "subscribe" means to elect to become a subscriber.

(As amended, Pub.L. 99–397, 100 Stat. 848 (1986); Pub.L. 100–667, 102 Stat. 3949 (1988); Pub.L. 101–318, 104 Stat. 287 (1990); Pub.L. 103–198, 107 Stat. 2304 (1993); Pub.L. 103–369, 108 Stat. 3477 (1994); Pub.L. 104–39, 109 Stat. 336 (1995); Pub.L. 106–113, 113 Stat. 1501A (1999); Pub.L. 108–419, 118 Stat. 2341 (2004); Pub.L. 108–447, 118 Stat. 2809 (2004); Pub.L. 109–303, 120 Stat. 1478 (2006); Pub.L. 110–229, 122 Stat. 754 (2008); Pub.L. 110–403, 122 Stat. 4256 (2008); Pub.L. 111–175, 124 Stat. 1218 (2010); Pub.L. 113–200, 128 Stat. 2059 (2014)).

## Sec. 112.     Limitations on Exclusive Rights: Ephemeral Recordings

(a)(1) Notwithstanding the provisions of section 106, and except in the case of a motion picture or other audiovisual work, it is not an infringement of copyright for a transmitting organization entitled to transmit to the public a performance or display of a work, under a license, including a statutory license under section 114(f), or transfer of the copyright or under the limitations on exclusive rights in sound recordings specified by section 114(a), or for a transmitting organization that is a broadcast radio or television station licensed as such by the Federal Communications Commission and that makes a broadcast transmission of a performance of a sound recording in a digital format on a nonsubscription basis, to make no more than one copy or phonorecord of a particular transmission program embodying the performance or display, if—

    (A) the copy or phonorecord is retained and used solely by the transmitting organization that made it, and no further copies or phonorecords are reproduced from it; and

    (B) the copy or phonorecord is used solely for the transmitting organization's own transmissions within its local service area, or for purposes of archival preservation or security; and

    (C) unless preserved exclusively for archival purposes, the copy or phonorecord is destroyed within six months from the date the transmission program was first transmitted to the public.

(2) In a case in which a transmitting organization entitled to make a copy or phonorecord under paragraph (1) in connection with the transmission to the public of a performance or display of a work is prevented from making such copy or phonorecord by reason of the application by the copyright owner of technical measures that prevent the reproduction of the work, the copyright owner shall make available to the transmitting organization the necessary means for permitting the making of such copy or phonorecord as permitted under that paragraph, if it is technologically feasible and economically reasonable for the copyright owner to do so. If the copyright owner fails to do so in a timely manner in light of the transmitting organization's reasonable business requirements, the transmitting organization shall not be liable for a violation of section 1201(a)(1) of this title for engaging in such

activities as are necessary to make such copies or phonorecords as permitted under paragraph (1) of this subsection.

(b)   Notwithstanding the provisions of section 106, it is not an infringement of copyright for a governmental body or other nonprofit organization entitled to transmit a performance or display of a work, under section 110(2) or under the limitations on exclusive rights in sound recordings specified by section 114(a), to make no more than thirty copies or phonorecords of a particular transmission program embodying the performance or display, if—

(1)   no further copies or phonorecords are reproduced from the copies or phonorecords made under this clause; and

(2)   except for one copy or phonorecord that may be preserved exclusively for archival purposes, the copies or phonorecords are destroyed within seven years from the date the transmission program was first transmitted to the public.

(c)   Notwithstanding the provisions of section 106, it is not an infringement of copyright for a governmental body or other nonprofit organization to make for distribution no more than one copy or phonorecord, for each transmitting organization specified in clause (2) of this subsection, of a particular transmission program embodying a performance of a nondramatic musical work of a religious nature, or of a sound recording of such a musical work, if—

(1)   there is no direct or indirect charge for making or distributing any such copies or phonorecords; and

(2)   none of such copies or phonorecords is used for any performance other than a single transmission to the public by a transmitting organization entitled to transmit to the public a performance of the work under a license or transfer of the copyright; and

(3)   except for one copy or phonorecord that may be preserved exclusively for archival purposes, the copies or phonorecords are all destroyed within one year from the date the transmission program was first transmitted to the public.

(d)   Notwithstanding the provisions of section 106, it is not an infringement of copyright for a governmental body or other nonprofit organization entitled to transmit a performance of a work under section 110(8) to make no more than ten copies or phonorecords embodying the performance, or to permit the use of any such copy or phonorecord by any governmental body or nonprofit organization entitled to transmit a performance of a work under section 110(8), if—

(1)   any such copy or phonorecord is retained and used solely by the organization that made it, or by a governmental body or nonprofit organization entitled to transmit a performance of a work under section 110(8), and no further copies or phonorecords are reproduced from it; and

(2)   any such copy or phonorecord is used solely for transmissions authorized under section 110(8), or for purposes of archival preservation or security; and

(3)   the governmental body or nonprofit organization permitting any use of any such copy or phonorecord by any governmental body or nonprofit organization under this subsection does not make any charge for such use.

**(e)   Statutory license.—**

(1)   A transmitting organization entitled to transmit to the public a performance of a sound recording under the limitation on exclusive rights specified by section 114(d)(1)(C)(iv) or under a statutory license in accordance with section 114(f) is entitled to a statutory license, under the conditions specified by this subsection, to make no more than 1 phonorecord of the sound recording (unless the terms and conditions of the statutory license allow for more), if the following conditions are satisfied:

(A)   The phonorecord is retained and used solely by the transmitting organization that made it, and no further phonorecords are reproduced from it.

(B)  The phonorecord is used solely for the transmitting organization's own transmissions originating in the United States under a statutory license in accordance with section 114(f) or the limitation on exclusive rights specified by section 114(d)(1)(C)(iv).

(C)  Unless preserved exclusively for purposes of archival preservation, the phonorecord is destroyed within 6 months from the date the sound recording was first transmitted to the public using the phonorecord.

(D)  Phonorecords of the sound recording have been distributed to the public under the authority of the copyright owner or the copyright owner authorizes the transmitting entity to transmit the sound recording, and the transmitting entity makes the phonorecord under this subsection from a phonorecord lawfully made and acquired under the authority of the copyright owner.

(2)  Notwithstanding any provision of the antitrust laws, any copyright owners of sound recordings and any transmitting organizations entitled to a statutory license under this subsection may negotiate and agree upon royalty rates and license terms and conditions for making phonorecords of such sound recordings under this section and the proportionate division of fees paid among copyright owners, and may designate common agents to negotiate, agree to, pay, or receive such royalty payments.

(3)  Proceedings under chapter 8 shall determine reasonable rates and terms of royalty payments for the activities specified by paragraph (1) during the 5-year period beginning on January 1 of the second year following the year in which the proceedings are to be commenced, or such other period as the parties may agree. Such rates shall include a minimum fee for each type of service offered by transmitting organizations. Any copyright owners of sound recordings or any transmitting organizations entitled to a statutory license under this subsection may submit to the Copyright Royalty Judges licenses covering such activities with respect to such sound recordings. The parties to each proceeding shall bear their own costs.

(4)  The schedule of reasonable rates and terms determined by the Copyright Royalty Judges shall, subject to paragraph (5), be binding on all copyright owners of sound recordings and transmitting organizations entitled to a statutory license under this subsection during the 5-year period specified in paragraph (3), or such other period as the parties may agree. Such rates shall include a minimum fee for each type of service offered by transmitting organizations. The Copyright Royalty Judges shall establish rates that most clearly represent the fees that would have been negotiated in the marketplace between a willing buyer and a willing seller. In determining such rates and terms, the Copyright Royalty Judges shall base their decision on economic, competitive, and programming information presented by the parties, including—

(A)  whether use of the service may substitute for or may promote the sales of phonorecords or otherwise interferes with or enhances the copyright owner's traditional streams of revenue; and

(B)  the relative roles of the copyright owner and the transmitting organization in the copyrighted work and the service made available to the public with respect to relative creative contribution, technological contribution, capital investment, cost, and risk.

In establishing such rates and terms, the Copyright Royalty Judges may consider the rates and terms under voluntary license agreements described in paragraphs (2) and (3). The Copyright Royalty Judges shall also establish requirements by which copyright owners may receive reasonable notice of the use of their sound recordings under this section, and under which records of such use shall be kept and made available by transmitting organizations entitled to obtain a statutory license under this subsection.

(5)  License agreements voluntarily negotiated at any time between 1 or more copyright owners of sound recordings and 1 or more transmitting organizations entitled to obtain a

statutory license under this subsection shall be given effect in lieu of any decision by the Librarian of Congress or determination by the Copyright Royalty Judges.

(6)(A) Any person who wishes to make a phonorecord of a sound recording under a statutory license in accordance with this subsection may do so without infringing the exclusive right of the copyright owner of the sound recording under section 106(1)—

 (i) by complying with such notice requirements as the Copyright Royalty Judges shall prescribe by regulation and by paying royalty fees in accordance with this subsection; or

 (ii) if such royalty fees have not been set, by agreeing to pay such royalty fees as shall be determined in accordance with this subsection.

(B) Any royalty payments in arrears shall be made on or before the 20th day of the month next succeeding the month in which the royalty fees are set.

(7) If a transmitting organization entitled to make a phonorecord under this subsection is prevented from making such phonorecord by reason of the application by the copyright owner of technical measures that prevent the reproduction of the sound recording, the copyright owner shall make available to the transmitting organization the necessary means for permitting the making of such phonorecord as permitted under this subsection, if it is technologically feasible and economically reasonable for the copyright owner to do so. If the copyright owner fails to do so in a timely manner in light of the transmitting organization's reasonable business requirements, the transmitting organization shall not be liable for a violation of section 1201(a)(1) of this title for engaging in such activities as are necessary to make such phonorecords as permitted under this subsection.

(8) Nothing in this subsection annuls, limits, impairs, or otherwise affects in any way the existence or value of any of the exclusive rights of the copyright owners in a sound recording, except as otherwise provided in this subsection, or in a musical work, including the exclusive rights to reproduce and distribute a sound recording or musical work, including by means of a digital phonorecord delivery, under sections 106(1), 106(3), and 115, and the right to perform publicly a sound recording or musical work, including by means of a digital audio transmission, under sections 106(4) and 106(6).

(f)(1) Notwithstanding the provisions of section 106, and without limiting the application of subsection (b), it is not an infringement of copyright for a governmental body or other nonprofit educational institution entitled under section 110(2) to transmit a performance or display to make copies or phonorecords of a work that is in digital form and, solely to the extent permitted in paragraph (2), of a work that is in analog form, embodying the performance or display to be used for making transmissions authorized under section 110(2), if—

 (A) such copies or phonorecords are retained and used solely by the body or institution that made them, and no further copies or phonorecords are reproduced from them, except as authorized under section 110(2); and

 (B) such copies or phonorecords are used solely for transmissions authorized under section 110(2).

(2) This subsection does not authorize the conversion of print or other analog versions of works into digital formats, except that such conversion is permitted hereunder, only with respect to the amount of such works authorized to be performed or displayed under section 110(2), if—

 (A) no digital version of the work is available to the institution; or

 (B) the digital version of the work that is available to the institution is subject to technological protection measures that prevent its use for section 110(2).

(g)   The transmission program embodied in a copy or phonorecord made under this section is not subject to protection as a derivative work under this title except with the express consent of the owners of copyright in the preexisting works employed in the program.

(As amended, Pub.L. 105–304, 112 Stat. 2860 (1998); Pub.L. 106–44, 113 Stat. 221 (1999); Pub.L. 107–273, 116 Stat. 1758 (2002); Pub.L. 108–419, 118 Stat. 2341 (2004)).

## Sec. 113.    Scope of Exclusive Rights in Pictorial, Graphic, and Sculptural Works

(a)   Subject to the provisions of subsections (b) and (c) of this section, the exclusive right to reproduce a copyrighted pictorial, graphic, or sculptural work in copies under section 106 includes the right to reproduce the work in or on any kind of article, whether useful or otherwise.

(b)   This title does not afford, to the owner of copyright in a work that portrays a useful article as such, any greater or lesser rights with respect to the making, distribution, or display of the useful article so portrayed than those afforded to such works under the law, whether title 17 or the common law or statutes of a State, in effect on December 31, 1977, as held applicable and construed by a court in an action brought under this title.

(c)   In the case of a work lawfully reproduced in useful articles that have been offered for sale or other distribution to the public, copyright does not include any right to prevent the making, distribution, or display of pictures or photographs of such articles in connection with advertisements or commentaries related to the distribution or display of such articles, or in connection with news reports.

(d)(1)   In a case in which—

(A)   a work of visual art has been incorporated in or made part of a building in such a way that removing the work from the building will cause the destruction, distortion, mutilation, or other modification of the work as described in section 106A(a)(3), and

(B)   the author consented to the installation of the work in the building either before the effective date set forth in section 9(a) of the Visual Artists Rights Act of 1990, or in a written instrument executed on or after such effective date that is signed by the owner of the building and the author and that specifies that installation of the work may subject the work to destruction, distortion, mutilation, or other modification, by reason of its removal,

then the rights conferred by paragraphs (2) and (3) of section 106A(a) shall not apply.

(2)   If the owner of a building wishes to remove a work of visual art which is a part of such building and which can be removed from the building without the destruction, distortion, mutilation, or other modification of the work as described in section 106A(a)(3), the author's rights under paragraphs (2) and (3) of section 106A(a) shall apply unless—

(A)   the owner has made a diligent, good faith attempt without success to notify the author of the owner's intended action affecting the work of visual art, or

(B)   the owner did provide such notice in writing and the person so notified failed, within 90 days after receiving such notice, either to remove the work or to pay for its removal.

For purposes of subparagraph (A), an owner shall be presumed to have made a diligent, good faith attempt to send notice if the owner sent such notice by registered mail to the author at the most recent address of the author that was recorded with the Register of Copyrights pursuant to paragraph (3). If the work is removed at the expense of the author, title to that copy of the work shall be deemed to be in the author.

(3)   The Register of Copyrights shall establish a system of records whereby any author of a work of visual art that has been incorporated in or made part of a building, may record his identity and address with the Copyright Office. The Register shall also establish procedures under which any such author may update the information so recorded, and procedures under which owners of buildings may record with the Copyright Office evidence of their efforts to comply with this subsection.

(As amended, Pub.L. 101–650, 104 Stat. 5089 (1990)).

## Sec. 114.    Scope of Exclusive Rights in Sound Recordings

**(a)**  The exclusive rights of the owner of copyright in a sound recording are limited to the rights specified by clauses (1), (2), (3) and (6) of section 106, and do not include any right of performance under section 106(4).

**(b)**  The exclusive right of the owner of copyright in a sound recording under clause (1) of section 106 is limited to the right to duplicate the sound recording in the form of phonorecords or copies that directly or indirectly recapture the actual sounds fixed in the recording. The exclusive right of the owner of copyright in a sound recording under clause (2) of section 106 is limited to the right to prepare a derivative work in which the actual sounds fixed in the sound recording are rearranged, remixed, or otherwise altered in sequence or quality. The exclusive rights of the owner of copyright in a sound recording under clauses (1) and (2) of section 106 do not extend to the making or duplication of another sound recording that consists entirely of an independent fixation of other sounds, even though such sounds imitate or simulate those in the copyrighted sound recording. The exclusive rights of the owner of copyright in a sound recording under clauses (1), (2), and (3) of section 106 do not apply to sound recordings included in educational television and radio programs (as defined in section 397 of title 47) distributed or transmitted by or through public broadcasting entities (as defined by section 118(f)): *Provided*, That copies or phonorecords of said programs are not commercially distributed by or through public broadcasting entities to the general public.

**(c)**  This section does not limit or impair the exclusive right to perform publicly, by means of a phonorecord, any of the works specified by section 106(4).

**(d)**  **Limitations on exclusive right.**—Notwithstanding the provisions of section 106(6)—

   **(1)  Exempt transmissions and retransmissions.**—The performance of a sound recording publicly by means of a digital audio transmission, other than as a part of an interactive service, is not an infringement of section 106(6) if the performance is part of—

   **(A)**  a nonsubscription broadcast transmission;

   **(B)**  a retransmission of a nonsubscription broadcast transmission: *Provided*, That, in the case of a retransmission of a radio station's broadcast transmission—

      **(i)**  the radio station's broadcast transmission is not willfully or repeatedly retransmitted more than a radius of 150 miles from the site of the radio broadcast transmitter, however—

         **(I)**  the 150 mile limitation under this clause shall not apply when a nonsubscription broadcast transmission by a radio station licensed by the Federal Communications Commission is retransmitted on a nonsubscription basis by a terrestrial broadcast station, terrestrial translator, or terrestrial repeater licensed by the Federal Communications Commission; and

         **(II)**  in the case of a subscription retransmission of a nonsubscription broadcast retransmission covered by subclause (I), the 150 mile radius shall be measured from the transmitter site of such broadcast retransmitter;

      **(ii)**  the retransmission is of radio station broadcast transmissions that are—

         **(I)**  obtained by the retransmitter over the air;

         **(II)**  not electronically processed by the retransmitter to deliver separate and discrete signals; and

         **(III)** retransmitted only within the local communities served by the retransmitter;

      **(iii)**  the radio station's broadcast transmission was being retransmitted to cable systems (as defined in section 111(f)) by a satellite carrier on January 1, 1995, and that retransmission was being retransmitted by cable systems as a separate and discrete signal, and the satellite carrier obtains the radio station's broadcast transmission in an analog format: *Provided*, That the broadcast transmission being retransmitted may embody the programming of no more than one radio station; or

**(iv)** the radio station's broadcast transmission is made by a noncommercial educational broadcast station funded on or after January 1, 1995, under section 396(k) of the Communications Act of 1934 (47 U.S.C. 396(k)), consists solely of noncommercial educational and cultural radio programs, and the retransmission, whether or not simultaneous, is a nonsubscription terrestrial broadcast retransmission; or

**(C)** a transmission that comes within any of the following categories—

**(i)** a prior or simultaneous transmission incidental to an exempt transmission, such as a feed received by and then retransmitted by an exempt transmitter: *Provided*, That such incidental transmissions do not include any subscription transmission directly for reception by members of the public;

**(ii)** a transmission within a business establishment, confined to its premises or the immediately surrounding vicinity;

**(iii)** a retransmission by any retransmitter, including a multichannel video programming distributor as defined in section 602(12) of the Communications Act of 1934 (47 U.S.C. 522(12)), of a transmission by a transmitter licensed to publicly perform the sound recording as a part of that transmission, if the retransmission is simultaneous with the licensed transmission and authorized by the transmitter; or

**(iv)** a transmission to a business establishment for use in the ordinary course of its business: *Provided*, That the business recipient does not retransmit the transmission outside of its premises or the immediately surrounding vicinity, and that the transmission does not exceed the sound recording performance complement. Nothing in this clause shall limit the scope of the exemption in clause (ii).

**(2) Statutory licensing of certain transmissions.**—The performance of a sound recording publicly by means of a subscription digital audio transmission not exempt under paragraph (1), an eligible nonsubscription transmission, or a transmission not exempt under paragraph (1) that is made by a preexisting satellite digital audio radio service shall be subject to statutory licensing, in accordance with subsection (f) if—

**(A)(i)** the transmission is not part of an interactive service;

**(ii)** except in the case of a transmission to a business establishment, the transmitting entity does not automatically and intentionally cause any device receiving the transmission to switch from one program channel to another; and

**(iii)** except as provided in section 1002(e), the transmission of the sound recording is accompanied, if technically feasible, by the information encoded in that sound recording, if any, by or under the authority of the copyright owner of that sound recording, that identifies the title of the sound recording, the featured recording artist who performs on the sound recording, and related information, including information concerning the underlying musical work and its writer;

**(B)** in the case of a subscription transmission not exempt under paragraph (1) that is made by a preexisting subscription service in the same transmission medium used by such service on July 31, 1998, or in the case of a transmission not exempt under paragraph (1) that is made by a preexisting satellite digital audio radio service—

**(i)** the transmission does not exceed the sound recording performance complement; and

**(ii)** the transmitting entity does not cause to be published by means of an advance program schedule or prior announcement the titles of the specific sound recordings or phonorecords embodying such sound recordings to be transmitted; and

**(C)** in the case of an eligible nonsubscription transmission or a subscription transmission not exempt under paragraph (1) that is made by a new subscription service or by a preexisting subscription service other than in the same transmission medium used by such service on July 31, 1998—

**(i)** the transmission does not exceed the sound recording performance complement, except that this requirement shall not apply in the case of a retransmission of a broadcast transmission if the retransmission is made by a transmitting entity that does not have the right or ability to control the programming of the broadcast station making the broadcast transmission, unless—

**(I)** the broadcast station makes broadcast transmissions—

**(aa)** in digital format that regularly exceed the sound recording performance complement; or

**(bb)** in analog format, a substantial portion of which, on a weekly basis, exceed the sound recording performance complement; and

**(II)** the sound recording copyright owner or its representative has notified the transmitting entity in writing that broadcast transmissions of the copyright owner's sound recordings exceed the sound recording performance complement as provided in this clause;

**(ii)** the transmitting entity does not cause to be published, or induce or facilitate the publication, by means of an advance program schedule or prior announcement, the titles of the specific sound recordings to be transmitted, the phonorecords embodying such sound recordings, or, other than for illustrative purposes, the names of the featured recording artists, except that this clause does not disqualify a transmitting entity that makes a prior announcement that a particular artist will be featured within an unspecified future time period, and in the case of a retransmission of a broadcast transmission by a transmitting entity that does not have the right or ability to control the programming of the broadcast transmission, the requirement of this clause shall not apply to a prior oral announcement by the broadcast station, or to an advance program schedule published, induced, or facilitated by the broadcast station, if the transmitting entity does not have actual knowledge and has not received written notice from the copyright owner or its representative that the broadcast station publishes or induces or facilitates the publication of such advance program schedule, or if such advance program schedule is a schedule of classical music programming published by the broadcast station in the same manner as published by that broadcast station on or before September 30, 1998;

**(iii)** the transmission—

**(I)** is not part of an archived program of less than 5 hours duration;

**(II)** is not part of an archived program of 5 hours or greater in duration that is made available for a period exceeding 2 weeks;

**(III)** is not part of a continuous program which is of less than 3 hours duration; or

**(IV)** is not part of an identifiable program in which performances of sound recordings are rendered in a predetermined order, other than an archived or continuous program, that is transmitted at—

**(aa)** more than 3 times in any 2-week period that have been publicly announced in advance, in the case of a program of less than 1 hour in duration, or

**(bb)** more than 4 times in any 2-week period that have been publicly announced in advance, in the case of a program of 1 hour or more in duration,

except that the requirement of this subclause shall not apply in the case of a retransmission of a broadcast transmission by a transmitting entity that does not have the right or ability to control the programming of the broadcast transmission, unless the transmitting entity is given notice in writing by the copyright owner of the sound recording that the broadcast station makes broadcast transmissions that regularly violate such requirement;

**(iv)** the transmitting entity does not knowingly perform the sound recording, as part of a service that offers transmissions of visual images contemporaneously with transmissions of sound recordings, in a manner that is likely to cause confusion, to cause mistake, or to deceive, as to the affiliation, connection, or association of the copyright owner or featured recording artist with the transmitting entity or a particular product or service advertised by the transmitting entity, or as to the origin, sponsorship, or approval by the copyright owner or featured recording artist of the activities of the transmitting entity other than the performance of the sound recording itself;

**(v)** the transmitting entity cooperates to prevent, to the extent feasible without imposing substantial costs or burdens, a transmission recipient or any other person or entity from automatically scanning the transmitting entity's transmissions alone or together with transmissions by other transmitting entities in order to select a particular sound recording to be transmitted to the transmission recipient, except that the requirement of this clause shall not apply to a satellite digital audio service that is in operation, or that is licensed by the Federal Communications Commission, on or before July 31, 1998;

**(vi)** the transmitting entity takes no affirmative steps to cause or induce the making of a phonorecord by the transmission recipient, and if the technology used by the transmitting entity enables the transmitting entity to limit the making by the transmission recipient of phonorecords of the transmission directly in a digital format, the transmitting entity sets such technology to limit such making of phonorecords to the extent permitted by such technology;

**(vii)** phonorecords of the sound recording have been distributed to the public under the authority of the copyright owner or the copyright owner authorizes the transmitting entity to transmit the sound recording, and the transmitting entity makes the transmission from a phonorecord lawfully made under the authority of the copyright owner, except that the requirement of this clause shall not apply to a retransmission of a broadcast transmission by a transmitting entity that does not have the right or ability to control the programming of the broadcast transmission, unless the transmitting entity is given notice in writing by the copyright owner of the sound recording that the broadcast station makes broadcast transmissions that regularly violate such requirement;

**(viii)** the transmitting entity accommodates and does not interfere with the transmission of technical measures that are widely used by sound recording copyright owners to identify or protect copyrighted works, and that are technically feasible of being transmitted by the transmitting entity without imposing substantial costs on the transmitting entity or resulting in perceptible aural or visual degradation of the digital signal, except that the requirement of this clause shall not apply to a satellite digital audio service that is in operation, or that is licensed under the authority of the Federal

Communications Commission, on or before July 31, 1998, to the extent that such service has designed, developed, or made commitments to procure equipment or technology that is not compatible with such technical measures before such technical measures are widely adopted by sound recording copyright owners; and

**(ix)** the transmitting entity identifies in textual data the sound recording during, but not before, the time it is performed, including the title of the sound recording, the title of the phonorecord embodying such sound recording, if any, and the featured recording artist, in a manner to permit it to be displayed to the transmission recipient by the device or technology intended for receiving the service provided by the transmitting entity, except that the obligation in this clause shall not take effect until 1 year after the date of the enactment of the Digital Millennium Copyright Act and shall not apply in the case of a retransmission of a broadcast transmission by a transmitting entity that does not have the right or ability to control the programming of the broadcast transmission, or in the case in which devices or technology intended for receiving the service provided by the transmitting entity that have the capability to display such textual data are not common in the marketplace.

**(3) Licenses for transmissions by interactive services.—**

**(A)** No interactive service shall be granted an exclusive license under section 106(6) for the performance of a sound recording publicly by means of digital audio transmission for a period in excess of 12 months, except that with respect to an exclusive license granted to an interactive service by a licensor that holds the copyright to 1,000 or fewer sound recordings, the period of such license shall not exceed 24 months: *Provided*, however, That the grantee of such exclusive license shall be ineligible to receive another exclusive license for the performance of that sound recording for a period of 13 months from the expiration of the prior exclusive license.

**(B)** The limitation set forth in subparagraph (A) of this paragraph shall not apply if—

**(i)** the licensor has granted and there remain in effect licenses under section 106(6) for the public performance of sound recordings by means of digital audio transmission by at least 5 different interactive services: *Provided*, however, That each such license must be for a minimum of 10 percent of the copyrighted sound recordings owned by the licensor that have been licensed to interactive services, but in no event less than 50 sound recordings; or

**(ii)** the exclusive license is granted to perform publicly up to 45 seconds of a sound recording and the sole purpose of the performance is to promote the distribution or performance of that sound recording.

**(C)** Notwithstanding the grant of an exclusive or nonexclusive license of the right of public performance under section 106(6), an interactive service may not publicly perform a sound recording unless a license has been granted for the public performance of any copyrighted musical work contained in the sound recording: *Provided*, That such license to publicly perform the copyrighted musical work may be granted either by a performing rights society representing the copyright owner or by the copyright owner.

**(D)** The performance of a sound recording by means of a retransmission of a digital audio transmission is not an infringement of section 106(6) if—

**(i)** the retransmission is of a transmission by an interactive service licensed to publicly perform the sound recording to a particular member of the public as part of that transmission; and

**(ii)** the retransmission is simultaneous with the licensed transmission, authorized by the transmitter, and limited to that particular member of the public intended by the interactive service to be the recipient of the transmission.

**(E)** For the purposes of this paragraph—

**(i)** a "licensor" shall include the licensing entity and any other entity under any material degree of common ownership, management, or control that owns copyrights in sound recordings; and

**(ii)** a "performing rights society" is an association or corporation that licenses the public performance of nondramatic musical works on behalf of the copyright owner, such as the American Society of Composers, Authors and Publishers, Broadcast Music, Inc., and SESAC, Inc.

**(4) Rights not otherwise limited.—**

**(A)** Except as expressly provided in this section, this section does not limit or impair the exclusive right to perform a sound recording publicly by means of a digital audio transmission under section 106(6).

**(B)** Nothing in this section annuls or limits in any way—

**(i)** the exclusive right to publicly perform a musical work, including by means of a digital audio transmission, under section 106(4);

**(ii)** the exclusive rights in a sound recording or the musical work embodied therein under sections 106(1), 106(2) and 106(3); or

**(iii)** any other rights under any other clause of section 106, or remedies available under this title, as such rights or remedies exist either before or after the date of enactment of the Digital Performance Right in Sound Recordings Act of 1995.

**(C)** Any limitations in this section on the exclusive right under section 106(6) apply only to the exclusive right under section 106(6) and not to any other exclusive rights under section 106. Nothing in this section shall be construed to annul, limit, impair or otherwise affect in any way the ability of the owner of a copyright in a sound recording to exercise the rights under sections 106(1), 106(2) and 106(3), or to obtain the remedies available under this title pursuant to such rights, as such rights and remedies exist either before or after the date of enactment of the Digital Performance Right in Sound Recordings Act of 1995.

**(e) Authority for Negotiations.—**

**(1)** Notwithstanding any provision of the antitrust laws, in negotiating statutory licenses in accordance with subsection (f), any copyright owners of sound recordings and any entities performing sound recordings affected by this section may negotiate and agree upon the royalty rates and license terms and conditions for the performance of such sound recordings and the proportionate division of fees paid among copyright owners, and may designate common agents on a nonexclusive basis to negotiate, agree to, pay, or receive payments.

**(2)** For licenses granted under section 106(6), other than statutory licenses, such as for performances by interactive services or performances that exceed the sound recording performance complement—

**(A)** copyright owners of sound recordings affected by this section may designate common agents to act on their behalf to grant licenses and receive and remit royalty payments: *Provided,* That each copyright owner shall establish the royalty rates and material license terms and conditions unilaterally, that is, not in agreement, combination, or concert with other copyright owners of sound recordings; and

**(B)** entities performing sound recordings affected by this section may designate common agents to act on their behalf to obtain licenses and collect and pay royalty fees: *Provided,* That each entity performing sound recordings shall determine the royalty rates and material license terms and conditions unilaterally, that is, not in agreement, combination, or concert with other entities performing sound recordings.

**(f)   Licenses for certain nonexempt transmissions.—**

**(1)(A)**   Proceedings under chapter 8 shall determine reasonable rates and terms of royalty payments for transmissions subject to statutory licensing under subsection (d)(2) during the 5-year period beginning on January 1 of the second year following the year in which the proceedings are to be commenced pursuant to subparagraph (A) or (B) of section 804(b)(3), as the case may be, or such other period as the parties may agree. The parties to each proceeding shall bear their own costs.

**(B)**   The schedule of reasonable rates and terms determined by the Copyright Royalty Judges shall, subject to paragraph (2), be binding on all copyright owners of sound recordings and entities performing sound recordings affected by this paragraph during the 5-year period specified in subparagraph (A), or such other period as the parties may agree. Such rates and terms shall distinguish among the different types of services then in operation and shall include a minimum fee for each such type of service, such differences to be based on criteria including the quantity and nature of the use of sound recordings and the degree to which use of the service may substitute for or may promote the purchase of phonorecords by consumers. The Copyright Royalty Judges shall establish rates and terms that most clearly represent the rates and terms that would have been negotiated in the marketplace between a willing buyer and a willing seller. In determining such rates and terms, the Copyright Royalty Judges—

> **(i)**   shall base their decision on economic, competitive, and programming information presented by the parties, including—
>
>> **(I)**   whether use of the service may substitute for or may promote the sales of phonorecords or otherwise may interfere with or may enhance the sound recording copyright owner's other streams of revenue from the copyright owner's sound recordings; and
>>
>> **(II)**   the relative roles of the copyright owner and the transmitting entity in the copyrighted work and the service made available to the public with respect to relative creative contribution, technological contribution, capital investment, cost, and risk; and
>
> **(ii)**   may consider the rates and terms for comparable types of audio transmission services and comparable circumstances under voluntary license agreements.

**(C)**   The procedures under subparagraphs (A) and (B) shall also be initiated pursuant to a petition filed by any sound recording copyright owner or any transmitting entity indicating that a new type of service on which sound recordings are performed is or is about to become operational, for the purpose of determining reasonable terms and rates of royalty payments with respect to such new type of service for the period beginning with the inception of such new type of service and ending on the date on which the royalty rates and terms for eligible nonsubscription services and new subscription services, or preexisting subscription services and preexisting satellite digital audio radio services, as the case may be, most recently determined under subparagraph (A) or (B) and chapter 8 expire, or such other period as the parties may agree.

**(2)**   License agreements voluntarily negotiated at any time between 1 or more copyright owners of sound recordings and 1 or more entities performing sound recordings shall be given effect in lieu of any decision by the Librarian of Congress or determination by the Copyright Royalty Judges.

**(3)(A)**   The Copyright Royalty Judges shall also establish requirements by which copyright owners may receive reasonable notice of the use of their sound recordings under this section, and under which records of such use shall be kept and made available by entities performing sound recordings. The notice and recordkeeping rules in effect on the day before the effective date of the Copyright Royalty and Distribution Reform Act of 2004 shall remain in effect unless and until new regulations are promulgated by the Copyright Royalty Judges. If new regulations are promulgated under this subparagraph, the Copyright Royalty Judges shall take into account the substance and effect of the rules in effect on the day before the effective date of the Copyright Royalty and Distribution Reform Act of 2004 and shall, to the extent practicable, avoid significant disruption of the functions of any designated agent authorized to collect and distribute royalty fees.

**(B)** Any person who wishes to perform a sound recording publicly by means of a transmission eligible for statutory licensing under this subsection may do so without infringing the exclusive right of the copyright owner of the sound recording—

    **(i)** by complying with such notice requirements as the Copyright Royalty Judges shall prescribe by regulation and by paying royalty fees in accordance with this subsection; or

    **(ii)** if such royalty fees have not been set, by agreeing to pay such royalty fees as shall be determined in accordance with this subsection.

**(C)** Any royalty payments in arrears shall be made on or before the twentieth day of the month next succeeding the month in which the royalty fees are set.

**(4)(A)** Notwithstanding section 112(e) and the other provisions of this subsection, the receiving agent may enter into agreements for the reproduction and performance of sound recordings under section 112(e) and this section by any 1 or more commercial webcasters or noncommercial webcasters for a period of not more than 11 years beginning on January 1, 2005, that, once published in the Federal Register pursuant to subparagraph (B), shall be binding on all copyright owners of sound recordings and other persons entitled to payment under this section, in lieu of any determination by the Copyright Royalty Judges. Any such agreement for commercial webcasters may include provisions for payment of royalties on the basis of a percentage of revenue or expenses, or both, and include a minimum fee. Any such agreement may include other terms and conditions, including requirements by which copyright owners may receive notice of the use of their sound recordings and under which records of such use shall be kept and made available by commercial webcasters or noncommercial webcasters. The receiving agent shall be under no obligation to negotiate any such agreement. The receiving agent shall have no obligation to any copyright owner of sound recordings or any other person entitled to payment under this section in negotiating any such agreement, and no liability to any copyright owner of sound recordings or any other person entitled to payment under this section for having entered into such agreement.

**(B)** The Copyright Office shall cause to be published in the Federal Register any agreement entered into pursuant to subparagraph (A). Such publication shall include a statement containing the substance of subparagraph (C). Such agreements shall not be included in the Code of Federal Regulations. Thereafter, the terms of such agreement shall be available, as an option, to any commercial webcaster or noncommercial webcaster meeting the eligibility conditions of such agreement.

**(C)** Neither subparagraph (A) nor any provisions of any agreement entered into pursuant to subparagraph (A), including any rate structure, fees, terms, conditions, or notice and recordkeeping requirements set forth therein, shall be admissible as evidence or otherwise taken into account in any administrative, judicial, or other government proceeding involving the setting or adjustment of the royalties payable for the public performance or reproduction in ephemeral phonorecords or copies of sound recordings, the determination of terms or conditions related thereto, or the establishment of notice or recordkeeping requirements by the Copyright Royalty Judges under paragraph (3) or section 112(e)(4). It is the intent of Congress that any royalty rates, rate structure, definitions, terms, conditions, or notice and recordkeeping requirements, included in such agreements shall be considered as a compromise motivated by the unique business, economic and political circumstances of webcasters, copyright owners, and performers rather than as matters that would have been negotiated in the marketplace between a willing buyer and a willing seller, or otherwise meet the objectives set forth in section 801(b). This subparagraph shall not apply to the extent that the receiving agent and a webcaster that is party to an agreement entered into pursuant to subparagraph (A) expressly authorize the submission of the agreement in a proceeding under this subsection.

**(D)** Nothing in the Webcaster Settlement Act of 2008, the Webcaster Settlement Act of 2009, or any agreement entered into pursuant to subparagraph (A) shall be taken into account by the United States Court of Appeals for the District of Columbia Circuit in its review of the determination by the Copyright Royalty Judges of May 1, 2007, of rates and terms for the digital performance of sound recordings and ephemeral recordings, pursuant to sections 112 and 114.

**(E)** As used in this paragraph—

    **(i)** the term "noncommercial webcaster" means a webcaster that—

        **(I)** is exempt from taxation under section 501 of the Internal Revenue Code of 1986 (26 U.S.C. 501);

        **(II)** has applied in good faith to the Internal Revenue Service for exemption from taxation under section 501 of the Internal Revenue Code and has a commercially reasonable expectation that such exemption shall be granted; or

        **(III)** is operated by a State or possession or any governmental entity or subordinate thereof, or by the United States or District of Columbia, for exclusively public purposes;

    **(ii)** the term "receiving agent" shall have the meaning given that term in section 261.2 of title 37, Code of Federal Regulations, as published in the Federal Register on July 8, 2002; and

    **(iii)** the term "webcaster" means a person or entity that has obtained a compulsory license under section 112 or 114 and the implementing regulations therefor.

**(F)** The authority to make settlements pursuant to subparagraph (A) shall expire at 11:59 p.m. Eastern time on the 30th day after the date of the enactment of the Webcaster Settlement Act of 2009.

**(g) Proceeds from licensing of transmissions.—**

**(1)** Except in the case of a transmission licensed under a statutory license in accordance with subsection (f) of this section—

    **(A)** a featured recording artist who performs on a sound recording that has been licensed for a transmission shall be entitled to receive payments from the copyright owner of the sound recording in accordance with the terms of the artist's contract; and

    **(B)** a nonfeatured recording artist who performs on a sound recording that has been licensed for a transmission shall be entitled to receive payments from the copyright owner of the sound recording in accordance with the terms of the nonfeatured recording artist's applicable contract or other applicable agreement.

**(2)** Except as provided for in paragraph (6), a nonprofit collective designated by the Copyright Royalty Judges to distribute receipts from the licensing of transmissions in accordance with subsection (f) shall distribute such receipts as follows:

    **(A)** 50 percent of the receipts shall be paid to the copyright owner of the exclusive right under section 106(6) of this title to publicly perform a sound recording by means of a digital audio transmission.

    **(B)** 2 ½ percent of the receipts shall be deposited in an escrow account managed by an independent administrator jointly appointed by copyright owners of sound recordings and the American Federation of Musicians (or any successor entity) to be distributed to nonfeatured musicians (whether or not members of the American Federation of Musicians) who have performed on sound recordings.

**(C)** 2 ½ percent of the receipts shall be deposited in an escrow account managed by an independent administrator jointly appointed by copyright owners of sound recordings and the American Federation of Television and Radio Artists (or any successor entity) to be distributed to nonfeatured vocalists (whether or not members of the American Federation of Television and Radio Artists) who have performed on sound recordings.

**(D)** 45 percent of the receipts shall be paid, on a per sound recording basis, to the recording artist or artists featured on such sound recording (or the persons conveying rights in the artists' performance in the sound recordings).

**(3)** A nonprofit collective designated by the Copyright Royalty Judges to distribute receipts from the licensing of transmissions in accordance with subsection (f) may deduct from any of its receipts, prior to the distribution of such receipts to any person or entity entitled thereto other than copyright owners and performers who have elected to receive royalties from another designated nonprofit collective and have notified such nonprofit collective in writing of such election, the reasonable costs of such collective incurred after November 1, 1995, in—

**(A)** the administration of the collection, distribution, and calculation of the royalties;

**(B)** the settlement of disputes relating to the collection and calculation of the royalties; and

**(C)** the licensing and enforcement of rights with respect to the making of ephemeral recordings and performances subject to licensing under section 112 and this section, including those incurred in participating in negotiations or arbitration proceedings under section 112 and this section, except that all costs incurred relating to the section 112 ephemeral recordings right may only be deducted from the royalties received pursuant to section 112.

**(4)** Notwithstanding paragraph (3), any nonprofit collective designated to distribute receipts from the licensing of transmissions in accordance with subsection (f) may deduct from any of its receipts, prior to the distribution of such receipts, the reasonable costs identified in paragraph (3) of such collective incurred after November 1, 1995, with respect to such copyright owners and performers who have entered with such collective a contractual relationship that specifies that such costs may be deducted from such royalty receipts.

**(5) Letter of direction.—**

**(A) In general.—**A nonprofit collective designated by the Copyright Royalty Judges to distribute receipts from the licensing of transmissions in accordance with subsection (f) shall adopt and reasonably implement a policy that provides, in circumstances determined by the collective to be appropriate, for acceptance of instructions from a payee identified under subparagraph (A) or (D) of paragraph (2) to distribute, to a producer, mixer, or sound engineer who was part of the creative process that created a sound recording, a portion of the payments to which the payee would otherwise be entitled from the licensing of transmissions of the sound recording. In this section, such instructions shall be referred to as a "letter of direction".

**(B) Acceptance of letter.—**To the extent that a collective described in subparagraph (A) accepts a letter of direction under that subparagraph, the person entitled to payment pursuant to the letter of direction shall, during the period in which the letter of direction is in effect and carried out by the collective, be treated for all purposes as the owner of the right to receive such payment, and the payee providing the letter of direction to the collective shall be treated as having no interest in such payment.

**(C) Authority of collective.—**This paragraph shall not be construed in such a manner so that the collective is not authorized to accept or act upon payment instructions in circumstances other than those to which this paragraph applies.

**(6) Sound recordings fixed before November 1, 1995.—**

**(A) Payment absent letter of direction.**—A nonprofit collective designated by the Copyright Royalty Judges to distribute receipts from the licensing of transmissions in accordance with subsection (f) (in this paragraph referred to as the "collective") shall adopt and reasonably implement a policy that provides, in circumstances determined by the collective to be appropriate, for the deduction of 2 percent of all the receipts that are collected from the licensing of transmissions of a sound recording fixed before November 1, 1995, but which is withdrawn from the amount otherwise payable under paragraph (2)(D) to the recording artist or artists featured on the sound recording (or the persons conveying rights in the artists' performance in the sound recording), and the distribution of such amount to 1 or more persons described in subparagraph (B) of this paragraph, after deduction of costs described in paragraph (3) or (4), as applicable, if each of the following requirements is met:

**(i) Certification of attempt to obtain a letter of direction.**—The person described in subparagraph (B) who is to receive the distribution has certified to the collective, under penalty of perjury, that—

**(I)** for a period of not less than 120 days, that person made reasonable efforts to contact the artist payee for such sound recording to request and obtain a letter of direction instructing the collective to pay to that person a portion of the royalties payable to the featured recording artist or artists; and

**(II)** during the period beginning on the date on which that person began the reasonable efforts described in subclause (I) and ending on the date of that person's certification to the collective, the artist payee did not affirm or deny in writing the request for a letter of direction.

**(ii) Collective attempt to contact artist.**—After receipt of the certification described in clause (i) and for a period of not less than 120 days before the first distribution by the collective to the person described in subparagraph (B), the collective attempts, in a reasonable manner as determined by the collective, to notify the artist payee of the certification made by the person described in subparagraph (B).

**(iii) No objection received.**—The artist payee does not, as of the date that was 10 business days before the date on which the first distribution is made, submit to the collective in writing an objection to the distribution.

**(B) Eligibility for payment.**—A person shall be eligible for payment under subparagraph (A) if the person—

**(i)** is a producer, mixer, or sound engineer of the sound recording;

**(ii)** has entered into a written contract with a record company involved in the creation or lawful exploitation of the sound recording, or with the recording artist or artists featured on the sound recording (or the persons conveying rights in the artists' performance in the sound recording), under which the person seeking payment is entitled to participate in royalty payments that are based on the exploitation of the sound recording and are payable from royalties otherwise payable to the recording artist or artists featured on the sound recording (or the persons conveying rights in the artists' performance in the sound recording);

**(iii)** made a creative contribution to the creation of the sound recording; and

**(iv)** submits to the collective—

**(I)** a written certification stating, under penalty of perjury, that the person meets the requirements in clauses (i) through (iii); and

**(II)** a true copy of the contract described in clause (ii).

**(C) Multiple certifications.**—Subject to subparagraph (D), in a case in which more than 1 person described in subparagraph (B) has met the requirements for a distribution under subparagraph (A) with respect to a sound recording as of the date that is 10 business days before the date on which the distribution is made, the collective shall divide the 2 percent distribution equally among all such persons.

**(D) Objection to payment.**—Not later than 10 business days after the date on which the collective receives from the artist payee a written objection to a distribution made pursuant to subparagraph (A), the collective shall cease making any further payment relating to such distribution. In any case in which the collective has made 1 or more distributions pursuant to subparagraph (A) to a person described in subparagraph (B) before the date that is 10 business days after the date on which the collective receives from the artist payee an objection to such distribution, the objection shall not affect that person's entitlement to any distribution made before the collective ceases such distribution under this subparagraph.

**(E) Ownership of the right to receive payments.**—To the extent that the collective determines that a distribution will be made under subparagraph (A) to a person described in subparagraph (B), such person shall, during the period covered by such distribution, be treated for all purposes as the owner of the right to receive such payments, and the artist payee to whom such payments would otherwise be payable shall be treated as having no interest in such payments.

**(F) Artist payee defined.**—In this paragraph, the term "artist payee" means a person, other than a person described in subparagraph (B), who owns the right to receive all or part of the receipts payable under paragraph (2)(D) with respect to a sound recording. In a case in which there are multiple artist payees with respect to a sound recording, an objection by 1 such payee shall apply only to that payee's share of the receipts payable under paragraph (2)(D), and shall not preclude payment under subparagraph (A) from the share of an artist payee that does not so object.

**(7) Preemption of State property laws.**—The holding and distribution of receipts under section 112 and this section by a nonprofit collective designated by the Copyright Royalty Judges in accordance with this subsection and regulations adopted by the Copyright Royalty Judges, or by an independent administrator pursuant to subparagraphs (B) and (C) of section 114(g)(2), shall supersede and preempt any State law (including common law) concerning escheatment or abandoned property, or any analogous provision, that might otherwise apply.

**(h) Licensing to Affiliates.—**

**(1)** If the copyright owner of a sound recording licenses an affiliated entity the right to publicly perform a sound recording by means of a digital audio transmission under section 106(6), the copyright owner shall make the licensed sound recording available under section 106(6) on no less favorable terms and conditions to all bona fide entities that offer similar services, except that, if there are material differences in the scope of the requested license with respect to the type of service, the particular sound recordings licensed, the frequency of use, the number of subscribers served, or the duration, then the copyright owner may establish different terms and conditions for such other services.

**(2)** The limitation set forth in paragraph (1) of this subsection shall not apply in the case where the copyright owner of a sound recording licenses—

**(A)** an interactive service; or

**(B)** an entity to perform publicly up to 45 seconds of the sound recording and the sole purpose of the performance is to promote the distribution or performance of that sound recording.

**(i)** **[Repealed]**

**(j)** **Definitions.**—As used in this section, the following terms have the following meanings:

**(1)** An "affiliated entity" is an entity engaging in digital audio transmissions covered by section 106(6), other than an interactive service, in which the licensor has any direct or indirect partnership or any ownership interest amounting to 5 percent or more of the outstanding voting or non-voting stock.

**(2)** An "archived program" is a predetermined program that is available repeatedly on the demand of the transmission recipient and that is performed in the same order from the beginning, except that an archived program shall not include a recorded event or broadcast transmission that makes no more than an incidental use of sound recordings, as long as such recorded event or broadcast transmission does not contain an entire sound recording or feature a particular sound recording.

**(3)** A "broadcast" transmission is a transmission made by a terrestrial broadcast station licensed as such by the Federal Communications Commission.

**(4)** A "continuous program" is a predetermined program that is continuously performed in the same order and that is accessed at a point in the program that is beyond the control of the transmission recipient.

**(5)** A "digital audio transmission" is a digital transmission as defined in section 101, that embodies the transmission of a sound recording. This term does not include the transmission of any audiovisual work.

**(6)** An "eligible nonsubscription transmission" is a noninteractive nonsubscription digital audio transmission not exempt under subsection (d)(1) that is made as part of a service that provides audio programming consisting, in whole or in part, of performances of sound recordings, including retransmissions of broadcast transmissions, if the primary purpose of the service is to provide to the public such audio or other entertainment programming, and the primary purpose of the service is not to sell, advertise, or promote particular products or services other than sound recordings, live concerts, or other music-related events.

**(7)** An "interactive service" is one that enables a member of the public to receive a transmission of a program specially created for the recipient, or on request, a transmission of a particular sound recording, whether or not as part of a program, which is selected by or on behalf of the recipient. The ability of individuals to request that particular sound recordings be performed for reception by the public at large, or in the case of a subscription service, by all subscribers of the service, does not make a service interactive, if the programming on each channel of the service does not substantially consist of sound recordings that are performed within 1 hour of the request or at a time designated by either the transmitting entity or the individual making such request. If an entity offers both interactive and noninteractive services (either concurrently or at different times), the noninteractive component shall not be treated as part of an interactive service.

**(8)** A "new subscription service" is a service that performs sound recordings by means of noninteractive subscription digital audio transmissions and that is not a preexisting subscription service or a preexisting satellite digital audio radio service.

**(9)** A "nonsubscription" transmission is any transmission that is not a subscription transmission.

**(10)** A "preexisting satellite digital audio radio service" is a subscription satellite digital audio radio service provided pursuant to a satellite digital audio radio service license issued by the Federal Communications Commission on or before July 31, 1998, and any renewal of such license to the extent of the scope of the original license, and may include a limited number of sample channels representative of the subscription service that are made available on a nonsubscription basis in order to promote the subscription service.

**(11)** A "preexisting subscription service" is a service that performs sound recordings by means of noninteractive audio-only subscription digital audio transmissions, which was in existence and was making such transmissions to the public for a fee on or before July 31, 1998, and may include a limited number of sample channels representative of the subscription service that are made available on a nonsubscription basis in order to promote the subscription service.

**(12)** A "retransmission" is a further transmission of an initial transmission, and includes any further retransmission of the same transmission. Except as provided in this section, a transmission qualifies as a "retransmission" only if it is simultaneous with the initial transmission. Nothing in this definition shall be construed to exempt a transmission that fails to satisfy a separate element required to qualify for an exemption under section 114(d)(1).

**(13)** The "sound recording performance complement" is the transmission during any 3-hour period, on a particular channel used by a transmitting entity, of no more than—

> **(A)** 3 different selections of sound recordings from any one phonorecord lawfully distributed for public performance or sale in the United States, if no more than 2 such selections are transmitted consecutively; or

> **(B)** 4 different selections of sound recordings—

>> **(i)** by the same featured recording artist; or

>> **(ii)** from any set or compilation of phonorecords lawfully distributed together as a unit for public performance or sale in the United States,

> if no more than three such selections are transmitted consecutively:

*Provided*, That the transmission of selections in excess of the numerical limits provided for in clauses (A) and (B) from multiple phonorecords shall nonetheless qualify as a sound recording performance complement if the programming of the multiple phonorecords was not willfully intended to avoid the numerical limitations prescribed in such clauses.

**(14)** A "subscription" transmission is a transmission that is controlled and limited to particular recipients, and for which consideration is required to be paid or otherwise given by or on behalf of the recipient to receive the transmission or a package of transmissions including the transmission.

**(15)** A "transmission" is either an initial transmission or a retransmission.

(As amended, Pub.L. 104–39, 109 Stat. 336 (1995); Pub.L. 105–80, 111 Stat. 1529 (1997); Pub.L. 105–304, 112 Stat. 2860 (1998); Pub.L. 107–321, 116 Stat. 2780 (2002); Pub.L. 108–419, 118 Stat. 2341 (2004); Pub.L. 109–303, 120 Stat. 1478 (2006); Pub.L. 110–435, 122 Stat. 4974 (2008); Pub.L. 111–36, 123 Stat. 1926 (2009); Pub.L. 111–295, 124 Stat. 3180 (2010); Pub.L. 115–264, 132 Stat. 3676 (2018)).

## Sec. 115.   Scope of Exclusive Rights in Nondramatic Musical Works: Compulsory License for Making and Distributing Phonorecords

In the case of nondramatic musical works, the exclusive rights provided by clauses (1) and (3) of section 106, to make and to distribute phonorecords of such works, are subject to compulsory licensing under the conditions specified by this section.

**(a) Availability and scope of compulsory license in general.—**

> **(1) Eligibility for compulsory license.—**

>> **(A) Conditions for compulsory license.—**A person may by complying with the provisions of this section obtain a compulsory license to make and distribute phonorecords of a nondramatic musical work, including by means of digital phonorecord delivery. A person may obtain a compulsory license only if the primary purpose in making phonorecords of the musical work is to distribute them to the public for private use, including by means of digital phonorecord delivery, and—

**(i)** phonorecords of such musical work have previously been distributed to the public in the United States under the authority of the copyright owner of the work, including by means of digital phonorecord delivery; or

**(ii)** in the case of a digital music provider seeking to make and distribute digital phonorecord deliveries of a sound recording embodying a musical work under a compulsory license for which clause (i) does not apply—

**(I)** the first fixation of such sound recording was made under the authority of the musical work copyright owner, and the sound recording copyright owner has the authority of the musical work copyright owner to make and distribute digital phonorecord deliveries embodying such work to the public in the United States; and

**(II)** the sound recording copyright owner, or the authorized distributor of the sound recording copyright owner, has authorized the digital music provider to make and distribute digital phonorecord deliveries of the sound recording to the public in the United States.

**(B) Duplication of sound recording.**—A person may not obtain a compulsory license for the use of the work in the making of phonorecords duplicating a sound recording fixed by another, including by means of digital phonorecord delivery, unless—

**(i)** such sound recording was fixed lawfully; and

**(ii)** the making of the phonorecords was authorized by the owner of the copyright in the sound recording or, if the sound recording was fixed before February 15, 1972, by any person who fixed the sound recording pursuant to an express license from the owner of the copyright in the musical work or pursuant to a valid compulsory license for use of such work in a sound recording.

**(2) Musical arrangement.**—A compulsory license includes the privilege of making a musical arrangement of the work to the extent necessary to conform it to the style or manner of interpretation of the performance involved, but the arrangement shall not change the basic melody or fundamental character of the work, and shall not be subject to protection as a derivative work under this title, except with the express consent of the copyright owner.

**(b) Procedures to obtain a compulsory license.**—

**(1) Phonorecords other than digital phonorecord deliveries.**—A person who seeks to obtain a compulsory license under subsection (a) to make and distribute phonorecords of a musical work other than by means of digital phonorecord delivery shall, before, or not later than 30 calendar days after, making, and before distributing, any phonorecord of the work, serve notice of intention to do so on the copyright owner. If the registration or other public records of the Copyright Office do not identify the copyright owner and include an address at which notice can be served, it shall be sufficient to file the notice of intention with the Copyright Office. The notice shall comply, in form, content, and manner of service, with requirements that the Register of Copyrights shall prescribe by regulation.

**(2) Digital phonorecord deliveries.**—A person who seeks to obtain a compulsory license under subsection (a) to make and distribute phonorecords of a musical work by means of digital phonorecord delivery—

**(A)** prior to the license availability date, shall, before, or not later than 30 calendar days after, first making any such digital phonorecord delivery, serve a notice of intention to do so on the copyright owner (but may not file the notice with the Copyright Office, even if the public records of the Office do not identify the owner or the owner's address), and such notice shall comply, in form, content, and manner of service, with requirements that the Register of Copyrights shall prescribe by regulation; or

**(B)** on or after the license availability date, shall, before making any such digital phonorecord delivery, follow the procedure described in subsection (d)(2), except as provided in paragraph (3).

**(3) Record company individual download licenses.**—Notwithstanding paragraph (2)(B), a record company may, on or after the license availability date, obtain an individual download license in accordance with the notice requirements described in paragraph (2)(A) (except for the requirement that notice occur prior to the license availability date). A record company that obtains an individual download license as permitted under this paragraph shall provide statements of account and pay royalties as provided in subsection (c)(2)(I).

**(4) Failure to obtain license.**—

**(A) Phonorecords other than digital phonorecord deliveries.**—In the case of phonorecords made and distributed other than by means of digital phonorecord delivery, the failure to serve or file the notice of intention required by paragraph (1) forecloses the possibility of a compulsory license under paragraph (1). In the absence of a voluntary license, the failure to obtain a compulsory license renders the making and distribution of phonorecords actionable as acts of infringement under section 501 and subject to the remedies provided by sections 502 through 506.

**(B) Digital phonorecord deliveries.**—

**(i) In general.**—In the case of phonorecords made and distributed by means of digital phonorecord delivery:

**(I)** The failure to serve the notice of intention required by paragraph (2)(A) or paragraph (3), as applicable, forecloses the possibility of a compulsory license under such paragraph.

**(II)** The failure to comply with paragraph (2)(B) forecloses the possibility of a blanket license for a period of 3 years after the last calendar day on which the notice of license was required to be submitted to the mechanical licensing collective under such paragraph.

**(ii) Effect of failure.**—In either case described in subclause (I) or (II) of clause (i), in the absence of a voluntary license, the failure to obtain a compulsory license renders the making and distribution of phonorecords by means of digital phonorecord delivery actionable as acts of infringement under section 501 and subject to the remedies provided by sections 502 through 506.

**(c) General conditions applicable to compulsory license.**—

**(1) Royalty payable under compulsory license.**—

**(A) Identification requirement.**—To be entitled to receive royalties under a compulsory license obtained under subsection (b)(1) the copyright owner must be identified in the registration or other public records of the Copyright Office. The owner is entitled to royalties for phonorecords made and distributed after being so identified, but is not entitled to recover for any phonorecords previously made and distributed.

**(B) Royalty for phonorecords other than digital phonorecord deliveries.**—Except as provided by subparagraph (A), for every phonorecord made and distributed under a compulsory license under subsection (a) other than by means of digital phonorecord delivery, with respect to each work embodied in the phonorecord, the royalty shall be the royalty prescribed under subparagraphs (D) through (F), paragraph (2)(A), and chapter 8. For purposes of this subparagraph, a phonorecord is considered 'distributed' if the person exercising the compulsory license has voluntarily and permanently parted with its possession.

**(C) Royalty for digital phonorecord deliveries.**—For every digital phonorecord delivery of a musical work made under a compulsory license under this section, the royalty payable shall be the royalty prescribed under subparagraphs (D) through (F), paragraph (2)(A), and chapter 8.

**(D) Authority to negotiate.**—Notwithstanding any provision of the antitrust laws, any copyright owners of nondramatic musical works and any persons entitled to obtain a compulsory license under subsection (a) may negotiate and agree upon the terms and rates of royalty payments under this section and the proportionate division of fees paid among copyright owners, and may designate common agents on a nonexclusive basis to negotiate, agree to, pay or receive such royalty payments. Such authority to negotiate the terms and rates of royalty payments includes, but is not limited to, the authority to negotiate the year during which the royalty rates prescribed under this subparagraph, subparagraphs (E) and (F), paragraph (2)(A), and chapter 8 shall next be determined.

**(E) Determination of reasonable rates and terms.**—Proceedings under chapter 8 shall determine reasonable rates and terms of royalty payments for the activities specified by this section during the period beginning with the effective date of such rates and terms, but not earlier than January 1 of the second year following the year in which the petition requesting the proceeding is filed, and ending on the effective date of successor rates and terms, or such other period as the parties may agree. Any copyright owners of nondramatic musical works and any persons entitled to obtain a compulsory license under subsection (a) may submit to the Copyright Royalty Judges licenses covering such activities. The parties to each proceeding shall bear their own costs.

**(F) Schedule of reasonable rates.**—The schedule of reasonable rates and terms determined by the Copyright Royalty Judges shall, subject to paragraph (2)(A), be binding on all copyright owners of nondramatic musical works and persons entitled to obtain a compulsory license under subsection (a) during the period specified in subparagraph (E), such other period as may be determined pursuant to subparagraphs (D) and (E), or such other period as the parties may agree. The Copyright Royalty Judges shall establish rates and terms that most clearly represent the rates and terms that would have been negotiated in the marketplace between a willing buyer and a willing seller. In determining such rates and terms for digital phonorecord deliveries, the Copyright Royalty Judges shall base their decision on economic, competitive, and programming information presented by the parties, including—

(i) whether use of the compulsory licensee's service may substitute for or may promote the sales of phonorecords or otherwise may interfere with or may enhance the musical work copyright owner's other streams of revenue from its musical works; and

(ii) the relative roles of the copyright owner and the compulsory licensee in the copyrighted work and the service made available to the public with respect to the relative creative contribution, technological contribution, capital investment, cost, and risk.

**(2) Additional terms and conditions.—**

**(A) Voluntary licenses and contractual royalty rates.—**

(i) **In general.**—License agreements voluntarily negotiated at any time between one or more copyright owners of nondramatic musical works and one or more persons entitled to obtain a compulsory license under subsection (a) shall be given effect in lieu of any determination by the Copyright Royalty Judges. Subject to clause (ii), the royalty rates determined pursuant to subparagraphs (E) and (F) of paragraph (1) shall be given effect as to digital phonorecord deliveries in lieu of any contrary royalty rates specified in a contract pursuant to which a recording artist who is the author of a nondramatic musical work grants a license under that person's exclusive rights in the musical work under paragraphs (1) and (3) of section 106 or commits another person to grant a license in that musical work under paragraphs (1) and (3) of section 106, to a person desiring to fix in a tangible medium of expression a sound recording embodying the musical work.

**(ii)  Applicability.**—The second sentence of clause (i) shall not apply to—

**(I)**  a contract entered into on or before June 22, 1995, and not modified thereafter for the purpose of reducing the royalty rates determined pursuant to subparagraphs (E) and (F) of paragraph (1) or of increasing the number of musical works within the scope of the contract covered by the reduced rates, except if a contract entered into on or before June 22, 1995, is modified thereafter for the purpose of increasing the number of musical works within the scope of the contract, any contrary royalty rates specified in the contract shall be given effect in lieu of royalty rates determined pursuant to subparagraphs (E) and (F) of paragraph (1) for the number of musical works within the scope of the contract as of June 22, 1995; and

**(II)**  a contract entered into after the date that the sound recording is fixed in a tangible medium of expression substantially in a form intended for commercial release, if at the time the contract is entered into, the recording artist retains the right to grant licenses as to the musical work under paragraphs (1) and (3) of section 106.

**(B)  Sound recording information.**—Except as provided in section 1002(e), a digital phonorecord delivery licensed under this paragraph shall be accompanied by the information encoded in the sound recording, if any, by or under the authority of the copyright owner of that sound recording, that identifies the title of the sound recording, the featured recording artist who performs on the sound recording, and related information, including information concerning the underlying musical work and its writer.

**(C)  Infringement remedies.—**

**(i)  In general.**—A digital phonorecord delivery of a sound recording is actionable as an act of infringement under section 501, and is fully subject to the remedies provided by sections 502 through 506, unless—

**(I)**  the digital phonorecord delivery has been authorized by the sound recording copyright owner; and

**(II)**  the entity making the digital phonorecord delivery has obtained a compulsory license under subsection (a) or has otherwise been authorized by the musical work copyright owner, or by a record company pursuant to an individual download license, to make and distribute phonorecords of each musical work embodied in the sound recording by means of digital phonorecord delivery.

**(ii)  Other remedies.**—Any cause of action under this subparagraph shall be in addition to those available to the owner of the copyright in the nondramatic musical work under subparagraph (J) and section 106(4) and the owner of the copyright in the sound recording under section 106(6).

**(D)  Liability of sound recording owners.**—The liability of the copyright owner of a sound recording for infringement of the copyright in a nondramatic musical work embodied in the sound recording shall be determined in accordance with applicable law, except that the owner of a copyright in a sound recording shall not be liable for a digital phonorecord delivery by a third party if the owner of the copyright in the sound recording does not license the distribution of a phonorecord of the nondramatic musical work.

**(E) Recording devices and media.**—Nothing in section 1008 shall be construed to prevent the exercise of the rights and remedies allowed by this paragraph, subparagraph (J), and chapter 5 in the event of a digital phonorecord delivery, except that no action alleging infringement of copyright may be brought under this title against a manufacturer, importer or distributor of a digital audio recording device, a digital audio recording medium, an analog recording device, or an analog recording medium, or against a consumer, based on the actions described in such section.

**(F) Preservation of rights.**—Nothing in this section annuls or limits—

> **(i)** the exclusive right to publicly perform a sound recording or the musical work embodied therein, including by means of a digital transmission, under paragraphs (4) and (6) of section 106;

> **(ii)** except for compulsory licensing under the conditions specified by this section, the exclusive rights to reproduce and distribute the sound recording and the musical work embodied therein under paragraphs (1) and (3) of section 106, including by means of a digital phonorecord delivery; or

> **(iii)** any other rights under any other provision of section 106, or remedies available under this title, as such rights or remedies exist before, on, or after the date of enactment of the Digital Performance Right in Sound Recordings Act of 1995.

**(G) Exempt transmissions and retransmissions.**—The provisions of this section concerning digital phonorecord deliveries shall not apply to any exempt transmissions or retransmissions under section 114(d)(1). The exemptions created in section 114(d)(1) do not expand or reduce the rights of copyright owners under paragraphs (1) through (5) of section 106 with respect to such transmissions and retransmissions.

**(H) Distribution by rental, lease, or lending.**—A compulsory license obtained under subsection (b)(1) to make and distribute phonorecords includes the right of the maker of such a phonorecord to distribute or authorize distribution of such phonorecord, other than by means of a digital phonorecord delivery, by rental, lease, or lending (or by acts or practices in the nature of rental, lease, or lending). With respect to each nondramatic musical work embodied in the phonorecord, the royalty shall be a proportion of the revenue received by the compulsory licensee from every such act of distribution of the phonorecord under this clause equal to the proportion of the revenue received by the compulsory licensee from distribution of the phonorecord under subsection (a)(1)(A)(ii)(II) that is payable by a compulsory licensee under that clause and under chapter 8. The Register of Copyrights shall issue regulations to carry out the purpose of this subparagraph.

**(I) Payment of royalties and statements of account.**—Except as provided in paragraphs (4)(A)(i) and (10)(B) of subsection (d), royalty payments shall be made on or before the twentieth day of each month and shall include all royalties for the month next preceding. Each monthly payment shall be made under oath and shall comply with requirements that the Register of Copyrights shall prescribe by regulation. The Register shall also prescribe regulations under which detailed cumulative annual statements of account, certified by a certified public accountant, shall be filed for every compulsory license under subsection (a). The regulations covering both the monthly and the annual statements of account shall prescribe the form, content, and manner of certification with respect to the number of records made and the number of records distributed.

**(J) Notice of default and termination of compulsory license.**—In the case of a license obtained under paragraph (1), (2)(A), or (3) of subsection (b), if the copyright owner does not receive the monthly payment and the monthly and annual statements of account when due, the owner may give written notice to the licensee that, unless the default is remedied not later than 30 days after the date on which the notice is sent, the compulsory license will be automatically terminated. Such termination renders either the making or the distribution, or both, of all phonorecords for which the royalty has not been paid, actionable as acts of infringement under section 501 and fully subject to the remedies provided by sections 502 through 506. In the case of a license obtained under subsection (b)(2)(B), license authority under the compulsory license may be terminated as provided in subsection (d)(4)(E).

**(d)  Blanket license for digital uses, mechanical licensing collective, and digital licensee coordinator.—**

   **(1)  Blanket license for digital uses.—**

   **(A)  In general.**—A digital music provider that qualifies for a compulsory license under subsection (a) may, by complying with the terms and conditions of this subsection, obtain a blanket license from copyright owners through the mechanical licensing collective to make and distribute digital phonorecord deliveries of musical works through one or more covered activities.

   **(B)  Included activities.**—A blanket license—

   **(i)**  covers all musical works (or shares of such works) available for compulsory licensing under this section for purposes of engaging in covered activities, except as provided in subparagraph (C);

   **(ii)**  includes the making and distribution of server, intermediate, archival, and incidental reproductions of musical works that are reasonable and necessary for the digital music provider to engage in covered activities licensed under this subsection, solely for the purpose of engaging in such covered activities; and

   **(iii)**  does not cover or include any rights or uses other than those described in clauses (i) and (ii).

   **(C)  Other licenses.**—A voluntary license for covered activities entered into by or under the authority of 1 or more copyright owners and 1 or more digital music providers, or authority to make and distribute permanent downloads of a musical work obtained by a digital music provider from a sound recording copyright owner pursuant to an individual download license, shall be given effect in lieu of a blanket license under this subsection with respect to the musical works (or shares thereof) covered by such voluntary license or individual download authority and the following conditions apply:

   **(i)**  Where a voluntary license or individual download license applies, the license authority provided under the blanket license shall exclude any musical works (or shares thereof) subject to the voluntary license or individual download license.

   **(ii)**  An entity engaged in covered activities under a voluntary license or authority obtained pursuant to an individual download license that is a significant nonblanket licensee shall comply with paragraph (6)(A).

   **(iii)**  The rates and terms of any voluntary license shall be subject to the second sentence of clause (i) and clause (ii) of subsection (c)(2)(A) and paragraph (9)(C), as applicable.

   **(D)  Protection against infringement actions.**—A digital music provider that obtains and complies with the terms of a valid blanket license under this subsection shall not be subject to an action for infringement of the exclusive rights provided by paragraphs (1) and (3) of section 106 under this title arising from use of a musical work (or share thereof) to engage in covered activities authorized by such license, subject to paragraph (4)(E).

   **(E)  Other requirements and conditions apply.**—Except as expressly provided in this subsection, each requirement, limitation, condition, privilege, right, and remedy otherwise applicable to compulsory licenses under this section shall apply to compulsory blanket licenses under this subsection.

**(2) Availability of blanket license.—**

**(A) Procedure for obtaining license.**—A digital music provider may obtain a blanket license by submitting a notice of license to the mechanical licensing collective that specifies the particular covered activities in which the digital music provider seeks to engage, as follows:

**(i)** The notice of license shall comply in form and substance with requirements that the Register of Copyrights shall establish by regulation.

**(ii)** Unless rejected in writing by the mechanical licensing collective not later than 30 calendar days after the date on which the mechanical licensing collective receives the notice, the blanket license shall be effective as of the date on which the notice of license was sent by the digital music provider, as shown by a physical or electronic record.

**(iii)** A notice of license may only be rejected by the mechanical licensing collective if—

**(I)** the digital music provider or notice of license does not meet the requirements of this section or applicable regulations, in which case the requirements at issue shall be specified with reasonable particularity in the notice of rejection; or

**(II)** the digital music provider has had a blanket license terminated by the mechanical licensing collective during the 3-year period preceding the date on which the mechanical licensing collective receives the notice pursuant to paragraph (4)(E).

**(iv)** If a notice of license is rejected under clause (iii)(I), the digital music provider shall have 30 calendar days after receipt of the notice of rejection to cure any deficiency and submit an amended notice of license to the mechanical licensing collective. If the deficiency has been cured, the mechanical licensing collective shall so confirm in writing, and the license shall be effective as of the date that the original notice of license was provided by the digital music provider.

**(v)** A digital music provider that believes a notice of license was improperly rejected by the mechanical licensing collective may seek review of such rejection in an appropriate district court of the United States. The district court shall determine the matter de novo based on the record before the mechanical licensing collective and any additional evidence presented by the parties.

**(B) Blanket license effective date.**—Blanket licenses shall be made available by the mechanical licensing collective on and after the license availability date. No such license shall be effective prior to the license availability date.

**(3) Mechanical licensing collective.—**

**(A) In general.**—The mechanical licensing collective shall be a single entity that—

**(i)** is a nonprofit entity, not owned by any other entity, that is created by copyright owners to carry out responsibilities under this subsection;

**(ii)** is endorsed by, and enjoys substantial support from, musical work copyright owners that together represent the greatest percentage of the licensor market for uses of such works in covered activities, as measured over the preceding 3 full calendar years;

**(iii)** is able to demonstrate to the Register of Copyrights that the entity has, or will have prior to the license availability date, the administrative and technological capabilities to perform the required functions of the mechanical licensing collective under this subsection and that is governed by a board of directors in accordance with subparagraph (D)(i); and

**(iv)** has been designated by the Register of Copyrights, with the approval of the Librarian of Congress pursuant to section 702, in accordance with subparagraph (B).

**(B) Designation of mechanical licensing collective.—**

**(i) Initial designation.—**Not later than 270 days after the enactment date, the Register of Copyrights shall initially designate the mechanical licensing collective as follows:

**(I)** Not later than 90 calendar days after the enactment date, the Register shall publish notice in the Federal Register soliciting information to assist in identifying the appropriate entity to serve as the mechanical licensing collective, including the name and affiliation of each member of the board of directors described under subparagraph (D)(i) and each committee established pursuant to clauses (iii), (iv), and (v) of subparagraph (D).

**(II)** After reviewing the information requested under subclause (I) and making a designation, the Register shall publish notice in the Federal Register setting forth—

**(aa)** the identity of and contact information for the mechanical licensing collective; and

**(bb)** the reasons for the designation.

**(ii) Periodic review of designation.—**Following the initial designation of the mechanical licensing collective, the Register shall, every 5 years, beginning with the fifth full calendar year to commence after the initial designation, publish notice in the Federal Register in the month of January soliciting information concerning whether the existing designation should be continued, or a different entity meeting the criteria described in clauses (i) through (iii) of subparagraph (A) shall be designated. Following publication of such notice, the Register shall—

**(I)** after reviewing the information submitted and conducting additional proceedings as appropriate, publish notice in the Federal Register of a continuing designation or new designation of the mechanical licensing collective, as the case may be, and the reasons for such a designation, with any new designation to be effective as of the first day of a month that is not less than 6 months and not longer than 9 months after the date on which the Register publishes the notice, as specified by the Register; and

**(II)** if a new entity is designated as the mechanical licensing collective, adopt regulations to govern the transfer of licenses, funds, records, data, and administrative responsibilities from the existing mechanical licensing collective to the new entity.

**(iii) Closest alternative designation.—**If the Register is unable to identify an entity that fulfills each of the qualifications set forth in clauses (i) through (iii) of subparagraph (A), the Register shall designate the entity that most nearly fulfills such qualifications for purposes of carrying out the responsibilities of the mechanical licensing collective.

**(C) Authorities and functions.—**

**(i) In general.—**The mechanical licensing collective is authorized to perform the following functions, subject to more particular requirements as described in this subsection:

**(I)** Offer and administer blanket licenses, including receipt of notices of license and reports of usage from digital music providers.

**(II)** Collect and distribute royalties from digital music providers for covered activities.

**(III)** Engage in efforts to identify musical works (and shares of such works) embodied in particular sound recordings, and to identify and locate the copyright owners of such musical works (and shares of such works).

**(IV)** Maintain the musical works database and other information relevant to the administration of licensing activities under this section.

**(V)** Administer a process by which copyright owners can claim ownership of musical works (and shares of such works), and a process by which royalties for works for which the owner is not identified or located are equitably distributed to known copyright owners.

**(VI)** Administer collections of the administrative assessment from digital music providers and significant nonblanket licensees, including receipt of notices of nonblanket activity.

**(VII)** Invest in relevant resources, and arrange for services of outside vendors and others, to support the activities of the mechanical licensing collective.

**(VIII)** Engage in legal and other efforts to enforce rights and obligations under this subsection, including by filing bankruptcy proofs of claims for amounts owed under licenses, and acting in coordination with the digital licensee coordinator.

**(IX)** Initiate and participate in proceedings before the Copyright Royalty Judges to establish the administrative assessment under this subsection.

**(X)** Initiate and participate in proceedings before the Copyright Office with respect to activities under this subsection.

**(XI)** Gather and provide documentation for use in proceedings before the Copyright Royalty Judges to set rates and terms under this section.

**(XII)** Maintain records of the activities of the mechanical licensing collective and engage in and respond to audits described in this subsection.

**(XIII)** Engage in such other activities as may be necessary or appropriate to fulfill the responsibilities of the mechanical licensing collective under this subsection.

**(ii) Restrictions concerning licensing and administrative activities.**—With respect to the administration of licenses, except as provided in clauses (i) and (iii) and subparagraph (E)(v), the mechanical licensing collective may only—

**(I)** issue blanket licenses pursuant to subsection (d)(1); and

**(II)** administer blanket licenses for reproduction or distribution rights in musical works for covered activities, including collecting and distributing royalties, pursuant to blanket licenses.

**(iii) Additional administrative activities.**—Subject to paragraph (11)(C), the mechanical licensing collective may also administer, including by collecting and distributing royalties, voluntary licenses issued by, or individual download licenses obtained from, copyright owners only for reproduction or distribution rights in musical works for covered activities, for which the mechanical licensing collective shall charge reasonable fees for such services.

**(iv) Restriction on lobbying.**—The mechanical licensing collective may not engage in government lobbying activities, but may engage in the activities described in subclauses (IX), (X), and (XI) of clause (i).

**(D) Governance.**—

61

**(i)  Board of directors.**—The mechanical licensing collective shall have a board of directors consisting of 14 voting members and 3 nonvoting members, as follows:

**(I)**  Ten voting members shall be representatives of music publishers—

**(aa)** to which songwriters have assigned exclusive rights of reproduction and distribution of musical works with respect to covered activities; and

**(bb)** none of which may be owned by, or under common control with, any other board member.

**(II)**  Four voting members shall be professional songwriters who have retained and exercise exclusive rights of reproduction and distribution with respect to covered activities with respect to musical works they have authored.

**(III)** One nonvoting member shall be a representative of the nonprofit trade association of music publishers that represents the greatest percentage of the licensor market for uses of musical works in covered activities, as measured for the 3-year period preceding the date on which the member is appointed.

**(IV)** One nonvoting member shall be a representative of the digital licensee coordinator, provided that a digital licensee coordinator has been designated pursuant to paragraph (5)(B). Otherwise, the nonvoting member shall be the nonprofit trade association of digital licensees that represents the greatest percentage of the licensee market for uses of musical works in covered activities, as measured over the preceding 3 full calendar years.

**(V)**  One nonvoting member shall be a representative of a nationally recognized nonprofit trade association whose primary mission is advocacy on behalf of songwriters in the United States.

**(ii)  Bylaws.**—

**(I)  Establishment.**—Not later than 1 year after the date on which the mechanical licensing collective is initially designated by the Register of Copyrights under subparagraph (B)(i), the collective shall establish bylaws to determine issues relating to the governance of the collective, including, but not limited to—

**(aa)** the length of the term for each member of the board of directors;

**(bb)** the staggering of the terms of the members of the board of directors;

**(cc)** a process for filling a seat on the board of directors that is vacated before the end of the term with respect to that seat;

**(dd)** a process for electing a member to the board of directors; and

**(ee)** a management structure for daily operation of the collective.

**(II)  Public availability.**—The mechanical licensing collective shall make the bylaws established under subclause (I) available to the public.

**(iii) Board meetings.**—The board of directors shall meet not less frequently than biannually and discuss matters pertinent to the operations of the mechanical licensing collective, including the mechanical licensing collective budget.

**(iv) Operations advisory committee.**—The board of directors of the mechanical licensing collective shall establish an operations advisory committee consisting of not fewer than 6 members to make recommendations to the board of directors concerning the operations of the mechanical licensing collective, including the efficient investment in and deployment of information technology and data resources. Such committee shall have an equal number of members of the committee who are—

(I)   musical work copyright owners who are appointed by the board of directors of the mechanical licensing collective; and

(II)   representatives of digital music providers who are appointed by the digital licensee coordinator.

**(v) Unclaimed royalties oversight committee.**—The board of directors of the mechanical licensing collective shall establish and appoint an unclaimed royalties oversight committee consisting of 10 members, 5 of which shall be musical work copyright owners and 5 of which shall be professional songwriters whose works are used in covered activities.

**(vi) Dispute resolution committee.**—The board of directors of the mechanical licensing collective shall establish and appoint a dispute resolution committee that shall—

(I)   consist of not fewer than 6 members; and

(II)   include an equal number of representatives of musical work copyright owners and professional songwriters.

**(vii) Mechanical licensing collective annual report.**—

(I)   **In general.**—Not later than June 30 of each year commencing after the license availability date, the mechanical licensing collective shall post, and make available online for a period of not less than 3 years, an annual report that sets forth information regarding—

(aa) the operational and licensing practices of the collective;

(bb) how royalties are collected and distributed;

(cc) budgeting and expenditures;

(dd) the collective total costs for the preceding calendar year;

(ee) the projected annual mechanical licensing collective budget;

(ff)  aggregated royalty receipts and payments;

(gg) expenses that are more than 10 percent of the annual mechanical licensing collective budget; and

(hh) the efforts of the collective to locate and identify copyright owners of unmatched musical works (and shares of works).

(II)   **Submission.**—On the date on which the mechanical licensing collective posts each report required under subclause (I), the collective shall provide a copy of the report to the Register of Copyrights.

**(viii) Independent officers.**—An individual serving as an officer of the mechanical licensing collective may not, at the same time, also be an employee or agent of any member of the board of directors of the collective or any entity represented by a member of the board of directors, as described in clause (i).

**(ix) Oversight and accountability.**—

(I)   **In general.**—The mechanical licensing collective shall—

(aa) ensure that the policies and practices of the collective are transparent and accountable;

(bb) identify a point of contact for publisher inquiries and complaints with timely redress; and

**(cc)** establish an anti-comingling policy for funds not collected under this section and royalties collected under this section.

**(II) Audits.—**

**(aa) In general.—**Beginning in the fourth full calendar year that begins after the initial designation of the mechanical licensing collective by the Register of Copyrights under subparagraph (B)(i), and in every fifth calendar year thereafter, the collective shall retain a qualified auditor that shall—

**(AA)** examine the books, records, and operations of the collective;

**(BB)** prepare a report for the board of directors of the collective with respect to the matters described in item (bb); and

**(CC)** not later than December 31 of the year in which the qualified auditor is retained, deliver the report described in subitem (BB) to the board of directors of the collective.

**(bb) Matters addressed.—**Each report prepared under item (aa) shall address the implementation and efficacy of procedures of the mechanical licensing collective—

**(AA)** for the receipt, handling, and distribution of royalty funds, including any amounts held as unclaimed royalties;

**(BB)** to guard against fraud, abuse, waste, and the unreasonable use of funds; and

**(CC)** to protect the confidentiality of financial, proprietary, and other sensitive information.

**(cc) Public availability.—**With respect to each report prepared under item (aa), the mechanical licensing collective shall—

**(AA)** submit the report to the Register of Copyrights; and

**(BB)** make the report available to the public.

**(E) Musical works database.—**

**(i) Establishment and maintenance of database.—**The mechanical licensing collective shall establish and maintain a database containing information relating to musical works (and shares of such works) and, to the extent known, the identity and location of the copyright owners of such works (and shares thereof) and the sound recordings in which the musical works are embodied. In furtherance of maintaining such database, the mechanical licensing collective shall engage in efforts to identify the musical works embodied in particular sound recordings, as well as to identify and locate the copyright owners of such works (and shares thereof), and update such data as appropriate.

**(ii) Matched works.—**With respect to musical works (and shares thereof) that have been matched to copyright owners, the musical works database shall include—

**(I)** the title of the musical work;

**(II)** the copyright owner of the work (or share thereof), and the ownership percentage of that owner;

**(III)** contact information for such copyright owner;

**(IV)** to the extent reasonably available to the mechanical licensing collective—

**(aa)** the international standard musical work code for the work; and

**(bb)** identifying information for sound recordings in which the musical work is embodied, including the name of the sound recording, featured artist, sound recording copyright owner, producer, international standard recording code, and other information commonly used to assist in associating sound recordings with musical works; and

**(V)** such other information as the Register of Copyrights may prescribe by regulation.

**(iii) Unmatched works.**—With respect to unmatched musical works (and shares of works) in the database, the musical works database shall include—

**(I)** to the extent reasonably available to the mechanical licensing collective—

**(aa)** the title of the musical work;

**(bb)** the ownership percentage for which an owner has not been identified;

**(cc)** if a copyright owner has been identified but not located, the identity of such owner and the ownership percentage of that owner;

**(dd)** identifying information for sound recordings in which the work is embodied, including sound recording name, featured artist, sound recording copyright owner, producer, international standard recording code, and other information commonly used to assist in associating sound recordings with musical works; and

**(ee)** any additional information reported to the mechanical licensing collective that may assist in identifying the work; and

**(II)** such other information relating to the identity and ownership of musical works (and shares of such works) as the Register of Copyrights may prescribe by regulation.

**(iv) Sound recording information.**—Each musical work copyright owner with any musical work listed in the musical works database shall engage in commercially reasonable efforts to deliver to the mechanical licensing collective, including for use in the musical works database, to the extent such information is not then available in the database, information regarding the names of the sound recordings in which that copyright owner's musical works (or shares thereof) are embodied, to the extent practicable.

**(v) Accessibility of database.**—The musical works database shall be made available to members of the public in a searchable, online format, free of charge. The mechanical licensing collective shall make such database available in a bulk, machine-readable format, through a widely available software application, to the following entities:

**(I)** Digital music providers operating under the authority of valid notices of license, free of charge.

**(II)** Significant nonblanket licensees in compliance with their obligations under paragraph (6), free of charge.

**(III)** Authorized vendors of the entities described in subclauses (I) and (II), free of charge.

**(IV)** The Register of Copyrights, free of charge (but the Register shall not treat such database or any information therein as a Government record).

**(V)** Any other person or entity for a fee not to exceed the marginal cost to the mechanical licensing collective of providing the database to such person or entity.

**(vi) Additional requirements.**—The Register of Copyrights shall establish requirements by regulations to ensure the usability, interoperability, and usage restrictions of the musical works database.

**(F) Notices of license and nonblanket activity.—**

**(i) Notices of licenses.**—The mechanical licensing collective shall receive, review, and confirm or reject notices of license from digital music providers, as provided in paragraph (2)(A). The collective shall maintain a current, publicly accessible list of blanket licenses that includes contact information for the licensees and the effective dates of such licenses.

**(ii) Notices of nonblanket activity.**—The mechanical licensing collective shall receive notices of nonblanket activity from significant nonblanket licensees, as provided in paragraph (6)(A). The collective shall maintain a current, publicly accessible list of notices of nonblanket activity that includes contact information for significant nonblanket licensees and the dates of receipt of such notices.

**(G) Collection and distribution of royalties.—**

**(i) In general.**—Upon receiving reports of usage and payments of royalties from digital music providers for covered activities, the mechanical licensing collective shall—

**(I)** engage in efforts to—

**(aa)** identify the musical works embodied in sound recordings reflected in such reports, and the copyright owners of such musical works (and shares thereof);

**(bb)** confirm uses of musical works subject to voluntary licenses and individual download licenses, and the corresponding pro rata amounts to be deducted from royalties that would otherwise be due under the blanket license; and

**(cc)** confirm proper payment of royalties due;

**(II)** distribute royalties to copyright owners in accordance with the usage and other information contained in such reports, as well as the ownership and other information contained in the records of the collective; and

**(III)** deposit into an interest-bearing account, as provided in subparagraph (H)(ii), royalties that cannot be distributed due to—

**(aa)** an inability to identify or locate a copyright owner of a musical work (or share thereof); or

**(bb)** a pending dispute before the dispute resolution committee of the mechanical licensing collective.

**(ii) Other collection efforts.**—Any royalties recovered by the mechanical licensing collective as a result of efforts to enforce rights or obligations under a blanket license, including through a bankruptcy proceeding or other legal action, shall be distributed to copyright owners based on available usage information and in accordance with the procedures described in subclauses (I) and (II) of clause (i), on a pro rata basis in proportion to the overall percentage recovery of the total royalties owed, with any pro rata share of royalties that cannot be distributed deposited in an interest-bearing account as provided in subparagraph (H)(ii).

**(H) Holding of accrued royalties.—**

**(i) Holding period.**—The mechanical licensing collective shall hold accrued royalties associated with particular musical works (and shares of works) that remain unmatched for a period of not less than 3 years after the date on which the funds were received by the mechanical licensing collective, or not less than 3 years after the date on which the funds were accrued by a digital music provider that subsequently transferred such funds to the mechanical licensing collective pursuant to paragraph (10)(B), whichever period expires sooner.

**(ii) Interest-bearing account.**—Accrued royalties for unmatched works (and shares thereof) shall be maintained by the mechanical licensing collective in an interest-bearing account that earns monthly interest—

**(I)** at the Federal, short-term rate; and

**(II)** that accrues for the benefit of copyright owners entitled to payment of such accrued royalties.

**(I) Musical works claiming process.**—When a copyright owner of an unmatched work (or share of a work) has been identified and located in accordance with the procedures of the mechanical licensing collective, the collective shall—

**(i)** update the musical works database and the other records of the collective accordingly; and

**(ii)** provided that accrued royalties for the musical work (or share thereof) have not yet been included in a distribution pursuant to subparagraph (J)(i), pay such accrued royalties and a proportionate amount of accrued interest associated with that work (or share thereof) to the copyright owner, accompanied by a cumulative statement of account reflecting usage of such work and accrued royalties based on information provided by digital music providers to the mechanical licensing collective.

**(J) Distribution of unclaimed accrued royalties.**—

**(i) Distribution procedures.**—After the expiration of the prescribed holding period for accrued royalties provided in subparagraph (H)(i), the mechanical licensing collective shall distribute such accrued royalties, along with a proportionate share of accrued interest, to copyright owners identified in the records of the collective, subject to the following requirements, and in accordance with the policies and procedures established under clause (ii):

**(I)** The first such distribution shall occur on or after January 1 of the second full calendar year to commence after the license availability date, with not less than 1 such distribution to take place during each calendar year thereafter.

**(II)** Copyright owners' payment shares for unclaimed accrued royalties for particular reporting periods shall be determined in a transparent and equitable manner based on data indicating the relative market shares of such copyright owners as reflected in reports of usage provided by digital music providers for covered activities for the periods in question, including, in addition to usage data provided to the mechanical licensing collective, usage data provided to copyright owners under voluntary licenses and individual download licenses for covered activities, to the extent such information is available to the mechanical licensing collective. In furtherance of the determination of equitable market shares under this subparagraph—

**(aa)** the mechanical licensing collective may require copyright owners seeking distributions of unclaimed accrued royalties to provide, or direct the provision of, information concerning the usage of musical works under voluntary licenses and individual download licenses for covered activities; and

**(bb)** the mechanical licensing collective shall take appropriate steps to safeguard the confidentiality and security of usage, financial, and other sensitive data used to compute market shares in accordance with the confidentiality provisions prescribed by the Register of Copyrights under paragraph (12)(C).

**(ii) Establishment of distribution policies.**—The unclaimed royalties oversight committee established under subparagraph (D)(v) shall establish policies and procedures for the distribution of unclaimed accrued royalties and accrued interest in accordance with this subparagraph, including the provision of usage data to copyright owners to allocate payments and credits to songwriters pursuant to clause (iv), subject to the approval of the board of directors of the mechanical licensing collective.

**(iii) Public notice of unclaimed accrued royalties.**—The mechanical licensing collective shall—

**(I)** maintain a publicly accessible online facility with contact information for the collective that lists unmatched musical works (and shares of works), through which a copyright owner may assert an ownership claim with respect to such a work (and a share of such a work);

**(II)** engage in diligent, good-faith efforts to publicize, throughout the music industry—

**(aa)** the existence of the collective and the ability to claim unclaimed accrued royalties for unmatched musical works (and shares of such works) held by the collective;

**(bb)** the procedures by which copyright owners may identify themselves and provide contact, ownership, and other relevant information to the collective in order to receive payments of accrued royalties;

**(cc)** any transfer of accrued royalties for musical works under paragraph (10)(B), not later than 180 days after the date on which the transfer is received; and

**(dd)** any pending distribution of unclaimed accrued royalties and accrued interest, not less than 90 days before the date on which the distribution is made; and

**(III)** as appropriate, participate in music industry conferences and events for the purpose of publicizing the matters described in subclause (II).

**(iv) Songwriter payments.**—Copyright owners that receive a distribution of unclaimed accrued royalties and accrued interest shall pay or credit a portion to songwriters (or the authorized agents of songwriters) on whose behalf the copyright owners license or administer musical works for covered activities, in accordance with applicable contractual terms, but notwithstanding any agreement to the contrary—

**(I)** such payments and credits to songwriters shall be allocated in proportion to reported usage of individual musical works by digital music providers during the reporting periods covered by the distribution from the mechanical licensing collective; and

**(II)** in no case shall the payment or credit to an individual songwriter be less than 50 percent of the payment received by the copyright owner attributable to usage of musical works (or shares of works) of that songwriter.

**(K) Dispute resolution.**—The dispute resolution committee established under subparagraph (D)(vi) shall establish policies and procedures—

**(i)** for copyright owners to address in a timely and equitable manner disputes relating to ownership interests in musical works licensed under this section and allocation and distribution of royalties by the mechanical licensing collective, subject to the approval of the board of directors of the mechanical licensing collective;

**(ii)** that shall include a mechanism to hold disputed funds in accordance with the requirements described in subparagraph (H)(ii) pending resolution of the dispute; and

**(iii)** except as provided in paragraph (11)(D), that shall not affect any legal or equitable rights or remedies available to any copyright owner or songwriter concerning ownership of, and entitlement to royalties for, a musical work.

**(L) Verification of payments by mechanical licensing collective.—**

**(i) Verification process.—**A copyright owner entitled to receive payments of royalties for covered activities from the mechanical licensing collective may, individually or with other copyright owners, conduct an audit of the mechanical licensing collective to verify the accuracy of royalty payments by the mechanical licensing collective to such copyright owner, as follows:

**(I)** A copyright owner may audit the mechanical licensing collective only once in a year for any or all of the 3 calendar years preceding the year in which the audit is commenced, and may not audit records for any calendar year more than once.

**(II)** The audit shall be conducted by a qualified auditor, who shall perform the audit during the ordinary course of business by examining the books, records, and data of the mechanical licensing collective, according to generally accepted auditing standards and subject to applicable confidentiality requirements prescribed by the Register of Copyrights under paragraph (12)(C).

**(III)** The mechanical licensing collective shall make such books, records, and data available to the qualified auditor and respond to reasonable requests for relevant information, and shall use commercially reasonable efforts to facilitate access to relevant information maintained by third parties.

**(IV)** To commence the audit, any copyright owner shall file with the Copyright Office a notice of intent to conduct an audit of the mechanical licensing collective, identifying the period of time to be audited, and shall simultaneously deliver a copy of such notice to the mechanical licensing collective. The Register of Copyrights shall cause the notice of audit to be published in the Federal Register not later than 45 calendar days after the date on which the notice is received.

**(V)** The qualified auditor shall determine the accuracy of royalty payments, including whether an underpayment or overpayment of royalties was made by the mechanical licensing collective to each auditing copyright owner, except that, before providing a final audit report to any such copyright owner, the qualified auditor shall provide a tentative draft of the report to the mechanical licensing collective and allow the mechanical licensing collective a reasonable opportunity to respond to the findings, including by clarifying issues and correcting factual errors.

**(VI)** The auditing copyright owner or owners shall bear the cost of the audit. In case of an underpayment to any copyright owner, the mechanical licensing collective shall pay the amounts of any such underpayment to such auditing copyright owner, as appropriate. In case of an overpayment by the mechanical licensing collective, the mechanical licensing collective may debit the account of the auditing copyright owner or owners for such overpaid amounts, or such owner or owners shall refund overpaid amounts to the mechanical licensing collective, as appropriate.

**(ii) Alternative verification procedures.**—Nothing in this subparagraph shall preclude a copyright owner and the mechanical licensing collective from agreeing to audit procedures different from those described in this subparagraph, except that a notice of the audit shall be provided to and published by the Copyright Office as described in clause (i)(IV).

**(M) Records of mechanical licensing collective.**—

**(i) Records maintenance.**—The mechanical licensing collective shall ensure that all material records of the operations of the mechanical licensing collective, including those relating to notices of license, the administration of the claims process of the mechanical licensing collective, reports of usage, royalty payments, receipt and maintenance of accrued royalties, royalty distribution processes, and legal matters, are preserved and maintained in a secure and reliable manner, with appropriate commercially reasonable safeguards against unauthorized access, copying, and disclosure, and subject to the confidentiality requirements prescribed by the Register of Copyrights under paragraph (12)(C) for a period of not less than 7 years after the date of creation or receipt, whichever occurs later.

**(ii) Records access.**—The mechanical licensing collective shall provide prompt access to electronic and other records pertaining to the administration of a copyright owner's musical works upon reasonable written request of the owner or the authorized representative of the owner.

**(4) Terms and conditions of blanket license.**—A blanket license is subject to, and conditioned upon, the following requirements:

**(A) Royalty reporting and payments.**—

**(i) Monthly reports and payment.**—A digital music provider shall report and pay royalties to the mechanical licensing collective under the blanket license on a monthly basis in accordance with clause (ii) and subsection (c)(2)(I), except that the monthly reporting shall be due on the date that is 45 calendar days, rather than 20 calendar days, after the end of the monthly reporting period.

**(ii) Data to be reported.**—In reporting usage of musical works to the mechanical licensing collective, a digital music provider shall provide usage data for musical works used under the blanket license and usage data for musical works used in covered activities under voluntary licenses and individual download licenses. In the report of usage, the digital music provider shall—

**(I)** with respect to each sound recording embodying a musical work—

**(aa)** provide identifying information for the sound recording, including sound recording name, featured artist, and, to the extent acquired by the digital music provider in connection with its use of sound recordings of musical works to engage in covered activities, including pursuant to subparagraph (B), sound recording copyright owner, producer, international standard recording code, and other information commonly used in the industry to identify sound recordings and match them to the musical works the sound recordings embody;

**(bb)** to the extent acquired by the digital music provider in the metadata provided by sound recording copyright owners or other licensors of sound recordings in connection with the use of sound recordings of musical works to engage in covered activities, including pursuant to subparagraph (B), provide information concerning authorship and ownership of the applicable rights in the musical work embodied in the sound recording (including each songwriter, publisher name, and respective ownership share) and the international standard musical work code; and

**(cc)** provide the number of digital phonorecord deliveries of the sound recording, including limited downloads and interactive streams;

**(II)** identify and provide contact information for all musical work copyright owners for works embodied in sound recordings as to which a voluntary license, rather than the blanket license, is in effect with respect to the uses being reported; and

**(III)** provide such other information as the Register of Copyrights shall require by regulation.

**(iii) Format and maintenance of reports.**—Reports of usage provided by digital music providers to the mechanical licensing collective shall be in a machine-readable format that is compatible with the information technology systems of the mechanical licensing collective and meets the requirements of regulations adopted by the Register of Copyrights. The Register shall also adopt regulations setting forth requirements under which records of use shall be maintained and made available to the mechanical licensing collective by digital music providers engaged in covered activities under a blanket license.

**(iv) Adoption of regulations.**—The Register of Copyrights shall adopt regulations—

**(I)** setting forth requirements under which records of use shall be maintained and made available to the mechanical licensing collective by digital music providers engaged in covered activities under a blanket license; and

**(II)** regarding adjustments to reports of usage by digital music providers, including mechanisms to account for overpayment and underpayment of royalties in prior periods.

**(B) Collection of sound recording information.**—A digital music provider shall engage in good-faith, commercially reasonable efforts to obtain from sound recording copyright owners and other licensors of sound recordings made available through the service of such digital music provider information concerning—

**(i)** sound recording copyright owners, producers, international standard recording codes, and other information commonly used in the industry to identify sound recordings and match them to the musical works the sound recordings embody; and

**(ii)** the authorship and ownership of musical works, including songwriters, publisher names, ownership shares, and international standard musical work codes.

**(C) Payment of administrative assessment.**—A digital music provider and any significant nonblanket licensee shall pay the administrative assessment established under paragraph (7)(D) in accordance with this subsection and applicable regulations.

**(D) Verification of payments by digital music providers.**—

**(i) Verification process.**—The mechanical licensing collective may conduct an audit of a digital music provider operating under the blanket license to verify the accuracy of royalty payments by the digital music provider to the mechanical licensing collective as follows:

**(I)** The mechanical licensing collective may commence an audit of a digital music provider not more frequently than once in any 3-calendar-year period to cover a verification period of not more than the 3 full calendar years preceding the date of commencement of the audit, and such audit may not audit records for any such 3-year verification period more than once.

71

**(II)** The audit shall be conducted by a qualified auditor, who shall perform the audit during the ordinary course of business by examining the books, records, and data of the digital music provider, according to generally accepted auditing standards and subject to applicable confidentiality requirements prescribed by the Register of Copyrights under paragraph (12)(C).

**(III)** The digital music provider shall make such books, records, and data available to the qualified auditor and respond to reasonable requests for relevant information, and shall use commercially reasonable efforts to provide access to relevant information maintained with respect to a digital music provider by third parties.

**(IV)** To commence the audit, the mechanical licensing collective shall file with the Copyright Office a notice of intent to conduct an audit of the digital music provider, identifying the period of time to be audited, and shall simultaneously deliver a copy of such notice to the digital music provider. The Register of Copyrights shall cause the notice of audit to be published in the Federal Register not later than 45 calendar days after the date on which notice is received.

**(V)** The qualified auditor shall determine the accuracy of royalty payments, including whether an underpayment or overpayment of royalties was made by the digital music provider to the mechanical licensing collective, except that, before providing a final audit report to the mechanical licensing collective, the qualified auditor shall provide a tentative draft of the report to the digital music provider and allow the digital music provider a reasonable opportunity to respond to the findings, including by clarifying issues and correcting factual errors.

**(VI)** The mechanical licensing collective shall pay the cost of the audit, unless the qualified auditor determines that there was an underpayment by the digital music provider of not less than 10 percent, in which case the digital music provider shall bear the reasonable costs of the audit, in addition to paying the amount of any underpayment to the mechanical licensing collective. In case of an overpayment by the digital music provider, the mechanical licensing collective shall provide a credit to the account of the digital music provider.

**(VII)** A digital music provider may not assert section 507 or any other Federal or State statute of limitations, doctrine of laches or estoppel, or similar provision as a defense to a legal action arising from an audit under this subparagraph if such legal action is commenced not more than 6 years after the commencement of the audit that is the basis for such action.

**(ii) Alternative verification procedures.**—Nothing in this subparagraph shall preclude the mechanical licensing collective and a digital music provider from agreeing to audit procedures different from those described in this subparagraph, except that a notice of the audit shall be provided to and published by the Copyright Office as described in clause (i)(IV).

**(E) Default under blanket license.**—

**(i) Conditions of default.**—A digital music provider shall be in default under a blanket license if the digital music provider—

**(I)** fails to provide 1 or more monthly reports of usage to the mechanical licensing collective when due;

**(II)** fails to make a monthly royalty or late fee payment to the mechanical licensing collective when due, in all or material part;

(III) provides 1 or more monthly reports of usage to the mechanical licensing collective that, on the whole, is or are materially deficient as a result of inaccurate, missing, or unreadable data, where the correct data was available to the digital music provider and required to be reported under this section and applicable regulations;

(IV) fails to pay the administrative assessment as required under this subsection and applicable regulations; or

(V) after being provided written notice by the mechanical licensing collective, refuses to comply with any other material term or condition of the blanket license under this section for a period of not less than 60 calendar days.

(ii) **Notice of default and termination.**—In case of a default by a digital music provider, the mechanical licensing collective may proceed to terminate the blanket license of the digital music provider as follows:

(I) The mechanical licensing collective shall provide written notice to the digital music provider describing with reasonable particularity the default and advising that unless such default is cured not later than 60 calendar days after the date of the notice, the blanket license will automatically terminate at the end of that period.

(II) If the digital music provider fails to remedy the default before the end of the 60-day period described in subclause (I), the license shall terminate without any further action on the part of the mechanical licensing collective. Such termination renders the making of all digital phonorecord deliveries of all musical works (and shares thereof) covered by the blanket license for which the royalty or administrative assessment has not been paid actionable as acts of infringement under section 501 and subject to the remedies provided by sections 502 through 506.

(iii) **Notice to copyright owners.**—The mechanical licensing collective shall provide written notice of any termination under this subparagraph to copyright owners of affected works.

(iv) **Review by Federal district court.**—A digital music provider that believes a blanket license was improperly terminated by the mechanical licensing collective may seek review of such termination in an appropriate district court of the United States. The district court shall determine the matter de novo based on the record before the mechanical licensing collective and any additional supporting evidence presented by the parties.

(5) **Digital licensee coordinator.**—

(A) **In general.**—The digital licensee coordinator shall be a single entity that—

(i) is a nonprofit, not owned by any other entity, that is created to carry out responsibilities under this subsection;

(ii) is endorsed by and enjoys substantial support from digital music providers and significant nonblanket licensees that together represent the greatest percentage of the licensee market for uses of musical works in covered activities, as measured over the preceding 3 calendar years;

(iii) is able to demonstrate that it has, or will have prior to the license availability date, the administrative capabilities to perform the required functions of the digital licensee coordinator under this subsection; and

(iv) has been designated by the Register of Copyrights, with the approval of the Librarian of Congress pursuant to section 702, in accordance with subparagraph (B).

**(B) Designation of digital licensee coordinator.—**

**(i) Initial designation.**—The Register of Copyrights shall initially designate the digital licensee coordinator not later than 270 days after the enactment date, in accordance with the same procedure described for designation of the mechanical licensing collective in paragraph (3)(B)(i).

**(ii) Periodic review of designation.**—Following the initial designation of the digital licensee coordinator, the Register of Copyrights shall, every 5 years, beginning with the fifth full calendar year to commence after the initial designation, determine whether the existing designation should be continued, or a different entity meeting the criteria described in clauses (i) through (iii) of subparagraph (A) should be designated, in accordance with the same procedure described for the mechanical licensing collective in paragraph (3)(B)(ii).

**(iii) Inability to designate.**—If the Register of Copyrights is unable to identify an entity that fulfills each of the qualifications described in clauses (i) through (iii) of subparagraph (A) to serve as the digital licensee coordinator, the Register may decline to designate a digital licensee coordinator. The determination of the Register not to designate a digital licensee coordinator shall not negate or otherwise affect any provision of this subsection except to the limited extent that a provision references the digital licensee coordinator. In such case, the reference to the digital licensee coordinator shall be without effect unless and until a new digital licensee coordinator is designated.

**(C) Authorities and functions.—**

**(i) In general.**—The digital licensee coordinator is authorized to perform the following functions, subject to more particular requirements as described in this subsection:

**(I)** Establish a governance structure, criteria for membership, and any dues to be paid by its members.

**(II)** Engage in efforts to enforce notice and payment obligations with respect to the administrative assessment, including by receiving information from and coordinating with the mechanical licensing collective.

**(III)** Initiate and participate in proceedings before the Copyright Royalty Judges to establish the administrative assessment under this subsection.

**(IV)** Initiate and participate in proceedings before the Copyright Office with respect to activities under this subsection.

**(V)** Gather and provide documentation for use in proceedings before the Copyright Royalty Judges to set rates and terms under this section.

**(VI)** Maintain records of its activities.

**(VII)** Assist in publicizing the existence of the mechanical licensing collective and the ability of copyright owners to claim royalties for unmatched musical works (and shares of works) through the collective.

**(VIII)** Engage in such other activities as may be necessary or appropriate to fulfill its responsibilities under this subsection.

**(ii) Restriction on lobbying.**—The digital licensee coordinator may not engage in government lobbying activities, but may engage in the activities described in subclauses (III), (IV), and (V) of clause (i).

**(iii) Assistance with publicity for unclaimed royalties.**—The digital licensee coordinator shall make reasonable, good-faith efforts to assist the mechanical licensing collective in the efforts of the collective to locate and identify copyright owners of unmatched musical works (and shares of such works) by encouraging digital music providers to publicize the existence of the collective and the ability of copyright owners to claim unclaimed accrued royalties, including by—

    **(I)** posting contact information for the collective at reasonably prominent locations on digital music provider websites and applications; and

    **(II)** conducting in-person outreach activities with songwriters.

**(6) Requirements for significant nonblanket licensees.—**

**(A) In general.—**

    **(i) Notice of activity.**—Not later than 45 calendar days after the license availability date, or 45 calendar days after the end of the first full calendar month in which an entity initially qualifies as a significant nonblanket licensee, whichever occurs later, a significant nonblanket licensee shall submit a notice of nonblanket activity to the mechanical licensing collective. The notice of nonblanket activity shall comply in form and substance with requirements that the Register of Copyrights shall establish by regulation, and a copy shall be made available to the digital licensee coordinator.

    **(ii) Reporting and payment obligations.**—The notice of nonblanket activity submitted to the mechanical licensing collective shall be accompanied by a report of usage that contains the information described in paragraph (4)(A)(ii), as well as any payment of the administrative assessment required under this subsection and applicable regulations. Thereafter, subject to clause (iii), a significant nonblanket licensee shall continue to provide monthly reports of usage, accompanied by any required payment of the administrative assessment, to the mechanical licensing collective. Such reports and payments shall be submitted not later than 45 calendar days after the end of the calendar month being reported.

    **(iii) Discontinuation of obligations.**—An entity that has submitted a notice of nonblanket activity to the mechanical licensing collective that has ceased to qualify as a significant nonblanket licensee may so notify the collective in writing. In such case, as of the calendar month in which such notice is provided, such entity shall no longer be required to provide reports of usage or pay the administrative assessment, but if such entity later qualifies as a significant nonblanket licensee, such entity shall again be required to comply with clauses (i) and (ii).

**(B) Reporting by mechanical licensing collective to digital licensee coordinator.—**

    **(i) Monthly reports of noncompliant licensees.**—The mechanical licensing collective shall provide monthly reports to the digital licensee coordinator setting forth any significant nonblanket licensees of which the collective is aware that have failed to comply with subparagraph (A).

    **(ii) Treatment of confidential information.**—The mechanical licensing collective and digital licensee coordinator shall take appropriate steps to safeguard the confidentiality and security of financial and other sensitive data shared under this subparagraph, in accordance with the confidentiality requirements prescribed by the Register of Copyrights under paragraph (12)(C).

**(C) Legal enforcement efforts.—**

    **(i) Federal court action.**—Should the mechanical licensing collective or digital licensee coordinator become aware that a significant nonblanket licensee has failed to comply with subparagraph (A), either may commence an action in an appropriate district court of the United States for damages and injunctive relief. If the significant nonblanket licensee is found liable, the court shall, absent a finding of excusable neglect, award damages in an amount equal to three times the total amount of the unpaid administrative assessment and, notwithstanding anything to the contrary in section 505, reasonable attorney's fees and costs, as well as such other relief as the court determines appropriate. In all other cases, the court shall award relief as appropriate. Any recovery of damages shall be payable to the mechanical licensing collective as an offset to the collective total costs.

**(ii) Statute of limitations for enforcement action.**—Any action described in this subparagraph shall be commenced within the time period described in section 507(b).

**(iii) Other rights and remedies preserved.**—The ability of the mechanical licensing collective or digital licensee coordinator to bring an action under this subparagraph shall in no way alter, limit or negate any other right or remedy that may be available to any party at law or in equity.

**(7) Funding of mechanical licensing collective.**—

**(A) In general.**—The collective total costs shall be funded by—

**(i)** an administrative assessment, as such assessment is established by the Copyright Royalty Judges pursuant to subparagraph (D) from time to time, to be paid by—

**(I)** digital music providers that are engaged, in all or in part, in covered activities pursuant to a blanket license; and

**(II)** significant nonblanket licensees; and

**(ii)** voluntary contributions from digital music providers and significant nonblanket licensees as may be agreed with copyright owners.

**(B) Voluntary contributions.**—

**(i) Agreements concerning contributions.**—Except as provided in clause (ii), voluntary contributions by digital music providers and significant nonblanket licensees shall be determined by private negotiation and agreement, and the following conditions apply:

**(I)** The date and amount of each voluntary contribution to the mechanical licensing collective shall be documented in a writing signed by an authorized agent of the mechanical licensing collective and the contributing party.

**(II)** Such agreement shall be made available as required in proceedings before the Copyright Royalty Judges to establish or adjust the administrative assessment in accordance with applicable statutory and regulatory provisions and rulings of the Copyright Royalty Judges.

**(ii) Treatment of contributions.**—Each voluntary contribution described in clause (i) shall be treated for purposes of an administrative assessment proceeding as an offset to the collective total costs that would otherwise be recovered through the administrative assessment. Any allocation or reallocation of voluntary contributions between or among individual digital music providers or significant nonblanket licensees shall be a matter of private negotiation and agreement among such parties and outside the scope of the administrative assessment proceeding.

**(C) Interim application of accrued royalties.**—In the event that the administrative assessment, together with any funding from voluntary contributions as provided in subparagraphs (A) and (B), is inadequate to cover current collective total costs, the collective, with approval of its board of directors, may apply unclaimed accrued royalties on an interim basis to defray such costs, subject to future reimbursement of such royalties from future collections of the assessment.

**(D) Determination of administrative assessment.—**

**(i) Administrative assessment to cover collective total costs.**—The administrative assessment shall be used solely and exclusively to fund the collective total costs.

**(ii) Separate proceeding before Copyright Royalty Judges.**—The amount and terms of the administrative assessment shall be determined and established in a separate and independent proceeding before the Copyright Royalty Judges, according to the procedures described in clauses (iii) and (iv). The administrative assessment determined in such proceeding shall—

**(I)** be wholly independent of royalty rates and terms applicable to digital music providers, which shall not be taken into consideration in any manner in establishing the administrative assessment;

**(II)** be established by the Copyright Royalty Judges in an amount that is calculated to defray the reasonable collective total costs;

**(III)** be assessed based on usage of musical works by digital music providers and significant nonblanket licensees in covered activities under both compulsory and nonblanket licenses;

**(IV)** may be in the form of a percentage of royalties payable under this section for usage of musical works in covered activities (regardless of whether a different rate applies under a voluntary license), or any other usage-based metric reasonably calculated to equitably allocate the collective total costs across digital music providers and significant nonblanket licensees engaged in covered activities, and shall include as a component a minimum fee for all digital music providers and significant nonblanket licensees; and

**(V)** take into consideration anticipated future collective total costs and collections of the administrative assessment, including, as applicable—

**(aa)** any portion of past actual collective total costs of the mechanical licensing collective not funded by previous collections of the administrative assessment or voluntary contributions because such collections or contributions together were insufficient to fund such costs;

**(bb)** any past collections of the administrative assessment and voluntary contributions that exceeded past actual collective total costs, resulting in a surplus; and

**(cc)** the amount of any voluntary contributions by digital music providers or significant nonblanket licensees in relevant periods, described in subparagraphs (A) and (B) of paragraph (7).

**(iii) Initial administrative assessment.**—The procedure for establishing the initial administrative assessment shall be as follows:

**(I)** Not later than 270 days after the enactment date, the Copyright Royalty Judges shall commence a proceeding to establish the initial administrative assessment by publishing a notice in the Federal Register seeking petitions to participate.

**(II)** The mechanical licensing collective and digital licensee coordinator shall participate in the proceeding described in subclause (I), along with any interested copyright owners, digital music providers or significant nonblanket licensees that have notified the Copyright Royalty Judges of their desire to participate.

**(III)** The Copyright Royalty Judges shall establish a schedule for submission by the parties of information that may be relevant to establishing the administrative assessment, including actual and anticipated collective total costs of the mechanical licensing collective, actual and anticipated collections from digital music providers and significant nonblanket licensees, and documentation of voluntary contributions, as well as a schedule for further proceedings, which shall include a hearing, as the Copyright Royalty Judges determine appropriate.

**(IV)** The initial administrative assessment shall be determined, and such determination shall be published in the Federal Register by the Copyright Royalty Judges, not later than 1 year after commencement of the proceeding described in this clause. The determination shall be supported by a written record. The initial administrative assessment shall be effective as of the license availability date, and shall continue in effect unless and until an adjusted administrative assessment is established pursuant to an adjustment proceeding under clause (iv).

**(iv) Adjustment of administrative assessment.**—The administrative assessment may be adjusted by the Copyright Royalty Judges periodically, in accordance with the following procedures:

**(I)** Not earlier than 1 year after the most recent publication of a determination of the administrative assessment by the Copyright Royalty Judges, the mechanical licensing collective, the digital licensee coordinator, or one or more interested copyright owners, digital music providers, or significant nonblanket licensees, may file a petition with the Copyright Royalty Judges in the month of May to commence a proceeding to adjust the administrative assessment.

**(II)** Notice of the commencement of such proceeding shall be published in the Federal Register in the month of June following the filing of any petition, with a schedule of requested information and additional proceedings, as described in clause (iii)(III). The mechanical licensing collective and digital licensee coordinator shall participate in such proceeding, along with any interested copyright owners, digital music providers, or significant nonblanket licensees that have notified the Copyright Royalty Judges of their desire to participate.

**(III)** The determination of the adjusted administrative assessment, which shall be supported by a written record, shall be published in the Federal Register during June of the calendar year following the commencement of the proceeding. The adjusted administrative assessment shall take effect January 1 of the year following such publication.

**(v) Adoption of voluntary agreements.**—In lieu of reaching their own determination based on evaluation of relevant data, the Copyright Royalty Judges shall approve and adopt a negotiated agreement to establish the amount and terms of the administrative assessment that has been agreed to by the mechanical licensing collective and the digital licensee coordinator (or if none has been designated, interested digital music providers and significant nonblanket licensees representing more than half of the market for uses of musical works in covered activities), except that the Copyright Royalty Judges shall have the discretion to reject any such agreement for good cause shown. An administrative assessment adopted under this clause shall apply to all digital music providers and significant nonblanket licensees engaged in covered activities during the period the administrative assessment is in effect.

**(vi) Continuing authority to amend.**—The Copyright Royalty Judges shall retain continuing authority to amend a determination of an administrative assessment to correct technical or clerical errors, or modify the terms of implementation, for good cause, with any such amendment to be published in the Federal Register.

**(vii) Appeal of administrative assessment.**—The determination of an administrative assessment by the Copyright Royalty Judges shall be appealable, not later than 30 calendar days after publication in the Federal Register, to the Court of Appeals for the District of Columbia Circuit by any party that fully participated in the proceeding. The administrative assessment as established by the Copyright Royalty Judges shall remain in effect pending the final outcome of any such appeal, and the mechanical licensing collective, digital licensee coordinator, digital music providers, and significant nonblanket licensees shall implement appropriate financial or other measures not later than 90 days after any modification of the assessment to reflect and account for such outcome.

**(viii) Regulations.**—The Copyright Royalty Judges may adopt regulations to govern the conduct of proceedings under this paragraph.

(8) **Establishment of rates and terms under blanket license.**—

**(A) Restrictions on ratesetting participation.**—Neither the mechanical licensing collective nor the digital licensee coordinator shall be a party to a proceeding described in subsection (c)(1)(E), except that the mechanical licensing collective or the digital licensee coordinator may gather and provide financial and other information for the use of a party to such a proceeding and comply with requests for information as required under applicable statutory and regulatory provisions and rulings of the Copyright Royalty Judges.

**(B) Application of late fees.**—In any proceeding described in subparagraph (A) in which the Copyright Royalty Judges establish a late fee for late payment of royalties for uses of musical works under this section, such fee shall apply to covered activities under blanket licenses, as follows:

**(i)** Late fees for past due royalty payments shall accrue from the due date for payment until payment is received by the mechanical licensing collective.

**(ii)** The availability of late fees shall in no way prevent a copyright owner or the mechanical licensing collective from asserting any other rights or remedies to which such copyright owner or the mechanical licensing collective may be entitled under this title.

**(C) Interim rate agreements in general.**—For any covered activity for which no rate or terms have been established by the Copyright Royalty Judges, the mechanical licensing collective and any digital music provider may agree to an interim rate and terms for such activity under the blanket license, and any such rate and terms—

**(i)** shall be treated as nonprecedential and not cited or relied upon in any ratesetting proceeding before the Copyright Royalty Judges or any other tribunal; and

**(ii)** shall automatically expire upon the establishment of a rate and terms for such covered activity by the Copyright Royalty Judges, under subsection (c)(1)(E).

**(D) Adjustments for interim rates.**—The rate and terms established by the Copyright Royalty Judges for a covered activity to which an interim rate and terms have been agreed under subparagraph (C) shall supersede the interim rate and terms and apply retroactively to the inception of the activity under the blanket license. In such case, not later than 90 days after the effective date of the rate and terms established by the Copyright Royalty Judges—

**(i)** if the rate established by the Copyright Royalty Judges exceeds the interim rate, the digital music provider shall pay to the mechanical licensing collective the amount of any underpayment of royalties due; or

**(ii)** if the interim rate exceeds the rate established by the Copyright Royalty Judges, the mechanical licensing collective shall credit the account of the digital music provider for the amount of any overpayment of royalties due.

**(9) Transition to blanket licenses.—**

**(A) Substitution of blanket license.—**On the license availability date, a blanket license shall, without any interruption in license authority enjoyed by such digital music provider, be automatically substituted for and supersede any existing compulsory license previously obtained under this section by the digital music provider from a copyright owner to engage in 1 or more covered activities with respect to a musical work, except that such substitution shall not apply to any authority obtained from a record company pursuant to a compulsory license to make and distribute permanent downloads unless and until such record company terminates such authority in writing to take effect at the end of a monthly reporting period, with a copy to the mechanical licensing collective.

**(B) Expiration of existing licenses.—**Except to the extent provided in subparagraph (A), on and after the license availability date, licenses other than individual download licenses obtained under this section for covered activities prior to the license availability date shall no longer continue in effect.

**(C) Treatment of voluntary licenses.—**A voluntary license for a covered activity in effect on the license availability date will remain in effect unless and until the voluntary license expires according to the terms of the voluntary license, or the parties agree to amend or terminate the voluntary license. In a case where a voluntary license for a covered activity entered into before the license availability date incorporates the terms of this section by reference, the terms so incorporated (but not the rates) shall be those in effect immediately prior to the license availability date, and those terms shall continue to apply unless and until such voluntary license is terminated or amended, or the parties enter into a new voluntary license.

**(D) Further acceptance of notices for covered activities by Copyright Office.—**On and after the enactment date—

    **(i)** the Copyright Office shall no longer accept notices of intention with respect to covered activities; and

    **(ii)** notices of intention filed before the enactment date will no longer be effective or provide license authority with respect to covered activities, except that, before the license availability date, there shall be no liability under section 501 for the reproduction or distribution of a musical work (or share thereof) in covered activities if a valid notice of intention was filed for such work (or share) before the enactment date.

**(10) Prior unlicensed uses.—**

**(A) Limitation on liability in general.—**A copyright owner that commences an action under section 501 on or after January 1, 2018, against a digital music provider for the infringement of the exclusive rights provided by paragraph (1) or (3) of section 106 arising from the unauthorized reproduction or distribution of a musical work by such digital music provider in the course of engaging in covered activities prior to the license availability date, shall, as the copyright owner's sole and exclusive remedy against the digital music provider, be eligible to recover the royalty prescribed under subsection (c)(1)(C) and chapter 8, from the digital music provider, provided that such digital music provider can demonstrate compliance with the requirements of subparagraph (B), as applicable. In all other cases the limitation on liability under this subparagraph shall not apply.

**(B) Requirements for limitation on liability.—**The following requirements shall apply on the enactment date and through the end of the period that expires 90 days after the license availability date to digital music providers seeking to avail themselves of the limitation on liability described in subparagraph (A):

    **(i)** Not later than 30 calendar days after first making a particular sound recording of a musical work available through its service via one or more covered activities, or 30 calendar days after the enactment date, whichever occurs later, a digital music provider shall engage in good-faith, commercially reasonable efforts to identify and locate each copyright owner of such musical work (or share thereof). Such required matching efforts shall include the following:

**(I)** Good-faith, commercially reasonable efforts to obtain from the owner of the corresponding sound recording made available through the digital music provider's service the following information:

**(aa)** Sound recording name, featured artist, sound recording copyright owner, producer, international standard recording code, and other information commonly used in the industry to identify sound recordings and match them to the musical works they embody.

**(bb)** Any available musical work ownership information, including each songwriter and publisher name, percentage ownership share, and international standard musical work code.

**(II)** Employment of 1 or more bulk electronic matching processes that are available to the digital music provider through a third-party vendor on commercially reasonable terms, except that a digital music provider may rely on its own bulk electronic matching process if that process has capabilities comparable to or better than those available from a third-party vendor on commercially reasonable terms.

**(ii)** The required matching efforts shall be repeated by the digital music provider not less than once per month for so long as the copyright owner remains unidentified or has not been located.

**(iii)** If the required matching efforts are successful in identifying and locating a copyright owner of a musical work (or share thereof) by the end of the calendar month in which the digital music provider first makes use of the work, the digital music provider shall provide statements of account and pay royalties to such copyright owner in accordance with this section and applicable regulations.

**(iv)** If the copyright owner is not identified or located by the end of the calendar month in which the digital music provider first makes use of the work, the digital music provider shall accrue and hold royalties calculated under the applicable statutory rate in accordance with usage of the work, from initial use of the work until the accrued royalties can be paid to the copyright owner or are required to be transferred to the mechanical licensing collective, as follows:

**(I)** Accrued royalties shall be maintained by the digital music provider in accordance with generally accepted accounting principles.

**(II)** If a copyright owner of an unmatched musical work (or share thereof) is identified and located by or to the digital music provider before the license availability date, the digital music provider shall—

**(aa)** not later than 45 calendar days after the end of the calendar month during which the copyright owner was identified and located, pay the copyright owner all accrued royalties, such payment to be accompanied by a cumulative statement of account that includes all of the information that would have been provided to the copyright owner had the digital music provider been providing monthly statements of account to the copyright owner from initial use of the work in accordance with this section and applicable regulations, including the requisite certification under subsection (c)(2)(I);

**(bb)** beginning with the accounting period following the calendar month in which the copyright owner was identified and located, and for all other accounting periods prior to the license availability date, provide monthly statements of account and pay royalties to the copyright owner as required under this section and applicable regulations; and

**(cc)** beginning with the monthly royalty reporting period commencing on the license availability date, report usage and pay royalties for such musical work (or share thereof) for such reporting period and reporting periods thereafter to the mechanical licensing collective, as required under this subsection and applicable regulations.

**(III)** If a copyright owner of an unmatched musical work (or share thereof) is not identified and located by the license availability date, the digital music provider shall—

**(aa)** not later than 45 calendar days after the license availability date, transfer all accrued royalties to the mechanical licensing collective, such payment to be accompanied by a cumulative statement of account that includes all of the information that would have been provided to the copyright owner had the digital music provider been serving monthly statements of account on the copyright owner from initial use of the work in accordance with this section and applicable regulations, including the requisite certification under subsection (c)(2)(I), and accompanied by an additional certification by a duly authorized officer of the digital music provider that the digital music provider has fulfilled the requirements of clauses (i) and (ii) of subparagraph (B) but has not been successful in locating or identifying the copyright owner; and

**(bb)** beginning with the monthly royalty reporting period commencing on the license availability date, report usage and pay royalties for such musical work (or share thereof) for such period and reporting periods thereafter to the mechanical licensing collective, as required under this subsection and applicable regulations.

**(v)** A digital music provider that complies with the requirements of this subparagraph with respect to unmatched musical works (or shares of works) shall not be liable for or accrue late fees for late payments of royalties for such works until such time as the digital music provider is required to begin paying monthly royalties to the copyright owner or the mechanical licensing collective, as applicable.

**(C) Adjusted statute of limitations.**—Notwithstanding anything to the contrary in section 507(b), with respect to any claim of infringement of the exclusive rights provided by paragraphs (1) and (3) of section 106 against a digital music provider arising from the unauthorized reproduction or distribution of a musical work by such digital music provider in the course of engaging in covered activities that accrued not more than 3 years prior to the license availability date, such action may be commenced not later than the later of—

**(i)** 3 years after the date on which the claim accrued; or

**(ii)** 2 years after the license availability date.

**(D) Other rights and remedies preserved.**—Except as expressly provided in this paragraph, nothing in this paragraph shall be construed to alter, limit, or negate any right or remedy of a copyright owner with respect to unauthorized use of a musical work.

**(11) Legal protections for licensing activities.**—

**(A) Exemption for compulsory license activities.**—The antitrust exemption described in subsection (c)(1)(D) shall apply to negotiations and agreements between and among copyright owners and persons entitled to obtain a compulsory license for covered activities, and common agents acting on behalf of such copyright owners or persons, including with respect to the administrative assessment established under this subsection.

**(B) Limitation on common agent exemption.**—Notwithstanding the antitrust exemption provided in subsection (c)(1)(D) and subparagraph (A) of this paragraph (except for the administrative assessment referenced in such subparagraph (A) and except as provided in paragraph (8)(C)), neither the mechanical licensing collective nor the digital licensee coordinator shall serve as a common agent with respect to the establishment of royalty rates or terms under this section.

**(C) Antitrust exemption for administrative activities.**—Notwithstanding any provision of the antitrust laws, copyright owners and persons entitled to obtain a compulsory license under this section may designate the mechanical licensing collective to administer voluntary licenses for the reproduction or distribution of musical works in covered activities on behalf of such copyright owners and persons, subject to the following conditions:

**(i)** Each copyright owner shall establish the royalty rates and material terms of any such voluntary license individually and not in agreement, combination, or concert with any other copyright owner.

**(ii)** Each person entitled to obtain a compulsory license under this section shall establish the royalty rates and material terms of any such voluntary license individually and not in agreement, combination, or concert with any other digital music provider.

**(iii)** The mechanical licensing collective shall maintain the confidentiality of the voluntary licenses in accordance with the confidentiality provisions prescribed by the Register of Copyrights under paragraph (12)(C).

**(D) Liability for good-faith activities.**—The mechanical licensing collective shall not be liable to any person or entity based on a claim arising from its good-faith administration of policies and procedures adopted and implemented to carry out the responsibilities described in subparagraphs (J) and (K) of paragraph (3), except to the extent of correcting an underpayment or overpayment of royalties as provided in paragraph (3)(L)(i)(VI), but the collective may participate in a legal proceeding as a stakeholder party if the collective is holding funds that are the subject of a dispute between copyright owners. For purposes of this subparagraph, the term "good-faith administration" means administration in a manner that is not grossly negligent.

**(E) Preemption of State property laws.**—The holding and distribution of funds by the mechanical licensing collective in accordance with this subsection shall supersede and preempt any State law (including common law) concerning escheatment or abandoned property, or any analogous provision, that might otherwise apply.

**(F) Rule of construction.**—Except as expressly provided in this subsection, nothing in this subsection shall negate or limit the ability of any person to pursue an action in Federal court against the mechanical licensing collective or any other person based upon a claim arising under this title or other applicable law.

**(12) Regulations.**—

**(A) Adoption by Register of Copyrights and Copyright Royalty Judges.**—The Register of Copyrights may conduct such proceedings and adopt such regulations as may be necessary or appropriate to effectuate the provisions of this subsection, except for regulations concerning proceedings before the Copyright Royalty Judges to establish the administrative assessment, which shall be adopted by the Copyright Royalty Judges.

(B) **Judicial review of regulations.**—Except as provided in paragraph (7)(D)(vii), regulations adopted under this subsection shall be subject to judicial review pursuant to chapter 7 of title 5.

(C) **Protection of confidential information.**—The Register of Copyrights shall adopt regulations to provide for the appropriate procedures to ensure that confidential, private, proprietary, or privileged information contained in the records of the mechanical licensing collective and digital licensee coordinator is not improperly disclosed or used, including through any disclosure or use by the board of directors or personnel of either entity, and specifically including the unclaimed royalties oversight committee and the dispute resolution committee of the mechanical licensing collective.

(13) **Savings clauses.**—

(A) **Limitation on activities and rights covered.**—This subsection applies solely to uses of musical works subject to licensing under this section. The blanket license shall not be construed to extend or apply to activities other than covered activities or to rights other than the exclusive rights of reproduction and distribution licensed under this section, or serve or act as the basis to extend or expand the compulsory license under this section to activities and rights not covered by this section on the day before the enactment date.

(B) **Rights of public performance not affected.**—The rights, protections, and immunities granted under this subsection, the data concerning musical works collected and made available under this subsection, and the definitions under subsection (e) shall not extend to, limit, or otherwise affect any right of public performance in a musical work.

(e) **Definitions.**—As used in this section:

(1) **Accrued interest.**—The term "accrued interest" means interest accrued on accrued royalties, as described in subsection (d)(3)(H)(ii).

(2) **Accrued royalties.**—The term "accrued royalties" means royalties accrued for the reproduction or distribution of a musical work (or share thereof) in a covered activity, calculated in accordance with the applicable royalty rate under this section.

(3) **Administrative assessment.**—The term "administrative assessment" means the fee established pursuant to subsection (d)(7)(D).

(4) **Audit.**—The term "audit" means a royalty compliance examination to verify the accuracy of royalty payments, or the conduct of such an examination, as applicable.

(5) **Blanket license.**—The term "blanket license" means a compulsory license described in subsection (d)(1)(A) to engage in covered activities.

(6) **Collective total costs.**—The term "collective total costs"—

(A) means the total costs of establishing, maintaining, and operating the mechanical licensing collective to fulfill its statutory functions, including—

(i) startup costs;

(ii) financing, legal, audit, and insurance costs;

(iii) investments in information technology, infrastructure, and other long-term resources;

(iv) outside vendor costs;

(v) costs of licensing, royalty administration, and enforcement of rights;

(vi) costs of bad debt; and

(vii) costs of automated and manual efforts to identify and locate copyright owners of musical works (and shares of such musical works) and match sound recordings to the musical works the sound recordings embody; and

**(B)** does not include any added costs incurred by the mechanical licensing collective to provide services under voluntary licenses.

**(7) Covered activity.**—The term "covered activity" means the activity of making a digital phonorecord delivery of a musical work, including in the form of a permanent download, limited download, or interactive stream, where such activity qualifies for a compulsory license under this section.

**(8) Digital music provider.**—The term "digital music provider" means a person (or persons operating under the authority of that person) that, with respect to a service engaged in covered activities—

**(A)** has a direct contractual, subscription, or other economic relationship with end users of the service, or, if no such relationship with end users exists, exercises direct control over the provision of the service to end users;

**(B)** is able to fully report on any revenues and consideration generated by the service; and

**(C)** is able to fully report on usage of sound recordings of musical works by the service (or procure such reporting).

**(9) Digital licensee coordinator.**—The term "digital licensee coordinator" means the entity most recently designated pursuant to subsection (d)(5).

**(10) Digital phonorecord delivery.**—The term "digital phonorecord delivery" means each individual delivery of a phonorecord by digital transmission of a sound recording that results in a specifically identifiable reproduction by or for any transmission recipient of a phonorecord of that sound recording, regardless of whether the digital transmission is also a public performance of the sound recording or any musical work embodied therein, and includes a permanent download, a limited download, or an interactive stream. A digital phonorecord delivery does not result from a real-time, noninteractive subscription transmission of a sound recording where no reproduction of the sound recording or the musical work embodied therein is made from the inception of the transmission through to its receipt by the transmission recipient in order to make the sound recording audible. A digital phonorecord delivery does not include the digital transmission of sounds accompanying a motion picture or other audiovisual work as defined in section 101.

**(11) Enactment date.**—The term "enactment date" means the date of the enactment of the Musical Works Modernization Act.

**(12) Individual download license.**—The term "individual download license" means a compulsory license obtained by a record company to make and distribute, or authorize the making and distribution of, permanent downloads embodying a specific individual musical work.

**(13) Interactive stream.**—The term "interactive stream" means a digital transmission of a sound recording of a musical work in the form of a stream, where the performance of the sound recording by means of such transmission is not exempt under section 114(d)(1) and does not in itself, or as a result of a program in which it is included, qualify for statutory licensing under section 114(d)(2). An interactive stream is a digital phonorecord delivery.

**(14) Interested.**—The term "interested", as applied to a party seeking to participate in a proceeding under subsection (d)(7)(D), is a party as to which the Copyright Royalty Judges have not determined that the party lacks a significant interest in such proceeding.

**(15) License availability date.**—The term "license availability date" means January 1 following the expiration of the 2-year period beginning on the enactment date.

**(16) Limited download.**—The term "limited download" means a digital transmission of a sound recording of a musical work in the form of a download, where such sound recording is accessible for listening only for a limited amount of time or specified number of times.

**(17) Matched.**—The term "matched", as applied to a musical work (or share thereof), means that the copyright owner of such work (or share thereof) has been identified and located.

**(18) Mechanical licensing collective.**—The term "mechanical licensing collective" means the entity most recently designated as such by the Register of Copyrights under subsection (d)(3).

**(19) Mechanical licensing collective budget.**—The term "mechanical licensing collective budget" means a statement of the financial position of the mechanical licensing collective for a fiscal year or quarter thereof based on estimates of expenditures during the period and proposals for financing those expenditures, including a calculation of the collective total costs.

**(20) Musical works database.**—The term "musical works database" means the database described in subsection (d)(3)(E).

**(21) Nonprofit.**—The term "nonprofit" means a nonprofit created or organized in a State.

**(22) Notice of license.**—The term "notice of license" means a notice from a digital music provider provided under subsection (d)(2)(A) for purposes of obtaining a blanket license.

**(23) Notice of nonblanket activity.**—The term "notice of nonblanket activity" means a notice from a significant nonblanket licensee provided under subsection (d)(6)(A) for purposes of notifying the mechanical licensing collective that the licensee has been engaging in covered activities.

**(24) Permanent download.**—The term "permanent download" means a digital transmission of a sound recording of a musical work in the form of a download, where such sound recording is accessible for listening without restriction as to the amount of time or number of times it may be accessed.

**(25) Qualified auditor.**—The term "qualified auditor" means an independent, certified public accountant with experience performing music royalty audits.

**(26) Record company.**—The term "record company" means an entity that invests in, produces, and markets sound recordings of musical works, and distributes such sound recordings for remuneration through multiple sales channels, including a corporate affiliate of such an entity engaged in distribution of sound recordings.

**(27) Report of usage.**—The term "report of usage" means a report reflecting an entity's usage of musical works in covered activities described in subsection (d)(4)(A).

**(28) Required matching efforts.**—The term "required matching efforts" means efforts to identify and locate copyright owners of musical works as described in subsection (d)(10)(B)(i).

**(29) Service.**—The term "service", as used in relation to covered activities, means any site, facility, or offering by or through which sound recordings of musical works are digitally transmitted to members of the public.

**(30) Share.**—The term "share", as applied to a musical work, means a fractional ownership interest in such work.

**(31) Significant nonblanket licensee.**—The term "significant nonblanket licensee"—

   **(A)** means an entity, including a group of entities under common ownership or control that, acting under the authority of one or more voluntary licenses or individual download licenses, offers a service engaged in covered activities, and such entity or group of entities—

      **(i)** is not currently operating under a blanket license and is not obligated to provide reports of usage reflecting covered activities under subsection (d)(4)(A);

**(ii)** has a direct contractual, subscription, or other economic relationship with end users of the service or, if no such relationship with end users exists, exercises direct control over the provision of the service to end users; and

**(iii)** either—

**(I)** on any day in a calendar month, makes more than 5,000 different sound recordings of musical works available through such service; or

**(II)** derives revenue or other consideration in connection with such covered activities greater than $50,000 in a calendar month, or total revenue or other consideration greater than $500,000 during the preceding 12 calendar months; and

**(B)** does not include—

**(i)** an entity whose covered activity consists solely of free-to-the-user streams of segments of sound recordings of musical works that do not exceed 90 seconds in length, are offered only to facilitate a licensed use of musical works that is not a covered activity, and have no revenue directly attributable to such streams constituting the covered activity; or

**(ii)** a "public broadcasting entity" as defined in section 118(f).

**(32) Songwriter.**—The term "songwriter" means the author of all or part of a musical work, including a composer or lyricist.

**(33) State.**—The term "State" means each State of the United States, the District of Columbia, and each territory or possession of the United States.

**(34) Unclaimed accrued royalties.**—The term "unclaimed accrued royalties" means accrued royalties eligible for distribution under subsection (d)(3)(J).

**(35) Unmatched.**—The term "unmatched", as applied to a musical work (or share thereof), means that the copyright owner of such work (or share thereof) has not been identified or located.

**(36) Voluntary license.**—The term "voluntary license" means a license for use of a musical work (or share thereof) other than a compulsory license obtained under this section.

(As amended, Pub.L. 98–450, 98 Stat. 1727 (1984); Pub.L. 104–39, 109 Stat. 336 (1995); Pub.L. 105–80, Stat. 1529 (1997); Pub.L. 108–419, 118 Stat. 2341 (2004); Pub.L. 109–303, 120 Stat. 1478 (2006); Pub.L. 110–403, 122 Stat. 4256 (2008); Pub.L. 115–264, 132 Stat. 3676 (2018)).

## Sec. 116.    Negotiated Licenses for Public Performances by Means of Coin-Operated Phonorecord Players

**(a) Applicability of Section.**—This section applies to any nondramatic musical work embodied in a phonorecord.

**(b) Negotiated Licenses.—**

**(1) Authority for Negotiations.**—Any owners of copyright in works to which this section applies and any operators of coin-operated phonorecord players may negotiate and agree upon the terms and rates of royalty payments for the performance of such works and the proportionate division of fees paid among copyright owners, and may designate common agents to negotiate, agree to, pay, or receive such royalty payments.

**(2) Chapter 8 Proceeding.**—Parties not subject to such a negotiation may have the terms and rates and the division of fees described in paragraph (1) determined in a proceeding in accordance with the provisions of chapter 8.

**(c) License Agreements Superior to Determinations by Copyright Royalty Judges.—** License agreements between one or more copyright owners and one or more operators of coin-operated phonorecord players, which are negotiated in accordance with subsection (b), shall be given effect in lieu of any otherwise applicable determination by the Copyright Royalty Judges.

    (d)  **Definitions.**—As used in this section, the following terms mean the following:

      (1)  A "coin-operated phonorecord player" is a machine or device that—

        (A)  is employed solely for the performance of nondramatic musical works by means of phonorecords upon being activated by the insertion of coins, currency, tokens, or other monetary units or their equivalent;

        (B)  is located in an establishment making no direct or indirect charge for admission;

        (C)  is accompanied by a list which is comprised of the titles of all the musical works available for performance on it, and is affixed to the phonorecord player or posted in the establishment in a prominent position where it can be readily examined by the public; and

        (D)  affords a choice of works available for performance and permits the choice to be made by the patrons of the establishment in which it is located.

      (2)  An "operator" is any person who, alone or jointly with others—

        (A)  owns a coin-operated phonorecord player;

        (B)  has the power to make a coin-operated phonorecord player available for placement in an establishment for purposes of public performance; or

        (C)  has the power to exercise primary control over the selection of the musical works made available for public performance on a coin-operated phonorecord player.

(Added by Pub.L. 100–568, 102 Stat. 2853 (1988); as amended, Pub.L. 103–198, 107 Stat. 2304 (1993); Pub.L. 105–80, 111 Stat. 1529 (1997); Pub.L. 108–419, 118 Stat. 2341 (2004)).

## Sec. 117.    Limitations on Exclusive Rights: Computer Programs

    (a)  **Making of Additional Copy or Adaptation by Owner of Copy.**—Notwithstanding the provisions of section 106, it is not an infringement for the owner of a copy of a computer program to make or authorize the making of another copy or adaptation of that computer program provided:

      (1)  that such a new copy or adaptation is created as an essential step in the utilization of the computer program in conjunction with a machine and that it is used in no other manner, or

      (2)  that such new copy or adaptation is for archival purposes only and that all archival copies are destroyed in the event that continued possession of the computer program should cease to be rightful.

    (b)  **Leases, Sale, or Other Transfer of Additional Copy or Adaptation.**—Any exact copies prepared in accordance with the provisions of this section may be leased, sold, or otherwise transferred, along with the copy from which such copies were prepared, only as part of the lease, sale, or other transfer of all rights in the program. Adaptations so prepared may be transferred only with the authorization of the copyright owner.

    (c)  **Machine Maintenance or Repair.**—Notwithstanding the provisions of section 106, it is not an infringement for the owner or lessee of a machine to make or authorize the making of a copy of a computer program if such copy is made solely by virtue of the activation of a machine that lawfully contains an authorized copy of the computer program, for purposes only of maintenance or repair of that machine, if—

      (1)  such new copy is used in no other manner and is destroyed immediately after the maintenance or repair is completed; and

(2)   with respect to any computer program or part thereof that is not necessary for that machine to be activated, such program or part thereof is not accessed or used other than to make such new copy by virtue of the activation of the machine.

(d)   **Definitions.**—For purposes of this section—

(1)   the "maintenance" of a machine is the servicing of the machine in order to make it work in accordance with its original specifications and any changes to those specifications authorized for that machine; and

(2)   the "repair" of a machine is the restoring of the machine to the state of working in accordance with its original specifications and any changes to those specifications authorized for that machine.

(As amended, Pub.L. 96–517, 94 Stat. 3028 (1980); Pub.L. 105–304, 112 Stat. 2860 (1998)).

## Sec. 118.    Scope of Exclusive Rights: Use of Certain Works in Connection With Noncommercial Broadcasting

(a)   The exclusive rights provided by section 106 shall, with respect to the works specified by subsection (b) and the activities specified by subsection (d), be subject to the conditions and limitations prescribed by this section.

(b)   Notwithstanding any provision of the antitrust laws, any owners of copyright in published nondramatic musical works and published pictorial, graphic, and sculptural works and any public broadcasting entities, respectively, may negotiate and agree upon the terms and rates of royalty payments and the proportionate division of fees paid among various copyright owners, and may designate common agents to negotiate, agree to, pay, or receive payments.

(1)   Any owner of copyright in a work specified in this subsection or any public broadcasting entity may submit to the Copyright Royalty Judges proposed licenses covering such activities with respect to such works.

(2)   License agreements voluntarily negotiated at any time between one or more copyright owners and one or more public broadcasting entities shall be given effect in lieu of any determination by the Librarian of Congress or the Copyright Royalty Judges, if copies of such agreements are filed with the Copyright Royalty Judges within 30 days of execution in accordance with regulations that the Copyright Royalty Judges shall issue.

(3)   Voluntary negotiation proceedings initiated pursuant to a petition filed under section 804(a) for the purpose of determining a schedule of terms and rates of royalty payments by public broadcasting entities to owners of copyright in works specified by this subsection and the proportionate division of fees paid among various copyright owners shall cover the 5-year period beginning on January 1 of the second year following the year in which the petition is filed. The parties to each negotiation proceeding shall bear their own costs. In establishing such rates and terms the Copyright Royalty Judges may consider the rates for comparable circumstances under voluntary license agreements negotiated as provided in paragraph (2) or (3). The Copyright Royalty Judges shall also establish requirements by which copyright owners may receive reasonable notice of the use of their works under this section, and under which records of such use shall be kept by public broadcasting entities.

(4)   In the absence of license agreements negotiated under paragraph (2) or (3), the Copyright Royalty Judges shall, pursuant to chapter 8, conduct a proceeding to determine and publish in the Federal Register a schedule of rates and terms which, subject to paragraph (2), shall be binding on all owners of copyright in works specified by this subsection and public broadcasting entities, regardless of whether such copyright owners have submitted proposals to the Copyright Royalty Judges.

(c)   Subject to the terms of any voluntary license agreements that have been negotiated as provided by subsection (b)(2) or (3), a public broadcasting entity may, upon compliance with the provisions of this section, including the rates and terms established by the Copyright Royalty Judges under subsection (b)(4), engage in the following activities with respect to published nondramatic musical works and published pictorial, graphic, and sculptural works:

(1)   performance or display of a work by or in the course of a transmission made by a noncommercial educational broadcast station referred to in subsection (f); and

(2)   production of a transmission program, reproduction of copies or phonorecords of such a transmission program, and distribution of such copies or phonorecords, where such production, reproduction, or distribution is made by a nonprofit institution or organization solely for the purpose of transmissions specified in paragraph (1); and

(3)   the making of reproductions by a governmental body or a nonprofit institution of a transmission program simultaneously with its transmission as specified in paragraph (1), and the performance or display of the contents of such program under the conditions specified by paragraph (1) of section 110, but only if the reproductions are used for performances or displays for a period of no more than seven days from the date of the transmission specified in paragraph (1), and are destroyed before or at the end of such period. No person supplying, in accordance with paragraph (2), a reproduction of a transmission program to governmental bodies or nonprofit institutions under this paragraph shall have any liability as a result of failure of such body or institution to destroy such reproduction: *Provided,* That it shall have notified such body or institution of the requirement for such destruction pursuant to this paragraph: *And provided further,* That if such body or institution itself fails to destroy such reproduction it shall be deemed to have infringed.

(d)   Except as expressly provided in this subsection, this section shall have no applicability to works other than those specified in subsection (b). Owners of copyright in nondramatic literary works and public broadcasting entities may, during the course of voluntary negotiations, agree among themselves, respectively, as to the terms and rates of royalty payments without liability under the antitrust laws. Any such terms and rates of royalty payments shall be effective upon filing with the Copyright Royalty Judges, in accordance with regulations that the Copyright Royalty Judges shall prescribe as provided in section 803(b)(6).

(e)   Nothing in this section shall be construed to permit, beyond the limits of fair use as provided by section 107, the unauthorized dramatization of a nondramatic musical work, the production of a transmission program drawn to any substantial extent from a published compilation of pictorial, graphic, or sculptural works, or the unauthorized use of any portion of an audiovisual work.

(f)   As used in this section, the term "public broadcasting entity" means a noncommercial educational broadcast station as defined in section 397 of title 47 and any nonprofit institution or organization engaged in the activities described in paragraph (2) of subsection (c).

(As amended, Pub.L. 103–198, 107 Stat. 2304 (1993); Pub.L. 106–44, 113 Stat. 223 (1999); Pub.L. 108–419, 118 Stat. 2341 (2004); Pub.L. 109–303, 120 Stat. 1478 (2006)).

## Sec. 119.   Limitations on Exclusive Rights: Secondary Transmissions of Distant Television Programming by Satellite

### (a)   Secondary transmissions by satellite carriers.—

**(1)   Non-network stations.**—Subject to the provisions of paragraphs (3), (4), and (6) of this subsection and section 114(d), secondary transmissions of a performance or display of a work embodied in a primary transmission made by a non-network station shall be subject to statutory licensing under this section if the secondary transmission is made by a satellite carrier to the public for private home viewing or for viewing in a commercial establishment, with regard to secondary transmissions the satellite carrier is in compliance with the rules, regulations, or authorizations of the Federal

Communications Commission governing the carriage of television broadcast station signals, and the carrier makes a direct or indirect charge for each retransmission service to each subscriber receiving the secondary transmission or to a distributor that has contracted with the carrier for direct or indirect delivery of the secondary transmission to the public for private home viewing or for viewing in a commercial establishment.

**(2) Network stations.—**

**(A) In general.—**Subject to the provisions of subparagraph (B) of this paragraph and paragraphs (3), (4), (5), and (6) of this subsection and section 114(d), secondary transmissions of a performance or display of a work embodied in a primary transmission made by a network station shall be subject to statutory licensing under this section if the secondary transmission is made by a satellite carrier to the public for private home viewing, with regard to secondary transmissions the satellite carrier is in compliance with the rules, regulations, or authorizations of the Federal Communications Commission governing the carriage of television broadcast station signals, the carrier makes a direct or indirect charge for such retransmission service to each subscriber receiving the secondary transmission, and the carrier provides local-into-local service to all DMAs. Failure to reach an agreement with a network station to retransmit the signals of the station shall not be construed to affect compliance with providing local-into-local service to all DMAs if the satellite carrier has the capability to retransmit such signals when an agreement is reached.

**(B) Secondary transmissions to unserved households.—**

**(i) In general.—**The statutory license provided for in subparagraph (A) shall be limited to secondary transmissions of the signals of no more than two network stations in a single day for each television network to persons who reside in unserved households.

**(ii) Short Markets.—**In the case of secondary transmissions to households located in short markets, subject to clause (i), the statutory license shall be further limited to secondary transmissions of only those primary transmissions of network stations that embody the programming of networks not offered on the primary stream or the multicast stream transmitted by any network station in that market.

**(C) Submission of subscriber lists to networks.—**

**(i) Initial lists.—**A satellite carrier that makes secondary transmissions of a primary transmission made by a network station pursuant to subparagraph (A) shall, not later than 90 days after commencing such secondary transmissions, submit to the network that owns or is affiliated with the network station a list identifying (by name and address, including street or rural route number, city, State, and 9-digit zip code) all subscribers to which the satellite carrier makes secondary transmissions of that primary transmission to subscribers in unserved households.

**(ii) Monthly lists.—**After the submission of the initial lists under clause (i), the satellite carrier shall, not later than the 15th of each month, submit to the network a list, aggregated by designated market area, identifying (by name and address, including street or rural route number, city, State, and 9-digit zip code) any persons who have been added or dropped as subscribers under clause (i) since the last submission under this subparagraph.

**(iii) Use of subscriber information.—**Subscriber information submitted by a satellite carrier under this subparagraph may be used only for purposes of monitoring compliance by the satellite carrier with this subsection.

**(iv) Applicability.—**The submission requirements of this subparagraph shall apply to a satellite carrier only if the network to which the submissions are to be made places on file with the Register of Copyrights a document identifying the name and address of the person to whom such submissions are to be made. The Register shall maintain for public inspection a file of all such documents.

**(3) Noncompliance with reporting and payment requirements.**—Notwithstanding the provisions of paragraphs (1) and (2), the willful or repeated secondary transmission to the public by a satellite carrier of a primary transmission made by a superstation or a network station and embodying a performance or display of a work is actionable as an act of infringement under section 501, and is fully subject to the remedies provided by sections 502 through 506, where the satellite carrier has not deposited the statement of account and royalty fee required by subsection (b), or has failed to make the submissions to networks required by paragraph (2)(C).

**(4) Willful alterations.**—Notwithstanding the provisions of paragraphs (1) and (2), the secondary transmission to the public by a satellite carrier of a performance or display of a work embodied in a primary transmission made by a non-network station or a network station is actionable as an act of infringement under section 501, and is fully subject to the remedies provided by sections 502 through 506 and section 510, if the content of the particular program in which the performance or display is embodied, or any commercial advertising or station announcement transmitted by the primary transmitter during, or immediately before or after, the transmission of such program, is in any way willfully altered by the satellite carrier through changes, deletions, or additions, or is combined with programming from any other broadcast signal.

**(5) Violation of territorial restrictions on statutory license for network stations.**—

**(A) Individual violations.**—The willful or repeated secondary transmission by a satellite carrier of a primary transmission made by a network station and embodying a performance or display of a work to a subscriber who is not eligible to receive the transmission under this section is actionable as an act of infringement under section 501 and is fully subject to the remedies provided by sections 502 through 506, except that—

(i) no damages shall be awarded for such act of infringement if the satellite carrier took corrective action by promptly withdrawing service from the ineligible subscriber, and

(ii) any statutory damages shall not exceed $250 for such subscriber for each month during which the violation occurred.

**(B) Pattern of violations.**—If a satellite carrier engages in a willful or repeated pattern or practice of delivering a primary transmission made by a network station and embodying a performance or display of a work to subscribers who are not eligible to receive the transmission under this section, then in addition to the remedies set forth in subparagraph (A)—

(i) if the pattern or practice has been carried out on a substantially nationwide basis, the court shall order a permanent injunction barring the secondary transmission by the satellite carrier, for private home viewing, of the primary transmissions of any primary network station affiliated with the same network, and the court may order statutory damages of not to exceed $2,500,000 for each 3-month period during which the pattern or practice was carried out; and

(ii) if the pattern or practice has been carried out on a local or regional basis, the court shall order a permanent injunction barring the secondary transmission, for private home viewing in that locality or region, by the satellite carrier of the primary transmissions of any primary network station affiliated with the same network, and the court may order statutory damages of not to exceed $2,500,000 for each 6-month period during which the pattern or practice was carried out.

The court shall direct one half of any statutory damages ordered under clause (i) to be deposited with the Register of Copyrights for distribution to copyright owners pursuant to subsection (b). The Copyright Royalty Judges shall issue regulations establishing procedures for distributing such funds, on a proportional basis, to copyright owners whose works were included in the secondary transmissions that were the subject of the statutory damages.

**(C)  Previous subscribers excluded.**—Subparagraphs (A) and (B) do not apply to secondary transmissions by a satellite carrier to persons who subscribed to receive such secondary transmissions from the satellite carrier or a distributor before November 16, 1988.

**(D)  Burden of proof.**—In any action brought under this paragraph, the satellite carrier shall have the burden of proving that its secondary transmission of a primary transmission by a network station is to a subscriber who is eligible to receive the secondary transmission under this section.

**(6)  Discrimination by a satellite carrier.**—Notwithstanding the provisions of paragraph (1), the willful or repeated secondary transmission to the public by a satellite carrier of a performance or display of a work embodied in a primary transmission made by a superstation or a network station is actionable as an act of infringement under section 501, and is fully subject to the remedies provided by sections 502 through 506, if the satellite carrier unlawfully discriminates against a distributor.

**(7)  Geographic limitation on secondary transmissions.**—The statutory license created by this section shall apply only to secondary transmissions to households located in the United States.

**(8)  Service to recreational vehicles and commercial trucks.**—

**(A)  Exemption.**—

**(i)  In general.**—For purposes of this subsection, and subject to clauses (ii) and (iii), the term "unserved household" shall include—

**(I)**  recreational vehicles as defined in regulations of the Secretary of Housing and Urban Development under section 3282.8 of title 24, Code of Federal Regulations; and

**(II)**  commercial trucks that qualify as commercial motor vehicles under regulations of the Secretary of Transportation under section 383.5 of title 49, Code of Federal Regulations.

**(ii)  Limitation.**—Clause (i) shall apply only to a recreational vehicle or commercial truck if any satellite carrier that proposes to make a secondary transmission of a network station to the operator of such a recreational vehicle or commercial truck complies with the documentation requirements under subparagraphs (B) and (C).

**(iii)  Exclusion.**—For purposes of this subparagraph, the terms "recreational vehicle" and "commercial truck" shall not include any fixed dwelling, whether a mobile home or otherwise.

**(B)  Documentation requirements.**—A recreational vehicle or commercial truck shall be deemed to be an unserved household beginning 10 days after the relevant satellite carrier provides to the network that owns or is affiliated with the network station that will be secondarily transmitted to the recreational vehicle or commercial truck the following documents:

**(i)  Declaration.**—A signed declaration by the operator of the recreational vehicle or commercial truck that the satellite dish is permanently attached to the recreational vehicle or commercial truck, and will not be used to receive satellite programming at any fixed dwelling.

**(ii)  Registration.**—In the case of a recreational vehicle, a copy of the current State vehicle registration for the recreational vehicle.

**(iii)  Registration and license.**—In the case of a commercial truck, a copy of—

**(I)**  the current State vehicle registration for the truck; and

**(II)**  a copy of a valid, current commercial driver's license, as defined in regulations of the Secretary of Transportation under section 383 of title 49, Code of Federal Regulations, issued to the operator.

(C) **Updated documentation requirements.**—If a satellite carrier wishes to continue to make secondary transmissions to a recreational vehicle or commercial truck for more than a 2-year period, that carrier shall provide each network, upon request, with updated documentation in the form described under subparagraph (B) during the 90 days before expiration of that 2-year period.

**(9) Statutory license contingent on compliance with FCC rules and remedial steps.**—Notwithstanding any other provision of this section, the willful or repeated secondary transmission to the public by a satellite carrier of a primary transmission embodying a performance or display of a work made by a broadcast station licensed by the Federal Communications Commission is actionable as an act of infringement under section 501, and is fully subject to the remedies provided by sections 502 through 506, if, at the time of such transmission, the satellite carrier is not in compliance with the rules, regulations, and authorizations of the Federal Communications Commission concerning the carriage of television broadcast station signals.

**(10) Restricted transmission of out-of-State distant network signals into certain markets.**—

(A) **Out-of-State network affiliates.**—Notwithstanding any other provision of this title, the statutory license in this subsection and subsection (b) shall not apply to any secondary transmission of the primary transmission of a network station located outside of the State of Alaska to any subscriber in that State to whom the secondary transmission of the primary transmission of a television station located in that State is made available by the satellite carrier pursuant to section 122.

(B) **Exception.**—The limitation in subparagraph (A) shall not apply to the secondary transmission of the primary transmission of a digital signal of a network station located outside of the State of Alaska if at the time that the secondary transmission is made, no television station licensed to a community in the State and affiliated with the same network makes primary transmissions of a digital signal.

**(b) Statutory license for secondary transmissions.**—

**(1) Deposits of statements and fees; verification procedures.**—A satellite carrier whose secondary transmissions are subject to statutory licensing under subsection (a) shall, on a semiannual basis, deposit with the Register of Copyrights, in accordance with requirements that the Register shall prescribe by regulation—

(A) a statement of account, covering the preceding 6-month period, specifying the names and locations of all non-network stations and network stations whose signals were retransmitted, at any time during that period, to subscribers as described in subsections (a)(1) and (a)(2), the total number of subscribers that received such retransmissions, and such other data as the Register of Copyrights may from time to time prescribe by regulation;

(B) a royalty fee payable to copyright owners pursuant to paragraph (4) for that 6-month period, computed by multiplying the total number of subscribers receiving each secondary transmission of a primary stream or multicast stream of each non-network station or network station during each calendar year month by the appropriate rate in effect under this subsection; and

(C) a filing fee, as determined by the Register of Copyrights pursuant to section 708(a).

**(2) Verification of accounts and fee payments.**—The Register of Copyrights shall issue regulations to permit interested parties to verify and audit the statements of account and royalty fees submitted by satellite carriers under this subsection.

**(3) Investment of fees.**—The Register of Copyrights shall receive all fees (including the fee specified in paragraph (1)(C)) deposited under this section and, after deducting the reasonable costs incurred by the Copyright Office under this section (other than the costs deducted under

94

paragraph (5)), shall deposit the balance in the Treasury of the United States, in such manner as the Secretary of the Treasury directs. All funds held by the Secretary of the Treasury shall be invested in interest-bearing securities of the United States for later distribution with interest by the Librarian of Congress as provided by this title.

**(4) Persons to whom fees are distributed.**—The royalty fees deposited under paragraph (3) shall, in accordance with the procedures provided by paragraph (5), be distributed to those copyright owners whose works were included in a secondary transmission made by a satellite carrier during the applicable 6-month accounting period and who file a claim with the Copyright Royalty Judges under paragraph (5).

**(5) Procedures for distribution.**—The royalty fees deposited under paragraph (3) shall be distributed in accordance with the following procedures:

**(A) Filing of claims for fees.**—During the month of July in each year, each person claiming to be entitled to statutory license fees for secondary transmissions shall file a claim with the Copyright Royalty Judges, in accordance with requirements that the Copyright Royalty Judges shall prescribe by regulation. For purposes of this paragraph, any claimants may agree among themselves as to the proportionate division of statutory license fees among them, may lump their claims together and file them jointly or as a single claim, or may designate a common agent to receive payment on their behalf.

**(B) Determination of controversy; distributions.**—After the first day of August of each year, the Copyright Royalty Judges shall determine whether there exists a controversy concerning the distribution of royalty fees. If the Copyright Royalty Judges determine that no such controversy exists, the Copyright Royalty Judges shall authorize the Librarian of Congress to proceed to distribute such fees to the copyright owners entitled to receive them, or to their designated agents, subject to the deduction of reasonable administrative costs under this section. If the Copyright Royalty Judges find the existence of a controversy, the Copyright Royalty Judges shall, pursuant to chapter 8 of this title, conduct a proceeding to determine the distribution of royalty fees.

**(C) Withholding of fees during controversy.**—During the pendency of any proceeding under this subsection, the Copyright Royalty Judges shall have the discretion to authorize the Librarian of Congress to proceed to distribute any amounts that are not in controversy.

**(c) Adjustment of royalty fees.**—

**(1) Applicability and determination of royalty fees for signals.**—

**(A) Initial fee.**—The appropriate fee for purposes of determining the royalty fee under subsection (b)(1)(B) for the secondary transmission of the primary transmissions of network stations and non-network stations shall be the appropriate fee set forth in part 258 of title 37, Code of Federal Regulations, as in effect on July 1, 2009, as modified under this paragraph.

**(B) Fee set by voluntary negotiation.**—On or before June 1, 2010, the Copyright Royalty Judges shall cause to be published in the Federal Register of the initiation of voluntary negotiation proceedings for the purpose of determining the royalty fee to be paid by satellite carriers for the secondary transmission of the primary transmissions of network stations and non-network stations under subsection (b)(1)(B).

**(C) Negotiations.**—Satellite carriers, distributors, and copyright owners entitled to royalty fees under this section shall negotiate in good faith in an effort to reach a voluntary agreement or agreements for the payment of royalty fees. Any such satellite carriers, distributors and copyright owners may at any time negotiate and agree to the royalty fee, and may designate common agents to negotiate, agree to, or pay such fees. If the parties fail to identify common agents, the Copyright Royalty Judges shall do so, after requesting recommendations from the parties to the negotiation proceeding. The parties to each negotiation proceeding shall bear the cost thereof.

**(D)  Agreements binding on parties; filing of agreements; public notice.—**

**(i)   Voluntary agreements; Filings.—**Voluntary agreements negotiated at any time in accordance with this paragraph shall be binding upon all satellite carriers, distributors, and copyright owners that are parties thereto. Copies of such agreements shall be filed with the Copyright Office within 30 days after execution in accordance with regulations that the Register of Copyrights shall prescribe.

**(ii)  Procedure for adoption of fees.—**

**(I)   Publication of notice.—**Within 10 days after publication in the Federal Register of a notice of the initiation of voluntary negotiation proceedings, parties who have reached a voluntary agreement may request that the royalty fees in that agreement be applied to all satellite carriers, distributors, and copyright owners without convening a proceeding under subparagraph (F).

**(II)  Public notice of fees.—**Upon receiving a request under subclause (I), the Copyright Royalty Judges shall immediately provide public notice of the royalty fees from the voluntary agreement and afford parties an opportunity to state that they object to those fees.

**(III) Adoption of fees.—**The Copyright Royalty Judges shall adopt the royalty fees from the voluntary agreement for all satellite carriers, distributors, and copyright owners without convening the proceeding under subparagraph (F) unless a party with an intent to participate in that proceeding and a significant interest in the outcome of that proceeding objects under subclause (II).

**(E)  Period agreement is in effect.—**The obligation to pay the royalty fees established under a voluntary agreement which has been filed with the Copyright Royalty Judges in accordance with this paragraph shall become effective on the date specified in the agreement and shall remain in effect in accordance with the terms of the agreement until the subscriber for which the royalty is payable is no longer eligible to receive a secondary transmission pursuant to the license under this section.

**(F)  Fee set by Copyright Royalty Judges proceeding.—**

**(i)   Notice of initiation of proceedings.—**On or before September 1, 2010, the Copyright Royalty Judges shall cause notice to be published in the Federal Register of the initiation of a proceeding for the purpose of determining the royalty fees to be paid for the secondary transmission of the primary transmissions of network stations and non-network stations under subsection (b)(1)(B) by satellite carriers and distributors

**(I)   in** the absence of a voluntary agreement filed in accordance with subparagraph (D) that establishes royalty fees to be paid by all satellite carriers and distributors; or

**(II)  if** an objection to the fees from a voluntary agreement submitted for adoption by the Copyright Royalty Judges to apply to all satellite carriers, distributors, and copyright owners is received under subparagraph (D) from a party with an intent to participate in the proceeding and a significant interest in the outcome of that proceeding.

Such proceeding shall be conducted under chapter 8.

**(ii)  Establishment of royalty fees.—**In determining royalty fees under this subparagraph, the Copyright Royalty Judges shall establish fees for the secondary transmissions of the primary transmissions of network stations and non-network stations that most clearly represent the fair market value of secondary transmissions, except that the Copyright Royalty Judges shall adjust royalty fees to account for the obligations of the parties under any applicable voluntary agreement filed with the Copyright Royalty Judges in accordance with subparagraph (D). In determining the fair market value, the Judges shall base their decision on economic, competitive, and programming information presented by the parties, including—

(I)   the competitive environment in which such programming is distributed, the cost of similar signals in similar private and compulsory license marketplaces, and any special features and conditions of the retransmission marketplace;

(II)   the economic impact of such fees on copyright owners and satellite carriers; and

(III) the impact on the continued availability of secondary transmissions to the public.

**(iii) Effective date for decision of Copyright Royalty Judges.**—The obligation to pay the royalty fees established under a determination that is made by the Copyright Royalty Judges in a proceeding under this paragraph shall be effective as of January 1, 2010.

**(iv)  Persons subject to royalty fees.**—The royalty fees referred to in clause (iii) shall be binding on all satellite carriers, distributors and copyright owners, who are not party to a voluntary agreement filed with the Copyright Office under subparagraph (D).

**(2)  Annual royalty fee adjustment.**—Effective January 1 of each year, the royalty fee payable under subsection (b)(1)(B) for the secondary transmission of the primary transmissions of network stations and non-network stations shall be adjusted by the Copyright Royalty Judges to reflect any changes occurring in the cost of living as determined by the most recent Consumer Price Index (for all consumers and for all items) published by the Secretary of Labor before December 1 of the preceding year. Notification of the adjusted fees shall be published in the Federal Register at least 25 days before January 1.

**(d)  Definitions.**—As used in this section—

**(1)  Distributor.**—The term "distributor" means an entity that contracts to distribute secondary transmissions from a satellite carrier and, either as a single channel or in a package with other programming, provides the secondary transmission either directly to individual subscribers or indirectly through other program distribution entities in accordance with the provisions of this section.

**(2)  Network station.**—The term "network station" means—

(A) a television station licensed by the Federal Communications Commission, including any translator station or terrestrial satellite station that rebroadcasts all or substantially all of the programming broadcast by a network station, that is owned or operated by, or affiliated with, one or more of the television networks in the United States that offer an interconnected program service on a regular basis for 15 or more hours per week to at least 25 of its affiliated television licensees in 10 or more States; or

(B) a noncommercial educational broadcast station (as defined in section 397 of the Communications Act of 1934);

except that the term does not include the signal of the Alaska Rural Communications Service, or any successor entity to that service.

**(3)  Primary network station.**—The term "primary network station" means a network station that broadcasts or rebroadcasts the basic programming service of a particular national network.

(4) **Primary transmission.**—The term "primary transmission" has the meaning given that term in section 111(f) of this title.

(5) **Private home viewing.**—The term "private home viewing" means the viewing, for private use in a household by means of satellite reception equipment that is operated by an individual in that household and that serves only such household, of a secondary transmission delivered by a satellite carrier of a primary transmission of a television station licensed by the Federal Communications Commission.

(6) **Satellite carrier.**—The term "satellite carrier" means an entity that uses the facilities of a satellite or satellite service licensed by the Federal Communications Commission and operates in the Fixed-Satellite Service under part 25 of title 47, Code of Federal Regulations, or the Direct Broadcast Satellite Service under part 100 of title 47, Code of Federal Regulations, to establish and operate a channel of communications for point-to-multipoint distribution of television station signals, and that owns or leases a capacity or service on a satellite in order to provide such point-to-multipoint distribution, except to the extent that such entity provides such distribution pursuant to tariff under the Communications Act of 1934, other than for private home viewing pursuant to this section.

(7) **Secondary transmission.**—The term "secondary transmission" has the meaning given that term in section 111(f) of this title.

(8) **Subscriber; Subscribe.**—

(A) **Subscriber**. The term "subscriber" means a person or entity that receives a secondary transmission service from a satellite carrier and pays a fee for the service, directly or indirectly, to the satellite carrier or to a distributor.

(B) **Subscribe.** The term "subscribe" means to elect to become a subscriber.

(9) **Non-network station.**—The term "non-network station" means a television station, other than a network station, licensed by the Federal Communications Commission, that is secondarily transmitted by a satellite carrier.

(10) **Unserved household.**—The term "unserved household", with respect to a particular television network, means a household that—

(A) is a subscriber to whom subsection (a)(8) applies; or

(B) is a subscriber located in a short market.

(11) **Local market.**—The term "local market" has the meaning given such term under section 122(j).

(12) **Commercial establishment.**—The term "commercial establishment"—

(A) means an establishment used for commercial purposes, such as a bar, restaurant, private office, fitness club, oil rig, retail store, bank or other financial institution, supermarket, automobile or boat dealership, or any other establishment with a common business area; and

(B) does not include a multi-unit permanent or temporary dwelling where private home viewing occurs, such as a hotel, dormitory, hospital, apartment, condominium, or prison.

(13) **Multicast stream.**—The term "multicast stream" means a digital stream containing programming and program-related material affiliated with a television network, other than the primary stream.

(14) **Primary stream.**—The term "primary stream" means

(A)  the single digital stream of programming as to which a television broadcast station has the right to mandatory carriage with a satellite carrier under the rules of the Federal Communications Commission in effect on July 1, 2009; or

(B)  if there is no stream described in subparagraph (A), then either—

(i)  the single digital stream of programming associated with the network last transmitted by the station as an analog signal; or

(ii)  if there is no stream described in clause (i), then the single digital stream of programming affiliated with the network that, as of July 1, 2009, had been offered by the television broadcast station for the longest period of time.

**(15) Local-into-local service to all DMAs.**—The term "local-into-local service to all DMAs" has the meaning given such term in subsection (f)(7).

**(16) Short market.**—The term "short market" means a local market in which programming of one or more of the four most widely viewed television networks nationwide is not offered on either the primary stream or multicast stream transmitted by any network station in that market or is temporarily or permanently unavailable as a result of an act of god or other force majeure event beyond the control of the carrier.

**(e)  Expedited consideration by Justice Department of voluntary agreements to provide satellite secondary transmissions to local markets.**—

**(1)  In general.**—In a case in which no satellite carrier makes available, to subscribers located in a local market, as defined in section 122(j)(2), the secondary transmission into that market of a primary transmission of one or more television broadcast stations licensed by the Federal Communications Commission, and two or more satellite carriers request a business review letter in accordance with section 50.6 of title 28, Code of Federal Regulations (as in effect on July 7, 2004), in order to assess the legality under the antitrust laws of proposed business conduct to make or carry out an agreement to provide such secondary transmission into such local market, the appropriate official of the Department of Justice shall respond to the request no later than 90 days after the date on which the request is received.

**(2)  Definition.**—For purposes of this subsection, the term "antitrust laws"—

(A)  has the meaning given that term in subsection (a) of the first section of the Clayton Act (15 U.S.C. 12(a)), except that such term includes section 5 of the Federal Trade Commission Act (15 U.S.C. 45) to the extent such section 5 applies to unfair methods of competition; and

(B)  includes any State law similar to the laws referred to in paragraph (1).

**(f)  Certain waivers granted to providers of local-into-local service to all DMAs.**—

**(1)  Injunction waiver.**—A court that issued an injunction pursuant to subsection (a)(5)(B) before the date of the enactment of this subsection shall waive such injunction if the court recognizes the entity against which the injunction was issued as a qualified carrier.

**(2)  Limited temporary waiver.**—

**(A)  In general.**—Upon a request made by a satellite carrier, a court that issued an injunction against such carrier under subsection (a)(5)(B) before the date of the enactment of this subsection shall waive such injunction with respect to the statutory license provided under subsection (a)(2) to the extent necessary to allow such carrier to make secondary transmissions of primary transmissions made by a network station to unserved households located in short markets in which such carrier was not providing local service pursuant to the license under section 122 as of December 31, 2009.

**(B)  Expiration of temporary waiver.**—A temporary waiver of an injunction under subparagraph (A) shall expire after the end of the 120-day period beginning on the date such temporary waiver is issued unless extended for good cause by the court making the temporary waiver.

**(C) Failure to provide local-into-local service to all DMAs.—**

**(i) Failure to act reasonably and in good faith.—**If the court issuing a temporary waiver under subparagraph (A) determines that the satellite carrier that made the request for such waiver has failed to act reasonably or has failed to make a good faith effort to provide local-into-local service to all DMAs, such failure—

(I)   is actionable as an act of infringement under section 501 and the court may in its discretion impose the remedies provided for in sections 502 through 506 and subsection (a)(6)(B) of this section; and

(II)   shall result in the termination of the waiver issued under subparagraph (A).

**(ii) Failure to provide local-into-local service.—**If the court issuing a temporary waiver under subparagraph (A) determines that the satellite carrier that made the request for such waiver has failed to provide local-into-local service to all DMAs, but determines that the carrier acted reasonably and in good faith, the court may in its discretion impose financial penalties that reflect—

(I)   the degree of control the carrier had over the circumstances that resulted in the failure;

(II)   the quality of the carrier's efforts to remedy the failure; and

(III)  the severity and duration of any service interruption.

**(D) Single temporary waiver available.—**An entity may only receive one temporary waiver under this paragraph.

**(E) Short market defined.—**For purposes of this paragraph, the term "short market" means a local market in which programming of one or more of the four most widely viewed television networks nationwide as measured on the date of the enactment of this subsection is not offered on the primary stream transmitted by any local television broadcast station.

**(3) Establishment of qualified carrier recognition.—**

**(A) Statement of eligibility.—**An entity seeking to be recognized as a qualified carrier under this subsection shall file a statement of eligibility with the court that imposed the injunction. A statement of eligibility must include—

(i)   an affidavit that the entity is providing local-into-local service to all DMAs;

(ii)  a motion for a waiver of the injunction;

(iii)  a motion that the court appoint a special master under Rule 53 of the Federal Rules of Civil Procedure;

(iv)  an agreement by the carrier to pay all expenses incurred by the special master under paragraph (4)(B)(ii); and

(v)   a certification issued pursuant to section 342(a) of Communications Act of 1934.

**(B) Grant of recognition as a qualified carrier.—**Upon receipt of a statement of eligibility, the court shall recognize the entity as a qualified carrier and issue the waiver under paragraph (1). Upon motion pursuant to subparagraph (A)(iii), the court shall appoint a special master to conduct the examination and provide a report to the court as provided in paragraph (4)(B).

**(C) Voluntary termination.**—At any time, an entity recognized as a qualified carrier may file a statement of voluntary termination with the court certifying that it no longer wishes to be recognized as a qualified carrier. Upon receipt of such statement, the court shall reinstate the injunction waived under paragraph (1).

**(D) Loss of recognition prevents future recognition.**—No entity may be recognized as a qualified carrier if such entity had previously been recognized as a qualified carrier and subsequently lost such recognition or voluntarily terminated such recognition under subparagraph (C).

**(4) Qualified carrier obligations and compliance.**—

**(A) Continuing obligations.**—

**(i) In general.**—An entity recognized as a qualified carrier shall continue to provide local-into-local service to all DMAs.

**(ii) Cooperation with compliance examination.**—An entity recognized as a qualified carrier shall fully cooperate with the special master appointed by the court under paragraph (3)(B) in an examination set forth in subparagraph (B).

**(B) Qualified carrier compliance examination.**—

**(i) Examination and report.**—A special master appointed by the court under paragraph (3)(B) shall conduct an examination of, and file a report on, the qualified carrier's compliance with the royalty payment and household eligibility requirements of the license under this section. The report shall address the qualified carrier's conduct during the period beginning on the date on which the qualified carrier is recognized as such under paragraph (3)(B) and ending on April 30, 2012.

**(ii) Records of qualified carrier.**—Beginning on the date that is one year after the date on which the qualified carrier is recognized as such under paragraph (3)(B), but not later than December 1, 2011, the qualified carrier shall provide the special master with all records that the special master considers to be directly pertinent to the following requirements under this section:

(I)  Proper calculation and payment of royalties under the statutory license under this section.

(II)  Provision of service under this license to eligible subscribers only.

**(iii) Submission of report.**—The special master shall file the report required by clause (i) not later than July 24, 2012, with the court referred to in paragraph (1) that issued the injunction, and the court shall transmit a copy of the report to the Register of Copyrights, the Committees on the Judiciary and on Energy and Commerce of the House of Representatives, and the Committees on the Judiciary and on Commerce, Science, and Transportation of the Senate.

**(iv) Evidence of infringement.**—The special master shall include in the report a statement of whether an examination by the special master indicated that there is substantial evidence that a copyright holder could bring a successful action under this section against the qualified carrier for infringement.

**(v) Subsequent examination.**—If the special master's report includes a statement that its examination indicated the existence of substantial evidence that a copyright holder could bring a successful action under this section against the qualified carrier for infringement, the special master shall, not later than 6 months after the report under clause (i) is filed, initiate another examination of the qualified carrier's compliance with the royalty payment and household eligibility requirements of the license under this section since the last report was filed under clause (iii). The special master shall file a report on the results of the examination conducted under this clause with the court referred to in paragraph (1) that issued the injunction, and the court shall transmit a copy to the Register of Copyrights, the Committees on the Judiciary and on Energy and Commerce of the House of Representatives, and the Committees on the Judiciary and on Commerce, Science, and Transportation of the Senate. The report shall include a statement described in clause (iv).

(vi) **Compliance.**—Upon motion filed by an aggrieved copyright owner, the court recognizing an entity as a qualified carrier shall terminate such designation upon finding that the entity has failed to cooperate with the examinations required by this subparagraph.

(vii) **Oversight.**—During the period of time that the special master is conducting an examination under this subparagraph, the Comptroller General shall monitor the degree to which the entity seeking to be recognized or recognized as a qualified carrier under paragraph (3) is complying with the special master's examination. The qualified carrier shall make available to the Comptroller General all records and individuals that the Comptroller General considers necessary to meet the Comptroller General's obligations under this clause. The Comptroller General shall report the results of the monitoring required by this clause to the Committees on the Judiciary and on Energy and Commerce of the House of Representatives and the Committees on the Judiciary and on Commerce, Science, and Transportation of the Senate at intervals of not less than six months during such period.

(C) **Affirmation.**—A qualified carrier shall file an affidavit with the district court and the Register of Copyrights 30 months after such status was granted stating that, to the best of the affiant's knowledge, it is in compliance with the requirements for a qualified carrier. The qualified carrier shall attach to its affidavit copies of all reports or orders issued by the court, the special master, and the Comptroller General.

(D) **Compliance determination.**—Upon the motion of an aggrieved television broadcast station, the court recognizing an entity as a qualified carrier may make a determination of whether the entity is providing local-into-local service to all DMAs.

(E) **Pleading requirement.**—In any motion brought under subparagraph (D), the party making such motion shall specify one or more designated market areas (as such term is defined in section 122(j)(2)(C)) for which the failure to provide service is being alleged, and, for each such designated market area, shall plead with particularity the circumstances of the alleged failure.

(F) **Burden of proof.**—In any proceeding to make a determination under subparagraph (D), and with respect to a designated market area for which failure to provide service is alleged, the entity recognized as a qualified carrier shall have the burden of proving that the entity provided local-into-local service with a good quality satellite signal to at least 90 percent of the households in such designated market area (based on the most recent census data released by the United States Census Bureau) at the time and place alleged.

(5) **Failure to provide service.**—

(A) **Penalties.**—If the court recognizing an entity as a qualified carrier finds that such entity has willfully failed to provide local-into-local service to all DMAs, such finding shall result in the loss of recognition of the entity as a qualified carrier and the termination of the waiver provided under paragraph (1), and the court may, in its discretion—

(i)   treat such failure as an act of infringement under section 501, and subject such infringement to the remedies provided for in sections 502 through 506 and subsection (a)(6)(B) of this section; and

(ii)   impose a fine of not less than $250,000 and not more than $5,000,000.

**(B) Exception for nonwillful violation.**—If the court determines that the failure to provide local-into-local service to all DMAs is nonwillful, the court may in its discretion impose financial penalties for noncompliance that reflect—

   (i)   the degree of control the entity had over the circumstances that resulted in the failure;

   (ii)  the quality of the entity's efforts to remedy the failure and restore service; and

   (iii) the severity and duration of any service interruption.

**(6) Penalties for violations of license.**—A court that finds, under subsection (a)(6)(A), that an entity recognized as a qualified carrier has willfully made a secondary transmission of a primary transmission made by a network station and embodying a performance or display of a work to a subscriber who is not eligible to receive the transmission under this section shall reinstate the injunction waived under paragraph (1), and the court may order statutory damages of not more than $2,500,000.

**(7) Local-into-local service to all DMAs defined.**—For purposes of this subsection:

   **(A) In general.**—An entity provides "local-into-local service to all DMAs" if the entity provides local service in all designated market areas (as such term is defined in section 122(j)(2)(C)) pursuant to the license under section 122, except for designated market areas where the entity is temporarily or permanently unable to provide local service as a result of an act of god or other force majeure event beyond the control of the entity.

   **(B) Household coverage.**—For purposes of subparagraph (A), an entity that makes available local-into-local service with a good quality satellite signal to at least 90 percent of the households in a designated market area based on the most recent census data released by the United States Census Bureau shall be considered to be providing local service to such designated market area.

   **(C) Good quality satellite signal defined.**—The term "good quality satellite signal" has the meaning given such term under section 342(e)(2) of Communications Act of 1934.

(Added by Pub.L. 100–667, 102 Stat. 3949 (1988); as amended, Pub.L. 103–198, 107 Stat. 2304 (1993); Pub.L. 103–369, 108 Stat. 3477 (1994); Pub.L. 104–39, 109 Stat. 336 (1995); Pub.L. 105–80, 111 Stat. 1529 (1997); Pub.L. 106–113, 113 Stat. 1501A (1999); Pub.L. 107–273, 116 Stat. 1758 (2002); Pub.L. 108–419, 118 Stat. 2341 (2004); Pub.L. 108–447, 118 Stat. 2809 (2004); Pub.L. 109–303, 120 Stat. 1478 (2006); Pub.L. 110–403, 122 Stat. 4256 (2008); Pub.L. 111–118, 123 Stat. 3409 (2009); Pub.L. 111–144, 124 Stat. 42 (2010); Pub.L. 111–151, 124 Stat. 1027 (2010); Pub.L. 111–157, 124 Stat. 1116 (2010); Pub. L. 111–175, 124 Stat. 1218 (2010); Pub.L. 113–1200, 128 Stat. 2059 (2014); Pub.L. 116–94, 133 Stat. 2534 (2019)).

## Sec. 120.     Scope of Exclusive Rights in Architectural Works

**(a) Pictorial Representations Permitted.**—The copyright in an architectural work that has been constructed does not include the right to prevent the making, distributing, or public display of pictures, paintings, photographs, or other pictorial representations of the work, if the building in which the work is embodied is located in or ordinarily visible from a public place.

**(b) Alterations to and Destruction of Buildings.**—Notwithstanding the provisions of section 106(2), the owners of a building embodying an architectural work may, without the consent of the author or copyright owner of the architectural work, make or authorize the making of alterations to such building, and destroy or authorize the destruction of such building.

(Added by Pub.L. 101–650, 104 Stat. 5089 (1990)).

**Sec. 121.  Limitations on Exclusive Rights: Reproduction for Blind or Other People with Disabilities**

(a)  Notwithstanding the provisions of section 106, it is not an infringement of copyright for an authorized entity to reproduce or to distribute in the United States copies or phonorecords of a previously published literary work or of a previously published musical work that has been fixed in the form of text or notation if such copies or phonorecords are reproduced or distributed in accessible formats exclusively for use by eligible persons.

(b)(1)  Copies or phonorecords to which this section applies shall—

(A)  not be reproduced or distributed in the United States in a format other than an accessible format exclusively for use by eligible persons;

(B)  bear a notice that any further reproduction or distribution in a format other than an accessible format is an infringement; and

(C)  include a copyright notice identifying the copyright owner and the date of the original publication.

(2)  The provisions of this subsection shall not apply to standardized, secure, or norm-referenced tests and related testing material, or to computer programs, except the portions thereof that are in conventional human language (including descriptions of pictorial works) and displayed to users in the ordinary course of using the computer programs.

(c)  Notwithstanding the provisions of section 106, it is not an infringement of copyright for a publisher of print instructional materials for use in elementary or secondary schools to create and distribute to the National Instructional Materials Access Center copies of the electronic files described in sections 612(a)(23)(C), 613(a)(6), and section 674(e) of the Individuals with Disabilities Education Act that contain the contents of print instructional materials using the National Instructional Material Accessibility Standard (as defined in section 674(e)(3) of that Act), if—

(1)  the inclusion of the contents of such print instructional materials is required by any State educational agency or local educational agency;

(2)  the publisher had the right to publish such print instructional materials in print formats; and

(3)  such copies are used solely for reproduction or distribution of the contents of such print instructional materials in accessible formats.

(d)  For purposes of this section, the term—

(1)  "accessible format" means an alternative manner or form that gives an eligible person access to the work when the copy or phonorecord in the accessible format is used exclusively by the eligible person to permit him or her to have access as feasibly and comfortably as a person without such disability as described in paragraph (3);

(2)  "authorized entity" means a nonprofit organization or a governmental agency that has a primary mission to provide specialized services relating to training, education, or adaptive reading or information access needs of blind or other persons with disabilities;

(3)  "eligible person" means an individual who, regardless of any other disability—

(A)  is blind;

(B)  has a visual impairment or perceptual or reading disability that cannot be improved to give visual function substantially equivalent to that of a person who has no such impairment or disability and so is unable to read printed works to substantially the same degree as a person without an impairment or disability; or

(C) is otherwise unable, through physical disability, to hold or manipulate a book or to focus or move the eyes to the extent that would be normally acceptable for reading; and

(4) "print instructional materials" has the meaning given under section 674(e)(3)(C) of the Individuals with Disabilities Education Act.

(Added by P.L. 104–197, 110 Stat. 2416 (1996); as amended, Pub.L. 106–379, 114 Stat. 1444 (2000); Pub.L. 108–446, 118 Stat. 2807 (2004); Pub.L. 115–261, 132 Stat. 3667 (2018)).

### Sec. 121A.    Limitations on Exclusive Rights: Reproduction for Blind or Other People with Disabilities in Marrakesh Treaty Countries

(a) Notwithstanding the provisions of sections 106 and 602, it is not an infringement of copyright for an authorized entity, acting pursuant to this section, to export copies or phonorecords of a previously published literary work or of a previously published musical work that has been fixed in the form of text or notation in accessible formats to another country when the exportation is made either to—

(1) an authorized entity located in a country that is a Party to the Marrakesh Treaty; or

(2) an eligible person in a country that is a Party to the Marrakesh Treaty,

if prior to the exportation of such copies or phonorecords, the authorized entity engaged in the exportation did not know or have reasonable grounds to know that the copies or phonorecords would be used other than by eligible persons.

(b) Notwithstanding the provisions of sections 106 and 602, it is not an infringement of copyright for an authorized entity or an eligible person, or someone acting on behalf of an eligible person, acting pursuant to this section, to import copies or phonorecords of a previously published literary work or of a previously published musical work that has been fixed in the form of text or notation in accessible formats.

(c) In conducting activities under subsection (a) or (b), an authorized entity shall establish and follow its own practices, in keeping with its particular circumstances, to—

(1) establish that the persons the authorized entity serves are eligible persons;

(2) limit to eligible persons and authorized entities the distribution of accessible format copies by the authorized entity;

(3) discourage the reproduction and distribution of unauthorized copies;

(4) maintain due care in, and records of, the handling of copies of works by the authorized entity, while respecting the privacy of eligible persons on an equal basis with others; and

(5) facilitate effective cross-border exchange of accessible format copies by making publicly available—

(A) the titles of works for which the authorized entity has accessible format copies or phonorecords and the specific accessible formats in which they are available; and

(B) information on the policies, practices, and authorized entity partners of the authorized entity for the cross-border exchange of accessible format copies.

(d) Nothing in this section shall be construed to establish—

(1) a cause of action under this title; or

(2) a basis for regulation by any Federal agency.

(e) Nothing in this section shall be construed to limit the ability to engage in any activity otherwise permitted under this title.

(f) For purposes of this section—

(1) the terms "accessible format", "authorized entity", and "eligible person" have the meanings given those terms in section 121; and

(2) the term "Marrakesh Treaty" means the Marrakesh Treaty to Facilitate Access to Published Works by Visually Impaired Persons and Persons with Print Disabilities concluded at Marrakesh, Morocco, on June 28, 2013.

(Added by Pub. L. 115–261, 132 Stat. 3667 (2018)).

## Sec. 122. Limitations on Exclusive Rights: Secondary Transmissions of Local Television Programming by Satellite

**(a) Secondary Transmissions Into Local Markets.—**

**(1) Secondary transmissions of television broadcast stations within a local market.**—A secondary transmission of a performance or display of a work embodied in a primary transmission of a television broadcast station into the station's local market shall be subject to statutory licensing under this section if—

(A) the secondary transmission is made by a satellite carrier to the public;

(B) with regard to secondary transmissions, the satellite carrier is in compliance with the rules, regulations, or authorizations of the Federal Communications Commission governing the carriage of television broadcast station signals; and

(C) the satellite carrier makes a direct or indirect charge for the secondary transmission to—

(i) each subscriber receiving the secondary transmission; or

(ii) a distributor that has contracted with the satellite carrier for direct or indirect delivery of the secondary transmission to the public.

**(2) Significantly viewed stations.—**

**(A) In general.**—A secondary transmission of a performance or display of a work embodied in a primary transmission of a television broadcast station to subscribers who receive secondary transmissions of primary transmissions under paragraph (1) shall be subject to statutory licensing under this paragraph if the secondary transmission is of the primary transmission of a network station or a non-network station to a subscriber who resides outside the station's local market but within a community in which the signal has been determined by the Federal Communications Commission to be significantly viewed in such community, pursuant to the rules, regulations, and authorizations of the Federal Communications Commission in effect on April 15, 1976, applicable to determining with respect to a cable system whether signals are significantly viewed in a community.

**(B) Waiver.**—A subscriber who is denied the secondary transmission of the primary transmission of a network station or a non-network station under subparagraph (A) may request a waiver from such denial by submitting a request, through the subscriber's satellite carrier, to the network station or non-network station in the local market affiliated with the same network or non-network where the subscriber is located. The network station or non-network station shall accept or reject the subscriber's request for a waiver within 30 days after receipt of the request. If the network station or non-network station fails to accept or reject the subscriber's request for a waiver within that 30-day period, that network station or non-network station shall be deemed to agree to the waiver request.

**(3) Secondary transmission of low power programming.—**

**(A) In general.**—Subject to subparagraphs (B) and (C), a secondary transmission of a performance or display of a work embodied in a primary transmission of a television broadcast station to subscribers who receive secondary transmissions of primary transmissions under paragraph (1) shall be subject to statutory licensing under this paragraph if the secondary transmission is of the primary transmission of a television broadcast station that is licensed as a low power television station, to a subscriber who resides within the same designated market area as the station that originates the transmission.

**(B) No applicability to repeaters and translators.**—Secondary transmissions provided for in subparagraph (A) shall not apply to any low power television station that retransmits the programs and signals of another television station for more than 2 hours each day.

**(C) No impact on other secondary transmissions obligations.**—A satellite carrier that makes secondary transmissions of a primary transmission of a low power television station under a statutory license provided under this section is not required, by reason of such secondary transmissions, to make any other secondary transmissions.

**(4) Special exceptions.**—A secondary transmission of a performance or display of a work embodied in a primary transmission of a television broadcast station to subscribers who receive secondary transmissions of primary transmissions under paragraph (1) shall, if the secondary transmission is made by a satellite carrier that complies with the requirements of paragraph (1), be subject to statutory licensing under this paragraph as follows:

**(A) States with single full-power network station.**—In a State in which there is licensed by the Federal Communications Commission a single full-power station that was a network station on January 1, 1995, the statutory license provided for in this paragraph shall apply to the secondary transmission by a satellite carrier of the primary transmission of that station to any subscriber in a community that is located within that State and that is not within the first 50 television markets as listed in the regulations of the Commission as in effect on such date (47 C.F.R. 76.51).

**(B) States with all network stations and non-network stations in same local market.**—In a State in which all network stations and non-network stations licensed by the Federal Communications Commission within that State as of January 1, 1995, are assigned to the same local market and that local market does not encompass all counties of that State, the statutory license provided under this paragraph shall apply to the secondary transmission by a satellite carrier of the primary transmissions of such station to all subscribers in the State who reside in a local market that is within the first 50 major television markets as listed in the regulations of the Commission as in effect on such date (section 76.51 of title 47, Code of Federal Regulations).

**(C) Additional stations.**—In the case of that State in which are located 4 counties that—

(i) on January 1, 2004, were in local markets principally comprised of counties in another State, and

(ii) had a combined total of 41,340 television households, according to the U.S. Television Household Estimates by Nielsen Media Research for 2004,

the statutory license provided under this paragraph shall apply to secondary transmissions by a satellite carrier to subscribers in any such county of the primary transmissions of any network station located in that State, if the satellite carrier was making such secondary transmissions to any subscribers in that county on January 1, 2004.

**(D) Certain additional stations.**—If 2 adjacent counties in a single State are in a local market comprised principally of counties located in another State, the statutory license provided for in this paragraph shall apply to the secondary transmission by a satellite carrier to subscribers in those 2 counties of the primary transmissions of any network station located in the capital of the State in which such 2 counties are located, if—

(i)   the 2 counties are located in a local market that is in the top 100 markets for the year 2003 according to Nielsen Media Research; and

(ii)   the total number of television households in the 2 counties combined did not exceed 10,000 for the year 2003 according to Nielsen Media Research.

(E)  **Networks of noncommercial educational broadcast stations.**—In the case of a system of three or more noncommercial educational broadcast stations licensed to a single State, public agency, or political, educational, or special purpose subdivision of a State, the statutory license provided for in this paragraph shall apply to the secondary transmission of the primary transmission of such system to any subscriber in any county or county equivalent within such State, if such subscriber is located in a designated market area that is not otherwise eligible to receive the secondary transmission of the primary transmission of a noncommercial educational broadcast station located within the State pursuant to paragraph (1).

(5)  **Applicability of royalty rates and procedures.**—The royalty rates and procedures under section 119(b) shall apply to the secondary transmissions to which the statutory license under paragraph (4) applies.

(b)  **Reporting Requirements.**—

(1)  **Initial Lists.**—A satellite carrier that makes secondary transmissions of a primary transmission made by a network station under subsection (a) shall, within 90 days after commencing such secondary transmissions, submit to the network station—

(A)  a list identifying (by name in alphabetical order and street address, including county and 9-digit zip code) all subscribers to which the satellite carrier makes secondary transmissions of that primary transmission under subsection (a); and

(B)  a separate list, aggregated by designated market area (by name and address, including street or rural route number, city, State, and 9-digit zip code), which shall indicate those subscribers being served pursuant to paragraph (2) of subsection (a).

(2)  **Subsequent Lists.**—After the list is submitted under paragraph (1), the satellite carrier shall, on the 15th of each month, submit to the network—

(A)  a list identifying (by name in alphabetical order and street address, including county and 9-digit zip code) any subscribers who have been added or dropped as subscribers since the last submission under this subsection; and

(B)  a separate list, aggregated by designated market area (by name and street address, including street or rural route number, city, State, and 9-digit zip code), identifying those subscribers whose service pursuant to paragraph (2) of subsection (a) has been added or dropped since the last submission under this subsection.

(3)  **Use of Subscriber Information.**—Subscriber information submitted by a satellite carrier under this subsection may be used only for the purposes of monitoring compliance by the satellite carrier with this section.

(4)  **Requirements of Networks.**—The submission requirements of this subsection shall apply to a satellite carrier only if the network to which the submissions are to be made places on file with the Register of Copyrights a document identifying the name and address of the person to whom such submissions are to be made. The Register of Copyrights shall maintain for public inspection a file of all such documents.

(c)  **No Royalty Fee Required for Certain Secondary Transmissions.**—A satellite carrier whose secondary transmissions are subject to statutory licensing under paragraphs (1), (2), and (3) of subsection (a) shall have no royalty obligation for such secondary transmissions.

**(d) Noncompliance with Reporting and Regulatory Requirements.**—Notwithstanding subsection (a), the willful or repeated secondary transmission to the public by a satellite carrier into the local market of a television broadcast station of a primary transmission embodying a performance or display of a work made by that television broadcast station is actionable as an act of infringement under section 501, and is fully subject to the remedies provided under sections 502 through 506, if the satellite carrier has not complied with the reporting requirements of subsection (b) or with the rules, regulations, and authorizations of the Federal Communications Commission concerning the carriage of television broadcast signals.

**(e) Willful Alterations.**—Notwithstanding subsection (a), the secondary transmission to the public by a satellite carrier into the local market of a television broadcast station of a performance or display of a work embodied in a primary transmission made by that television broadcast station is actionable as an act of infringement under section 501, and is fully subject to the remedies provided by sections 502 through 506 and section 510, if the content of the particular program in which the performance or display is embodied, or any commercial advertising or station announcement transmitted by the primary transmitter during, or immediately before or after, the transmission of such program, is in any way willfully altered by the satellite carrier through changes, deletions, or additions, or is combined with programming from any other broadcast signal.

**(f) Violation of Territorial Restrictions on Statutory License for Television Broadcast Stations.**—

**(1) Individual Violations.**—The willful or repeated secondary transmission to the public by a satellite carrier of a primary transmission embodying a performance or display of a work made by a television broadcast station to a subscriber who does not reside in that station's local market, and is not subject to statutory licensing under section 119, subject to statutory licensing by reason of paragraph (2)(A), (3), or (4) of subsection (a), or subject to a private licensing agreement, is actionable as an act of infringement under section 501 and is fully subject to the remedies provided by sections 502 through 506, except that—

(A) no damages shall be awarded for such act of infringement if the satellite carrier took corrective action by promptly withdrawing service from the ineligible subscriber; and

(B) any statutory damages shall not exceed $250 for such subscriber for each month during which the violation occurred.

**(2) Pattern of Violations.**—If a satellite carrier engages in a willful or repeated pattern or practice of secondarily transmitting to the public a primary transmission embodying a performance or display of a work made by a television broadcast station to subscribers who do not reside in that station's local market, and are not subject to statutory licensing under section 119, subject to statutory licensing by reason of paragraph (2)(A), (3), or (4) of subsection (a), or subject to a private licensing agreement, then in addition to the remedies under paragraph (1)—

(A) if the pattern or practice has been carried out on a substantially nationwide basis, the court—

(i) shall order a permanent injunction barring the secondary transmission by the satellite carrier of the primary transmissions of that television broadcast station (and if such television broadcast station is a network station, all other television broadcast stations affiliated with such network); and

(ii) may order statutory damages not exceeding $2,500,000 for each 6-month period during which the pattern or practice was carried out; and

(B) if the pattern or practice has been carried out on a local or regional basis with respect to more than one television broadcast station, the court—

(i)   shall order a permanent injunction barring the secondary transmission in that locality or region by the satellite carrier of the primary transmissions of any television broadcast station; and

(ii)   may order statutory damages not exceeding $2,500,000 for each 6-month period during which the pattern or practice was carried out.

**(g)   Burden of Proof.**—In any action brought under subsection (f), the satellite carrier shall have the burden of proving that its secondary transmission of a primary transmission by a television broadcast station is made only to subscribers located within that station's local market or subscribers being served in compliance with section 119, paragraph (2)(A), (3), or (4) of subsection (a), or a private licensing agreement.

**(h)   Geographic Limitations on Secondary Transmissions.**—The statutory license created by this section shall apply to secondary transmissions to locations in the United States.

**(i)   Exclusivity with Respect to Secondary Transmissions of Broadcast Stations by Satellite to Members of the Public.**—No provision of section 111 or any other law (other than this section and section 119) shall be construed to contain any authorization, exemption, or license through which secondary transmissions by satellite carriers of programming contained in a primary transmission made by a television broadcast station may be made without obtaining the consent of the copyright owner.

**(j)   Definitions.**—In this section—

**(1)   Distributor.**—The term "distributor" means an entity that contracts to distribute secondary transmissions from a satellite carrier and, either as a single channel or in a package with other programming, provides the secondary transmission either directly to individual subscribers or indirectly through other program distribution entities.

**(2)   Local Market.**—

**(A)   In General.**—The term "local market", in the case of both commercial and noncommercial television broadcast stations, means the designated market area in which a station is located, and—

(i)   in the case of a commercial television broadcast station, all commercial television broadcast stations licensed to a community within the same designated market area are within the same local market; and

(ii)   in the case of a noncommercial educational television broadcast station, the market includes any station that is licensed to a community within the same designated market area as the noncommercial educational television broadcast station.

**(B)   County of License.**—In addition to the area described in subparagraph (A), a station's local market includes the county in which the station's community of license is located.

**(C)   Designated Market Area.**—For purposes of subparagraph (A), the term "designated market area" means a designated market area, as determined by Nielsen Media Research and published in the 1999–2000 Nielsen Station Index Directory and Nielsen Station Index United States Television Household Estimates or any successor publication.

**(D)   Certain Areas Outside of Any Designated Market Area.**—Any census area, borough, or other area in the State of Alaska that is outside of a designated market area, as determined by Nielsen Media Research, shall be deemed to be part of one of the local markets in the State of Alaska. A satellite carrier may determine which local market in the State of Alaska will be deemed to be the relevant local market in connection with each subscriber in such census area, borough, or other area.

**(E) Market Determinations.**—The local market of a commercial television broadcast station may be modified by the Federal Communications Commission in accordance with section 338(*l*) of the Communications Act of 1934 (47 U.S.C. 338).

**(3) Low Power Television Station.**—The term "low power television station" means a low power TV station as defined in section 74.701(f) of title 47, Code of Federal Regulations, as in effect on June 1, 2004. For purposes of this paragraph, the term "low power television station" includes a low power television station that has been accorded primary status as a Class A television licensee under section 73.6001(a) of title 47, Code of Federal Regulations.

**(4) Network Station; Non-network Station; Satellite Carrier; Secondary Transmission.**—The terms "network station", "non-network station", "satellite carrier", and "secondary transmission" have the meanings given such terms under section 119(d).

**(5) Noncommercial Educational Broadcast Station.**—The term "noncommercial educational broadcast station" means a television broadcast station that is a noncommercial educational broadcast station as defined in section 397 of the Communications Act of 1934, as in effect on the date of the enactment of the Satellite Television Extension and Localism Act of 2010.

**(6) Subscriber.**—The term "subscriber" means a person or entity that receives a secondary transmission service from a satellite carrier and pays a fee for the service, directly or indirectly, to the satellite carrier or to a distributor.

**(7) Television Broadcast Station.**—The term "television broadcast station"—

(A) means an over-the-air, commercial or noncommercial television broadcast station licensed by the Federal Communications Commission under subpart E of part 73 of title 47, Code of Federal Regulations, except that such term does not include a low-power or translator television station; and

(B) includes a television broadcast station licensed by an appropriate governmental authority of Canada or Mexico if the station broadcasts primarily in the English language and is a network station as defined in section 119(d)(2)(A).

(Added by Pub.L. 106–113, 113 Stat. 1501A (1999); Pub.L. 108–447, 118 Stat. 2809 (2004); Pub.L. 110–403, 122 Stat. 4256 (2008); Pub.L. 111–175, 124 Stat. 1218 (2010); Pub.L. 113–200, 128 Stat. 2059 (2014)).

## CHAPTER 2.—COPYRIGHT OWNERSHIP AND TRANSFER

## Sec. 201.     Ownership of Copyright

**(a) Initial Ownership.**—Copyright in a work protected under this title vests initially in the author or authors of the work. The authors of a joint work are coowners of copyright in the work.

**(b) Works Made for Hire.**—In the case of a work made for hire, the employer or other person for whom the work was prepared is considered the author for purposes of this title, and, unless the parties have expressly agreed otherwise in a written instrument signed by them, owns all of the rights comprised in the copyright.

**(c) Contributions to Collective Works.**—Copyright in each separate contribution to a collective work is distinct from copyright in the collective work as a whole, and vests initially in the author of the contribution. In the absence of an express transfer of the copyright or of any rights under it, the owner of copyright in the collective work is presumed to have acquired only the privilege of reproducing and distributing the contribution as part of that particular collective work, any revision of that collective work, and any later collective work in the same series.

   **(d)  Transfer of Ownership.—**

   (1)   The ownership of a copyright may be transferred in whole or in part by any means of conveyance or by operation of law, and may be bequeathed by will or pass as personal property by the applicable laws of intestate succession.

   (2)   Any of the exclusive rights comprised in a copyright, including any subdivision of any of the rights specified by section 106, may be transferred as provided by clause (1) and owned separately. The owner of any particular exclusive right is entitled, to the extent of that right, to all of the protection and remedies accorded to the copyright owner by this title.

   **(e)  Involuntary Transfer.—**When an individual author's ownership of a copyright, or of any of the exclusive rights under a copyright, has not previously been transferred voluntarily by that individual author, no action by any governmental body or other official or organization purporting to seize, expropriate, transfer, or exercise rights of ownership with respect to the copyright, or any of the exclusive rights under a copyright, shall be given effect under this title, except as provided under Title 11.

(As amended, Pub.L. 95–598, 92 Stat. 2676 (1978)).

## Sec. 202.    Ownership of Copyright as Distinct From Ownership of Material Object

   Ownership of a copyright, or of any of the exclusive rights under a copyright, is distinct from ownership of any material object in which the work is embodied. Transfer of ownership of any material object, including the copy or phonorecord in which the work is first fixed, does not of itself convey any rights in the copyrighted work embodied in the object; nor, in the absence of an agreement, does transfer of ownership of a copyright or of any exclusive rights under a copyright convey property rights in any material object.

## Sec. 203.    Termination of Transfers and Licenses Granted by the Author

   **(a)  Conditions for Termination.—**In the case of any work other than a work made for hire, the exclusive or nonexclusive grant of a transfer or license of copyright or of any right under a copyright, executed by the author on or after January 1, 1978, otherwise than by will, is subject to termination under the following conditions:

   (1)   In the case of a grant executed by one author, termination of the grant may be effected by that author or, if the author is dead, by the person or persons who, under clause (2) of this subsection, own and are entitled to exercise a total of more than one-half of that author's termination interest. In the case of a grant executed by two or more authors of a joint work, termination of the grant may be effected by a majority of the authors who executed it; if any of such authors is dead, the termination interest of any such author may be exercised as a unit by the person or persons who, under clause (2) of this subsection, own and are entitled to exercise a total of more than one-half of that author's interest.

   (2)   Where an author is dead, his or her termination interest is owned, and may be exercised, as follows:

      (A)   The widow or widower owns the author's entire termination interest unless there are any surviving children or grandchildren of the author, in which case the widow or widower owns one-half of the author's interest.

      (B)   The author's surviving children, and the surviving children of any dead child of the author, own the author's entire termination interest unless there is a widow or widower, in which case the ownership of one-half of the author's interest is divided among them.

(C)  The rights of the author's children and grandchildren are in all cases divided among them and exercised on a per stirpes basis according to the number of such author's children represented; the share of the children of a dead child in a termination interest can be exercised only by the action of a majority of them.

(D)  In the event that the author's widow or widower, children, and grandchildren are not living, the author's executor, administrator, personal representative, or trustee shall own the author's entire termination interest.

(3)  Termination of the grant may be effected at any time during a period of five years beginning at the end of thirty-five years from the date of execution of the grant; or, if the grant covers the right of publication of the work, the period begins at the end of thirty-five years from the date of publication of the work under the grant or at the end of forty years from the date of execution of the grant, whichever term ends earlier.

(4)  The termination shall be effected by serving an advance notice in writing, signed by the number and proportion of owners of termination interests required under clauses (1) and (2) of this subsection, or by their duly authorized agents, upon the grantee or the grantee's successor in title.

(A)  The notice shall state the effective date of the termination, which shall fall within the five-year period specified by clause (3) of this subsection, and the notice shall be served not less than two or more than ten years before that date. A copy of the notice shall be recorded in the Copyright Office before the effective date of termination, as a condition to its taking effect.

(B)  The notice shall comply, in form, content, and manner of service, with requirements that the Register of Copyrights shall prescribe by regulation.

(5)  Termination of the grant may be effected notwithstanding any agreement to the contrary, including an agreement to make a will or to make any future grant.

**(b)  Effect of Termination.**—Upon the effective date of termination, all rights under this title that were covered by the terminated grants revert to the author, authors, and other persons owning termination interests under clauses (1) and (2) of subsection (a), including those owners who did not join in signing the notice of termination under clause (4) of subsection (a), but with the following limitations:

(1)  A derivative work prepared under authority of the grant before its termination may continue to be utilized under the terms of the grant after its termination, but this privilege does not extend to the preparation after the termination of other derivative works based upon the copyrighted work covered by the terminated grant.

(2)  The future rights that will revert upon termination of the grant become vested on the date the notice of termination has been served as provided by clause (4) of subsection (a). The rights vest in the author, authors, and other persons named in, and in the proportionate shares provided by, clauses (1) and (2) of subsection (a).

(3)  Subject to the provisions of clause (4) of this subsection, a further grant, or agreement to make a further grant, of any right covered by a terminated grant is valid only if it is signed by the same number and proportion of the owners, in whom the right has vested under clause (2) of this subsection, as are required to terminate the grant under clauses (1) and (2) of subsection (a). Such further grant or agreement is effective with respect to all of the persons in whom the right it covers has vested under clause (2) of this subsection, including those who did not join in signing it. If any person dies after rights under a terminated grant have vested in him or her, that person's legal representatives, legatees, or heirs at law represent him or her for purposes of this clause.

(4) A further grant, or agreement to make a further grant, of any right covered by a terminated grant is valid only if it is made after the effective date of the termination. As an exception, however, an agreement for such a further grant may be made between the persons provided by clause (3) of this subsection and the original grantee or such grantee's successor in title, after the notice of termination has been served as provided by clause (4) of subsection (a).

(5) Termination of a grant under this section affects only those rights covered by the grants that arise under this title, and in no way affects rights arising under any other Federal, State, or foreign laws.

(6) Unless and until termination is effected under this section, the grant, if it does not provide otherwise, continues in effect for the term of copyright provided by this title.

(As amended, Pub.L. 105–298, 112 Stat. 2827 (1998)).

## Sec. 204. Execution of Transfers of Copyright Ownership

(a) A transfer of copyright ownership, other than by operation of law, is not valid unless an instrument of conveyance, or a note or memorandum of the transfer, is in writing and signed by the owner of the rights conveyed or such owner's duly authorized agent.

(b) A certificate of acknowledgement is not required for the validity of a transfer, but is prima facie evidence of the execution of the transfer if—

(1) in the case of a transfer executed in the United States, the certificate is issued by a person authorized to administer oaths within the United States; or

(2) in the case of a transfer executed in a foreign country, the certificate is issued by a diplomatic or consular officer of the United States, or by a person authorized to administer oaths whose authority is proved by a certificate of such an officer.

## Sec. 205. Recordation of Transfers and Other Documents

(a) **Conditions for Recordation.**—Any transfer of copyright ownership or other document pertaining to a copyright may be recorded in the Copyright Office if the document filed for recordation bears the actual signature of the person who executed it, or if it is accompanied by a sworn or official certification that it is a true copy of the original, signed document. A sworn or official certification may be submitted to the Copyright Office electronically, pursuant to regulations established by the Register of Copyrights.

(b) **Certificate of Recordation.**—The Register of Copyrights shall, upon receipt of a document as provided by subsection (a) and of the fee provided by section 708, record the document and return it with a certificate of recordation.

(c) **Recordation as Constructive Notice.**—Recordation of a document in the Copyright Office gives all persons constructive notice of the facts stated in the recorded document, but only if—

(1) the document, or material attached to it, specifically identifies the work to which it pertains so that, after the document is indexed by the Register of Copyrights, it would be revealed by a reasonable search under the title or registration number of the work; and

(2) registration has been made for the work.

(d) **Priority Between Conflicting Transfers.**—As between two conflicting transfers, the one executed first prevails if it is recorded, in the manner required to give constructive notice under subsection (c), within one month after its execution in the United States or within two months after its execution outside the United States, or at any time before recordation in such manner of the later transfer. Otherwise the later transfer prevails if recorded first in such manner, and if taken in good faith, for valuable consideration or on the basis of a binding promise to pay royalties, and without notice of the earlier transfer.

(e)  **Priority Between Conflicting Transfer of Ownership and Nonexclusive License.**— A nonexclusive license, whether recorded or not, prevails over a conflicting transfer of copyright ownership if the license is evidenced by a written instrument signed by the owner of the rights licensed or such owner's duly authorized agent; and if—

(1)  the license was taken before execution of the transfer; or

(2)  the license was taken in good faith before recordation of the transfer and without notice of it.

(As amended, Pub.L. 100–568, 102 Stat. 2853 (1988); Pub.L. 111–295, 124 Stat. 3180 (2010)).

## CHAPTER 3.—DURATION OF COPYRIGHT

## Sec. 301.    Preemption With Respect to Other Laws

(a)  On and after January 1, 1978, all legal or equitable rights that are equivalent to any of the exclusive rights within the general scope of copyright as specified by section 106 in works of authorship that are fixed in a tangible medium of expression and come within the subject matter of copyright as specified by sections 102 and 103, whether created before or after that date and whether published or unpublished, are governed exclusively by this title. Thereafter, no person is entitled to any such right or equivalent right in any such work under the common law or statutes of any State.

(b)  Nothing in this title annuls or limits any rights or remedies under the common law or statutes of any State with respect to—

(1)  subject matter that does not come within the subject matter of copyright as specified by sections 102 and 103, including works of authorship not fixed in any tangible medium of expression; or

(2)  any cause of action arising from undertakings commenced before January 1, 1978;

(3)  activities violating legal or equitable rights that are not equivalent to any of the exclusive rights within the general scope of copyright as specified by section 106; or

(4)  State and local landmarks, historic preservation, zoning, or building codes, relating to architectural works protected under section 102(a)(8).

(c)  Notwithstanding the provisions of section 303, and in accordance with chapter 14, no sound recording fixed before February 15, 1972, shall be subject to copyright under this title. With respect to sound recordings fixed before February 15, 1972, the preemptive provisions of subsection (a) shall apply to activities that are commenced on and after the date of enactment of the Classics Protection and Access Act. Nothing in this subsection may be construed to affirm or negate the preemption of rights and remedies pertaining to any cause of action arising from the nonsubscription broadcast transmission of sound recordings under the common law or statutes of any State for activities that do not qualify as covered activities under chapter 14 undertaken during the period between the date of enactment of the Classics Protection and Access Act and the date on which the term of prohibition on unauthorized acts under section 1401(a)(2) expires for such sound recordings. Any potential preemption of rights and remedies related to such activities undertaken during that period shall apply in all respects as it did the day before the date of enactment of the Classics Protection and Access Act.

(d)  Nothing in this title annuls or limits any rights or remedies under any other Federal statute.

(e)   The scope of Federal preemption under this section is not affected by the adherence of the United States to the Berne Convention or the satisfaction of obligations of the United States thereunder.

(f)(1)   On or after the effective date set forth in section 9(a) of the Visual Artists Rights Act of 1990, all legal or equitable rights that are equivalent to any of the rights conferred by section 106A with respect to works of visual art to which the rights conferred by section 106A apply are governed exclusively by section 106A and section 113(d) and the provisions of this title relating to such sections. Thereafter, no person is entitled to any such right or equivalent right in any work of visual art under the common law or statutes of any State.

(2)   Nothing in paragraph (1) annuls or limits any rights or remedies under the common law or statutes of any State with respect to—

(A)   any cause of action from undertakings commenced before the effective date set forth in section 9(a) of the Visual Artists Rights Act of 1990;

(B)   activities violating legal or equitable rights that are not equivalent to any of the rights conferred by section 106A with respect to works of visual art; or

(C)   activities violating legal or equitable rights which extend beyond the life of the author.

(As amended, Pub.L. 100–568, 102 Stat. 2853 (1988); Pub.L. 101–650, 104 Stat. 5089 (1990); Pub.L. 105–298, 112 Stat. 2827 (1998); Pub.L. 115–264, 132 Stat. 3676 (2018)).

## Sec. 302.    Duration of Copyright: Works Created on or After January 1, 1978

(a)   **In General.**—Copyright in a work created on or after January 1, 1978, subsists from its creation and, except as provided by the following subsections, endures for a term consisting of the life of the author and 70 years after the author's death.

(b)   **Joint Works.**—In the case of a joint work prepared by two or more authors who did not work for hire, the copyright endures for a term consisting of the life of the last surviving author and 70 years after such last surviving author's death.

(c)   **Anonymous Works, Pseudonymous Works, and Works Made for Hire.**—In the case of an anonymous work, a pseudonymous work, or a work made for hire, the copyright endures for a term of 95 years from the year of its first publication, or a term of 120 years from the year of its creation, whichever expires first. If, before the end of such term, the identity of one or more of the authors of an anonymous or pseudonymous work is revealed in the records of a registration made for that work under subsections (a) or (d) of section 408, or in the records provided by this subsection, the copyright in the work endures for the term specified by subsection (a) or (b), based on the life of the author or authors whose identity has been revealed. Any person having an interest in the copyright in an anonymous or pseudonymous work may at any time record, in records to be maintained by the Copyright Office for that purpose, a statement identifying one or more authors of the work; the statement shall also identify the person filing it, the nature of that person's interest, the source of the information recorded, and the particular work affected, and shall comply in form and content with requirements that the Register of Copyrights shall prescribe by regulation.

(d)   **Records Relating to Death of Authors.**—Any person having an interest in a copyright may at any time record in the Copyright Office a statement of the date of death of the author of the copyrighted work, or a statement that the author is still living on a particular date. The statement shall identify the person filing it, the nature of that person's interest, and the source of the information recorded, and shall comply in form and content with requirements that the Register of Copyrights shall prescribe by regulation. The Register shall maintain current records of information relating to the death of authors of copyrighted works, based on such recorded statements and, to the extent the Register considers practicable, on data contained in any of the records of the Copyright Office or in other reference sources.

(e)  **Presumption as to Author's Death.**—After a period of 95 years from the year of first publication of a work, or a period of 120 years from the year of its creation, whichever expires first, any person who obtains from the Copyright Office a certified report that the records provided by subsection (d) disclose nothing to indicate that the author of the work is living, or died less than 70 years before, is entitled to the benefit of a presumption that the author has been dead for at least 70 years. Reliance in good faith upon this presumption shall be a complete defense to any action for infringement under this title.

(As amended, Pub.L. 105–298, 112 Stat. 2827 (1998)).

## Sec. 303.    Duration of Copyright: Works Created But Not Published or Copyrighted Before January 1, 1978

(a)  Copyright in a work created before January 1, 1978, but not theretofore in the public domain or copyrighted, subsists from January 1, 1978, and endures for the term provided by section 302. In no case, however, shall the term of copyright in such a work expire before December 31, 2002; and, if the work is published on or before December 31, 2002, the term of copyright shall not expire before December 31, 2047.

(b)  The distribution before January 1, 1978, of a phonorecord shall not for any purpose constitute a publication of any musical work, dramatic work, or literary work embodied therein.

(As amended, Pub.L. 105–80, 111 Stat. 1529 (1997); Pub.L. 105–298, 112 Stat. 2827 (1998); Pub.L. 111–295, 124 Stat. 3180 (2010)).

## Sec. 304.    Duration of Copyright: Subsisting Copyrights

**(a)  Copyrights in Their First Term on January 1, 1978.—**

(1)(A)  Any copyright, the first term of which is subsisting on January 1, 1978, shall endure for 28 years from the date it was originally secured.

(B)  In the case of—

(i)  any posthumous work or of any periodical, cyclopedic, or other composite work upon which the copyright was originally secured by the proprietor thereof, or

(ii)  any work copyrighted by a corporate body (otherwise than as assignee or licensee of the individual author) or by an employer for whom such work is made for hire,

the proprietor of such copyright shall be entitled to a renewal and extension of the copyright in such work for the further term of 67 years.

(C)  In the case of any other copyrighted work, including a contribution by an individual author to a periodical or to a cyclopedic or other composite work—

(i)  the author of such work, if the author is still living,

(ii)  the widow, widower, or children of the author, if the author is not living,

(iii)  the author's executors, if such author, widow, widower, or children are not living, or

(iv)  the author's next of kin, in the absence of a will of the author,

shall be entitled to a renewal and extension of the copyright in such work for a further term of 67 years.

(2)(A)  At the expiration of the original term of copyright in a work specified in paragraph (1)(B) of this subsection, the copyright shall endure for a renewed and extended further term of 67 years, which—

(i)  if an application to register a claim to such further term has been made to the Copyright Office within 1 year before the expiration of the original term of copyright, and the claim is registered, shall vest, upon the beginning of such further term, in the proprietor of the copyright who is entitled to claim the renewal of copyright at the time the application is made; or

(ii)   if no such application is made or the claim pursuant to such application is not registered, shall vest, upon the beginning of such further term, in the person or entity that was the proprietor of the copyright as of the last day of the original term of copyright.

(B)   At the expiration of the original term of copyright in a work specified in paragraph (1)(C) of this subsection, the copyright shall endure for a renewed and extended further term of 67 years, which—

(i)   if an application to register a claim to such further term has been made to the Copyright Office within 1 year before the expiration of the original term of copyright, and the claim is registered, shall vest, upon the beginning of such further term, in any person who is entitled under paragraph (1)(C) to the renewal and extension of the copyright at the time the application is made; or

(ii)   if no such application is made or the claim pursuant to such application is not registered, shall vest, upon the beginning of such further term, in any person entitled under paragraph (1)(C), as of the last day of the original term of copyright, to the renewal and extension of the copyright.

(3)(A)   An application to register a claim to the renewed and extended term of copyright in a work may be made to the Copyright Office—

(i)   within 1 year before the expiration of the original term of copyright by any person entitled under paragraph (1)(B) or (C) to such further term of 67 years; and

(ii)   at any time during the renewed and extended term by any person in whom such further term vested, under paragraph (2)(A) or (B), or by any successor or assign of such person, if the application is made in the name of such person.

(B)   Such an application is not a condition of the renewal and extension of the copyright in a work for a further term of 67 years.

(4)(A)   If an application to register a claim to the renewed and extended term of copyright in a work is not made within 1 year before the expiration of the original term of copyright in a work, or if the claim pursuant to such application is not registered, then a derivative work prepared under authority of a grant of a transfer or license of the copyright that is made before the expiration of the original term of copyright may continue to be used under the terms of the grant during the renewed and extended term of copyright without infringing the copyright, except that such use does not extend to the preparation during such renewed and extended term of other derivative works based upon the copyrighted work covered by such grant.

(B)   If an application to register a claim to the renewed and extended term of copyright in a work is made within 1 year before its expiration, and the claim is registered, the certificate of such registration shall constitute prima facie evidence as to the validity of the copyright during its renewed and extended term and of the facts stated in the certificate. The evidentiary weight to be accorded the certificates of a registration of a renewed and extended term of copyright made after the end of that 1-year period shall be within the discretion of the court.

(b)   **Copyrights in their Renewal Term at the Time of the Effective Date of the Sonny Bono Copyright Term Extension Act.**—Any copyright still in its renewal term at the time that the Sonny Bono Copyright Term Extension Act becomes effective shall have a copyright term of 95 years from the date copyright was originally secured.

(c)   **Termination of Transfers and Licenses Covering Extended Renewal Term.**—In the case of any copyright subsisting in either its first or renewal term on January 1, 1978, other than a copyright in a work made for hire, the exclusive or nonexclusive grant of a transfer or license of the renewal copyright or any right under it, executed before January 1, 1978, by any of the persons designated by subsection (a)(1)(C) of this section, otherwise than by will, is subject to termination under the following conditions:

(1)  In the case of a grant executed by a person or persons other than the author, termination of the grant may be effected by the surviving person or persons who executed it. In the case of a grant executed by one or more of the authors of the work, termination of the grant may be effected, to the extent of a particular author's share in the ownership of the renewal copyright, by the author who executed it or, if such author is dead, by the person or persons who, under clause (2) of this subsection, own and are entitled to exercise a total of more than one-half of that author's termination interest.

(2)  Where an author is dead, his or her termination interest is owned, and may be exercised, as follows:

(A)  The widow or widower owns the author's entire termination interest unless there are any surviving children or grandchildren of the author, in which case the widow or widower owns one-half of the author's interest.

(B)  The author's surviving children, and the surviving children of any dead child of the author, own the author's entire termination interest unless there is a widow or widower, in which case the ownership of one-half of the author's interest is divided among them.

(C)  The rights of the author's children and grandchildren are in all cases divided among them and exercised on a per stirpes basis according to the number of such author's children represented; the share of the children of a dead child in a termination interest can be exercised only by the action of a majority of them.

(D)  In the event that the author's widow or widower, children, and grandchildren are not living, the author's executor, administrator, personal representative, or trustee shall own the author's entire termination interest.

(3)  Termination of the grant may be effected at any time during a period of five years beginning at the end of fifty-six years from the date copyright was originally secured, or beginning on January 1, 1978, whichever is later.

(4)  The termination shall be effected by serving an advance notice in writing upon the grantee or the grantee's successor in title. In the case of a grant executed by a person or persons other than the author, the notice shall be signed by all of those entitled to terminate the grant under clause (1) of this subsection, or by their duly authorized agents. In the case of a grant executed by one or more of the authors of the work, the notice as to any one author's share shall be signed by that author or his or her duly authorized agent or, if that author is dead, by the number and proportion of the owners of his or her termination interest required under clauses (1) and (2) of this subsection, or by their duly authorized agents.

(A)  The notice shall state the effective date of the termination, which shall fall within the five-year period specified by clause (3) of this subsection, or, in the case of a termination under subsection (d), within the five-year period specified by subsection (d)(2), and the notice shall be served not less than two or more than ten years before that date. A copy of the notice shall be recorded in the Copyright Office before the effective date of termination, as a condition to its taking effect.

(B)  The notice shall comply, in form, content, and manner of service, with requirements that the Register of Copyrights shall prescribe by regulation.

(5)  Termination of the grant may be effected notwithstanding any agreement to the contrary, including an agreement to make a will or to make any future grant.

(6)  In the case of a grant executed by a person or persons other than the author, all rights under this title that were covered by the terminated grant revert, upon the effective date of termination, to all of those entitled to terminate the grant under clause (1) of this subsection. In

the case of a grant executed by one or more of the authors of the work, all of a particular author's rights under this title that were covered by the terminated grant revert, upon the effective date of termination, to that author or, if that author is dead, to the persons owning his or her termination interest under clause (2) of this subsection, including those owners who did not join in signing the notice of termination under clause (4) of this subsection. In all cases the reversion of rights is subject to the following limitations:

(A)  A derivative work prepared under authority of the grant before its termination may continue to be utilized under the terms of the grant after its termination, but this privilege does not extend to the preparation after the termination of other derivative works based upon the copyrighted work covered by the terminated grant.

(B)  The future rights that will revert upon termination of the grant become vested on the date the notice of termination has been served as provided by clause (4) of this subsection.

(C)  Where the author's rights revert to two or more persons under clause (2) of this subsection, they shall vest in those persons in the proportionate shares provided by that clause. In such a case, and subject to the provisions of subclause (D) of this clause, a further grant, or agreement to make a further grant, of a particular author's share with respect to any right covered by a terminated grant is valid only if it is signed by the same number and proportion of the owners, in whom the right has vested under this clause, as are required to terminate the grant under clause (2) of this subsection. Such further grant or agreement is effective with respect to all of the persons in whom the right it covers has vested under this subclause, including those who did not join in signing it. If any person dies after rights under a terminated grant have vested in him or her, that person's legal representatives, legatees, or heirs at law represent him or her for purposes of this subclause.

(D)  A further grant, or agreement to make a further grant, of any right covered by a terminated grant is valid only if it is made after the effective date of the termination. As an exception, however, an agreement for such a further grant may be made between the author or any of the persons provided by the first sentence of clause (6) of this subsection, or between the persons provided by subclause (C) of this clause, and the original grantee or such grantee's successor in title, after the notice of termination has been served as provided by clause (4) of this subsection.

(E)  Termination of a grant under this subsection affects only those rights covered by the grant that arise under this title, and in no way affects rights arising under any other Federal, State, or foreign laws.

(F)  Unless and until termination is effected under this subsection, the grant, if it does not provide otherwise, continues in effect for the remainder of the extended renewal term.

**(d)  Termination Rights Provided in Subsection (c) which have Expired On or Before the Effective Date of the Sonny Bono Copyright Term Extension Act.**—In the case of any copyright other than a work made for hire, subsisting in its renewal term on the effective date of the Sonny Bono Copyright Term Extension Act for which the termination right provided in subsection (c) has expired by such date, where the author or owner of the termination right has not previously exercised such termination right, the exclusive or nonexclusive grant of a transfer or license of the renewal copyright or any right under it, executed before January 1, 1978, by any of the persons designated in subsection (a)(1)(C) of this section, other than by will, is subject to termination under the following conditions:

(1)  The conditions specified in subsections (c)(1), (2), (4), (5), and (6) of this section apply to terminations of the last 20 years of copyright term as provided by the amendments made by the Sonny Bono Copyright Term Extension Act.

(2)  Termination of the grant may be effected at any time during a period of 5 years beginning at the end of 75 years from the date copyright was originally secured.

(As amended, Pub.L. 102–307, 106 Stat. 264 (1992); Pub.L. 105–298, 112 Stat. 2827 (1998)).

## Sec. 305.    Duration of Copyright: Terminal Date

All terms of copyright provided by sections 302 through 304 run to the end of the calendar year in which they would otherwise expire.

### CHAPTER 4.—COPYRIGHT NOTICE, DEPOSIT, AND REGISTRATION

## Sec. 401.    Notice of Copyright: Visually Perceptible Copies

(a)  **General Provisions.**—Whenever a work protected under this title is published in the United States or elsewhere by authority of the copyright owner, a notice of copyright as provided by this section may be placed on publicly distributed copies from which the work can be visually perceived, either directly or with the aid of a machine or device.

(b)  **Form of Notice.**—If a notice appears on the copies, it shall consist of the following three elements:

(1)  the symbol © (the letter C in a circle), or the word "Copyright", or the abbreviation "Copr."; and

(2)  the year of first publication of the work; in the case of compilations or derivative works incorporating previously published material, the year date of first publication of the compilation or derivative work is sufficient. The year date may be omitted where a pictorial, graphic, or sculptural work, with accompanying text matter, if any, is reproduced in or on greeting cards, postcards, stationery, jewelry, dolls, toys, or any useful articles; and

(3)  the name of the owner of copyright in the work, or an abbreviation by which the name can be recognized, or a generally known alternative designation of the owner.

(c)  **Position of Notice.**—The notice shall be affixed to the copies in such manner and location as to give reasonable notice of the claim of copyright. The Register of Copyrights shall prescribe by regulation, as examples, specific methods of affixation and positions of the notice on various types of works that will satisfy this requirement, but these specifications shall not be considered exhaustive.

(d)  **Evidentiary Weight of Notice.**—If a notice of copyright in the form and position specified by this section appears on the published copy or copies to which a defendant in a copyright infringement suit had access, then no weight shall be given to such a defendant's interposition of a defense based on innocent infringement in mitigation of actual or statutory damages, except as provided in the last sentence of section 504(c)(2).

(As amended, Pub.L. 100–568, 102 Stat. 2853 (1988)).

## Sec. 402.    Notice of Copyright: Phonorecords of Sound Recordings

(a)  **General Provisions.**—Whenever a sound recording protected under this title is published in the United States or elsewhere by authority of the copyright owner, a notice of copyright as provided by this section may be placed on publicly distributed phonorecords of the sound recording.

(b)  **Form of Notice.**—If a notice appears on the phonorecords, it shall consist of the following three elements:

(1)  the symbol ℗ (the letter P in a circle); and

(2)  the year of first publication of the sound recording; and

(3)  the name of the owner of copyright in the sound recording, or an abbreviation by which the name can be recognized, or a generally known alternative designation of the owner; if the producer of the sound recording is named on the phonorecord labels or containers, and if no other name appears in conjunction with the notice, the producer's name shall be considered a part of the notice.

(c)  **Position of Notice.**—The notice shall be placed on the surface of the phonorecord, or on the phonorecord label or container, in such manner and location as to give reasonable notice of the claim of copyright.

(d)  **Evidentiary Weight of Notice.**—If a notice of copyright in the form and position specified by this section appears on the published phonorecord or phonorecords to which a defendant in a copyright infringement suit had access, then no weight shall be given to such a defendant's interposition of a defense based on innocent infringement in mitigation of actual or statutory damages, except as provided in the last sentence of section 504(c)(2).

(As amended, Pub.L. 100–568, 102 Stat. 2853 (1988)).

## Sec.  403.  Notice  of  Copyright:  Publications  Incorporating  United  States Government Works

Sections 401(d) and 402(d) shall not apply to a work published in copies or phonorecords consisting predominantly of one or more works of the United States Government unless the notice of copyright appearing on the published copies or phonorecords to which a defendant in the copyright infringement suit had access includes a statement identifying, either affirmatively or negatively, those portions of the copies or phonorecords embodying any work or works protected under this title.

(As amended, Pub.L. 100–568, 102 Stat. 2853 (1988)).

## Sec. 404.    Notice of Copyright: Contributions to Collective Works

(a)  A separate contribution to a collective work may bear its own notice of copyright, as provided by sections 401 through 403. However, a single notice applicable to the collective work as a whole is sufficient to invoke the provisions of section 401(d) or 402(d), as applicable with respect to the separate contributions it contains (not including advertisements inserted on behalf of persons other than the owner of copyright in the collective work), regardless of the ownership of copyright in the contributions and whether or not they have been previously published.

(b)  With respect to copies and phonorecords publicly distributed by authority of the copyright owner before the effective date of the Berne Convention Implementation Act of 1988, where the person named in a single notice applicable to a collective work as a whole is not the owner of copyright in a separate contribution that does not bear its own notice, the case is governed by the provisions of section 406(a).

(As amended, Pub.L. 100–568, 102 Stat. 2853 (1988)).

## Sec. 405. Notice of Copyright: Omission of Notice on Certain Copies and Phonorecords

(a) **Effect of Omission on Copyright.**—With respect to copies and phonorecords publicly distributed by authority of the copyright owner before the effective date of the Berne Convention Implementation Act of 1988, the omission of the copyright notice described in sections 401 through 403 from copies or phonorecords publicly distributed by authority of the copyright owner does not invalidate the copyright in a work if—

(1) the notice has been omitted from no more than a relatively small number of copies or phonorecords distributed to the public; or

(2) registration for the work has been made before or is made within five years after the publication without notice, and a reasonable effort is made to add notice to all copies or phonorecords that are distributed to the public in the United States after the omission has been discovered; or

(3) the notice has been omitted in violation of an express requirement in writing that, as a condition of the copyright owner's authorization of the public distribution of copies or phonorecords, they bear the prescribed notice.

(b) **Effect of Omission on Innocent Infringers.**—Any person who innocently infringes a copyright, in reliance upon an authorized copy or phonorecord from which the copyright notice has been omitted and which was publicly distributed by authority of the copyright owner before the effective date of the Berne Convention Implementation Act of 1988, incurs no liability for actual or statutory damages under section 504 for any infringing acts committed before receiving actual notice that registration for the work has been made under section 408, if such person proves that he or she was misled by the omission of notice. In a suit for infringement in such a case the court may allow or disallow recovery of any of the infringer's profits attributable to the infringement, and may enjoin the continuation of the infringing undertaking or may require, as a condition for permitting the continuation of the infringing undertaking, that the infringer pay the copyright owner a reasonable license fee in an amount and on terms fixed by the court.

(c) **Removal of Notice.**—Protection under this title is not affected by the removal, destruction, or obliteration of the notice, without the authorization of the copyright owner, from any publicly distributed copies or phonorecords.

(As amended, Pub.L. 100–568, 102 Stat. 2853 (1988)).

## Sec. 406. Notice of Copyright: Error in Name or Date on Certain Copies and Phonorecords

(a) **Error in Name.**—With respect to copies and phonorecords publicly distributed by authority of the copyright owner before the effective date of the Berne Convention Implementation Act of 1988, where the person named in the copyright notice on copies or phonorecords publicly distributed by authority of the copyright owner is not the owner of copyright, the validity and ownership of the copyright are not affected. In such a case, however, any person who innocently begins an undertaking that infringes the copyright has a complete defense to any action for such infringement if such person proves that he or she was misled by the notice and began the undertaking in good faith under a purported transfer or license from the person named therein, unless before the undertaking was begun—

(1) registration for the work had been made in the name of the owner of copyright; or

(2)   a document executed by the person named in the notice and showing the ownership of the copyright had been recorded.

The person named in the notice is liable to account to the copyright owner for all receipts from transfers or licenses purportedly made under the copyright by the person named in the notice.

   **(b)   Error in Date.**—When the year date in the notice on copies or phonorecords distributed before the effective date of the Berne Convention Implementation Act of 1988 by authority of the copyright owner is earlier than the year in which publication first occurred, any period computed from the year of first publication under section 302 is to be computed from the year in the notice. Where the year date is more than one year later than the year in which publication first occurred, the work is considered to have been published without any notice and is governed by the provisions of section 405.

   **(c)   Omission of Name or Date.**—Where copies or phonorecords publicly distributed before the effective date of the Berne Convention Implementation Act of 1988 by authority of the copyright owner contain no name or no date that could reasonably be considered a part of the notice, the work is considered to have been published without any notice and is governed by the provisions of section 405 as in effect on the day before the effective date of the Berne Convention Implementation Act of 1988.

(As amended, Pub.L. 100–568, 102 Stat. 2853 (1988)).

## Sec. 407.    Deposit of Copies or Phonorecords for Library of Congress

   (a)   Except as provided by subsection (c), and subject to the provisions of subsection (e), the owner of copyright or of the exclusive right of publication in a work published in the United States shall deposit, within three months after the date of such publication—

   (1)   two complete copies of the best edition; or

   (2)   if the work is a sound recording, two complete phonorecords of the best edition, together with any printed or other visually perceptible material published with such phonorecords.

Neither the deposit requirements of this subsection nor the acquisition provisions of subsection (e) are conditions of copyright protection.

   (b)   The required copies or phonorecords shall be deposited in the Copyright Office for the use or disposition of the Library of Congress. The Register of Copyrights shall, when requested by the depositor and upon payment of the fee prescribed by section 708, issue a receipt for the deposit.

   (c)   The Register of Copyrights may by regulation exempt any categories of material from the deposit requirements of this section, or require deposit of only one copy or phonorecord with respect to any categories. Such regulations shall provide either for complete exemption from the deposit requirements of this section, or for alternative forms of deposit aimed at providing a satisfactory archival record of a work without imposing practical or financial hardships on the depositor, where the individual author is the owner of copyright in a pictorial, graphic, or sculptural work and (i) less than five copies of the work have been published, or (ii) the work has been published in a limited edition consisting of numbered copies, the monetary value of which would make the mandatory deposit of two copies of the best edition of the work burdensome, unfair, or unreasonable.

   (d)   At any time after publication of a work as provided by subsection (a), the Register of Copyrights may make written demand for the required deposit on any of the persons obligated to make the deposit under subsection (a). Unless deposit is made within three months after the demand is received, the person or persons on whom the demand was made are liable—

   (1)   to a fine of not more than $250 for each work; and

   (2)   to pay into a specially designated fund in the Library of Congress the total retail price of the copies or phonorecords demanded, or, if no retail price has been fixed, the reasonable cost to the Library of Congress of acquiring them; and

(3)   to pay a fine of $2,500, in addition to any fine or liability imposed under clauses (1) and (2), if such person willfully or repeatedly fails or refuses to comply with such a demand.

(e)   With respect to transmission programs that have been fixed and transmitted to the public in the United States but have not been published, the Register of Copyrights shall, after consulting with the Librarian of Congress and other interested organizations and officials, establish regulations governing the acquisition, through deposit or otherwise, of copies or phonorecords of such programs for the collections of the Library of Congress.

(1)   The Librarian of Congress shall be permitted, under the standards and conditions set forth in such regulations, to make a fixation of a transmission program directly from a transmission to the public, and to reproduce one copy or phonorecord from such fixation for archival purposes.

(2)   Such regulations shall also provide standards and procedures by which the Register of Copyrights may make written demand upon the owner of the right of transmission in the United States, for the deposit of a copy or phonorecord of a specific transmission program. Such deposit may, at the option of the owner of the right of transmission in the United States, be accomplished by gift, by loan for purposes of reproduction, or by sale at a price not to exceed the cost of reproducing and supplying the copy or phonorecord. The regulations established under this clause shall provide reasonable periods of not less than three months for compliance with a demand, and shall allow for extensions of such periods and adjustments in the scope of the demand or the methods for fulfilling it, as reasonably warranted by the circumstances. Willful failure or refusal to comply with the conditions prescribed by such regulations shall subject the owner of the right of transmission in the United States to liability for an amount, not to exceed the cost of reproducing and supplying the copy or phonorecord in question, to be paid into a specially designated fund in the Library of Congress.

(3)   Nothing in this subsection shall be construed to require the making or retention, for purposes of deposit, of any copy or phonorecord of an unpublished transmission program, the transmission of which occurs before the receipt of a specific written demand as provided by clause (2).

(4)   No activity undertaken in compliance with regulations prescribed under clauses (1) or (2) of this subsection shall result in liability if intended solely to assist in the acquisition of copies or phonorecords under this subsection.

(As amended, Pub.L. 100–568, 102 Stat. 2853 (1988)).

## Sec. 408.     Copyright Registration in General

(a)   **Registration Permissive.**—At any time during the subsistence of the first term of copyright in any published or unpublished work in which the copyright was secured before January 1, 1978, and during the subsistence of any copyright secured on or after that date, the owner of copyright or of any exclusive right in the work may obtain registration of the copyright claim by delivering to the Copyright Office the deposit specified by this section, together with the application and fee specified by sections 409 and 708. Such registration is not a condition of copyright protection.

(b)   **Deposit for Copyright Registration.**—Except as provided by subsection (c), the material deposited for registration shall include—

(1)   in the case of an unpublished work, one complete copy or phonorecord;

(2)   in the case of a published work, two complete copies or phonorecords of the best edition;

(3)   in the case of a work first published outside the United States, one complete copy or phonorecord as so published;

(4)   in the case of a contribution to a collective work, one complete copy or phonorecord of the best edition of the collective work.

Copies or phonorecords deposited for the Library of Congress under section 407 may be used to satisfy the deposit provisions of this section, if they are accompanied by the prescribed application and fee, and by any additional identifying material that the Register may, by regulation, require. The Register shall also prescribe regulations establishing requirements under which copies or phonorecords acquired for the Library of Congress under subsection (e) of section 407, otherwise than by deposit, may be used to satisfy the deposit provisions of this section.

**(c)  Administrative Classification and Optional Deposit.—**

(1)  The Register of Copyrights is authorized to specify by regulation the administrative classes into which works are to be placed for purposes of deposit and registration, and the nature of the copies or phonorecords to be deposited in the various classes specified. The regulations may require or permit, for particular classes, the deposit of identifying material instead of copies or phonorecords, the deposit of only one copy or phonorecord where two would normally be required, or a single registration for a group of related works. This administrative classification of works has no significance with respect to the subject matter of copyright or the exclusive rights provided by this title.

(2)  Without prejudice to the general authority provided under clause (1), the Register of Copyrights shall establish regulations specifically permitting a single registration for a group of works by the same individual author, all first published as contributions to periodicals, including newspapers, within a twelve-month period, on the basis of a single deposit, application, and registration fee, under the following conditions—

(A)  if the deposit consists of one copy of the entire issue of the periodical, or of the entire section in the case of a newspaper, in which each contribution was first published; and

(B)  if the application identifies each work separately, including the periodical containing it and its date of first publication.

(3)  As an alternative to separate renewal registrations under subsection (a) of section 304, a single renewal registration may be made for a group of works by the same individual author, all first published as contributions to periodicals, including newspapers, upon the filing of a single application and fee, under all of the following conditions:

(A)  the renewal claimant or claimants, and the basis of claim or claims under section 304(a), is the same for each of the works; and

(B)  the works were all copyrighted upon their first publication, either through separate copyright notice and registration or by virtue of a general copyright notice in the periodical issue as a whole; and

(C)  the renewal application and fee are received not more than twenty-eight or less than twenty-seven years after the thirty-first day of December of the calendar year in which all of the works were first published; and

(D)  the renewal application identifies each work separately, including the periodical containing it and its date of first publication.

**(d)  Corrections and Amplifications.**—The Register may also establish, by regulation, formal procedures for the filing of an application for supplementary registration, to correct an error in a copyright registration or to amplify the information given in a registration. Such application shall be accompanied by the fee provided by section 708, and shall clearly identify the registration to be corrected or amplified. The information contained in a supplementary registration augments but does not supersede that contained in the earlier registration.

**(e)  Published Edition of Previously Registered Work.**—Registration for the first published edition of a work previously registered in unpublished form may be made even though the work as published is substantially the same as the unpublished version.

**(f)  Preregistration of Works Being Prepared for Commercial Distribution.—**

**(1)  Rulemaking.—**Not later than 180 days after the date of enactment of this subsection, the Register of Copyrights shall issue regulations to establish procedures for preregistration of a work that is being prepared for commercial distribution and has not been published.

**(2)  Class of Works.—**The regulations established under paragraph (1) shall permit preregistration for any work that is in a class of works that the Register determines has had a history of infringement prior to authorized commercial distribution.

**(3)  Application for Registration.—**Not later than 3 months after the first publication of a work preregistered under this subsection, the applicant shall submit to the Copyright Office—

(A)  an application for registration of the work;

(B)  a deposit; and

(C)  the applicable fee.

**(4)  Effect of Untimely Application.—**An action under this chapter for infringement of a work preregistered under this subsection, in a case in which the infringement commenced no later than 2 months after the first publication of the work, shall be dismissed if the items described in paragraph (3) are not submitted to the Copyright Office in proper form within the earlier of—

(A)  3 months after the first publication of the work; or

(B)  1 month after the copyright owner has learned of the infringement.

(As amended, Pub.L. 100–568, 102 Stat. 2853 (1988); Pub.L. 102–307, 106 Stat. 264 (1992); Pub.L. 109–9, 119 Stat. 218 (2005)).

## Sec. 409.    Application for Copyright Registration

The application for copyright registration shall be made on a form prescribed by the Register of Copyrights and shall include—

(1)  the name and address of the copyright claimant;

(2)  in the case of a work other than an anonymous or pseudonymous work, the name and nationality or domicile of the author or authors, and, if one or more of the authors is dead, the dates of their deaths;

(3)  if the work is anonymous or pseudonymous, the nationality or domicile of the author or authors;

(4)  in the case of a work made for hire, a statement to this effect;

(5)  if the copyright claimant is not the author, a brief statement of how the claimant obtained ownership of the copyright;

(6)  the title of the work, together with any previous or alternative titles under which the work can be identified;

(7)  the year in which creation of the work was completed;

(8)  if the work has been published, the date and nation of its first publication;

(9)  in the case of a compilation or derivative work, an identification of any preexisting work or works that it is based on or incorporates, and a brief, general statement of the additional material covered by the copyright claim being registered; and

(10) any other information regarded by the Register of Copyrights as bearing upon the preparation or identification of the work or the existence, ownership, or duration of the copyright.

If an application is submitted for the renewed and extended term provided for in section 304(a)(3)(A) and an original term registration has not been made, the Register may request information with respect to the existence, ownership, or duration of the copyright for the original term.

(As amended, Pub.L. 102–307, 106 Stat. 264 (1992); Pub.L. 111–295, 124 Stat. 3180 (2010)).

## Sec. 410.    Registration of Claim and Issuance of Certificate

(a)   When, after examination, the Register of Copyrights determines that, in accordance with the provisions of this title, the material deposited constitutes copyrightable subject matter and that the other legal and formal requirements of this title have been met, the Register shall register the claim and issue to the applicant a certificate of registration under the seal of the Copyright Office. The certificate shall contain the information given in the application, together with the number and effective date of the registration.

(b)   In any case in which the Register of Copyrights determines that, in accordance with the provisions of this title, the material deposited does not constitute copyrightable subject matter or that the claim is invalid for any other reason, the Register shall refuse registration and shall notify the applicant in writing of the reasons for such refusal.

(c)   In any judicial proceedings the certificate of a registration made before or within five years after first publication of the work shall constitute prima facie evidence of the validity of the copyright and of the facts stated in the certificate. The evidentiary weight to be accorded the certificate of a registration made thereafter shall be within the discretion of the court.

(d)   The effective date of a copyright registration is the day on which an application, deposit, and fee, which are later determined by the Register of Copyrights or by a court of competent jurisdiction to be acceptable for registration, have all been received in the Copyright Office.

## Sec. 411.    Registration and Civil Infringement Actions

(a)   Except for an action brought for violation of the rights of the author under section 106A(a), and subject to the provisions of subsection (b), no civil action for infringement of the copyright in any United States work shall be instituted until preregistration or registration of the copyright claim has been made in accordance with this title. In any case, however, where the deposit, application, and fee required for registration have been delivered to the Copyright Office in proper form and registration has been refused, the applicant is entitled to institute a civil action for infringement if notice thereof, with a copy of the complaint, is served on the Register of Copyrights. The Register may, at his or her option, become a party to the action with respect to the issue of registrability of the copyright claim by entering an appearance within sixty days after such service, but the Register's failure to become a party shall not deprive the court of jurisdiction to determine that issue.

(b)(1)   A certificate of registration satisfies the requirements of this section and section 412, regardless of whether the certificate contains any inaccurate information, unless—

(A)   the inaccurate information was included on the application for copyright registration with knowledge that it was inaccurate; and

(B)   the inaccuracy of the information, if known, would have caused the Register of Copyrights to refuse registration.

(2)   In any case in which inaccurate information described under paragraph (1) is alleged, the court shall request the Register of Copyrights to advise the court whether the inaccurate information, if known, would have caused the Register of Copyrights to refuse registration.

(3)   Nothing in this subsection shall affect any rights, obligations, or requirements of a person related to information contained in a registration certificate, except for the institution of and remedies in infringement actions under this section and section 412.

(c)   In the case of a work consisting of sounds, images, or both, the first fixation of which is made simultaneously with its transmission, the copyright owner may, either before or after such fixation takes place, institute an action for infringement under section 501, fully subject to the remedies provided by sections 502 through 505 and section 510, if, in accordance with requirements that the Register of Copyrights shall prescribe by regulation, the copyright owner—

> (1)   serves notice upon the infringer, not less than 48 hours before such fixation, identifying the work and the specific time and source of its first transmission, and declaring an intention to secure copyright in the work; and

> (2)   makes registration for the work, if required by subsection (a), within three months after its first transmission.

(As amended, Pub.L. 100–568, 102 Stat. 2853 (1988); Pub.L. 101–650, 104 Stat. 5089 (1990); Pub.L. 105–80, 111 Stat. 1529 (1997); Pub.L. 105–304, 112 Stat. 2860 (1998); Pub.L. 109–9, 119 Stat. 218 (2005); Pub.L. 110–403, 122 Stat. 4256 (2008)).

### Sec. 412.   Registration as Prerequisite to Certain Remedies for Infringement

In any action under this title, other than an action brought for a violation of the rights of the author under section 106A(a), an action for infringement of the copyright of a work that has been preregistered under section 408(f) before the commencement of the infringement and that has an effective date of registration not later than the earlier of 3 months after the first publication of the work or 1 month after the copyright owner has learned of the infringement, or an action instituted under section 411(c), no award of statutory damages or of attorney's fees, as provided by sections 504 and 505, shall be made for—

> (1)   any infringement of copyright in an unpublished work commenced before the effective date of its registration; or

> (2)   any infringement of copyright commenced after first publication of the work and before the effective date of its registration, unless such registration is made within three months after the first publication of the work.

(As amended, Pub.L. 101–650, 104 Stat. 5089 (1990); Pub.L. 109–9, 119 Stat. 218 (2005); Pub.L. 110–403, 122 Stat. 4256 (2008)).

### CHAPTER 5.—COPYRIGHT INFRINGEMENT AND REMEDIES

Sec.
| | |
|---|---|
| 501. | Infringement of Copyright. |
| 502. | Remedies for Infringement: Injunctions. |
| 503. | Remedies for Infringement: Impounding and Disposition of Infringing Articles. |
| 504. | Remedies for Infringement: Damages and Profits. |
| 505. | Remedies for Infringement: Costs and Attorney's Fees. |
| 506. | Criminal Offenses. |
| 507. | Limitations on Actions. |
| 508. | Notification of Filing and Determination of Actions. |
| 509. | [Repealed]. |
| 510. | Remedies for Alteration of Programming by Cable Systems. |
| 511. | Liability of States, Instrumentalities of States, and State Officials for Infringement of Copyright. |
| 512. | Limitations on Liability Relating to Material Online. |
| 513. | Determination of Reasonable License Fees for Individual Proprietors. |

### Sec. 501.   Infringement of Copyright

(a)   Anyone who violates any of the exclusive rights of the copyright owner as provided by sections 106 through 122 or of the author as provided in section 106A(a), or who imports copies or phonorecords into the United States in violation of section 602, is an infringer of the copyright or right of the author, as the case may be. For purposes of this chapter (other than section 506), any reference to copyright shall be deemed to include the rights conferred by section 106A(a). As used in this subsection, the term "anyone" includes any State, any instrumentality of a State, and any officer or employee of a State or instrumentality of a State acting in his or her official capacity. Any State, and any such instrumentality, officer, or employee, shall be subject to the provisions of this title in the same manner and to the same extent as any nongovernmental entity.

(b)   The legal or beneficial owner of an exclusive right under a copyright is entitled, subject to the requirements of section 411, to institute an action for any infringement of that particular right committed while he or she is the owner of it. The court may require such owner to serve written notice of the action with a copy of the complaint upon any person shown, by the records of the Copyright Office or otherwise, to have or claim an interest in the copyright, and shall require that such notice be served upon any person whose interest is likely to be affected by a decision in the case. The court may require the joinder, and shall permit the intervention, of any person having or claiming an interest in the copyright.

(c)   For any secondary transmission by a cable system that embodies a performance or a display of a work which is actionable as an act of infringement under subsection (c) of section 111, a television broadcast station holding a copyright or other license to transmit or perform the same version of that work shall, for purposes of subsection (b) of this section, be treated as a legal or beneficial owner if such secondary transmission occurs within the local service area of that television station.

(d)   For any secondary transmission by a cable system that is actionable as an act of infringement pursuant to section 111(c)(3), the following shall also have standing to sue: (i) the primary transmitter whose transmission has been altered by the cable system; and (ii) any broadcast station within whose local service area the secondary transmission occurs.

(e)   With respect to any secondary transmission that is made by a satellite carrier of a performance or display of a work embodied in a primary transmission and is actionable as an act of infringement under section 119(a)(3), a network station holding a copyright or other license to transmit or perform the same version of that work shall, for purposes of subsection (b) of this section, be treated as a legal or beneficial owner if such secondary transmission occurs within the local service area of that station.

(f)(1)   With respect to any secondary transmission that is made by a satellite carrier of a performance or display of a work embodied in a primary transmission and is actionable as an act of infringement under section 122, a television broadcast station holding a copyright or other license to transmit or perform the same version of that work shall, for purposes of subsection (b) of this section, be treated as a legal or beneficial owner if such secondary transmission occurs within the local market of that station.

(2)   A television broadcast station may file a civil action against any satellite carrier that has refused to carry television broadcast signals, as required under section 122(a)(2), to enforce that television broadcast station's rights under section 338(a) of the Communications Act of 1934 [47 U.S.C.A. § 338(a)].

(As amended, Pub.L. 100–568, 102 Stat. 2853 (1988); Pub.L. 100–667, 102 Stat. 3935 (1988); Pub.L. 101–553, 104 Stat. 2749 (1990); Pub.L. 101–650, 104 Stat. 5089 (1990); Pub.L. 106–44, 113 Stat. 221 (1999); Pub.L. 106–113, 113 Stat. 1051A (1999); Pub.L. 107–273, 116 Stat. 1758 (2002)).

## Sec. 502.   Remedies for Infringement: Injunctions

(a)   Any court having jurisdiction of a civil action arising under this title may, subject to the provisions of section 1498 of title 28, grant temporary and final injunctions on such terms as it may deem reasonable to prevent or restrain infringement of a copyright.

(b)   Any such injunction may be served anywhere in the United States on the person enjoined; it shall be operative throughout the United States and shall be enforceable, by proceedings in contempt or otherwise, by any United States court having jurisdiction of that person. The clerk of the court granting the injunction shall, when requested by any other court in which enforcement of the injunction is sought, transmit promptly to the other court a certified copy of all the papers in the case on file in such clerk's office.

## Sec. 503.    Remedies for Infringement: Impounding and Disposition of Infringing Articles

(a)(1)   At any time while an action under this title is pending, the court may order the impounding, on such terms as it may deem reasonable—

(A)   of all copies or phonorecords claimed to have been made or used in violation of the exclusive right of the copyright owner;

(B)   of all plates, molds, matrices, masters, tapes, film negatives, or other articles by means of which such copies or phonorecords may be reproduced; and

(C)   of records documenting the manufacture, sale, or receipt of things involved in any such violation, provided that any records seized under this subparagraph shall be taken into the custody of the court.

(2)   For impoundments of records ordered under paragraph (1)(C), the court shall enter an appropriate protective order with respect to discovery and use of any records or information that has been impounded. The protective order shall provide for appropriate procedures to ensure that confidential, private, proprietary, or privileged information contained in such records is not improperly disclosed or used.

(3)   The relevant provisions of paragraphs (2) through (11) of section 34(d) of the Trademark Act (15 U.S.C. 1116(d)(2) through (11)) shall extend to any impoundment of records ordered under paragraph (1)(C) that is based upon an ex parte application, notwithstanding the provisions of rule 65 of the Federal Rules of Civil Procedure. Any references in paragraphs (2) through (11) of section 34(d) of the Trademark Act to section 32 of such Act shall be read as references to section 501 of this title, and references to use of a counterfeit mark in connection with the sale, offering for sale, or distribution of goods or services shall be read as references to infringement of a copyright.

(b)   As part of a final judgment or decree, the court may order the destruction or other reasonable disposition of all copies or phonorecords found to have been made or used in violation of the copyright owner's exclusive rights, and of all plates, molds, matrices, masters, tapes, film negatives, or other articles by means of which such copies or phonorecords may be reproduced.

(As amended, Pub.L. 110–403, 122 Stat. 4256 (2008)).

## Sec. 504.    Remedies for Infringement: Damages and Profits

(a)  In General.—Except as otherwise provided by this title, an infringer of copyright is liable for either—

(1)   the copyright owner's actual damages and any additional profits of the infringer, as provided by subsection (b); or

(2)   statutory damages, as provided by subsection (c).

(b)  Actual Damages and Profits.—The copyright owner is entitled to recover the actual damages suffered by him or her as a result of the infringement, and any profits of the infringer that are attributable to the infringement and are not taken into account in computing the actual damages. In establishing the infringer's profits, the copyright owner is required to present proof only of the infringer's gross revenue, and the infringer is required to prove his or her deductible expenses and the elements of profit attributable to factors other than the copyrighted work.

**(c) Statutory Damages.—**

(1)   Except as provided by clause (2) of this subsection, the copyright owner may elect, at any time before final judgment is rendered, to recover, instead of actual damages and profits, an award of statutory damages for all infringements involved in the action, with respect to any one work, for which any one infringer is liable individually, or for which any two or more infringers are liable jointly and severally, in a sum of not less than $750 or more than $30,000 as the court considers just. For the purposes of this subsection, all the parts of a compilation or derivative work constitute one work.

(2)   In a case where the copyright owner sustains the burden of proving, and the court finds, that infringement was committed willfully, the court in its discretion may increase the award of statutory damages to a sum of not more than $150,000. In a case where the infringer sustains the burden of proving, and the court finds, that such infringer was not aware and had no reason to believe that his or her acts constituted an infringement of copyright, the court in its discretion may reduce the award of statutory damages to a sum of not less than $200. The court shall remit statutory damages in any case where an infringer believed and had reasonable grounds for believing that his or her use of the copyrighted work was a fair use under section 107, if the infringer was: (i) an employee or agent of a nonprofit educational institution, library, or archives acting within the scope of his or her employment who, or such institution, library, or archives itself, which infringed by reproducing the work in copies or phonorecords; or (ii) a public broadcasting entity which or a person who, as a regular part of the nonprofit activities of a public broadcasting entity (as defined in section 118(f)) infringed by performing a published nondramatic literary work or by reproducing a transmission program embodying a performance of such a work.

(3)(A)   In a case of infringement, it shall be a rebuttable presumption that the infringement was committed willfully for purposes of determining relief if the violator, or a person acting in concert with the violator, knowingly provided or knowingly caused to be provided materially false contact information to a domain name registrar, domain name registry, or other domain name registration authority in registering, maintaining, or renewing a domain name used in connection with the infringement.

(B)   Nothing in this paragraph limits what may be considered willful infringement under this subsection.

(C)   For purposes of this paragraph, the term "domain name" has the meaning given that term in section 45 of the Act entitled "An Act to provide for the registration and protection of trademarks used in commerce, to carry out the provisions of certain international conventions, and for other purposes" approved July 5, 1946 (commonly referred to as the "Trademark Act of 1946"; 15 U.S.C. 1127).

**(d) Additional Damages in Certain Cases.**—In any case in which the court finds that a defendant proprietor of an establishment who claims as a defense that its activities were exempt under section 110(5) did not have reasonable grounds to believe that its use of a copyrighted work was exempt under such section, the plaintiff shall be entitled to, in addition to any award of damages under this section, an additional award of two times the amount of the license fee that the proprietor of the establishment concerned should have paid the plaintiff for such use during the preceding period of up to 3 years.

(As amended, Pub.L. 100–568, 102 Stat. 2853 (1988); Pub.L. 105–298, 112 Stat. 2827 (1998); Pub.L. 106–160, 113 Stat. 1774 (1999); Pub.L. 108–482, 118 Stat. 3916 (2004)).

**Sec. 505.**     **Remedies for Infringement: Costs and Attorney's Fees**

In any civil action under this title, the court in its discretion may allow the recovery of full costs by or against any party other than the United States or an officer thereof. Except as otherwise provided by this title, the court may also award a reasonable attorney's fee to the prevailing party as part of the costs.

**Sec. 506.**     **Criminal Offenses**

**(a) Criminal Infringement.—**

**(1) In General.—**Any person who willfully infringes a copyright shall be punished as provided under section 2319 of title 18, if the infringement was committed—

(A)   for purposes of commercial advantage or private financial gain;

(B)   by the reproduction or distribution, including by electronic means, during any 180-day period, of 1 or more copies or phonorecords of 1 or more copyrighted works, which have a total retail value of more than $1,000; or

(C)   by the distribution of a work being prepared for commercial distribution, by making it available on a computer network accessible to members of the public, if such person knew or should have known that the work was intended for commercial distribution.

**(2) Evidence.—**For purposes of this subsection, evidence of reproduction or distribution of a copyrighted work, by itself, shall not be sufficient to establish willful infringement of a copyright.

**(3) Definition.—**In this subsection, the term "work being prepared for commercial distribution" means—

(A)   a computer program, a musical work, a motion picture or other audiovisual work, or a sound recording, if, at the time of unauthorized distribution—

(i)   the copyright owner has a reasonable expectation of commercial distribution; and

(ii)   the copies or phonorecords of the work have not been commercially distributed; or

(B)   a motion picture, if, at the time of unauthorized distribution, the motion picture—

(i)   has been made available for viewing in a motion picture exhibition facility; and

(ii)   has not been made available in copies for sale to the general public in the United States in a format intended to permit viewing outside a motion picture exhibition facility.

**(b) Forfeiture, Destruction, and Restitution.—**Forfeiture, destruction, and restitution relating to this section shall be subject to section 2323 of title 18, to the extent provided in that section, in addition to any other similar remedies provided by law.

**(c) Fraudulent Copyright Notice.—**Any person who, with fraudulent intent, places on any article a notice of copyright or words of the same purport that such person knows to be false, or who, with fraudulent intent, publicly distributes or imports for public distribution any article bearing such notice or words that such person knows to be false, shall be fined not more than $2,500.

**(d) Fraudulent Removal of Copyright Notice.—**Any person who, with fraudulent intent, removes or alters any notice of copyright appearing on a copy of a copyrighted work shall be fined not more than $2,500.

(e)   **False Representation.**—Any person who knowingly makes a false representation of a material fact in the application for copyright registration provided for by section 409, or in any written statement filed in connection with the application, shall be fined not more than $2,500.

(f)   **Rights of Attribution and Integrity.**—Nothing in this section applies to infringement of the rights conferred by section 106A(a).

(As amended, Pub.L. 97–180, 96 Stat. 93 (1982); Pub.L. 101–650, 104 Stat. 5089 (1990); Pub.L. 105–147, 111 Stat. 2678 (1997); Pub.L. 109–9, 119 Stat. 218 (2005); Pub.L. 110–403, 122 Stat. 4256 (2008)).

## Sec. 507.   Limitations on Actions

(a)   **Criminal Proceedings.**—Except as expressly provided otherwise in this title, no criminal proceeding shall be maintained under the provisions of this title unless it is commenced within five years after the cause of action arose.

(b)   **Civil Actions.**—No civil action shall be maintained under the provisions of this title unless it is commenced within three years after the claim accrued.

(As amended, Pub.L. 105–147, 111 Stat. 2678 (1997); Pub.L. 105–304, 112 Stat. 2860 (1998)).

## Sec. 508.   Notification of Filing and Determination of Actions

(a)   Within one month after the filing of any action under this title, the clerks of the courts of the United States shall send written notification to the Register of Copyrights setting forth, as far as is shown by the papers filed in the court, the names and addresses of the parties and the title, author, and registration number of each work involved in the action. If any other copyrighted work is later included in the action by amendment, answer, or other pleading, the clerk shall also send a notification concerning it to the Register within one month after the pleading is filed.

(b)   Within one month after any final order or judgment is issued in the case, the clerk of the court shall notify the Register of it, sending with the notification a copy of the order or judgment together with the written opinion, if any, of the court.

(c)   Upon receiving the notifications specified in this section, the Register shall make them a part of the public records of the Copyright Office.

## Sec. 509.   [Repealed]

## Sec. 510.   Remedies for Alteration of Programming by Cable Systems

(a)   In any action filed pursuant to section 111(c)(3), the following remedies shall be available:

(1)   Where an action is brought by a party identified in subsections (b) or (c) of section 501, the remedies provided by sections 502 through 505, and the remedy provided by subsection (b) of this section; and

(2)   When an action is brought by a party identified in subsection (d) of section 501, the remedies provided by sections 502 and 505, together with any actual damages suffered by such party as a result of the infringement, and the remedy provided by subsection (b) of this section.

(b)   In any action filed pursuant to section 111(c)(3), the court may decree that, for a period not to exceed thirty days, the cable system shall be deprived of the benefit of a statutory license for one or more distant signals carried by such cable system.

(As amended, Pub.L. 106–113, 113 Stat. 1501A (1999)).

## Sec. 511.    Liability of States, Instrumentalities of States, and State Officials for Infringement of Copyright

(a)  **In General.**—Any State, any instrumentality of a State, and any officer or employee of a State or instrumentality of a State acting in his or her official capacity, shall not be immune, under the Eleventh Amendment of the Constitution of the United States or under any other doctrine of sovereign immunity, from suit in Federal court by any person, including any governmental or nongovernmental entity, for a violation of any of the exclusive rights of a copyright owner provided by sections 106 through 122, for importing copies or phonorecords in violation of section 602, or for any other violation under this title.

(b)  **Remedies.**—In a suit described in subsection (a) for a violation described in that subsection, remedies (including remedies both at law and in equity) are available for the violation to the same extent as such remedies are available for such a violation in a suit against any public or private entity other than a State, instrumentality of a State, or officer or employee of a State acting in his or her official capacity. Such remedies include impounding and disposition of infringing articles under section 503, actual damages and profits and statutory damages under section 504, costs and attorney's fees under section 505, and the remedies provided in section 510.

(Added by Pub.L. 101–553, 104 Stat. 2749 (1990); as amended, Pub.L. 106–44, 113 Stat. 221 (1999); Pub.L. 107–273, 116 Stat. 1758 (2002)).

## Sec. 512.    Limitations on Liability Relating to Material Online

(a)  **Transitory Digital Network Communications.**—A service provider shall not be liable for monetary relief, or, except as provided in subsection (j), for injunctive or other equitable relief, for infringement of copyright by reason of the provider's transmitting, routing, or providing connections for, material through a system or network controlled or operated by or for the service provider, or by reason of the intermediate and transient storage of that material in the course of such transmitting, routing, or providing connections, if—

(1)  the transmission of the material was initiated by or at the direction of a person other than the service provider;

(2)  the transmission, routing, provision of connections, or storage is carried out through an automatic technical process without selection of the material by the service provider;

(3)  the service provider does not select the recipients of the material except as an automatic response to the request of another person;

(4)  no copy of the material made by the service provider in the course of such intermediate or transient storage is maintained on the system or network in a manner ordinarily accessible to anyone other than anticipated recipients, and no such copy is maintained on the system or network in a manner ordinarily accessible to such anticipated recipients for a longer period than is reasonably necessary for the transmission, routing, or provision of connections; and

(5)  the material is transmitted through the system or network without modification of its content.

(b)  **System Caching.**—

(1)  **Limitation on Liability.**—A service provider shall not be liable for monetary relief, or, except as provided in subsection (j), for injunctive or other equitable relief, for infringement of copyright by reason of the intermediate and temporary storage of material on a system or network controlled or operated by or for the service provider in a case in which—

(A)  the material is made available online by a person other than the service provider;

(B) the material is transmitted from the person described in subparagraph (A) through the system or network to a person other than the person described in subparagraph (A) at the direction of that other person; and

(C) the storage is carried out through an automatic technical process for the purpose of making the material available to users of the system or network who, after the material is transmitted as described in subparagraph (B), request access to the material from the person described in subparagraph (A), if the conditions set forth in paragraph (2) are met.

(2) Conditions.—The conditions referred to in paragraph (1) are that—

(A) the material described in paragraph (1) is transmitted to the subsequent users described in paragraph (1)(C) without modification to its content from the manner in which the material was transmitted from the person described in paragraph (1)(A);

(B) the service provider described in paragraph (1) complies with rules concerning the refreshing, reloading, or other updating of the material when specified by the person making the material available online in accordance with a generally accepted industry standard data communications protocol for the system or network through which that person makes the material available, except that this subparagraph applies only if those rules are not used by the person described in paragraph (1)(A) to prevent or unreasonably impair the intermediate storage to which this subsection applies;

(C) the service provider does not interfere with the ability of technology associated with the material to return to the person described in paragraph (1)(A) the information that would have been available to that person if the material had been obtained by the subsequent users described in paragraph (1)(C) directly from that person, except that this subparagraph applies only if that technology—

(i) does not significantly interfere with the performance of the provider's system or network or with the intermediate storage of the material;

(ii) is consistent with generally accepted industry standard communications protocols; and

(iii) does not extract information from the provider's system or network other than the information that would have been available to the person described in paragraph (1)(A) if the subsequent users had gained access to the material directly from that person;

(D) if the person described in paragraph (1)(A) has in effect a condition that a person must meet prior to having access to the material, such as a condition based on payment of a fee or provision of a password or other information, the service provider permits access to the stored material in significant part only to users of its system or network that have met those conditions and only in accordance with those conditions; and

(E) if the person described in paragraph (1)(A) makes that material available online without the authorization of the copyright owner of the material, the service provider responds expeditiously to remove, or disable access to, the material that is claimed to be infringing upon notification of claimed infringement as described in subsection (c)(3), except that this subparagraph applies only if—

(i) the material has previously been removed from the originating site or access to it has been disabled, or a court has ordered that the material be removed from the originating site or that access to the material on the originating site be disabled; and

(ii) the party giving the notification includes in the notification a statement confirming that the material has been removed from the originating site or access to it has been disabled or that a court has ordered that the material be removed from the originating site or that access to the material on the originating site be disabled.

**(c)  Information Residing on Systems or Networks at Direction of Users.—**

**(1)  In General.—**A service provider shall not be liable for monetary relief, or, except as provided in subsection (j), for injunctive or other equitable relief, for infringement of copyright by reason of the storage at the direction of a user of material that resides on a system or network controlled or operated by or for the service provider, if the service provider—

(A)(i)  does not have actual knowledge that the material or an activity using the material on the system or network is infringing;

(ii)  in the absence of such actual knowledge, is not aware of facts or circumstances from which infringing activity is apparent; or

(iii)  upon obtaining such knowledge or awareness, acts expeditiously to remove, or disable access to, the material;

(B)  does not receive a financial benefit directly attributable to the infringing activity, in a case in which the service provider has the right and ability to control such activity; and

(C)  upon notification of claimed infringement as described in paragraph (3), responds expeditiously to remove, or disable access to, the material that is claimed to be infringing or to be the subject of infringing activity.

**(2)  Designated Agent.—**The limitations on liability established in this subsection apply to a service provider only if the service provider has designated an agent to receive notifications of claimed infringement described in paragraph (3), by making available through its service, including on its website in a location accessible to the public, and by providing to the Copyright Office, substantially the following information:

(A)  the name, address, phone number, and electronic mail address of the agent.

(B)  other contact information which the Register of Copyrights may deem appropriate.

The Register of Copyrights shall maintain a current directory of agents available to the public for inspection, including through the Internet, and may require payment of a fee by service providers to cover the costs of maintaining the directory.

**(3)  Elements of Notification.—**

(A)  To be effective under this subsection, a notification of claimed infringement must be a written communication provided to the designated agent of a service provider that includes substantially the following:

(i)  A physical or electronic signature of a person authorized to act on behalf of the owner of an exclusive right that is allegedly infringed.

(ii)  Identification of the copyrighted work claimed to have been infringed, or, if multiple copyrighted works at a single online site are covered by a single notification, a representative list of such works at that site.

(iii)  Identification of the material that is claimed to be infringing or to be the subject of infringing activity and that is to be removed or access to which is to be disabled, and information reasonably sufficient to permit the service provider to locate the material.

(iv)  Information reasonably sufficient to permit the service provider to contact the complaining party, such as an address, telephone number, and, if available, an electronic mail address at which the complaining party may be contacted.

(v)  A statement that the complaining party has a good faith belief that use of the material in the manner complained of is not authorized by the copyright owner, its agent, or the law.

(vi)  A statement that the information in the notification is accurate, and under penalty of perjury, that the complaining party is authorized to act on behalf of the owner of an exclusive right that is allegedly infringed.

(B)(i)  Subject to clause (ii), a notification from a copyright owner or from a person authorized to act on behalf of the copyright owner that fails to comply substantially with the provisions of subparagraph (A) shall not be considered under paragraph (1)(A) in determining whether a service provider has actual knowledge or is aware of facts or circumstances from which infringing activity is apparent.

(ii)  In a case in which the notification that is provided to the service provider's designated agent fails to comply substantially with all the provisions of subparagraph (A) but substantially complies with clauses (ii), (iii), and (iv) of subparagraph (A), clause (i) of this subparagraph applies only if the service provider promptly attempts to contact the person making the notification or takes other reasonable steps to assist in the receipt of notification that substantially complies with all the provisions of subparagraph (A).

(d)  **Information Location Tools.**—A service provider shall not be liable for monetary relief, or, except as provided in subsection (j), for injunctive or other equitable relief, for infringement of copyright by reason of the provider referring or linking users to an online location containing infringing material or infringing activity, by using information location tools, including a directory, index, reference, pointer, or hypertext link, if the service provider—

(1)(A)  does not have actual knowledge that the material or activity is infringing;

(B)  in the absence of such actual knowledge, is not aware of facts or circumstances from which infringing activity is apparent; or

(C)  upon obtaining such knowledge or awareness, acts expeditiously to remove, or disable access to, the material;

(2)  does not receive a financial benefit directly attributable to the infringing activity, in a case in which the service provider has the right and ability to control such activity; and

(3)  upon notification of claimed infringement as described in subsection (c)(3), responds expeditiously to remove, or disable access to, the material that is claimed to be infringing or to be the subject of infringing activity, except that, for purposes of this paragraph, the information described in subsection (c)(3)(A)(iii) shall be identification of the reference or link, to material or activity claimed to be infringing, that is to be removed or access to which is to be disabled, and information reasonably sufficient to permit the service provider to locate that reference or link.

(e)  **Limitation on Liability of Nonprofit Educational Institutions.**—

(1)  When a public or other nonprofit institution of higher education is a service provider, and when a faculty member or graduate student who is an employee of such institution is performing a teaching or research function, for the purposes of subsections (a) and (b) such faculty member or graduate student shall be considered to be a person other than the institution, and for the purposes of subsections (c) and (d) such faculty member's or graduate student's knowledge or awareness of his or her infringing activities shall not be attributed to the institution, if—

(A)  such faculty member's or graduate student's infringing activities do not involve the provision of online access to instructional materials that are or were required or recommended, within the preceding 3-year period, for a course taught at the institution by such faculty member or graduate student;

(B)  the institution has not, within the preceding 3-year period, received more than two notifications described in subsection (c)(3) of claimed infringement by such faculty member or graduate student, and such notifications of claimed infringement were not actionable under subsection (f); and

(C) the institution provides to all users of its system or network informational materials that accurately describe, and promote compliance with, the laws of the United States relating to copyright.

(2) For the purposes of this subsection, the limitations on injunctive relief contained in subsections (j)(2) and (j)(3), but not those in (j)(1), shall apply.

**(f) Misrepresentations.**—Any person who knowingly materially misrepresents under this section—

(1) that material or activity is infringing, or

(2) that material or activity was removed or disabled by mistake or misidentification,

shall be liable for any damages, including costs and attorneys' fees, incurred by the alleged infringer, by any copyright owner or copyright owner's authorized licensee, or by a service provider, who is injured by such misrepresentation, as the result of the service provider relying upon such misrepresentation in removing or disabling access to the material or activity claimed to be infringing, or in replacing the removed material or ceasing to disable access to it

**(g) Replacement of Removed or Disabled Material and Limitation on Other Liability.**—

**(1) No Liability for Taking Down Generally.**—Subject to paragraph (2), a service provider shall not be liable to any person for any claim based on the service provider's good faith disabling of access to, or removal of, material or activity claimed to be infringing or based on facts or circumstances from which infringing activity is apparent, regardless of whether the material or activity is ultimately determined to be infringing.

**(2) Exception.**—Paragraph (1) shall not apply with respect to material residing at the direction of a subscriber of the service provider on a system or network controlled or operated by or for the service provider that is removed, or to which access is disabled by the service provider, pursuant to a notice provided under subsection (c)(1)(C), unless the service provider—

(A) takes reasonable steps promptly to notify the subscriber that it has removed or disabled access to the material;

(B) upon receipt of a counter notification described in paragraph (3), promptly provides the person who provided the notification under subsection (c)(1)(C) with a copy of the counter notification, and informs that person that it will replace the removed material or cease disabling access to it in 10 business days; and

(C) replaces the removed material and ceases disabling access to it not less than 10, nor more than 14, business days following receipt of the counter notice, unless its designated agent first receives notice from the person who submitted the notification under subsection (c)(1)(C) that such person has filed an action seeking a court order to restrain the subscriber from engaging in infringing activity relating to the material on the service provider's system or network.

**(3) Contents of Counter Notification.**—To be effective under this subsection, a counter notification must be a written communication provided to the service provider's designated agent that includes substantially the following:

(A) A physical or electronic signature of the subscriber.

(B) Identification of the material that has been removed or to which access has been disabled and the location at which the material appeared before it was removed or access to it was disabled.

(C) A statement under penalty of perjury that the subscriber has a good faith belief that the material was removed or disabled as a result of mistake or misidentification of the material to be removed or disabled.

(D)  The subscriber's name, address, and telephone number, and a statement that the subscriber consents to the jurisdiction of Federal District Court for the judicial district in which the address is located, or if the subscriber's address is outside of the United States, for any judicial district in which the service provider may be found, and that the subscriber will accept service of process from the person who provided notification under subsection (c)(1)(C) or an agent of such person.

**(4)  Limitation on Other Liability.**—A service provider's compliance with paragraph (2) shall not subject the service provider to liability for copyright infringement with respect to the material identified in the notice provided under subsection (c)(1)(C).

**(h)  Subpoena to Identify Infringer.**—

**(1)  Request.**—A copyright owner or a person authorized to act on the owner's behalf may request the clerk of any United States district court to issue a subpoena to a service provider for identification of an alleged infringer in accordance with this subsection.

**(2)  Contents of Request.**—The request may be made by filing with the clerk—

(A)  a copy of a notification described in subsection (c)(3)(A);

(B)  a proposed subpoena; and

(C)  a sworn declaration to the effect that the purpose for which the subpoena is sought is to obtain the identity of an alleged infringer and that such information will only be used for the purpose of protecting rights under this title.

**(3)  Contents of Subpoena.**—The subpoena shall authorize and order the service provider receiving the notification and the subpoena to expeditiously disclose to the copyright owner or person authorized by the copyright owner information sufficient to identify the alleged infringer of the material described in the notification to the extent such information is available to the service provider.

**(4)  Basis for Granting Subpoena.**—If the notification filed satisfies the provisions of subsection (c)(3)(A), the proposed subpoena is in proper form, and the accompanying declaration is properly executed, the clerk shall expeditiously issue and sign the proposed subpoena and return it to the requester for delivery to the service provider.

**(5)  Actions of Service Provider Receiving Subpoena.**—Upon receipt of the issued subpoena, either accompanying or subsequent to the receipt of a notification described in subsection (c)(3)(A), the service provider shall expeditiously disclose to the copyright owner or person authorized by the copyright owner the information required by the subpoena, notwithstanding any other provision of law and regardless of whether the service provider responds to the notification.

**(6)  Rules Applicable to Subpoena.**—Unless otherwise provided by this section or by applicable rules of the court, the procedure for issuance and delivery of the subpoena, and the remedies for noncompliance with the subpoena, shall be governed to the greatest extent practicable by those provisions of the Federal Rules of Civil Procedure governing the issuance, service, and enforcement of a subpoena duces tecum.

**(i)  Conditions for Eligibility.**—

**(1)  Accommodation of Technology.**—The limitations on liability established by this section shall apply to a service provider only if the service provider—

(A)  has adopted and reasonably implemented, and informs subscribers and account holders of the service provider's system or network of, a policy that provides for the termination in appropriate circumstances of subscribers and account holders of the service provider's system or network who are repeat infringers; and

(B)  accommodates and does not interfere with standard technical measures.

(2) **Definition.**—As used in this subsection, the term "standard technical measures" means technical measures that are used by copyright owners to identify or protect copyrighted works and—

(A) have been developed pursuant to a broad consensus of copyright owners and service providers in an open, fair, voluntary, multi-industry standards process;

(B) are available to any person on reasonable and nondiscriminatory terms; and

(C) do not impose substantial costs on service providers or substantial burdens on their systems or networks.

(j) **Injunctions.**—The following rules shall apply in the case of any application for an injunction under section 502 against a service provider that is not subject to monetary remedies under this section:

(1) **Scope of Relief.**—

(A) With respect to conduct other than that which qualifies for the limitation on remedies set forth in subsection (a), the court may grant injunctive relief with respect to a service provider only in one or more of the following forms:

(i) An order restraining the service provider from providing access to infringing material or activity residing at a particular online site on the provider's system or network.

(ii) An order restraining the service provider from providing access to a subscriber or account holder of the service provider's system or network who is engaging in infringing activity and is identified in the order, by terminating the accounts of the subscriber or account holder that are specified in the order.

(iii) Such other injunctive relief as the court may consider necessary to prevent or restrain infringement of copyrighted material specified in the order of the court at a particular online location, if such relief is the least burdensome to the service provider among the forms of relief comparably effective for that purpose.

(B) If the service provider qualifies for the limitation on remedies described in subsection (a), the court may only grant injunctive relief in one or both of the following forms:

(i) An order restraining the service provider from providing access to a subscriber or account holder of the service provider's system or network who is using the provider's service to engage in infringing activity and is identified in the order, by terminating the accounts of the subscriber or account holder that are specified in the order.

(ii) An order restraining the service provider from providing access, by taking reasonable steps specified in the order to block access, to a specific, identified, online location outside the United States.

(2) **Considerations.**—The court, in considering the relevant criteria for injunctive relief under applicable law, shall consider—

(A) whether such an injunction, either alone or in combination with other such injunctions issued against the same service provider under this subsection, would significantly burden either the provider or the operation of the provider's system or network;

(B) the magnitude of the harm likely to be suffered by the copyright owner in the digital network environment if steps are not taken to prevent or restrain the infringement;

(C) whether implementation of such an injunction would be technically feasible and effective, and would not interfere with access to noninfringing material at other online locations; and

141

(D) whether other less burdensome and comparably effective means of preventing or restraining access to the infringing material are available.

**(3) Notice and Ex Parte Orders.**—Injunctive relief under this subsection shall be available only after notice to the service provider and an opportunity for the service provider to appear are provided, except for orders ensuring the preservation of evidence or other orders having no material adverse effect on the operation of the service provider's communications network.

**(k) Definitions.**—

**(1) Service Provider.**—

(A) As used in subsection (a), the term "service provider" means an entity offering the transmission, routing, or providing of connections for digital online communications, between or among points specified by a user, of material of the user's choosing, without modification to the content of the material as sent or received.

(B) As used in this section, other than subsection (a), the term "service provider" means a provider of online services or network access, or the operator of facilities therefor, and includes an entity described in subparagraph (A).

**(2) Monetary Relief.**—As used in this section, the term "monetary relief" means damages, costs, attorneys' fees, and any other form of monetary payment.

**(*l*) Other Defenses Not Affected.**—The failure of a service provider's conduct to qualify for limitation of liability under this section shall not bear adversely upon the consideration of a defense by the service provider that the service provider's conduct is not infringing under this title or any other defense.

**(m) Protection of Privacy.**—Nothing in this section shall be construed to condition the applicability of subsections (a) through (d) on—

(1) a service provider monitoring its service or affirmatively seeking facts indicating infringing activity, except to the extent consistent with a standard technical measure complying with the provisions of subsection (i); or

(2) a service provider gaining access to, removing, or disabling access to material in cases in which such conduct is prohibited by law.

**(n) Construction.**—Subsections (a), (b), (c), and (d) describe separate and distinct functions for purposes of applying this section. Whether a service provider qualifies for the limitation on liability in any one of those subsections shall be based solely on the criteria in that subsection, and shall not affect a determination of whether that service provider qualifies for the limitations on liability under any other such subsection.

(Added by Pub.L. 105–304, 112 Stat. 2860 (1998); as amended, Pub.L. 106–44, 113 Stat. 222 (1999); Pub.L. 111–295, 124 Stat. 3180 (2010)).

## Sec. 513.    Determination of Reasonable License Fees for Individual Proprietors

In the case of any performing rights society subject to a consent decree which provides for the determination of reasonable license rates or fees to be charged by the performing rights society, notwithstanding the provisions of that consent decree, an individual proprietor who owns or operates fewer than 7 non-publicly traded establishments in which nondramatic musical works are performed publicly and who claims that any license agreement offered by that performing rights society is unreasonable in its license rate or fee as to that individual proprietor, shall be entitled to determination of a reasonable license rate or fee as follows:

(1) The individual proprietor may commence such proceeding for determination of a reasonable license rate or fee by filing an application in the applicable district court under

paragraph (2) that a rate disagreement exists and by serving a copy of the application on the performing rights society. Such proceeding shall commence in the applicable district court within 90 days after the service of such copy, except that such 90-day requirement shall be subject to the administrative requirements of the court.

(2)   The proceeding under paragraph (1) shall be held, at the individual proprietor's election, in the judicial district of the district court with jurisdiction over the applicable consent decree or in that place of holding court of a district court that is the seat of the Federal circuit (other than the Court of Appeals for the Federal Circuit) in which the proprietor's establishment is located.

(3)   Such proceeding shall be held before the judge of the court with jurisdiction over the consent decree governing the performing rights society. At the discretion of the court, the proceeding shall be held before a special master or magistrate judge appointed by such judge. Should that consent decree provide for the appointment of an advisor or advisors to the court for any purpose, any such advisor shall be the special master so named by the court.

(4)   In any such proceeding, the industry rate shall be presumed to have been reasonable at the time it was agreed to or determined by the court. Such presumption shall in no way affect a determination of whether the rate is being correctly applied to the individual proprietor.

(5)   Pending the completion of such proceeding, the individual proprietor shall have the right to perform publicly the copyrighted musical compositions in the repertoire of the performing rights society by paying an interim license rate or fee into an interest bearing escrow account with the clerk of the court, subject to retroactive adjustment when a final rate or fee has been determined, in an amount equal to the industry rate, or, in the absence of an industry rate, the amount of the most recent license rate or fee agreed to by the parties.

(6)   Any decision rendered in such proceeding by a special master or magistrate judge named under paragraph (3) shall be reviewed by the judge of the court with jurisdiction over the consent decree governing the performing rights society. Such proceeding, including such review, shall be concluded within 6 months after its commencement.

(7)   Any such final determination shall be binding only as to the individual proprietor commencing the proceeding, and shall not be applicable to any other proprietor or any other performing rights society, and the performing rights society shall be relieved of any obligation of nondiscrimination among similarly situated music users that may be imposed by the consent decree governing its operations.

(8)   An individual proprietor may not bring more than one proceeding provided for in this section for the determination of a reasonable license rate or fee under any license agreement with respect to any one performing rights society.

(9)   For purposes of this section, the term "industry rate" means the license fee a performing rights society has agreed to with, or which has been determined by the court for, a significant segment of the music user industry to which the individual proprietor belongs.

(Added by Pub.L. 105–298, 112 Stat. 2827 (1998); as amended, Pub.L. 106–44, 113 Stat. 221 (1999)).

## CHAPTER 6.—IMPORTATION AND EXPORTATION

## Sec. 601.   Manufacture, Importation, and Public Distribution of Certain Copies [Repealed, Pub.L. 111–295, 124 Stat. 3180 (2010)]

## Sec. 602. Infringing Importation or Exportation of Copies or Phonorecords

### (a) Infringing Importation or Exportation.—

**(1) Importation.**—Importation into the United States, without the authority of the owner of copyright under this title, of copies or phonorecords of a work that have been acquired outside the United States is an infringement of the exclusive right to distribute copies or phonorecords under section 106, actionable under section 501.

**(2) Importation or Exportation of Infringing Items.**—Importation into the United States or exportation from the United States, without the authority of the owner of copyright under this title, of copies or phonorecords, the making of which either constituted an infringement of copyright, or which would have constituted an infringement of copyright if this title had been applicable, is an infringement of the exclusive right to distribute copies or phonorecords under section 106, actionable under sections 501 and 506.

**(3) Exceptions.**—This subsection does not apply to—

(A) importation or exportation of copies or phonorecords under the authority or for the use of the Government of the United States or of any State or political subdivision of a State, but not including copies or phonorecords for use in schools, or copies of any audiovisual work imported for purposes other than archival use;

(B) importation or exportation, for the private use of the importer or exporter and not for distribution, by any person with respect to no more than one copy or phonorecord of any one work at any one time, or by any person arriving from outside the United States or departing from the United States with respect to copies or phonorecords forming part of such person's personal baggage; or

(C) importation by or for an organization operated for scholarly, educational, or religious purposes and not for private gain, with respect to no more than one copy of an audiovisual work solely for its archival purposes, and no more than five copies or phonorecords of any other work for its library lending or archival purposes, unless the importation of such copies or phonorecords is part of an activity consisting of systematic reproduction or distribution, engaged in by such organization in violation of the provisions of section 108(g)(2).

**(b) Import Prohibition.**—In a case where the making of the copies or phonorecords would have constituted an infringement of copyright if this title had been applicable, their importation is prohibited. In a case where the copies or phonorecords were lawfully made, United States Customs and Border Protection has no authority to prevent their importation. In either case, the Secretary of the Treasury is authorized to prescribe, by regulation, a procedure under which any person claiming an interest in the copyright in a particular work may, upon payment of a specified fee, be entitled to notification by United States Customs and Border Protection of the importation of articles that appear to be copies or phonorecords of the work.

(As amended, Pub.L. 110–403, 122 Stat. 4256 (2008); Pub.L. 111–295, 124 Stat. 3180 (2010)).

## Sec. 603. Importation Prohibitions: Enforcement and Disposition of Excluded Articles

(a) The Secretary of the Treasury and the United States Postal Service shall separately or jointly make regulations for the enforcement of the provisions of this title prohibiting importation.

(b) These regulations may require, as a condition for the exclusion of articles under section 602—

(1) that the person seeking exclusion obtain a court order enjoining importation of the articles; or

(2) that the person seeking exclusion furnish proof, of a specified nature and in accordance with prescribed procedures, that the copyright in which such person claims an interest is valid

and that the importation would violate the prohibition in section 602; the person seeking exclusion may also be required to post a surety bond for any injury that may result if the detention or exclusion of the articles proves to be unjustified.

(c)   Articles imported in violation of the importation prohibitions of this title are subject to seizure and forfeiture in the same manner as property imported in violation of the customs revenue laws. Forfeited articles shall be destroyed as directed by the Secretary of the Treasury or the court, as the case may be.

(As amended, Pub.L. 104–153, 110 Stat. 1386 (1996)).

## CHAPTER 7.—COPYRIGHT OFFICE

## Sec. 701.   The Copyright Office: General Responsibilities and Organization

(a)   All administrative functions and duties under this title, except as otherwise specified, are the responsibility of the Register of Copyrights as director of the Copyright Office of the Library of Congress. The Register of Copyrights, together with the subordinate officers and employees of the Copyright Office, shall be appointed by the Librarian of Congress, and shall act under the Librarian's general direction and supervision.

(b)   In addition to the functions and duties set out elsewhere in this chapter, the Register of Copyrights shall perform the following functions:

(1)   Advise Congress on national and international issues relating to copyright, other matters arising under this title, and related matters.

(2)   Provide information and assistance to Federal departments and agencies and the Judiciary on national and international issues relating to copyright, other matters arising under this title, and related matters.

(3)   Participate in meetings of international intergovernmental organizations and meetings with foreign government officials relating to copyright, other matters arising under this title, and related matters, including as a member of United States delegations as authorized by the appropriate Executive branch authority.

(4)   Conduct studies and programs regarding copyright, other matters arising under this title, and related matters, the administration of the Copyright Office, or any function vested in the Copyright Office by law, including educational programs conducted cooperatively with foreign intellectual property offices and international intergovernmental organizations.

(5)   Perform such other functions as Congress may direct, or as may be appropriate in furtherance of the functions and duties specifically set forth in this title.

(c)   The Register of Copyrights shall adopt a seal to be used on and after January 1, 1978, to authenticate all certified documents issued by the Copyright Office.

(d)   The Register of Copyrights shall make an annual report to the Librarian of Congress of the work and accomplishments of the Copyright Office during the previous fiscal year. The annual report of the Register of Copyrights shall be published separately and as a part of the annual report of the Librarian of Congress.

(e)   Except as provided by section 706(b) and the regulations issued thereunder, all actions taken by the Register of Copyrights under this title are subject to the provisions of the Administrative Procedure Act of June 11, 1946, as amended (c. 324, 60 Stat. 237, title 5, United States Code, Chapter 5, Subchapter II and Chapter 7).

(f)   The Register of Copyrights shall be compensated at the greater of the rate of pay in effect for level III of the Executive Schedule under section 5314 of title 5 or the maximum annual rate of basic pay payable under section 5376 of such title for positions at agencies with a performance appraisal system certified under section 5307(d) of such title. The Librarian of Congress shall establish not more than four positions for Associate Registers of Copyrights, in accordance with the recommendations of the Register of Copyrights. The Librarian shall make appointments to such positions after consultation with the Register of Copyrights. The rate of basic pay for each Associate Register of Copyrights shall be fixed in accordance with section 5376 of title 5.

(As amended, Pub.L. 101–319, 104 Stat. 290 (1990); Pub.L. 105–304, 112 Stat. 2860 (1998); Pub.L. 116–94, 133 Stat. 2534 (2019)).

## Sec. 702.    Copyright Office Regulations

The Register of Copyrights is authorized to establish regulations not inconsistent with law for the administration of the functions and duties made the responsibility of the Register under this title. All regulations established by the Register under this title are subject to the approval of the Librarian of Congress.

## Sec. 703.    Effective Date of Actions in Copyright Office

In any case in which time limits are prescribed under this title for the performance of an action in the Copyright Office, and in which the last day of the prescribed period falls on a Saturday, Sunday, holiday, or other nonbusiness day within the District of Columbia or the Federal Government, the action may be taken on the next succeeding business day, and is effective as of the date when the period expired.

## Sec. 704.    Retention and Disposition of Articles Deposited in Copyright Office

(a)   Upon their deposit in the Copyright Office under sections 407 and 408, all copies, phonorecords, and identifying material, including those deposited in connection with claims that have been refused registration, are the property of the United States Government.

(b)   In the case of published works, all copies, phonorecords, and identifying material deposited are available to the Library of Congress for its collections, or for exchange or transfer to any other library. In the case of unpublished works, the Library is entitled, under regulations that the Register of Copyrights shall prescribe, to select any deposits for its collections or for transfer to the National Archives of the United States or to a Federal records center, as defined in section 2901 of title 44.

(c)   The Register of Copyrights is authorized, for specific or general categories of works, to make a facsimile reproduction of all or any part of the material deposited under section 408, and to make such reproduction a part of the Copyright Office records of the registration, before transferring such material to the Library of Congress as provided by subsection (b), or before destroying or otherwise disposing of such material as provided by subsection (d).

(d)   Deposits not selected by the Library under subsection (b), or identifying portions or reproductions of them, shall be retained under the control of the Copyright Office, including retention in Government storage facilities, for the longest period considered practicable and desirable by the

Register of Copyrights and the Librarian of Congress. After that period it is within the joint discretion of the Register and the Librarian to order their destruction or other disposition; but, in the case of unpublished works, no deposit shall be knowingly or intentionally destroyed or otherwise disposed of during its term of copyright unless a facsimile reproduction of the entire deposit has been made a part of the Copyright Office records as provided by subsection (c).

(e)   The depositor of copies, phonorecords, or identifying material under section 408, or the copyright owner of record, may request retention, under the control of the Copyright Office, of one or more of such articles for the full term of copyright in the work. The Register of Copyrights shall prescribe, by regulation, the conditions under which such requests are to be made and granted, and shall fix the fee to be charged under section 708(a) if the request is granted.

(As amended, Pub.L. 101–318, 104 Stat. 288 (1990)).

## Sec. 705.   Copyright Office Records: Preparation, Maintenance, Public Inspection, and Searching

(a)   The Register of Copyrights shall ensure that records of deposits, registrations, recordations, and other actions taken under this title are maintained, and that indexes of such records are prepared.

(b)   Such records and indexes, as well as the articles deposited in connection with completed copyright registrations and retained under the control of the Copyright Office, shall be open to public inspection.

(c)   Upon request and payment of the fee specified by section 708, the Copyright Office shall make a search of its public records, indexes, and deposits, and shall furnish a report of the information they disclose with respect to any particular deposits, registrations, or recorded documents.

(As amended, Pub.L. 106–379, 114 Stat. 1444 (2000)).

## Sec. 706.   Copies of Copyright Office Records

(a)   Copies may be made of any public records or indexes of the Copyright Office; additional certificates of copyright registration and copies of any public records or indexes may be furnished upon request and payment of the fees specified by section 708.

(b)   Copies or reproductions of deposited articles retained under the control of the Copyright Office shall be authorized or furnished only under the conditions specified by the Copyright Office regulations.

## Sec. 707.   Copyright Office Forms and Publications

(a)   **Catalog of Copyright Entries.**—The Register of Copyrights shall compile and publish at periodic intervals catalogs of all copyright registrations. These catalogs shall be divided into parts in accordance with the various classes of works, and the Register has discretion to determine, on the basis of practicability and usefulness, the form and frequency of publication of each particular part.

(b)   **Other Publications.**—The Register shall furnish, free of charge upon request, application forms for copyright registration and general informational material in connection with the functions of the Copyright Office. The Register also has the authority to publish compilations of information, bibliographies, and other material he or she considers to be of value to the public.

(c)   **Distribution of Publications.**—All publications of the Copyright Office shall be furnished to depository libraries as specified under section 1905 of title 44, and, aside from those furnished free of charge, shall be offered for sale to the public at prices based on the cost of reproduction and distribution.

## Sec. 708.   Copyright Office Fees

(a)   **Fees.**—Fees shall be paid to the Register of Copyrights—

(1)  on filing each application under section 408 for registration of a copyright claim or for a supplementary registration, including the issuance of a certificate of registration if registration is made;

(2)  on filing each application for registration of a claim for renewal of a subsisting copyright under section 304(a), including the issuance of a certificate of registration if registration is made;

(3)  for the issuance of a receipt for a deposit under section 407;

(4)  for the recordation, as provided by section 205, of a transfer of copyright ownership or other document;

(5)  for the filing, under section 115(b), of a notice of intention to obtain a compulsory license;

(6)  for the recordation, under section 302(c), of a statement revealing the identity of an author of an anonymous or pseudonymous work, or for the recordation, under section 302(d), of a statement relating to the death of an author;

(7)  for the issuance, under section 706, of an additional certificate of registration;

(8)  for the issuance of any other certification;

(9)  for the making and reporting of a search as provided by section 705, and for any related services;

(10) on filing a statement of account based on secondary transmissions of primary transmissions pursuant to section 119 or 122; and

(11) on filing a statement of account based on secondary transmissions of primary transmissions pursuant to section 111.

The Register is authorized to fix fees for other services, including the cost of preparing copies of Copyright Office records, whether or not such copies are certified, based on the cost of providing the service. Fees established under paragraphs (10) and (11) shall be reasonable and may not exceed one-half of the cost necessary to cover reasonable expenses incurred by the Copyright Office for the collection and administration of the statements of account and any royalty fees deposited with such statements.

**(b)  Adjustment of Fees.**—The Register of Copyrights may, by regulation, adjust the fees for the services specified in paragraphs (1) through (9) of subsection (a) in the following manner:

(1)  The Register shall conduct a study of the costs incurred by the Copyright Office for the registration of claims, the recordation of documents, and the provision of services. The study shall also consider the timing of any adjustment in fees and the authority to use such fees consistent with the budget.

(2)  The Register may, on the basis of the study under paragraph (1), and subject to paragraph (5), adjust fees to not more than that necessary to cover the reasonable costs incurred by the Copyright Office for the services described in paragraph (1), plus a reasonable inflation adjustment to account for any estimated increase in costs.

(3)  Any fee established under paragraph (2) shall be rounded off to the nearest dollar, or for a fee less than $12, rounded off to the nearest 50 cents.

(4)  Fees established under this subsection shall be fair and equitable and give due consideration to the objectives of the copyright system.

(5)  If the Register determines under paragraph (2) that fees should be adjusted, the Register shall prepare a proposed fee schedule and submit the schedule with the accompanying economic analysis to the Congress. The fees proposed by the Register may be instituted after the end of 120 days after the schedule is submitted to the Congress unless, within that 120-day period, a law is enacted stating in substance that the Congress does not approve the schedule.

(c)   The fees prescribed by or under this section are applicable to the United States Government and any of its agencies, employees, or officers, but the Register of Copyrights has discretion to waive the requirement of this subsection in occasional or isolated cases involving relatively small amounts.

(d)(1)   Except as provided in paragraph (2), all fees received under this section shall be deposited by the Register of Copyrights in the Treasury of the United States and shall be credited to the appropriations for necessary expenses of the Copyright Office. Such fees that are collected shall remain available until expended. The Register may, in accordance with regulations that he or she shall prescribe, refund any sum paid by mistake or in excess of the fee required by this section.

(2)   In the case of fees deposited against future services, the Register of Copyrights shall request the Secretary of the Treasury to invest in interest-bearing securities in the United States Treasury any portion of the fees that, as determined by the Register, is not required to meet current deposit account demands. Funds from such portion of fees shall be invested in securities that permit funds to be available to the Copyright Office at all times if they are determined to be necessary to meet current deposit account demands. Such investments shall be in public debt securities with maturities suitable to the needs of the Copyright Office, as determined by the Register of Copyrights, and bearing interest at rates determined by the Secretary of the Treasury, taking into consideration current market yields on outstanding marketable obligations of the United States of comparable maturities.

(3)   The income on such investments shall be deposited in the Treasury of the United States and shall be credited to the appropriations for necessary expenses of the Copyright Office.

(As amended, Pub.L. 95–94, 91 Stat. 682 (1977); Pub.L. 97–366, 96 Stat. 1759 (1982); Pub.L. 101–318, 104 Stat. 287 (1990); Pub.L. 102–307, 106 Stat. 264 (1992); Pub.L. 105–80, 111 Stat. 1529 (1997); Pub.L. 106–379, 114 Stat. 1444 (2000); Pub.L. 111–175, 124 Stat. 1218 (2010)).

## Sec. 709.   Delay in Delivery Caused by Disruption of Postal or Other Services

In any case in which the Register of Copyrights determines, on the basis of such evidence as the Register may by regulation require, that a deposit, application, fee, or any other material to be delivered to the Copyright Office by a particular date, would have been received in the Copyright Office in due time except for a general disruption or suspension of postal or other transportation or communications services, the actual receipt of such material in the Copyright Office within one month after the date on which the Register determines that the disruption or suspension of such services has terminated, shall be considered timely.

## Sec. 710.   Emergency Relief Authority

(a)  Emergency Action.—If, on or before December 31, 2021, the Register of Copyrights determines that a national emergency declared by the President under the National Emergencies Act (50 U.S.C. 1601 et seq.) generally disrupts or suspends the ordinary functioning of the copyright system under this title, or any component thereof, including on a regional basis, the Register may, on a temporary basis, toll, waive, adjust, or modify any timing provision (including any deadline or effective period, except as provided in subsection (c)) or procedural provision contained in this title or chapters II or III of title 37, Code of Federal Regulations, for no longer than the Register reasonably determines to be appropriate to mitigate the impact of the disruption caused by the national emergency. In taking such action, the Register shall consider the scope and severity of the particular national emergency, and its specific effect with respect to the particular provision, and shall tailor any remedy accordingly.

(b)  Notice and Effect.—Any action taken by the Register in response to a national emergency pursuant to subsection (a) shall not be subject to section 701(e) or subchapter II of chapter 5 of title 5, United States Code, and chapter 7 of title 5, United States Code. The provision of general public notice detailing the action being taken by the Register in response to the national emergency under subsection (a) is sufficient to effectuate such action. The Register may make such action effective both prospectively and retroactively in relation to a particular provision as the Register determines to be appropriate based on the timing, scope, and nature of the public emergency, but any action by the Register may only be retroactive with respect to a deadline that has not already passed before the declaration described in subsection (a).

(c) **Statement Required**.—Except as provided in subsection (d), not later than 20 days after taking any action that results in a provision being modified for a cumulative total of longer than 120 days, the Register shall submit to Congress a statement detailing the action taken, the relevant background, and rationale for the action.

(d) **Exceptions**.—The authority of the Register to act under subsection (a) does not extend provisions under this title requiring the commencement of an action or proceeding in Federal court within a specified period of time, except that if the Register adjusts the license availability date defined in section 115(e)(15), such adjustment shall not affect the ability to commence actions for any claim of infringement of exclusive rights provided by paragraphs (1) and (3) of section 106 against a digital music provider arising from the unauthorized reproduction or distribution of a musical work by such digital music provider in the course of engaging in covered activities that accrued after January 1, 2018, provided that such action is commenced within the time periods prescribed under section 115(d)(10)(C)(i) or 115(d)(10)(C)(ii) as calculated from the adjusted license availability date. If the Register adjusts the license availability date, the Register must provide the statement to Congress under subsection (c) at the same time as the public notice of such adjustment with a detailed explanation of why such adjustment is needed.

(e) **Copyright Term Exception**.—The authority of the Register to act under subsection (a) does not extend to provisions under chapter 3, except section 304(c), or section 1401(a)(2).

(f) **Other Laws**.—Notwithstanding section 301 of the National Emergencies Act (50 U.S.C. 1631), the authority of the Register under subsection (a) is not contingent on a specification made by the President under such section or any other requirement under that Act (other than the emergency declaration under section 201(a) of such Act (50 U.S.C. 1621(a))). The authority described in this section supersedes the authority of title II of the National Emergencies Act (50 U.S.C. 1621 et seq.).

(Added by Pub.L. 116–136, 134 Stat. 281 (2020)).

## CHAPTER 8.—PROCEEDINGS BY COPYRIGHT ROYALTY JUDGES

## Sec. 801.    Copyright Royalty Judges; Appointment and Functions

(a) **Appointment**.—The Librarian of Congress shall appoint 3 full-time Copyright Royalty Judges, and shall appoint 1 of the 3 as the Chief Copyright Royalty Judge. The Librarian shall make appointments to such positions after consultation with the Register of Copyrights.

(b) **Functions**.—Subject to the provisions of this chapter, the functions of the Copyright Royalty Judges shall be as follows:

(1) To make determinations and adjustments of reasonable terms and rates of royalty payments as provided in sections 112(e), 114, 115, 116, 118, 119, and 1004.

(2) To make determinations concerning the adjustment of the copyright royalty rates under section 111 solely in accordance with the following provisions:

(A) The rates established by section 111(d)(1)(B) may be adjusted to reflect—

    (i)   national monetary inflation or deflation; or

    (ii)   changes in the average rates charged cable subscribers for the basic service of providing secondary transmissions to maintain the real constant dollar level of the royalty fee per subscriber which existed as of the date of October 19, 1976, except that—

    (I)   if the average rates charged cable system subscribers for the basic service of providing secondary transmissions are changed so that the average rates exceed national monetary inflation, no change in the rates established by section 111(d)(1)(B) shall be permitted; and

    (II)   no increase in the royalty fee shall be permitted based on any reduction in the average number of distant signal equivalents per subscriber.

The Copyright Royalty Judges may consider all factors relating to the maintenance of such level of payments, including, as an extenuating factor, whether the industry has been restrained by subscriber rate regulating authorities from increasing the rates for the basic service of providing secondary transmissions.

    (B)   In the event that the rules and regulations of the Federal Communications Commission are amended at any time after April 15, 1976, to permit the carriage by cable systems of additional television broadcast signals beyond the local service area of the primary transmitters of such signals, the royalty rates established by section 111(d)(1)(B) may be adjusted to ensure that the rates for the additional distant signal equivalents resulting from such carriage are reasonable in the light of the changes effected by the amendment to such rules and regulations. In determining the reasonableness of rates proposed following an amendment of Federal Communications Commission rules and regulations, the Copyright Royalty Judges shall consider, among other factors, the economic impact on copyright owners and users; except that no adjustment in royalty rates shall be made under this subparagraph with respect to any distant signal equivalent or fraction thereof represented by—

    (i)   carriage of any signal permitted under the rules and regulations of the Federal Communications Commission in effect on April 15, 1976, or the carriage of a signal of the same type (that is, independent, network, or noncommercial educational) substituted for such permitted signal; or

    (ii)   a television broadcast signal first carried after April 15, 1976, pursuant to an individual waiver of the rules and regulations of the Federal Communications Commission, as such rules and regulations were in effect on April 15, 1976.

    (C)   In the event of any change in the rules and regulations of the Federal Communications Commission with respect to syndicated and sports program exclusivity after April 15, 1976, the rates established by section 111(d)(1)(B) may be adjusted to assure that such rates are reasonable in light of the changes to such rules and regulations, but any such adjustment shall apply only to the affected television broadcast signals carried on those systems affected by the change.

    (D)   The gross receipts limitations established by section 111(d)(1)(C) and (D) shall be adjusted to reflect national monetary inflation or deflation or changes in the average rates charged cable system subscribers for the basic service of providing secondary transmissions to maintain the real constant dollar value of the exemption provided by such section, and the royalty rate specified therein shall not be subject to adjustment.

    (3)(A)   To authorize the distribution, under sections 111, 119, and 1007, of those royalty fees collected under sections 111, 119, and 1005, as the case may be, to the extent that the Copyright Royalty Judges have found that the distribution of such fees is not subject to controversy.

(B)   In cases where the Copyright Royalty Judges determine that controversy exists, the Copyright Royalty Judges shall determine the distribution of such fees, including partial distributions, in accordance with section 111, 119, or 1007, as the case may be.

(C)   Notwithstanding section 804(b)(8), the Copyright Royalty Judges, at any time after the filing of claims under section 111, 119, or 1007, may, upon motion of one or more of the claimants and after publication in the Federal Register of a request for responses to the motion from interested claimants, make a partial distribution of such fees, if, based upon all responses received during the 30-day period beginning on the date of such publication, the Copyright Royalty Judges conclude that no claimant entitled to receive such fees has stated a reasonable objection to the partial distribution, and all such claimants—

   (i)   agree to the partial distribution;

   (ii)   sign an agreement obligating them to return any excess amounts to the extent necessary to comply with the final determination on the distribution of the fees made under subparagraph (B);

   (iii)   file the agreement with the Copyright Royalty Judges; and

   (iv)   agree that such funds are available for distribution.

(D)   The Copyright Royalty Judges and any other officer or employee acting in good faith in distributing funds under subparagraph (C) shall not be held liable for the payment of any excess fees under subparagraph (C). The Copyright Royalty Judges shall, at the time the final determination is made, calculate any such excess amounts.

(4)   To accept or reject royalty claims filed under sections 111, 119, and 1007, on the basis of timeliness or the failure to establish the basis for a claim.

(5)   To accept or reject rate adjustment petitions as provided in section 804 and petitions to participate as provided in section 803(b)(1) and (2).

(6)   To determine the status of a digital audio recording device or a digital audio interface device under sections 1002 and 1003, as provided in section 1010.

(7)(A)   To adopt as a basis for statutory terms and rates or as a basis for the distribution of statutory royalty payments, an agreement concerning such matters reached among some or all of the participants in a proceeding at any time during the proceeding, except that—

   (i)   the Copyright Royalty Judges shall provide to those that would be bound by the terms, rates, or other determination set by any agreement in a proceeding to determine royalty rates an opportunity to comment on the agreement and shall provide to participants in the proceeding under section 803(b)(2) that would be bound by the terms, rates, or other determination set by the agreement an opportunity to comment on the agreement and object to its adoption as a basis for statutory terms and rates; and

   (ii)   the Copyright Royalty Judges may decline to adopt the agreement as a basis for statutory terms and rates for participants that are not parties to the agreement, if any participant described in clause (i) objects to the agreement and the Copyright Royalty Judges conclude, based on the record before them if one exists, that the agreement does not provide a reasonable basis for setting statutory terms or rates.

(B)   License agreements voluntarily negotiated pursuant to section 112(e)(5), 114(f)(2), 115(c)(3)(E)(i), 116(c), or 118(b)(2) that do not result in statutory terms and rates shall not be subject to clauses (i) and (ii) of subparagraph (A).

(C)   Interested parties may negotiate and agree to, and the Copyright Royalty Judges may adopt, an agreement that specifies as terms notice and recordkeeping requirements that apply in lieu of those that would otherwise apply under regulations.

(8)   To determine the administrative assessment to be paid by digital music providers under section 115(d). The provisions of section 115(d) shall apply to the conduct of proceedings by the Copyright Royalty Judges under section 115(d) and not the procedures described in this section, or section 803, 804, or 805.

(9)   To perform other duties, as assigned by the Register of Copyrights within the Library of Congress, except as provided in section 802(g), at times when Copyright Royalty Judges are not engaged in performing the other duties set forth in this section.

(c)  **Rulings.**—The Copyright Royalty Judges may make any necessary procedural or evidentiary rulings in any proceeding under this chapter and may, before commencing a proceeding under this chapter, make any such rulings that would apply to the proceedings conducted by the Copyright Royalty Judges.

(d)  **Administrative Support.**—The Librarian of Congress shall provide the Copyright Royalty Judges with the necessary administrative services related to proceedings under this chapter.

(e)  **Location in Library of Congress.**—The offices of the Copyright Royalty Judges and staff shall be in the Library of Congress.

(f)  **Effective Date of Actions.**—On and after the date of the enactment of the Copyright Royalty and Distribution Reform Act of 2004 [enacted Nov. 30, 2004], in any case in which time limits are prescribed under this title for performance of an action with or by the Copyright Royalty Judges, and in which the last day of the prescribed period falls on a Saturday, Sunday, holiday, or other nonbusiness day within the District of Columbia or the Federal Government, the action may be taken on the next succeeding business day, and is effective as of the date when the period expired.

(As amended, Pub.L. 99–397, 100 Stat. 848 (1986); Pub.L. 100–568, 102 Stat. 2853 (1988); Pub.L. 100–667, 102 Stat. 3935 (1988); Pub.L. 101–318, 104 Stat. 288 (1990); Pub.L. 102–563, 106 Stat. 4247 (1992); Pub.L. 103–198, 107 Stat. 2304 (1993); Pub.L. 104–39, 109 Stat. 336 (1995); Pub.L. 105–80, 111 Stat. 1529 (1997); Pub.L. 105–304, 112 Stat. 2860 (1998); Pub.L. 108–419, 118 Stat. 2341 (2004); Pub.L. 109–303, 120 Stat. 1478 (2006; Pub.L. 115–264, 132 Stat. 3676 (2018)).

## Sec. 802.    Copyright Royalty Judgeships; Staff

(a)  **Qualifications of Copyright Royalty Judges.**—

(1)  **In general.**—Each Copyright Royalty Judge shall be an attorney who has at least 7 years of legal experience. The Chief Copyright Royalty Judge shall have at least 5 years of experience in adjudications, arbitrations, or court trials. Of the other 2 Copyright Royalty Judges, 1 shall have significant knowledge of copyright law, and the other shall have significant knowledge of economics. An individual may serve as a Copyright Royalty Judge only if the individual is free of any financial conflict of interest under subsection (h).

(2)  **Definition.**—In this subsection, the term "adjudication" has the meaning given that term in section 551 of title 5, but does not include mediation.

(b)  **Staff.**—The Chief Copyright Royalty Judge shall hire full-time staff members to assist the Copyright Royalty Judges in performing their functions.

(c)  **Terms.**—The individual first appointed as the Chief Copyright Royalty Judge shall be appointed to a term of 6 years, and of the remaining individuals first appointed as Copyright Royalty Judges, 1 shall be appointed to a term of 4 years, and the other shall be appointed to a term of 2 years. Thereafter, the terms of succeeding Copyright Royalty Judges shall each be 6 years. An individual serving as a Copyright Royalty Judge may be reappointed to subsequent terms. The term of a Copyright Royalty Judge shall begin when the term of the predecessor of that Copyright Royalty Judge ends. When the term of office of a Copyright Royalty Judge ends, the individual serving that term may continue to serve until a successor is selected.

(d)  **Vacancies or incapacity.**—

(1) **Vacancies.**—If a vacancy should occur in the position of Copyright Royalty Judge, the Librarian of Congress shall act expeditiously to fill the vacancy, and may appoint an interim Copyright Royalty Judge to serve until another Copyright Royalty Judge is appointed under this section. An individual appointed to fill the vacancy occurring before the expiration of the term for which the predecessor of that individual was appointed shall be appointed for the remainder of that term.

(2) **Incapacity.**—In the case in which a Copyright Royalty Judge is temporarily unable to perform his or her duties, the Librarian of Congress may appoint an interim Copyright Royalty Judge to perform such duties during the period of such incapacity.

**(e) Compensation.—**

(1) **Judges.**—The Chief Copyright Royalty Judge shall receive compensation at the rate of basic pay payable for level AL-1 for administrative law judges pursuant to section 5372(b) of title 5, and each of the other two Copyright Royalty Judges shall receive compensation at the rate of basic pay payable for level AL-2 for administrative law judges pursuant to such section. The compensation of the Copyright Royalty Judges shall not be subject to any regulations adopted by the Office of Personnel Management pursuant to its authority under section 5376(b)(1) of title 5.

(2) **Staff members.**—Staff members appointed under subsection (b) shall be compensated at a rate not more than the basic rate of pay payable for level 10 of GS-15 of the General Schedule.

(3) **Locality pay.**—All rates of pay referred to under this subsection shall include locality pay.

**(f) Independence of Copyright Royalty Judge.—**

(1) **In making determinations.—**

(A) **In general.—**

(i) Subject to subparagraph (B) and clause (ii) of this subparagraph, the Copyright Royalty Judges shall have full independence in making determinations concerning adjustments and determinations of copyright royalty rates and terms, the distribution of copyright royalties, the acceptance or rejection of royalty claims, rate adjustment petitions, and petitions to participate, and in issuing other rulings under this title, except that the Copyright Royalty Judges may consult with the Register of Copyrights on any matter other than a question of fact.

(ii) One or more Copyright Royalty Judges may, or by motion to the Copyright Royalty Judges, any participant in a proceeding may, request from the Register of Copyrights an interpretation of any material questions of substantive law that relate to the construction of provisions of this title and arise in the course of the proceeding. Any request for a written interpretation shall be in writing and on the record, and reasonable provision shall be made to permit participants in the proceeding to comment on the material questions of substantive law in a manner that minimizes duplication and delay. Except as provided in subparagraph (B), the Register of Copyrights shall deliver to the Copyright Royalty Judges a written response within 14 days after the receipt of all briefs and comments from the participants. The Copyright Royalty Judges shall apply the legal interpretation embodied in the response of the Register of Copyrights if it is timely delivered, and the response shall be included in the record that accompanies the final determination. The authority under this clause shall not be construed to authorize the Register of Copyrights to provide an interpretation of questions of procedure before the Copyright Royalty Judges, the ultimate adjustments and determinations of copyright royalty rates and terms, the ultimate distribution of copyright royalties, or the acceptance or rejection of royalty claims, rate adjustment petitions, or petitions to participate in a proceeding.

**(B) Novel questions.—**

(i)   In any case in which a novel material question of substantive law concerning an interpretation of those provisions of this title that are the subject of the proceeding is presented, the Copyright Royalty Judges shall request a decision of the Register of Copyrights, in writing, to resolve such novel question. Reasonable provision shall be made for comment on such request by the participants in the proceeding, in such a way as to minimize duplication and delay. The Register of Copyrights shall transmit his or her decision to the Copyright Royalty Judges within 30 days after the Register of Copyrights receives all of the briefs or comments of the participants. Such decision shall be in writing and included by the Copyright Royalty Judges in the record that accompanies their final determination. If such a decision is timely delivered to the Copyright Royalty Judges, the Copyright Royalty Judges shall apply the legal determinations embodied in the decision of the Register of Copyrights in resolving material questions of substantive law.

(ii)   In clause (i), a "novel question of law" is a question of law that has not been determined in prior decisions, determinations, and rulings described in section 803(a).

**(C)  Consultation.—**Notwithstanding the provisions of subparagraph (A), the Copyright Royalty Judges shall consult with the Register of Copyrights with respect to any determination or ruling that would require that any act be performed by the Copyright Office, and any such determination or ruling shall not be binding upon the Register of Copyrights.

**(D)  Review of legal conclusions by the Register of Copyrights.—**The Register of Copyrights may review for legal error the resolution by the Copyright Royalty Judges of a material question of substantive law under this title that underlies or is contained in a final determination of the Copyright Royalty Judges. If the Register of Copyrights concludes, after taking into consideration the views of the participants in the proceeding, that any resolution reached by the Copyright Royalty Judges was in material error, the Register of Copyrights shall issue a written decision correcting such legal error, which shall be made part of the record of the proceeding. The Register of Copyrights shall issue such written decision not later than 60 days after the date on which the final determination by the Copyright Royalty Judges is issued. Additionally, the Register of Copyrights shall cause to be published in the Federal Register such written decision, together with a specific identification of the legal conclusion of the Copyright Royalty Judges that is determined to be erroneous. As to conclusions of substantive law involving an interpretation of the statutory provisions of this title, the decision of the Register of Copyrights shall be binding as precedent upon the Copyright Royalty Judges in subsequent proceedings under this chapter. When a decision has been rendered pursuant to this subparagraph, the Register of Copyrights may, on the basis of and in accordance with such decision, intervene as of right in any appeal of a final determination of the Copyright Royalty Judges pursuant to section 803(d) in the United States Court of Appeals for the District of Columbia Circuit. If, prior to intervening in such an appeal, the Register of Copyrights gives notification to, and undertakes to consult with, the Attorney General with respect to such intervention, and the Attorney General fails, within a reasonable period after receiving such notification, to intervene in such appeal, the Register of Copyrights may intervene in such appeal in his or her own name by any attorney designated by the Register of Copyrights for such purpose. Intervention by the Register of Copyrights in his or her own name shall not preclude the Attorney General from intervening on behalf of the United States in such an appeal as may be otherwise provided or required by law.

**(E)  Effect on judicial review.—**Nothing in this section shall be interpreted to alter the standard applied by a court in reviewing legal determinations involving an interpretation or construction of the provisions of this title or to affect the extent to which any construction or interpretation of the provisions of this title shall be accorded deference by a reviewing court.

**(2) Performance appraisals.—**

**(A) In general.—**Notwithstanding any other provision of law or any regulation of the Library of Congress, and subject to subparagraph (B), the Copyright Royalty Judges shall not receive performance appraisals.

**(B) Relating to sanction or removal.—**To the extent that the Librarian of Congress adopts regulations under subsection (h) relating to the sanction or removal of a Copyright Royalty Judge and such regulations require documentation to establish the cause of such sanction or removal, the Copyright Royalty Judge may receive an appraisal related specifically to the cause of the sanction or removal.

**(g) Inconsistent duties barred.—**No Copyright Royalty Judge may undertake duties that conflict with his or her duties and responsibilities as a Copyright Royalty Judge.

**(h) Standards of conduct.—**The Librarian of Congress shall adopt regulations regarding the standards of conduct, including financial conflict of interest and restrictions against ex parte communications, which shall govern the Copyright Royalty Judges and the proceedings under this chapter.

**(i) Removal or sanction.—**The Librarian of Congress may sanction or remove a Copyright Royalty Judge for violation of the standards of conduct adopted under subsection (h), misconduct, neglect of duty, or any disqualifying physical or mental disability. Any such sanction or removal may be made only after notice and opportunity for a hearing, but the Librarian of Congress may suspend the Copyright Royalty Judge during the pendency of such hearing. The Librarian shall appoint an interim Copyright Royalty Judge during the period of any such suspension.

(As amended, Pub.L. 101–319, 104 Stat. 290 (1990); Pub.L. 103–198, 107 Stat. 2304 (1993); Pub.L. 104–39, 109 Stat. 336 (1995); Pub.L. 105–80, 111 Stat. 1529 (1997); Pub.L. 105–304, 112 Stat. 2860 (1998); Pub.L. 107–273, 116 Stat. 1758 (2002); Pub.L. 108–419, 118 Stat. 2341 (2004); Pub.L. 109–303, 120 Stat. 1478 (2006); Pub.L. 116–94, 133 Stat. 2534 (2019)).

## Sec. 803.    Proceedings of Copyright Royalty Judges

**(a) Proceedings.—**

**(1) In general.—**The Copyright Royalty Judges shall act in accordance with this title, and to the extent not inconsistent with this title, in accordance with subchapter II of chapter 5 of title 5, in carrying out the purposes set forth in section 801. The Copyright Royalty Judges shall act in accordance with regulations issued by the Copyright Royalty Judges and the Librarian of Congress, and on the basis of a written record, prior determinations and interpretations of the Copyright Royalty Tribunal, Librarian of Congress, the Register of Copyrights, copyright arbitration royalty panels (to the extent those determinations are not inconsistent with a decision of the Librarian of Congress or the Register of Copyrights), and the Copyright Royalty Judges (to the extent those determinations are not inconsistent with a decision of the Register of Copyrights that was timely delivered to the Copyright Royalty Judges pursuant to section 802(f)(1)(A) or (B), or with a decision of the Register of Copyrights pursuant to section 802(f)(1)(D)), under this chapter, and decisions of the court of appeals under this chapter before, on, or after the effective date of the Copyright Royalty and Distribution Reform Act of 2004.

**(2) Judges acting as panel and individually.—**The Copyright Royalty Judges shall preside over hearings in proceedings under this chapter en banc. The Chief Copyright Royalty Judge may designate a Copyright Royalty Judge to preside individually over such collateral and administrative proceedings, and over such proceedings under paragraphs (1) through (5) of subsection (b), as the Chief Judge considers appropriate.

**(3) Determinations.**—Final determinations of the Copyright Royalty Judges in proceedings under this chapter shall be made by majority vote. A Copyright Royalty Judge dissenting from the majority on any determination under this chapter may issue his or her dissenting opinion, which shall be included with the determination.

**(b) Procedures.—**

**(1) Initiation.—**

**(A) Call for petitions to participate.—**

(i)　The Copyright Royalty Judges shall cause to be published in the Federal Register notice of commencement of proceedings under this chapter, calling for the filing of petitions to participate in a proceeding under this chapter for the purpose of making the relevant determination under section 111, 112, 114, 115, 116, 118, 119, 1004, or 1007, as the case may be—

(I)　promptly upon a determination made under section 804(a);

(II)　by no later than January 5 of a year specified in paragraph (2) of section 804(b) for the commencement of proceedings;

(III)　by no later than January 5 of a year specified in subparagraph (A) or (B) of paragraph (3) of section 804(b) for the commencement of proceedings, or as otherwise provided in subparagraph (A) or (C) of such paragraph for the commencement of proceedings;

(IV)　as provided under section 804(b)(8); or

(V)　by no later than January 5 of a year specified in any other provision of section 804(b) for the filing of petitions for the commencement of proceedings, if a petition has not been filed by that date, except that the publication of notice requirement shall not apply in the case of proceedings under section 111 that are scheduled to commence in 2005.

(ii)　Petitions to participate shall be filed by no later than 30 days after publication of notice of commencement of a proceeding under clause (i), except that the Copyright Royalty Judges may, for substantial good cause shown and if there is no prejudice to the participants that have already filed petitions, accept late petitions to participate at any time up to the date that is 90 days before the date on which participants in the proceeding are to file their written direct statements. Notwithstanding the preceding sentence, petitioners whose petitions are filed more than 30 days after publication of notice of commencement of a proceeding are not eligible to object to a settlement reached during the voluntary negotiation period under paragraph (3), and any objection filed by such a petitioner shall not be taken into account by the Copyright Royalty Judges.

**(B) Petitions to participate.** Each petition to participate in a proceeding shall describe the petitioner's interest in the subject matter of the proceeding. Parties with similar interests may file a single petition to participate.

**(2) Participation in general.**—Subject to paragraph (4), a person may participate in a proceeding under this chapter, including through the submission of briefs or other information, only if—

(A)　that person has filed a petition to participate in accordance with paragraph (1) (either individually or as a group under paragraph (1)(B));

(B)　the Copyright Royalty Judges have not determined that the petition to participate is facially invalid;

(C) the Copyright Royalty Judges have not determined, sua sponte or on the motion of another participant in the proceeding, that the person lacks a significant interest in the proceeding; and

(D) the petition to participate is accompanied by either—

(i) in a proceeding to determine royalty rates, a filing fee of $150; or

(ii) in a proceeding to determine distribution of royalty fees—

(I) a filing fee of $150; or

(II) a statement that the petitioner (individually or as a group) will not seek a distribution of more than $1000, in which case the amount distributed to the petitioner shall not exceed $1000.

**(3) Voluntary negotiation period.—**

**(A) Commencement of proceedings.—**

**(i) Rate adjustment proceeding.—**Promptly after the date for filing of petitions to participate in a proceeding, the Copyright Royalty Judges shall make available to all participants in the proceeding a list of such participants and shall initiate a voluntary negotiation period among the participants.

**(ii) Distribution proceeding.—**Promptly after the date for filing of petitions to participate in a proceeding to determine the distribution of royalties, the Copyright Royalty Judges shall make available to all participants in the proceeding a list of such participants. The initiation of a voluntary negotiation period among the participants shall be set at a time determined by the Copyright Royalty Judges.

**(B) Length of proceedings.—**The voluntary negotiation period initiated under subparagraph (A) shall be 3 months.

**(C) Determination of subsequent proceedings.—**At the close of the voluntary negotiation proceedings, the Copyright Royalty Judges shall, if further proceedings under this chapter are necessary, determine whether and to what extent paragraphs (4) and (5) will apply to the parties.

**(4) Small claims procedure in distribution proceedings.—**

**(A) In general.—**If, in a proceeding under this chapter to determine the distribution of royalties, the contested amount of a claim is $10,000 or less, the Copyright Royalty Judges shall decide the controversy on the basis of the filing of the written direct statement by the participant, the response by any opposing participant, and 1 additional response by each such party.

**(B) Bad faith inflation of claim.—**If the Copyright Royalty Judges determine that a participant asserts in bad faith an amount in controversy in excess of $10,000 for the purpose of avoiding a determination under the procedure set forth in subparagraph (A), the Copyright Royalty Judges shall impose a fine on that participant in an amount not to exceed the difference between the actual amount distributed and the amount asserted by the participant.

**(5) Paper proceedings.—**The Copyright Royalty Judges in proceedings under this chapter may decide, sua sponte or upon motion of a participant, to determine issues on the basis of the filing of the written direct statement by the participant, the response by any opposing participant, and one additional response by each such participant. Prior to making such decision to proceed on such a paper record only, the Copyright Royalty Judges shall offer to all parties to the proceeding the opportunity to comment on the decision. The procedure under this paragraph—

(A) shall be applied in cases in which there is no genuine issue of material fact, there is no need for evidentiary hearings, and all participants in the proceeding agree in writing to the procedure; and

(B) may be applied under such other circumstances as the Copyright Royalty Judges consider appropriate.

**(6) Regulations.—**

**(A) In general.**—The Copyright Royalty Judges may issue regulations to carry out their functions under this title. All regulations issued by the Copyright Royalty Judges are subject to the approval of the Librarian of Congress and are subject to judicial review pursuant to chapter 7 of title 5, except as set forth in subsection (d). Not later than 120 days after Copyright Royalty Judges or interim Copyright Royalty Judges, as the case may be, are first appointed after the enactment of the Copyright Royalty and Distribution Reform Act of 2004, such judges shall issue regulations to govern proceedings under this chapter.

**(B) Interim regulations.**—Until regulations are adopted under subparagraph (A), the Copyright Royalty Judges shall apply the regulations in effect under this chapter on the day before the effective date of the Copyright Royalty and Distribution Reform Act of 2004, to the extent such regulations are not inconsistent with this chapter, except that functions carried out under such regulations by the Librarian of Congress, the Register of Copyrights, or copyright arbitration royalty panels that, as of such date of enactment, are to be carried out by the Copyright Royalty Judges under this chapter, shall be carried out by the Copyright Royalty Judges under such regulations.

**(C) Requirements.**—Regulations issued under subparagraph (A) shall include the following:

(i) The written direct statements and written rebuttal statements of all participants in a proceeding under paragraph (2) shall be filed by a date specified by the Copyright Royalty Judges, which, in the case of written direct statements, may be not earlier than 4 months, and not later than 5 months, after the end of the voluntary negotiation period under paragraph (3). Notwithstanding the preceding sentence, the Copyright Royalty Judges may allow a participant in a proceeding to file an amended written direct statement based on new information received during the discovery process, within 15 days after the end of the discovery period specified in clause (iv).

(ii)(I) Following the submission to the Copyright Royalty Judges of written direct statements and written rebuttal statements by the participants in a proceeding under paragraph (2), the Copyright Royalty Judges, after taking into consideration the views of the participants in the proceeding, shall determine a schedule for conducting and completing discovery.

(II) In this chapter, the term "written direct statements" means witness statements, testimony, and exhibits to be presented in the proceedings, and such other information that is necessary to establish terms and rates, or the distribution of royalty payments, as the case may be, as set forth in regulations issued by the Copyright Royalty Judges.

(iii) Hearsay may be admitted in proceedings under this chapter to the extent deemed appropriate by the Copyright Royalty Judges.

(iv) Discovery in connection with written direct statements shall be permitted for a period of 60 days, except for discovery ordered by the Copyright Royalty Judges in connection with the resolution of motions, orders, and disputes pending at the end of such period. The Copyright Royalty Judges may order a discovery schedule in connection with written rebuttal statements.

(v) Any participant under paragraph (2) in a proceeding under this chapter to determine royalty rates may request of an opposing participant nonprivileged documents directly related to the written direct statement or written rebuttal statement of that participant. Any objection to such a request shall be resolved by a motion or request to compel production made to the Copyright Royalty Judges in accordance with regulations adopted by the Copyright Royalty Judges. Each motion or request to compel discovery shall be determined by the Copyright Royalty Judges, or by a Copyright Royalty Judge when permitted under subsection (a)(2). Upon such motion, the Copyright Royalty Judges may order discovery pursuant to regulations established under this paragraph.

(vi)(I) Any participant under paragraph (2) in a proceeding under this chapter to determine royalty rates may, by means of written motion or on the record, request of an opposing participant or witness other relevant information and materials if, absent the discovery sought, the Copyright Royalty Judges' resolution of the proceeding would be substantially impaired. In determining whether discovery will be granted under this clause, the Copyright Royalty Judges may consider—

(aa) whether the burden or expense of producing the requested information or materials outweighs the likely benefit, taking into account the needs and resources of the participants, the importance of the issues at stake, and the probative value of the requested information or materials in resolving such issues;

(bb) whether the requested information or materials would be unreasonably cumulative or duplicative, or are obtainable from another source that is more convenient, less burdensome, or less expensive; and

(cc) whether the participant seeking discovery has had ample opportunity by discovery in the proceeding or by other means to obtain the information sought.

(II) This clause shall not apply to any proceeding scheduled to commence after December 31, 2010.

(vii) In a proceeding under this chapter to determine royalty rates, the participants entitled to receive royalties shall collectively be permitted to take no more than 10 depositions and secure responses to no more than 25 interrogatories, and the participants obligated to pay royalties shall collectively be permitted to take no more than 10 depositions and secure responses to no more than 25 interrogatories. The Copyright Royalty Judges shall resolve any disputes among similarly aligned participants to allocate the number of depositions or interrogatories permitted under this clause.

(viii) The rules and practices in effect on the day before the effective date of the Copyright Royalty and Distribution Reform Act of 2004, relating to discovery in proceedings under this chapter to determine the distribution of royalty fees, shall continue to apply to such proceedings on and after such effective date.

(ix) In proceedings to determine royalty rates, the Copyright Royalty Judges may issue a subpoena commanding a participant or witness to appear and give testimony, or to produce and permit inspection of documents or tangible things, if the Copyright Royalty Judges' resolution of the proceeding would be substantially impaired by the absence of such testimony or production of documents or tangible things. Such subpoena shall specify with reasonable particularity the materials to be produced or the scope and nature of the required testimony. Nothing in this clause shall preclude the Copyright Royalty Judges from requesting the production by a nonparticipant of information or materials relevant to the resolution by the Copyright Royalty Judges of a material issue of fact.

(x) The Copyright Royalty Judges shall order a settlement conference among the participants in the proceeding to facilitate the presentation of offers of settlement among the participants. The settlement conference shall be held during a 21-day period following the 60-day discovery period specified in clause (iv) and shall take place outside the presence of the Copyright Royalty Judges.

(xi) No evidence, including exhibits, may be submitted in the written direct statement or written rebuttal statement of a participant without a sponsoring witness, except where the Copyright Royalty Judges have taken official notice, or in the case of incorporation by reference of past records, or for good cause shown.

**(c) Determination of Copyright Royalty Judges.—**

**(1) Timing.—**The Copyright Royalty Judges shall issue their determination in a proceeding not later than 11 months after the conclusion of the 21-day settlement conference period under subsection (b)(6)(C)(x), but, in the case of a proceeding to determine successors to rates or terms that expire on a specified date, in no event later than 15 days before the expiration of the then current statutory rates and terms.

**(2) Rehearings.—**

**(A) In general.—**The Copyright Royalty Judges may, in exceptional cases, upon motion of a participant in a proceeding under subsection (b)(2), order a rehearing, after the determination in the proceeding is issued under paragraph (1), on such matters as the Copyright Royalty Judges determine to be appropriate.

**(B) Timing for filing motion.—**Any motion for a rehearing under subparagraph (A) may only be filed within 15 days after the date on which the Copyright Royalty Judges deliver to the participants in the proceeding their initial determination.

**(C) Participation by opposing party not required.—**In any case in which a rehearing is ordered, any opposing party shall not be required to participate in the rehearing, except that nonparticipation may give rise to the limitations with respect to judicial review provided for in subsection (d)(1).

**(D) No negative inference.—**No negative inference shall be drawn from lack of participation in a rehearing.

**(E) Continuity of rates and terms.—**

(i) If the decision of the Copyright Royalty Judges on any motion for a rehearing is not rendered before the expiration of the statutory rates and terms that were previously in effect, in the case of a proceeding to determine successors to rates and terms that expire on a specified date, then—

(I) the initial determination of the Copyright Royalty Judges that is the subject of the rehearing motion shall be effective as of the day following the date on which the rates and terms that were previously in effect expire; and

(II) in the case of a proceeding under section 114(f)(1)(C), royalty rates and terms shall, for purposes of section 114(f)(3)(B), be deemed to have been set at those rates and terms contained in the initial determination of the Copyright Royalty Judges that is the subject of the rehearing motion, as of the date of that determination.

(ii) The pendency of a motion for a rehearing under this paragraph shall not relieve persons obligated to make royalty payments who would be affected by the determination on that motion from providing the statements of account and any reports of use, to the extent required, and paying the royalties required under the relevant determination or regulations.

(iii) Notwithstanding clause (ii), whenever royalties described in clause (ii) are paid to a person other than the Copyright Office, the entity designated by the Copyright Royalty Judges to which such royalties are paid by the copyright user (and any successor thereto) shall, within 60 days after the motion for rehearing is resolved or, if the motion is granted, within 60 days after the rehearing is concluded, return any excess amounts previously paid to the extent necessary to comply with the final determination of royalty rates by the Copyright Royalty Judges. Any underpayment of royalties resulting from a rehearing shall be paid within the same period.

(3) **Contents of determination.**—A determination of the Copyright Royalty Judges shall be supported by the written record and shall set forth the findings of fact relied on by the Copyright Royalty Judges. Among other terms adopted in a determination, the Copyright Royalty Judges may specify notice and recordkeeping requirements of users of the copyrights at issue that apply in lieu of those that would otherwise apply under regulations.

(4) **Continuing jurisdiction.**—The Copyright Royalty Judges may issue an amendment to a written determination to correct any technical or clerical errors in the determination or to modify the terms, but not the rates, of royalty payments in response to unforeseen circumstances that would frustrate the proper implementation of such determination. Such amendment shall be set forth in a written addendum to the determination that shall be distributed to the participants of the proceeding and shall be published in the Federal Register.

(5) **Protective order.**—The Copyright Royalty Judges may issue such orders as may be appropriate to protect confidential information, including orders excluding confidential information from the record of the determination that is published or made available to the public, except that any terms or rates of royalty payments or distributions may not be excluded.

(6) **Publication of determination.**—By no later than the end of the 60-day period provided in section 802(f)(1)(D), the Librarian of Congress shall cause the determination, and any corrections thereto, to be published in the Federal Register. The Librarian of Congress shall also publicize the determination and corrections in such other manner as the Librarian considers appropriate, including, but not limited to, publication on the Internet. The Librarian of Congress shall also make the determination, corrections, and the accompanying record available for public inspection and copying.

(7) **Late payment.**—A determination of the Copyright Royalty Judges may include terms with respect to late payment, but in no way shall such terms prevent the copyright holder from asserting other rights or remedies provided under this title.

**(d) Judicial Review.—**

(1) **Appeal.**—Any determination of the Copyright Royalty Judges under subsection (c) may, within 30 days after the publication of the determination in the Federal Register, be appealed, to the United States Court of Appeals for the District of Columbia Circuit, by any aggrieved participant in the proceeding under subsection (b)(2) who fully participated in the proceeding and who would be bound by the determination. Any participant that did not participate in a rehearing may not raise any issue that was the subject of that rehearing at any stage of judicial review of the hearing determination. If no appeal is brought within that 30-day period, the determination of the Copyright Royalty Judges shall be final, and the royalty fee or determination with respect to the distribution of fees, as the case may be, shall take effect as set forth in paragraph (2).

(2) **Effect of rates.—**

(A) **Expiration on specified date.**—When this title provides that the royalty rates and terms that were previously in effect are to expire on a specified date, any adjustment or determination by the Copyright Royalty Judges of successor rates and terms for an ensuing statutory license period shall be effective as of the day following the date of expiration of the rates and terms that were previously in effect, even if the determination of the Copyright Royalty Judges is rendered on a later date. A licensee shall be obligated to continue making payments under the rates and terms previously in effect until such time as rates and terms for the successor period are established. Whenever royalties pursuant to this section are paid to a person other than the Copyright Office, the entity designated by the Copyright Royalty Judges to which such royalties are paid by the copyright user (and any successor thereto) shall, within 60 days after the final determination of the Copyright Royalty Judges establishing rates and terms for a successor period or the exhaustion of all rehearings or appeals of such determination, if any, return any excess amounts previously paid to the extent necessary to comply with the final determination of royalty rates. Any underpayment of royalties by a copyright user shall be paid to the entity designated by the Copyright Royalty Judges within the same period.

(B) **Other cases.**—In cases where rates and terms have not, prior to the inception of an activity, been established for that particular activity under the relevant license, such rates and terms shall be retroactive to the inception of activity under the relevant license covered by such rates and terms. In other cases where rates and terms do not expire on a specified date, successor rates and terms shall take effect on the first day of the second month that begins after the publication of the determination of the Copyright Royalty Judges in the Federal Register, except as otherwise provided in this title, or by the Copyright Royalty Judges, or as agreed by the participants in a proceeding that would be bound by the rates and terms. Except as otherwise provided in this title, the rates and terms, to the extent applicable, shall remain in effect until such successor rates and terms become effective.

(C) **Obligation to make payments.**—

(i) The pendency of an appeal under this subsection shall not relieve persons obligated to make royalty payments under section 111, 112, 114, 115, 116, 118, 119, or 1003, who would be affected by the determination on appeal, from—

(I) providing the applicable statements of accounts and reports of use; and

(II) paying the royalties required under the relevant determination or regulations.

(ii) Notwithstanding clause (i), whenever royalties described in clause (i) are paid to a person other than the Copyright Office, the entity designated by the Copyright Royalty Judges to which such royalties are paid by the copyright user (and any successor thereto) shall, within 60 days after the final resolution of the appeal, return any excess amounts previously paid (and interest thereon, if ordered pursuant to paragraph (3)) to the extent necessary to comply with the final determination of royalty rates on appeal. Any underpayment of royalties resulting from an appeal (and interest thereon, if ordered pursuant to paragraph (3)) shall be paid within the same period.

(3) **Jurisdiction of court.**—Section 706 of the title 5 shall apply with respect to review by the court of appeals under this subsection. If the court modifies or vacates a determination of the Copyright Royalty Judges, the court may enter its own determination with respect to the amount or distribution of royalty fees and costs, and order the repayment of any excess fees, the payment of any underpaid fees, and the payment of interest pertaining respectively thereto, in accordance with its final judgment. The court may also vacate the determination of the Copyright Royalty Judges and remand the case to the Copyright Royalty Judges for further proceedings in accordance with subsection (a).

(e) **Administrative matters.**—

(1) **Deduction of costs of Library of Congress and Copyright Office from filing fees.**—

(A) **Deduction from filing fees.**—The Librarian of Congress may, to the extent not otherwise provided under this title, deduct from the filing fees collected under subsection (b) for a particular proceeding under this chapter the reasonable costs incurred by the Librarian of Congress, the Copyright Office, and the Copyright Royalty Judges in conducting that proceeding, other than the salaries of the Copyright Royalty Judges and the staff members appointed under section 802(b).

(B) **Authorization of appropriations.**—There are authorized to be appropriated such sums as may be necessary to pay the costs incurred under this chapter not covered by the filing fees collected under subsection (b). All funds made available pursuant to this subparagraph shall remain available until expended.

(2) **Positions required for administration of compulsory licensing.**—Section 307 of the Legislative Branch Appropriations Act, 1994, shall not apply to employee positions in the Library of Congress that are required to be filled in order to carry out section 111, 112, 114, 115, 116, 118, or 119 or chapter 10.

(As amended, Pub.L. 100–568, 102 Stat. 2853 (1988); Pub.L. 100–667, 102 Stat. 3935 (1988); Pub.L. 101–318, 104 Stat. 288 (1990); Pub.L. 102–563, 106 Stat. 4248 (1992); Pub.L. 103–198, 107 Stat. 2304 (1993); Pub.L. 104–39, 109 Stat. 336 (1995); Pub.L. 105–304, 112 Stat. 2860 (1998); Pub.L. 108–419, 118 Stat. 2341 (2004); Pub.L. 108–447, 118 Stat. 2809 (2004); Pub.L. 109–303, 120 Stat. 1478 (2006); Pub.L. 111–295, 124 Stat. 3180 (2010); Pub.L. 115–264, 132 Stat. 3676 (2018); Pub.L. 116–94, 113 Stat 2534 (2019)).

## Sec. 804.    Institution of Proceedings

(a) **Filing of petition.**—With respect to proceedings referred to in paragraphs (1) and (2) of section 801(b) concerning the determination or adjustment of royalty rates as provided in sections 111, 112, 114, 115, 116, 118, 119, and 1004, during the calendar years specified in the schedule set forth in subsection (b), any owner or user of a copyrighted work whose royalty rates are specified by this title, or are established under this chapter before or after the enactment of the Copyright Royalty and Distribution Reform Act of 2004, may file a petition with the Copyright Royalty Judges declaring that the petitioner requests a determination or adjustment of the rate. The Copyright Royalty Judges shall make a determination as to whether the petitioner has such a significant interest in the royalty rate in which a determination or adjustment is requested. If the Copyright Royalty Judges determine that the petitioner has such a significant interest, the Copyright Royalty Judges shall cause notice of this determination, with the reasons for such determination, to be published in the Federal Register, together with the notice of commencement of proceedings under this chapter. With respect to proceedings under paragraph (1) of section 801(b) concerning the determination or adjustment of royalty rates as provided in sections 112 and 114, during the calendar years specified in the schedule set forth in subsection (b), the Copyright Royalty Judges shall cause notice of commencement of proceedings under this chapter to be published in the Federal Register as provided in section 803(b)(1)(A).

(b) **Timing of proceedings.—**

(1) **Section 111 proceedings.—**

(A) A petition described in subsection (a) to initiate proceedings under section 801(b)(2) concerning the adjustment of royalty rates under section 111 to which subparagraph (A) or (D) of section 801(b)(2) applies may be filed during the year 2015 and in each subsequent fifth calendar year.

(B) In order to initiate proceedings under section 801(b)(2) concerning the adjustment of royalty rates under section 111 to which subparagraph (B) or (C) of section 801(b)(2) applies, within 12 months after an event described in either of those subsections, any owner or user of a copyrighted work whose royalty rates are specified by section 111, or by a rate established under this chapter before or after the enactment of the Copyright Royalty and Distribution Reform Act of 2004, may file a petition with the Copyright Royalty Judges declaring that the petitioner requests an adjustment of the rate. The Copyright Royalty Judges shall then proceed as set forth in subsection (a) of this section. Any change in royalty rates made under this chapter pursuant to this subparagraph may be reconsidered in the year 2015, and each fifth calendar year thereafter, in accordance with the provisions in section 801(b)(2)(B) or (C), as the case may be. A petition for adjustment of rates established by section 111(d)(1)(B) as a result of a change in the rules and regulations of the Federal Communications Commission shall set forth the change on which the petition is based.

(C)  Any adjustment of royalty rates under section 111 shall take effect as of the first accounting period commencing after the publication of the determination of the Copyright Royalty Judges in the Federal Register, or on such other date as is specified in that determination.

**(2)  Certain section 112 proceedings.**—Proceedings under this chapter shall be commenced in the year 2007 to determine reasonable terms and rates of royalty payments for the activities described in section 112(e)(1) relating to the limitation on exclusive rights specified by section 114(d)(1)(C)(iv), to become effective on January 1, 2009. Such proceedings shall be repeated in each subsequent fifth calendar year.

**(3)  Section 114 and corresponding 112 proceedings.**—

(A)  For eligible nonsubscription services and new subscription services. Proceedings under this chapter shall be commenced as soon as practicable after the date of enactment of the Copyright Royalty and Distribution Reform Act of 2004 to determine reasonable terms and rates of royalty payments under sections 114 and 112 for the activities of eligible nonsubscription transmission services and new subscription services, to be effective for the period beginning on January 1, 2006, and ending on December 31, 2010. Such proceedings shall next be commenced in January 2009 to determine reasonable terms and rates of royalty payments, to become effective on January 1, 2011. Thereafter, such proceedings shall be repeated in each subsequent fifth calendar year.

(B)  For preexisting subscription and satellite digital audio radio services. Proceedings under this chapter shall be commenced in January 2006 to determine reasonable terms and rates of royalty payments under sections 114 and 112 for the activities of preexisting subscription services, to be effective during the period beginning on January 1, 2008, and ending on December 31, 2012, and preexisting satellite digital audio radio services, to be effective during the period beginning on January 1, 2007, and ending on December 31, 2012. Such proceedings shall next be commenced in 2011 to determine reasonable terms and rates of royalty payments, to become effective on January 1, 2013. Thereafter, such proceedings shall be repeated in each subsequent fifth calendar year, except that—

(i)  with respect to preexisting subscription services, the terms and rates finally determined for the rate period ending on December 31, 2022, shall remain in effect through December 31, 2027, and there shall be no proceeding to determine terms and rates for preexisting subscription services for the period beginning on January 1, 2023, and ending on December 31, 2027; and

(ii)  with respect to pre-existing satellite digital audio radio services, the terms and rates set forth by the Copyright Royalty Judges on December 14, 2017, in their initial determination for the rate period ending on December 31, 2022, shall be in effect through December 31, 2027, without any change based on a rehearing under section 803(c)(2) and without the possibility of appeal under section 803(d), and there shall be no proceeding to determine terms and rates for preexisting satellite digital audio radio services for the period beginning on January 1, 2023, and ending on December 31, 2027.

(C)(i)  Notwithstanding any other provision of this chapter, this subparagraph shall govern proceedings commenced pursuant to section 114(f)(1)(C) concerning new types of services.

(ii) Not later than 30 days after a petition to determine rates and terms for a new type of service is filed by any copyright owner of sound recordings, or such new type of service, indicating that such new type of service is or is about to become operational, the Copyright Royalty Judges shall issue a notice for a proceeding to determine rates and terms for such service.

(iii) The proceeding shall follow the schedule set forth in subsections (b), (c), and (d) of section 803, except that—

(I) the determination shall be issued by not later than 24 months after the publication of the notice under clause (ii); and

(II) the decision shall take effect as provided in subsections (c)(2) and (d)(2) of section 803 and section 114(f)(3)(B)(ii) and (C).

(iv) The rates and terms shall remain in effect for the period set forth in section 114(f)(1)(C).

**(4) Section 115 proceedings.**—A petition described in subsection (a) to initiate proceedings under section 801(b)(1) concerning the adjustment or determination of royalty rates as provided in section 115 may be filed in the year 2006 and in each subsequent fifth calendar year, or at such other times as the parties have agreed under section 115(c)(3)(B) and (C).

**(5) Section 116 proceedings.—**

(A) A petition described in subsection (a) to initiate proceedings under section 801(b) concerning the determination of royalty rates and terms as provided in section 116 may be filed at any time within 1 year after negotiated licenses authorized by section 116 are terminated or expire and are not replaced by subsequent agreements.

(B) If a negotiated license authorized by section 116 is terminated or expires and is not replaced by another such license agreement which provides permission to use a quantity of musical works not substantially smaller than the quantity of such works performed on coin-operated phonorecord players during the 1-year period ending March 1, 1989, the Copyright Royalty Judges shall, upon petition filed under paragraph (1) within 1 year after such termination or expiration, commence a proceeding to promptly establish an interim royalty rate or rates for the public performance by means of a coin-operated phonorecord player of nondramatic musical works embodied in phonorecords which had been subject to the terminated or expired negotiated license agreement. Such rate or rates shall be the same as the last such rate or rates and shall remain in force until the conclusion of proceedings by the Copyright Royalty Judges, in accordance with section 803, to adjust the royalty rates applicable to such works, or until superseded by a new negotiated license agreement, as provided in section 116(b).

**(6) Section 118 proceedings.**—A petition described in subsection (a) to initiate proceedings under section 801(b)(1) concerning the determination of reasonable terms and rates of royalty payments as provided in section 118 may be filed in the year 2006 and in each subsequent fifth calendar year.

**(7) Section 1004 proceedings.**—A petition described in subsection (a) to initiate proceedings under section 801(b)(1) concerning the adjustment of reasonable royalty rates under section 1004 may be filed as provided in section 1004(a)(3).

**(8) Proceedings concerning distribution of royalty fees.**—With respect to proceedings under section 801(b)(3) concerning the distribution of royalty fees in certain circumstances under section 111, 119, or 1007, the Copyright Royalty Judges shall, upon a determination that a controversy exists concerning such distribution, cause to be published in the Federal Register notice of commencement of proceedings under this chapter.

(Added, Pub.L. 108–419, 118 Stat. 2341 (2004); as amended, Pub.L. 109–303, 120 Stat. 1478 (2006); Pub.L. 111–175, 124 Stat. 1218 (2010); Pub.L. 115–264, 132 Stat. 3676 (2018)).

## Sec. 805.   General Rule for Voluntarily Negotiated Agreements

Any rates or terms under this title that—

(1)   are agreed to by participants to a proceeding under section 803(b)(3),

(2)   are adopted by the Copyright Royalty Judges as part of a determination under this chapter, and

(3)   are in effect for a period shorter than would otherwise apply under a determination pursuant to this chapter,

shall remain in effect for such period of time as would otherwise apply under such determination, except that the Copyright Royalty Judges shall adjust the rates pursuant to the voluntary negotiations to reflect national monetary inflation during the additional period the rates remain in effect.

(Added, Pub.L. 108–419, 118 Stat. 2341 (2004)).

## CHAPTER 9.—PROTECTION OF SEMICONDUCTOR CHIP PRODUCTS

(Pub.L. 98–620, 98 Stat. 3347 (1984)).

## Sec. 901.   Definitions

(a)   As used in this chapter—

(1)   a "semiconductor chip product" is the final or intermediate form of any product—

(A)   having two or more layers of metallic, insulating, or semiconductor material, deposited or otherwise placed on, or etched away or otherwise removed from, a piece of semiconductor material in accordance with a predetermined pattern; and

(B)   intended to perform electronic circuitry functions;

(2)   a "mask work" is a series of related images, however fixed or encoded—

(A)   having or representing the predetermined, three-dimensional pattern of metallic, insulating, or semiconductor material present or removed from the layers of a semiconductor chip product; and

(B)  in which series the relation of the images to one another is that each image has the pattern of the surface of one form of the semiconductor chip product;

(3)  a mask work is "fixed" in a semiconductor chip product when its embodiment in the product is sufficiently permanent or stable to permit the mask work to be perceived or reproduced from the product for a period of more than transitory duration;

(4)  to "distribute" means to sell, or to lease, bail, or otherwise transfer, or to offer to sell, lease, bail, or otherwise transfer;

(5)  to "commercially exploit" a mask work is to distribute to the public for commercial purposes a semiconductor chip product embodying the mask work; except that such term includes an offer to sell or transfer a semiconductor chip product only when the offer is in writing and occurs after the mask work is fixed in the semiconductor chip product;

(6)  the "owner" of a mask work is the person who created the mask work, the legal representative of that person if that person is deceased or under a legal incapacity, or a party to whom all the rights under this chapter of such person or representative are transferred in accordance with section 903(b); except that, in the case of a work made within the scope of a person's employment, the owner is the employer for whom the person created the mask work or a party to whom all the rights under this chapter of the employer are transferred in accordance with section 903(b);

(7)  an "innocent purchaser" is a person who purchases a semiconductor chip product in good faith and without having notice of protection with respect to the semiconductor chip product;

(8)  having "notice of protection" means having actual knowledge that, or reasonable grounds to believe that, a mask work is protected under this chapter; and

(9)  an "infringing semiconductor chip product" is a semiconductor chip product which is made, imported, or distributed in violation of the exclusive rights of the owner of a mask work under this chapter.

(b)  For purposes of this chapter, the distribution or importation of a product incorporating a semiconductor chip product as a part thereof is a distribution or importation of that semiconductor chip product.

## Sec. 902.    Subject Matter of Protection

(a)(1)  Subject to the provisions of subsection (b), a mask work fixed in a semiconductor chip product, by or under the authority of the owner of the mask work, is eligible for protection under this chapter if—

(A)  on the date on which the mask work is registered under section 908, or is first commercially exploited anywhere in the world, whichever occurs first, the owner of the mask work is (i) a national or domiciliary of the United States, (ii) a national, domiciliary, or sovereign authority of a foreign nation that is a party to a treaty affording protection to mask works to which the United States is also a party, or (iii) a stateless person, wherever that person may be domiciled;

(B)  the mask work is first commercially exploited in the United States; or

(C)  the mask work comes within the scope of a Presidential proclamation issued under paragraph (2).

(2)  Whenever the President finds that a foreign nation extends, to mask works of owners who are nationals or domiciliaries of the United States protection (A) on substantially the same basis as that on which the foreign nation extends protection to mask works of its own nationals and domiciliaries and mask works first commercially exploited in that nation, or (B) on substantially the same basis as provided in this chapter, the President may by proclamation extend protection under

this chapter to mask works (i) of owners who are, on the date on which the mask works are registered under section 908, or the date on which the mask works are first commercially exploited anywhere in the world, whichever occurs first, nationals, domiciliaries, or sovereign authorities of that nation, or (ii) which are first commercially exploited in that nation. The President may revise, suspend, or revoke any such proclamation or impose any conditions or limitations on protection extended under any such proclamation.

(b) Protection under this chapter shall not be available for a mask work that—

(1) is not original; or

(2) consists of designs that are staple, commonplace, or familiar in the semiconductor industry, or variations of such designs, combined in a way that, considered as a whole, is not original.

(c) In no case does protection under this chapter for a mask work extend to any idea, procedure, process, system, method of operation, concept, principle, or discovery, regardless of the form in which it is described, explained, illustrated, or embodied in such work.

(As amended, Pub.L. 100–159, 100 Stat. 900 (1987)).

## Sec. 903. Ownership, Transfer, Licensing, and Recordation

(a) The exclusive rights in a mask work subject to protection under this chapter belong to the owner of the mask work.

(b) The owner of the exclusive rights in a mask work may transfer all of those rights, or license all or less than all of those rights, by any written instrument signed by such owner or a duly authorized agent of the owner. Such rights may be transferred or licensed by operation of law, may be bequeathed by will, and may pass as personal property by the applicable laws of intestate succession.

(c)(1) Any document pertaining to a mask work may be recorded in the Copyright Office if the document filed for recordation bears the actual signature of the person who executed it, or if it is accompanied by a sworn or official certification that it is a true copy of the original, signed document. The Register of Copyrights shall, upon receipt of the document and the fee specified pursuant to section 908(d), record the document and return it with a certificate of recordation. The recordation of any transfer or license under this paragraph gives all persons constructive notice of the facts stated in the recorded document concerning the transfer or license.

(2) In any case in which conflicting transfers of the exclusive rights in a mask work are made, the transfer first executed shall be void as against a subsequent transfer which is made for a valuable consideration and without notice of the first transfer, unless the first transfer is recorded in accordance with paragraph (1) within three months after the date on which it is executed, but in no case later than the day before the date of such subsequent transfer.

(d) Mask works prepared by an officer or employee of the United States Government as part of that person's official duties are not protected under this chapter, but the United States Government is not precluded from receiving and holding exclusive rights in mask works transferred to the Government under subsection (b).

## Sec. 904. Duration of Protection

(a) The protection provided for a mask work under this chapter shall commence on the date on which the mask work is registered under section 908, or the date on which the mask work is first commercially exploited anywhere in the world, whichever occurs first.

(b) Subject to subsection (c) and the provisions of this chapter, the protection provided under this chapter to a mask work shall end ten years after the date on which such protection commences under subsection (a).

(c)   All terms of protection provided in this section shall run to the end of the calendar year in which they would otherwise expire.

## Sec. 905.    Exclusive Rights in Mask Works

The owner of a mask work provided protection under this chapter has the exclusive rights to do and to authorize any of the following:

(1)   to reproduce the mask work by optical, electronic, or any other means;

(2)   to import or distribute a semiconductor chip product in which the mask work is embodied; and

(3)   to induce or knowingly to cause another person to do any of the acts described in paragraphs (1) and (2).

## Sec. 906.    Limitation on Exclusive Rights: Reverse Engineering; First Sale

(a)   Notwithstanding the provisions of section 905, it is not an infringement of the exclusive rights of the owner of a mask work for—

(1)   a person to reproduce the mask work solely for the purpose of teaching, analyzing, or evaluating the concepts or techniques embodied in the mask work or the circuitry, logic flow, or organization of components used in the mask work; or

(2)   a person who performs the analysis or evaluation described in paragraph (1) to incorporate the results of such conduct in an original mask work which is made to be distributed.

(b)   Notwithstanding the provisions of section 905(2), the owner of a particular semiconductor chip product made by the owner of the mask work, or by any person authorized by the owner of the mask work, may import, distribute, or otherwise dispose of or use, but not reproduce, that particular semiconductor chip product without the authority of the owner of the mask work.

## Sec. 907.    Limitation on Exclusive Rights: Innocent Infringement

(a)   Notwithstanding any other provision of this chapter, an innocent purchaser of an infringing semiconductor chip product—

(1)   shall incur no liability under this chapter with respect to the importation or distribution of units of the infringing semiconductor chip product that occurs before the innocent purchaser has notice of protection with respect to the mask work embodied in the semiconductor chip product; and

(2)   shall be liable only for a reasonable royalty on each unit of the infringing semiconductor chip product that the innocent purchaser imports or distributes after having notice of protection with respect to the mask work embodied in the semiconductor chip product.

(b)   The amount of the royalty referred to in subsection (a)(2) shall be determined by the court in a civil action for infringement unless the parties resolve the issue by voluntary negotiation, mediation, or binding arbitration.

(c)   The immunity of an innocent purchaser from liability referred to in subsection (a)(1) and the limitation of remedies with respect to an innocent purchaser referred to in subsection (a)(2) shall extend to any person who directly or indirectly purchases an infringing semiconductor chip product from an innocent purchaser.

(d)   The provisions of subsections (a), (b), and (c) apply only with respect to those units of an infringing semiconductor chip product that an innocent purchaser purchased before having notice of protection with respect to the mask work embodied in the semiconductor chip product.

## Sec. 908.    Registration of Claims of Protection

(a)    The owner of a mask work may apply to the Register of Copyrights for registration of a claim of protection in a mask work. Protection of a mask work under this chapter shall terminate if application for registration of a claim of protection in the mask work is not made as provided in this chapter within two years after the date on which the mask work is first commercially exploited anywhere in the world.

(b)    The Register of Copyrights shall be responsible for all administrative functions and duties under this chapter. Except for section 708, the provisions of chapter 7 of this title relating to the general responsibilities, organization, regulatory authority, actions, records, and publications of the Copyright Office shall apply to this chapter, except that the Register of Copyrights may make such changes as may be necessary in applying those provisions to this chapter.

(c)    The application for registration of a mask work shall be made on a form prescribed by the Register of Copyrights. Such form may require any information regarded by the Register as bearing upon the preparation or identification of the mask work, the existence or duration of protection of the mask work under this chapter, or ownership of the mask work. The application shall be accompanied by the fee set pursuant to subsection (d) and the identifying material specified pursuant to such subsection.

(d)    The Register of Copyrights shall by regulation set reasonable fees for the filing of applications to register claims of protection in mask works under this chapter, and for other services relating to the administration of this chapter or the rights under this chapter, taking into consideration the cost of providing those services, the benefits of a public record, and statutory fee schedules under this title. The Register shall also specify the identifying material to be deposited in connection with the claim for registration.

(e)    If the Register of Copyrights, after examining an application for registration, determines, in accordance with the provisions of this chapter, that the application relates to a mask work which is entitled to protection under this chapter, then the Register shall register the claim of protection and issue to the applicant a certificate of registration of the claim of protection under the seal of the Copyright Office. The effective date of registration of a claim of protection shall be the date on which an application, deposit of identifying material, and fee, which are determined by the Register of Copyrights or by a court of competent jurisdiction to be acceptable for registration of the claim, have all been received in the Copyright Office.

(f)    In any action for infringement under this chapter, the certificate of registration of a mask work shall constitute prima facie evidence (1) of the facts stated in the certificate, and (2) that the applicant issued the certificate has met the requirements of this chapter, and the regulations issued under this chapter, with respect to the registration of claims.

(g)    Any applicant for registration under this section who is dissatisfied with the refusal of the Register of Copyrights to issue a certificate of registration under this section may seek judicial review of that refusal by bringing an action for such review in an appropriate United States district court not later than sixty days after the refusal. The provisions of chapter 7 of title 5 shall apply to such judicial review. The failure of the Register of Copyrights to issue a certificate of registration within four months after an application for registration is filed shall be deemed to be a refusal to issue a certificate of registration for purposes of this subsection and section 910(b)(2), except that, upon a showing of good cause, the district court may shorten such four-month period.

## Sec. 909.    Mask Work Notice

(a)    The owner of a mask work provided protection under this chapter may affix notice to the mask work, and to masks and semiconductor chip products embodying the mask work, in such manner and location as to give reasonable notice of such protection. The Register of Copyrights shall prescribe by regulation, as examples, specific methods of affixation and positions of notice for purposes of this section, but these specifications shall not be considered exhaustive. The affixation of such notice is not a condition of protection under this chapter, but shall constitute prima facie evidence of notice of protection.

(b)   the notice referred to in subsection (a) shall consist of—

(1)   the words "mask work", the symbol *M*, or the symbol Ⓜ (the letter M in a circle); and

(2)   the name of the owner or owners of the mask work or an abbreviation by which the name is recognized or is generally known.

(As amended, Pub.L. 105–80, 111 Stat. 1535 (1997)).

## Sec. 910.      Enforcement of Exclusive Rights

(a)   Except as otherwise provided in this chapter, any person who violates any of the exclusive rights of the owner of a mask work under this chapter, by conduct in or affecting commerce, shall be liable as an infringer of such rights. As used in this subsection, the term "any person" includes any State, any instrumentality of a State, and any officer or employee of a State or instrumentality of a State acting in his or her official capacity. Any State, and any such instrumentality, officer, or employee, shall be subject to the provisions of this chapter in the same manner and to the same extent as any nongovernmental entity.

(b)(1)   The owner of a mask work protected under this chapter, or the exclusive licensee of all rights under this chapter with respect to the mask work, shall, after a certificate of registration of a claim of protection in that mask work has been issued under section 908, be entitled to institute a civil action for any infringement with respect to the mask work which is committed after the commencement of protection of the mask work under section 904(a).

(2)   In any case in which an application for registration of a claim of protection in a mask work and the required deposit of identifying material and fee have been received in the Copyright Office in proper form and registration of the mask work has been refused, the applicant is entitled to institute a civil action for infringement under this chapter with respect to the mask work if notice of the action, together with a copy of the complaint, is served on the Register of Copyrights, in accordance with the Federal Rules of Civil Procedure. The Register may, at his or her option, become a party to the action with respect to the issue of whether the claim of protection is eligible for registration by entering an appearance within sixty days after such service, but the failure of the Register to become a party to the action shall not deprive the court of jurisdiction to determine that issue.

(c)(1)   The Secretary of the Treasury and the United States Postal Service shall separately or jointly issue regulations for the enforcement of the rights set forth in section 905 with respect to importation. These regulations may require, as a condition for the exclusion of articles from the United States, that the person seeking exclusion take any one or more of the following actions:

(A)   Obtain a court order enjoining, or an order of the International Trade Commission under section 337 of the Tariff Act of 1930 excluding, importation of the articles.

(B)   Furnish proof that the mask work involved is protected under this chapter and that the importation of the articles would infringe the rights in the mask work under this chapter.

(C)   Post a surety bond for any injury that may result if the detention or exclusion of the articles proves to be unjustified.

(2)   Articles imported in violation of the rights set forth in section 905 are subject to seizure and forfeiture in the same manner as property imported in violation of the customs laws. Any such forfeited articles shall be destroyed as directed by the Secretary of the Treasury or the court, as the case may be, except that the articles may be returned to the country of export whenever it is shown to the satisfaction of the Secretary of the Treasury that the importer had no reasonable grounds for believing that his or her acts constituted a violation of the law.

(As amended, Pub.L. 101–553, 104 Stat. 2749 (1990); Pub.L. 105–80, 111 Stat. 1535 (1997)).

## Sec. 911.    Civil Actions

(a)  Any court having jurisdiction of a civil action arising under this chapter may grant temporary restraining orders, preliminary injunctions, and permanent injunctions on such terms as the court may deem reasonable to prevent or restrain infringement of the exclusive rights in a mask work under this chapter.

(b)  Upon finding an infringer liable, to a person entitled under section 910(b)(1) to institute a civil action, for an infringement of any exclusive right under this chapter, the court shall award such person actual damages suffered by the person as a result of the infringement. The court shall also award such person the infringer's profits that are attributable to the infringement and are not taken into account in computing the award of actual damages. In establishing the infringer's profits, such person is required to present proof only of the infringer's gross revenue, and the infringer is required to prove his or her deductible expenses and the elements of profit attributable to factors other than the mask work.

(c)  At any time before final judgment is rendered, a person entitled to institute a civil action for infringement may elect, instead of actual damages and profits as provided by subsection (b), an award of statutory damages for all infringements involved in the action, with respect to any one mask work for which any one infringer is liable individually, or for which any two or more infringers are liable jointly and severally, in an amount not more than $250,000 as the court considers just.

(d)  An action for infringement under this chapter shall be barred unless the action is commenced within three years after the claim accrues.

(e)(1)  At any time while an action for infringement of the exclusive rights in a mask work under this chapter is pending, the court may order the impounding, on such terms as it may deem reasonable, of all semiconductor chip products, and any drawings, tapes, masks, or other products by means of which such products may be reproduced, that are claimed to have been made, imported, or used in violation of those exclusive rights. Insofar as practicable, applications for orders under this paragraph shall be heard and determined in the same manner as an application for a temporary restraining order or preliminary injunction.

(2)  As part of a final judgment or decree, the court may order the destruction or other disposition of any infringing semiconductor chip products, and any masks, tapes, or other articles by means of which such products may be reproduced.

(f)  In any civil action arising under this chapter, the court in its discretion may allow the recovery of full costs, including reasonable attorneys' fees, to the prevailing party.

(g)(1)  Any State, any instrumentality of a State, and any officer or employee of a State or instrumentality of a State acting in his or her official capacity, shall not be immune, under the Eleventh Amendment of the Constitution of the United States or under any other doctrine of sovereign immunity, from suit in Federal court by any person, including any governmental or nongovernmental entity, for a violation of any of the exclusive rights of the owner of a mask work under this chapter, or for any other violation under this chapter.

(2)  In a suit described in paragraph (1) for a violation described in that paragraph, remedies (including remedies both at law and in equity) are available for the violation to the same extent as such remedies are available for such a violation in a suit against any public or private entity other than a State, instrumentality of a State, or officer or employee of a State acting in his or her official capacity. Such remedies include actual damages and profits under subsection (b), statutory damages under subsection (c), impounding and disposition of infringing articles under subsection (e), and costs and attorney's fees under subsection (f).

(As amended, Pub.L. 101–553, 104 Stat. 2749 (1990)).

## Sec. 912.    Relation to Other Laws

(a)   Nothing in this chapter shall affect any right or remedy held by any person under chapters 1 through 8 or 10 of this title, or under title 35.

(b)   Except as provided in section 908(b) of this title, references to "this title" or "title 17" in chapters 1 through 8 or 10 of this title shall be deemed not to apply to this chapter.

(c)   The provisions of this chapter shall preempt the laws of any State to the extent those laws provide any rights or remedies with respect to a mask work which are equivalent to those rights or remedies provided by this chapter, except that such preemption shall be effective only with respect to actions filed on or after January 1, 1986.

(d)   Notwithstanding subsection (c), nothing in this chapter shall detract from any rights of a mask work owner, whether under Federal law (exclusive of this chapter) or under the common law or the statutes of a State, heretofore or hereafter declared or enacted, with respect to any mask work first commercially exploited before July 1, 1983.

(As amended, Pub.L. 100–702, 102 Stat. 4672 (1988); Pub.L. 102–563, 106 Stat. 4248 (1992)).

## Sec. 913.    Transitional Provisions

(a)   No application for registration under section 908 may be filed, and no civil action under section 910 or other enforcement proceeding under this chapter may be instituted, until sixty days after the date of the enactment of this chapter.

(b)   No monetary relief under section 911 may be granted with respect to any conduct that occurred before the date of the enactment of this chapter, except as provided in subsection (d).

(c)   Subject to subsection (a), the provisions of this chapter apply to all mask works that are first commercially exploited or are registered under this chapter, or both, on or after the date of the enactment of this chapter.

(d)(1)   Subject to subsection (a), protection is available under this chapter to any mask work that was first commercially exploited on or after July 1, 1983, and before the date of the enactment of this chapter, if a claim of protection in the mask work is registered in the Copyright Office before July 1, 1985, under section 908.

(2)   In the case of any mask work described in paragraph (1) that is provided protection under this chapter, infringing semiconductor chip product units manufactured before the date of the enactment of this chapter may, without liability under sections 910 and 911, be imported into or distributed in the United States, or both, until two years after the date of registration of the mask work under section 908, but only if the importer or distributor, as the case may be, first pays or offers to pay the reasonable royalty referred to in section 907(a)(2) to the mask work owner, on all such units imported or distributed, or both, after the date of the enactment of this chapter.

(3)   In the event that a person imports or distributes infringing semiconductor chip product units described in paragraph (2) of this subsection without first paying or offering to pay the reasonable royalty specified in such paragraph, or if the person refuses or fails to make such payment, the mask work owner shall be entitled to the relief provided in sections 910 and 911.

## Sec. 914.    International Transitional Provisions

(a)   Notwithstanding the conditions set forth in subparagraphs (A) and (C) of section 902(a)(1) with respect to the availability of protection under this chapter to nationals, domiciliaries, and sovereign authorities of a foreign nation, the Secretary of Commerce may, upon the petition of any person, or upon the Secretary's own motion, issue an order extending protection under this chapter to such foreign nationals, domiciliaries, and sovereign authorities if the Secretary finds—

(1)   that the foreign nation is making good faith efforts and reasonable progress toward—

(A)   entering into a treaty described in section 902(a)(1)(A); or

(B)   enacting or implementing legislation that would be in compliance with subparagraphs (A) or (B) of section 902(a)(2); and

(2)   that the nationals, domiciliaries, and sovereign authorities of the foreign nation, and persons controlled by them, are not engaged in the misappropriation, or unauthorized distribution or commercial exploitation, of mask works; and

(3)   that issuing the order would promote the purposes of this chapter and international comity with respect to the protection of mask works.

(b)   While an order under subsection (a) is in effect with respect to a foreign nation, no application for registration of a claim for protection in a mask work under this chapter may be denied solely because the owner of the mask work is a national, domiciliary, or sovereign authority of that foreign nation, or solely because the mask work was first commercially exploited in that foreign nation.

(c)   Any order issued by the Secretary of Commerce under subsection (a) shall be effective for such period as the Secretary designates in the order, except that no such order may be effective after the date on which the authority of the Secretary of Commerce terminates under subsection (e). The effective date of any such order shall also be designated in the order. In the case of an order issued upon the petition of a person, such effective date may be no earlier than the date on which the Secretary receives such petition.

(d)(1)   Any order issued under this section shall terminate if—

(A)   the Secretary of Commerce finds that any of the conditions set forth in paragraphs (1), (2), and (3) of subsection (a) no longer exist; or

(B)   mask works of nationals, domiciliaries, and sovereign authorities of that foreign nation or mask works first commercially exploited in that foreign nation become eligible for protection under subparagraph (A) or (C) of section 902(a)(1).

(2)   Upon the termination or expiration of an order issued under this section, registrations of claims of protection in mask works made pursuant to that order shall remain valid for the period specified in section 904.

(e)   The authority of the Secretary of Commerce under this section shall commence on the date of the enactment of this chapter, and shall terminate on July 1, 1995.

(f)(1)   The Secretary of Commerce shall promptly notify the Register of Copyrights and the Committees on the Judiciary of the Senate and the House of Representatives of the issuance or termination of any order under this section, together with a statement of the reasons for such action. The Secretary shall also publish such notification and statement of reasons in the Federal Register.

(2)   Two years after the date of the enactment of this chapter, the Secretary of Commerce, in consultation with the Register of Copyrights, shall transmit to the Committees on the Judiciary of the Senate and the House of Representatives a report on the actions taken under this section and on the current status of international recognition of mask work protection. The report shall include such recommendations for modifications of the protection accorded under this chapter to mask works owned by nationals, domiciliaries, or sovereign authorities of foreign nations as the Secretary, in consultation with the Register of Copyrights, considers would promote the purposes of this chapter and international comity with respect to mask work protection. Not later than July 1, 1994, the Secretary of Commerce, in consultation with the Register of Copyrights, shall transmit to the Committees on the Judiciary of the Senate and the House of Representatives a report updating the matters contained in the report transmitted under the preceding sentence.

(As amended, Pub.L. 100–159, 101 Stat. 899 (1987); Pub.L. 102–64, 105 Stat. 320 (1991)).

## CHAPTER 10.—DIGITAL AUDIO RECORDING
## DEVICES AND MEDIA

(Pub.L. 102–563, 106 Stat. 4237 (1992)).

### SUBCHAPTER A—DEFINITIONS

### SUBCHAPTER B—COPYING CONTROLS

### SUBCHAPTER C—ROYALTY PAYMENTS

### SUBCHAPTER D—PROHIBITION ON CERTAIN INFRINGEMENT
### ACTIONS, REMEDIES, AND ARBITRATION

### SUBCHAPTER A—DEFINITIONS

## Sec. 1001.   Definitions

As used in this chapter, the following terms have the following meanings:

(1)   A "digital audio copied recording" is a reproduction in a digital recording format of a digital musical recording, whether that reproduction is made directly from another digital musical recording or indirectly from a transmission.

(2)   A "digital audio interface device" is any machine or device that is designed specifically to communicate digital audio information and related interface data to a digital audio recording device through a nonprofessional interface.

(3)   A "digital audio recording device" is any machine or device of a type commonly distributed to individuals for use by individuals, whether or not included with or as part of some other machine or device, the digital recording function of which is designed or marketed for the primary purpose of, and that is capable of, making a digital audio copied recording for private use, except for—

(A)   professional model products, and

(B)   dictation machines, answering machines, and other audio recording equipment that is designed and marketed primarily for the creation of sound recordings resulting from the fixation of nonmusical sounds.

(4)(A)   A "digital audio recording medium" is any material object in a form commonly distributed for use by individuals, that is primarily marketed or most commonly used by consumers for the purpose of making digital audio copied recordings by use of a digital audio recording device.

(B)   Such term does not include any material object—

(i)   that embodies a sound recording at the time it is first distributed by the importer or manufacturer; or

(ii) that is primarily marketed and most commonly used by consumers either for the purpose of making copies of motion pictures or other audiovisual works or for the purpose of making copies of nonmusical literary works, including computer programs or data bases.

(5)(A) A "digital musical recording" is a material object—

(i) in which are fixed, in a digital recording format, only sounds, and material, statements, or instructions incidental to those fixed sounds, if any, and

(ii) from which the sounds and material can be perceived, reproduced, or otherwise communicated, either directly or with the aid of a machine or device.

(B) A "digital musical recording" does not include a material object—

(i) in which the fixed sounds consist entirely of spoken word recordings, or

(ii) in which one or more computer programs are fixed, except that a digital musical recording may contain statements or instructions constituting the fixed sounds and incidental material, and statements or instructions to be used directly or indirectly in order to bring about the perception, reproduction, or communication of the fixed sounds and incidental material.

(C) For purposes of this paragraph—

(i) a "spoken word recording" is a sound recording in which are fixed only a series of spoken words, except that the spoken words may be accompanied by incidental musical or other sounds, and

(ii) the term "incidental" means related to and relatively minor by comparison.

(6) "Distribute" means to sell, lease, or assign a product to consumers in the United States, or to sell, lease, or assign a product in the United States for ultimate transfer to consumers in the United States.

(7) An "interested copyright party" is—

(A) the owner of the exclusive right under section 106(1) of this title to reproduce a sound recording of a musical work that has been embodied in a digital musical recording or analog musical recording lawfully made under this title that has been distributed;

(B) the legal or beneficial owner of, or the person that controls, the right to reproduce in a digital musical recording or analog musical recording a musical work that has been embodied in a digital musical recording or analog musical recording lawfully made under this title that has been distributed;

(C) a featured recording artist who performs on a sound recording that has been distributed; or

(D) any association or other organization—

(i) representing persons specified in subparagraph (A), (B), or (C), or

(ii) engaged in licensing rights in musical works to music users on behalf of writers and publishers.

(8) To "manufacture" means to produce or assemble a product in the United States. A "manufacturer" is a person who manufactures.

(9) A "music publisher" is a person that is authorized to license the reproduction of a particular musical work in a sound recording.

(10) A "professional model product" is an audio recording device that is designed, manufactured, marketed, and intended for use by recording professionals in the ordinary course of a lawful business, in accordance with such requirements as the Secretary of Commerce shall establish by regulation.

(11) The term "serial copying" means the duplication in a digital format of a copyrighted musical work or sound recording from a digital reproduction of a digital musical recording. The term "digital reproduction of a digital musical recording" does not include a digital musical recording as distributed, by authority of the copyright owner, for ultimate sale to consumers.

(12) The "transfer price" of a digital audio recording device or a digital audio recording medium—

(A)   is, subject to subparagraph (B)—

(i)   in the case of an imported product, the actual entered value at United States Customs (exclusive of any freight, insurance, and applicable duty), and

(ii)   in the case of a domestic product, the manufacturer's transfer price (FOB the manufacturer, and exclusive of any direct sales taxes or excise taxes incurred in connection with the sale); and

(B)   shall, in a case in which the transferor and transferee are related entities or within a single entity, not be less than a reasonable arms-length price under the principles of the regulations adopted pursuant to section 482 of the Internal Revenue Code of 1986, or any successor provision to such section.

(13) A "writer" is the composer or lyricist of a particular musical work.

## SUBCHAPTER B—COPYING CONTROLS

### Sec. 1002.    Incorporation of Copying Controls

(a) **Prohibition on Importation, Manufacture, and Distribution.**—No person shall import, manufacture, or distribute any digital audio recording device or digital audio interface device that does not conform to—

(1)   the Serial Copy Management System;

(2)   a system that has the same functional characteristics as the Serial Copy Management System and requires that copyright and generation status information be accurately sent, received, and acted upon between devices using the system's method of serial copying regulation and devices using the Serial Copy Management System; or

(3)   any other system certified by the Secretary of Commerce as prohibiting unauthorized serial copying.

(b) **Development of Verification Procedure.**—The Secretary of Commerce shall establish a procedure to verify, upon the petition of an interested party, that a system meets the standards set forth in subsection (a)(2).

(c) **Prohibition on Circumvention of the System.**—No person shall import, manufacture, or distribute any device, or offer or perform any service, the primary purpose or effect of which is to avoid, bypass, remove, deactivate, or otherwise circumvent any program or circuit which implements, in whole or in part, a system described in subsection (a).

(d) **Encoding of Information on Digital Musical Recordings.**—

(1) **Prohibition on encoding inaccurate information.**—No person shall encode a digital musical recording of a sound recording with inaccurate information relating to the category code, copyright status, or generation status of the source material for the recording.

(2) **Encoding of copyright status not required.**—Nothing in this chapter requires any person engaged in the importation or manufacture of digital musical recordings to encode any such digital musical recording with respect to its copyright status.

(e) **Information Accompanying Transmissions in Digital Format.**—Any person who transmits or otherwise communicates to the public any sound recording in digital format is not required under this chapter to transmit or otherwise communicate the information relating to the copyright status of the sound recording. Any such person who does transmit or otherwise communicate such copyright status information shall transmit or communicate such information accurately.

## SUBCHAPTER C—ROYALTY PAYMENTS

### Sec. 1003.    Obligation to Make Royalty Payments

**(a) Prohibition on Importation and Manufacture.**—No person shall import into and distribute, or manufacture and distribute, any digital audio recording device or digital audio recording medium unless such person records the notice specified by this section and subsequently deposits the statements of account and applicable royalty payments for such device or medium specified in section 1004.

**(b) Filing of Notice.**—The importer or manufacturer of any digital audio recording device or digital audio recording medium, within a product category or utilizing a technology with respect to which such manufacturer or importer has not previously filed a notice under this subsection, shall file with the Register of Copyrights a notice with respect to such device or medium, in such form and content as the Register shall prescribe by regulation.

**(c) Filing of Quarterly and Annual Statements of Account.—**

**(1) Generally.**—Any importer or manufacturer that distributes any digital audio recording device or digital audio recording medium that it manufactured or imported shall file with the Register of Copyrights, in such form and content as the Register shall prescribe by regulation, such quarterly and annual statements of account with respect to such distribution as the Register shall prescribe by regulation.

**(2) Certification, verification, and confidentiality.**—Each such statement shall be certified as accurate by an authorized officer or principal of the importer or manufacturer. The Register shall issue regulations to provide for the verification and audit of such statements and to protect the confidentiality of the information contained in such statements. Such regulations shall provide for the disclosure, in confidence, of such statements to interested copyright parties.

**(3) Royalty payments.**—Each such statement shall be accompanied by the royalty payments specified in section 1004.

### Sec. 1004.    Royalty Payments

**(a) Digital Audio Recording Devices.—**

**(1) Amount of payment.**—The royalty payment due under section 1003 for each digital audio recording device imported into and distributed in the United States, or manufactured and distributed in the United States, shall be 2 percent of the transfer price. Only the first person to manufacture and distribute or import and distribute such device shall be required to pay the royalty with respect to such device.

**(2) Calculation for devices distributed with other devices.**—With respect to a digital audio recording device first distributed in combination with one or more devices, either as a physically integrated unit or as separate components, the royalty payment shall be calculated as follows:

(A) If the digital audio recording device and such other devices are part of a physically integrated unit, the royalty payment shall be based on the transfer price of the unit, but shall be reduced by any royalty payment made on any digital audio recording device included within the unit that was not first distributed in combination with the unit.

(B) If the digital audio recording device is not part of a physically integrated unit and substantially similar devices have been distributed separately at any time during the preceding 4 calendar quarters, the royalty payment shall be based on the average transfer price of such devices during those 4 quarters.

(C) If the digital audio recording device is not part of a physically integrated unit and substantially similar devices have not been distributed separately at any time during the preceding 4 calendar quarters, the royalty payment shall be based on a constructed price reflecting the proportional value of such device to the combination as a whole.

**(3) Limits on Royalties.**—Notwithstanding paragraph (1) or (2), the amount of the royalty payment for each digital audio recording device shall not be less than $1 nor more than the royalty maximum. The royalty maximum shall be $8 per device, except that in the case of a physically integrated unit containing more than 1 digital audio recording device, the royalty maximum for such unit shall be $12. During the 6th year after the effective date of this chapter, and not more than once each year thereafter, any interested copyright party may petition the Copyright Royalty Judges to increase the royalty maximum and, if more than 20 percent of the royalty payments are at the relevant royalty maximum, the Copyright Royalty Judges shall prospectively increase such royalty maximum with the goal of having no more than 10 percent of such payments at the new royalty maximum; however the amount of any such increase as a percentage of the royalty maximum shall in no event exceed the percentage increase in the Consumer Price Index during the period under review.

**(b) Digital Audio Recording Media.**—The royalty payment due under section 1003 for each digital audio recording medium imported into and distributed in the United States, or manufactured and distributed in the United States, shall be 3 percent of the transfer price. Only the first person to manufacture and distribute or import and distribute such medium shall be required to pay the royalty with respect to such medium.

(As amended, Pub.L. 103–198, 107 Stat. 2304 (1993); Pub.L. 108–419, 118 Stat. 2341 (2004)).

## Sec. 1005.    Deposit of Royalty Payments and Deduction of Expenses

The Register of Copyrights shall receive all royalty payments deposited under this chapter and, after deducting the reasonable costs incurred by the Copyright Office under this chapter, shall deposit the balance in the Treasury of the United States as offsetting receipts, in such manner as the Secretary of the Treasury directs. All funds held by the Secretary of the Treasury shall be invested in interest-bearing United States securities for later distribution with interest under section 1007. The Register may, in the Register's discretion, 4 years after the close of any calendar year, close out the royalty payments account for that calendar year, and may treat any funds remaining in such account and any subsequent deposits that would otherwise be attributable to that calendar year as attributable to the succeeding calendar year.

(As amended, Pub.L. 103–198, 107 Stat. 2304 (1993)).

## Sec. 1006.    Entitlement to Royalty Payments

**(a) Interested Copyright Parties.**—The royalty payments deposited pursuant to section 1005 shall, in accordance with the procedures specified in section 1007, be distributed to any interested copyright party—

(1) whose musical work or sound recording has been—

(A) embodied in a digital musical recording or an analog musical recording lawfully made under this title that has been distributed, and

(B) distributed in the form of digital musical recordings or analog musical recordings or disseminated to the public in transmissions, during the period to which such payments pertain; and

(2) who has filed a claim under section 1007.

**(b)  Allocation of Royalty Payments to Groups.**—The royalty payments shall be divided into 2 funds as follows:

**(1)  The sound recordings fund.**—$66^2/_3$ percent of the royalty payments shall be allocated to the Sound Recordings Fund. $2^5/_8$ percent of the royalty payments allocated to the Sound Recordings Fund shall be placed in an escrow account managed by an independent administrator jointly appointed by the interested copyright parties described in section 1001(7)(A) and the American Federation of Musicians (or any successor entity) to be distributed to nonfeatured musicians (whether or not members of the American Federation of Musicians or any successor entity) who have performed on sound recordings distributed in the United States. $1^3/_8$ percent of the royalty payments allocated to the Sound Recordings Fund shall be placed in an escrow account managed by an independent administrator jointly appointed by the interested copyright parties described in section 1001(7)(A) and the American Federation of Television and Radio Artists (or any successor entity) to be distributed to nonfeatured vocalists (whether or not members of the American Federation of Television and Radio Artists or any successor entity) who have performed on sound recordings distributed in the United States. 40 percent of the remaining royalty payments in the Sound Recordings Fund shall be distributed to the interested copyright parties described in section 1001(7)(C), and 60 percent of such remaining royalty payments shall be distributed to the interested copyright parties described in section 1001(7)(A).

**(2)  The musical works fund.—**

(A)  $33^1/_3$ percent of the royalty payments shall be allocated to the Musical Works Fund for distribution to interested copyright parties described in section 1001(7)(B).

(B)(i)  Music publishers shall be entitled to 50 percent of the royalty payments allocated to the Musical Works Fund.

(ii)  Writers shall be entitled to the other 50 percent of the royalty payments allocated to the Musical Works Fund.

**(c)  Allocation of Royalty Payments Within Groups.**—If all interested copyright parties within a group specified in subsection (b) do not agree on a voluntary proposal for the distribution of the royalty payments within each group, the Copyright Royalty Judges shall, pursuant to the procedures specified under section 1007(c), allocate royalty payments under this section based on the extent to which, during the relevant period—

(1)  for the Sound Recordings Fund, each sound recording was distributed in the form of digital musical recordings or analog musical recordings; and

(2)  for the Musical Works Fund, each musical work was distributed in the form of digital musical recordings or analog musical recordings or disseminated to the public in transmissions.

(As amended, Pub.L. 103–198, 107 Stat. 2304 (1993); Pub.L. 108–419, 118 Stat. 2341 (2004)).

## Sec. 1007.  Procedures for Distributing Royalty Payments

**(a)  Filing of Claims and Negotiations.—**

**(1)  Filing of Claims.**—During the first two months of each calendar year, every interested copyright party seeking to receive royalty payments to which such party is entitled under section 1006 shall file with the Copyright Royalty Judges a claim for payments collected during the preceding year in such form and manner as the Copyright Royalty Judges shall prescribe by regulation.

**(2)  Negotiations.**—Notwithstanding any provision of the antitrust laws, for purposes of this section interested copyright parties within each group specified in section 1006(b) may agree among themselves to the proportionate division of royalty payments, may lump their claims together and file them jointly or as a single claim, or may designate a common agent, including any organization described in section 1001(7)(D), to negotiate or receive payment on their behalf;

except that no agreement under this subsection may modify the allocation of royalties specified in section 1006(b).

**(b) Distribution of Payments in the Absence of a Dispute.**—After the period established for the filing of claims under subsection (a), in each year, the Copyright Royalty Judges shall determine whether there exists a controversy concerning the distribution of royalty payments under section 1006(c). If the Copyright Royalty Judges determine that no such controversy exists, the Copyright Royalty Judges shall, within 30 days after such determination, authorize the distribution of the royalty payments as set forth in the agreements regarding the distribution of royalty payments entered into pursuant to subsection (a). The Librarian of Congress shall, before such royalty payments are distributed, deduct the reasonable administrative cost incurred under this section.

**(c) Resolution of Disputes.**—If the Copyright Royalty Judges find the existence of a controversy, the Copyright Royalty Judges shall, pursuant to chapter 8 of this title, conduct a proceeding to determine the distribution of royalty payments. During the pendency of such a proceeding, the Copyright Royalty Judges shall withhold from distribution an amount sufficient to satisfy all claims with respect to which a controversy exists, but shall, to the extent feasible, authorize the distribution of any amounts that are not in controversy. The Librarian of Congress shall, before such royalty payments are distributed, deduct the reasonable administrative costs incurred by the Librarian under this section.

(As amended, Pub.L. 103–198, 107 Stat. 2304 (1993); Pub.L. 105–80, 111 Stat. 1529 (1997); Pub.L. 108–419, 118 Stat. 2341 (2004); Pub.L. 109–303, 120 Stat. 1478 (2006)).

## SUBCHAPTER D—PROHIBITION ON CERTAIN INFRINGEMENT ACTIONS, REMEDIES, AND ARBITRATION

## Sec. 1008.    Prohibition on Certain Infringement Actions

No action may be brought under this title alleging infringement of copyright based on the manufacture, importation, or distribution of a digital audio recording device, a digital audio recording medium, an analog recording device, or an analog recording medium, or based on the noncommercial use by a consumer of such a device or medium for making digital musical recordings or analog musical recordings.

## Sec. 1009.    Civil Remedies

**(a) Civil Actions.**—Any interested copyright party injured by a violation of section 1002 or 1003 may bring a civil action in an appropriate United States district court against any person for such violation.

**(b) Other Civil Actions.**—Any person injured by a violation of this chapter may bring a civil action in an appropriate United States district court for actual damages incurred as a result of such violation.

**(c) Powers of the Court.**—In an action brought under subsection (a), the court—

    (1) may grant temporary and permanent injunctions on such terms as it deems reasonable to prevent or restrain such violation;

    (2) in the case of a violation of section 1002, or in the case of an injury resulting from a failure to make royalty payments required by section 1003, shall award damages under subsection (d);

    (3) in its discretion may allow the recovery of costs by or against any party other than the United States or an officer thereof; and

    (4) in its discretion may award a reasonable attorney's fee to the prevailing party.

**(d) Award of Damages.**—

    (1) **Damages for section 1002 or 1003 violations.**—

      (A) **Actual damages.**—

        (i) In an action brought under subsection (a), if the court finds that a violation of section 1002 or 1003 has occurred, the court shall award to the complaining party its actual damages if the complaining party elects such damages at any time before final judgment is entered.

        (ii) In the case of section 1003, actual damages shall constitute the royalty payments that should have been paid under section 1004 and deposited under section 1005. In such a case, the court, in its discretion, may award an additional amount of not to exceed 50 percent of the actual damages.

      (B) **Statutory damages for section 1002 violations.**—

        (i) **Device.**—A complaining party may recover an award of statutory damages for each violation of section 1002(a) or (c) in the sum of not more than $2,500 per device involved in such violation or per device on which a service prohibited by section 1002(c) has been performed, as the court considers just.

        (ii) **Digital musical recording.**—A complaining party may recover an award of statutory damages for each violation of section 1002(d) in the sum of not more than $25 per digital musical recording involved in such violation, as the court considers just.

        (iii) **Transmission.**—A complaining party may recover an award of damages for each transmission or communication that violates section 1002(e) in the sum of not more than $10,000, as the court considers just.

    (2) **Repeated violations.**—In any case in which the court finds that a person has violated section 1002 or 1003 within 3 years after a final judgment against that person for another such violation was entered, the court may increase the award of damages to not more than double the amounts that would otherwise be awarded under paragraph (1), as the court considers just.

    (3) **Innocent violations of section 1002.**—The court in its discretion may reduce the total award of damages against a person violating section 1002 to a sum of not less than $250 in any case in which the court finds that the violator was not aware and had no reason to believe that its acts constituted a violation of section 1002.

    (e) **Payment of Damages.**—Any award of damages under subsection (d) shall be deposited with the Register pursuant to section 1005 for distribution to interested copyright parties as though such funds were royalty payments made pursuant to section 1003.

    (f) **Impounding of Articles.**—At any time while an action under subsection (a) is pending, the court may order the impounding, on such terms as it deems reasonable, of any digital audio recording device, digital musical recording, or device specified in section 1002(c) that is in the custody or control of the alleged violator and that the court has reasonable cause to believe does not comply with, or was involved in a violation of, section 1002.

    (g) **Remedial Modification and Destruction of Articles.**—In an action brought under subsection (a), the court may, as part of a final judgment or decree finding a violation of section 1002, order the remedial modification or the destruction of any digital audio recording device, digital musical recording, or device specified in section 1002(c) that

    (1) does not comply with, or was involved in a violation of, section 1002, and

    (2) is in the custody or control of the violator or has been impounded under subsection (f).

## Sec. 1010.    Determination of Certain Disputes

    (a) **Scope of determination.**—Before the date of first distribution in the United States of a digital audio recording device or a digital audio interface device, any party manufacturing, importing, or distributing such device, and any interested copyright party may mutually agree to petition the Copyright Royalty Judges to determine whether such device is subject to section 1002, or the basis on which royalty payments for such device are to be made under section 1003.

**(b) Initiation of proceedings.**—The parties under subsection (a) shall file the petition with the Copyright Royalty Judges requesting the commencement of a proceeding. Within 2 weeks after receiving such a petition, the Chief Copyright Royalty Judge shall cause notice to be published in the Federal Register of the initiation of the proceeding.

**(c) Stay of judicial proceedings.**—Any civil action brought under section 1009 against a party to a proceeding under this section shall, on application of one of the parties to the proceeding, be stayed until completion of the proceeding.

**(d) Proceeding.**—The Copyright Royalty Judges shall conduct a proceeding with respect to the matter concerned, in accordance with such procedures as the Copyright Royalty Judges may adopt. The Copyright Royalty Judges shall act on the basis of a fully documented written record. Any party to the proceeding may submit relevant information and proposals to the Copyright Royalty Judges. The parties to the proceeding shall each bear their respective costs of participation.

**(e) Judicial review.**—Any determination of the Copyright Royalty Judges under subsection (d) may be appealed, by a party to the proceeding, in accordance with section 803(d) of this title. The pendency of an appeal under this subsection shall not stay the determination of the Copyright Royalty Judges. If the court modifies the determination of the Copyright Royalty Judges, the court shall have jurisdiction to enter its own decision in accordance with its final judgment. The court may further vacate the determination of the Copyright Royalty Judges and remand the case for proceedings as provided in this section.

(As amended, Pub.L. 103–198, 107 Stat. 2304 (1993); Pub.L. 108–419, 118 Stat. 2341 (2004)).

## CHAPTER 11.—SOUND RECORDINGS AND MUSIC VIDEOS

## Sec. 1101. Unauthorized Fixation and Trafficking in Sound Recordings and Music Videos

**(a) Unauthorized Acts.**—Anyone who, without the consent of the performer or performers involved—

(1) fixes the sounds or sounds and images of a live musical performance in a copy or phonorecord, or reproduces copies or phonorecords of such a performance from an unauthorized fixation,

(2) transmits or otherwise communicates to the public the sounds or sounds and images of a live musical performance, or

(3) distributes or offers to distribute, sells or offers to sell, rents or offers to rent, or traffics in any copy or phonorecord fixed as described in paragraph (1), regardless of whether the fixations occurred in the United States,

shall be subject to the remedies provided in sections 502 through 505, to the same extent as an infringer of copyright.

**(b) Definition.**—In this section, the term "traffic" has the same meaning as in section 2320(e) of title 18.

**(c) Applicability.**—This section shall apply to any act or acts that occur on or after the date of the enactment of the Uruguay Round Agreements Act.

(d)  **State Law Not Preempted.**—Nothing in this section may be construed to annul or limit any rights or remedies under the common law or statutes of any State.

(Added by Pub.L. 103–465, 108 Stat. 4974 (1994); as amended, Pub.L. 109–181, 120 Stat. 285 (2006)).

## CHAPTER 12.—COPYRIGHT PROTECTION AND MANAGEMENT SYSTEMS

### (Pub.L. 105–304, 112 Stat. 2863 (1998)).

## Sec. 1201.    Circumvention of Copyright Protection Systems

### (a)  Violations Regarding Circumvention of Technological Measures.—

(1)(A)  No person shall circumvent a technological measure that effectively controls access to a work protected under this title. The prohibition contained in the preceding sentence shall take effect at the end of the 2-year period beginning on the date of the enactment of this chapter.

(B)  The prohibition contained in subparagraph (A) shall not apply to persons who are users of a copyrighted work which is in a particular class of works, if such persons are, or are likely to be in the succeeding 3-year period, adversely affected by virtue of such prohibition in their ability to make noninfringing uses of that particular class of works under this title, as determined under subparagraph (C).

(C)  During the 2-year period described in subparagraph (A), and during each succeeding 3-year period, the Librarian of Congress, upon the recommendation of the Register of Copyrights, who shall consult with the Assistant Secretary for Communications and Information of the Department of Commerce and report and comment on his or her views in making such recommendation, shall make the determination in a rulemaking proceeding for purposes of subparagraph (B) of whether persons who are users of a copyrighted work are, or are likely to be in the succeeding 3-year period, adversely affected by the prohibition under subparagraph (A) in their ability to make noninfringing uses under this title of a particular class of copyrighted works. In conducting such rulemaking, the Librarian shall examine—

(i)  the availability for use of copyrighted works;

(ii)  the availability for use of works for nonprofit archival, preservation, and educational purposes;

(iii)  the impact that the prohibition on the circumvention of technological measures applied to copyrighted works has on criticism, comment, news reporting, teaching, scholarship, or research;

(iv)  the effect of circumvention of technological measures on the market for or value of copyrighted works; and

(v)  such other factors as the Librarian considers appropriate.

(D)  The Librarian shall publish any class of copyrighted works for which the Librarian has determined, pursuant to the rulemaking conducted under subparagraph (C), that noninfringing uses by persons who are users of a copyrighted work are, or are likely to be, adversely affected, and the prohibition contained in subparagraph (A) shall not apply to such users with respect to such class of works for the ensuing 3-year period.

(E)  Neither the exception under subparagraph (B) from the applicability of the prohibition contained in subparagraph (A), nor any determination made in a rulemaking conducted under subparagraph (C), may be used as a defense in any action to enforce any provision of this title other than this paragraph.

(2)  No person shall manufacture, import, offer to the public, provide, or otherwise traffic in any technology, product, service, device, component, or part thereof, that—

(A)  is primarily designed or produced for the purpose of circumventing a technological measure that effectively controls access to a work protected under this title;

(B)  has only limited commercially significant purpose or use other than to circumvent a technological measure that effectively controls access to a work protected under this title; or

(C)  is marketed by that person or another acting in concert with that person with that person's knowledge for use in circumventing a technological measure that effectively controls access to a work protected under this title.

(3)  As used in this subsection—

(A)  to "circumvent a technological measure" means to descramble a scrambled work, to decrypt an encrypted work, or otherwise to avoid, bypass, remove, deactivate, or impair a technological measure, without the authority of the copyright owner; and

(B)  a technological measure "effectively controls access to a work" if the measure, in the ordinary course of its operation, requires the application of information, or a process or a treatment, with the authority of the copyright owner, to gain access to the work.

**(b)  Additional Violations.—**

(1)  No person shall manufacture, import, offer to the public, provide, or otherwise traffic in any technology, product, service, device, component, or part thereof, that—

(A)  is primarily designed or produced for the purpose of circumventing protection afforded by a technological measure that effectively protects a right of a copyright owner under this title in a work or a portion thereof;

(B)  has only limited commercially significant purpose or use other than to circumvent protection afforded by a technological measure that effectively protects a right of a copyright owner under this title in a work or a portion thereof; or

(C)  is marketed by that person or another acting in concert with that person with that person's knowledge for use in circumventing protection afforded by a technological measure that effectively protects a right of a copyright owner under this title in a work or a portion thereof.

(2)  As used in this subsection—

(A)  to "circumvent protection afforded by a technological measure" means avoiding, bypassing, removing, deactivating, or otherwise impairing a technological measure; and

(B)  a technological measure "effectively protects a right of a copyright owner under this title" if the measure, in the ordinary course of its operation, prevents, restricts, or otherwise limits the exercise of a right of a copyright owner under this title.

**(c)  Other Rights, Etc., Not Affected.—**

(1)  Nothing in this section shall affect rights, remedies, limitations, or defenses to copyright infringement, including fair use, under this title.

(2)   Nothing in this section shall enlarge or diminish vicarious or contributory liability for copyright infringement in connection with any technology, product, service, device, component, or part thereof.

(3)   Nothing in this section shall require that the design of, or design and selection of parts and components for, a consumer electronics, telecommunications, or computing product provide for a response to any particular technological measure, so long as such part or component, or the product in which such part or component is integrated, does not otherwise fall within the prohibitions of subsection (a)(2) or (b)(1).

(4)   Nothing in this section shall enlarge or diminish any rights of free speech or the press for activities using consumer electronics, telecommunications, or computing products.

**(d)   Exemption for Nonprofit Libraries, Archives, and Educational Institutions.—**

(1)   A nonprofit library, archives, or educational institution which gains access to a commercially exploited copyrighted work solely in order to make a good faith determination of whether to acquire a copy of that work for the sole purpose of engaging in conduct permitted under this title shall not be in violation of subsection (a)(1)(A). A copy of a work to which access has been gained under this paragraph—

(A)   may not be retained longer than necessary to make such good faith determination; and

(B)   may not be used for any other purpose.

(2)   The exemption made available under paragraph (1) shall only apply with respect to a work when an identical copy of that work is not reasonably available in another form.

(3)   A nonprofit library, archives, or educational institution that willfully for the purpose of commercial advantage or financial gain violates paragraph (1)—

(A)   shall, for the first offense, be subject to the civil remedies under section 1203; and

(B)   shall, for repeated or subsequent offenses, in addition to the civil remedies under section 1203, forfeit the exemption provided under paragraph (1).

(4)   This subsection may not be used as a defense to a claim under subsection (a)(2) or (b), nor may this subsection permit a nonprofit library, archives, or educational institution to manufacture, import, offer to the public, provide, or otherwise traffic in any technology, product, service, component, or part thereof, which circumvents a technological measure.

(5)   In order for a library or archives to qualify for the exemption under this subsection, the collections of that library or archives shall be—

(A)   open to the public; or

(B)   available not only to researchers affiliated with the library or archives or with the institution of which it is a part, but also to other persons doing research in a specialized field.

**(e)   Law Enforcement, Intelligence, and Other Government Activities.**—This section does not prohibit any lawfully authorized investigative, protective, information security, or intelligence activity of an officer, agent, or employee of the United States, a State, or a political subdivision of a State, or a person acting pursuant to a contract with the United States, a State, or a political subdivision of a State. For purposes of this subsection, the term "information security" means activities carried out in order to identify and address the vulnerabilities of a government computer, computer system, or computer network.

**(f)   Reverse Engineering.—**

(1)   Notwithstanding the provisions of subsection (a)(1)(A), a person who has lawfully obtained the right to use a copy of a computer program may circumvent a technological measure that effectively controls access to a particular portion of that program for the sole purpose of

identifying and analyzing those elements of the program that are necessary to achieve interoperability of an independently created computer program with other programs, and that have not previously been readily available to the person engaging in the circumvention, to the extent any such acts of identification and analysis do not constitute infringement under this title.

(2)   Notwithstanding the provisions of subsections (a)(2) and (b), a person may develop and employ technological means to circumvent a technological measure, or to circumvent protection afforded by a technological measure, in order to enable the identification and analysis under paragraph (1), or for the purpose of enabling interoperability of an independently created computer program with other programs, if such means are necessary to achieve such interoperability, to the extent that doing so does not constitute infringement under this title.

(3)   The information acquired through the acts permitted under paragraph (1), and the means permitted under paragraph (2), may be made available to others if the person referred to in paragraph (1) or (2), as the case may be, provides such information or means solely for the purpose of enabling interoperability of an independently created computer program with other programs, and to the extent that doing so does not constitute infringement under this title or violate applicable law other than this section.

(4)   For purposes of this subsection, the term "interoperability" means the ability of computer programs to exchange information, and of such programs mutually to use the information which has been exchanged.

(g)   **Encryption Research.**—

(1)   **Definitions.**—For purposes of this subsection—

(A)   the term "encryption research" means activities necessary to identify and analyze flaws and vulnerabilities of encryption technologies applied to copyrighted works, if these activities are conducted to advance the state of knowledge in the field of encryption technology or to assist in the development of encryption products; and

(B)   the term "encryption technology" means the scrambling and descrambling of information using mathematical formulas or algorithms.

(2)   **Permissible Acts of Encryption Research.**—Notwithstanding the provisions of subsection (a)(1)(A), it is not a violation of that subsection for a person to circumvent a technological measure as applied to a copy, phonorecord, performance, or display of a published work in the course of an act of good faith encryption research if—

(A)   the person lawfully obtained the encrypted copy, phonorecord, performance, or display of the published work;

(B)   such act is necessary to conduct such encryption research;

(C)   the person made a good faith effort to obtain authorization before the circumvention; and

(D)   such act does not constitute infringement under this title or a violation of applicable law other than this section, including section 1030 of title 18 and those provisions of title 18 amended by the Computer Fraud and Abuse Act of 1986.

(3)   **Factors in Determining Exemption.**—In determining whether a person qualifies for the exemption under paragraph (2), the factors to be considered shall include—

(A)   whether the information derived from the encryption research was disseminated, and if so, whether it was disseminated in a manner reasonably calculated to advance the state of knowledge or development of encryption technology, versus whether it was disseminated in a manner that facilitates infringement under this title or a violation of applicable law other than this section including a violation of privacy or breach of security;

(B) whether the person is engaged in a legitimate course of study, is employed, or is appropriately trained or experienced, in the field of encryption technology; and

(C) whether the person provides the copyright owner of the work to which the technological measure is applied with notice of the findings and documentation of the research, and the time when such notice is provided.

**(4) Use of Technological Means for Research Activities.**—Notwithstanding the provisions of subsection (a)(2), it is not a violation of that subsection for a person to—

(A) develop and employ technological means to circumvent a technological measure for the sole purpose of that person performing the acts of good faith encryption research described in paragraph (2); and

(B) provide the technological means to another person with whom he or she is working collaboratively for the purpose of conducting the acts of good faith encryption research described in paragraph (2) or for the purpose of having that other person verify his or her acts of good faith encryption research described in paragraph (2).

**(5) Report to Congress.**—Not later than 1 year after the date of the enactment of this chapter, the Register of Copyrights and the Assistant Secretary for Communications and Information of the Department of Commerce shall jointly report to the Congress on the effect this subsection has had on—

(A) encryption research and the development of encryption technology;

(B) the adequacy and effectiveness of technological measures designed to protect copyrighted works; and

(C) protection of copyright owners against the unauthorized access to their encrypted copyrighted works.

The report shall include legislative recommendations, if any.

**(h) Exceptions Regarding Minors.**—In applying subsection (a) to a component or part, the court may consider the necessity for its intended and actual incorporation in a technology, product, service, or device, which—

(1) does not itself violate the provisions of this title; and

(2) has the sole purpose to prevent the access of minors to material on the Internet.

**(i) Protection of Personally Identifying Information.—**

**(1) Circumvention Permitted.**—Notwithstanding the provisions of subsection (a)(1)(A), it is not a violation of that subsection for a person to circumvent a technological measure that effectively controls access to a work protected under this title, if—

(A) the technological measure, or the work it protects, contains the capability of collecting or disseminating personally identifying information reflecting the online activities of a natural person who seeks to gain access to the work protected;

(B) in the normal course of its operation, the technological measure, or the work it protects, collects or disseminates personally identifying information about the person who seeks to gain access to the work protected, without providing conspicuous notice of such collection or dissemination to such person, and without providing such person with the capability to prevent or restrict such collection or dissemination;

(C) the act of circumvention has the sole effect of identifying and disabling the capability described in subparagraph (A), and has no other effect on the ability of any person to gain access to any work; and

(D)   the act of circumvention is carried out solely for the purpose of preventing the collection or dissemination of personally identifying information about a natural person who seeks to gain access to the work protected, and is not in violation of any other law.

**(2)   Inapplicability to Certain Technological Measures.**—This subsection does not apply to a technological measure, or a work it protects, that does not collect or disseminate personally identifying information and that is disclosed to a user as not having or using such capability.

**(j)   Security Testing.—**

**(1)   Definition.**—For purposes of this subsection, the term "security testing" means accessing a computer network, solely for the purpose of good faith testing, investigating, or correcting, a security flaw or vulnerability, with the authorization of the owner or operator of such computer, computer system, or computer network.

**(2)   Permissible Acts of Security Testing.**—Notwithstanding the provisions of subsection (a)(1)(A), it is not a violation of that subsection for a person to engage in an act of security testing, if such act does not constitute infringement under this title or a violation of applicable law other than this section, including section 1030 of title 18 and those provisions of title 18 amended by the Computer Fraud and Abuse Act of 1986.

**(3)   Factors in Determining Exemption.**—In determining whether a person qualifies for the exemption under paragraph (2), the factors to be considered shall include—

(A)   whether the information derived from the security testing was used solely to promote the security of the owner or operator of such computer, computer system or computer network, or shared directly with the developer of such computer, computer system, or computer network; and

(B)   whether the information derived from the security testing was used or maintained in a manner that does not facilitate infringement under this title or a violation of applicable law other than this section, including a violation of privacy or breach of security.

**(4)   Use of Technological Means for Security Testing.**—Notwithstanding the provisions of subsection (a)(2), it is not a violation of that subsection for a person to develop, produce, distribute or employ technological means for the sole purpose of performing the acts of security testing described in subsection (2), provided such technological means does not otherwise violate section (a)(2).

**(k)   Certain Analog Devices and Certain Technological Measures.—**

**(1)   Certain Analog Devices.—**

(A)   Effective 18 months after the date of the enactment of this chapter, no person shall manufacture, import, offer to the public, provide or otherwise traffic in any—

(i)   VHS format analog video cassette recorder unless such recorder conforms to the automatic gain control copy control technology;

(ii)   8mm format analog video cassette camcorder unless such camcorder conforms to the automatic gain control technology;

(iii)   Beta format analog video cassette recorder, unless such recorder conforms to the automatic gain control copy control technology, except that this requirement shall not apply until there are 1,000 Beta format analog video cassette recorders sold in the United States in any one calendar year after the date of the enactment of this chapter;

(iv)   8mm format analog video cassette recorder that is not an analog video cassette camcorder, unless such recorder conforms to the automatic gain control copy control technology, except that this requirement shall not apply until there are 20,000 such recorders sold in the United States in any one calendar year after the date of the enactment of this chapter; or

(v) analog video cassette recorder that records using an NTSC format video input and that is not otherwise covered under clauses (i) through (iv), unless such device conforms to the automatic gain control copy control technology.

(B) Effective on the date of the enactment of this chapter, no person shall manufacture, import, offer to the public, provide or otherwise traffic in—

(i) any VHS format analog video cassette recorder or any 8mm format analog video cassette recorder if the design of the model of such recorder has been modified after such date of enactment so that a model of recorder that previously conformed to the automatic gain control copy control technology no longer conforms to such technology; or

(ii) any VHS format analog video cassette recorder, or any 8mm format analog video cassette recorder that is not an 8mm analog video cassette camcorder, if the design of the model of such recorder has been modified after such date of enactment so that a model of recorder that previously conformed to the four-line colorstripe copy control technology no longer conforms to such technology.

Manufacturers that have not previously manufactured or sold a VHS format analog video cassette recorder, or an 8mm format analog cassette recorder, shall be required to conform to the four-line colorstripe copy control technology in the initial model of any such recorder manufactured after the date of the enactment of this chapter, and thereafter to continue conforming to the four-line colorstripe copy control technology. For purposes of this subparagraph, an analog video cassette recorder "conforms to" the four-line colorstripe copy control technology if it records a signal that, when played back by the playback function of that recorder in the normal viewing mode, exhibits, on a reference display device, a display containing distracting visible lines through portions of the viewable picture.

**(2) Certain Encoding Restrictions.**—No person shall apply the automatic gain control copy control technology or colorstripe copy control technology to prevent or limit consumer copying except such copying—

(A) of a single transmission, or specified group of transmissions, of live events or of audiovisual works for which a member of the public has exercised choice in selecting the transmissions, including the content of the transmissions or the time of receipt of such transmissions, or both, and as to which such member is charged a separate fee for each such transmission or specified group of transmissions;

(B) from a copy of a transmission of a live event or an audiovisual work if such transmission is provided by a channel or service where payment is made by a member of the public for such channel or service in the form of a subscription fee that entitles the member of the public to receive all of the programming contained in such channel or service;

(C) from a physical medium containing one or more prerecorded audiovisual works; or

(D) from a copy of a transmission described in subparagraph (A) or from a copy made from a physical medium described in subparagraph (C).

In the event that a transmission meets both the conditions set forth in subparagraph (A) and those set forth in subparagraph (B), the transmission shall be treated as a transmission described in subparagraph (A).

**(3) Inapplicability.**—This subsection shall not—

(A) require any analog video cassette camcorder to conform to the automatic gain control copy control technology with respect to any video signal received through a camera lens;

(B) apply to the manufacture, importation, offer for sale, provision of, or other trafficking in, any professional analog video cassette recorder; or

(C) apply to the offer for sale or provision of, or other trafficking in, any previously owned analog video cassette recorder, if such recorder was legally manufactured and sold when new and not subsequently modified in violation of paragraph (1)(B).

**(4) Definitions.**—For purposes of this subsection:

(A) An "analog video cassette recorder" means a device that records, or a device that includes a function that records, on electromagnetic tape in an analog format the electronic impulses produced by the video and audio portions of a television program, motion picture, or other form of audiovisual work.

(B) An "analog video cassette camcorder" means an analog video cassette recorder that contains a recording function that operates through a camera lens and through a video input that may be connected with a television or other video playback device.

(C) An analog video cassette recorder "conforms" to the automatic gain control copy control technology if it—

(i) detects one or more of the elements of such technology and does not record the motion picture or transmission protected by such technology; or

(ii) records a signal that, when played back, exhibits a meaningfully distorted or degraded display.

(D) The term "professional analog video cassette recorder" means an analog video cassette recorder that is designed, manufactured, marketed, and intended for use by a person who regularly employs such a device for a lawful business or industrial use, including making, performing, displaying, distributing, or transmitting copies of motion pictures on a commercial scale.

(E) The terms "VHS format", "8mm format", "Beta format", "automatic gain control copy control technology", "colorstripe copy control technology", "four-line version of the colorstripe copy control technology", and "NTSC" have the meanings that are commonly understood in the consumer electronics and motion picture industries as of the date of the enactment of this chapter.

**(5) Violations.**—Any violation of paragraph (1) of this subsection shall be treated as a violation of subsection (b)(1) of this section. Any violation of paragraph (2) of this subsection shall be deemed an "act of circumvention" for the purposes of section 1203(c)(3)(A) of this chapter.

(As amended, Pub.L. 106–113, 113 Stat. 1501A (1999)).

## Sec. 1202.   Integrity of Copyright Management Information

**(a) False Copyright Management Information.**—No person shall knowingly and with the intent to induce, enable, facilitate, or conceal infringement—

(1)   provide copyright management information that is false, or

(2)   distribute or import for distribution copyright management information that is false.

**(b) Removal or Alteration of Copyright Management Information.**—No person shall, without the authority of the copyright owner or the law—

(1)   intentionally remove or alter any copyright management information,

(2)   distribute or import for distribution copyright management information knowing that the copyright management information has been removed or altered without authority of the copyright owner or the law, or

(3) distribute, import for distribution, or publicly perform works, copies of works, or phonorecords, knowing that copyright management information has been removed or altered without authority of the copyright owner or the law,

knowing, or, with respect to civil remedies under section 1203, having reasonable grounds to know, that it will induce, enable, facilitate, or conceal an infringement of any right under this title.

(c) **Definition.**—As used in this section, the term "copyright management information" means any of the following information conveyed in connection with copies or phonorecords of a work or performances or displays of a work, including in digital form, except that such term does not include any personally identifying information about a user of a work or of a copy, phonorecord, performance, or display of a work:

(1) The title and other information identifying the work, including the information set forth on a notice of copyright.

(2) The name of, and other identifying information about, the author of a work.

(3) The name of, and other identifying information about, the copyright owner of the work, including the information set forth in a notice of copyright.

(4) With the exception of public performances of works by radio and television broadcast stations, the name of, and other identifying information about, a performer whose performance is fixed in a work other than an audiovisual work.

(5) With the exception of public performances of works by radio and television broadcast stations, in the case of an audiovisual work, the name of, and other identifying information about, a writer, performer, or director who is credited in the audiovisual work.

(6) Terms and conditions for use of the work.

(7) Identifying numbers or symbols referring to such information or links to such information.

(8) Such other information as the Register of Copyrights may prescribe by regulation, except that the Register of Copyrights may not require the provision of any information concerning the user of a copyrighted work.

(d) **Law Enforcement, Intelligence, and Other Government Activities.**—This section does not prohibit any lawfully authorized investigative, protective, information security, or intelligence activity of an officer, agent, or employee of the United States, a State, or a political subdivision of a State, or a person acting pursuant to a contract with the United States, a State, or a political subdivision of a State. For purposes of this subsection, the term "information security" means activities carried out in order to identify and address the vulnerabilities of a government computer, computer system, or computer network.

(e) **Limitations on Liability.**—

(1) **Analog Transmissions.**—In the case of an analog transmission, a person who is making transmissions in its capacity as a broadcast station, or as a cable system, or someone who provides programming to such station or system, shall not be liable for a violation of subsection (b) if—

(A) avoiding the activity that constitutes such violation is not technically feasible or would create an undue financial hardship on such person; and

(B) such person did not intend, by engaging in such activity, to induce, enable, facilitate, or conceal infringement of a right under this title.

(2) **Digital Transmissions.**—

(A) If a digital transmission standard for the placement of copyright management information for a category of works is set in a voluntary, consensus standard-setting process involving a representative cross-section of broadcast stations or cable systems and copyright owners of a category of works that are intended for public performance by such stations or systems, a person identified in paragraph (1) shall not be liable for a violation of subsection (b) with respect to the particular copyright management information addressed by such standard if—

> (i)   the placement of such information by someone other than such person is not in accordance with such standard; and

> (ii)   the activity that constitutes such violation is not intended to induce, enable, facilitate, or conceal infringement of a right under this title.

(B)   Until a digital transmission standard has been set pursuant to subparagraph (A) with respect to the placement of copyright management information for a category of works, a person identified in paragraph (1) shall not be liable for a violation of subsection (b) with respect to such copyright management information, if the activity that constitutes such violation is not intended to induce, enable, facilitate, or conceal infringement of a right under this title, and if—

> (i)   the transmission of such information by such person would result in a perceptible visual or aural degradation of the digital signal; or

> (ii)   the transmission of such information by such person would conflict with—

>> (I)   an applicable government regulation relating to transmission of information in a digital signal;

>> (II)   an applicable industry-wide standard relating to the transmission of information in a digital signal that was adopted by a voluntary consensus standards body prior to the effective date of this chapter; or

>> (III) an applicable industry-wide standard relating to the transmission of information in a digital signal that was adopted in a voluntary, consensus standards-setting process open to participation by a representative cross-section of broadcast stations or cable systems and copyright owners of a category of works that are intended for public performance by such stations or systems.

(3)   **Definitions.**—As used in this subsection—

(A)   the term "broadcast station" has the meaning given that term in section 3 of the Communications Act of 1934 (47 U.S.C. 153); and

(B)   the term "cable system" has the meaning given that term in section 602 of the Communications Act of 1934 (47 U.S.C. 522).

## Sec. 1203.   Civil Remedies

(a)   **Civil Actions.**—Any person injured by a violation of section 1201 or 1202 may bring a civil action in an appropriate United States district court for such violation.

(b)   **Powers of the Court.**—In an action brought under subsection (a), the court—

(1)   may grant temporary and permanent injunctions on such terms as it deems reasonable to prevent or restrain a violation, but in no event shall impose a prior restraint on free speech or the press protected under the 1st amendment to the Constitution;

(2)   at any time while an action is pending, may order the impounding, on such terms as it deems reasonable, of any device or product that is in the custody or control of the alleged violator and that the court has reasonable cause to believe was involved in a violation;

(3)   may award damages under subsection (c);

(4)   in its discretion may allow the recovery of costs by or against any party other than the United States or an officer thereof;

(5)   in its discretion may award reasonable attorney's fees to the prevailing party; and

(6)   may, as part of a final judgment or decree finding a violation, order the remedial modification or the destruction of any device or product involved in the violation that is in the custody or control of the violator or has been impounded under paragraph (2).

**(c)   Award of Damages.—**

**(1)   In General.**—Except as otherwise provided in this title, a person committing a violation of section 1201 or 1202 is liable for either—

(A)   the actual damages and any additional profits of the violator, as provided in paragraph (2), or

(B)   statutory damages, as provided in paragraph (3).

**(2)   Actual Damages.**—The court shall award to the complaining party the actual damages suffered by the party as a result of the violation, and any profits of the violator that are attributable to the violation and are not taken into account in computing the actual damages, if the complaining party elects such damages at any time before final judgment is entered.

**(3)   Statutory Damages.—**

(A) At any time before final judgment is entered, a complaining party may elect to recover an award of statutory damages for each violation of section 1201 in the sum of not less than $200 or more than $2,500 per act of circumvention, device, product, component, offer, or performance of service, as the court considers just.

(B)   At any time before final judgment is entered, a complaining party may elect to recover an award of statutory damages for each violation of section 1202 in the sum of not less than $2,500 or more than $25,000.

**(4)   Repeated Violations.**—In any case in which the injured party sustains the burden of proving, and the court finds, that a person has violated section 1201 or 1202 within 3 years after a final judgment was entered against the person for another such violation, the court may increase the award of damages up to triple the amount that would otherwise be awarded, as the court considers just.

**(5)   Innocent Violations.—**

**(A)   In General.**—The court in its discretion may reduce or remit the total award of damages in any case in which the violator sustains the burden of proving, and the court finds, that the violator was not aware and had no reason to believe that its acts constituted a violation.

**(B) Nonprofit Library, Archives, Educational Institutions, or Public Broadcasting Entities.—**

**(i)   Definition.**—In this subparagraph, the term "public broadcasting entity" has the meaning given such term under section 118(f).

**(ii) In general.**—In the case of a nonprofit library, archives, educational institution, or public broadcasting entity, the court shall remit damages in any case in which the library, archives, educational institution, or public broadcasting entity sustains the burden of proving, and the court finds, that the library, archives, educational institution, or public broadcasting entity was not aware and had no reason to believe that its acts constituted a violation.

(As amended, Pub.L. 106–113, 113 Stat. 1501A (1999)).

## Sec. 1204.   Criminal Offenses and Penalties

(a)  **In General.**—Any person who violates section 1201 or 1202 willfully and for purposes of commercial advantage or private financial gain—

(1)   shall be fined not more than $500,000 or imprisoned for not more than 5 years, or both, for the first offense; and

(2)   shall be fined not more than $1,000,000 or imprisoned for not more than 10 years, or both, for any subsequent offense.

(b)  **Limitation for Nonprofit Library, Archives, Educational Institution, or Public Broadcasting Entity.**—Subsection (a) shall not apply to a nonprofit library, archives, educational institution, or public broadcasting entity (as defined under section 118(f)).

(c)  **Statute of Limitations.**—No criminal proceeding shall be brought under this section unless such proceeding is commenced within 5 years after the cause of action arose.

(As amended, Pub.L. 106–113, 113 Stat. 1501A (1999)).

## Sec. 1205.   Savings Clause

Nothing in this chapter abrogates, diminishes, or weakens the provisions of, nor provides any defense or element of mitigation in a criminal prosecution or civil action under, any Federal or State law that prevents the violation of the privacy of an individual in connection with the individual's use of the Internet.

## CHAPTER 13.—PROTECTION OF ORIGINAL DESIGNS
### (Pub.L. 105–304, 112 Stat. 2905 (1998)).

## Sec. 1301.   Designs Protected

**(a)  Designs Protected.—**

**(1)  In General.—**The designer or other owner of an original design of a useful article which makes the article attractive or distinctive in appearance to the purchasing or using public may secure the protection provided by this chapter upon complying with and subject to this chapter.

**(2)  Vessel Features.—**The design of a vessel hull, deck, or combination of a hull and deck, including a plug or mold, is subject to protection under this chapter, notwithstanding section 1302(4).

**(3)  Exceptions.—**Department of Defense rights in a registered design under this chapter, including the right to build to such registered design, shall be determined solely by operation of section 2320 of title 10 or by the instrument under which the design was developed for the United States Government.

**(b)  Definitions.—**For the purpose of this chapter, the following terms have the following meanings:

(1)   A design is "original" if it is the result of the designer's creative endeavor that provides a distinguishable variation over prior work pertaining to similar articles which is more than merely trivial and has not been copied from another source.

(2)   A "useful article" is a vessel hull or deck, including a plug or mold, which in normal use has an intrinsic utilitarian function that is not merely to portray the appearance of the article or to convey information. An article which normally is part of a useful article shall be deemed to be a useful article.

(3)   A "vessel" is a craft—

(A)   that is designed and capable of independently steering a course on or through water through its own means of propulsion; and

(B)   that is designed and capable of carrying and transporting one or more passengers.

(4)   A "hull" is the exterior frame or body of a vessel, exclusive of the deck, superstructure, masts, sails, yards, rigging, hardware, fixtures, and other attachments.

(5)   A "plug" means a device or model used to make a mold for the purpose of exact duplication, regardless of whether the device or model has an intrinsic utilitarian function that is not only to portray the appearance of the product or to convey information.

(6)   A "mold" means a matrix or form in which a substance for material is used, regardless of whether the matrix or form has an intrinsic utilitarian function that is not only to portray the appearance of the product or to convey information.

(7)   A "deck" is the horizontal surface of a vessel that covers the hull, including exterior cabin and cockpit surfaces, and exclusive of masts, yards, rigging, hardware, fixtures, and other attachments.

(As amended, Pub.L. 106–113, 113 Stat. 1501A (1999); Pub.L. 110–434, 122 Stat. 4972 (2008)).

## Sec. 1302.    Designs not Subject to Protection

Protection under this chapter shall not be available for a design that is—

(1)   not original;

(2)   staple or commonplace, such as a standard geometric figure, a familiar symbol, an emblem, or a motif, or another shape, pattern, or configuration which has become standard, common, prevalent, or ordinary;

(3)   different from a design excluded by paragraph (2) only in insignificant details or in elements which are variants commonly used in the relevant trades;

(4)   dictated solely by a utilitarian function of the article that embodies it; or

(5)   embodied in a useful article that was made public by the designer or owner in the United States or a foreign country more than 2 years before the date of the application for registration under this chapter.

(As amended, Pub.L. 106–44, 113 Stat. 221 (1999)).

## Sec. 1303.    Revisions, Adaptations, and Rearrangements

Protection for a design under this chapter shall be available notwithstanding the employment in the design of subject matter excluded from protection under section 1302 if the design is a substantial revision, adaptation, or rearrangement of such subject matter. Such protection shall be independent of any subsisting protection in subject matter employed in the design, and shall not be construed as securing any right to subject matter excluded from protection under this chapter or as extending any subsisting protection under this chapter.

## Sec. 1304.    Commencement of Protection

The protection provided for a design under this chapter shall commence upon the earlier of the date of publication of the registration under section 1313(a) or the date the design is first made public as defined by section 1310(b).

## Sec. 1305.    Term of Protection

(a)  In General.—Subject to subsection (b), the protection provided under this chapter for a design shall continue for a term of 10 years beginning on the date of the commencement of protection under section 1304.

(b)  Expiration.—All terms of protection provided in this section shall run to the end of the calendar year in which they would otherwise expire.

(c)  Termination of Rights.—Upon expiration or termination of protection in a particular design under this chapter, all rights under this chapter in the design shall terminate, regardless of the number of different articles in which the design may have been used during the term of its protection.

## Sec. 1306.    Design Notice

(a)  Contents of Design Notice.—

(1)   Whenever any design for which protection is sought under this chapter is made public under section 1310(b), the owner of the design shall, subject to the provisions of section 1307, mark it or have it marked legibly with a design notice consisting of—

(A)   the words "Protected Design", the abbreviation "Prot'd Des.", or the letter "D" with a circle, or the symbol " *D* ";

(B)   the year of the date on which protection for the design commenced; and

(C)   the name of the owner, an abbreviation by which the name can be recognized, or a generally accepted alternative designation of the owner.

Any distinctive identification of the owner may be used for purposes of subparagraph (C) if it has been recorded by the Administrator before the design marked with such identification is registered

(2)   After registration, the registration number may be used instead of the elements specified in subparagraphs (B) and (C) of paragraph (1).

**(b)   Location of Notice.**—The design notice shall be so located and applied as to give reasonable notice of design protection while the useful article embodying the design is passing through its normal channels of commerce.

**(c)   Subsequent Removal of Notice.**—When the owner of a design has complied with the provisions of this section, protection under this chapter shall not be affected by the removal, destruction, or obliteration by others of the design notice on an article.

## Sec. 1307.   Effect of Omission of Notice

**(a)   Actions with Notice.**—Except as provided in subsection (b), the omission of the notice prescribed in section 1306 shall not cause loss of the protection under this chapter or prevent recovery for infringement under this chapter against any person who, after receiving written notice of the design protection, begins an undertaking leading to infringement under this chapter.

**(b)   Actions Without Notice.**—The omission of the notice prescribed in section 1306 shall prevent any recovery under section 1323 against a person who began an undertaking leading to infringement under this chapter before receiving written notice of the design protection. No injunction shall be issued under this chapter with respect to such undertaking unless the owner of the design reimburses that person for any reasonable expenditure or contractual obligation in connection with such undertaking that was incurred before receiving written notice of the design protection, as the court in its discretion directs. The burden of providing written notice of design protection shall be on the owner of the design.

## Sec. 1308.   Exclusive Rights

The owner of a design protected under this chapter has the exclusive right to—

(1)   make, have made, or import, for sale or for use in trade, any useful article embodying that design; and

(2)   sell or distribute for sale or for use in trade any useful article embodying that design.

## Sec. 1309.   Infringement

**(a)   Acts of Infringement.**—Except as provided in subsection (b), it shall be infringement of the exclusive rights in a design protected under this chapter for any person, without the consent of the owner of the design, within the United States and during the term of such protection, to—

(1)   make, have made, or import, for sale or for use in trade, any infringing article as defined in subsection (e); or

(2)   sell or distribute for sale or for use in trade any such infringing article.

**(b)   Acts of Sellers and Distributors.**—A seller or distributor of an infringing article who did not make or import the article shall be deemed to have infringed on a design protected under this chapter only if that person—

(1)   induced or acted in collusion with a manufacturer to make, or an importer to import such article, except that merely purchasing or giving an order to purchase such article in the ordinary course of business shall not of itself constitute such inducement or collusion; or

(2)   refused or failed, upon the request of the owner of the design, to make a prompt and full disclosure of that person's source of such article, and that person orders or reorders such article after receiving notice by registered or certified mail of the protection subsisting in the design.

(c)  **Acts Without Knowledge.**—It shall not be infringement under this section to make, have made, import, sell, or distribute, any article embodying a design which was created without knowledge that a design was protected under this chapter and was copied from such protected design.

(d)  **Acts in Ordinary Course of Business.**—A person who incorporates into that person's product of manufacture an infringing article acquired from others in the ordinary course of business, or who, without knowledge of the protected design embodied in an infringing article, makes or processes the infringing article for the account of another person in the ordinary course of business, shall not be deemed to have infringed the rights in that design under this chapter except under a condition contained in paragraph (1) or (2) of subsection (b). Accepting an order or reorder from the source of the infringing article shall be deemed ordering or reordering within the meaning of subsection (b)(2).

(e)  **Infringing Article Defined.**—As used in this section, an "infringing article" is any article the design of which has been copied from a design protected under this chapter, without the consent of the owner of the protected design. An infringing article is not an illustration or picture of a protected design in an advertisement, book, periodical, newspaper, photograph, broadcast, motion picture, or similar medium. A design shall not be deemed to have been copied from a protected design if it is original and not substantially similar in appearance to a protected design.

(f)  **Establishing Originality.**—The party to any action or proceeding under this chapter who alleges rights under this chapter in a design shall have the burden of establishing the design's originality whenever the opposing party introduces an earlier work which is identical to such design, or so similar as to make prima facie showing that such design was copied from such work.

(g)  **Reproduction for Teaching or Analysis.**—It is not an infringement of the exclusive rights of a design owner for a person to reproduce the design in a useful article or in any other form solely for the purpose of teaching, analyzing, or evaluating the appearance, concepts, or techniques embodied in the design, or the function of the useful article embodying the design.

## Sec. 1310.   Application for Registration

(a)  **Time Limit for Application for Registration.**—Protection under this chapter shall be lost if application for registration of the design is not made within 2 years after the date on which the design is first made public.

(b)  **When Design is Made Public.**—A design is made public when an existing useful article embodying the design is anywhere publicly exhibited, publicly distributed, or offered for sale or sold to the public by the owner of the design or with the owner's consent.

(c)  **Application by Owner of Design.**—Application for registration may be made by the owner of the design.

(d)  **Contents of Application.**—The application for registration shall be made to the Administrator and shall state—

(1)   the name and address of the designer or designers of the design;

(2)   the name and address of the owner if different from the designer;

(3)   the specific name of the useful article embodying the design;

    (4)   the date, if any, that the design was first made public, if such date was earlier than the date of the application;

    (5)   affirmation that the design has been fixed in a useful article; and

    (6)   such other information as may be required by the Administrator.

The application for registration may include a description setting forth the salient features of the design, but the absence of such a description shall not prevent registration under this chapter

    **(e)  Sworn Statement.**—The application for registration shall be accompanied by a statement under oath by the applicant or the applicant's duly authorized agent or representative, setting forth, to the best of the applicant's knowledge and belief—

    (1)   that the design is original and was created by the designer or designers named in the application;

    (2)   that the design has not previously been registered on behalf of the applicant or the applicant's predecessor in title; and

    (3)   that the applicant is the person entitled to protection and to registration under this chapter.

If the design has been made public with the design notice prescribed in section 1306, the statement shall also describe the exact form and position of the design notice

    **(f)  Effect of Errors.**—

    (1)   Error in any statement or assertion as to the utility of the useful article named in the application under this section, the design of which is sought to be registered, shall not affect the protection secured under this chapter.

    (2)   Errors in omitting a joint designer or in naming an alleged joint designer shall not affect the validity of the registration, or the actual ownership or the protection of the design, unless it is shown that the error occurred with deceptive intent.

    **(g)  Design Made in Scope of Employment.**—In a case in which the design was made within the regular scope of the designer's employment and individual authorship of the design is difficult or impossible to ascribe and the application so states, the name and address of the employer for whom the design was made may be stated instead of that of the individual designer.

    **(h)  Pictorial Representation of Design.**—The application for registration shall be accompanied by two copies of a drawing or other pictorial representation of the useful article embodying the design, having one or more views, adequate to show the design, in a form and style suitable for reproduction, which shall be deemed a part of the application.

    **(i)  Design in More Than One Useful Article.**—If the distinguishing elements of a design are in substantially the same form in different useful articles, the design shall be protected as to all such useful articles when protected as to one of them, but not more than one registration shall be required for the design.

    **(j)  Application for More Than One Design.**—More than one design may be included in the same application under such conditions as may be prescribed by the Administrator. For each design included in an application the fee prescribed for a single design shall be paid.

## Sec. 1311.   Benefit of Earlier Filing Date in Foreign Country

    An application for registration of a design filed in the United States by any person who has, or whose legal representative or predecessor or successor in title has, previously filed an application for registration of the same design in a foreign country which extends to designs of owners who are citizens of the United States, or to applications filed under this chapter, similar protection to that provided under this chapter shall have that same effect as if filed in the United States on the date on which the application was first filed in such foreign country, if the application in the United States is filed within 6 months after the earliest date on which any such foreign application was filed.

## Sec. 1312.    Oaths and Acknowledgments

(a)  In General.—Oaths and acknowledgments required by this chapter—

(1)  may be made—

(A)  before any person in the United States authorized by law to administer oaths; or

(B)  when made in a foreign country, before any diplomatic or consular officer of the United States authorized to administer oaths, or before any official authorized to administer oaths in the foreign country concerned, whose authority shall be proved by a certificate of a diplomatic or consular officer of the United States; and

(2)  shall be valid if they comply with the laws of the State or country where made.

(b)  Written Declaration in Lieu of Oath.—

(1)  The Administrator may by rule prescribe that any document which is to be filed under this chapter in the Office of the Administrator and which is required by any law, rule, or other regulation to be under oath, may be subscribed to by a written declaration in such form as the Administrator may prescribe, and such declaration shall be in lieu of the oath otherwise required.

(2)  Whenever a written declaration under paragraph (1) is used, the document containing the declaration shall state that willful false statements are punishable by fine or imprisonment, or both, pursuant to section 1001 of title 18, and may jeopardize the validity of the application or document or a registration resulting therefrom.

## Sec. 1313.    Examination of Application and Issue or Refusal of Registration

(a)  Determination of Registrability of Design; Registration.—Upon the filing of an application for registration in proper form under section 1310, and upon payment of the fee prescribed under section 1316, the Administrator shall determine whether or not the application relates to a design which on its face appears to be subject to protection under this chapter, and, if so, the Register shall register the design. Registration under this subsection shall be announced by publication. The date of registration shall be the date of publication.

(b)  Refusal to Register; Reconsideration.—If, in the judgment of the Administrator, the application for registration relates to a design which on its face is not subject to protection under this chapter, the Administrator shall send to the applicant a notice of refusal to register and the grounds for the refusal. Within 3 months after the date on which the notice of refusal is sent, the applicant may, by written request, seek reconsideration of the application. After consideration of such a request, the Administrator shall either register the design or send to the applicant a notice of final refusal to register.

(c)  Application to Cancel Registration.—Any person who believes he or she is or will be damaged by a registration under this chapter may, upon payment of the prescribed fee, apply to the Administrator at any time to cancel the registration on the ground that the design is not subject to protection under this chapter, stating the reasons for the request. Upon receipt of an application for cancellation, the Administrator shall send to the owner of the design, as shown in the records of the Office of the Administrator, a notice of the application, and the owner shall have a period of 3 months after the date on which such notice is mailed in which to present arguments to the Administrator for support of the validity of the registration. The Administrator shall also have the authority to establish, by regulation, conditions under which the opposing parties may appear and be heard in support of their arguments. If, after the periods provided for the presentation of arguments have expired, the Administrator determines that the applicant for cancellation has established that the design is not subject to protection under this chapter, the Administrator shall order the registration stricken from the record. Cancellation under this subsection shall be announced by publication, and notice of the Administrator's final determination with respect to any application for cancellation shall be sent to the applicant and to the owner of record. Costs of the cancellation procedure under this subsection shall be borne by the nonprevailing party or parties, and the Administrator shall have the authority to assess and collect such costs.

(As amended, Pub.L. 106–113, 113 Stat. 1501A (1999)).

### Sec. 1314.    Certification of Registration

Certificates of registration shall be issued in the name of the United States under the seal of the Office of the Administrator and shall be recorded in the official records of the Office. The certificate shall state the name of the useful article, the date of filing of the application, the date of registration, and the date the design was made public, if earlier than the date of filing of the application, and shall contain a reproduction of the drawing or other pictorial representation of the design. If a description of the salient features of the design appears in the application, the description shall also appear in the certificate. A certificate of registration shall be admitted in any court as prima facie evidence of the facts stated in the certificate.

### Sec. 1315.    Publication of Announcements and Indexes

(a)  **Publications of the Administrator.**—The Administrator shall publish lists and indexes of registered designs and cancellations of designs and may also publish the drawings or other pictorial representations of registered designs for sale or other distribution.

(b)  **File of Representatives of Registered Designs.**—The Administrator shall establish and maintain a file of the drawings or other pictorial representations of registered designs. The file shall be available for use by the public under such conditions as the Administrator may prescribe.

### Sec. 1316.    Fees

The Administrator shall by regulation set reasonable fees for the filing of applications to register designs under this chapter and for other services relating to the administration of this chapter, taking into consideration the cost of providing these services and the benefit of a public record.

### Sec. 1317.    Regulations

The Administrator may establish regulations for the administration of this chapter.

### Sec. 1318.    Copies of Records

Upon payment of the prescribed fee, any person may obtain a certified copy of any official record of the Office of the Administrator that relates to this chapter. That copy shall be admissible in evidence with the same effect as the original.

### Sec. 1319.    Correction of Errors in Certificates

The Administrator may, by a certificate of correction under seal, correct any error in a registration incurred through the fault of the Office, or, upon payment of the required fee, any error of a clerical or typographical nature occurring in good faith but not through the fault of the Office. Such registration, together with the certificate, shall thereafter have the same effect as if it had been originally issued in such corrected form.

### Sec. 1320.    Ownership and Transfer

(a)  **Property Right in Design.**—The property right in a design subject to protection under this chapter shall vest in the designer, the legal representatives of a deceased designer or of one under legal incapacity, the employer for whom the designer created the design in the case of a design made within the regular scope of the designer's employment, or a person to whom the rights of the designer or of such employer have been transferred. The person in whom the property right is vested shall be considered the owner of the design.

(b)  **Transfer of Property Right.**—The property right in a registered design, or a design for which an application for registration has been or may be filed, may be assigned, granted, conveyed, or mortgaged by an instrument in writing, signed by the owner, or may be bequeathed by will.

(c)  **Oath or Acknowledgment of Transfer.**—An oath or acknowledgment under section 1312 shall be prima facie evidence of the execution of an assignment, grant, conveyance, or mortgage under subsection (b).

(d)  **Recordation of Transfer.**—An assignment, grant, conveyance, or mortgage under subsection (b) shall be void as against any subsequent purchaser or mortgagee for a valuable consideration, unless it is recorded in the Office of the Administrator within 3 months after its date of execution or before the date of such subsequent purchase or mortgage.

## Sec. 1321.  Remedy for Infringement

(a)  **In General.**—The owner of a design is entitled, after issuance of a certificate of registration of the design under this chapter, to institute an action for any infringement of the design.

(b)  **Review of Refusal to Register.**—

(1)  Subject to paragraph (2), the owner of a design may seek judicial review of a final refusal of the Administrator to register the design under this chapter by bringing a civil action, and may in the same action, if the court adjudges the design subject to protection under this chapter, enforce the rights in that design under this chapter.

(2)  The owner of a design may seek judicial review under this section if—

(A)  the owner has previously duly filed and prosecuted to final refusal an application in proper form for registration of the design;

(B)  the owner causes a copy of the complaint in the action to be delivered to the Administrator within 10 days after the commencement of the action; and

(C)  the defendant has committed acts in respect to the design which would constitute infringement with respect to a design protected under this chapter.

(c)  **Administrator as Party to Action.**—The Administrator may, at the Administrator's option, become a party to the action with respect to the issue of registrability of the design claim by entering an appearance within 60 days after being served with the complaint, but the failure of the Administrator to become a party shall not deprive the court of jurisdiction to determine that issue.

(d)  **Use of Arbitration to Resolve Dispute.**—The parties to an infringement dispute under this chapter, within such time as may be specified by the Administrator by regulation, may determine the dispute, or any aspect of the dispute, by arbitration. Arbitration shall be governed by title 9. The parties shall give notice of any arbitration award to the Administrator, and such award shall, as between the parties to the arbitration, be dispositive of the issues to which it relates. The arbitration award shall be unenforceable until such notice is given. Nothing in this subsection shall preclude the Administrator from determining whether a design is subject to registration in a cancellation proceeding under section 1313(c).

## Sec. 1322.  Injunctions

(a)  **In General.**—A court having jurisdiction over actions under this chapter may grant injunctions in accordance with the principles of equity to prevent infringement of a design under this chapter, including, in its discretion, prompt relief by temporary restraining orders and preliminary injunctions.

**(b) Damages for Injunctive Relief Wrongfully Obtained.**—A seller or distributor who suffers damage by reason of injunctive relief wrongfully obtained under this section has a cause of action against the applicant for such injunctive relief and may recover such relief as may be appropriate, including damages for lost profits, cost of materials, loss of good will, and punitive damages in instances where the injunctive relief was sought in bad faith, and, unless the court finds extenuating circumstances, reasonable attorney's fees.

## Sec. 1323.    Recovery for Infringement

**(a) Damages.**—Upon a finding for the claimant in an action for infringement under this chapter, the court shall award the claimant damages adequate to compensate for the infringement. In addition, the court may increase the damages to such amount, not exceeding $50,000 or $1 per copy, whichever is greater, as the court determines to be just. The damages awarded shall constitute compensation and not a penalty. The court may receive expert testimony as an aid to the determination of damages.

**(b) Infringer's Profits.**—As an alternative to the remedies provided in subsection (a), the court may award the claimant the infringer's profits resulting from the sale of the copies if the court finds that the infringer's sales are reasonably related to the use of the claimant's design. In such a case, the claimant shall be required to prove only the amount of the infringer's sales and the infringer shall be required to prove its expenses against such sales.

**(c) Statute of Limitations.**—No recovery under subsection (a) or (b) shall be had for any infringement committed more than 3 years before the date on which the complaint is filed.

**(d) Attorney's Fees.**—In an action for infringement under this chapter, the court may award reasonable attorney's fees to the prevailing party.

**(e) Disposition of Infringing and Other Articles.**—The court may order that all infringing articles, and any plates, molds, patterns, models, or other means specifically adapted for making the articles, be delivered up for destruction or other disposition as the court may direct.

## Sec. 1324.    Power of Court Over Registration

In any action involving the protection of a design under this chapter, the court, when appropriate, may order registration of a design under this chapter or the cancellation of such a registration. Any such order shall be certified by the court to the Administrator, who shall make an appropriate entry upon the record.

## Sec. 1325.    Liability for Action on Registration Fraudulently Obtained

Any person who brings an action for infringement knowing that registration of the design was obtained by a false or fraudulent representation materially affecting the rights under this chapter, shall be liable in the sum of $10,000, or such part of that amount as the court may determine. That am amount shall be to compensate the defendant and shall be charged against the plaintiff and paid to the defendant, in addition to such costs and attorney's fees of the defendant as may be assessed by the court.

## Sec. 1326.    Penalty for False Marking

**(a) In General.**—Whoever, for the purpose of deceiving the public, marks upon, applies to, or uses in advertising in connection with an article made, used, distributed, or sold, a design which is not protected under this chapter, a design notice specified in section 1306, or any other words or symbols importing that the design is protected under this chapter, knowing that the design is not so protected, shall pay a civil fine of not more than $500 for each such offense.

**(b) Suit by Private Persons.**—Any person may sue for the penalty established by subsection (a), in which event one-half of the penalty shall be awarded to the person suing and the remainder shall be awarded to the United States.

## Sec. 1327.  Penalty for False Representation

Whoever knowingly makes a false representation materially affecting the rights obtainable under this chapter for the purpose of obtaining registration of a design under this chapter shall pay a penalty of not less than $500 and not more than $1,000, and any rights or privileges that individual may have in the design under this chapter shall be forfeited.

## Sec. 1328.  Enforcement by Treasury and Postal Service

**(a) Regulations.**—The Secretary of the Treasury and the United States Postal Service shall separately or jointly issue regulations for the enforcement of the rights set forth in section 1308 with respect to importation. Such regulations may require, as a condition for the exclusion of articles from the United States, that the person seeking exclusion take any one or more of the following actions:

(1)  Obtain a court order enjoining, or an order of the International Trade Commission under section 337 of the Tariff Act of 1930 excluding, importation of the articles.

(2)  Furnish proof that the design involved is protected under this chapter and that the importation of the articles would infringe the rights in the design under this chapter.

(3)  Post a surety bond for any injury that may result if the detention or exclusion of the articles proves to be unjustified.

**(b) Seizure and Forfeiture.**—Articles imported in violation of the rights set forth in section 1308 are subject to seizure and forfeiture in the same manner as property imported in violation of the customs laws. Any such forfeited articles shall be destroyed as directed by the Secretary of the Treasury or the court, as the case may be, except that the articles may be returned to the country of export whenever it is shown to the satisfaction of the Secretary of the Treasury that the importer had no reasonable grounds for believing that his or her acts constituted a violation of the law.

## Sec. 1329.  Relation to Design Patent Law

The issuance of a design patent under title 35, United States Code, for an original design for an article of manufacture shall terminate any protection of the original design under this chapter.

## Sec. 1330.  Common Law and Other Rights Unaffected

Nothing in this chapter shall annul or limit—

(1)  common law or other rights or remedies, if any, available to or held by any person with respect to a design which has not been registered under this chapter; or

(2)  any right under the trademark laws or any right protected against unfair competition.

## Sec. 1331.  Administrator; Office of the Administrator

In this chapter, the "Administrator" is the Register of Copyrights, and the "Office of the Administrator" and the "Office" refer to the Copyright Office of the Library of Congress.

## Sec. 1332.  No Retroactive Effect

Protection under this chapter shall not be available for any design that has been made public under section 1310(b) before the effective date of this chapter.

## CHAPTER 14.—UNAUTHORIZED USE OF PRE-1972 SOUND RECORDINGS

Sec.
1401.    Unauthorized Use of Pre-1972 Sound Recordings.

## Sec. 1401.    Unauthorized Use of Pre-1972 Sound Recordings

**(a)  In general.—**

**(1)  Unauthorized acts.—**Anyone who, on or before the last day of the applicable transition period under paragraph (2), and without the consent of the rights owner, engages in covered activity with respect to a sound recording fixed before February 15, 1972, shall be subject to the remedies provided in sections 502 through 505 and 1203 to the same extent as an infringer of copyright or a person that engages in unauthorized activity under chapter 12.

**(2)  Term of prohibition.—**

**(A)  In general.—**The prohibition under paragraph (1)—

**(i)**  subject to clause (ii), shall apply to a sound recording described in that paragraph—

**(I)**  through December 31 of the year that is 95 years after the year of first publication; and

**(II)**  for a further transition period as prescribed under subparagraph (B) of this paragraph; and

**(ii)**  shall not apply to any sound recording after February 15, 2067.

**(B)  Transition periods.—**

**(i)  Pre-1923 recordings.—**In the case of a sound recording first published before January 1, 1923, the transition period described in subparagraph (A)(i)(II) shall end on December 31 of the year that is 3 years after the date of enactment of this section.

**(ii)  1923–1946 recordings.—**In the case of a sound recording first published during the period beginning on January 1, 1923, and ending on December 31, 1946, the transition period described in subparagraph (A)(i)(II) shall end on the date that is 5 years after the last day of the period described in subparagraph (A)(i)(I).

**(iii)  1947–1956 recordings.—**In the case of a sound recording first published during the period beginning on January 1, 1947, and ending on December 31, 1956, the transition period described in subparagraph (A)(i)(II) shall end on the date that is 15 years after the last day of the period described in subparagraph (A)(i)(I).

**(iv)  Post-1956 recordings.—**In the case of a sound recording fixed before February 15, 1972, that is not described in clause (i), (ii), or (iii), the transition period described in subparagraph (A)(i)(II) shall end on February 15, 2067.

**(3)  Rule of construction.—**For the purposes of this subsection, the term "anyone" includes any State, any instrumentality of a State, and any officer or employee of a State or instrumentality of a State acting in the official capacity of the officer or employee, as applicable.

**(b)  Certain authorized transmissions and reproductions.—**A public performance by means of a digital audio transmission of a sound recording fixed before February 15, 1972, or a reproduction in an ephemeral phonorecord or copy of a sound recording fixed before February 15, 1972, shall, for purposes of subsection (a), be considered to be authorized and made with the consent of the rights owner if—

**(1)**  the transmission or reproduction would satisfy the requirements for statutory licensing under section 112(e)(1) or section 114(d)(2), or would be exempt under section 114(d)(1), as the case may be, if the sound recording were fixed on or after February 15, 1972; and

**(2)** the transmitting entity pays the statutory royalty for the transmission or reproduction pursuant to the rates and terms adopted under sections 112(e) and 114(f), and complies with other obligations, in the same manner as required by regulations adopted by the Copyright Royalty Judges under sections 112(e) and 114(f) for sound recordings that are fixed on or after February 15, 1972, except in the case of a transmission that would be exempt under section 114(d)(1).

**(c) Certain noncommercial uses of sound recordings that are not being commercially exploited.—**

**(1) In general.—**Noncommercial use of a sound recording fixed before February 15, 1972, that is not being commercially exploited by or under the authority of the rights owner shall not violate subsection (a) if—

**(A)** the person engaging in the noncommercial use, in order to determine whether the sound recording is being commercially exploited by or under the authority of the rights owner, makes a good faith, reasonable search for, but does not find, the sound recording—

**(i)** in the records of schedules filed in the Copyright Office as described in subsection (f)(5)(A); and

**(ii)** on services offering a comprehensive set of sound recordings for sale or streaming;

**(B)** the person engaging in the noncommercial use files a notice identifying the sound recording and the nature of the use in the Copyright Office in accordance with the regulations issued under paragraph (3)(B); and

**(C)** during the 90-day period beginning on the date on which the notice described in subparagraph (B) is indexed into the public records of the Copyright Office, the rights owner of the sound recording does not, in its discretion, opt out of the noncommercial use by filing notice thereof in the Copyright Office in accordance with the regulations issued under paragraph (5).

**(2) Rules of construction.—**For purposes of this subsection—

**(A)** merely recovering costs of production and distribution of a sound recording resulting from a use otherwise permitted under this subsection does not itself necessarily constitute a commercial use of the sound recording;

**(B)** the fact that a person engaging in the use of a sound recording also engages in commercial activities does not itself necessarily render the use commercial; and

**(C)** the fact that a person files notice of a noncommercial use of a sound recording in accordance with the regulations issued under paragraph (3)(B) does not itself affect any limitation on the exclusive rights of a copyright owner described in section 107, 108, 109, 110, or 112(f) as applied to a claim under subsection (a) of this section pursuant to subsection (f)(1)(A) of this section.

**(3) Notice of covered activity.—**Not later than 180 days after the date of enactment of this section, the Register of Copyrights shall issue regulations that—

**(A)** provide specific, reasonable steps that, if taken by a filer, are sufficient to constitute a good faith, reasonable search under paragraph (1)(A) to determine whether a recording is being commercially exploited, including the services that satisfy the good faith, reasonable search requirement under paragraph (1)(A) for purposes of the safe harbor described in paragraph (4)(A); and

**(B)** establish the form, content, and procedures for the filing of notices under paragraph (1)(B).

**(4) Safe harbor.—**

**(A) In general.**—A person engaging in a noncommercial use of a sound recording otherwise permitted under this subsection who establishes that the person made a good faith, reasonable search under paragraph (1)(A) without finding commercial exploitation of the sound recording by or under the authority of the rights owner shall not be found to be in violation of subsection (a).

**(B) Steps sufficient but not necessary.**—Taking the specific, reasonable steps identified by the Register of Copyrights in the regulations issued under paragraph (3)(A) shall be sufficient, but not necessary, for a filer to satisfy the requirement to conduct a good faith, reasonable search under paragraph (1)(A) for purposes of subparagraph (A) of this paragraph.

**(5) Opting out of covered activity.—**

**(A) In general.**—Not later than 180 days after the date of enactment of this section, the Register of Copyrights shall issue regulations establishing the form, content, and procedures for the rights owner of a sound recording that is the subject of a notice under paragraph (1)(B) to, in its discretion, file notice opting out of the covered activity described in the notice under paragraph (1)(B) during the 90-day period beginning on the date on which the notice under paragraph (1)(B) is indexed into the public records of the Copyright Office.

**(B) Rule of construction.**—The fact that a rights holder opts out of a noncommercial use of a sound recording by filing notice thereof in the Copyright Office in accordance with the regulations issued under subparagraph (A) does not itself enlarge or diminish any limitation on the exclusive rights of a copyright owner described in section 107, 108, 109, 110, or 112(f) as applied to a claim under subsection (a) of this section pursuant to subsection (f)(1)(A) of this section.

**(6) Civil penalties for certain acts.—**

**(A) Filing of notices of noncommercial use.**—Any person who willfully engages in a pattern or practice of filing a notice of noncommercial use of a sound recording as described in paragraph (1)(B) fraudulently describing the use proposed, or knowing that the use proposed is not permitted under this subsection, shall be assessed a civil penalty in an amount that is not less than $250, and not more than $1000, for each such notice, in addition to any other remedies that may be available under this title based on the actual use made.

**(B) Filing of opt-out notices.—**

**(i) In general.**—Any person who files an opt-out notice as described in paragraph (1)(C), knowing that the person is not the rights owner or authorized to act on behalf of the rights owner of the sound recording to which the notice pertains, shall be assessed a civil penalty in an amount not less than $250, and not more than $1,000, for each such notice.

**(ii) Pattern or practice.**—Any person who engages in a pattern or practice of making filings as described in clause (i) shall be assessed a civil penalty in an amount not less than $10,000 for each such filing.

**(C) Definition.**—For purposes of this paragraph, the term "knowing"—

**(i)** does not require specific intent to defraud; and

**(ii)** with respect to information about ownership of the sound recording in question, means that the person—

**(I)** has actual knowledge of the information;

**(II)** acts in deliberate ignorance of the truth or falsity of the information; or

**(III)** acts in grossly negligent disregard of the truth or falsity of the information.

**(d)  Payment of royalties for transmissions of performances by direct licensing of statutory services.—**

**(1)**  In general.—A public performance by means of a digital audio transmission of a sound recording fixed before February 15, 1972, shall, for purposes of subsection (a), be considered to be authorized and made with the consent of the rights owner if the transmission is made pursuant to a license agreement voluntarily negotiated at any time between the rights owner and the entity performing the sound recording.

**(2)  Payment of royalties to nonprofit collective under certain license agreements.—**

**(A)  Licenses entered into on or after date of enactment.**—To the extent that a license agreement described in paragraph (1) entered into on or after the date of enactment of this section extends to a public performance by means of a digital audio transmission of a sound recording fixed before February 15, 1972, that meets the conditions of subsection (b)—

**(i)**  the licensee shall, with respect to such transmission, pay to the collective designated to distribute receipts from the licensing of transmissions in accordance with section 114(f), 50 percent of the performance royalties for that transmission due under the license; and

**(ii)**  the royalties paid under clause (i) shall be fully credited as payments due under the license.

**(B)  Certain agreements entered into before enactment.**—To the extent that a license agreement described in paragraph (1), entered into during the period beginning on January 1 of the year in which this section is enacted and ending on the day before the date of enactment of this section, or a settlement agreement with a preexisting satellite digital audio radio service (as defined in section 114(j)) entered into during the period beginning on January 1, 2015, and ending on the day before the date of enactment of this section, extends to a public performance by means of a digital audio transmission of a sound recording fixed before February 15, 1972, that meets the conditions of subsection (b)—

**(i)**  the rights owner shall, with respect to such transmission, pay to the collective designated to distribute receipts from the licensing of transmissions in accordance with section 114(f) an amount that is equal to the difference between—

**(I)**  50 percent of the difference between—

**(aa)** the rights owner's total gross performance royalty fee receipts or settlement monies received for all such transmissions covered under the license or settlement agreement, as applicable; and

**(bb)** the rights owner's total payments for outside legal expenses, including any payments of third-party claims, that are directly attributable to the license or settlement agreement, as applicable; and

**(II)**  the amount of any royalty receipts or settlement monies under the agreement that are distributed by the rights owner to featured and nonfeatured artists before the date of enactment of this section; and

**(ii)**  the royalties paid under clause (i) shall be fully credited as payments due under the license or settlement agreement, as applicable.

**(3)  Distribution of royalties and settlement monies by collective.**—The collective described in paragraph (2) shall, in accordance with subparagraphs (B) through (D) of section 114(g)(2), and paragraphs (5) and (6) of section 114(g), distribute the royalties or settlement monies received under paragraph (2) under a license or settlement described in paragraph (2), which shall be the only payments to which featured and nonfeatured artists are entitled by virtue of the transmissions described in paragraph (2), except for settlement monies described in paragraph (2) that are distributed by the rights owner to featured and nonfeatured artists before the date of enactment of this section.

**(4) Payment of royalties under license agreements entered before enactment or not otherwise described in paragraph (2).—**

**(A) In general.**—To the extent that a license agreement described in paragraph (1) entered into before the date of enactment of this section, or any other license agreement not as described in paragraph (2), extends to a public performance by means of a digital audio transmission of a sound recording fixed before February 15, 1972, that meets the conditions of subsection (b), the payments made by the licensee pursuant to the license shall be made in accordance with the agreement.

**(B) Additional payments not required.**—To the extent that a licensee has made, or will make in the future, payments pursuant to a license as described in subparagraph (A), the provisions of paragraphs (2) and (3) shall not require any additional payments from, or additional financial obligations on the part of, the licensee.

**(C) Rule of construction.**—Nothing in this subsection may be construed to prohibit the collective designated to distribute receipts from the licensing of transmissions in accordance with section 114(f) from administering royalty payments under any license not described in paragraph (2).

**(e) Preemption with respect to certain past acts.—**

**(1) In general.**—This section preempts any claim of common law copyright or equivalent right under the laws of any State arising from a digital audio transmission or reproduction that is made before the date of enactment of this section of a sound recording fixed before February 15, 1972, if—

**(A)** the digital audio transmission would have satisfied the requirements for statutory licensing under section 114(d)(2) or been exempt under section 114(d)(1), or the reproduction would have satisfied the requirements of section 112(e)(1), as the case may be, if the sound recording were fixed on or after February 15, 1972; and

**(B)** either—

**(i)** except in the case of a transmission that would have been exempt under section 114(d)(1), not later than 270 days after the date of enactment of this section, the transmitting entity pays statutory royalties and provides notice of the use of the relevant sound recordings in the same manner as required by regulations adopted by the Copyright Royalty Judges for sound recordings that are fixed on or after February 15, 1972, for all the digital audio transmissions and reproductions satisfying the requirements for statutory licensing under sections 112(e)(1) and 114(d)(2) during the 3 years before that date of enactment; or

**(ii)** an agreement voluntarily negotiated between the rights owner and the entity performing the sound recording (including a litigation settlement agreement entered into before the date of enactment of this section) authorizes or waives liability for any such transmission or reproduction and the transmitting entity has paid for and reported such digital audio transmission under that agreement.

**(2) Rule of construction for common law copyright.**—For purposes of paragraph (1), a claim of common law copyright or equivalent right under the laws of any State includes a claim that characterizes conduct subject to that paragraph as an unlawful distribution, act of record piracy, or similar violation.

**(3) Rule of construction for public performance rights.**—Nothing in this section may be construed to recognize or negate the existence of public performance rights in sound recordings under the laws of any State.

**(f)  Limitations on remedies.—**

**(1)  Fair use; uses by libraries, archives, and educational institutions.—**

**(A)  In general.**—The limitations on the exclusive rights of a copyright owner described in sections 107, 108, 109, 110, and 112(f) shall apply to a claim under subsection (a) with respect to a sound recording fixed before February 15, 1972.

**(B)  Rule of construction for section 108(h).**—With respect to the application of section 108(h) to a claim under subsection (a) with respect to a sound recording fixed before February 15, 1972, the phrase "during the last 20 years of any term of copyright of a published work" in such section 108(h) shall be construed to mean at any time after the date of enactment of this section.

**(2)  Actions.**—The limitations on actions described in section 507 shall apply to a claim under subsection (a) with respect to a sound recording fixed before February 15, 1972.

**(3)  Material online.**—Section 512 shall apply to a claim under subsection (a) with respect to a sound recording fixed before February 15, 1972.

**(4)  Principles of equity.**—Principles of equity apply to remedies for a violation of this section to the same extent as such principles apply to remedies for infringement of copyright.

**(5)  Filing requirement for statutory damages and attorneys' fees.—**

**(A)  Filing of information on sound recordings.—**

**(i)  Filing requirement.**—Except in the case of a transmitting entity that has filed contact information for that transmitting entity under subparagraph (B), in any action under this section, an award of statutory damages or of attorneys' fees under section 504 or 505 may be made with respect to an unauthorized use of a sound recording under subsection (a) only if—

**(I)**  the rights owner has filed with the Copyright Office a schedule that specifies the title, artist, and rights owner of the sound recording and contains such other information, as practicable, as the Register of Copyrights prescribes by regulation; and

**(II)**  the use occurs after the end of the 90-day period beginning on the date on which the information described in subclause (I) is indexed into the public records of the Copyright Office.

**(ii)  Regulations.**—Not later than 180 days after the date of enactment of this section, the Register of Copyrights shall issue regulations that—

**(I)**  establish the form, content, and procedures for the filing of schedules under clause (i);

**(II)**  provide that a person may request that the person receive timely notification of a filing described in subclause (I); and

**(III)** set forth the manner in which a person may make a request under subclause (II).

**(B)  Filing of contact information for transmitting entities.—**

**(i)  Filing requirement.**—Not later than 30 days after the date of enactment of this section, the Register of Copyrights shall issue regulations establishing the form, content, and procedures for the filing of contact information by any entity that, as of the date of enactment of this section, performs a sound recording fixed before February 15, 1972, by means of a digital audio transmission.

(ii) **Time limit on filings.**—The Register of Copyrights may accept filings under clause (i) only until the 180th day after the date of enactment of this section.

(iii) **Limitation on statutory damages and attorneys' fees.**—

(I) **Limitation.**—An award of statutory damages or of attorneys' fees under section 504 or 505 may not be made against an entity that has filed contact information for that entity under clause (i) with respect to an unauthorized use by that entity of a sound recording under subsection (a) if the use occurs before the end of the 90-day period beginning on the date on which the entity receives a notice that—

(aa) is sent by or on behalf of the rights owner of the sound recording;

(bb) states that the entity is not legally authorized to use that sound recording under subsection (a); and

(cc) identifies the sound recording in a schedule conforming to the requirements prescribed by the regulations issued under subparagraph (A)(ii).

(II) **Undeliverable notices.**—In any case in which a notice under subclause (I) is sent to an entity by mail or courier service and the notice is returned to the sender because the entity either is no longer located at the address provided in the contact information filed under clause (i) or has refused to accept delivery, or the notice is sent by electronic mail and is undeliverable, the 90-day period under subclause (I) shall begin on the date of the attempted delivery.

(C) **Section 412.**—Section 412 shall not limit an award of statutory damages under section 504(c) or attorneys' fees under section 505 with respect to a covered activity in violation of subsection (a).

(6) **Applicability of other provisions.**—

(A) **In general.**—Subject to subparagraph (B), no provision of this title shall apply to or limit the remedies available under this section except as otherwise provided in this section.

(B) **Applicability of definitions.**—Any term used in this section that is defined in section 101 shall have the meaning given that term in section 101.

(g) **Application of section 230 safe harbor.**—For purposes of section 230 of the Communications Act of 1934 (47 U.S.C. 230), subsection (a) shall be considered to be a "law pertaining to intellectual property" under subsection (e)(2) of such section 230.

(h) **Application to rights owners.**—

(1) **Transfers.**—With respect to a rights owner described in subsection (*l*)(2)(B)—

(A) subsections (d) and (e) of section 201 and section 204 shall apply to a transfer described in subsection (*l*)(2)(B) to the same extent as with respect to a transfer of copyright ownership; and

(B) notwithstanding section 411, that rights owner may institute an action with respect to a violation of this section to the same extent as the owner of an exclusive right under a copyright may institute an action under section 501(b).

(2) **Application of other provisions.**—The following provisions shall apply to a rights owner under this section to the same extent as any copyright owner:

(A) Section 112(e)(2).

(B) Section 112(e)(7).

(C) Section 114(e).

**(D)** Section 114(h).

**(i) Ephemeral recordings.**—An authorized reproduction made under this section shall be subject to section 112(g) to the same extent as a reproduction of a sound recording fixed on or after February 15, 1972.

**(j) Rule of construction.**—A rights owner of, or featured recording artist who performs on, a sound recording under this chapter shall be deemed to be an interested copyright party, as defined in section 1001, to the same extent as a copyright owner or featured recording artist under chapter 10.

**(k) Treatment of States and State instrumentalities, officers, and employees.**—Any State, and any instrumentality, officer, or employee described in subsection (a)(3), shall be subject to the provisions of this section in the same manner and to the same extent as any nongovernmental entity.

**(*l*) Definitions.**—In this section:

    **(1) Covered activity.**—The term "covered activity" means any activity that the copyright owner of a sound recording would have the exclusive right to do or authorize under section 106 or 602, or that would violate section 1201 or 1202, if the sound recording were fixed on or after February 15, 1972.

    **(2) Rights owner.**—The term "rights owner" means—

        **(A)** the person that has the exclusive right to reproduce a sound recording under the laws of any State, as of the day before the date of enactment of this section; or

        **(B)** any person to which a right to enforce a violation of this section may be transferred, in whole or in part, after the date of enactment of this section, under—

            **(i)** subsections (d) and (e) of section 201; and

            **(ii)** section 204.

(Added by Pub.L. 115–264, Title II, 132 Stat. 3728 (2018)).

---

## TRANSITIONAL AND SUPPLEMENTARY PROVISIONS OF THE 1976 COPYRIGHT ACT

SEC. 102. This Act becomes effective on January 1, 1978, except as otherwise expressly provided by this Act, including provisions of the first section of this Act. The provisions of sections 118, 304(b), and chapter 8 of title 17, as amended by the first section of this Act, take effect upon enactment of this Act.

SEC. 103. This Act does not provide copyright protection for any work that goes into the public domain before January 1, 1978. The exclusive rights, as provided by section 106 of title 17 as amended by the first section of this Act, to reproduce a work in phonorecords and to distribute phonorecords of the work, do not extend to any non-dramatic musical work copyrighted before July 1, 1909.

    \* \* \*

SEC. 108. The notice provisions of sections 401 through 403 of title 17 as amended by the first section of this Act apply to all copies or phonorecords publicly distributed on or after January 1, 1978. However, in the case of a work published before January 1, 1978, compliance with the notice provisions of title 17 either as it existed on December 31, 1977, or as amended by the first section of this Act, is adequate with respect to copies publicly distributed after December 31, 1977.

    \* \* \*

SEC. 112. All causes of action that arose under title 17 before January 1, 1978, shall be governed by title 17 as it existed when the cause of action arose.

    \* \* \*

## THE COPYRIGHT ACT OF 1976

Sec. 115. If any provision of title 17, as amended by the first section of this Act, is declared unconstitutional, the validity of the remainder of this title is not affected.

Approved October 19, 1976.

## LEGISLATIVE HISTORY

HOUSE REPORTS: No. 94–1476 (Comm. on the Judiciary) and No. 94–1733 (Comm. of Conference).

SENATE REPORT No. 94–473 (Comm. on the Judiciary).

CONGRESSIONAL RECORD, Vol. 122 (1976):

Feb. 6, 16–19, considered and passed Senate.

Sept. 22, considered and passed Senate, amended.

Sept. 30, Senate and House agreed to conference report.

# APPENDIX B

---

# CRIMINAL PENALTIES

**18 U.S.C.A. § 2318.** **Trafficking in counterfeit labels, illicit labels, or counterfeit documentation or packaging**

(a)(1)   Whoever, in any of the circumstances described in subsection (c), knowingly traffics in—

(A)   a counterfeit label or illicit label affixed to, enclosing, or accompanying, or designed to be affixed to, enclose, or accompany—

(i)     a phonorecord;

(ii)    a copy of a computer program;

(iii)   a copy of a motion picture or other audiovisual work;

(iv)    a copy of a literary work;

(v)     a copy of a pictorial, graphic, or sculptural work;

(vi)    a work of visual art; or

(vii)  documentation or packaging; or

(B)   counterfeit documentation or packaging,

shall be fined under this title or imprisoned for not more than 5 years, or both.

(b)   As used in this section—

(1)   the term "counterfeit label" means an identifying label or container that appears to be genuine, but is not;

(2)   the term "traffic" has the same meaning as in section 2320(f) of this title;

(3)   the terms "copy", "phonorecord", "motion picture", "computer program", "audiovisual work", "literary work", "pictorial, graphic, or sculptural work", "sound recording", "work of visual art", and "copyright owner" have, respectively, the meanings given those terms in section 101 (relating to definitions) of title 17;

(4)   the term "illicit label" means a genuine certificate, licensing document, registration card, or similar labeling component—

(A)   that is used by the copyright owner to verify that a phonorecord, a copy of a computer program, a copy of a motion picture or other audiovisual work, a copy of a literary work, a copy of a pictorial, graphic, or sculptural work, a work of visual art, or documentation or packaging is not counterfeit or infringing of any copyright; and

(B)   that is, without the authorization of the copyright owner—

(i)     distributed or intended for distribution not in connection with the copy, phonorecord, or work of visual art to which such labeling component was intended to be affixed by the respective copyright owner; or

(ii)    in connection with a genuine certificate or licensing document, knowingly falsified in order to designate a higher number of licensed users or copies than authorized by the copyright owner, unless that certificate or document is used by the copyright owner solely for the purpose of monitoring or tracking the copyright owner's

217

distribution channel and not for the purpose of verifying that a copy or phonorecord is noninfringing;

(5)   the term "documentation or packaging" means documentation or packaging, in physical form, for a phonorecord, copy of a computer program, copy of a motion picture or other audiovisual work, copy of a literary work, copy of a pictorial, graphic, or sculptural work, or work of visual art; and

(6)   the term "counterfeit documentation or packaging" means documentation or packaging that appears to be genuine, but is not.

(c)   The circumstances referred to in subsection (a) of this section are—

(1)   the offense is committed within the special maritime and territorial jurisdiction of the United States; or within the special aircraft jurisdiction of the United States (as defined in section 46501 of title 49);

(2)   the mail or a facility of interstate or foreign commerce is used or intended to be used in the commission of the offense;

(3)   the counterfeit label or illicit label is affixed to, encloses, or accompanies, or is designed to be affixed to, enclose, or accompany—

(A)   a phonorecord of a copyrighted sound recording or copyrighted musical work;

(B)   a copy of a copyrighted computer program;

(C)   a copy of a copyrighted motion picture or other audiovisual work;

(D)   a copy of a literary work;

(E)   a copy of a pictorial, graphic, or sculptural work;

(F)   a work of visual art; or

(G)   copyrighted documentation or packaging; or

(4)   the counterfeited documentation or packaging is copyrighted.

(d)   Forfeiture and Destruction of Property; Restitution.—Forfeiture, destruction, and restitution relating to this section shall be subject to section 2323, to the extent provided in that section, in addition to any other similar remedies provided by law.

(e)   Civil remedies.

(1)   In general. Any copyright owner who is injured, or is threatened with injury, by a violation of subsection (a) may bring a civil action in an appropriate United States district court.

(2)   Discretion of court. In any action brought under paragraph (1), the court—

(A)   may grant 1 or more temporary or permanent injunctions on such terms as the court determines to be reasonable to prevent or restrain a violation of subsection (a);

(B)   at any time while the action is pending, may order the impounding, on such terms as the court determines to be reasonable, of any article that is in the custody or control of the alleged violator and that the court has reasonable cause to believe was involved in a violation of subsection (a); and

(C)   may award to the injured party—

(i)   reasonable attorney fees and costs; and

(ii)(I) actual damages and any additional profits of the violator, as provided in paragraph (3); or

(II)  statutory damages, as provided in paragraph (4).

(3)   Actual damages and profits.

(A)   In general. The injured party is entitled to recover—

(i)   the actual damages suffered by the injured party as a result of a violation of subsection (a), as provided in subparagraph (B) of this paragraph; and

(ii)   any profits of the violator that are attributable to a violation of subsection (a) and are not taken into account in computing the actual damages.

(B)   Calculation of damages. The court shall calculate actual damages by multiplying—

(i)   the value of the phonorecords, copies, or works of visual art which are, or are intended to be, affixed with, enclosed in, or accompanied by any counterfeit labels, illicit labels, or counterfeit documentation or packaging, by

(ii)   the number of phonorecords, copies, or works of visual art which are, or are intended to be, affixed with, enclosed in, or accompanied by any counterfeit labels, illicit labels, or counterfeit documentation or packaging.

(C)   Definition. For purposes of this paragraph, the "value" of a phonorecord, copy, or work of visual art is—

(i)   in the case of a copyrighted sound recording or copyrighted musical work, the retail value of an authorized phonorecord of that sound recording or musical work;

(ii)   in the case of a copyrighted computer program, the retail value of an authorized copy of that computer program;

(iii)   in the case of a copyrighted motion picture or other audiovisual work, the retail value of an authorized copy of that motion picture or audiovisual work;

(iv)   in the case of a copyrighted literary work, the retail value of an authorized copy of that literary work;

(v)   in the case of a pictorial, graphic, or sculptural work, the retail value of an authorized copy of that work; and

(vi)   in the case of a work of visual art, the retail value of that work.

(4)   Statutory damages. The injured party may elect, at any time before final judgment is rendered, to recover, instead of actual damages and profits, an award of statutory damages for each violation of subsection (a) in a sum of not less than $2,500 or more than $25,000, as the court considers appropriate.

(5)   Subsequent violation. The court may increase an award of damages under this subsection by 3 times the amount that would otherwise be awarded, as the court considers appropriate, if the court finds that a person has subsequently violated subsection (a) within 3 years after a final judgment was entered against that person for a violation of that subsection.

(6)   Limitation on actions. A civil action may not be commenced under this subsection unless it is commenced within 3 years after the date on which the claimant discovers the violation of subsection (a).

## 18 U.S.C.A. § 2319.   Criminal Infringement of a Copyright

(a)   Any person who violates section 506(a) (relating to criminal offenses) of title 17 shall be punished as provided in subsections (b), (c), and (d) and such penalties shall be in addition to any other provisions of title 17 or any other law.

(b)   Any person who commits an offense under section 506(a)(1)(A) of title 17—

(1)   shall be imprisoned not more than 5 years, or fined in the amount set forth in this title, or both, if the offense consists of the reproduction or distribution, including by electronic means,

during any 180-day period, of at least 10 copies or phonorecords, of 1 or more copyrighted works, which have a total retail value of more than $2,500;

(2)   shall be imprisoned not more than 10 years, or fined in the amount set forth in this title, or both, if the offense is a felony and is a second or subsequent offense under subsection (a); and

(3)   shall be imprisoned not more than 1 year, or fined in the amount set forth in this title, or both, in any other case.

(c)   Any person who commits an offense under section 506(a)(1)(B) of title 17—

(1)   shall be imprisoned not more than 3 years, or fined in the amount set forth in this title, or both, if the offense consists of the reproduction or distribution of 10 or more copies or phonorecords of 1 or more copyrighted works, which have a total retail value of $2,500 or more;

(2)   shall be imprisoned not more than 6 years, or fined in the amount set forth in this title, or both, if the offense is a felony and is a second or subsequent offense under subsection (a); and

(3)   shall be imprisoned not more than 1 year, or fined in the amount set forth in this title, or both, if the offense consists of the reproduction or distribution of 1 or more copies or phonorecords of 1 or more copyrighted works, which have a total retail value of more than $1,000.

(d)   Any person who commits an offense under section 506(a)(1)(C) of title 17—

(1)   shall be imprisoned not more than 3 years, fined under this title, or both;

(2)   shall be imprisoned not more than 5 years, fined under this title, or both, if the offense was committed for purposes of commercial advantage or private commercial gain;

(3)   shall be imprisoned not more than 6 years, fined under this title, or both, if the offense is a felony and is a second or subsequent offense under subsection (a); and

(4)   shall be imprisoned not more than 10 years, fined under this title, or both, if the offense is a felony and is a second or subsequent offense under paragraph (2).

(e)(1)   During preparation of the presentence report pursuant to Rule 32(c) of the Federal Rules of Criminal Procedure, victims of the offense shall be permitted to submit, and the probation officer shall receive, a victim impact statement that identifies the victim of the offense and the extent and scope of the injury and loss suffered by the victim, including the estimated economic impact of the offense on that victim.

(2)   Persons permitted to submit victim impact statements shall include—

(A)   producers and sellers of legitimate works affected by conduct involved in the offense;

(B)   holders of intellectual property rights in such works; and

(C)   the legal representatives of such producers, sellers, and holders.

(f)   As used in this section—

(1)   the terms "phonorecord" and "copies" have, respectively, the meanings set forth in section 101 (relating to definitions) of title 17;

(2)   the terms "reproduction" and "distribution" refer to the exclusive rights of a copyright owner under clauses (1) and (3) respectively of section 106 (relating to exclusive rights in copyrighted works), as limited by sections 107 through 122, of title 17;

(3)   the term "financial gain" has the meaning given the term in section 101 of title 17; and

(4)   the term "work being prepared for commercial distribution" has the meaning given the term in section 506(a) of title 17.

## 18 U.S.C.A. § 2319A. Unauthorized Fixation of and Trafficking in Sound Recordings and Music Videos of Live Musical Performances

**(a) Offense.**—Whoever, without the consent of the performer or performers involved, knowingly and for purposes of commercial advantage or private financial gain—

(1) fixes the sounds or sounds and images of a live musical performance in a copy or phonorecord, or reproduces copies or phonorecords of such a performance from an unauthorized fixation;

(2) transmits or otherwise communicates to the public the sounds or sounds and images of a live musical performance; or

(3) distributes or offers to distribute, sells or offers to sell, rents or offers to rent, or traffics in any copy or phonorecord fixed as described in paragraph (1), regardless of whether the fixations occurred in the United States;

shall be imprisoned for not more than 5 years or fined in the amount set forth in this title, or both, or if the offense is a second or subsequent offense, shall be imprisoned for not more than 10 years or fined in the amount set forth in this title, or both.

**(b) Forfeiture and Destruction of Property; Restitution.**—Forfeiture, destruction, and restitution relating to this section shall be subject to section 2323, to the extent provided in that section, in addition to any other similar remedies provided by law.

**(c) Seizure and Forfeiture.**—If copies or phonorecords of sounds or sounds and images of a live musical performance are fixed outside of the United States without the consent of the performer or performers involved, such copies or phonorecords are subject to seizure and forfeiture in the United States in the same manner as property imported in violation of the customs laws. The Secretary of Homeland Security shall issue regulations by which any performer may, upon payment of a specified fee, be entitled to notification by United States Customs and Border Protection of the importation of copies or phonorecords that appear to consist of unauthorized fixations of the sounds or sounds and images of a live musical performance.

**(d) Victim Impact Statement.**—

(1) During preparation of the presentence report pursuant to Rule 32(c) of the Federal Rules of Criminal Procedure, victims of the offense shall be permitted to submit, and the probation officer shall receive, a victim impact statement that identifies the victim of the offense and the extent and scope of the injury and loss suffered by the victim, including the estimated economic impact of the offense on that victim.

(2) Persons permitted to submit victim impact statements shall include—

(A) producers and sellers of legitimate works affected by conduct involved in the offense;

(B) holders of intellectual property rights in such works; and

(C) the legal representatives of such producers, sellers, and holders.

**(e) Definitions.**—As used in this section—

(1) the terms "copy", "fixed", "musical work", "phonorecord", "reproduce", "sound recordings", and "transmit" mean those terms within the meaning of title 17; and

(2) the term "traffic" has the same meaning as in section 2320(e) of this title.

**(f) Applicability.**—This section shall apply to any act or acts that occur on or after the date of the enactment of the Uruguay Round Agreements Act.

## 18 U.S.C.A. § 2319B. Unauthorized Recording of Motion Pictures in a Motion Picture Exhibition Facility

(a) **Offense.**—Any person who, without the authorization of the copyright owner, knowingly uses or attempts to use an audiovisual recording device to transmit or make a copy of a motion picture or other audiovisual work protected under title 17, or any part thereof, from a performance of such work in a motion picture exhibition facility, shall—

(1)   be imprisoned for not more than 3 years, fined under this title, or both; or

(2)   if the offense is a second or subsequent offense, be imprisoned for no more than 6 years, fined under this title, or both. The possession by a person of an audiovisual recording device in a motion picture exhibition facility may be considered as evidence in any proceeding to determine whether that person committed an offense under this subsection, but shall not, by itself, be sufficient to support a conviction of that person for such offense.

(b) **Forfeiture and Destruction of Property; Restitution.**—Forfeiture, destruction, and restitution relating to this section shall be subject to section 2323, to the extent provided in that section, in addition to any other similar remedies provided by law.

(c) **Authorized Activities.**—This section does not prevent any lawfully authorized investigative, protective, or intelligence activity by an officer, agent, or employee of the United States, a State, or a political subdivision of a State, or by a person acting under a contract with the United States, a State, or a political subdivision of a State.

(d) **Immunity for Theaters**.—With reasonable cause, the owner or lessee of a motion picture exhibition facility where a motion picture or other audiovisual work is being exhibited, the authorized agent or employee of such owner or lessee, the licensor of the motion picture or other audiovisual work being exhibited, or the agent or employee of such licensor—

(1)   may detain, in a reasonable manner and for a reasonable time, any person suspected of a violation of this section with respect to that motion picture or audiovisual work for the purpose of questioning or summoning a law enforcement officer; and

(2)   shall not be held liable in any civil or criminal action arising out of a detention under paragraph (1).

(e) **Victim Impact Statement.**—

(1)   **In General.**—During the preparation of the presentence report under rule 32(c) of the Federal Rules of Criminal Procedure, victims of an offense under this section shall be permitted to submit to the probation officer a victim impact statement that identifies the victim of the offense and the extent and scope of the injury and loss suffered by the victim, including the estimated economic impact of the offense on that victim.

(2)   **Contents.**—A victim impact statement submitted under this subsection shall include—

(A)   producers and sellers of legitimate works affected by conduct involved in the offense;

(B)   holders of intellectual property rights in the works described in subparagraph (A); and

(C)   the legal representatives of such producers, sellers, and holders.

(f)   **State Law Not Preempted.**—Nothing in this section may be construed to annul or limit any rights or remedies under the laws of any State.

(g)   **Definitions.**—In this section, the following definitions shall apply:

**(1)  Title 17 Definitions.**—The terms "audiovisual work", "copy", "copyright owner", "motion picture", "motion picture exhibition facility", and "transmit" have, respectively, the meanings given those terms in section 101 of title 17.

**(2)  Audiovisual Recording Device.**—The term "audiovisual recording device" means a digital or analog photographic or video camera, or any other technology or device capable of enabling the recording or transmission of a copyrighted motion picture or other audiovisual work, or any part thereof, regardless of whether audiovisual recording is the sole or primary purpose of the device.

## 18 U.S.C.A. § 2323.    Forfeiture, Destruction, and Restitution

**(a)  Civil Forfeiture.**—

**(1)  Property Subject to Forfeiture.**—The following property is subject to forfeiture to the United States Government:

**(A)**  Any article, the making or trafficking of which is, prohibited under section 506 of title 17, or section 2318, 2319, 2319A, 2319B, or 2320, or chapter 90, of this title.

**(B)**  Any property used, or intended to be used, in any manner or part to commit or facilitate the commission of an offense referred to in subparagraph (A).

**(C)**  Any property constituting or derived from any proceeds obtained directly or indirectly as a result of the commission of an offense referred to in subparagraph (A).

**(2)  Procedures.**—The provisions of chapter 46 relating to civil forfeitures shall extend to any seizure or civil forfeiture under this section. For seizures made under this section, the court shall enter an appropriate protective order with respect to discovery and use of any records or information that has been seized. The protective order shall provide for appropriate procedures to ensure that confidential, private, proprietary, or privileged information contained in such records is not improperly disclosed or used. At the conclusion of the forfeiture proceedings, unless otherwise requested by an agency of the United States, the court shall order that any property forfeited under paragraph (1) be destroyed, or otherwise disposed of according to law.

**(b)  Criminal Forfeiture.**—

**(1)  Property Subject to Forfeiture.**—The court, in imposing sentence on a person convicted of an offense under section 506 of title 17, or section 2318, 2319, 2319A, 2319B, or 2320, or chapter 90, of this title, shall order, in addition to any other sentence imposed, that the person forfeit to the United States Government any property subject to forfeiture under subsection (a) for that offense.

**(2)  Procedures.**—

**(A)  In General.**—The forfeiture of property under paragraph (1), including any seizure and disposition of the property and any related judicial or administrative proceeding, shall be governed by the procedures set forth in section 413 of the Comprehensive Drug Abuse Prevention and Control Act of 1970 (21 U.S.C. 853), other than subsection (d) of that section.

**(B)  Destruction.**—At the conclusion of the forfeiture proceedings, the court, unless otherwise requested by an agency of the United States shall order that any—

**(i)**  forfeited article or component of an article bearing or consisting of a counterfeit mark be destroyed or otherwise disposed of according to law; and

**(ii)**  infringing items or other property described in subsection (a)(1)(A) and forfeited under paragraph (1) of this subsection be destroyed or otherwise disposed of according to law.

**(c) Restitution.**—When a person is convicted of an offense under section 506 of title 17 or section 2318, 2319, 2319A, 2319B, or 2320, or chapter 90, of this title, the court, pursuant to sections 3556, 3663A, and 3664 of this title, shall order the person to pay restitution to any victim of the offense as an offense against property referred to in section 3663A(c)(1)(A)(ii) of this title.

# APPENDIX C

# COPYRIGHT ACT OF 1909, AS AMENDED

## CHAPTER 1.—REGISTRATION OF COPYRIGHTS

## § 1.    Exclusive rights as to copyrighted works

Any person entitled thereto, upon complying with the provisions of this title, shall have the exclusive right:

(a)  To print, reprint, publish, copy, and vend the copyrighted work;

(b)  To translate the copyrighted work into other languages or dialects, or make any other version thereof, if it be a literary work; to dramatize it if it be a nondramatic work; to convert it into a novel or other nondramatic work if it be a drama; to arrange or adapt it if it be a musical work; to complete, execute, and finish it if it be a model or design for a work of art;

(c)  To deliver, authorize the delivery of, read, or present the copyrighted work in public for profit if it be a lecture, sermon, address or similar production, or other nondramatic literary work; to make or procure the making of any transcription or record thereof by or from which, in whole or in part, it may in any manner or by any method be exhibited, delivered, presented, produced, or reproduced; and to play or perform it in public for profit, and to exhibit, represent, produce, or reproduce it in any manner or by any method whatsoever. The damages for the infringement by broadcast of any work referred to in this subsection shall not exceed the sum of $100 where the infringing broadcaster shows that he was not aware that he was infringing and that such infringement could not have been reasonably foreseen; and

(d)  To perform or represent the copyrighted work publicly if it be a drama or, if it be a dramatic work and not reproduced in copies for sale, to vend any manuscript or any record whatsoever thereof; to make or to procure the making of any transcription or record thereof by or from which, in whole or in part, it may in any manner or by any method be exhibited, performed, represented, produced, or reproduced; and to exhibit, perform, represent, produce, or reproduce it in any manner or by any method whatsoever; and

(e)  To perform the copyrighted work publicly for profit if it be a musical composition; and for the purpose of public performance for profit, and for the purposes set forth in subsection (a) hereof, to make any arrangement or setting of it or of the melody of it in any system of notation or any form of record in which the thought of an author may be recorded and from which it may be read or reproduced: *Provided*, That the provisions of this title, so far as they secure copyright controlling the parts of instruments serving to reproduce mechanically the musical work, shall include only compositions published and copyrighted after July 1, 1909, and shall not include the works of a foreign author or composer unless the foreign state or nation of which such author or composer is a citizen or subject grants, either by treaty, convention, agreement, or law, to citizens of the United States similar rights. And as a condition of extending the copyrighted control to such mechanical reproductions, that whenever the owner of a musical copyright has used or permitted or knowingly acquiesced in the use of the copyrighted work upon the parts of instruments serving to reproduce mechanically the musical work, any other person may make similar use of the copyrighted work upon the payment to the copyright proprietor of a royalty of 2 cents on each such part manufactured, to be paid by the manufacturer thereof; and the copyright proprietor may require, and if so the manufacturer shall furnish, a report under oath on the 20th day of each month on the number of parts of instruments manufactured during the previous month serving to reproduce mechanically said musical work, and royalties shall be due on the parts manufactured during any month upon the 20th of the next succeeding month. The payment of the royalty provided for by this section shall free the articles or devices for which such royalty has been paid from further contribution to the copyright except in case of public performance for profit. It shall be the duty of the copyright owner, if he uses the musical composition himself for the manufacture of parts of instruments serving to reproduce mechanically the musical work, or licenses others to do so, to file notice thereof, accompanied by a recording fee, in the Copyright Office, and any failure to file such notice shall be a complete defense to any suit, action, or proceeding for any infringement of such copyright.

In case of failure of such manufacturer to pay to the copyright proprietor within thirty days after demand in writing the full sum of royalties due at said rate at the date of such demand, the court may award taxable costs to the plaintiff and a reasonable counsel fee, and the court may, in its discretion, enter judgment therein for any sum in addition over the amount found to be due as royalty in accordance with the terms of this title, not exceeding three times such amount.

The reproduction or rendition of a musical composition by or upon coin-operated machines shall not be deemed a public performance for profit unless a fee is charged for admission to the place where such reproduction or rendition occurs.

(f)  To reproduce and distribute to the public by sale or other transfer of ownership, or by rental, lease, or lending, reproductions of the copyrighted work if it be a sound recording: *Provided,* That the exclusive right of the owner of a copyright in a sound recording to reproduce it is limited to the right to duplicate the sound recording in a tangible form that directly or indirectly recaptures the actual sounds fixed in the recording: *Provided further,* That this right does not extend to the making or duplication of another sound recording that is an independent fixation of other sounds, even though such sounds imitate or simulate those in the copyrighted sound recording; or to reproductions made by transmitting organizations exclusively for their own use. July 30, 1947, c. 391, 61 Stat. 652; July 17, 1952, c. 923, § 1, 66 Stat. 752; Oct. 15, 1971, Pub.L. 92–140, § 1(a), 85 Stat. 391.

## § 2.  Rights of author or proprietor of unpublished work

Nothing in this title shall be construed to annul or limit the right of the author or proprietor of an unpublished work, at common law or in equity, to prevent the copying, publication, or use of such unpublished work without his consent, and to obtain damages therefor. July 30, 1947, c. 391, 61 Stat. 654.

## § 3.  Protection of component parts of work copyrighted; composite works or periodicals

The copyright provided by this title shall protect all the copyrightable component parts of the work copyrighted, and all matter therein in which copyright is already subsisting, but without extending the duration or scope of such copyright. The copyright upon composite works or periodicals shall give to the proprietor thereof all the rights in respect thereto which he would have if each part were individually copyrighted under this title. July 30, 1947, c. 391, 61 Stat. 654; Oct. 31, 1951, c. 655, § 16(a), 65 Stat. 716.

## § 4.  All writings of author included

The works for which copyright may be secured under this title shall include all the writings of an author. July 30, 1947, c. 391, 61 Stat. 654.

## § 5.  Classification of works for registration

The application for registration shall specify to which of the following classes the work in which copyright is claimed belongs:

(a)  Books, including composite and cyclopedic works, directories, gazetteers, and other compilations.

(b)  Periodicals, including newspapers.

(c)  Lectures, sermons, addresses (prepared for oral delivery).

(d)  Dramatic or dramatico-musical compositions.

(e)  Musical compositions.

(f)  Maps.

(g)  Works of art; models or designs for works of art.

(h)  Reproductions of a work of art.

(i)   Drawings or plastic works of a scientific or technical character.

(j)   Photographs.

(k)   Prints and pictorial illustrations including prints or labels used for articles of merchandise.

(l)   Motion-picture photoplays.

(m)  Motion pictures other than photoplays.

(n)   Sound recordings.

The above specifications shall not be held to limit the subject matter of copyright as defined in section 4 of this title, nor shall any error in classification invalidate or impair the copyright protection secured under this title. July 30, 1947, c. 391, 61 Stat. 654; Oct. 15, 1971, Pub.L. 92–140, § 1(b), 85 Stat. 391.

## § 6.    Registration of prints and labels

Commencing July 1, 1940, the Register of Copyrights is charged with the registration of claims to copyright properly presented, in all prints and labels published in connection with the sale or advertisement of articles of merchandise, including all claims to copyright in prints and labels pending in the Patent Office and uncleared at the close of business June 30, 1940. There shall be paid for registering a claim of copyright in any such print or label not a trade-mark $6, which sum shall cover the expense of furnishing a certificate of such registration, under the seal of the Copyright Office, to the claimant of copyright. July 30, 1947, c. 391, 61 Stat. 654.

## § 7.    Copyright on compilations of works in public domain or of copyrighted works; subsisting copyrights not affected

Compilations or abridgements, adaptations, arrangements, dramatizations, translations, or other versions of works in the public domain or of copyrighted works when produced with the consent of the proprietor of the copyright in such works, or works republished with new matter, shall be regarded as new works subject to copyright under the provisions of this title; but the publication of any such new works shall not affect the force or validity of any subsisting copyright upon the matter employed or any part thereof, or be construed to imply an exclusive right to such use of the original works, or to secure or extend copyright in such original works. July 30, 1947, c. 391, 61 Stat. 655.

## § 8.    Copyright not to subsist in works in public domain, or published prior to July 1, 1909, and not already copyrighted, or Government publications; publication by Government of copyrighted material

No copyright shall subsist in the original text of any work which is in the public domain, or in any work which was published in this country or any foreign country prior to July 1, 1909, and has not been already copyrighted in the United States, or in any publication of the United States Government, or any reprint, in whole or in part, thereof, except that the United States Postal Service may secure copyright on behalf of the United States in the whole or any part of the publications authorized by section 405 of title 39.

The publication or republication by the Government, either separately or in a public document, of any material in which copyright is subsisting shall not be taken to cause any abridgment or annulment of the copyright or to authorize any use or appropriation of such copyright material without the consent of the copyright proprietor. July 30, 1947, c. 391, 61 Stat. 655; Oct. 31, 1951, c. 655, § 16(b), 65 Stat. 716; Sept. 7, 1962, Pub.L. 87–646, § 21, 76 Stat. 446; Aug. 12, 1970, Pub.L. 91–375, § 6(i), 84 Stat. 777.

## § 9.   Authors or proprietors, entitled; aliens

The author or proprietor of any work made the subject of copyright by this title, or his executors, administrators, or assigns, shall have copyright for such work under the conditions and for the terms specified in this title: *Provided, however,* That the copyright secured by this title shall extend to the work of an author or proprietor who is a citizen or subject of a foreign state or nation only under the conditions described in subsections (a), (b), or (c) below:

(a)   When an alien author or proprietor shall be domiciled within the United States at the time of the first publication of his work; or

(b)   When the foreign state or nation of which such author or proprietor is a citizen or subject grants, either by treaty, convention, agreement, or law, to citizens of the United States the benefit of copyright on substantially the same basis as to its own citizens, or copyright protection, substantially equal to the protection secured to such foreign author under this title or by treaty; or when such foreign state or nation is a party to an international agreement which provides for reciprocity in the granting of copyright, by the terms of which agreement the United States may, at its pleasure, become a party thereto.

The existence of the reciprocal conditions aforesaid shall be determined by the President of the United States, by proclamation made from time to time, as the purposes of this title may require: *Provided,* That whenever the President shall find that the authors, copyright owners, or proprietors of works first produced or published abroad and subject to copyright or to renewal of copyright under the laws of the United States, including works subject to ad interim copyright, are or may have been temporarily unable to comply with the conditions and formalities prescribed with respect to such works by the copyright laws of the United States, because of the disruption or suspension of facilities essential for such compliance, he may by proclamation grant such extension of time as he may deem appropriate for the fulfillment of such conditions or formalities by authors, copyright owners, or proprietors who are citizens of the United States or who are nationals of countries which accord substantially equal treatment in this respect to authors, copyright owners, or proprietors who are citizens of the United States: *Provided further,* That no liability shall attach under this title for lawful uses made or acts done prior to the effective date of such proclamation in connection with such works, or in respect to the continuance for one year subsequent to such date of any business undertaking or enterprise lawfully undertaken prior to such date involving expenditure or contractual obligation in connection with the exploitation, production, reproduction, circulation, or performance of any such work.

The President may at any time terminate any proclamation authorized herein or any part thereof or suspend or extend its operation for such period or periods of time as in his judgment the interests of the United States may require.

(c)   When the Universal Copyright Convention, signed at Geneva on September 6, 1952, shall be in force between the United States of America and the foreign state or nation of which such author is a citizen or subject, or in which the work was first published. Any work to which copyright is extended pursuant to this subsection shall be exempt from the following provisions of this title: (1) The requirement in section 1(e) that a foreign state or nation must grant to United States citizens mechanical reproduction rights similar to those specified therein; (2) the obligatory deposit requirements of the first sentence of section 13; (3) the provisions of sections 14, 16, 17, and 18; (4) the import prohibitions of section 107, to the extent that they are related to the manufacturing requirements of section 16; and (5) the requirements of sections 19 and 20: *Provided, however,* That such exemptions shall apply only if from the time of first publication all the copies of the work published with the authority of the author or other copyright proprietor shall bear the symbol © accompanied by the name of the copyright proprietor and the year of first publication placed in such manner and location as to give reasonable notice of claim of copyright.

Upon the coming into force of the Universal Copyright Convention in a foreign state or nation as hereinbefore provided, every book or periodical of a citizen or subject thereof in which ad interim copyright was subsisting on the effective date of said coming into force shall have copyright for twenty-eight years from the date of first publication abroad without the necessity of complying with the further formalities specified in section 23 of this title.

The provisions of this subsection shall not be extended to works of an author who is a citizen of, or domiciled in the United States of America regardless of place of first publication, or to works first published in the United States. July 30, 1947, c. 391, 61 Stat. 655; Aug. 31, 1954, c. 1161, § 1, 68 Stat. 1030.

### § 10.     Publication of work with notice

Any person entitled thereto by this title may secure copyright for his work by publication thereof with the notice of copyright required by this title; and such notice shall be affixed to each copy thereof published or offered for sale in the United States by authority of the copyright proprietor, except in the case of books seeking ad interim protection under section 22 of this title. July 30, 1947, c. 391, 61 Stat. 656.

### § 11.     Registration of claim and issuance of certificate

Such person may obtain registration of his claim to copyright by complying with the provisions of this title, including the deposit of copies, and upon such compliance the Register of Copyrights shall issue to him the certificates provided for in section 209 of this title. July 30, 1947, c. 391, 61 Stat. 656.

### § 12.     Works not reproduced for sale

Copyright may also be had of the works of an author, of which copies are not reproduced for sale, by the deposit, with claim of copyright, of one complete copy of such work if it be a lecture or similar production or a dramatic, musical, or dramatico-musical composition; of a title and description, with one print taken from each scene or act, if the work be a motion-picture photoplay; of a photographic print if the work be a photograph; of a title and description, with not less than two prints taken from different sections of a complete motion picture, if the work be a motion picture other than a photoplay; or of a photograph or other identifying reproduction thereof, if it be a work of art or a plastic work or drawing. But the privilege of registration of copyright secured hereunder shall not exempt the copyright proprietor from the deposit of copies, under sections 13 and 14 of this title, where the work is later reproduced in copies for sale. July 30, 1947, c. 391, 61 Stat. 656.

### § 13.     Deposit of copies after publication; action or proceeding for infringement

After copyright has been secured by publication of the work with the notice of copyright as provided in section 10 of this title, there shall be promptly deposited in the Copyright Office or in the mail addressed to the Register of Copyrights, Washington, District of Columbia, two complete copies of the best edition thereof then published, or if the work is by an author who is a citizen or subject of a foreign state or nation and has been published in a foreign country, one complete copy of the best edition then published in such foreign country, which copies or copy, if the work be a book or periodical, shall have been produced in accordance with the manufacturing provisions specified in section 16 of this title; or if such work be a contribution to a periodical, for which contribution special registration is requested, one copy of the issue or issues containing such contribution; or if the work belongs to a class specified in subsections (g), (h), (i) or (k) of section 5 of this title, and if the Register of Copyrights determines that it is impracticable to deposit copies because of their size, weight, fragility, or monetary value he may permit the deposit of photographs or other identifying reproductions in lieu of copies of the work as published under such rules and regulations as he may prescribe with the approval of the Librarian of Congress; or if the work is not reproduced in copies for sale there shall be deposited the copy, print, photograph, or other identifying reproduction provided by section 12 of this title, such copies or copy, print, photograph, or other reproduction to be accompanied in each case by a claim of copyright. No action or proceeding shall be maintained for infringement of copyright in any work until the provisions of this title with respect to the deposit of copies and registration of such work shall have been complied with. July 30, 1947, c. 391, 61 Stat. 656; Mar. 29, 1956, c. 109, 70 Stat. 63.

## § 14. Deposit of copies after publication; failure to deposit; demand; penalty

Should the copies called for by section 13 of this title not be promptly deposited as provided in this title, the Register of Copyrights may at any time after the publication of the work, upon actual notice, require the proprietor of the copyright to deposit them, and after the said demand shall have been made, in default of the deposit of copies of the work within three months from any part of the United States, except an outlying territorial possession of the United States, or within six months from any outlying territorial possession of the United States, or from any foreign country, the proprietor of the copyright shall be liable to a fine of $100 and to pay to the Library of Congress twice the amount of the retail price of the best edition of the work, and the copyright shall become void. July 30, 1947, c. 391, 61 Stat. 657.

## § 15. Deposit of copies after publication; postmaster's receipt; transmission by mail without cost

The postmaster to whom are delivered the articles deposited as provided in sections 12 and 13 of this title shall, if requested, give a receipt therefor and shall mail them to their destination without cost to the copyright claimant. July 30, 1947, c. 391, 61 Stat. 657.

## § 16. Mechanical work to be done in United States

Of the printed book or periodical specified in section 5, subsections (a) and (b), of this title, except the original text of a book or periodical of foreign origin in a language or languages other than English, the text of all copies accorded protection under this title, except as below provided, shall be printed from type set within the limits of the United States, either by hand or by the aid of any kind of typesetting machine, or from plates made within the limits of the United States from type set therein, or, if the text be produced by lithographic process, or photoengraving process, then by a process wholly performed within the limits of the United States, and the printing of the text and binding of the said book shall be performed within the limits of the United States; which requirements shall extend also to the illustrations within a book consisting of printed text and illustrations produced by lithographic process, or photoengraving process, and also to separate lithographs or photoengravings, except where in either case the subjects represented are located in a foreign country and illustrate a scientific work or reproduce a work of art: *Provided, however,* That said requirements shall not apply to works in raised characters for the use of the blind, or to books or periodicals of foreign origin in a language or languages other than English, or to works printed or produced in the United States by any other process than those above specified in this section, or to copies of books or periodicals, first published abroad in the English language, imported into the United States within five years after first publication in a foreign state or nation up to the number of fifteen hundred copies of each such book or periodical if said copies shall contain notice of copyright in accordance with sections 10, 19, and 20 of this title and if ad interim copyright in said work shall have been obtained pursuant to section 22 of this title prior to the importation into the United States of any copy except those permitted by the provisions of section 107 of this title: *Provided further,* That the provisions of this section shall not affect the right of importation under the provisions of section 107 of this title. July 30, 1947, c. 391, 61 Stat. 657; June 3, 1949, c. 171, § 1, 63 Stat. 153; Aug. 31, 1954, c. 1161, § 2, 68 Stat. 1031.

## § 17. Affidavit to accompany copies

In the case of the book the copies so deposited shall be accompanied by an affidavit under the official seal of any officer authorized to administer oaths within the United States, duly made by the person claiming copyright or by his duly authorized agent or representative residing in the United States, or by the printer who has printed the book, setting forth that the copies deposited have been printed from type set within the limits of the United States or from plates made within the limits of the United States from type set therein; or, if the text be produced by lithographic process, or photoengraving process, that such process was wholly performed within the limits of the United States and that the printing of the text and binding of the said book have also been performed within the limits of the United States. Such affidavit shall state also the place where and the establishment or establishments in which such type was set or plates were made or lithographic process, or photoengraving process or printing and binding were performed and the date of the completion of the printing of the book or the date of publication. July 30, 1947, c. 391, 61 Stat. 657.

### § 18.    Making false affidavit

Any person who, for the purpose of obtaining registration of a claim to copyright, shall knowingly make a false affidavit as to his having complied with the above conditions shall be deemed guilty of a misdemeanor, and upon conviction thereof shall be punished by a fine of not more than $1,000, and all of his rights and privileges under said copyright shall thereafter be forfeited. July 30, 1947, c. 391, 61 Stat. 658.

### § 19.    Notice; form

The notice of copyright required by section 10 of this title shall consist either of the word "Copyright", the abbreviation "Copr.", or the symbol ©, accompanied by the name of the copyright proprietor, and if the work be a printed literary, musical, or dramatic work, the notice shall include also the year in which the copyright was secured by publication. In the case, however, of copies of works specified in subsections (f) to (k), inclusive, of section 5 of this title, the notice may consist of the letter C enclosed within a circle, thus ©, accompanied by the initials, monogram, mark, or symbol of the copyright proprietor: *Provided,* That on some accessible portion of such copies or of the margin, back, permanent base, or pedestal, or of the substance on which such copies shall be mounted, his name shall appear. But in the case of works in which copyright was subsisting on July 1, 1909, the notice of copyright may be either in one of the forms prescribed herein or may consist of the following words: "Entered according to Act of Congress, in the year __, by A.B., and in the office of the Librarian of Congress, at Washington, D.C.," or, at his option the word "Copyright", together with the year the copyright was entered and the name of the party by whom it was taken out; thus, "Copyright, 19__, by A.B."

In the case of reproductions of works specified in subsection (n) of section 5 of this title, the notice shall consist of the symbol Ⓟ (the letter P in a circle), the year of first publication of the sound recording, and the name of the owner of copyright in the sound recording, or an abbreviation by which the name can be recognized, or a generally known alternative designation of the owner: *Provided,* That if the producer of the sound recording is named on the labels or containers of the reproduction, and if no other name appears in conjunction with the notice, his name shall be considered a part of the notice. July 30, 1947, c. 391, 61 Stat. 658; Aug. 31, 1954, c. 1161, § 3, 68 Stat. 1032; Oct. 15, 1971, Pub.L. 92–140, § 1(c), 85 Stat. 391.

### § 20.    Notice; place of application of; one notice in each volume or number of newspaper or periodical

The notice of copyright shall be applied, in the case of a book or other printed publication, upon its title page or the page immediately following, or if a periodical either upon the title page or upon the first page of text of each separate number or under the title heading, or if a musical work either upon its title page or the first page of music, or if a sound recording on the surface of reproductions thereof or on the label or container in such manner and location as to give reasonable notice of the claim of copyright. One notice of copyright in each volume or in each number of a newspaper or periodical published shall suffice. July 30, 1947, c. 391, 61 Stat. 658; Oct. 15, 1971, Pub.L. 92–140, § 1(d), 85 Stat. 391.

## § 21.    Notice; effect of accidental omission from copy or copies

Where the copyright proprietor has sought to comply with the provisions of this title with respect to notice, the omission by accident or mistake of the prescribed notice from a particular copy or copies shall not invalidate the copyright or prevent recovery for infringement against any person who, after actual notice of the copyright, begins an undertaking to infringe it, but shall prevent the recovery of damages against an innocent infringer who has been misled by the omission of the notice; and in a suit for infringement no permanent injunction shall be had unless the copyright proprietor shall reimburse to the innocent infringer his reasonable outlay innocently incurred if the court, in its discretion, shall so direct. July 30, 1947, c. 391, 61 Stat. 658.

## § 22.    Ad interim protection of book or periodical published abroad

In the case of a book or periodical first published abroad in the English language the deposit in the Copyright Office, not later than six months after its publication abroad, of one complete copy of the foreign edition, with a request for the reservation of the copyright and a statement of the name and nationality of the author and of the copyright proprietor and of the date of publication of the said book or periodical, shall secure to the author or proprietor an ad interim copyright therein, which shall have all the force and effect given to copyright by this title, and shall endure until the expiration of five years after the date of first publication abroad. July 30, 1947, c. 391, 61 Stat. 659; June 3, 1949, c. 171, § 2, 63 Stat. 154.

## § 23.    Ad interim protection of book or periodical published abroad; extension to full term

Whenever within the period of such ad interim protection an authorized edition of such books or periodicals shall be published within the United States, in accordance with the manufacturing provisions specified in section 16 of this title, and whenever the provisions of this title as to deposit of copies, registration, filing of affidavits, and the printing of the copyright notice shall have been duly complied with, the copyright shall be extended to endure in such book or periodical for the term provided in this title. July 30, 1947, c. 391, 61 Stat. 659; June 3, 1949, c. 171, § 3, 63 Stat. 154.

## § 24.    Duration, renewal and extension

The copyright secured by this title shall endure for twenty-eight years from the date of first publication, whether the copyrighted work bears the author's true name or is published anonymously or under an assumed name: *Provided,* That in the case of any posthumous work or of any periodical, cyclopedic, or other composite work upon which the copyright was originally secured by the proprietor thereof, or of any work copyrighted by a corporate body (otherwise than as assignee or licensee of the individual author) or by an employer for whom such work is made for hire, the proprietor of such copyright shall be entitled to a renewal and extension of the copyright in such work for the further term of twenty-eight years when application for such renewal and extension shall have been made to the Copyright Office and duly registered therein within one year prior to the expiration of the original term of copyright: *And provided further,* That in the case of any other copyrighted work, including a contribution by an individual author to a periodical or to a cyclopedic or other composite work, the author of such work, if still living, or the widow, widower, or children of the author, if the author be not living, or if such author, widow, widower or children be not living, then the author's executors, or in the absence of a will, his next of kin shall be entitled to a renewal and extension of the copyright in such work for a further term of twenty-eight years when application for such renewal and extension shall have been made to the Copyright Office and duly registered therein within one year prior to the expiration of the original term of copyright: *And provided further,* That in default of the registration of such application for renewal and extension, the copyright in any work shall determine at the expiration of twenty-eight years from first publication. July 30, 1947, c. 391, 61 Stat. 659.

### § 25.    Renewal of copyrights registered in Patent Office under repealed law

Subsisting copyrights originally registered in the Patent Office prior to July 1, 1940, under section 3 of the act of June 18, 1874, shall be subject to renewal in behalf of the proprietor upon application made to the Register of Copyrights within one year prior to the expiration of the original term of twenty-eight years. July 30, 1947, c. 391, 61 Stat. 659.

### § 26.    Terms defined

In the interpretation and construction of this title "the date of publication" shall in the case of a work of which copies are reproduced for sale or distribution be held to be the earliest date when copies of the first authorized edition were placed on sale, sold, or publicly distributed by the proprietor of the copyright or under his authority, and the word "author" shall include an employer in the case of works made for hire.

For the purposes of this section and sections 10, 11, 13, 14, 21, 101, 106, 109, 209, 215, but not for any other purpose, a reproduction of a work described in subsection 5(n) shall be considered to be a copy thereof. "Sound recordings" are works that result from the fixation of a series of musical, spoken, or other sounds, but not including the sounds accompanying a motion picture. "Reproductions of sound recordings" are material objects in which sounds other than those accompanying a motion picture are fixed by any method now known or later developed, and from which the sounds can be perceived, reproduced, or otherwise communicated, either directly or with the aid of a machine or device, and include the "parts of instruments serving to reproduce mechanically the musical work", "mechanical reproductions", and "interchangeable parts, such as discs or tapes for use in mechanical music-producing machines" referred to in sections 1(e) and 101(e) of this title. July 30, 1947, c. 391, 61 Stat. 659; Oct. 15, 1971, Pub.L. 92–140, § 1(e), 85 Stat. 391.

### § 27.    Copyright distinct from property in object copyrighted; effect of sale of object, and of assignment of copyright

The copyright is distinct from the property in the material object copyrighted, and the sale or conveyance, by gift or otherwise, of the material object shall not of itself constitute a transfer of the copyright, nor shall the assignment of the copyright constitute a transfer of the title to the material object; but nothing in this title shall be deemed to forbid, prevent, or restrict the transfer of any copy of a copyrighted work the possession of which has been lawfully obtained. July 30, 1947, c. 391, 61 Stat. 660.

### § 28.    Assignments and bequests

Copyright secured under this title or previous copyright laws of the United States may be assigned, granted, or mortgaged by an instrument in writing signed by the proprietor of the copyright, or may be bequeathed by will. July 30, 1947, c. 391, 61 Stat. 660.

### § 29.    Assignments and bequests; executed in foreign country; acknowledgment and certificate

Every assignment of copyright executed in a foreign country shall be acknowledged by the assignor before a consular officer or secretary of legation of the United States authorized by law to administer oaths or perform notarial acts. The certificate of such acknowledgment under the hand and official seal of such consular officer or secretary of legation shall be prima facie evidence of the execution of the instrument. July 30, 1947, c. 391, 61 Stat. 660.

### § 30.    Assignments and bequests; record

Every assignment of copyright shall be recorded in the Copyright Office within three calendar months after its execution in the United States or within six calendar months after its execution without the limits of the United States, in default of which it shall be void as against any subsequent purchaser or mortgagee for a valuable consideration, without notice, whose assignment has been duly recorded. July 30, 1947, c. 391, 61 Stat. 660.

## § 31. Assignments and bequests; certificate of record

The Register of Copyrights shall, upon payment of the prescribed fee, record such assignment, and shall return it to the sender with a certificate of record attached under seal of the Copyright Office, and upon the payment of the fee prescribed by this title he shall furnish to any person requesting the same a certified copy thereof under the said seal. July 30, 1947, c. 391, 61 Stat. 660.

## § 32. Assignments and bequests; use of name of assignee in notice

When an assignment of the copyright in a specified book or other work has been recorded the assignee may substitute his name for that of the assignor in the statutory notice of copyright prescribed by this title. July 30, 1947, c. 391, 61 Stat. 660.

## CHAPTER 2.—INFRINGEMENT PROCEEDINGS

Sec.
101.     Infringement.
    (a)     Injunction.
    (b)     Damages and profits; amount; other remedies.
    (c)     Impounding during action.
    (d)     Destruction of infringing copies and plates.
    (e)     Interchangeable parts for use in mechanical music-producing machines.
102, 103.     [Repealed.]
104.     Willful infringement for profit.
105.     Fraudulent notice of copyright, or removal or alteration of notice.
106.     Importation of article bearing false notice or piratical copies of copyrighted work.
107.     Importation, during existence of copyright, or piratical copies, or of copies not produced in accordance with Section 16 of this title.
108.     Forfeiture and destruction of articles prohibited importation.
109.     Importation of prohibited articles; regulations; proof of deposit of copies by complainants.
110, 111.     [Repealed.]
112.     Injunctions; service and enforcement.
113.     Transmission of certified copies of papers for enforcement of injunction by other court.
114.     Review of orders, judgments, or decrees.
115.     Limitations.
    (a)     Criminal proceedings.
    (b)     Civil actions.
116.     Costs; attorney's fees.

## § 101. Infringement

If any person shall infringe the copyright in any work protected under the copyright laws of the United States such person shall be liable:

### (a) Injunction

To an injunction restraining such infringement;

### (b) Damages and profits; amount; other remedies

To pay to the copyright proprietor such damages as the copyright proprietor may have suffered due to the infringement, as well as all the profits which the infringer shall have made from such infringement, and in proving profits the plaintiff shall be required to prove sales only, and the defendant shall be required to prove every element of cost which he claims, or in lieu of actual damages and profits, such damages as to the court shall appear to be just, and in assessing such damages the court may, in its discretion, allow the amounts as hereinafter stated, but in case of a newspaper reproduction of a copyrighted photograph, such damages shall not exceed the sum of $200 nor be less than the sum of $50, and in the case of the infringement of an undramatized or nondramatic work by means of motion pictures, where the infringer shall show that he was not aware that he was infringing, and that such infringement could not have been reasonably foreseen, such damages shall not exceed the sum of $100; and in the case of an infringement of a copyrighted dramatic or dramatico-musical work by a maker of motion pictures and his agencies for distribution thereof to exhibitors, where such infringer shows that he was not aware that he was infringing a copyrighted work, and that such infringements could not reasonably have been foreseen, the entire sum of such damages recoverable by the copyright proprietor from such infringing maker and his agencies for the distribution to exhibitors of such infringing motion picture shall not exceed the sum of $5,000 nor be less than $250, and such damages shall in no other case exceed the sum of $5,000 nor be less than the sum of $250, and shall not be regarded as a penalty. But the foregoing exceptions shall not deprive the copyright proprietor of any other remedy given him under this law, nor shall the limitation as to the amount of recovery apply to infringements occurring after the actual notice to a defendant, either by service of process in a suit or other written notice served upon him.

First. In the case of a painting, statue, or sculpture, $10 for every infringing copy made or sold by or found in the possession of the infringer or his agents or employees;

Second. In the case of any work enumerated in section 5 of this title, except a painting, statue, or sculpture, $1 for every infringing copy made or sold by or found in the possession of the infringer or his agents or employees;

Third. In the case of a lecture, sermon, or address, $50 for every infringing delivery;

Fourth. In the case of a dramatic or dramatico-musical or a choral or orchestral composition, $100 for the first and $50 for every subsequent infringing performance; in the case of other musical compositions $10 for every infringing performance;

### (c)  Impounding during action

To deliver up on oath, to be impounded during the pendency of the action, upon such terms and conditions as the court may prescribe, all articles alleged to infringe a copyright;

### (d)  Destruction of infringing copies and plates

To deliver up on oath for destruction all the infringing copies or devices, as well as all plates, molds, matrices, or other means for making such infringing copies as the court may order.

### (e)  Interchangeable parts for use in mechanical music-producing machines

Interchangeable parts, such as discs or tapes for use in mechanical music-producing machines adapted to reproduce copyrighted musical works, shall be considered copies of the copyrighted musical works which they serve to reproduce mechanically for the purposes of this section 101 and sections 106 and 109 of this title, and the unauthorized manufacture, use, or sale of such interchangeable parts shall constitute an infringement of the copyrighted work rendering the infringer liable in accordance with all provisions of this title dealing with infringements of copyright and, in a case of willful infringement for profit, to criminal prosecution pursuant to section 104 of this title. Whenever any person, in the absence of a license agreement, intends to use a copyrighted musical composition upon the parts of instruments serving to reproduce mechanically the musical work, relying upon the compulsory license provision of this title, he shall serve notice of such intention, by registered mail, upon the copyright proprietor at his last address disclosed by the records of the Copyright Office, sending to the Copyright Office a duplicate of such notice. July 30, 1947, c. 391, 61 Stat. 661; June 25, 1948, c. 646, § 39, 62 Stat. 992; Oct. 15, 1971, Pub.L. 92–140, § 2, 85 Stat. 392.

**§§ 102, 103.  Repealed. June 25, 1948, c. 646, § 39, 62 Stat. 992**

## § 104. Willful infringement for profit

(a)   Except as provided in subsection (b), any person who willfully and for profit shall infringe any copyright secured by this title, or who shall knowingly and willfully aid or abet such infringement, shall be deemed guilty of a misdemeanor, and upon conviction thereof shall be punished by imprisonment for not exceeding one year or by a fine of not less than $100 nor more than $1,000, or both, in the discretion of the court: *Provided, however,* That nothing in this title shall be so construed as to prevent the performance of religious or secular works such as oratorios, cantatas, masses, or octavo choruses by public schools, church choirs, or vocal societies, rented, borrowed, or obtained from some public library, public school, church choir, school choir, or vocal society, provided the performance is given for charitable or educational purposes and not for profit.

(b)   Any person who willfully and for profit shall infringe any copyright provided by section 1(f) of this title, or who should knowingly and willfully aid or abet such infringement, shall be fined not more than $25,000 or imprisoned not more than one year, or both, for the first offense and shall be fined not more than $50,000 or imprisoned not more than two years, or both for any subsequent offense. July 30, 1947, c. 391, 61 Stat. 662; Dec. 31, 1974, Pub.L. 93–573, Title I, § 102, 88 Stat. 1873.

## § 105. Fraudulent notice of copyright, or removal or alteration of notice

Any person who, with fraudulent intent, shall insert or impress any notice of copyright required by this title, or words of the same purport, in or upon any uncopyrighted article or with fraudulent intent shall remove or alter the copyright notice upon any article duly copyrighted shall be guilty of a misdemeanor, punishable by a fine of not less than $100 and not more than $1,000. Any person who shall knowingly issue or sell any article bearing a notice of United States copyright which has not been copyrighted in this country, or who shall knowingly import any article bearing such notice or words of the same purport, which has not been copyrighted in this country, shall be liable to a fine of $100. July 30, 1947, c. 391, 61 Stat. 662.

## § 106. Importation of article bearing false notice or piratical copies of copyrighted work

The importation into the United States of any article bearing a false notice of copyright when there is no existing copyright thereon in the United States, or of any piratical copies of any work copyrighted in the United States, is prohibited. July 30, 1947, c. 391, 61 Stat. 663.

## § 107. Importation, during existence of copyright, of piratical copies, or of copies not produced in accordance with Section 16 of this title

During the existence of the American copyright in any book, the importation into the United States of any piratical copies thereof or of any copies thereof (although authorized by the author or proprietor) which have not been produced in accordance with the manufacturing provisions specified in section 16 of this title, or any plates of the same not made from type set within the limits of the United States, or any copies thereof produced by lithographic or photoengraving process not performed within the limits of the United States, in accordance with the provisions of section 16 of this title, is prohibited: *Provided, however,* That, except as regards piratical copies, such prohibition shall not apply:

(a)   To works in raised characters for the use of the blind.

(b)   To a foreign newspaper or magazine, although containing matter copyrighted in the United States printed or reprinted by authority of the copyright proprietor, unless such newspaper or magazine contains also copyright matter printed or reprinted without such authorization.

(c)   To the authorized edition of a book in a foreign language or languages of which only a translation into English has been copyrighted in this country.

(d)   To any book published abroad with the authorization of the author or copyright proprietor when imported under the circumstances stated in one of the four subdivisions following, that is to say:

First. When imported, not more than one copy at one time, for individual use and not for sale; but such privilege of importation shall not extend to a foreign reprint of a book by an American author copyrighted in the United States.

Second. When imported by the authority or for the use of the United States.

Third. When imported, for use and not for sale, not more than one copy of any such book in any one invoice, in good faith by or for any society or institution incorporated for educational, literary, philosophical, scientific, or religious purposes, or for the encouragement of the fine arts, or for any college, academy, school, or seminary of learning, or for any State, school, college, university, or free public library in the United States.

Fourth. When such books form parts of libraries or collections purchased en bloc for the use of societies, institutions, or libraries designated in the foregoing paragraph, or form parts of the libraries or personal baggage belonging to persons or families arriving from foreign countries and are not intended for sale: *Provided,* That copies imported as above may not lawfully be used in any way to violate the rights of the proprietor of the American copyright or annul or limit the copyright protection secured by this title, and such unlawful use shall be deemed an infringement of copyright. July 30, 1947, c. 391, 61 Stat. 663.

## § 108.   Forfeiture and destruction of articles prohibited importation

Any and all articles prohibited importation by this title which are brought into the United States from any foreign country (except in the mails) shall be seized and forfeited by like proceedings as those provided by law for the seizure and condemnation of property imported into the United States in violation of the customs revenue laws. Such articles when forfeited shall be destroyed in such manner as the Secretary of the Treasury or the court, as the case may be, shall direct: *Provided, however,* That all copies of authorized editions of copyright books imported in the mails or otherwise in violation of the provisions of this title may be exported and returned to the country of export whenever it is shown to the satisfaction of the Secretary of the Treasury, in a written application, that such importation does not involve willful negligence or fraud. July 30, 1947, c. 391, 61 Stat. 664.

## § 109.   Importation of prohibited articles; regulations; proof of deposit of copies by complainants

The Secretary of the Treasury and the Postmaster General are hereby empowered and required to make and enforce individually or jointly such rules and regulations as shall prevent the importation into the United States of articles prohibited importation by this title, and may require, as conditions precedent to exclusion of any work in which copyright is claimed, the copyright proprietor or any person claiming actual or potential injury by reason of actual or contemplated importations of copies of such work to file with the Post Office Department or the Treasury Department a certificate of the Register of Copyrights that the provisions of section 13 of this title have been fully complied with, and to give notice of such compliance to postmasters or to customs officers at the ports of entry in the United States in such form and accompanied by such exhibits as may be deemed necessary for the practical and efficient administration and enforcement of the provisions of sections 106 and 107 of this title. July 30, 1947, c. 391, 61 Stat. 664.

## §§ 110, 111.   Repealed. June 25, 1948, c. 646, § 39, 62 Stat. 992

## § 112.   Injunctions; service and enforcement

Any court mentioned in section 1338 of Title 28 or judge thereof shall have power, upon complaint filed by any party aggrieved, to grant injunctions to prevent and restrain the violation of any right secured by this title, according to the course and principles of courts of equity, on such terms as said court or judge may deem reasonable. Any injunction that may be granted restraining and enjoining the doing of anything forbidden by this title may be served on the part against whom such injunction may be granted anywhere in the United States, and shall be operative throughout the United States and be enforceable by proceedings in contempt or otherwise by any other court or judge possessing jurisdiction of the defendants. July 30, 1947, c. 391, 61 Stat. 664; Oct. 31, 1951, c. 655, § 16(c), 65 Stat. 716.

## § 113. Transmission of certified copies of papers for enforcement of injunction by other court

The clerk of the court, or judge granting the injunction, shall when required so to do by the court hearing the application to enforce said injunction, transmit without delay to said court a certified copy of all the papers in said cause that are on file in his office. July 30, 1947, c. 391, 61 Stat. 664.

## § 114. Review of orders, judgments, or decrees

The orders, judgments, or decrees of any court mentioned in section 1338 of Title 28 arising under the copyright laws of the United States may be reviewed on appeal in the manner and to the extent now provided by law for the review of cases determined in said courts, respectively. July 30, 1947, c. 391, 61 Stat. 665; Oct. 31, 1951, c. 655, § 17, 65 Stat. 717.

## § 115. Limitations

### (a) Criminal proceedings

No criminal proceedings shall be maintained under the provisions of this title unless the same is commenced within three years after the cause of action arose.

### (b) Civil actions

No civil action shall be maintained under the provisions of this title unless the same is commenced within three years after the claim accrued. July 30, 1947, c. 391, 61 Stat. 665; Sept. 7, 1957, Pub.L. 85–313, § 1, 71 Stat. 633.

## § 116. Costs; attorney's fees

In all actions, suits, or proceedings under this title, except when brought by or against the United States or any officer thereof, full costs shall be allowed, and the court may award to the prevailing party a reasonable attorney's fee as part of the costs. July 30, 1947, c. 391, 61 Stat. 665.

## CHAPTER 3.—COPYRIGHT OFFICE

## § 201.   Copyright Office; preservation of records

All records and other things relating to copyrights required by law to be preserved shall be kept and preserved in the Copyright Office, Library of Congress, District of Columbia, and shall be under the control of the register of copyrights, who shall under the direction and supervision of the Librarian of Congress, perform all the duties relating to the registration of copyrights. July 30, 1947, c. 391, 61 Stat. 665.

## § 202.   Register, assistant register, and subordinates

There shall be appointed by the Librarian of Congress a Register of Copyrights, and one Assistant Register of Copyrights, who shall have authority during the absence of the Register of Copyrights to attach the Copyright Office seal to all papers issued from the said office and to sign such certificates and other papers as may be necessary. There shall also be appointed by the Librarian such subordinate assistants to the register as may from time to time be authorized by law. July 30, 1947, c. 391, 61 Stat. 665.

## § 203.   Register; deposit of moneys received; reports

The Register of Copyrights shall make daily deposits in some bank in the District of Columbia, designated for this purpose by the Secretary of the Treasury as a national depository, of all moneys received to be applied as copyright fees, and shall make weekly deposits with the Secretary of the Treasury, in such manner as the latter shall direct, of all copyright fees actually applied under the provisions of this title, and annual deposits of sums received which it has not been possible to apply as copyright fees or to return to the remitters, and shall also make monthly reports to the Secretary of the Treasury and to the Librarian of Congress of the applied copyright fees for each calendar month, together with a statement of all remittances received, trust funds on hand, moneys refunded, and unapplied balances.

All moneys deposited with the Secretary of the Treasury under this section shall be credited to the appropriation for necessary expenses of the Copyright Office. July 30, 1947, c. 391, 61 Stat. 665; Aug. 5, 1977, Pub.L. 95–94, § 406, 91 Stat. 682.

## § 204.   Repealed. Pub.L. 92–310, Title II, § 205(a), June 6, 1972, 86 Stat. 203

## § 205.   Register; annual report

The Register of Copyrights shall make an annual report to the Librarian of Congress, to be printed in the annual report on the Library of Congress, of all copyright business for the previous fiscal year, including the number and kind of works which have been deposited in the Copyright Office during the fiscal year, under the provisions of this title. July 30, 1947, c. 391, 61 Stat. 666.

## § 206.   Seal of Copyright Office

The seal used in the Copyright Office on July 1, 1909, shall be the seal of the Copyright Office, and by it all papers issued from the Copyright Office requiring authentication shall be authenticated. July 30, 1947, c. 391, 61 Stat. 666.

## § 207. Rules for registration of claims

Subject to the approval of the Librarian of Congress, the Register of Copyrights shall be authorized to make rules and regulations for the registration of claims to copyright as provided by this title. July 30, 1947, c. 391, 61 Stat. 666.

## § 208. Record books in Copyright Office

The Register of Copyrights shall provide and keep such record books in the Copyright Office as are required to carry out the provisions of this title, and whenever deposit has been made in the Copyright Office of a copy of any work under the provisions of this title he shall make entry thereof. July 30, 1947, c. 391, 61 Stat. 666.

## § 209. Certificate of registration; effect as evidence; receipt for copies deposited

In the case of each entry the person recorded as the claimant of the copyright shall be entitled to a certificate of registration under seal of the Copyright Office, to contain the name and address of said claimant, the name of the country of which the author of the work is a citizen or subject, and when an alien author domiciled in the United States at the time of said registration, then a statement of that fact, including his place of domicile, the name of the author (when the records of the Copyright Office shall show the same), the title of the work which is registered for which copyright is claimed, the date of the deposit of the copies of such work, the date of publication if the work has been reproduced in copies for sale, or publicly distributed, and such marks as to class designation and entry number as shall fully identify the entry. In the case of a book, the certificate shall also state the receipt of the affidavit, as provided by section 17 of this title, and the date of the completion of the printing, or the date of the publication of the book, as stated in the said affidavit. The Register of Copyrights shall prepare a printed form for the said certificate, to be filled out in each case as above provided for in the case of all registrations made after July 1, 1909, and in the case of all previous registrations so far as the Copyright Office record books shall show such facts, which certificate, sealed with the seal of the Copyright Office, shall, upon payment of the prescribed fee, be given to any person making application for the same. Said certificate shall be admitted in any court as prima facie evidence of the facts stated therein. In addition to such certificate the register of copyrights shall furnish, upon request, without additional fee, a receipt for the copies of the work deposited to complete the registration. July 30, 1947, c. 391, 61 Stat. 666.

## § 210. Catalog of copyright entries; effect as evidence

The Register of Copyrights shall fully index all copyright registrations and assignments and shall print at periodic intervals a catalog of the titles of articles deposited and registered for copyright, together with suitable indexes, and at stated intervals shall print complete and indexed catalog for each class of copyright entries, and may thereupon, if expedient, destroy the original manuscript catalog cards containing the titles included in such printed volumes and representing the entries made during such intervals. The current catalog of copyright entries and the index volumes herein provided for shall be admitted in any court as prima facie evidence of the facts stated therein as regards any copyright registration. July 30, 1947, c. 391, 61 Stat. 666.

## § 211. Catalog of copyright entries; distribution and sale; disposal of proceeds

The said printed current catalogs as they are issued shall be promptly distributed by the Superintendent of Documents to the collectors of customs of the United States and to the postmasters of all exchange offices of receipt of foreign mails, in accordance with revised list of such collectors of customs and postmasters prepared by the Secretary of the Treasury and the Postmaster General, and they shall also be furnished in whole or in part to all parties desiring them at a price to be determined by the Register of Copyrights for each part of the catalog not exceeding $75 for the complete yearly catalog of copyright entries. The consolidated catalogs and indexes shall also be supplied to all persons ordering them at such prices as may be fixed by the Register of Copyrights, and all subscriptions for the catalogs shall be received by the Superintendent of Documents, who shall forward the said publications; and the moneys thus received shall be paid into the Treasury of the United States and accounted for under such laws and Treasury regulations as shall be in force at the time. July 30, 1947, c. 391, 61 Stat. 667; Apr. 27, 1948, c. 236, § 1, 62 Stat. 202; Oct. 27, 1965, Pub.L. 89–297, § 1, 79 Stat. 1072.

### § 212.   Records and works deposited in Copyright Office open to public inspection; taking copies of entries

The record books of the Copyright Office, together with the indexes to such record books, and all works deposited and retained in the Copyright Office, shall be open to public inspection; and copies may be taken of the copyright entries actually made in such record books, subject to such safeguards and regulations as shall be prescribed by the Register of Copyrights and approved by the Librarian of Congress. July 30, 1947, c. 391, 61 Stat. 667.

### § 213.   Disposition of articles deposited in office

Of the articles deposited in the Copyright Office under the provisions of the copyright laws of the United States, the Librarian of Congress shall determine what books and other articles shall be transferred to the permanent collections of the Library of Congress, including the law library, and what other books or articles shall be placed in the reserve collections of the Library of Congress for sale or exchange, or be transferred to other governmental libraries in the District of Columbia for use therein. July 30, 1947, c. 391, 61 Stat. 667.

### § 214.   Destruction of articles deposited in office remaining undisposed of; removal of by author or proprietor; manuscripts of unpublished works

Of any articles undisposed of as above provided, together with all titles and correspondence relating thereto, the Librarian of Congress and the Register of Copyrights jointly shall, at suitable intervals, determine what of these received during any period of years it is desirable or useful to preserve in the permanent files of the Copyright Office, and, after due notice as hereinafter provided, may within their discretion cause the remaining articles and other things to be destroyed: *Provided,* That there shall be printed in the Catalog of Copyright Entries from February to November, inclusive, a statement of the years of receipt of such articles and a notice to permit any author, copyright proprietor, or other lawful claimant to claim and remove before the expiration of the month of December of that year anything found which relates to any of his productions deposited or registered for copyright within the period of years stated, not reserved or disposed of as provided for in this title. No manuscript of an unpublished work shall be destroyed during its term of copyright without specific notice to the copyright proprietor of record, permitting him to claim and remove it. July 30, 1947, c. 391, 61 Stat. 667.

### § 215.   Fees

The Register of Copyrights shall receive, and the persons to whom the services designated are rendered shall pay, the following fees:

For the registration of a claim to copyright in any work, including a print or label used for articles of merchandise, $6; for the registration of a claim to renewal of copyright, $4; which fees shall include a certificate for each registration: *Provided,* That only one registration fee shall be required in the case of several volumes of the same book published and deposited at the same time: *And provided further,* That with respect to works of foreign origin, in lieu of payment of the copyright fee of $6 together with one copy of the work and application, the foreign author or proprietor may at any time within six months from the date of first publication abroad deposit in the Copyright Office an application for registration and two copies of the work which shall be accompanied by a catalog card in form and content satisfactory to the Register of Copyrights.

For every additional certificate of registration, $2.

For certifying a copy of an application for registration of copyright, and for all other certifications, $3.

For recording every assignment, agreement, power of attorney or other paper not exceeding six pages, $5; for each additional page or less, 50 cents; for each title over one in the paper recorded, 50 cents additional.

For recording a notice of use, or notice of intention to use, $3, for each notice of not more than five titles; and 50 cents for each additional title.

For any requested search of Copyright Office records, works deposited, or other available material, or services rendered in connection therewith, $5, for each hour of time consumed. July 30, 1947, c. 391, 61 Stat. 668; Apr. 27, 1948, c. 236, § 2, 62 Stat. 202; June 3, 1949, c. 171, § 4, 63 Stat. 154; Oct. 27, 1965, Pub.L. 89–297, § 2, 79 Stat. 1072.

## § 216.  When the day for taking action falls on Saturday, Sunday, or a holiday

When the last day for making any deposit or application, or for paying any fee, or for delivering any other material to the Copyright Office falls on Saturday, Sunday, or a holiday within the District of Columbia, such action may be taken on the next succeeding business day. Added Apr. 13, 1954, c. 137, § 1, 68 Stat. 52.

# APPENDIX D

## FIRST UNITED STATES COPYRIGHT ACT

(1 Stat. 124; 1st Cong., 2d Sess., c. 15 (1790))

An Act for the encouragement of learning, by securing the copies of maps, charts, and books, to the authors and proprietors of such copies, during the times therein mentioned.

SECTION 1. *Be it enacted by the Senate and House of Representatives of the United States of America in Congress assembled,* That from and after the passing of this act, the author and authors of any map, chart, book or books already printed within these United States, being a citizen or citizens thereof, or resident within the same, his or their executors, administrators or assigns, who hath or have not transferred to any other person the copyright of such map, chart, book or books, share or shares thereof; and any other person or persons, being a citizen or citizens of these United States, or residents therein, his or their executors, administrators or assigns, who hath or have purchased or legally acquired the copyright of any such map, chart, book or books, in order to print, reprint, publish or vend the same, shall have the sole right and liberty of printing, reprinting, publishing and vending such map, chart, book or books, for the term of fourteen years from the recording the title thereof in the clerk's office, as is herein after directed: And that the author and authors of any map, chart, book or books already made and composed, and not printed or published, or that shall hereafter be made and composed, being a citizen or citizens of these United States, or resident therein, and his or their executors, administrators or assigns, shall have the sole right and liberty of printing, reprinting, publishing and vending such map, chart, book or books, for the like term of fourteen years from the time of recording the title thereof in the clerk's office as aforesaid. And if, at the expiration of the said term, the author or authors, or any of them, be living, and a citizen or citizens of these United States, or resident therein, the same exclusive right shall be continued to him or them, his or their executors, administrators or assigns, for the further term of fourteen years: *Provided,* he or they shall cause the title thereof to be a second time recorded and published in the same manner as is herein after directed, and that within six months before the expiration of the first term of fourteen years aforesaid.

SEC. 2. *And be it further enacted,* That if any other person or persons, from and after the recording the title of any map, chart, book or books, and publishing the same as aforesaid, and within the times limited and granted by this act, shall print, reprint, publish, or import, or cause to be printed, reprinted, published, or imported from any foreign kingdom or state, any copy or copies of such map, chart, book or books, without the consent of the author or proprietor thereof, first had and obtained in writing, signed in the presence of two or more credible witnesses; or knowing the same to be so printed, reprinted, or imported, shall publish, sell, or expose to sale, or cause to be published, sold, or exposed to sale, any copy of such map, chart, book or books, without such consent first had and obtained in writing as aforesaid, then such offender or offenders shall forfeit all and every copy and copies of such map, chart, book or books, and all and every sheet and sheets, being part of the same, or either of them, to the author or proprietor of such map, chart, book or books, who shall forthwith destroy the same: And every such offender and offenders shall also forfeit and pay the sum of fifty cents for every sheet which shall be found in his or their possession, either printed or printing, published, imported or exposed to sale, contrary to the true intent and meaning of this act, the one moiety thereof to the author or proprietor of such map, chart, book or books who shall sue for the same, and the other moiety thereof to and for the use of the United States, to be recovered by action of debt in any court of record in the United States, wherein the same is cognizable. *Provided always,* That such action be commenced within one year after the cause of action shall arise, and not afterwards.

# FIRST UNITED STATES COPYRIGHT ACT

SEC. 3.    *And be it further enacted,* That no person shall be entitled to the benefit of this act, in cases where any map, chart, book or books, hath or have been already printed and published, unless he shall first deposit, and in all other cases, unless he shall before publication deposit a printed copy of the title of such map, chart, book or books, in the clerk's office of the district court where the author or proprietor shall reside: And the clerk of such court is hereby directed and required to record the same forthwith, in a book to be kept by him for that purpose, in the words following, (giving a copy thereof to the said author or proprietor, under the seal of the court, if he shall require the same). "District of _____ to wit: *Be it remembered,* that on the _____ day of _____ in the _____ year of the independence of the United States of America, A.B. of the said district, hath deposited in this office the title of a map, chart, book or books, (as the case may be) the right whereof he claims as author or proprietor, (as the case may be) in the words following, to wit: [here insert the title] in conformity to the act of the Congress of the United States, intituled 'An act for the encouragement of learning, by securing the copies of maps, charts, and books, to the authors and proprietors of such copies, during the times therein mentioned.' C.D. clerk of the district of _____." For which the said clerk shall be entitled to receive sixty cents from the said author or proprietor, and sixty cents for every copy under seal actually given to such author or proprietor as aforesaid. And such author or proprietor shall, within two months from the date thereof, cause a copy of the said record to be published in one or more of the newspapers printed in the United States, for the space of four weeks.

SEC. 4.    *And be it further enacted,* That the author or proprietor of any such map, chart, book or books, shall, within six months after the publishing thereof, deliver, or cause to be delivered to the Secretary of State a copy of the same, to be preserved in his office.

SEC. 5.    *And be it further enacted,* That nothing in this act shall be construed to extend to prohibit the importation or vending, reprinting or publishing within the United States, of any map, chart, book or books, written, printed, or published by any person not a citizen of the United States, in foreign parts or places without the jurisdiction of the United States.

SEC. 6.    *And be it further enacted,* That any person or persons who shall print or publish any manuscript, without the consent and approbation of the author or proprietor thereof, first had and obtained as aforesaid, (if such author or proprietor be a citizen of or resident in these United States) shall be liable to suffer and pay to the said author or proprietor all damages occasioned by such injury, to be recovered by a special action on the case founded upon this act, in any court having cognizance thereof.

SEC. 7.    *And be it further enacted,* That if any person or persons shall be sued or prosecuted for any matter, act or thing done under or by virtue of this act, he or they may plead the general issue, and give the special matter in evidence.

Approved, May 31, 1790.

# APPENDIX E

# STATUTE OF ANNE

### (8 Anne, c. 19 (1710))

*An act for the encouragement of learning, by vesting the copies of printed books in the authors or purchasers of such copies, during the times therein mentioned.*

I.     Whereas *printers, booksellers, and other persons have of late frequently taken the liberty of printing, reprinting, and publishing, or causing to be printed, reprinted, and published, books and other writings, without the consent of the authors or proprietors of such books and writings, to their very great detriment, and too often to the ruin of them and their families:* for preventing therefore such practices for the future, and for the encouragement of learned men to compose and write useful books; may it please your Majesty, that it may be enacted, and be it enacted by the Queen's most excellent majesty, by and with the advice and consent of the lords spiritual and temporal, and commons, in this present parliament assembled, and by the authority of the same; That from and after the tenth day of *April,* one thousand seven hundred and ten, the author of any book or books already printed, who hath not transferred to any other the copy or copies of such book or books, share or shares thereof, or the bookseller or booksellers, printer or printers, or other person or persons, who hath or have purchased or acquired the copy or copies of any book or books, in order to print or reprint the same, shall have the sole right and liberty of printing such book and books for the term of one and twenty years, to commence from the said tenth day of *April,* and no longer; and that the author of any book or books already composed, and not printed and published, or that shall hereafter be composed, and his assignee or assigns, shall have the sole liberty of printing and reprinting such book and books for the term of fourteen years, to commence from the day of the first publishing the same, and no longer; and that if any other bookseller, printer, or other person whatsoever, from and after the tenth day of *April,* one thousand seven hundred and ten, within the times granted and limited by this act, as aforesaid, shall print, reprint, or import, or cause to be printed, reprinted, or imported, any such book or books, without the consent of the proprietor or proprietors thereof first had and obtained in writing, signed in the presence of two or more credible witnesses; or knowing the same to be so printed or reprinted, without the consent of the proprietors, shall sell, publish, or expose to sale, or cause to be sold, published, or exposed to sale, any such book or books, without such consent first had and obtained, as aforesaid: then such offender or offenders shall forfeit such book or books, and all and every sheet or sheets, being part of such book or books, to the proprietor or proprietors of the copy thereof, who shall forthwith damask, and make waste paper of them; and further, That every such offender or offenders shall forfeit one penny for every sheet which shall be found in his, her, or their custody, either printed or printing, published, or exposed to sale, contrary to the true intent and meaning of this act; the one moiety thereof to the Queen's most excellent majesty, her heirs and successors, and the other moiety thereof to any person or persons that shall sue for the same, to be recovered in any of her Majesty's courts of record at *Westminster,* by action of debt, bill, plaint, or information, in which no wager of law, essoin, privilege, or protection, or more than one imparlance shall be allowed.

II.     *And whereas many persons may through ignorance offend against this act, unless some provision be made, whereby the property in every such book, as is intended by this act to be secured to the proprietor or proprietors thereof, may be ascertained, as likewise the consent of such proprietor or proprietors for the printing or reprinting of such book or books may from time to time be known;* be it therefore further enacted by the authority aforesaid, that nothing in this act contained shall be construed to extend to subject any bookseller, printer, or other person whatsoever, to the forfeitures or penalties therein mentioned, for or by reason of the printing or reprinting of any book or books without such consent, as aforesaid, unless the title to the copy of such book or books hereafter published shall, before such publication, be entered in the register book of the company of stationers, in such manner as hath been usual, which register book shall at all times be kept at the hall of the said company, and unless such consent of the proprietor or proprietors be in like manner entered as aforesaid, for every of which several entries, six pence shall be paid, and no more; which said register book may, at all seasonable and convenient time, be resorted to, and inspected by any bookseller, printer, or other person, for the purposes before-mentioned, without any fee or reward; and the clerk of the said company of stationers shall, when and as often as thereunto required, give a certificate under his hand of such entry or entries, and for every such certificate may take a fee not exceeding six pence.

III. Provided nevertheless, That if the clerk of the said company of stationers for the time being, shall refuse or neglect to register, or make such entry or entries, or to give such certificate, being thereunto required by the author or proprietor of such copy or copies, in the presence of two or more credible witnesses, That then such person and persons so refusing, notice being first duly given of such refusal, by an advertisement in the *Gazette*, shall have the like benefit, as if such entry or entries, certificate or certificates had been duly made and given; and that the clerks so refusing, shall, for any such offence, forfeit to the proprietor of such copy or copies the sum of twenty pounds, to be recovered in any of her Majesty's courts of record at *Westminster*, by action of debt, bill, plaint, or information, in which no wager of law, essoin, privilege or protection, or more than one imparlance shall be allowed.

IV. Provided nevertheless, and it is hereby further enacted by the authority aforesaid, That if any bookseller or booksellers, printer or printers, shall, after the said five and twentieth day of *March*, one thousand seven hundred and ten, set a price upon, or sell, or expose to sale, any book or books at such a price or rate as shall be conceived by any person or persons to be too high and unreasonable; it shall and may be lawful for any person or persons, to make complaint thereof to the lord archbishop of *Canterbury* for the time being, the lord chancellor, or lord keeper of the great seal of *Great Britain* for the time being, the lord bishop of *London* for the time being, the lord chief justice of the court of *Queen's Bench,* the lord chief justice of the court of *Common Pleas,* the lord chief baron of the court of *Exchequer* for the time being, the vice chancellors of the two universities for the time being, in that part of *Great Britain* called *England;* the lord president of the sessions for the time being, the lord chief justice general for the time being, the lord chief baron of the *Exchequer* for the time being, the rector of the college of *Edinburgh* for the time being, in that part of *Great Britain* called *Scotland;* who, or any one of them, shall and have hereby full power and authority, from time to time, to send for, summon, or call before him or them such bookseller or booksellers, printer or printers, and to examine and enquire of the reason of the dearness and inhauncement of the price or value of such book or books by him or them so sold or exposed to sale; and if upon such enquiry and examination it shall be found, that the price of such book or books is inhaunced, or any wise too high or unreasonable, then and in such case the said archbishop of *Canterbury,* lord chancellor or lord keeper, bishop of *London,* two chief justices, chief baron, vice chancellors of the universities, in that part of *Great Britain* called *England,* and the said lord president of the sessions, lord justice general, lord chief baron, and the rector of the college of *Edinburgh,* in that part of *Great Britain* called *Scotland,* or any one or more of them, so enquiring and examining, have hereby full power and authority to reform and redress the same, and to limit and settle the price of every such printed book and books, from time to time, according to the best of their judgments, and as to them shall seem just and reasonable; and in case of alteration of the rate or price from what was set or demanded by such bookseller or booksellers, printer or printers, to award and order such bookseller and booksellers, printer and printers, to pay all the costs and charges that the person or persons so complaining shall be put unto, by reason of such complaint, and of the causing such rate or price to be so limited and settled; all which shall be done by the said archbishop of *Canterbury,* lord chancellor or lord keeper, bishop of *London,* two chief justices, chief baron, vice chancellors of the two universities, in that part of *Great Britain* called *England,* and the said lord president of the sessions, lord justice general, lord chief baron, and rector of the college of *Edinburgh,* in that part of *Great Britain* called *Scotland,* or any one of them, by writing under their hands and seals, and thereof publick notice shall be forthwith given by the said bookseller or booksellers, printer or printers, by an advertisement in the *Gazette;* and if any bookseller or booksellers, printer or printers, shall, after such settlement made of the said rate and price, sell, or expose to sale, any book or books, at a higher or greater price, than what shall have been so limited and settled, as aforesaid, then, and in every such case such bookseller and booksellers, printer and printers, shall forfeit the sum of five pounds for every such book so by him, her, or them sold or exposed to sale; one moiety thereof to the Queen's most excellent majesty, her heirs and successors, and the other moiety to any person or persons that shall sue for the same, to be recovered, with costs of suit, in any of her Majesty's courts of record at *Westminster,* by action of debt, bill, plaint or information, in which no wager of law, essoin, privilege, or protection, or more than one imparlance shall be allowed.

V.    Provided always, and it is hereby enacted, That nine copies of each book or books, upon the best paper, that from and after the said tenth day of *April,* one thousand seven hundred and ten, shall be printed and published, as aforesaid, or reprinted and published with additions, shall, by the printer and printers thereof, be delivered to the warehouse keeper of the said company of stationers for the time being, at the hall of the said company, before such publication made, for the use of the royal library, the libraries of the universities of *Oxford* and *Cambridge,* the libraries of the four universities in *Scotland,* the library of *Sion College* in *London,* and the library commonly called the library belonging to the faculty of advocates at *Edinburgh* respectively; which said warehouse keeper is hereby required within ten days after demand by the keepers of the respective libraries, or any person or persons by them or any of them authorized to demand the said copy, to deliver the same, for the use of the aforesaid libraries; and if any proprietor, bookseller, or printer, or the said warehouse keeper of the said company of stationers, shall not observe the direction of this act therein, that then he and they so making default in not delivering the said printed copies, as aforesaid, shall forfeit, besides the value of the said printed copies, the sum of five pounds for every copy not so delivered, as also the value of the said printed copy not so delivered, the same to be recovered by the Queen's majesty, her heirs and successors, and by the chancellor, masters, and scholars of any of the said universities, and by the president and fellows of *Sion College,* and the said faculty of advocates at *Edinburgh,* with their full costs respectively.

VI.    Provided always, and be it further enacted, That if any person or persons incur the penalties contained in this act, in that part of *Great Britain* called *Scotland,* they shall be recoverable by any action before the court of session there.

VII. Provided, That nothing in this act contained, do extend, or shall be construed to extend to prohibit the importation, vending, or selling of any books in *Greek, Latin,* or any other foreign language printed beyond the seas; any thing in this act contained to the contrary notwithstanding.

VIII. And be it further enacted by the authority aforesaid, That if any action or suit shall be commenced or brought against any person or persons whatsoever, for doing or causing to be done any thing in pursuance of this act, the defendants in such action may plead the general issue, and give the special matter in evidence; and if upon such action a verdict be given for the defendant, or the plaintiff become nonsuited, or discontinue his action, then the defendant shall have and recover his full costs, for which he shall have the same remedy as a defendant in any case by law hath.

IX.    Provided, That nothing in this act contained shall extend, or be construed to extend, either to prejudice or confirm any right that the said universities, or any of them, or any person or persons have, or claim to have, to the printing or reprinting any book or copy already printed, or hereafter to be printed.

X.    Provided nevertheless, That all actions, suits, bills, indictments, or informations for any offence that shall be committed against this act, shall be brought, sued, and commenced within three months next after such offence committed, or else the same shall be void and of none effect.

XI.    Provided always, That after the expiration of the said term of fourteen years, the sole right of printing or disposing of copies shall return to the authors thereof, if they are then living, for another term of fourteen years.

# APPENDIX F

---

# UNIVERSAL COPYRIGHT CONVENTION
## AS REVISED AT
## PARIS ON 24 JULY 1971

The Contracting States,

Moved by the desire to ensure in all countries copyright protection of literary, scientific and artistic works,

Convinced that a system of copyright protection appropriate to all nations of the world and expressed in a universal convention, additional to, and without impairing international systems already in force, will ensure respect for the rights of the individual and encourage the development of literature, the sciences and the arts,

Persuaded that such a universal copyright system will facilitate a wider dissemination of works of the human mind and increase international understanding,

Have resolved to revise the Universal Copyright Convention as signed at Geneva on 6 September 1952 (hereinafter called "the 1952 Convention"), and consequently,

Have agreed as follows:

## ARTICLE I

Each Contracting State undertakes to provide for the adequate and effective protection of the rights of authors and other copyright proprietors in literary, scientific and artistic works, including writings, musical, dramatic and cinematographic works, and paintings, engravings and sculpture.

## ARTICLE II

1.  Published works of nationals of any Contracting State and works first published in that State shall enjoy in each other Contracting State the same protection as that other State accords to works of its nationals first published in its own territory, as well as the protection specially granted by this Convention.

2.  Unpublished works of nationals of each Contracting State shall enjoy in each other Contracting State the same protection as that other State accords to unpublished works of its own nationals, as well as the protection specially granted by this Convention.

3.  For the purpose of this Convention any Contracting State may, by domestic legislation, assimilate to its own nationals any person domiciled in that State.

## ARTICLE III

1.  Any Contracting State which, under its domestic law, requires as a condition of copyright, compliance with formalities such as deposit, registration, notice, notarial certificates, payment of fees or manufacture or publication in that Contracting State, shall regard these requirements as satisfied with respect to all works protected in accordance with this Convention and first published outside its territory and the author of which is not one of its nationals, if from the time of the first publication all the copies of the work published with the authority of the author or other copyright proprietor bear the symbol © accompanied by the name of the copyright proprietor and the year of first publication placed in such manner and location as to give reasonable notice of claim of copyright.

251

# UNIVERSAL COPYRIGHT CONVENTION (1971)

2.    The provisions of paragraph 1 shall not preclude any Contracting State from requiring formalities or other conditions for the acquisition and enjoyment of copyright in respect of works first published in its territory or works of its nationals wherever published.

3.    The provisions of paragraph 1 shall not preclude any Contracting State from providing that a person seeking judicial relief must, in bringing the action, comply with procedural requirements, such as that the complainant must appear through domestic counsel or that the complainant must deposit with the court or an administrative office, or both, a copy of the work involved in the litigation; provided that failure to comply with such requirements shall not affect the validity of the copyright, nor shall any such requirement be imposed upon a national of another Contracting State if such requirement is not imposed on nationals of the State in which protection is claimed.

4.    In each Contracting State there shall be legal means of protecting without formalities the unpublished works of nationals of other Contracting States.

5.    If a Contracting State grants protection for more than one term of copyright and the first term is for a period longer than one of the minimum periods prescribed in Article IV, such State shall not be required to comply with the provisions of paragraph 1 of this Article in respect of the second or any subsequent term of copyright.

## ARTICLE IV

1.    The duration of protection of a work shall be governed, in accordance with the provisions of Article II and this Article, by the law of the Contracting State in which protection is claimed.

2.    (a)    The term of protection for works protected under this Convention shall not be less than the life of the author and twenty-five years after his death. However, any Contracting State which, on the effective date of this Convention in that State, has limited this term for certain classes of works to a period computed from the first publication of the work, shall be entitled to maintain these exceptions and to extend them to other classes of works. For all these classes the term of protection shall not be less than twenty-five years from the date of first publication.

(b)    Any Contracting State which, upon the effective date of this Convention in that State, does not compute the term of protection upon the basis of the life of the author, shall be entitled to compute the term of protection from the date of the first publication of the work or from its registration prior to publication, as the case may be, provided the term of protection shall not be less than twenty-five years from the date of first publication or from its registration prior to publication, as the case may be.

(c)    If the legislation of a Contracting State grants two or more successive terms of protection, the duration of the first term shall not be less than one of the minimum periods specified in sub-paragraphs (a) and (b).

3.    The provisions of paragraph 2 shall not apply to photographic works or to works of applied art; provided, however, that the term of protection in those Contracting States which protect photographic works, or works of applied art in so far as they are protected as artistic works, shall not be less than ten years for each of said classes of works.

4.    (a)    No Contracting State shall be obliged to grant protection to a work for a period longer than that fixed for the class of works to which the work in question belongs, in the case of unpublished works by the law of the Contracting State of which the author is a national, and in the case of published works by the law of the Contracting State in which the work has been first published.

(b)    For the purposes of the application of sub-paragraph (a), if the law of any Contracting State grants two or more successive terms of protection, the period of protection of that State shall be considered to be the aggregate of those terms. However, if a specified work is not protected by such State during the second or any subsequent term for any reason, the other Contracting States shall not be obliged to protect it during the second or any subsequent term.

5.  For the purposes of the application of paragraph 4, the work of a national of a Contracting State, first published in a non-Contracting State, shall be treated as though first published in the Contracting State of which the author is a national.

6.  For the purposes of the application of paragraph 4, in case of simultaneous publication in two or more Contracting States, the work shall be treated as though first published in the State which affords the shortest term; any work published in two or more Contracting States within thirty days of its first publication shall be considered as having been published simultaneously in said Contracting States.

## Article IV*bis*

1.  The rights referred to in Article I shall include the basic rights ensuring the author's economic interests, including the exclusive right to authorize reproduction by any means, public performance and broadcasting. The provisions of this Article shall extend to works protected under this Convention either in their original form or in any form recognizably derived from the original.

2.  However, any Contracting State may, by its domestic legislation, make exceptions that do not conflict with the spirit and provisions of this Convention, to the rights mentioned in paragraph 1 of this Article. Any State whose legislation so provides, shall nevertheless accord a reasonable degree of effective protection to each of the rights to which exception has been made.

## Article V

1.  The rights referred to in Article I shall include the exclusive right of the author to make, publish and authorize the making and publication of translations of works protected under this Convention.

2.  However, any Contracting State may, by its domestic legislation, restrict the right of translation of writings, but only subject to the following provisions:

(a)  If, after the expiration of a period of seven years from the date of the first publication of a writing, a translation of such writing has not been published in a language in general use in the Contracting State, by the owner of the right of translation or with his authorization, any national of such Contracting State may obtain a non-exclusive licence from the competent authority thereof to translate the work into that language and publish the work so translated.

(b)  Such national shall in accordance with the procedure of the State concerned, establish either that he has requested, and been denied, authorization by the proprietor of the right to make and publish the translation, or that, after due diligence on his part, he was unable to find the owner of the right. A licence may also be granted on the same conditions if all previous editions of a translation in a language in general use in the Contracting State are out of print.

(c)  If the owner of the right of translation cannot be found, then the applicant for a licence shall send copies of his application to the publisher whose name appears on the work and, if the nationality of the owner of the right of translation is known, to the diplomatic or consular representative of the State of which such owner is a national, or to the organization which may have been designated by the government of that State. The licence shall not be granted before the expiration of a period of two months from the date of the dispatch of the copies of the application.

(d)  Due provision shall be made by domestic legislation to ensure to the owner of the right of translation a compensation which is just and conforms to international standards, to ensure payment and transmittal of such compensation, and to ensure a correct translation of the work.

(e)  The original title and the name of the author of the work shall be printed on all copies of the published translation. The licence shall be valid only for publication of the translation in the territory of the Contracting State where it has been applied for. Copies so published may be imported and sold in another Contracting State if a language in general use in such other State is the same language as that into which the work has been so translated, and if the domestic law in such other State makes provision for such licences and does not prohibit such importation and sale. Where the foregoing conditions do not exist, the importation and sale of such copies in a Contracting State shall be governed by its domestic law and its agreements. The licence shall not be transferred by the licencee.

(f)   The licence shall not be granted when the author has withdrawn from circulation all copies of the work.

### ARTICLE V*bis*

1.   Any Contracting State regarded as a developing country in conformity with the established practice of the General Assembly of the United Nations may, by a notification deposited with the Director-General of the United Nations Educational, Scientific and Cultural Organization (hereinafter called "the Director-General") at the time of its ratification, acceptance or accession or thereafter, avail itself of any or all of the exceptions provided for in Articles V*ter* and V*quater*.

2.   Any such notification shall be effective for ten years from the date of coming into force of this Convention, or for such part of that ten-year period as remains at the date of deposit of the notification, and may be renewed in whole or in part for further periods of ten years each if, not more than fifteen or less than three months before the expiration of the relevant ten-year period, the contracting State deposits a further notification with the Director-General. Initial notifications may also be made during these further periods of ten years in accordance with the provisions of this Article.

3.   Notwithstanding the provisions of paragraph 2, a Contracting State that has ceased to be regarded as a developing country as referred to in paragraph 1 shall no longer be entitled to renew its notification made under the provisions of paragraph 1 or 2, and whether or not it formally withdraws the notification such State shall be precluded from availing itself of the exceptions provided for in Articles V*ter* and V*quater* at the end of the current ten-year period, or at the end of three years after it has ceased to be regarded as a developing country, whichever period expires later.

4.   Any copies of a work already made under the exceptions provided for in Articles V*ter* and V*quater* may continue to be distributed after the expiration of the period for which notifications under this Article were effective until their stock is exhausted.

5.   Any Contracting State that has deposited a notification in accordance with Article XIII with respect to the application of this Convention to a particular country or territory, the situation of which can be regarded as analogous to that of the States referred to in paragraph 1 of this Article, may also deposit notifications and renew them in accordance with the provisions of this Article with respect to any such country or territory. During the effective period of such notifications, the provisions of Articles V*ter* and V*quater* may be applied with respect to such country or territory. The sending of copies from the country or territory to the Contracting State shall be considered as export within the meaning of Articles V*ter* and V*quater*.

### ARTICLE V*ter*

1.   (a)   Any Contracting State to which Article V*bis* (1) applies may substitute for the period of seven years provided for in Article V(2) a period of three years or any longer period prescribed by its legislation. However, in the case of a translation into a language not in general use in one or more developed countries that are party to this Convention or only the 1952 Convention, the period shall be one year instead of three.

(b)   A Contracting State to which Article V*bis* (1) applies may, with the unanimous agreement of the developed countries party to this Convention or only the 1952 Convention and in which the same language is in general use, substitute, in the case of translation into that language, for the period of three years provided for in sub-paragraph (a) another period as determined by such agreement but not shorter than one year. However, this sub-paragraph shall not apply where the language in question is English, French or Spanish. Notification of any such agreement shall be made to the Director-General.

(c)   The licence may only be granted if the applicant, in accordance with the procedure of the State concerned, establishes either that he has requested, and been denied, authorization by the owner of the right of translation, or that, after due diligence on his part, he was unable to find the owner of the right. At the same time as he makes his request he shall inform either the International Copyright Information Centre established by the United Nations Educational, Scientific and Cultural Organization or any national or regional information centre which may have been designated in a notification to that effect deposited with the Director-General by the government of the State in which the publisher is believed to have his principal place of business.

(d)   If the owner of the right of translation cannot be found, the applicant for a licence shall send, by registered airmail, copies of his application to the publisher whose name appears on the work and to any national or regional information centre as mentioned in sub-paragraph (c). If no such centre is notified he shall also send a copy to the international copyright information centre established by the United Nations Educational, Scientific and Cultural Organization.

2.   (a)   Licences obtainable after three years shall not be granted under this Article until a further period of six months has elapsed and licences obtainable after one year until a further period of nine months has elapsed. The further period shall begin either from the date of the request for permission to translate mentioned in paragraph 1(c) or, if the identity or address of the owner of the right of translation is not known, from the date of dispatch of the copies of the application for a licence mentioned in paragraph 1(d).

(b)   Licences shall not be granted if a translation has been published by the owner of the right of translation or with his authorization during the said period of six or nine months.

3.   Any licence under this Article shall be granted only for the purpose of teaching, scholarship or research.

4.   (a)   Any licence granted under this Article shall not extend to the export of copies and shall be valid only for publication in the territory of the Contracting State where it has been applied for.

(b)   Any copy published in accordance with a licence granted under this Article shall bear a notice in the appropriate language stating that the copy is available for distribution only in the Contracting State granting the licence. If the writing bears the notice specified in Article III(1) the copies shall bear the same notice.

(c)   The prohibition of export provided for in sub-paragraph (a) shall not apply where a governmental or other public entity of a State which has granted a licence under this Article to translate a work into a language other than English, French or Spanish sends copies of a translation prepared under such license to another country if:

(i)   the recipients are individuals who are nationals of the Contracting State granting the licence, or organizations grouping such individuals;

(ii)   the copies are to be used only for the purpose of teaching, scholarship or research;

(iii)   the sending of the copies and their subsequent distribution to recipients is without the object of commercial purpose; and

(iv)   the country to which the copies have been sent has agreed with the Contracting State to allow the receipt, distribution or both and the Director-General has been notified of such agreement by any one of the governments which have concluded it.

5.   Due provision shall be made at the national level to ensure:

(a)   that the licence provides for just compensation that is consistent with standards of royalties normally operating in the case of licences freely negotiated between persons in the two countries concerned; and

(b) payment and transmittal of the compensation; however, should national currency regulations intervene, the competent authority shall make all efforts, by the use of international machinery, to ensure transmittal in internationally convertible currency or its equivalent.

6. Any licence granted by a Contracting State under this Article shall terminate if a translation of the work in the same language with substantially the same content as the edition in respect of which the licence was granted is published in the said State by the owner of the right of translation or with his authorization, at a price reasonably related to that normally charged in the same State for comparable works. Any copies already made before the licence is terminated may continue to be distributed until their stock is exhausted.

7. For works which are composed mainly of illustrations a licence to translate the text and to reproduce the illustrations may be granted only if the conditions of Article V*quater* are also fulfilled.

8. (a) A licence to translate a work protected under this Convention, published in printed or analogous forms of reproduction, may also be granted to a broadcasting organization having its headquarters in a Contracting State to which Article V*bis* (1) applies, upon an application made in that State by the said organization under the following conditions:

(i) the translation is made from a copy made and acquired in accordance with the laws of the Contracting State;

(ii) the translation is for use only in broadcasts intended exclusively for teaching or for the dissemination of the results of specialized technical or scientific research to experts in a particular profession;

(iii) the translation is used exclusively for the purposes set out in condition (ii), through broadcasts lawfully made which are intended for recipients on the territory of the Contracting State, including broadcasts made through the medium of sound or visual recordings lawfully and exclusively made for the purpose of such broadcasts;

(iv) sound or visual recordings of the translation may be exchanged only between broadcasting organizations having their headquarters in the Contracting State granting the licence; and

(v) all uses made of the translation are without any commercial purpose.

(b) Provided all of the criteria and conditions set out in sub-paragraph (a) are met, a licence may also be granted to a broadcasting organization to translate any text incorporated in an audio-visual fixation which was itself prepared and published for the sole purpose of being used in connexion with systematic instructional activities.

(c) Subject to sub-paragraph (a) and (b), the other provisions of this Article shall apply to the grant and exercise of the licence.

9. Subject to the provisions of this Article, any license granted under this Article shall be governed by the provisions of Article V, and shall continue to be governed by the provisions of Article V and of this Article, even after the seven-year period provided for in Article V(2) has expired. However, after the said period has expired, the licencee shall be free to request that the said licence be replaced by a new licence governed exclusively by the provisions of Article V.

## ARTICLE V*quater*

1. Any Contracting State to which Article V*bis* (1) applies may adopt the following provisions:

(a) If, after the expiration of (i) the relevant period specified in sub-paragraph (c) commencing from the date of first publication of a particular edition of a literary, scientific or artistic work referred to in paragraph 3, or (ii) any longer period determined by national legislation of the State, copies of such edition have not been distributed in that State to the general public or in connexion with systematic instructional activities at a price reasonably related to that normally charged in the State for comparable works, by the owner of the right of reproduction or with his authorization, any national of such State may obtain a non-exclusive licence from the competent authority to publish such edition at that or a lower price for use in connexion with systematic instructional activities. The licence may only be granted if such national, in accordance with the procedure of the State concerned, establishes either that he has requested, and been denied, authorization by the proprietor of the right to publish such work, or that, after due diligence on his part, he was unable to find the owner of the right. At the same time as he makes his request he shall inform either the international copyright information centre established by the United Nations Educational, Scientific and Cultural Organization or any national or regional information centre referred to in sub-paragraph (d).

(b)  A licence may also be granted on the same conditions if, for a period of six months, no authorized copies of the edition in question have been on sale in the State concerned to the general public or in connexion with systematic instructional activities at a price reasonably related to that normally charged in the State for comparable works.

(c)  The period referred to in sub-paragraph (a) shall be five years except that:

(i)  for works of the natural and physical sciences, including mathematics, and of technology, the period shall be three years;

(ii)  for works of fiction, poetry, drama and music, and for art books, the period shall be seven years.

(d)  If the owner of the right of reproduction cannot be found, the applicant for a licence shall send, by registered air mail, copies of his application to the publisher whose name appears on the work and to any national or regional information centre identified as such in a notification deposited with the Director-General by the State in which the publisher is believed to have his principal place of business. In the absence of any such notification, he shall also send a copy to the international copyright information center established by the United Nations Educational, Scientific and Cultural Organization. The licence shall not be granted before the expiration of a period of three months from the date of dispatch of the copies of the application.

(e)  Licences obtainable after three years shall not be granted under this Article:

(i)  until a period of six months has elapsed from the date of the request for permission referred to in sub-paragraph (a) or, if the identity or address of the owner of the right of reproduction is unknown, from the date of the dispatch of the copies of the application for a licence referred to in sub-paragraph (d);

(ii)  if any such distribution of copies of the edition as is mentioned in sub-paragraph (a) has taken place during that period.

(f)  The name of the author and the title of the particular edition of the work shall be printed on all copies of the published reproduction. The licence shall not extend to the export of copies and shall be valid only for publication in the territory of the Contracting State where it has been applied for. The licence shall not be transferable by the licencee.

(g)  Due provision shall be made by domestic legislation to ensure an accurate reproduction of the particular edition in question.

(h)  A licence to reproduce and publish a translation of a work shall not be granted under this Article in the following cases:

(i)  where the translation was not published by the owner of the right of translation or with his authorization;

(ii)  where the translation is not in a language in general use in the State with power to grant the licence.

2.  The exceptions provided for in paragraph 1 are subject to the following additional provisions:

(a)   Any copy published in accordance with a licence granted under this Article shall bear a notice in the appropriate language stating that the copy is available for distribution only in the Contracting State to which the said licence applies. If the edition bears the notice specified in Article III(1), the copies shall bear the same notice.

(b)   Due provision shall be made at the national level to ensure:

(i)   that the licence provides for just compensation that is consistent with standards of royalties normally operating in the case of licences freely negotiated between persons in the two countries concerned; and

(ii)   payment and transmittal of the compensation; however, should national currency regulations intervene, the competent authority shall make all efforts, by the use of international machinery, to ensure transmittal in internationally convertible currency or its equivalent.

(c)   Whenever copies of an edition of a work are distributed in the Contracting State to the general public or in connexion with systematic instructional activities, by the owner of the right of reproduction or with his authorization, at a price reasonably related to that normally charged in the State for comparable works, any licence granted under this Article shall terminate if such edition is in the same language and is substantially the same in content as the edition published under the licence. Any copies already made before the licence is terminated may continue to be distributed until their stock is exhausted.

(d)   No licence shall be granted when the author has withdrawn from circulation all copies of the edition in question.

3.   (a)   Subject to sub-paragraph (b), the literary, scientific or artistic works to which this Article applies shall be limited to works published in printed or analogous forms of reproduction.

(b)   The provisions of this Article shall also apply to reproduction in audio-visual form of lawfully made audio-visual fixations including any protected works incorporated therein and to the translation of any incorporated text into a language in general use in the State with power to grant the licence; always provided that the audio-visual fixations in question were prepared and published for the sole purpose of being used in connexion with systematic instructional activities.

### ARTICLE VI

"Publication", as used in this Convention, means the reproduction in tangible form and the general distribution to the public of copies of a work from which it can be read or otherwise visually perceived.

### ARTICLE VII

This Convention shall not apply to works or rights in works which, at the effective date of this Convention in a Contracting State where protection is claimed, are permanently in the public domain in the said Contracting State.

### ARTICLE VIII

1.   This Convention, which shall bear the date of 24 July 1971, shall be deposited with the Director-General and shall remain open for signature by all States party to the 1952 Convention for a period of 120 days after the date of this Convention. It shall be subject to ratification or acceptance by the signatory States.

2.   Any State which has not signed this Convention may accede thereto.

3.   Ratification, acceptance or accession shall be effected by the deposit of an instrument to that effect with the Director-General.

## ARTICLE IX

1.    This Convention shall come into force three months after the deposit of twelve instruments of ratification, acceptance or accession.

2.    Subsequently, this Convention shall come into force in respect of each State three months after that State has deposited its instrument of ratification, acceptance or accession.

3.    Accession to this Convention by a State not party to the 1952 Convention shall also constitute accession to that Convention; however, if its instrument of accession is deposited before this Convention comes into force, such State may make its accession to the 1952 Convention conditional upon the coming into force of this Convention. After the coming into force of this Convention, no State may accede solely to the 1952 Convention.

4.    Relations between States party to this Convention and States that are party only to the 1952 Convention, shall be governed by the 1952 Convention. However, any State party only to the 1952 Convention may, by a notification deposited with the Director-General, declare that it will admit the application of the 1971 Convention to works of its nationals or works first published in its territory by all States party to this Convention.

## ARTICLE X

1.    Each Contracting State undertakes to adopt, in accordance with its Constitution, such measures as are necessary to ensure the application of this Convention.

2.    It is understood that at the date this Convention comes into force in respect of any State, that State must be in a position under its domestic law to give effect to the terms of this Convention.

## ARTICLE XI

1.    An Intergovernmental Committee is hereby established with the following duties:

(a)   to study the problems concerning the application and operation of the Universal Copyright Convention;

(b)   to make preparation for periodic revisions of this Convention;

(c)   to study any other problems concerning the international protection of copyright, in co-operation with the various interested international organizations, such as the United Nations Educational, Scientific and Cultural Organization, the International Union for the Protection of Literary and Artistic Works and the Organization of American States;

(d)   to inform States party to the Universal Copyright Convention as to its activities.

2.    The Committee shall consist of the representatives of eighteen States party to this Convention or only to the 1952 Convention.

3.    The Committee shall be selected with due consideration to a fair balance of national interests on the basis of geographical location, population, languages and stage of development.

4.    The Director-General of the United Nations Educational, Scientific and Cultural Organization, the Director-General of the World Intellectual Property Organization and the Secretary-General of the Organization of American States, or their representatives, may attend meetings of the Committee in an advisory capacity.

## ARTICLE XII

The Intergovernmental Committee shall convene a conference for revision whenever it deems necessary, or at the request of at least ten States party to this Convention.

## ARTICLE XIII

1.    Any Contracting State may, at the time of deposit of its instrument of ratification, acceptance or accession, or at any time thereafter, declare by notification addressed to the Director-

General that this Convention shall apply to all or any of the countries or territories for the international relations of which it is responsible and this Convention shall thereupon apply to the countries or territories named in such notification after the expiration of the term of three months provided for in Article IX. In the absence of such notification, this Convention shall not apply to any such country or territory.

2. However, nothing in this Article shall be understood as implying the recognition or tacit acceptance by a Contracting State of the factual situation concerning a country or territory to which this Convention is made applicable by another Contracting State in accordance with the provisions of this Article.

## ARTICLE XIV

1. Any Contracting State may denounce this Convention in its own name or on behalf of all or any of the countries or territories with respect to which a notification has been given under Article XIII. The denunciation shall be made by notification addressed to the Director-General. Such denunciation shall also constitute denunciation of the 1952 Convention.

2. Such denunciation shall operate only in respect of the State or of the country or territory on whose behalf it was made and shall not take effect until twelve months after the date of receipt of the notification.

## ARTICLE XV

A dispute between two or more Contracting States concerning the interpretation or application of this Convention, not settled by negotiation, shall, unless the States concerned agree on some other method of settlement, be brought before the International Court of Justice for determination by it.

## ARTICLE XVI

1. This Convention shall be established in English, French, and Spanish. The three texts shall be signed and shall be equally authoritative.

2. Official texts of this Convention shall be established by the Director-General, after consultation with the governments concerned, in Arabic, German, Italian and Portuguese.

3. Any Contracting State or group of Contracting States shall be entitled to have established by the Director-General other texts in the language of its choice by arrangement with the Director-General.

4. All such texts shall be annexed to the signed texts of this Convention.

## ARTICLE XVII

1. This Convention shall not in any way affect the provisions of the Berne Convention for the Protection of Literary and Artistic Works or membership in the Union created by that Convention.

2. In application of the foregoing paragraph, a declaration has been annexed to the present Article. This declaration is an integral part of this Convention for the States bound by the Berne Convention on 1 January 1951, or which have or may become bound to it at a later date. The signature of this Convention by such States shall also constitute signature of the said declaration, and ratification, acceptance or accession by such States shall include the declaration, as well as this Convention.

## ARTICLE XVIII

This Convention shall not abrogate multilateral or bilateral copyright conventions or arrangements that are or may be in effect exclusively between two or more American Republics. In the event of any difference either between the provisions of such existing conventions or arrangements and the provisions of this Convention, or between the provisions of this Convention and those of any new convention or arrangement which may be formulated between two or more American Republics after this Convention comes into force, the convention or arrangement most recently formulated shall prevail between the parties thereto. Rights in works acquired in any Contracting State under existing conventions or arrangements before the date this Convention comes into force in such State shall not be affected.

## ARTICLE XIX

This Convention shall not abrogate multilateral or bilateral conventions or arrangements in effect between two or more Contracting States. In the event of any difference between the provisions of such existing conventions or arrangements and the provisions of this Convention, the provisions of this Convention shall prevail. Rights in works acquired in any Contracting State under existing conventions or arrangements before the date on which this Convention comes into force in such State shall not be affected. Nothing in this Article shall affect the provisions of Articles XVII and XVIII.

## ARTICLE XX

Reservations to this Convention shall not be permitted.

## ARTICLE XXI

1.   The Director-General shall send duly certified copies of this Convention to the States interested and to the Secretary-General of the United Nations for registration by him.

2.   He shall also inform all interested States of the ratifications, acceptances and accessions which have been deposited, the date on which this Convention comes into force, the notifications under this Convention and denunciations under Article XIV.

## APPENDIX DECLARATION RELATING TO ARTICLE XVII

The States which are members of the International Union for the Protection of Literary and Artistic Works (hereinafter called "the Berne Union") and which are signatories to this Convention,

Desiring to reinforce their mutual relations on the basis of the said Union and to avoid any conflict which might result from the co-existence of the Berne Convention and the Universal Copyright Convention,

Recognizing the temporary need of some States to adjust their level of copyright protection in accordance with their stage of cultural, social and economic development,

Have, by common agreement, accepted the terms of the following declaration:

(a)   Except as provided by paragraph (b), works which, according to the Berne Convention, have as their country of origin a country which has withdrawn from the Berne Union after 1 January 1951, shall not be protected by the Universal Copyright Convention in the countries of the Berne Union;

(b)   Where a Contracting State is regarded as a developing country in conformity with the established practice of the General Assembly of the United Nations, and has deposited with the Director-General of the United Nations Educational, Scientific and Cultural Organization, at the time of its withdrawal from the Berne Union, a notification to the effect that it regards itself as a developing country, the provisions of paragraph (a) shall not be applicable as long as such State may avail itself of the exceptions provided for by this Convention in accordance with Article Vbis;

(c)   The Universal Copyright Convention shall not be applicable to the relationships among countries of the Berne Union in so far as it relates to the protection of works having as their country of origin, within the meaning of the Berne Convention, a country of the Berne Union.

## RESOLUTION CONCERNING ARTICLE XI

The Conference for Revision of the Universal Copyright Convention,

Having considered the problems relating to the Intergovernmental Committee provided for in Article XI of this Convention, to which this resolution is annexed,

Resolves that:

# UNIVERSAL COPYRIGHT CONVENTION (1971)

1. At its inception, the Committee shall include representatives of the twelve States members of the Intergovernmental Committee established under Article XI of the 1952 Convention and the resolution annexed to it, and, in addition, representatives of the following States: Algeria, Australia, Japan, Mexico, Senegal and Yugoslavia.

2. Any States that are not party to the 1952 Convention and have not acceded to this Convention before the first ordinary session of the Committee following the entry into force of this Convention shall be replaced by other States to be selected by the Committee at its first ordinary session in conformity with the provisions of Article XI(2) and (3).

3. As soon as this Convention comes into force the Committee as provided for in paragraph 1 shall be deemed to be constituted in accordance with Article XI of this Convention.

4. A session of the Committee shall take place within one year after the coming into force of this Convention; thereafter the Committee shall meet in ordinary session at intervals of not more than two years.

5. The Committee shall elect its Chairman and two Vice-Chairmen. It shall establish its Rules of Procedure having regard to the following principles:

(a) The normal duration of the term of office of the members represented on the Committee shall be six years with one-third retiring every two years, it being however understood that, of the original terms of office, one-third shall expire at the end of the Committee's second ordinary session which will follow the entry into force of this Convention, a further third at the end of its third ordinary session, and the remaining third at the end of its fourth ordinary session.

(b) The rules governing the procedure whereby the Committee shall fill vacancies, the order in which terms of membership expire, eligibility for re-election, and election procedures, shall be based upon a balancing of the needs for continuity of membership and rotation of representation, as well as the considerations set out in Article XI(3).

Expresses the wish that the United Nations Educational, Scientific and Cultural Organization provide its Secretariat.

In faith whereof the undersigned, having deposited their respective full powers, have signed this Convention.

Done at Paris, this twenty-fourth day of July 1971, in a single copy.

## PROTOCOL 1

*Annexed to the Universal Copyright Convention as revised at Paris on 24 July 1971 concerning the application of that Convention to works of Stateless persons and refugees*

The States party hereto, being also party to the Universal Copyright Convention as revised at Paris on 24 July 1971 (hereinafter called "the 1971 Convention"),

Have accepted the following provisions:

(1) Stateless persons and refugees who have their habitual residence in a State party to this Protocol shall, for the purposes of the 1971 Convention, be assimilated to the nationals of that State.

(2)(a) This Protocol shall be signed and shall be subject to ratification or acceptance, or may be acceded to, as if the provisions of Article VIII of the 1971 Convention applied hereto.

(b) This Protocol shall enter into force in respect of each State, on the date of deposit of the instrument of ratification, acceptance or accession of the State concerned or on the date of entry into force of the 1971 Convention with respect to such State, whichever is the later.

(c) On the entry into force of this Protocol in respect of a State not party to Protocol 1 annexed to the 1952 Convention, the latter Protocol shall be deemed to enter into force in respect of such State.

In faith whereof the undersigned, being duly authorized thereto, have signed this Protocol.

Done at Paris this twenty-fourth day of July 1971, in the English, French and Spanish languages, the three texts being equally authoritative, in a single copy which shall be deposited with the Director-General of the United Nations Educational, Scientific and Cultural Organization. The Director-General shall send certified copies to the signatory States, and to the Secretary-General of the United Nations for registration.

## PROTOCOL 2

*Annexed to the Universal Copyright Convention as revised at Paris on 24 July 1971 concerning the application of that Convention to the works of certain international organizations*

The States party hereto, being also party to the Universal Copyright Convention as revised at Paris on 24 July 1971 (hereinafter called "the 1971 Convention"),

Have accepted the following provisions:

(1)(a)   The protection provided for in Article II(1) of the 1971 Convention shall apply to works published for the first time by the United Nations, by the Specialized Agencies in relationship therewith, or by the Organization of American States.

(b)   Similarly, Article II(2) of the 1971 Convention shall apply to the said organization or agencies.

(2)(a)   This Protocol shall be signed and shall be subject to ratification or acceptance, or may be acceded to, as if the provisions of Article VIII of the 1971 Convention applied hereto.

(b)   This Protocol shall enter into force for each State on the date of deposit of the instrument of ratification, acceptance or accession of the State concerned or on the date of entry into force of the 1971 Convention with respect to such State, whichever is the later.

In faith whereof the undersigned, being duly authorized thereto, have signed this Protocol.

Done at Paris, this twenty-fourth day of July 1971, in the English, French and Spanish languages, the three texts being equally authoritative, in a single copy which shall be deposited with the Director-General of the United Nations Educational, Scientific and Cultural Organization. The Director-General shall send certified copies to the signatory States, and to the Secretary-General of the United Nations for registration.

# APPENDIX G

## BERNE CONVENTION FOR THE PROTECTION OF LITERARY AND ARTISTIC WORKS

(As Revised at Paris on July 24, 1971)

The countries of the Union, being equally animated by the desire to protect, in as effective and uniform a manner as possible, the rights of authors in their literary and artistic works,

Recognizing the importance of the work of the Revision Conference held at Stockholm in 1967,

Having resolved to revise the Act adopted by the Stockholm Conference, while maintaining without change Article 1 to 20 and 22 to 26 of that Act.

Consequently, the undersigned Plenipotentiaries, having presented their full powers, recognized as in good and due form, have agreed as follows:

### Article 1

The countries to which this Convention applies constitute a Union for the protection of the rights of authors in their literary and artistic works.

### Article 2

(1)   The expression "literary and artistic works" shall include every production in the literary, scientific and artistic domain, whatever may be the mode or form of its expression, such as books, pamphlets and other writings; lectures, addresses, sermons and other works of the same nature; dramatic or dramatico-musical works; choreographic works and entertainments in dumb show; musical compositions with or without words; cinematographic works to which are assimilated works expressed by a process analogous to cinematography; works of drawing, painting, architecture, sculpture, engraving and lithography; photographic works to which are assimilated works expressed by a process analogous to photography; works of applied art; illustrations, maps, plans, sketches and three-dimensional works relative to geography, topography, architecture or science.

(2)   It shall, however, be a matter for legislation in the countries of the Union to prescribe that works in general or any specified categories of works shall not be protected unless they have been fixed in some material form.

(3)   Translations, adaptations, arrangements of music and other alterations of a literary or artistic work shall be protected as original works without prejudice to the copyright in the original work.

(4)   It shall be a matter for legislation in the countries of the Union to determine the protection to be granted to official texts of a legislative, administrative and legal nature, and to official translations of such texts.

(5)   Collections of literary or artistic works such as encyclopaedias and anthologies which, by reason of the selection and arrangement of their contents, constitute intellectual creations shall be protected as such, without prejudice to the copyright in each of the works forming part of such collections.

(6)  The works mentioned in this Article shall enjoy protection in all countries of the Union. This protection shall operate for the benefit of the author and his successors in title.

(7)  Subject to the provisions of Article 7(4) of this Convention, it shall be a matter for legislation in the countries of the Union to determine the extent of the application of their laws to works of applied art and industrial designs and models, as well as the conditions under which such works, designs and models shall be protected. Works protected in the country of origin solely as designs and models shall be entitled in another country of the Union only to such special protection as is granted in that country to designs and models; however, if no such special protection is granted in that country, such works shall be protected as artistic works.

(8)  The protection of this Convention shall not apply to news of the day or to miscellaneous facts having the character of mere items of press information.

### Article 2$^{bis}$

(1)  It shall be a matter for legislation in the countries of the Union to exclude, wholly or in part, from the protection provided by the preceding Article political speeches and speeches delivered in the course of legal proceedings.

(2)  It shall also be a matter for legislation in the countries of the Union to determine the conditions under which lectures, addresses and other works of the same nature which are delivered in public may be reproduced by the press, broadcast, communicated to the public by wire and made the subject of public communication as envisaged in Article 11$^{bis}$(1) of this Convention, when such use is justified by the informatory purpose.

(3)  Nevertheless, the author shall enjoy the exclusive right of making a collection of his works mentioned in the preceding paragraphs.

### Article 3

(1)  The protection of this Convention shall apply to:

(a)  authors who are nationals of one of the countries of the Union, for their works, whether published or not;

(b)  authors who are not nationals of one of the countries of the Union, for their works first published in one of those countries, or simultaneously in a country outside the Union and in a country of the Union.

(2)  Authors who are not nationals of one of the countries of the Union but who have their habitual residence in one of them shall, for the purposes of this Convention, be assimilated to nationals of that country.

(3)  The expression "published works" means works published with the consent of their authors, whatever may be the means of manufacture of the copies, provided that the availability of such copies has been such as to satisfy the reasonable requirements of the public, having regard to the nature of the work. The performance of a dramatic, dramatico-musical, cinematographic or musical work, the public recitation of a literary work, the communication by wire or the broadcasting of literary or artistic works, the exhibition of a work of art and the construction of a work of architecture shall not constitute publication.

(4)  A work shall be considered as having been published simultaneously in several countries if it has been published in two or more countries within thirty days of its first publication.

### Article 4

The protection of this Convention shall apply, even if the conditions of Article 3 are not fulfilled, to:

(a)  authors of cinematographic works the maker of which has his headquarters or habitual residence in one of the countries of the Union;

(b) authors of works of architecture erected in a country of the Union or of other artistic works incorporated in a building or other structure located in a country of the Union.

## Article 5

(1) Authors shall enjoy, in respect of works for which they are protected under this Convention, in countries of the Union other than the country of origin, the rights which their respective laws do now or may hereafter grant to their nationals, as well as the rights specially granted by this Convention.

(2) The enjoyment and the exercise of these rights shall not be subject to any formality; such enjoyment and such exercise shall be independent of the existence of protection in the country of origin of the work. Consequently, apart from the provisions of this Convention, the extent of protection, as well as the means of redress afforded to the author to protect his rights, shall be governed exclusively by the laws of the country where protection is claimed.

(3) Protection in the country of origin is governed by domestic law. However, when the author is not a national of the country of origin of the work for which he is protected under this Convention, he shall enjoy in that country the same rights as national authors.

(4) The country of origin shall be considered to be:

(a) in the case of works first published in a country of the Union, that country; in the case of works published simultaneously in several countries of the Union which grant different terms of protection, the country whose legislation grants the shortest term of protection;

(b) in the case of works published simultaneously in a country outside the Union and in a country of the Union, the latter country;

(c) in the case of unpublished works or of works first published in a country outside the Union, without simultaneous publication in a country of the Union, the country of the Union of which the author is a national, provided that:

  (i) when these are cinematographic works the maker of which has his headquarters or his habitual residence in a country of the Union, the country of origin shall be that country, and

  (ii) when these are works of architecture erected in a country of the Union or other artistic works incorporated in a building or other structure located in a country of the Union, the country of origin shall be that country.

## Article 6

(1) Where any country outside the Union fails to protect in an adequate manner the works of authors who are nationals of one of the countries of the Union, the latter country may restrict the protection given to the works of authors who are, at the date of the first publication thereof, nationals of the other country and are not habitually resident in one of the countries of the Union. If the country of first publication avails itself of this right, the other countries of the Union shall not be required to grant to works thus subjected to special treatment a wider protection than that granted to them in the country of first publication.

(2) No restrictions introduced by virtue of the preceding paragraph shall affect the rights which an author may have acquired in respect of a work published in a country of the Union before such restrictions were put into force.

(3) The countries of the Union which restrict the grant of copyright in accordance with this Article shall give notice thereof to the Director General of the World Intellectual Property Organization (hereinafter designated as "the Director General") by a written declaration specifying the countries in regard to which protection is restricted, and the restrictions to which rights of authors who are nationals of those countries are subjected. The Director General shall immediately communicate this declaration to all the countries of the Union.

# BERNE CONVENTION (1971)

### Article 6<sup>bis</sup>

(1)   Independently of the author's economic rights, and even after the transfer of the said rights, the author shall have the right to claim authorship of the work and to object to any distortion, mutilation or other modification of, or other derogatory action in relation to, the said work, which would be prejudicial to his honor or reputation.

(2)   The rights granted to the author in accordance with the preceding paragraph shall, after his death, be maintained, at least until the expiry of the economic rights, and shall be exercisable by the persons or institutions authorized by the legislation of the country where protection is claimed. However, those countries whose legislation, at the moment of their ratification of or accession to this Act, does not provide for the protection after the death of the author of all the rights set out in the preceding paragraph may provide that some of these rights may, after his death, cease to be maintained.

(3)   The means of redress for safeguarding the rights granted by this Article shall be governed by the legislation of the country where protection is claimed.

### Article 7

(1)   The term of protection granted by this Convention shall be the life of the author and fifty years after his death.

(2)   However, in the case of cinematographic works, the countries of the Union may provide that the term of protection shall expire fifty years after the work has been made available to the public with the consent of the author, or, failing such an event within fifty years from the making of such a work, fifty years after the making.

(3)   In the case of anonymous or pseudonymous works, the terms of protection granted by this Convention shall expire fifty years after the work has been lawfully made available to the public. However, when the pseudonym adopted by the author leaves no doubt as to his identity, the term of protection shall be that provided in paragraph (1). If the author of an anonymous or pseudonymous work discloses his identity during the above-mentioned period, the term of protection applicable shall be that provided in paragraph (1). The countries of the Union shall not be required to protect anonymous or pseudonymous works in respect of which it is reasonable to presume that their author has been dead for fifty years.

(4)   It shall be a matter for legislation in the countries of the Union to determine the term of protection of photographic works and that of works of applied art in so far as they are protected as artistic works; however, this term shall last at least until the end of a period of twenty-five years from the making of such a work.

(5)   The term of protection subsequent to the death of the author and the terms provided by paragraphs (2), (3) and (4) shall run from the date of death or of the event referred to in those paragraphs, but such terms shall always be deemed to begin on the first of January of the year following the death or such event.

(6)   The countries of the Union may grant a term of protection in excess of those provided by the preceding paragraphs.

(7)   Those countries of the Union bound by the Rome Act of this Convention which grant, in their national legislation in force at the time of signature of the present Act, shorter terms of protection than those provided for in the preceding paragraphs shall have the right to maintain such terms when ratifying or acceding to the present Act.

(8)   In any case, the term shall be governed by the legislation of the country where protection is claimed; however, unless the legislation of that country otherwise provides, the term shall not exceed the term fixed in the country of origin of the work.

### Article 7<sup>bis</sup>

The provisions of the preceding Article shall also apply in the case of a work of joint authorship, provided that the terms measured from the death of the author shall be calculated from the death of the last surviving author.

### Article 8

Authors of literary and artistic works protected by this Convention shall enjoy the exclusive right of making and of authorizing the translation of their works throughout the term of protection of their rights in the original works.

### Article 9

(1) Authors of literary and artistic works protected by this Convention shall have the exclusive right of authorizing the reproduction of these works, in any manner or form.

(2) It shall be a matter for legislation in the countries of the Union to permit the reproduction of such works in certain special cases, provided that such reproduction does not conflict with a normal exploitation of the work and does not unreasonably prejudice the legitimate interests of the author.

(3) Any sound or visual recording shall be considered as a reproduction for the purposes of this Convention.

### Article 10

(1) It shall be permissible to make quotations from a work which has already been lawfully made available to the public, provided that their making is compatible with fair practice, and their extent does not exceed that justified by the purpose, including quotations from newspaper articles and periodicals in the form of press summaries.

(2) It shall be a matter for legislation in the countries of the Union, and for special agreements existing or to be concluded between them, to permit the utilization, to the extent justified by the purpose, of literary or artistic works by way of illustration in publications, broadcasts or sound or visual recordings for teaching, provided such utilization is compatible with fair practice.

(3) Where use is made of works in accordance with the preceding paragraphs of this Article, mention shall be made of the source, and of the name of the author if it appears thereon.

### Article 10<sup>bis</sup>

(1) It shall be a matter for legislation in the countries of the Union to permit the reproduction by the press, the broadcasting or the communication to the public by wire of articles published in newspapers or periodicals on current economic, political or religious topics, and of broadcast works of the same character, in cases in which the reproduction, broadcasting or such communication thereof is not expressly reserved. Nevertheless, the source must always be clearly indicated; the legal consequences of a breach of this obligation shall be determined by the legislation of the country where protection is claimed.

(2) It shall also be a matter for legislation in the countries of the Union to determine the conditions under which, for the purpose of reporting current events by means of photography, cinematography, broadcasting or communication to the public by wire, literary or artistic works seen or heard in the course of the event may, to the extent justified by the informatory purpose, be reproduced and made available to the public.

### Article 11

(1) Authors of dramatic, dramatico-musical and musical works shall enjoy the exclusive right of authorizing:

  (i)  the public performance of their works, including such public performance by any means or process;

    (ii)   any communication to the public of the performance of their works.

(2)   Authors of dramatic or dramatico-musical works shall enjoy, during the full term of their rights in the original works, the same rights with respect to translations thereof.

### Article 11*bis*

(1)   Authors of literary and artistic works shall enjoy the exclusive right of authorizing:

    (i)   the broadcasting of their works or the communication thereof to the public by any other means of wireless diffusion of signs, sounds or images;

    (ii)   any communication to the public by wire or by rebroadcasting of the broadcast of the work, when this communication is made by an organization other than the original one;

    (iii)   the public communication by loudspeaker or any other analogous instrument transmitting, by signs, sounds or images, the broadcast of the work.

(2)   It shall be a matter for legislation in the countries of the Union to determine the conditions under which the rights mentioned in the preceding paragraph may be exercised, but these conditions shall apply only in the countries where they have been prescribed. They shall not in any circumstances be prejudicial to the moral rights of the author, nor to his right to obtain equitable remuneration which, in the absence of agreement, shall be fixed by competent authority.

(3)   In the absence of any contrary stipulation, permission granted in accordance with paragraph (1) of this Article shall not imply permission to record, by means of instruments recording sounds or images, the work broadcast. It shall, however, be a matter for legislation in the countries of the Union to determine the regulations for ephemeral recordings made by a broadcasting organization by means of its own facilities and used for its own broadcasts. The preservation of these recordings in official archives may, on the ground of their exceptional documentary character, be authorized by such legislation.

### Article 11*ter*

(1)   Authors of literary works shall enjoy the exclusive right of authorizing:

    (i)   the public recitation of their words, including such public recitation by any means or process;

    (ii)   any communication to the public of the recitation of their works.

(2)   Authors of literary works shall enjoy, during the full term of their rights in the original works, the same rights with respect to translations thereof.

### Article 12

Authors of literary or artistic works shall enjoy the exclusive right of authorizing adaptations, arrangements and other alterations of their works.

### Article 13

(1)   Each country of the Union may impose for itself reservations and conditions on the exclusive right granted to the author of a musical work and to the author of any words, the recording of which together with the musical work has already been authorized by the latter, to authorize the sound recording of that musical work, together with such words, if any; but all such reservations and conditions shall apply only in the countries which have imposed them and shall not, in any circumstances, be prejudicial to the rights of these authors to obtain equitable remuneration which, in the absence of agreement, shall be fixed by competent authority.

(2)   Recordings of musical works made in a country of the Union in accordance with Article 13(3) of the Conventions signed at Rome on 2 June 1928, and at Brussels on 26 June 1948, may be reproduced in that country without the permission of the author of the musical work until a date two years after that country becomes bound by this Act.

(3)   Recordings made in accordance with paragraphs (1) and (2) of this Article and imported without permission from the parties concerned into a country where they are treated as infringing recordings shall be liable to seizure.

## Article 14

(1)   Authors of literary or artistic works shall have the exclusive right of authorizing:

    (i)   the cinematographic adaptation and reproduction of these works, and the distribution of the works thus adapted or reproduced;

    (ii)   the public performance and communication to the public by wire of the works thus adapted or reproduced.

(2)   The adaptation into any other artistic form of a cinematographic production derived from literary or artistic works shall, without prejudice to the authorization of the author of the cinematographic production, remain subject to the authorization of the authors of the original works.

(3)   The provisions of Article 13(1) shall not apply.

## Article 14$^{bis}$

(1)   Without prejudice to the copyright in any work which may have been adapted or reproduced, a cinematographic work shall be protected as an original work. The owner of copyright in a cinematographic work shall enjoy the same rights as the author of an original work, including the rights referred to in the preceding Article.

(2)(a)   Ownership of copyright in a cinematographic work shall be a matter for legislation in a country where protection is claimed.

(b)   However, in the countries of the Union which, by legislation, include among the owners of copyright in a cinematographic work authors who have brought contributions to the making of the work, such authors, if they have undertaken to bring such contributions, may not, in the absence of any contrary or special stipulation, object to the reproduction, distribution, public performance, communication to the public by wire, broadcasting or any other communication to the public, or to the subtitling or dubbing of texts, of the work.

(c)   The question whether or not the form of the undertaking referred to above should, for the application of the preceding subparagraph (b), be in a written agreement or a written act of the same effect shall be a matter for the legislation of the country where the maker of the cinematographic work has his headquarters or habitual residence. However, it shall be a matter for the legislation of the country of the Union where protection is claimed to provide that the said undertaking shall be in a written agreement or a written act of the same effect. The countries whose legislation so provides shall notify the Director General by means of a written declaration, which will be immediately communicated by him to all the other countries of the Union.

(d)   By "contrary or special stipulation" is meant any restrictive condition which is relevant to the aforesaid undertaking.

(3)   Unless the national legislation provides to the contrary, the provisions of paragraph (2)(b) above shall not be applicable to authors of scenarios, dialogues and musical works created for the making of the cinematographic work, or to the principal director thereof. However, those countries of the Union whose legislation does not contain rules providing for the application of the said paragraph (2)(b) to such director shall notify the Director General by means of a written declaration, which will be immediately communicated by him to all the other countries of the Union.

## Article 14$^{ter}$

(1)   The author, or after his death the persons or institutions authorized by national legislation, shall, with respect to original works of art and original manuscripts of writers and composers, enjoy the inalienable right to an interest in any sale of the work subsequent to the first transfer by the author of the work.

(2)   The protection provided by the preceding paragraph may be claimed in a country of the Union only if legislation in the country to which the author belongs so permits, and to the extent permitted by the country where this protection is claimed.

(3)   The procedure for collection and the amounts shall be matters for determination by national legislation.

### Article 15

(1)   In order that the author of a literary or artistic work protected by this Convention shall, in the absence of proof to the contrary, be regarded as such, and consequently be entitled to institute infringement proceedings in the countries of the Union, it shall be sufficient for his name to appear on the work in the usual manner. This paragraph shall be applicable even if this name is a pseudonym, where the pseudonym adopted by the author leaves no doubt as to his identity.

(2)   The person or body corporate whose name appears on a cinematographic work in the usual manner shall, in the absence of proof to the contrary, be presumed to be the maker of the said work.

(3)   In the case of anonymous and pseudonymous works, other than those referred to in paragraph (1) above, the publisher whose name appears on the work shall, in the absence of proof to the contrary, be deemed to represent the author, and in this capacity he shall be entitled to protect and enforce the author's rights. The provisions of this paragraph shall cease to apply when the author reveals his identity and establishes his claim to authorship of the work.

(4)(a)   In the case of unpublished works where the identity of the author is unknown, but where there is every ground to presume that he is a national of a country of the Union, it shall be a matter for legislation in that country to designate the competent authority which shall represent the author and shall be entitled to protect and enforce his rights in the countries of the Union.

(b)   Countries of the Union which makes such designation under the terms of this provision shall notify the Director General by means of a written declaration giving full information concerning the authority thus designated. The Director General shall at once communicate this declaration to all other countries of the Union.

### Article 16

(1)   Infringing copies of a work shall be liable to seizure in any country of the Union where the work enjoys legal protection.

(2)   The provisions of the preceding paragraph shall also apply to reproductions coming from a country where the work is not protected, or has ceased to be protected.

(3)   The seizure shall take place in accordance with the legislation of each country.

### Article 17

The provisions of this Convention cannot in any way affect the right of the Government of each country of the Union to permit, to control, or to prohibit, by legislation or regulation, the circulation, presentation, or exhibition of any work or production in regard to which the competent authority may find it necessary to exercise that right.

### Article 18

(1)   This Convention shall apply to all works which, at the moment of its coming into force, have not yet fallen into the public domain in the country of origin through the expiry of the term of protection.

(2)   If, however, through the expiry of the term of protection which was previously granted, a work has fallen into the public domain of the country where protection is claimed, that work shall not be protected anew.

(3)   The application of this principle shall be subject to any provisions contained in special conventions to that effect existing or to be concluded between countries of the Union. In the absence

of such provisions, the respective countries shall determine, each in so far as it is concerned, the conditions of application of this principle.

(4)   The preceding provisions shall also apply in the case of new accessions to the Union and to cases in which protection is extended by the application of Article 7 or by the abandonment of reservations.

### Article 19

The provisions of this Convention shall not preclude the making of a claim to the benefit of any greater protection which may be granted by legislation in a country of the Union.

### Article 20

The Governments of the countries of the Union reserve the right to enter into special agreements among themselves, in so far as such agreements grant to authors more extensive rights than those granted by the Convention, or contain other provisions not contrary to this Convention. The provisions of existing agreements which satisfy these conditions shall remain applicable.

### Article 21

(1)   Special provisions regarding developing countries are included in the Appendix.

(2)   Subject to the provisions of Article 28(1)(b), the Appendix forms an integral part of this Act.

### Article 22

(1)(a)   The Union shall have an Assembly consisting of those countries of the Union which are bound by Articles 22 to 26.

(b)   The Government of each country shall be represented by one delegate, who may be assisted by alternate delegates, advisers, and experts.

(c)   The expenses of each delegation shall be borne by the Government which has appointed it.

(2)(a)   The Assembly shall:

  (i)   deal with all matters concerning the maintenance and development of the Union and the implementation of this Convention;

  (ii)   give directions concerning the preparation for conferences of revision to the International Bureau of Intellectual Property (hereinafter designated as "the International Bureau") referred to in the Convention Establishing the World Intellectual Property Organization (hereinafter designed as "the Organization"), due account being taken of any comments made by those countries of the Union which are not bound by Articles 22 to 26;

  (iii)   review and approve the reports and activities of the Director General of the Organization concerning the Union, and give him all necessary instructions concerning matters within the competence of the Union;

  (iv)   elect the members of the Executive Committee of the Assembly;

  (v)   review and approve the reports and activities of its Executive Committee, and give instructions to such Committee;

  (vi)   determine the program and adopt the [triennial] * biennial ** budget of the Union, and approve its final accounts;

  (vii)   adopt the financial regulations of the Union;

---

*   Original wording in the Paris Act 1971.
**   Wording adopted by the Assembly of the Berne Union on 2 October 1979; entry into force 19 November 1984.

(viii)   establish such committees of experts and working groups as may be necessary for the work of the Union;

(ix)   determine which countries not members of the Union and which intergovernmental and international non-governmental organizations shall be admitted to its meetings as observers;

(x)   adopt amendments to Articles 22 to 26;

(xi)   take any other appropriate action designed to further the objectives of the Union;

(xii)   exercise such other functions as are appropriate under this Convention;

(xiii)   subject to its acceptance, exercise such rights as are given to it in the Convention establishing the Organization.

(b)   With respect to matters which are of interest also to other Unions administered by the Organization, the Assembly shall make its decisions after having heard the advice of the Coordination Committee of the Organization.

(3)(a)   Each country member of the Assembly shall have one vote.

(b)   One-half of the countries members of the Assembly shall constitute a quorum.

(c)   Notwithstanding the provisions of subparagraph (b), if, in any session, the number of countries represented is less than one-half but equal to or more than one-third of the countries members of the Assembly, the Assembly may make decisions but, with the exception of decisions concerning its own procedure, all such decisions shall take effect only if the following conditions are fulfilled. The International Bureau shall communicate the said decisions to the countries members of the Assembly which were not represented and shall invite them to express in writing their vote or abstention within a period of three months from the date of the communication. If, at the expiration of this period, the number of countries having thus expressed their vote or abstention attains the number of countries which was lacking for attaining the quorum in the session itself, such decisions shall take effect provided that at the same time the required majority still obtains.

(d)   Subject to the provisions of Article 26(2), the decisions of the Assembly shall require two-thirds of the votes cast.

(e)   Abstentions shall not be considered as votes.

(f)   A delegate may represent, and vote in the name of, one country only.

(g)   Countries of the Union not members of the Assembly shall be admitted to its meetings as observers.

(4)(a)   The Assembly shall meet once in every [third]* second** calendar year in ordinary session upon convocation by the Director General and, in the absence of exceptional circumstances, during the same period and at the same place as the General Assembly of the Organization.

(b)   The Assembly shall meet in extraordinary session upon convocation by the Director General, at the request of the Executive Committee or at the request of one-fourth of the countries members of the Assembly.

(5)   The Assembly shall adopt its own rules of procedure.

### Article 23

(1)   The Assembly shall have an Executive Committee.

(2)(a)   The Executive Committee shall consist of countries elected by the Assembly from among countries members of the Assembly. Furthermore, the country on whose territory the Organization has its headquarters shall, subject to the provisions of Article 25(7)(b), have an *ex officio* seat on the Committee.

(b)   The Government of each country member of the Executive Committee shall be represented by one delegate, who may be assisted by alternate delegates, advisers, and experts.

(c)   The expenses of each delegation shall be borne by the Government which has appointed it.

(3)   The number of countries members of the Executive Committee shall correspond to one-fourth of the number of countries members of the Assembly. In establishing the number of seats to be filled, remainders after division by four shall be disregarded.

(4)   In electing the members of the Executive Committee, the Assembly shall have due regard to an equitable geographical distribution and to the need for countries party to the Special Agreements which might be established in relation with the Union to be among the countries constituting the Executive Committee.

(5)(a)   Each member of the Executive Committee shall serve from the close of the session of the Assembly which elected it to the close of the next ordinary session of the Assembly.

(b)   Members of the Executive Committee may be re-elected, but not more than two-thirds of them.

(c)   The Assembly shall establish the details of the rules governing the election and possible re-election of the members of the Executive Committee.

(6)(a)   The Executive Committee shall:

  (i)   prepare the draft agenda of the Assembly

  (ii)   submit proposals to the Assembly respecting the draft program and [triennial]*** biennial**** budget of the Union prepared by the Director General;

  [(iii)   approve, within the limits of the program and the triennial budget, the specific yearly budgets and programs prepared by the Director General;]*****

  (iv)   submit, with appropriate comments, to the Assembly the periodical reports of the Director General and the yearly audit reports on the accounts;

  (v)   in accordance with the decisions of the Assembly and having regard to circumstances arising between two ordinary sessions of the Assembly, take all necessary measures to ensure the execution of the program of the Union by the Director General;

  (vi)   perform such other functions as are allocated to it under this Convention.

(b)   With respect to matters which are of interest also to other Unions administered by the Organization, the Executive Committee shall make its decisions after having heard the advice of the Coordination Committee of the Organization.

(7)(a)   The Executive Committee shall meet once a year in ordinary session upon convocation by the Director General, preferably during the same period and at the same place as the Coordination Committee of the Organization.

(b)   The Executive Committee shall meet in extraordinary session upon convocation by the Director General, either on his own initiative, or at the request of its Chairman or one-fourth of its members.

(8)(a)   Each country member of the Executive Committee shall have one vote.

(b)   One-half of the members of the Executive Committee shall constitute a quorum.

(c)   Decisions shall be made by a simple majority of the votes cast.

---

*** Original wording in the Paris Act 1971.
**** Wording adopted by the Assembly of the Berne Union on 2 October 1979; entry into force 19 November 1984.
***** Original wording deleted by Assembly on 2 October 1979; entry into force 19 November 1984.

(d)   Abstentions shall not be considered as votes.

(e)   A delegate may represent, and vote in the name of, one country only.

(9)   Countries of the Union not members of the Executive Committee shall be admitted to its meetings as observers.

(10)  The Executive Committee shall adopt its own rules of procedure.

**Article 24**

(1)(a)  The administrative tasks with respect to the Union shall be performed by the International Bureau, which is a continuation of the Bureau of the Union united with the Bureau of the Union established by the International Convention for the Protection of Industrial Property.

(b)   In particular, the International Bureau shall provide the secretariat of the various organs of the Union.

(c)   The Director General of the Organization shall be the chief executive of the Union and shall represent the Union.

(2)   The International Bureau shall assemble and publish information concerning the protection of copyright. Each country of the Union shall promptly communicate to the International Bureau all new laws and official texts concerning the protection of copyright.

(3)   The International Bureau shall publish a monthly periodical.

(4)   The International Bureau shall, on request, furnish information to any country of the Union on matters concerning the protection of copyright.

(5)   The International Bureau shall conduct studies, and shall provide services, designed to facilitate the protection of copyright.

(6)   The Director General and any staff member designated by him shall participate, without the right to vote, in all meetings of the Assembly, the Executive Committee and any other committee of experts or working group. The Director General, or a staff member designated by him, shall be *ex officio* secretary of these bodies.

(7)(a)  The International Bureau shall, in accordance with the directions of the Assembly and in cooperation with the Executive Committee, make the preparations for the conferences of revision of the provisions of the Convention other than Articles 22 to 26.

(b)   The International Bureau may consult with inter-governmental and international non-governmental organizations concerning preparations for conferences of revision.

(c)   The Director General and persons designated by him shall take part, without the right to vote, in the discussions at these conferences.

(8)   The International Bureau shall carry out any other tasks assigned to it.

**Article 25**

(1)(a)  The Union shall have a budget.

(b)   The budget of the Union shall include the income and expenses proper to the Union, its contribution to the budget of expenses common to the Unions, and, where applicable, the sum made available to the budget of the Conference of the Organization.

(c)   Expenses not attributable exclusively to the Union but also to one or more other Unions administered by the Organization shall be considered as expenses common to the Unions. The share of the Union in such common expenses shall be in proportion to the interest the Union has in them.

(2)   The budget of the Union shall be established with due regard to the requirements of coordination with the budgets of the other Unions administered by the Organization.

(3)   The budget of the Union shall be financed from the following sources:

   (i)    contributions of the countries of the Union;

   (ii)   fees and charges due for services performed by the International Bureau in relation to the Union;

   (iii)  sale of, or royalties on, the publications of the International Bureau concerning the Union;

   (iv)  gifts, bequests, and subventions;

   (v)   rents, interests, and other miscellaneous income.

   (4)(a)   For the purpose of establishing its contribution towards the budget, each country of the Union shall belong to a class, and shall pay its annual contributions on the basis of a number of units fixed as follows:

| | |
|---|---|
| Class I | 25 |
| Class II | 20 |
| Class III | 15 |
| Class IV | 10 |
| Class V | 5 |
| Class VI | 3 |
| Class VII | 1 |

   (b)   Unless it has already done so, each country shall indicate, concurrently with depositing its instrument of ratification or accession, the class to which it wishes to belong. Any country may change class. If it chooses a lower class, the country must announce it to the Assembly at one of its ordinary sessions. Any such change shall take effect at the beginning of the calendar year following the session.

   (c)   The annual contribution of each country shall be an amount in the same proportion to the total sum to be contributed to the annual budget of the Union by all countries as the number of its units is to the total of the units of all contributing countries.

   (d)   Contributions shall become due on the first of January of each year.

   (e)   A country which is in arrears in the payment of its contributions shall have no vote in any of the organs of the Union of which it is a member if the amount of its arrears equals or exceeds the amount of the contributions due from it for the preceding two full years. However, any organ of the Union may allow such a country to continue to exercise its vote in that organ if, and as long as, it is satisfied that the delay in payment is due to exceptional and unavoidable circumstances.

   (f)   If the budget is not adopted before the beginning of a new financial period, it shall be at the same level as the budget of the previous year, in accordance with the financial regulations.

   (5)   The amount of the fees and charges due for services rendered by the International Bureau in relation to the Union shall be established, and shall be reported to the Assembly and the Executive Committee, by the Director General.

   (6)(a)   The Union shall have a working capital fund which shall be constituted by a single payment made by each country of the Union. If the fund becomes insufficient, an increase shall be decided by the Assembly.

   (b)   The amount of the initial payment of each country to the said fund or of its participation in the increase thereof shall be a proportion of the contribution of that country for the year in which the fund is established or the increase decided.

(c)    The proportion and the terms of payment shall be fixed by the Assembly on the proposal of the Director General and after it has heard the advice of the Coordination Committee of the Organization.

(7)(a)   In the headquarters agreement concluded with the country on the territory of which the Organization has its headquarters, it shall be provided that, whenever the working capital fund is insufficient, such country shall grant advances. The amount of these advances and the conditions on which they are granted shall be the subject of separate agreements, in each case, between such country and the Organization. As long as it remains under the obligation to grant advances, such country shall have an *ex officio* seat on the Executive Committee.

(b)    The country referred to in subparagraph (a) and the Organization shall each have the right to denounce the obligation to grant advances, by written notification. Denunciation shall take effect three years after the end of the year in which it has been notified.

(8)    The auditing of the accounts shall be effected by one or more of the countries of the Union or by external auditors, as provided in the financial regulations. They shall be designated, with their agreement, by the Assembly.

### Article 26

(1)    Proposals for the amendment of Articles 22, 23, 24, 25, and the present Article, may be initiated by any country member of the Assembly, by the Executive Committee, or by the Director General. Such proposals shall be communicated by the Director General to the member countries of the Assembly at least six months in advance of their consideration by the Assembly.

(2)    Amendments to the Articles referred to in paragraph (1) shall be adopted by the Assembly. Adoption shall require three-fourths of the votes cast, provided that any amendment of Article 22, and of the present paragraph, shall require four-fifths of the votes cast.

(3)    Any amendment to the Articles referred to in paragraph (1) shall enter into force one month after written notifications of acceptance, effected in accordance with their respective constitutional processes, have been received by the Director General from three-fourths of the countries members of the Assembly at the time it adopted the amendment. Any amendment to the said Articles thus accepted shall bind all the countries which are members of the Assembly at the time the amendment enters into force, or which become members thereof at a subsequent date, provided that any amendment increasing the financial obligations of countries of the Union shall bind only those countries which have notified their acceptance of such amendment.

### Article 27

(1)    This Convention shall be submitted to revision with a view to the introduction of amendments designed to improve the system of the Union.

(2)    For this purpose, conferences shall be held successively in one of the countries of the Union among the delegates of the said countries.

(3)    Subject to the provisions of Article 26 which apply to the amendment of Articles 22 to 26, any revision of this Act, including the Appendix, shall require the unanimity of the votes cast.

### Article 28

(1)(a)   Any country of the Union which has signed this Act may ratify it, and, if it has not signed it, may accede to it. Instruments of ratification or accession shall be deposited with the Director General.

(b)    Any country of the Union may declare in its instrument of ratification or accession that its ratification or accession shall not apply to Articles 1 to 21 and the Appendix, provided that, if such country has previously made a declaration under Article VI(1) of the Appendix, then it may declare in the said instrument only that its ratification or accession shall not apply to Articles 1 to 20.

(c)   Any country of the Union which, in accordance with subparagraph (b), has excluded provisions therein referred to from the effects of its ratification or accession may at any later time declare that it extends the effects of its ratification or accession to those provisions. Such declaration shall be deposited with the Director General.

(2)(a)   Articles 1 to 21 and the Appendix shall enter into force three months after both of the following two conditions are fulfilled:

  (i)   at least five countries of the Union have ratified or acceded to this Act without making a declaration under paragraph (1)(b),

  (ii)   France, Spain, the United Kingdom of Great Britain and Northern Ireland, and the United States of America, have become bound by the Universal Copyright Convention as revised at Paris on July 24, 1971.

(b)   The entry into force referred to in subparagraph (a) shall apply to those countries of the Union which, at least three months before the said entry into force, have deposited instruments of ratification or accession not containing a declaration under paragraph (1)(b).

(c)   With respect to any country of the Union not covered by subparagraph (b) and which ratifies or accedes to this Act without making a declaration under paragraph (1)(b), Articles 1 to 21 and the Appendix shall enter into force three months after the date on which the Director General has notified the deposit of the relevant instrument of ratification or accession, unless a subsequent date has been indicated in the instrument deposited. In the latter case, Articles 1 to 21 and the Appendix shall enter into force with respect to that country on the date thus indicated.

(d)   The provisions of subparagraphs (a) to (c) do not affect the application of Article VI of the Appendix.

(3)   With respect to any country of the Union which ratifies or accedes to this Act with or without a declaration made under paragraph (1)(b), Articles 22 to 38 shall enter into force three months after the date on which the Director General has notified the deposit of the relevant instrument of ratification or accession, unless a subsequent date has been indicated in the instrument deposited. In the latter case, Articles 22 to 38 shall enter into force with respect to that country on the date thus indicated.

## Article 29

(1)   Any country outside the Union may accede to this Act and thereby become party to this Convention and a member of the Union. Instruments of accession shall be deposited with the Director General.

(2)(a)   Subject to subparagraph (b), this Convention shall enter into force with respect to any country outside the Union three months after the date on which the Director General has notified the deposit of its instrument of accession, unless a subsequent date has been indicated in the instrument deposited. In the latter case, this Convention shall enter into force with respect to that country on the date thus indicated.

(b)   If the entry into force according to subparagraph (a) precedes the entry into force of Articles 1 to 21 and the Appendix according to Article 28(2)(a), the said country shall, in the meantime, be bound, instead of by Articles 1 to 21 and the Appendix, by Articles 1 to 20 of the Brussels Act of this Convention.

## Article 29<sup>bis</sup>

Ratification of or accession to this Act by any country not bound by Articles 22 to 38 of the Stockholm Act of this Convention shall, for the sole purposes of Article 14(2) of the Convention establishing the Organization, amount to ratification of or accession to the said Stockholm Act with the limitation set forth in Article 28(1)(b)(i) thereof.

279

# BERNE CONVENTION (1971)

### Article 30

(1)   Subject to the exceptions permitted by paragraph (2) of this Article, by Article 28(1)(b), by Article 33(2), and by the Appendix, ratification or accession shall automatically entail acceptance of all the provisions and admission to all the advantages of this Convention.

(2)(a)   Any country of the Union ratifying or acceding to this Act may, subject to Article V(2) of the Appendix, retain the benefit of the reservations it has previously formulated on condition that it makes a declaration to that effect at the time of the deposit of its instrument of ratification or accession.

(b)   Any country outside the Union may declare, in acceding to this Convention and subject to Article V(2) of the Appendix, that it intends to substitute, temporarily at least, for Article 8 of this Act concerning the right of translation, the provisions of Article 5 of the Union Convention of 1886, as completed at Paris in 1896, on the clear understanding that the said provisions are applicable only to translations into a language in general use in the said country. Subject to Article I(6)(b) of the Appendix, any country has the right to apply, in relation to the right of translation of works whose country of origin is a country availing itself of such a reservation, a protection which is equivalent to the protection granted by the latter country.

(c)   Any country may withdraw such reservations at any time by notification addressed to the Director General.

### Article 31

(1)   Any country may declare in its instrument of ratification or accession, or may inform the Director General by written notification at any time thereafter, that this Convention shall be applicable to all or part of those territories, designated in the declaration or notification, for the external relations of which it is responsible.

(2)   Any country which has made such a declaration or given such a notification may, at any time, notify the Director General that this Convention shall cease to be applicable to all or part of such territories.

(3)(a)   Any declaration made under paragraph (1) shall take effect on the same date as the ratification or accession in which it was included, and any notification given under that paragraph shall take effect three months after its notification by the Director General.

(b)   Any notification given under paragraph (2) shall take effect twelve months after its receipt by the Director General.

(4)   This Article shall in no way be understood as implying the recognition or tacit acceptance by a country of the Union of the factual situation concerning a territory to which this Convention is made applicable by another country of the Union by virtue of a declaration under paragraph (1).

### Article 32

(1)   This Act shall, as regards relations between the countries of the Union, and to the extent that it applies, replace the Berne Convention of 9 September 1886, and the subsequent Acts of revision. The Acts previously in force shall continue to be applicable, in their entirety or to the extent that this Act does not replace them by virtue of the preceding sentence, in relations with countries of the Union which do not ratify or accede to this Act.

(2)   Countries outside the Union which become party to this Act shall, subject to paragraph (3), apply it with respect to any country of the Union not bound by this Act or which, although bound by this Act, has made a declaration pursuant to Article 28(1)(b). Such countries recognize that the said country of the Union, in its relations with them:

(i)    may apply the provisions of the most recent Act by which it is bound, and

(ii)   subject to Article I(6) of the Appendix, has the right to adapt the protection to the level provided for by this Act.

(3)   Any country which has availed itself of any of the faculties provided for in the Appendix may apply the provisions of the Appendix relating to the faculty or faculties of which it has availed itself in its relations with any other country of the Union which is not bound by this Act, provided that the latter country has accepted the application of the said provisions.

### Article 33

(1)   Any dispute between two or more countries of the Union concerning the interpretation or application of this Convention, not settled by negotiation, may, by any one of the countries concerned, be brought before the International Court of Justice by application in conformity with the Statute of the Court, unless the countries concerned agree on some other method of settlement. The country bringing the dispute before the Court shall inform the International Bureau; the International Bureau shall bring the matter to the attention of the other countries of the Union.

(2)   Each country may, at the time it signs this Act or deposits its instrument of ratification or accession, declare that it does not consider itself bound by the provisions of paragraph (1). With regard to any dispute between such country and any other country of the Union, the provisions of paragraph (1) shall not apply.

(3)   Any country having made a declaration in accordance with the provisions of paragraph (2) may, at any time, withdraw its declaration by notification addressed to the Director General.

### Article 34

(1)   Subject to Article 29$^{bis}$, no country may ratify or accede to earlier Acts of this Convention once Articles 1 to 21 and the Appendix have entered into force.

(2)   Once Articles 1 to 21 and the Appendix have entered into force, no country may make a declaration under Article 5 of the Protocol Regarding Developing Countries attached to the Stockholm Act.

### Article 35

(1)   This Convention shall remain in force without limitation as to time.

(2)   Any country may denounce this Act by notification addressed to the Director General. Such denunciation shall constitute also denunciation of all earlier Acts and shall affect only the country making it, the Convention remaining in full force and effect as regards the other countries of the Union.

(3)   Denunciation shall take effect one year after the day on which the Director General has received the notification.

(4)   The right of denunciation provided by this Article shall not be exercised by any country before the expiration of five years from the date upon which it becomes a member of the Union.

### Article 36

(1)   Any country party to this Convention undertakes to adopt, in accordance with its constitution, the measures necessary to ensure the application of this Convention.

(2)   It is understood that, at the time a country becomes bound by this Convention, it will be in a position under its domestic law to give effect to the provisions of this Convention.

### Article 37

(1)(a)   This Act shall be signed in a single copy in the French and English languages and, subject to paragraph (2), shall be deposited with the Director General.

(b)   Official texts shall be established by the Director General, after consultation with the interested Governments, in the Arabic, German, Italian, Portuguese and Spanish languages, and such other languages as the Assembly may designate.

281

# BERNE CONVENTION (1971)

(c)   In case of differences of opinion on the interpretation of the various texts, the French text shall prevail.

(2)   This Act shall remain open for signature until 31 January 1972. Until that date, the copy referred to in paragraph (1)(a) shall be deposited with the Government of the French Republic.

(3)   The Director General shall certify and transmit two copies of the signed text of this Act to the Governments of all countries of the Union and, on request, to the Government of any other country.

(4)   The Director General shall register this Act with the Secretariat of the United Nations.

(5)   The Director General shall notify the Governments of all countries of the Union of signatures, deposits of instruments of ratification or accession and any declarations included in such instruments or made pursuant to Articles 28(1)(c), 30(2)(a) and (b), and 33(2), entry into force of any provisions of this Act, notifications of denunciation, and notifications pursuant to Articles 30(2)(c), 31(1) and (2), 33(3), and 38(1), as well as the Appendix.

## Article 38

(1)   Countries of the Union which have not ratified or acceded to this Act and which are not bound by Articles 22 to 26 of the Stockholm Act of this Convention may, until 26 April 1975, exercise, if they so desire, the rights provided under the said Articles as if they were bound by them. Any country desiring to exercise such rights shall give written notification to this effect to the Director General; this notification shall be effective on the date of its receipt. Such countries shall be deemed to be members of the Assembly until the said date.

(2)   As long as all the countries of the Union have not become Members of the Organization, the International Bureau of the Organization shall also function as the Bureau of the Union, and the Director General as the Director of the said Bureau.

(3)   Once all the countries of the Union have become Members of the Organization, the rights, obligations, and property, of the Bureau of the Union shall devolve on the International Bureau of the Organization.

## Appendix

### Article I

(1)   Any country regarded as a developing country in conformity with the established practice of the General Assembly of the United Nations which ratifies or accedes to this Act, of which this Appendix forms an integral part, and which, having regard to its economic situation and its social or cultural needs, does not consider itself immediately in a position to make provision for the protection of all the rights as provided for in this Act, may, by a notification deposited with the Director General at the time of depositing its instrument of ratification or accession or, subject to Article V(1)(c), at any time thereafter, declare that it will avail itself of the faculty provided for in Article II, or of the faculty provided for in Article III, or of both of those faculties. It may, instead of availing itself of the faculty provided for in Article II, make a declaration according to Article V(1)(a).

(2)(a)   Any declaration under paragraph (1) notified before the expiration of the period of ten years from the entry into force of Articles 1 to 21 and this Appendix according to Article 28(2) shall be effective until the expiration of the said period. Any such declaration may be renewed in whole or in part for periods of ten years each by a notification deposited with the Director General not more than fifteen months and not less than three months before the expiration of the ten-year period then running.

(b)   Any declaration under paragraph (1) notified after the expiration of the period of ten years from the entry into force of Articles 1 to 21 and this Appendix according to Article 28(2) shall be effective until the expiration of the ten-year period then running. Any such declaration may be renewed as provided for in the second sentence of subparagraph (a).

(3)   Any country of the Union which has ceased to be regarded as a developing country as referred to in paragraph (1) shall no longer be entitled to renew its declaration as provided in paragraph (2), and, whether or not it formally withdraws its declaration, such country shall be precluded from availing itself of the facilities referred to in paragraph (1) from the expiration of the ten-year period then running or from the expiration of a period of three years after it has ceased to be regarded as a developing country, whichever period expires later.

(4)   Where, at the time when the declaration made under paragraph (1) or (2) ceases to be effective, there are copies in stock which were made under a licence granted by virtue of this Appendix, such copies may continue to be distributed until their stock is exhausted.

(5)   Any country which is bound by the provisions of this Act and which has deposited a declaration or a notification in accordance with Article 31(1) with respect to the application of this Act to a particular territory, the situation of which can be regarded as analogous to that of the countries referred to in paragraph (1), may, in respect of such territory, make the declaration referred to in paragraph (1) and the notification of renewal referred to in paragraph (2). As long as such declaration or notification remains in effect, the provisions of this Appendix shall be applicable to the territory in respect of which it was made.

(6)(a)   The fact that a country avails itself of any of the faculties referred to in paragraph (1) does not permit another country to give less protection to works of which the country of origin is the former country than it is obliged to grant under Articles 1 to 20.

(b)   The right to apply reciprocal treatment provided for in Article 30(2)(b), second sentence, shall not, until the date on which the period applicable under Article I(3) expires, be exercised in respect of works the country of origin of which is a country which has made a declaration according to Article V(1)(a).

### Article II

(1)   Any country which has declared that it will avail itself of the faculty provided for in this Article shall be entitled, so far as works published in printed or analogous forms of reproduction are concerned, to substitute for the exclusive right of translation provided for in Article 8 a system of non-exclusive and non-transferable licences, granted by the competent authority under the following conditions and subject to Article IV.

(2)(a)   Subject to paragraph (3), if, after the expiration of a period of three years, or of any longer period determined by the national legislation of the said country, commencing on the date of the first publication of the work, a translation of such work has not been published in a language in general use in that country by the owner of the right of translation, or with his authorization, any national of such country may obtain a licence to make a translation of the work in the said language and publish the translation in printed or analogous forms of reproduction.

(b)   A licence under the conditions provided for in this Article may also be granted if all the editions of the translation published in the language concerned are out of print.

(3)(a)   In the case of translations into a language which is not in general use in one or more developed countries which are members of the Union, a period of one year shall be substituted for the period of three years referred to in paragraph (2)(a).

(b)   Any country referred to in paragraph (1) may, with the unanimous agreement of the developed countries which are members of the Union and in which the same language is in general use, substitute, in the case of translations into that language, for the period of three years referred to in paragraph (2)(a) a shorter period as determined by such agreement but not less than one year. However, the provisions of the foregoing sentence shall not apply where the language in question is English, French or Spanish. The Director General shall be notified of any such agreement by the Governments which have concluded it.

(4)(a)   No licence obtainable after three years shall be granted under this Article until a further period of six months has elapsed, and no licence obtainable after one year shall be granted under this Article until a further period of nine months has elapsed

> (i)   from the date on which the applicant complies with the requirements mentioned in Article IV(1), or

> (ii)   where the identity or the address of the owner of the right of translation is unknown, from the date on which the applicant sends, as provided for in Article IV(2), copies of his application submitted to the authority competent to grant the licence.

(b)   If, during the said period of six or nine months, a translation in the language in respect of which the application was made is published by the owner of the right of translation or with his authorization, no licence under this Article shall be granted.

(5)   Any licence under this Article shall be granted only for the purpose of teaching, scholarship or research.

(6)   If a translation of a work is published by the owner of the right of translation or with his authorization at a price reasonably related to that normally charged in the country for comparable works, any licence granted under this Article shall terminate if such translation is in the same language and with substantially the same content as the translation published under the licence. Any copies already made before the licence terminates may continue to be distributed until their stock is exhausted.

(7)   For works which are composed mainly of illustrations, a licence to make and publish a translation of the text and to reproduce and publish the illustrations may be granted only if the conditions of Article III are also fulfilled.

(8)   No licence shall be granted under this Article when the author has withdrawn from circulation all copies of his work.

(9)(a)   A licence to make a translation of a work which has been published in printed or analogous forms of reproduction may also be granted to any broadcasting organization having its headquarters in a country referred to in paragraph (1), upon an application made to the competent authority of that country by the said organization, provided that all of the following conditions are met:

> (i)   the translation is made from a copy made and acquired in accordance with the laws of the said country;

> (ii)   the translation is only for use in broadcasts intended exclusively for teaching or for the dissemination of the results of specialized technical or scientific research to experts in a particular profession;

> (iii)   the translation is used exclusively for the purposes referred to in condition (ii) through broadcasts made lawfully and intended for recipients on the territory of the said country, including broadcasts made through the medium of sound or visual recordings lawfully and exclusively made for the purpose of such broadcasts;

> (iv)   all uses made of the translation are without any commercial purpose.

(b)   Sound or visual recordings of a translation which was made by a broadcasting organization under a licence granted by virtue of this paragraph may, for the purposes and subject to the conditions referred to in subparagraph (a) and with the agreement of that organization, also be used by any other broadcasting organization having its headquarters in the country whose competent authority granted the licence in question.

(c)   Provided that all of the criteria and conditions set out in subparagraph (a) are met, a licence may also be granted to a broadcasting organization to translate any text incorporated in an audio-visual fixation where such fixation was itself prepared and published for the sole purpose of being used in connection with systematic instructional activities.

(d)   Subject to subparagraphs (a) to (c), the provisions of the preceding paragraphs shall apply to the grant and exercise of any licence granted under this paragraph.

**Article III**

(1)   Any country which has declared that it will avail itself of the faculty provided for in this Article shall be entitled to substitute for the exclusive right of reproduction provided for in Article 9 a system of non-exclusive and non-transferable licences, granted by the competent authority under the following conditions and subject to Article IV.

(2)(a)   If, in relation to a work to which this Article applies by virtue of paragraph (7), after the expiration of

(i)   the relevant period specified in paragraph (3), commencing on the date of first publication of a particular edition of the work, or

(ii)   any longer period determined by national legislation of the country referred to in paragraph (1), commencing on the same date,

copies of such edition have not been distributed in that country to the general public or in connection with systematic instructional activities, by the owner of the right of reproduction or with his authorization, at a price reasonably related to that normally charged in the country for comparable works, any national of such country may obtain a licence to reproduce and publish such edition at that or a lower price for use in connection with systematic instructional activities.

(b)   A licence to reproduce and publish an edition which has been distributed as described in subparagraph (a) may also be granted under the conditions provided for in this Article if, after the expiration of the applicable period, no authorized copies of that edition have been on sale for a period of six months in the country concerned to the general public or in connection with systematic instructional activities at a price reasonably related to that normally charged in the country for comparable works.

(3)   The period referred to in paragraph (2)(a)(i) shall be five years, except that

(i)   for works of the natural and physical sciences, including mathematics, and of technology, the period shall be three years;

(ii)   for works of fiction, poetry, drama and music, and for art books, the period shall be seven years.

(4)(a)   No licence obtainable after three years shall be granted under this Article until a period of six months has elapsed

(i)   from the date on which the applicant complies with the requirements mentioned in Article IV(1), or

(ii)   where the identity or the address of the owner of the right of reproduction is unknown, from the date on which the applicant sends, as provided for in Article IV(2), copies of his application submitted to the authority competent to grant the licence.

(b)   Where licences are obtainable after other periods and Article IV(2) is applicable, no licence shall be granted until a period of three months has elapsed from the date of the dispatch of the copies of the application.

(c)   If, during the period of six or three months referred to in subparagraphs (a) and (b), a distribution as described in paragraph (2)(a) has taken place, no licence shall be granted under this Article.

(d)   No licence shall be granted if the author has withdrawn from circulation all copies of the edition for the reproduction and publication of which the licence has been applied for.

(5)   A licence to reproduce and publish a translation of a work shall not be granted under this Article in the following cases:

(i)    where the translation was not published by the owner of the right of translation or with this authorization, or

(ii)    where the translation is not in a language in general use in the country in which the licence is applied for.

(6)    If copies of an edition of a work are distributed in the country referred to in paragraph (1) to the general public or in connection with systematic instructional activities, by the owner of the right of reproduction or with his authorization, at a price reasonably related to that normally charged in the country for comparable works, any licence granted under this Article shall terminate if such edition is in the same language and with substantially the same content as the edition which was published under the said licence. Any copies already made before the licence terminates may continue to be distributed until their stock is exhausted.

(7)(a)    Subject to subparagraph (b), the works to which this Article applies shall be limited to works published in printed or analogous forms of reproduction.

(b)    This Article shall also apply to the reproduction in audio-visual form of lawfully made audio-visual fixations including any protected works incorporated therein and to the translation of any incorporated text into a language in general use in the country in which the licence is applied for, always provided that the audio-visual fixations in question were prepared and published for the sole purpose of being used in connection with systematic instructional activities.

## Article IV

(1)    A licence under Article II or Article III may be granted only if the applicant, in accordance with the procedure of the country concerned, establishes either that he has requested, and has been denied, authorization by the owner of the right to make and publish the translation or to reproduce and publish the edition, as the case may be, or that, after due diligence on his part, he was unable to find the owner of the right. At the same time as making the request, the applicant shall inform any national or international information centre referred to in paragraph (2).

(2)    If the owner of the right cannot be found, the applicant for a licence shall send, by registered airmail, copies of his application, submitted to the authority competent to grant the licence, to the publisher whose name appears on the work and to any national or international information centre which may have been designated, in a notification to that effect deposited with the Director General, by the Government of the country in which the publisher is believed to have his principal place of business.

(3)    The name of the author shall be indicated on all copies of the translation or reproduction published under a licence granted under Article II or Article III. The title of the work shall appear on all such copies. In the case of a translation, the original title of the work shall appear in any case on all the said copies.

(4)(a)    No licence granted under Article II or Article III shall extend to the export of copies, and any such licence shall be valid only for publication of the translation or of the reproduction, as the case may be, in the territory of the country in which it has been applied for.

(b)    For the purposes of subparagraph (a), the notion of export shall include the sending of copies from any territory to the country which, in respect of that territory, has made a declaration under Article I(5).

(c)    Where a governmental or other public entity of a country which has granted a licence to make a translation under Article II into a language other than English, French or Spanish sends copies of a translation published under such licence to another country, such sending of copies shall not, for the purposes of subparagraph (a), be considered to constitute export if all of the following conditions are met:

(i)    the recipients are individuals who are nationals of the country whose competent authority has granted the licence, or organizations grouping such individuals;

(ii) the copies are to be used only for the purpose of teaching, scholarship or research;

(iii) the sending of the copies and their subsequent distribution to recipients is without any commercial purpose; and

(iv) the country to which the copies have been sent has agreed with the country whose competent authority has granted the licence to allow the receipt, or distribution, or both, and the Director General has been notified of the agreement by the Government of the country in which the licence has been granted.

(5) All copies published under a licence granted by virtue of Article II or Article III shall bear a notice in the appropriate language stating that the copies are available for distribution only in the country or territory to which the said licence applies.

(6)(a) Due provision shall be made at the national level to ensure

(i) that the licence provides, in favour of the owner of the right of translation or of reproduction, as the case may be, for just compensation that is consistent with standards of royalties normally operating on licences freely negotiated between persons in the two countries concerned, and

(ii) payment and transmittal of the compensation: should national currency regulations intervene, the competent authority shall make all efforts, by the use of international machinery, to ensure transmittal in internationally convertible currency or its equivalent.

(b) Due provision shall be made by national legislation to ensure a correct translation of the work, or an accurate reproduction of the particular edition, as the case may be.

## Article V

(1)(a) Any county entitled to make a declaration that it will avail itself of the faculty provided for in Article II may, instead, at the time of ratifying or acceding to this Act:

(i) if it is a country to which Article 30(2)(a) applies, make a declaration under that provision as far as the right of translation is concerned;

(ii) if it is a country to which Article 30(2)(a) does not apply, and even if it is not a country outside the Union, make a declaration as provided for in Article 30(2)(b), first sentence.

(b) In the case of a country which ceases to be regarded as a developing country as referred to in Article I(1), a declaration made according to this paragraph shall be effective until the date on which the period applicable under Article I(3) expires.

(c) Any country which has made a declaration according to this paragraph may not subsequently avail itself of the faculty provided for in Article II even if it withdraws the said declaration.

(2) Subject to paragraph (3), any country which has availed itself of the faculty provided for in Article II may not subsequently make a declaration according to paragraph (1).

(3) Any country which has ceased to be regarded as a developing country as referred to in Article I(1) may, not later than two years prior to the expiration of the period applicable under Article I(3), make a declaration to the effect provided for in Article 30(2)(b), first sentence, notwithstanding the fact that it is not a country outside the Union. Such declaration shall take effect at the date on which the period applicable under Article I(3) expires.

## Article VI

(1) Any country of the Union may declare, as from the date of this Act, and at any time before becoming bound by Articles 1 to 21 and this Appendix:

(i)    if it is a country which, were it bound by Articles 1 to 21 and this Appendix, would be entitled to avail itself of the faculties referred to in Article I(1), that it will apply the provisions of Article II or of Article III or of both to works whose country of origin is a country which, pursuant to (ii) below, admits the application of those Articles to such works, or which is bound by Articles 1 to 21 and this Appendix; such declaration may, instead of referring to Article II, refer to Article V;

(ii)    that it admits the application of this Appendix to works of which it is the country of origin by countries which have made a declaration under (i) above or a notification under Article I.

(2)    Any declaration made under paragraph (1) shall be in writing and shall be deposited with the Director General. The declaration shall become effective from the date of its deposit.

# APPENDIX H

---

# AGREEMENT ON TRADE-RELATED ASPECTS OF INTELLECTUAL PROPERTY RIGHTS

Members,

*Desiring* to reduce distortions and impediments to international trade, and taking into account the need to promote effective and adequate protection of intellectual property rights, and to ensure that measures and procedures to enforce intellectual property rights do not themselves become barriers to legitimate trade;

*Recognizing,* to this end, the need for new rules and disciplines concerning:

(a)   the applicability of the basic principles of the GATT 1994 and of relevant international intellectual property agreements or conventions;

(b)   the provision of adequate standards and principles concerning the availability, scope and use of trade-related intellectual property rights;

(c)   the provision of effective and appropriate means for the enforcement of trade-related intellectual property rights, taking into account differences in national legal systems;

(d)   the provision of effective and expeditious procedures for the multilateral prevention and settlement of disputes between governments; and

(e)   transitional arrangements aiming at the fullest participation in the results of the negotiations;

# TRIPS AGREEMENT

*Recognizing* the need for a multilateral framework of principles, rules and disciplines dealing with international trade in counterfeit goods;

*Recognizing* that intellectual property rights are private rights;

*Recognizing* the underlying public policy objectives of national systems for the protection of intellectual property, including development and technological objectives;

*Recognizing* also the special needs of the least-developed country Members in respect of maximum flexibility in the domestic implementation of laws and regulations in order to enable them to create a sound and viable technological base;

*Emphasizing* the importance of reducing tensions by reaching strengthened commitments to resolve disputes on trade-related intellectual property issues through multilateral procedures;

*Desiring* to establish a mutually supportive relationship between the WTO and the World Intellectual Property Organization (WIPO) as well as other relevant international organizations;

*Hereby agree* as follows:

## PART I.   GENERAL PROVISIONS AND BASIC PRINCIPLES

### Article 1

### Nature and Scope of Obligations

1.    Members shall give effect to the provisions of this Agreement. Members may, but shall not be obliged to, implement in their domestic law more extensive protection than is required by this Agreement, provided that such protection does not contravene the provisions of this Agreement. Members shall be free to determine the appropriate method of implementing the provisions of this Agreement within their own legal system and practice.

2.    For the purposes of this Agreement, the term "intellectual property" refers to all categories of intellectual property that are the subject of Sections 1 to 7 of Part II.

3.    Members shall accord the treatment provided for in this Agreement to the nationals of other Members.[1] In respect for the relevant intellectual property right, the nationals of other Members shall be understood as those natural or legal persons that would meet the criteria for eligibility for protection provided for in the Paris Convention (1967), the Berne Convention (1971), the Rome Convention and the Treaty on Intellectual Property in Respect of Integrated Circuits, were all Members of the WTO members of those conventions.[2] Any Member availing itself of the possibilities provided in paragraph 3 of Article 5 or paragraph 2 of Article 6 of the Rome Convention shall make a notification as foreseen in those provisions to the Council for Trade-Related Aspects of Intellectual Property Rights.

### Article 2

### Intellectual Property Conventions

1.    In respect of Parts II, III and IV of this Agreement, Members shall comply with Articles 1–12 and 19 of the Paris Convention (1967).

---

[1]   When "nationals" are referred to in this Agreement, they shall be deemed, in the case of a separate customs territory Member of the WTO, to mean persons, natural or legal, who are domiciled or who have a real and effective industrial or commercial establishment in that customs territory.

[2]   In this Agreement, "Paris Convention" refers to the Paris Convention for the Protection of Industrial Property; "Paris Convention (1967)" refers to the Stockholm Act of this Convention of 14 July 1967. "Berne Convention" refers to the Berne Convention for the Protection of Literary and Artistic Works; "Berne Convention (1971)" refers to the Paris Act of this Convention of 24 July 1971. "Rome Convention" refers to the International Convention for the Protection of Performers, Producers of Phonograms and Broadcasting Organizations, adopted at Rome on 26 October 1961. "Treaty on Intellectual Property in Respect of Integrated Circuits" (IPIC Treaty) refers to the Treaty on Intellectual Property in Respect of Integrated Circuits, adopted at Washington on 26 May 1989.

2.    Nothing in Parts I to IV of this Agreement shall derogate from existing obligations that Members may have to each other under the Paris Convention, the Berne Convention, the Rome Convention and the Treaty on Intellectual Property in Respect of Integrated Circuits.

## Article 3

### National Treatment

1.    Each Member shall accord to the nationals of other Members treatment no less favourable than that it accords to its own nationals with regard to the protection[3] of intellectual property, subject to the exceptions already provided in, respectively, the Paris Convention (1967), the Berne Convention (1971), the Rome Convention and the Treaty on Intellectual Property in Respect of Integrated Circuits. In respect of performers, producers of phonograms and broadcasting organizations, this obligation only applies in respect of the rights provided under this Agreement. Any Member availing itself of the possibilities provided in Article 6 of the Berne Convention and paragraph 1(b) of Article 16 of the Rome Convention shall make a notification as foreseen in those provisions to the Council for Trade-Related Aspects of Intellectual Property Rights.

2.    Members may avail themselves of the exceptions permitted under paragraph 1 above in relation to judicial and administrative procedures, including the designation of an address for service or the appointment of an agent within the jurisdiction of a Member, only where such exceptions are necessary to secure compliance with laws and regulations which are not inconsistent with the provisions of this Agreement and where such practices are not applied in a manner which would constitute a disguised restriction on trade.

## Article 4

### Most-Favoured-Nation Treatment

With regard to the protection of intellectual property, any advantage, favour, privilege or immunity granted by a Member to the nationals of any other country shall be accorded immediately and unconditionally to the nationals of all other Members. Exempted from this obligation are any advantage, favour, privilege or immunity accorded by a Member:

(a)    deriving from international agreements on judicial assistance and law enforcement of a general nature and not particularly confined to the protection of intellectual property;

(b)    granted in accordance with the provisions of the Berne Convention (1971) or the Rome Convention authorizing that the treatment accorded be a function not of national treatment but of the treatment accorded in another country;

(c)    in respect of the rights of performers, producers of phonograms and broadcasting organizations not provided under this Agreement;

(d)    deriving from international agreements related to the protection of intellectual property which entered into force prior to the entry into force of the Agreement Establishing the WTO, provided that such agreements are notified to the Council for Trade-Related Aspects of Intellectual Property Rights and do not constitute an arbitrary or unjustifiable discrimination against nationals of other Members.

## Article 5

### Multilateral Agreements on Acquisition or Maintenance of Protection

The obligations under Articles 3 and 4 above do not apply to procedures provided in multilateral agreements concluded under the auspices of the World Intellectual Property Organization relating to the acquisition or maintenance of intellectual property rights.

---

[3]    For the purposes of Articles 3 and 4 of this Agreement, protection shall include matters affecting the availability, acquisition, scope, maintenance and enforcement of intellectual property rights as well as those matters affecting the use of intellectual property rights specifically addressed in this Agreement.

### Article 6

*Exhaustion*

For the purposes of dispute settlement under this Agreement, subject to the provisions of Articles 3 and 4 above nothing in this Agreement shall be used to address the issue of the exhaustion of intellectual property rights.

### Article 7

*Objectives*

The protection and enforcement of intellectual property rights should contribute to the promotion of technological innovation and to the transfer and dissemination of technology, to the mutual advantage of producers and users of technological knowledge and in a manner conducive to social and economic welfare, and to a balance of rights and obligations.

### Article 8

*Principles*

1.   Members may, in formulating or amending their national laws and regulations, adopt measures necessary to protect public health and nutrition, and to promote the public interest in sectors of vital importance to their socio-economic and technological development, provided that such measures are consistent with the provisions of this Agreement.

2.   Appropriate measures, provided that they are consistent with the provisions of this Agreement, may be used to prevent the abuse of intellectual property rights by right holders or the resort to practices which unreasonably restrain trade or adversely affect the international transfer of technology.

## PART II.   STANDARDS CONCERNING THE AVAILABILITY, SCOPE AND USE OF INTELLECTUAL PROPERTY RIGHTS

### Sec. 1.   Copyright and Related Rights

### Article 9

*Relation to Berne Convention*

1.   Members shall comply with Articles 1–21 and the Appendix of the Berne Convention (1971). However, Members shall not have rights or obligations under this Agreement in respect of the rights conferred under Article 6*bis* of that Convention or of the rights derived therefrom.

2.   Copyright protection shall extend to expressions and not to ideas, procedures, methods of operation or mathematical concepts as such.

### Article 10

*Computer Programs and Compilations of Data*

1.   Computer programs, whether in source or object code, shall be protected as literary works under the Berne Convention (1971).

2.   Compilations of data or other material, whether in machine readable or other form, which by reason of the selection or arrangement of their contents constitute intellectual creations shall be protected as such. Such protection, which shall not extend to the data or material itself, shall be without prejudice to any copyright subsisting in the data or material itself.

### Article 11

*Rental Rights*

In respect of at least computer programs and cinematographic works, a Member shall provide authors and their successors in title the right to authorize or to prohibit the commercial rental to the public of originals or copies of their copyright works. A Member shall be excepted from this obligation in respect of cinematographic works unless such rental has led to widespread copying of such works which is materially impairing the exclusive right of reproduction conferred in that Member on authors and their successors in title. In respect of computer programs, this obligation does not apply to rentals where the program itself is not the essential object of the rental.

## Article 12

### Term of Protection

Whenever the term of protection of a work, other than a photographic work or a work of applied art, is calculated on a basis other than the life of a natural person, such term shall be no less than fifty years from the end of the calendar year of authorized publication, or, failing such authorized publication within fifty years from the making of the work, fifty years from the end of the calendar year of making.

## Article 13

### Limitations and Exceptions

Members shall confine limitations or exceptions to exclusive rights to certain special cases which do not conflict with a normal exploitation of the work and do not unreasonably prejudice the legitimate interests of the right holder.

## Article 14

### Protection of Performers, Producers of Phonograms (Sound Recordings) and Broadcasting Organizations

1.   In respect of a fixation of their performance on a phonogram, performers shall have the possibility of preventing the following acts when undertaken without their authorization: the fixation of their unfixed performance and the reproduction of such fixation. Performers shall also have the possibility of preventing the following acts when undertaken without their authorization: the broadcasting by wireless means and the communication to the public of their live performance.

2.   Producers of phonograms shall enjoy the right to authorize or prohibit the direct or indirect reproduction of their phonograms.

3.   Broadcasting organizations shall have the right to prohibit the following acts when undertaken without their authorization: the fixation, the reproduction of fixations, and the rebroadcasting by wireless means of broadcasts, as well as the communication to the public of television broadcasts of the same. Where Members do not grant such rights to broadcasting organizations, they shall provide owners of copyright in the subject matter of broadcasts with the possibility of preventing the above acts, subject to the provisions of the Berne Convention (1971).

4.   The provisions of Article 11 in respect of computer programs shall apply *mutatis mutandis* to producers of phonograms and any other right holders in phonograms as determined in domestic law. If, on the date of the Ministerial Meeting concluding the Uruguay Round of Multilateral Trade Negotiations, a Member has in force a system of equitable remuneration of right holders in respect of the rental of phonograms, it may maintain such system provided that the commercial rental of phonograms is not giving rise to the material impairment of the exclusive rights of reproduction of right holders.

5.   The term of the protection available under this Agreement to performers and producers of phonograms shall last at least until the end of a period of fifty years computed from the end of the calendar year in which the fixation was made or the performance took place. The term of protection granted pursuant to paragraph 3 above shall last for at least twenty years from the end of the calendar year in which the broadcast took place.

6.   Any Member may, in relation to the rights conferred under paragraphs 1–3 above, provide for conditions, limitations, exceptions and reservations to the extent permitted by the Rome

TRIPS AGREEMENT

Convention. However, the provisions of Article 18 of the Berne Convention (1971) shall also apply, *mutatis mutandis,* to the rights of performers and producers of phonograms in phonograms.

## Sec. 2.   Trademarks

### Article 15

### *Protectable Subject Matter*

1.    Any sign, or any combination of signs, capable of distinguishing the goods or services of one undertaking from those of other undertakings, shall be capable of constituting a trademark. Such signs, in particular words including personal names, letters, numerals, figurative elements and combinations of colours as well as any combination of such signs, shall be eligible for registration as trademarks. Where signs are not inherently capable of distinguishing the relevant goods or services, Members may make registrability depend on distinctiveness acquired through use. Members may require, as a condition of registration, that signs be visually perceptible.

2.    Paragraph 1 above shall not be understood to prevent a Member from denying registration of a trademark on other grounds, provided that they do not derogate from the provisions of the Paris Convention (1967).

3.    Members may make registrability depend on use. However, actual use of a trademark shall not be a condition for filing an application for registration. An application shall not be refused solely on the ground that intended use has not taken place before the expiry of a period of three years from the date of application.

4.    The nature of the goods or services to which a trademark is to be applied shall in no case form an obstacle to registration of the trademark.

5.    Members shall publish each trademark either before it is registered or promptly after it is registered and shall afford a reasonable opportunity for petitions to cancel the registration. In addition, Members may afford an opportunity for the registration of a trademark to be opposed.

### Article 16

### *Rights Conferred*

1.    The owner of a registered trademark shall have the exclusive right to prevent all third parties not having his consent from using in the course of trade identical or similar signs for goods or services which are identical or similar to those in respect of which the trademark is registered where such use would result in a likelihood of confusion. In case of the use of an identical sign for identical goods or services, a likelihood of confusion shall be presumed. The rights described above shall not prejudice any existing prior rights, nor shall they affect the possibility of Members making rights available on the basis of use.

2.    Article 6*bis* of the Paris Convention (1967) shall apply, *mutatis mutandis,* to services. In determining whether a trademark is well-known, account shall be taken of the knowledge of the trademark in the relevant sector of the public, including knowledge in that Member obtained as a result of the promotion of the trademark.

3.    Article 6*bis* of the Paris Convention (1967) shall apply, *mutatis mutandis,* to goods or services which are not similar to those in respect of which a trademark is registered, provided that use of that trademark in relation to those goods or services would indicate a connection between those goods or services and the owner of the registered trademark and provided that the interests of the owner of the registered trademark are likely to be damaged by such use.

## Article 17

### Exceptions

Members may provide limited exceptions to the rights conferred by a trademark, such as fair use of descriptive terms, provided that such exceptions take account of the legitimate interests of the owner of the trademark and of third parties.

## Article 18

### Term of Protection

Initial registration, and each renewal of registration, of a trademark shall be for a term of no less than seven years. The registration of a trademark shall be renewable indefinitely.

## Article 19

### Requirement of Use

1. If use is required to maintain a registration, the registration may be cancelled only after an uninterrupted period of at least three years of non-use, unless valid reasons based on the existence of obstacles to such use are shown by the trademark owner. Circumstances arising independently of the will of the owner of the trademark which constitute an obstacle to the use of the trademark, such as import restrictions on or other government requirements for goods or services protected by the trademark, shall be recognized as valid reasons for non-use.

2. When subject to the control of its owner, use of a trademark by another person shall be recognized as use of the trademark for the purpose of maintaining the registration.

## Article 20

### Other Requirements

The use of a trademark in the course of trade shall not be unjustifiably encumbered by special requirements, such as use with another trademark, use in a special form or use in a manner detrimental to its capability to distinguish the goods or services of one undertaking from those of other undertakings. This will not preclude a requirement prescribing the use of the trademark identifying the undertaking producing the goods or services along with, but without linking it to, the trademark distinguishing the specific goods or services in question of that undertaking.

## Article 21

### Licensing and Assignment

Members may determine conditions on the licensing and assignment of trademarks, it being understood that the compulsory licensing of trademarks shall not be permitted and that the owner of a registered trademark shall have the right to assign his trademark with or without the transfer of the business to which the trademark belongs.

## Sec. 3. Geographical Indications

### Article 22

### Protection of Geographical Indications

1. Geographical indications are, for the purposes of this Agreement, indications which identify a good as originating in the territory of a Member, or a region or locality in that territory, where a given quality, reputation or other characteristic of the good is essentially attributable to its geographical origin.

2. In respect of geographical indications, Members shall provide the legal means for interested parties to prevent:

(a)   the use of any means in the designation or presentation of a good that indicates or suggests that the good in question originates in a geographical area other than the true place of origin in a manner which misleads the public as to the geographical origin of the good;

(b)   any use which constitutes an act of unfair competition within the meaning of Article 10*bis* of the Paris Convention (1967).

3.   A Member shall, *ex officio* if its legislation so permits or at the request of an interested party, refuse or invalidate the registration of a trademark which contains or consists of a geographical indication with respect to goods not originating in the territory indicated, if use of the indication in the trademark for such goods in that Member is of such a nature as to mislead the public as to the true place of origin.

4.   The provisions of the preceding paragraphs of this Article shall apply to a geographical indication which, although literally true as to the territory, region or locality in which the goods originate, falsely represents to the public that the goods originate in another territory.

*Article 23*

*Additional Protection for Geographical Indications for Wines and Spirits*

1.   Each Member shall provide the legal means for interested parties to prevent use of a geographical indication identifying wines not originating in the place indicated by the geographical indication in question or identifying spirits for spirits not originating in the place indicated by the geographical indication in question, even where the true origin of the goods is indicated or the geographical indication is used in translation or accompanied by expressions such as "kind", "type", "style", "imitation" or the like.[4]

2.   The registration of a trademark for wines which contains or consists of a geographical indication identifying wines or for spirits which contains or consists of a geographical indication identifying spirits shall be refused or invalidated, *ex officio* if domestic legislation so permits or at the request of an interested party, with respect to such wines or spirits not having this origin.

3.   In the case of homonymous geographical indications for wines, protection shall be accorded to each indication, subject to the provisions of paragraph 4 of Article 22 above. Each Member shall determine the practical conditions under which the homonymous indications in question will be differentiated from each other, taking into account the need to ensure equitable treatment of the producers concerned and that consumers are not misled.

4.   In order to facilitate the protection of geographical indications for wines, negotiations shall be undertaken in the Council for Trade-Related Aspects of Intellectual Property Rights concerning the establishment of a multilateral system of notification and registration of geographical indications for wines eligible for protection in those Members participating in the system.

*Article 24*

*International Negotiations; Exceptions*

1.   Members agree to enter into negotiations aimed at increasing the protection of individual geographical indications under Article 23. The provisions of paragraphs 4–8 below shall not be used by a Member to refuse to conduct negotiations or to conclude bilateral or multilateral agreements. In the context of such negotiations, Members shall be willing to consider the continued applicability of these provisions to individual geographical indications whose use was the subject of such negotiations.

2.   The Council for Trade-Related Aspects of Intellectual Property Rights shall keep under review the application of the provisions of this section; the first such review shall take place within two years of the entry into force of the Agreement Establishing the WTO. Any matter affecting the compliance with the obligations under these provisions may be drawn to the attention of the Council,

---

4   Notwithstanding the first sentence of Article 42, Members may, with respect to these obligations, instead provide for enforcement by administrative action.

which, at the request of a Member, shall consult with any Member or Members in respect of such matter in respect of which it has not been possible to find a satisfactory solution through bilateral or plurilateral consultations between the Members concerned. The Council shall take such action as may be agreed to facilitate the operation and further the objection of this Section.

3. In implementing this Section, a Member shall not diminish the protection of geographical indications that existed in that Member immediately prior to the date of entry into force of the Agreement Establishing the WTO.

4. Nothing in this Section shall require a Member to prevent continued and similar use of a particular geographical indication of another Member identifying wines or spirits in connection with goods or services by any of its nationals or domiciliaries who have used that geographical indication in a continuous manner with regard to the same or related goods or services in the territory of that Member either (a) for at least ten years preceding the date of the Ministerial Meeting concluding the Uruguay Round of Multilateral Trade Negotiations or (b) in good faith preceding that date.

5. Where a trademark has been applied for or registered in good faith, or where rights to a trademark have been acquired through use in good faith either:

(a) before the date of application of these provisions in that Member as defined in part VI below; or

(b) before the geographical indication is protected in its country of origin;

measures adopted to implement this Section shall not prejudice eligibility for or the validity of the registration of a trademark, or the right to use a trademark, on the basis that such a trademark is identical with, or similar to, a geographical indication.

6. Nothing in this section shall require a Member to apply its provisions in respect of a geographical indication of any other Member with respect to goods or services for which the relevant indication is identical with the term customary in common languages as the common name for such goods or services in the territory of that Member. Nothing in this Section shall require a Member to apply its provisions in respect of a geographical indication of any other Member with respect to products of the vine for which the relevant indication is identical with the customary name of a grape variety existing in the territory of that Member as of the date of entry into force of the Agreement establishing the WTO.

7. A Member may provide that any request made under this Section in connection with the use or registration of a trademark must be presented within five years after the adverse use of the protected indication has become generally known in that Member or after the date of registration of the trademark in that Member provided that the trademark has been published by that date, if such date is earlier than the date on which the adverse use became generally known in that Member, provided that the geographical indication is not used or registered in bad faith.

8. The provisions of this Section shall in no way prejudice the right of any person to use, in the course of trade, his name or the name of his predecessor in business, except where such name is used in such a manner as to mislead the public.

9. There shall be no obligation under this Agreement to protect geographical indications which are not or cease to be protected in their country of origin, or which have fallen into disuse in that country.

### Sec. 4. Industrial Designs

*Article 25*

*Requirements for Protection*

1. Members shall provide for the protection of independently created industrial designs that are new or original. Members may provide that designs are not new or original if they do not

significantly differ from known designs or combinations of known design features. Members may provide that such protection shall not extend to designs dictated essentially by technical or functional considerations.

2.   Each Member shall ensure that requirements for securing protection for textile designs, in particular in regard to any cost, examination or publication, do not unreasonably impair the opportunity to seek and obtain such protection. Members shall be free to meet this obligation through industrial design law or through copyright law.

### Article 26

### Protection

1.   The owner of a protected industrial design shall have the right to prevent third parties not having his consent from making, selling or importing articles bearing or embodying a design which is a copy, or substantially a copy, of the protected design, when such acts are undertaken for commercial purposes.

2.   Members may provide limited exceptions to the protection of industrial designs, provided that such exceptions do not unreasonably conflict with the normal exploitation of protected industrial designs and do not unreasonably prejudice the legitimate interests of the owner of the protected design, taking account of the legitimate interests of third parties.

3.   The duration of protection available shall amount to at least ten years.

## Sec. 5.  Patents

### Article 27

### Patentable Subject Matter

1.   Subject to the provisions of paragraphs 2 and 3 below, patents shall be available for any inventions, whether products or processes, in all fields of technology, provided that they are new, involve an inventive step and are capable of industrial application.[5] Subject to paragraph 4 of Article 65, paragraph 8 of Article 70 and paragraph 3 of this Article, patents shall be available and patent rights enjoyable without discrimination as to the place of invention, the field of technology and whether products are imported or locally produced.

2.   Members may exclude from patentability inventions, the prevention within their territory of the commercial exploitation of which is necessary to protect *ordre public* or morality, including to protect human, animal or plant life or health or to avoid serious prejudice to the environment, provided that such exclusion is not made merely because the exploitation is prohibited by domestic law.

3.   Members may also exclude from patentability:

   (a)   diagnostic, therapeutic and surgical methods for the treatment of humans or animals;

   (b)   plants and animals other than microorganisms, and essentially biological processes for the production of plants or animals other than nonbiological and microbiological processes. However, Members shall provide for the protection of plant varieties either by patents or by an effective *sui generis* system or by any combination thereof. The provisions of this sub-paragraph shall be reviewed four years after the entry into force of the Agreement Establishing the WTO.

### Article 28

### Rights Conferred

1.   A patent shall confer on its owner the following exclusive rights:

---

[5]   For the purposes of this Article, the terms "inventive step" and "capable of industrial application" may be deemed by a Member to be synonymous with the terms "non-obvious" and "useful" respectively.

(a)    where the subject matter of a patent is a product, to prevent third parties not having his consent from the acts of: making, using, offering for sale, selling, or importing[6] for these purposes that product;

(b)    where the subject matter of a patent is a process, to prevent third parties not having his consent from the act of using the process, and from the acts of: using, offering for sale, selling, or importing for these purposes at least the product obtained directly by that process.

2.    Patent owners shall also have the right to assign, or transfer by succession, the patent and to conclude licensing contracts.

## Article 29

### Conditions on Patent Applicants

1.    Members shall require that an applicant for a patent shall disclose the invention in a manner sufficiently clear and complete for the invention to be carried out by a person skilled in the art and may require the applicant to indicate the best mode for carrying out the invention known to the inventor at the filing date or, where priority is claimed, at the priority date of the application.

2.    Members may require an applicant for a patent to provide information concerning his corresponding foreign applications and grants.

## Article 30

### Exceptions to Rights Conferred

Members may provide limited exceptions to the exclusive rights conferred by a patent, provided that such exceptions do not unreasonably conflict with a normal exploitation of the patent and do not unreasonably prejudice the legitimate interests of the patent owner, taking account of the legitimate interests of third parties.

## Article 31

### Other Use Without Authorization of the Right Holder

Where the law of a Member allows for other use[7] of the subject matter of a patent without the authorization of the right holder, including use by the government or third parties authorized by the government, the following provisions shall be respected:

(a)    authorization of such use shall be considered on its individual merits;

(b)    such use may only be permitted if, prior to such use, the proposed user has made efforts to obtain authorization from the right holder on reasonable commercial terms and conditions and that such efforts have not been successful within a reasonable period of time. This requirement may be waived by a Member in the case of a national emergency or other circumstances of extreme urgency or in cases of public non-commercial use. In situations of national emergency or other circumstances of extreme urgency, the right holder shall, nevertheless, be notified as soon as reasonably practicable. In the case of public non-commercial use, where the government or contractor, without making a patent search, knows or has demonstrable grounds to know that a valid patent is or will be used by or for the government, the right holder shall be informed promptly;

(c)    the scope and duration of such use shall be limited to the purpose for which it was authorized, and in the case of semi-conductor technology shall only be for public non-commercial use or to remedy a practice determined after judicial or administrative process to be anti-competitive;

---

[6]    This right, like all other rights conferred under this Agreement in respect of the use, sale, importation or other distribution of goods, is subject to the provisions of Article 6 above.

[7]    "Other use" refers to use other than that allowed under Article 30.

(d)  such use shall be non-exclusive;

(e)  such use shall be non-assignable, except with that part of the enterprise or goodwill which enjoys such use;

(f)  any such use shall be authorized predominantly for the supply of the domestic market of the Member authorizing such use;

(g)  authorization for such use shall be liable, subject to adequate protection of the legitimate interests of the persons so authorized, to be terminated if and when the circumstances which led to it cease to exist and are unlikely to recur. The competent authority shall have the authority to review, upon motivated request, the continued existence of these circumstances;

(h)  the right holder shall be paid adequate remuneration in the circumstances of each case, taking into account the economic value of the authorization;

(i)  the legal validity of any decision relating to the authorization of such use shall be subject to judicial review or other independent review by a distinct higher authority in that Member;

(j)  any decision relating to the remuneration provided in respect of such use shall be subject to judicial review or other independent review by a distinct higher authority in that Member;

(k)  Members are not obliged to apply the conditions set forth in sub-paragraphs (b) and (f) above where such use is permitted to remedy a practice determined after judicial or administrative process to be anti-competitive. The need to correct anticompetitive practices may be taken into account in determining the amount of remuneration in such cases. Competent authorities shall have the authority to refuse termination of authorization if and when the conditions which led to such authorization are likely to recur;

(l)  where such use is authorized to permit the exploitation of a patent ("the second patent") which cannot be exploited without infringing another patent ("the first patent"), the following additional conditions shall apply:

(i)  the invention claimed in the second patent shall involve an important technical advance of considerable economic significance in relation to the invention claimed in the first patent;

(ii)  the owner of the first patent shall be entitled to a cross-licence on reasonable terms to use the invention claimed in the second patent; and

(iii)  the use authorized in respect of the first patent shall be non-assignable except with the assignment of the second patent.

### Article 32

#### Revocation/Forfeiture

An opportunity for judicial review of any decision to revoke or forfeit a patent shall be available.

### Article 33

#### Term of Protection

The term of protection available shall not end before the expiration of a period of twenty years counted from the filing date.[8]

---

[8]  It is understood that those Members which do not have a system of original grant may provide that the term of protection shall be computed from the filing date in the system of original grant.

## Article 34

### Process Patents: Burden of Proof

1.  For the purposes of civil proceedings in respect of the infringement of the rights of the owner referred to in paragraph 1(b) of Article 28 above, if the subject matter of a patent is a process for obtaining a product, the judicial authorities shall have the authority to order the defendant to prove that the process to obtain an identical product is different from the patented process. Therefore, Members shall provide, in at least one of the following circumstances, that any identical product when produced without the consent of the patent owner shall, in the absence of proof to the contrary, be deemed to have been obtained by the patented process:

   (a)   if the product obtained by the patented process is new;

   (b)   if there is a substantial likelihood that the identical product was made by the process and the owner of the patent has been unable through reasonable efforts to determine the process actually used.

2.  Any Member shall be free to provide that the burden of proof indicated in paragraph 1 shall be on the alleged infringer only if the condition referred to in sub-paragraph (a) is fulfilled or only if the condition referred to in sub-paragraph (b) is fulfilled.

3.  In the adduction of proof to the contrary, the legitimate interests of the defendant in protecting his manufacturing and business secrets shall be taken into account.

## Sec. 6.   Layout-Designs (Topographies) of Integrated Circuits

### Article 35

#### Relation to IPIC Treaty

Members agree to provide protection to the layout-designs (topographies) of integrated circuits (hereinafter referred to as "layout-designs") in accordance with Articles 2–7 (other than paragraph 3 of Article 6), Article 12 and paragraph 3 of Article 16 of the Treaty on Intellectual Property in Respect of Integrated Circuits and, in addition, to comply with the following provisions.

### Article 36

#### Scope of the Protection

Subject to the provisions of paragraph 1 of Article 37 below, Members shall consider unlawful the following acts if performed without the authorization of the right holder:[9] importing, selling, or otherwise distributing for commercial purposes a protected layout-design, an integrated circuit in which a protected layout-design is incorporated, or an article incorporating such an integrated circuit only insofar as it continues to contain an unlawfully reproduced layout-design.

### Article 37

#### Acts Not Requiring the Authorization of the Right Holder

1.  Notwithstanding Article 36 above, no Member shall consider unlawful the performance of any of the acts referred to in that Article in respect of an integrated circuit incorporating an unlawfully reproduced layout-design or any article incorporating such an integrated circuit where the person performing or ordering such acts did not know and had no reasonable ground to know, when acquiring the integrated circuit or article incorporating such an integrated circuit, that it incorporated an unlawfully reproduced layout-design. Members shall provide that, after the time that such person has received sufficient notice that the layout-design was unlawfully reproduced, he may perform any of the acts with respect to the stock on hand or ordered before such time, but shall be liable to pay to the

---

[9]   The term "right holder" in this Section shall be understood as having the same meaning as the term "holder of the right" in the IPIC Treaty.

right holder a sum equivalent to a reasonable royalty such as would be payable under a freely negotiated licence in respect of such a layout-design.

2.    The conditions set out in sub-paragraphs (a)–(k) of Article 31 above shall apply *mutatis mutandis* in the event of any non-voluntary licensing of a layout-design or of its use by or for the government without the authorization of the right holder.

### Article 38

### Term of Protection

1.    In Members requiring registration as a condition of protection, the term of protection of layout-designs shall not end before the expiration of a period of ten years counted from the date of filing an application for registration or from the first commercial exploitation wherever in the world it occurs.

2.    In Members not requiring registration as a condition for protection, layout-designs shall be protected for a term of no less than ten years from the date of the first commercial exploitation wherever in the world it occurs.

3.    Notwithstanding paragraphs 1 and 2 above, a Member may provide that protection shall lapse fifteen years after the creation of the layout-design.

### Sec. 7.   Protection of Undisclosed Information

### Article 39

1.    In the course of ensuring effective protection against unfair competition as provided in Article 10*bis* of the Paris Convention (1967), Members shall protect undisclosed information in accordance with paragraph 2 below and data submitted to governments or governmental agencies in accordance with paragraph 3 below.

2.    Natural and legal persons shall have the possibility of preventing information lawfully within their control from being disclosed to, acquired by, or used by others without their consent in a manner contrary to honest commercial practices[10] so long as such information:

(a)    is secret in the sense that is not, as a body or in the precise configuration and assembly of its components, generally known among or readily accessible to persons within the circles that normally deal with the kind of information in question;

(b)    has commercial value because it is secret; and

(c)    has been subject to reasonable steps under the circumstances, by the person lawfully in control of the information, to keep it secret.

3.    Members, when requiring, as a condition of approving the marketing of pharmaceutical or of agricultural chemical products which utilize new chemical entities, the submission of undisclosed test or other data, the origination of which involves a considerable effort, shall protect such data against unfair commercial use. In addition, Members shall protect such data against disclosure, except where necessary to protect the public, or unless steps are taken to ensure that the data are protected against unfair commercial use.

---

[10]    For the purpose of this provision, "a manner contrary to honest commercial practices" shall mean at least practices such as breach of contract, breach of confidence and inducement to breach, and includes the acquisition of undisclosed information by third parties who knew, or were grossly negligent in failing to know, that such practices were involved in the acquisition.

### Sec. 8. Control of Anti-Competitive Practices
### in Contractual Licences

*Article 40*

1.   Members agree that some licensing practices or conditions pertaining to intellectual property rights which restrain competition may have adverse effects on trade and may impede the transfer and dissemination of technology.

2.   Nothing in this Agreement shall prevent Members from specifying in their national legislation licensing practices or conditions that may in particular cases constitute an abuse of intellectual property rights having an adverse effect on competition in the relevant market. As provided above, a Member may adopt, consistently with the other provisions of this Agreement, appropriate measures to prevent or control such practices, which may include for example exclusive grantback conditions, conditions preventing challenges to validity and coercive package licensing, in the light of the relevant laws and regulations of that Member.

3.   Each Member shall enter, upon request, into consultations with any other Member which has cause to believe that an intellectual property right owner that is a national or domiciliary of the Member to which the request for consultations has been addressed is undertaking practices in violation of the requesting Member's laws and regulations on the subject matter of this Section, and which wishes to secure compliance with such legislation, without prejudice to any action under law and to the full freedom of an ultimate decision of either Member. The Member addressed shall accord full and sympathetic consideration to, and shall afford adequate opportunity for, consultations with the requesting Member, and shall co-operate through supply of publicly available nonconfidential information of relevance to the matter in question and of other information available to the Member, subject to domestic law and to the conclusion of mutually satisfactory agreements concerning the safeguarding of its confidentiality by the requesting Member.

4.   A Member whose nationals or domiciliaries are subject to proceedings in another member concerning alleged violation of that other Member's laws and regulations on the subject matter of this Section shall, upon request, be granted an opportunity for consultations by the other Member under the same conditions as those foreseen in paragraph 3 above.

## PART III.   ENFORCEMENT OF INTELLECTUAL PROPERTY RIGHTS

### Sec. 1.   General Obligations

*Article 41*

1.   Members shall ensure that enforcement procedures as specified in this Part are available under their national laws so as to permit effective action against any act of infringement of intellectual property rights covered by this Agreement, including expeditious remedies to prevent infringements and remedies which constitute a deterrent to further infringements. These procedures shall be applied in such a manner as to avoid the creation of barriers to legitimate trade and to provide for safeguards against their abuse.

2.   Procedures concerning the enforcement of intellectual property rights shall be fair and equitable. They shall not be unnecessarily complicated or costly, or entail unreasonable time-limits or unwarranted delays.

3.   Decisions on the merits of a case shall preferably be in writing and reasoned. They shall be made available at least to the parties to the proceeding without undue delay. Decisions on the merits of a case shall be based only on evidence in respect of which parties were offered the opportunity to be heard.

4.   Parties to a proceeding shall have an opportunity for review by a judicial authority of final administrative decisions and, subject to jurisdictional provisions in national laws concerning the importance of a case, of at least the legal aspects of initial judicial decisions on the merits of a case.

However, there shall be no obligation to provide an opportunity for review of acquittals in criminal cases.

5.    It is understood that this Part does not create any obligation to put in place a judicial system for the enforcement of intellectual property rights distinct from that for the enforcement of laws in general, nor does it affect the capacity of Members to enforce their laws in general. Nothing in this Part creates any obligations with respect to the distribution of resources as between enforcement of intellectual property rights and the enforcement of laws in general.

### Sec. 2.   Civil and Administrative Procedures and Remedies

#### Article 42

#### Fair and Equitable Procedures

Members shall make available to right holders[11] civil judicial procedures concerning the enforcement of any intellectual property right covered by this agreement. Defendants shall have the right to written notice which is timely and contains sufficient detail, including the basis of the claims. Parties shall be allowed to be represented by independent legal counsel, and procedures shall not impose overly burdensome requirements concerning mandatory personal appearances. All parties to such procedures shall be duly entitled to substantiate their claims and to present all relevant evidence. The procedure shall provide a means to identify and protect confidential information, unless this would be contrary to existing constitutional requirements.

#### Article 43

#### Evidence of Proof

1.    The judicial authorities shall have the authority, where a party has presented reasonably available evidence sufficient to support its claims and has specified evidence relevant to substantiation of its claims which lies in the control of the opposing party, to order that this evidence be produced by the opposing party, subject in appropriate cases to conditions which ensure the protection of confidential information.

2.    In cases in which a party to a proceeding voluntarily and without good reason refuses access to, or otherwise does not provide necessary information within a reasonable period, or significantly impedes a procedure relating to an enforcement action, a Member may accord judicial authorities the authority to make preliminary and final determinations, affirmative or negative, on the basis of the information presented to them, including the complaint or the allegation presented by the party adversely affected by the denial of access to information, subject to providing the parties an opportunity to be heard on the allegations or evidence.

#### Article 44

#### Injunctions

1.    The judicial authorities shall have the authority to order a party to desist from an infringement, *inter alia* to prevent the entry into the channels of commerce in their jurisdiction of imported goods that involve the infringement of an intellectual property right, immediately after customs clearance of such goods. Members are not obliged to accord such authority in respect of protected subject matter acquired or ordered by a person prior to knowing or having reasonable grounds to know that dealing in such subject matter would entail the infringement of an intellectual property right.

2.    Notwithstanding the other provisions of this Part and provided that the provisions of Part II specifically addressing use by governments, or by third parties authorized by a government, without the authorization of the right holder are complied with, Members may limit the remedies available against such use to payment of remuneration in accordance with sub-paragraph (h) of Article 31 above.

---

[11]  For the purpose of this Part, the term "right holder" includes federations and associations having legal standing to assert such rights.

In other cases, the remedies under this Part shall apply or, where these remedies are inconsistent with national law, declaratory judgments and adequate compensation shall be available.

## Article 45

### Damages

1.    The judicial authorities shall have the authority to order the infringer to pay the right holder damages adequate to compensate for the injury the right holder has suffered because of an infringement of his intellectual property right by an infringer who knew or had reasonable grounds to know that he was engaged in infringing activity.

2.    The judicial authorities shall also have the authority to order the infringer to pay the right holder expenses, which may include appropriate attorney's fees. In appropriate cases, Members may authorize the judicial authorities to order recovery of profits and/or payment of pre-established damages even where the infringer did not know or had no reasonable grounds to know that he was engaged in infringing activity.

## Article 46

### Other Remedies

In order to create an effective deterrent to infringement, the judicial authorities shall have the authority to order that goods that they have found to be infringing be, without compensation of any sort, disposed of outside the channels of commerce in such a manner as to avoid any harm caused to the right holder, or, unless this would be contrary to existing constitutional requirements, destroyed. The judicial authorities shall also have the authority to order that materials and implements the predominant use of which has been in the creation of the infringing goods be, without compensation of any sort, disposed of outside the channels of commerce in such a manner as to minimize the risks of further infringements. In considering such requests, the need for proportionality between the seriousness of the infringement and the remedies ordered as well as the interests of third parties shall be taken into account. In regard to counterfeit trademark goods, the simple removal of the trademark unlawfully affixed shall not be sufficient, other than in exceptional cases, to permit release of the goods into the channels of commerce.

## Article 47

### Right of Information

Members may provide that the judicial authorities shall have the authority, unless this would be out of proportion to the seriousness of the infringement, to order the infringer to inform the right holder of the identity of third persons involved in the production and distribution of the infringing goods or services and of their channels of distribution.

## Article 48

### Indemnification of the Defendant

1.    The judicial authorities shall have the authority to order a party at whose request measures were taken and who has abused enforcement procedures to provide to a party wrongfully enjoined or restrained adequate compensation for the injury suffered because of such abuse. The judicial authorities shall also have the authority to order the applicant to pay the defendant expenses, which may include appropriate attorney's fees.

2.    In respect of the administration of any law pertaining to the protection or enforcement of intellectual property rights, Members shall only exempt both public authorities and officials from liability to appropriate remedial measures where actions are taken or intended in good faith in the course of the administration of such laws.

## Article 49
### Administrative Procedures

To the extent that any civil remedy can be ordered as a result of administrative procedures on the merits of a case, such procedures shall conform to principles equivalent in substance to those set forth in this Section.

## Sec. 3.  Provisional Measures
### Article 50

1.    The judicial authorities shall have the authority to order prompt and effective provisional measures:

(a)   to prevent an infringement of any intellectual property right from occurring, and in particular to prevent the entry into the channels of commerce in their jurisdiction of goods, including imported goods immediately after customs clearance;

(b)   to preserve relevant evidence in regard to the alleged infringement.

2.    The judicial authorities shall have the authority to adopt provisional measures *inaudita altera parte* where appropriate, in particular where any delay is likely to cause irreparable harm to the right holder, or where there is a demonstrable risk of evidence being destroyed.

3.    The judicial authorities shall have the authority to require the applicant to provide any reasonably available evidence in order to satisfy themselves with a sufficient degree of certainty that the applicant is the right holder and that his right is being infringed or that such infringement is imminent, and to order the applicant to provide a security or equivalent assurance sufficient to protect the defendant and to prevent abuse.

4.    Where provisional measures have been adopted *inaudita altera parte,* the parties affected shall be given notice, without delay after the execution of the measures at the latest. A review, including a right to be heard, shall take place upon request of the defendant with a view to deciding, within a reasonable period after the notification of the measures, whether these measures shall be modified, revoked or confirmed.

5.    The applicant may be required to supply other information necessary for the identification of the goods concerned by the authority that will execute the provisional measures.

6.    Without prejudice to paragraph 4 above, provisional measures taken on the basis of paragraphs 1 and 2 above shall, upon request by the defendant, be revoked or otherwise cease to have effect, if proceedings leading to a decision on the merits of the case are not initiated within a reasonable period, to be determined by the judicial authority ordering the measures where national law so permits or, in the absence of such a determination, not to exceed twenty working days or thirty-one calendar days, whichever is the longer.

7.    Where the provisional measures are revoked or where they lapse due to any act or commission by the applicant, or where it is subsequently found that there has been no infringement or threat of infringement of an intellectual property right, the judicial authorities shall have the authority to order the applicant, upon request of the defendant, to provide the defendant appropriate compensation for any injury caused by these measures.

8.    To the extent that any provisional measure can be ordered as a result of administrative procedures, such procedures shall conform to principles equivalent in substance to those set forth in this Section.

## Sec. 4. Special Requirements Related to Border Measures[12]

### Article 51

*Suspension of Release by Customs Authorities*

Members shall, in conformity with the provisions set out below, adopt procedures[13] to enable a right holder, who has valid grounds for suspecting that the importation of counterfeit trademark or pirated copyright goods[14] may take place to lodge an application in writing with competent authorities, administrative or judicial, for the suspension by the customs authorities of the release into free circulation of such goods. Members may enable such an application to be made in respect of goods which involve other infringements of intellectual property rights, provided that the requirements of this Section are met. Members may also provide for corresponding procedures concerning the suspension by the customs authorities of the release of infringing goods destined for exportation from their territories.

### Article 52

*Application*

Any right holder initiating the procedures under Article 51 above shall be required to provide adequate evidence to satisfy the competent authorities that, under the laws of the country of importation there is prima facie an infringement of his intellectual property right and to supply a sufficiently detailed description of the goods to make them readily recognizable by the customs authorities. The competent authorities shall inform the applicant within a reasonable period whether they have accepted the application and, where determined by the competent authorities, the period for which the customs authorities will take action.

### Article 53

*Security or Equivalent Assurance*

1. The competent authorities shall have the authority to require an applicant to provide a security or equivalent assurance sufficient to protect the defendant and the competent authorities and to prevent abuse. Such security or equivalent assurance shall not unreasonably deter recourse to these procedures.

2. When pursuant to an application under this Section the release of goods involving industrial designs, patents, layout-designs or undisclosed information into free circulation has been suspended by customs authorities on the basis of a decision other than by a judicial or other independent authority, and the period provided for in Article 55 has expired without the granting of provisional relief by the duly empowered authority, and provided that all other conditions for importation have been complied with, the owner, importer, or consignee of such goods shall be entitled to their release on the posting of a security in an amount sufficient to protect the right holder for any infringement.

---

[12] Where a Member has dismantled substantially all controls over movement of goods across its border with another Member with which it forms part of a customs union, it shall not be required to apply the provisions of this Section at that border.

[13] It is understood that there shall be no obligations to apply such procedures to imports of goods put on the market in another country by or with the consent of the right holder, or to goods in transit.

[14] For the purposes of this Agreement:

(a) counterfeit trademark goods shall mean any goods, including packaging, bearing without authorization a trademark which is identical to the trademark validly registered in respect of such goods, or which cannot be distinguished in its essential aspects from such a trademark, and which thereby infringes the rights of the owner of the trademark in question under the law of the country of imposition;

(b) pirated copyright goods shall mean any goods which are copies made without the consent of the right holder or person duly authorized by him in the country of production and which are made directly or indirectly from an article where the making of that copy would have constituted an infringement of a copyright or a related right under the law of the country of importation.

Payment of such security shall be released if the right holder fails to pursue his right of action within a reasonable period of time.

### Article 54

#### Notice of Suspension

The importer and the applicant shall be promptly notified of the suspension of the release of goods according to Article 51 above.

### Article 55

#### Duration of Suspension

If, within a period not exceeding ten working days after the applicant has been served notice of the suspension, the customs authorities have not been informed that proceedings leading to a decision on the merits of the case have been initiated by a party other than the defendant, or that the duly empowered authority has taken provisional measures prolonging the suspension of the release of the goods, the goods shall be released, provided that all other conditions for importation or exportation have been complied with: in appropriate cases, this time-limit may be extended by another ten working days. If proceedings leading to a decision on the merits of the case have been initiated, a review, including a right to be heard, shall take place upon request of the defendant with a view to deciding, within a reasonable period, whether these measures shall be modified, revoked or confirmed. Notwithstanding the above, where the suspension of the release of goods is carried out or continued in accordance with a provisional judicial measure, the provisions of Article 50, paragraph 6 above shall apply.

### Article 56

#### Indemnification of the Importer and of the Owner of the Goods

Relevant authorities shall have the authority to order the applicant to pay the importer, the consignee and the owner of the goods appropriate compensation for any injury caused to them through the wrongful detention of goods or through the detention of goods released pursuant to Article 55 above.

### Article 57

#### Right of Inspection and Information

Without prejudice to the protection of confidential information, Members shall provide the competent authorities the authority to give the right holder sufficient opportunity to have any product detained by the customs authorities inspected in order to substantiate his claims. The competent authorities shall also have authority to give the importer an equivalent opportunity to have any such product inspected. Where a positive determination has been made on the merits of a case, Members may provide the competent authorities the authority to inform the right holder of the names and addresses of the consignor, the importer and the consignee and of the quantity of the goods in question.

### Article 58

#### Ex Officio Action

Where Members require competent authorities to act upon their own initiative and to suspend the release of goods in respect of which they have acquired *prima facie* evidence that an intellectual property right is being infringed:

(a) the competent authorities may at any time seek from the right holder any information that may assist them to exercise these powers;

(b) the importer and the right holder shall be promptly notified of the suspension. Where the importer has lodged an appeal against the suspension with the competent authorities, the suspension shall be subject to the conditions, *mutatis mutandis,* set out at Article 55 above;

(c) Members shall only exempt both public authorities and officials from liability to appropriate remedial measures where actions are taken or intended in good faith.

### Article 59

### Remedies

Without prejudice to other rights of action open to the right holder and subject to the right of the defendant to seek review by a judicial authority, competent authorities shall have the authority to order the destruction or disposal of infringing goods in accordance with the principles set out in Article 46 above. In regard to counterfeit trademark goods, the authorities shall not allow the reexportation of the infringing goods in an unaltered state or subject them to a different customs procedure, other than in exceptional circumstances.

### Article 60

### De Minimis Imports

Members may exclude from the application of the above provisions small quantities of goods of a noncommercial nature contained in traveller's personal luggage or sent in small consignments.

### Sec. 5.   Criminal Procedures

### Article 61

Members shall provide for criminal procedures and penalties to be applied at least in cases of wilful trademark counterfeiting or copyright piracy on a commercial scale. Remedies available shall include imprisonment and/or monetary fines sufficient to provide a deterrent, consistently with the level of penalties applied for crimes of a corresponding gravity. In appropriate cases, remedies available shall also include the seizure, forfeiture and destruction of the infringing goods and of any materials and implements the predominant use of which has been in the commission of the offence. Members may provide for criminal procedures and penalties to be applied in other cases of infringement of intellectual property rights, in particular where they are committed wilfully and on a commercial scale.

## PART IV.   ACQUISITION AND MAINTENANCE OF INTELLECTUAL PROPERTY RIGHTS AND RELATED *INTER-PARTES* PROCEDURES

### Article 62

1.    Members may require, as a condition of the acquisition or maintenance of the intellectual property rights provided for under Sections 2–6 of Part II of this Agreement, compliance with reasonable procedures and formalities. Such procedures and formalities shall be consistent with the provisions of this Agreement.

2.    Where the acquisition of an intellectual property right is subject to the right being granted or registered, Members shall ensure that the procedures for grant or registration, subject to compliance with the substantive conditions for acquisition of the right, permit the granting or registration of the right within a reasonable period of time so as to avoid unwarranted curtailment of the period of protection.

3.    Article 4 of the Paris Convention (1967) shall apply *mutatis mutandis* to service marks.

4.    Procedures concerning the acquisition or maintenance of intellectual property rights and, where the national law provides for such procedures, administrative revocation and *inter partes* procedures such as opposition, revocation and cancellation, shall be governed by the general principles set out in paragraphs 2 and 3 of Article 41.

5.    Final administrative decisions in any of the procedures referred to under paragraph 4 above shall be subject to review by a judicial or quasi-judicial authority. However, there shall be no obligation to provide an opportunity for such review of decisions in cases of unsuccessful opposition or

administrative revocation, provided that the grounds for such procedures can be the subject of invalidation procedures.

## PART V.   DISPUTE PREVENTION AND SETTLEMENT

### Article 63

#### Transparency

1.    Laws and regulations, and final judicial decisions and administrative rulings of general application, made effective by any Member pertaining to the subject matter of this Agreement (the availability, scope, acquisition, enforcement and prevention of the abuse of intellectual property rights) shall be published, or where such publication is not practicable made publicly available, in a national language, in such a manner as to enable governments and right holders to become acquainted with them. Agreements concerning the subject matter of this Agreement which are in force between the government or a governmental agency of any Member and the government or a governmental agency of any other Member shall also be published.

2.    Members shall notify the laws and regulations referred to in paragraph 1 above to the Council for Trade-Related Aspects of Intellectual Property Rights in order to assist that Council in its review of the operation of this Agreement. The Council shall attempt to minimize the burden on Members in carrying out this obligation and may decide to waive the obligation to notify such laws and regulations directly to the Council if consultations with the World Intellectual Property Organization on the establishment of a common register containing these laws and regulations are successful. The Council shall also consider in this connection any action required regarding notifications pursuant to the obligations under this Agreement stemming from the provisions of Article 6*ter* of the Paris Convention (1967).

3.    Each Member shall be prepared to supply, in response to a written request from another Member, information of the sort referred to in paragraph 1 above. A Member, having reason to believe that a specific judicial decision or administrative ruling or bilateral agreement in the area of intellectual property rights affects its rights under this Agreement, may also request in writing to be given access to or be informed in sufficient detail of such specific judicial decisions or administrative rulings or bilateral agreements.

4.    Nothing in paragraphs 1 to 3 above shall require Members to disclose confidential information which would impede law enforcement or otherwise be contrary to the public interest or would prejudice the legitimate commercial interests of particular enterprises, public or private.

### Article 64

#### Dispute Settlement

1.    The provisions of Articles XXII and XXIII of the Agreement on Tariffs and Trade 1994 as elaborated and applied by the Understanding on Rules and Procedures Governing the Settlement of Disputes shall apply to consultations and the settlement of disputes under this Agreement except as otherwise specifically provided herein.

2.    Sub-paragraphs XXIII:1(b) and XXIII:1(c) of the General Agreement on Tariffs and Trade 1994 shall not apply to the settlement of disputes under this Agreement for a period of five years from the entry into force of the Agreement establishing the WTO.

3.    During the time period referred to in paragraph 2, the TRIPS Council shall examine the scope and modalities for Article XXIII:1(b) and Article XXIII:1(c)-type complaints made pursuant to this Agreement, and submit its recommendations to the Ministerial Conference for approval. Any decision of the Ministerial Conference to approve such recommendations or to extend the period in paragraph 2 shall be made only by consensus, and approved recommendations shall be effective for all Members without further formal acceptance process.

## PART VI.   TRANSITIONAL ARRANGEMENTS

### Article 65

### *Transitional Arrangements*

1.    Subject to the provisions of paragraphs 2, 3 and 4 below, no Member shall be obliged to apply the provisions of this Agreement before the expiry of a general period of one year following the date of entry into force of the Agreement Establishing the WTO.

2.    Any developing country Member is entitled to delay for a further period of four years the date of application, as defined in paragraph 1 above, of the provisions of this Agreement other than Articles 3, 4 and 5 of Part I.

3.    Any other Member which is in the process of transformation from a centrally-planned into a market, free-enterprise economy and which is undertaking structural reform of its intellectual property system and facing special problems in the preparation and implementation of intellectual property laws, may also benefit from a period of delay as foreseen in paragraph 2 above.

4.    To the extent that a developing country Member is obliged by this Agreement to extend product patent protection to areas of technology not so protectable in its territory on the general date of application of this Agreement for that Member, as defined in paragraph 2 above, it may delay the application of the provisions on product patents of Section 5 of Part II of this Agreement to such areas of technology for an additional period of five years.

5.    Any Member availing itself of a transitional period under paragraphs 1, 2, 3 or 4 above shall ensure that any changes in its domestic laws, regulations and practice made during that period do not result in a lesser degree of consistency with the provisions of this Agreement.

### Article 66

### *Least-Developed Country Members*

1.    In view of their special needs and requirements, their economic, financial and administrative constraints, and their need for flexibility to create a viable technological base, least-developed country Members shall not be required to apply the provisions of this Agreement, other than Articles 3, 4 and 5, for a period of 10 years from the date of application as defined under paragraph 1 of Article 65 above. The Council shall, upon duly motivated request by a least-developed country Member, accord extensions of this period.

2.    Developed country Members shall provide incentives to enterprises and institutions in their territories for the purpose of promoting and encouraging technology transfer to least-developed country Members in order to enable them to create a sound and viable technological base.

### Article 67

### *Technical Cooperation*

In order to facilitate the implementation of this Agreement, developed country Members shall provide, on request and on mutually agreed terms and conditions, technical and financial cooperation in favour of developing and least-developed country Members. Such cooperation shall include assistance in the preparation of domestic legislation on the protection and enforcement of intellectual property rights as well as on the prevention of their abuse, and shall include support regarding the establishment or reinforcement of domestic offices and agencies relevant to these matters, including the training of personnel.

# TRIPS AGREEMENT

## PART VII.  INSTITUTIONAL ARRANGEMENTS; FINAL PROVISIONS

### Article 68

### Council for Trade-Related Aspects of Intellectual Property Rights

The Council for Trade-Related Aspects of Intellectual Property Rights shall monitor the operation of this Agreement and, in particular, Members' compliance with their obligations hereunder, and shall afford Members the opportunity of consulting on matters relating to the trade-related aspects of intellectual property rights. It shall carry out such other responsibilities as assigned to it by the Members, and it shall, in particular, provide any assistance requested by them in the context of dispute settlement procedures. In carrying out its functions, the Council may consult with and seek information from any source it deems appropriate. In consultation with the World Intellectual Property Organization, the Council shall seek to establish, within one year of its first meeting, appropriate arrangements for cooperation with bodies of that Organization.

### Article 69

### International Cooperation

Members agree to cooperate with each other with a view to eliminating international trade in goods infringing intellectual property rights. For this purpose, they shall establish and notify contact points in their national administrations and be ready to exchange information on trade in infringing goods. They shall, in particular, promote the exchange of information and cooperation between customs authorities with regard to trade in counterfeit trademark goods and pirated copyright goods.

### Article 70

### Protection of Existing Subject Matter

1.    This Agreement does not give rise to obligations in respect of acts which occurred before the date of application of the Agreement for the Member in question.

2.    Except as otherwise provided for in this Agreement, this Agreement gives rise to obligations in respect of all subject matter existing at the date of application of this Agreement for the Member in question, and which is protected in that Member on the said date, or which meets or comes subsequently to meet the criteria for protection under the terms of this Agreement. In respect of this paragraph and paragraphs 3 and 4 below, copyright obligations with respect to existing works shall be solely determined under Article 18 of the Berne Convention (1971), and obligations with respect to the rights of producers of phonograms and performers in existing phonograms shall be determined solely under Article 18 of the Berne Convention (1971) as made applicable under paragraph 6 of Article 14 of this Agreement.

3.    There shall be no obligation to restore protection to the subject matter which on the date of application of this Agreement for the Member in question has fallen into the public domain.

4.    In respect of any acts in respect of specific objects embodying protected subject matter which become infringing under the terms of legislation in conformity with this Agreement, and which were commenced, or in respect of which a significant investment was made, before the date of acceptance of the Agreement Establishing the WTO by that Member, any Member may provide for a limitation of the remedies available to the right holder as to the continued performance of such acts after the date of application of the Agreement for that Member. In such cases the Member shall, however, at least provide for the payment of equitable remuneration.

5.    A Member is not obliged to apply the provisions of Article 11 and of paragraph 4 of Article 14 with respect to originals or copies purchased prior to the date of application of this Agreement for that Member.

6.    Members shall not be required to apply Article 31, or the requirement in paragraph 1 of Article 27 that patent rights shall be enjoyable without discrimination as to the field of technology, to

312

use without the authorization of the right holder where authorization for such use was granted by the government before the date this Agreement became known.

7.   In the case of intellectual property rights for which protection is conditional upon registration, applications for protection which are pending on the date of application of this Agreement for the Member in question shall be permitted to be amended to claim any enhanced protection provided under the provisions of this Agreement. Such amendments shall not include new matter.

8.   Where a Member does not make available as of the date of entry into force of the Agreement Establishing the WTO patent protection for pharmaceutical and agricultural chemical products commensurate with its obligations under Article 27, that Member shall:

(i)   notwithstanding the provisions of Part VI above, provide as from the date of entry into force of the Agreement Establishing the WTO a means by which applications for patents for such inventions can be filed;

(ii)   apply to these applications, as of the date of application of this Agreement, the criteria for patentability as laid down in this Agreement as if those criteria were being applied on the date of filing in that Member or, where priority is available and claimed, the priority date of the application;

(iii)   provide patent protection in accordance with this Agreement as from the grant of the patent and for the remainder of the patent term, counted from the filing date in accordance with Article 33 of this Agreement, for those of these applications that meet the criteria for protection referred to in subparagraph (ii) above.

9.   Where a product is the subject of a patent application in a Member in accordance with paragraph 8(i) above, exclusive marketing rights shall be granted, notwithstanding the provisions of Part VI above, for a period of five years after obtaining market approval in that Member or until a product patent is granted or rejected in that Member, whichever period is shorter, provided that, subsequent to the entry into force of the Agreement Establishing the WTO, a patent application has been filed and a patent granted for that product in another Member and marketing approval obtained in such other Member.

### Article 71

### Review and Amendment

1.   The Council for Trade-Related Aspects of Intellectual Property Rights shall review the implementation of this Agreement after the expiration of the transitional period referred to in paragraph 2 of Article 65 above. The Council shall, having regard to the experience gained in its implementation, review it two years after that date, and at identical intervals thereafter. The Council may also undertake reviews in the light of any relevant new developments which might warrant modification or amendment of this Agreement.

2.   Amendments merely serving the purpose of adjusting to higher levels of protection of intellectual property rights achieved, and in force, in other multilateral agreements and accepted under those agreements by all Members of the WTO may be referred to the Ministerial Conference for action in accordance with Article X, paragraph 6, of the Agreement Establishing the WTO on the basis of a consensus proposal from the Council for Trade-Related Aspects of Intellectual Property Rights.

### Article 72

### Reservations

Reservations may not be entered in respect of any of the provisions of this Agreement without the consent of the other Members.

# TRIPS AGREEMENT

## Article 73

### Security Exceptions

Nothing in this Agreement shall be construed:

(a)   to require any Member to furnish any information the disclosure of which it considers contrary to its essential security interest; or

(b)   to prevent any Member from taking any action which it considers necessary for the protection of its essential security interests;

   (i)   relating to fissionable materials or the materials from which they are derived;

   (ii)   relating to the traffic in arms, ammunition and implements of war and to such traffic in other goods and materials as is carried on directly or indirectly for the purpose of supplying a military establishment;

   (iii)   taken in time of war or other emergency in international relations; or

(c)   to prevent any Member from taking any action in pursuance of its obligations under the United Nations Charter for the maintenance of international peace and security.

Signed by the Members of the General Agreement on Tariffs and Trade on April 15, 1994.

# APPENDIX I

---

# WORLD INTELLECTUAL PROPERTY ORGANIZATION COPYRIGHT TREATY

(Adopted on December 20, 1996)

## Preamble

*The Contracting Parties,*

*Desiring* to develop and maintain the protection of the rights of authors in their literary and artistic works in a manner as effective and uniform as possible,

*Recognizing* the need to introduce new international rules and clarify the interpretation of certain existing rules in order to provide adequate solutions to the questions raised by new economic, social, cultural and technological developments,

*Recognizing* the profound impact of the development and convergence of information and communication technologies on the creation and use of literary and artistic works,

*Emphasizing* the outstanding significance of copyright protection as an incentive for literary and artistic creation,

*Recognizing* the need to maintain a balance between the rights of authors and the larger public interest, particularly education, research and access to information, as reflected in the Berne Convention,

*Have agreed as follows:*

## Article 1

### Relation to the Berne Convention

(1)   This Treaty is a special agreement within the meaning of Article 20 of the Berne Convention for the Protection of Literary and Artistic Works, as regards Contracting Parties that are countries of the Union established by that Convention. This Treaty shall not have any connection with treaties other than the Berne Convention, nor shall it prejudice any rights and obligations under any other treaties.

(2)   Nothing in this Treaty shall derogate from existing obligations that Contracting Parties have to each other under the Berne Convention for the Protection of Literary and Artistic Works.

(3)   Hereinafter, "Berne Convention" shall refer to the Paris Act of July 24, 1971 of the Berne Convention for the Protection of Literary and Artistic Works.

(4)   Contracting Parties shall comply with Articles 1 to 21 and the Appendix of the Berne Convention.

## Article 2

### Scope of Copyright Protection

Copyright protection extends to expressions and not to ideas, procedures, methods of operation or mathematical concepts as such.

# COPYRIGHT TREATY

## Article 3

### Application of Articles 2 to 6 of the Berne Convention

Contracting Parties shall apply *mutatis mutandis* the provisions of Articles 2 to 6 of the Berne Convention in respect of the protection provided for in this Treaty.

## Article 4

### Computer Programs

Computer programs are protected as literary works within the meaning of Article 2 of the Berne Convention. Such protection applies to computer programs, whatever may be the mode or form of their expression.

## Article 5

### Compilations of Data (Databases)

Compilations of data or other material, in any form, which by reason of the selection or arrangement of their contents constitute intellectual creations, are protected as such. This protection does not extend to the data or the material itself and is without prejudice to any copyright subsisting in the data or material contained in the compilation.

## Article 6

### Right of Distribution

(1)   Authors of literary and artistic works shall enjoy the exclusive right of authorizing the making available to the public of the original and copies of their works through sale or other transfer of ownership.

(2)   Nothing in this Treaty shall affect the freedom of Contracting Parties to determine the conditions, if any, under which the exhaustion of the right in paragraph (1) applies after the first sale or other transfer of ownership of the original or a copy of the work with the authorization of the author.

## Article 7

### Right of Rental

(1)   Authors of

   (i)   computer programs;

   (ii)   cinematographic works; and

   (iii)   works embodied in phonograms, as determined in the national law of Contracting Parties,

shall enjoy the exclusive right of authorizing commercial rental to the public of the originals or copies of their works.

(2)   Paragraph (1) shall not apply

   (i)   in the case of computer programs, where the program itself is not the essential object of the rental; and

   (ii)   in the case of cinematographic works, unless such commercial rental has led to widespread copying of such works materially impairing the exclusive right of reproduction.

(3)   Notwithstanding the provisions of paragraph (1), a Contracting Party that, on April 15, 1994, had and continues to have in force a system of equitable remuneration of authors for the rental of copies of their works embodied in phonograms may maintain that system provided that the commercial rental of works embodied in phonograms is not giving rise to the material impairment of the exclusive right of reproduction of authors.

## Article 8
### Right of Communication to the Public

Without prejudice to the provisions of Articles 11(1)(ii), 11*bis*(1)(i) and (ii), 11*ter*(1)(ii), 14(1)(ii) and 14*bis*(1) of the Berne Convention, authors of literary and artistic works shall enjoy the exclusive right of authorizing any communication to the public of their works, by wire or wireless means, including the making available to the public of their works in such a way that members of the public may access these works from a place and at a time individually chosen by them.

## Article 9
### Duration of the Protection of Photographic Works

In respect of photographic works, the Contracting Parties shall not apply the provisions of Article 7(4) of the Berne Convention.

## Article 10
### Limitations and Exceptions

(1) Contracting Parties may, in their national legislation, provide for limitations of or exceptions to the rights granted to authors of literary and artistic works under this Treaty in certain special cases that do not conflict with a normal exploitation of the work and do not unreasonably prejudice the legitimate interests of the author.

(2) Contracting Parties shall, when applying the Berne Convention, confine any limitations of or exceptions to rights provided for therein to certain special cases that do not conflict with a normal exploitation of the work and do not unreasonably prejudice the legitimate interests of the author.

## Article 11
### Obligations concerning Technological Measures

Contracting Parties shall provide adequate legal protection and effective legal remedies against the circumvention of effective technological measures that are used by authors in connection with the exercise of their rights under this Treaty or the Berne Convention and that restrict acts, in respect of their works, which are not authorized by the authors concerned or permitted by law.

## Article 12
### Obligations concerning Rights Management Information

(1) Contracting Parties shall provide adequate and effective legal remedies against any person knowingly performing any of the following acts knowing, or with respect to civil remedies having reasonable grounds to know, that it will induce, enable, facilitate or conceal an infringement of any right covered by this Treaty or the Berne Convention:

  (i)  to remove or alter any electronic rights management information without authority;

  (ii)  to distribute, import for distribution, broadcast or communicate to the public, without authority, works or copies of works knowing that electronic rights management information has been removed or altered without authority.

(2) As used in this Article, "rights management information" means information which identifies the work, the author of the work, the owner of any right in the work, or information about the terms and conditions of use of the work, and any numbers or codes that represent such information, when any of these items of information is attached to a copy of a work or appears in connection with the communication of a work to the public.

# COPYRIGHT TREATY

## Article 13

### Application in Time

Contracting Parties shall apply the provisions of Article 18 of the Berne Convention to all protection provided for in this Treaty.

## Article 14

### Provisions on Enforcement of Rights

(1)   Contracting Parties undertake to adopt, in accordance with their legal systems, the measures necessary to ensure the application of this Treaty.

(2)   Contracting Parties shall ensure that enforcement procedures are available under their law so as to permit effective action against any act of infringement of rights covered by this Treaty, including expeditious remedies to prevent infringements and remedies which constitute a deterrent to further infringements.

## Article 15

### Assembly

(1)(a)   The Contracting Parties shall have an Assembly.

(b)   Each Contracting Party shall be represented by one delegate who may be assisted by alternate delegates, advisors and experts.

(c)   The expenses of each delegation shall be borne by the Contracting Party that has appointed the delegation. The Assembly may ask the World Intellectual Property Organization (hereinafter referred to as "WIPO") to grant financial assistance to facilitate the participation of delegations of Contracting Parties that are regarded as developing countries in conformity with the established practice of the General Assembly of the United Nations or that are countries in transition to a market economy.

(2)(a)   The Assembly shall deal with matters concerning the maintenance and development of this Treaty and the application and operation of this Treaty.

(b)   The Assembly shall perform the function allocated to it under Article 17(2) in respect of the admission of certain intergovernmental organizations to become party to this Treaty.

(c)   The Assembly shall decide the convocation of any diplomatic conference for the revision of this Treaty and give the necessary instructions to the Director General of WIPO for the preparation of such diplomatic conference.

(3)(a)   Each Contracting Party that is a State shall have one vote and shall vote only in its own name.

(b)   Any Contracting Party that is an intergovernmental organization may participate in the vote, in place of its Member States, with a number of votes equal to the number of its Member States which are party to this Treaty. No such intergovernmental organization shall participate in the vote if any one of its Member States exercises its right to vote and *vice versa*.

(4)   The Assembly shall meet in ordinary session once every two years upon convocation by the Director General of WIPO.

(5)   The Assembly shall establish its own rules of procedure, including the convocation of extraordinary sessions, the requirements of a quorum and, subject to the provisions of this Treaty, the required majority for various kinds of decisions.

## Article 16

### International Bureau

The International Bureau of WIPO shall perform the administrative tasks concerning the Treaty.

## Article 17

### Eligibility for Becoming Party to the Treaty

(1)   Any Member State of WIPO may become party to this Treaty.

(2)   The Assembly may decide to admit any intergovernmental organization to become party to this Treaty which declares that it is competent in respect of, and has its own legislation binding on all its Member States on, matters covered by this Treaty and that it has been duly authorized, in accordance with its internal procedures, to become party to this Treaty.

(3)   The European Community, having made the declaration referred to in the preceding paragraph in the Diplomatic Conference that has adopted this Treaty, may become party to this Treaty.

## Article 18

### Rights and Obligations under the Treaty

Subject to any specific provisions to the contrary in this Treaty, each Contracting Party shall enjoy all of the rights and assume all of the obligations under this Treaty.

## Article 19

### Signature of the Treaty

This Treaty shall be open for signature until December 31, 1997, by any Member State of WIPO and by the European Community.

## Article 20

### Entry into Force of the Treaty

This Treaty shall enter into force three months after 30 instruments of ratification or accession by States have been deposited with the Director General of WIPO.

## Article 21

### Effective Date of Becoming Party to the Treaty

This Treaty shall bind

(i)   the 30 States referred to in Article 20, from the date on which this Treaty has entered into force;

(ii)   each other State from the expiration of three months from the date on which the State has deposited its instrument with the Director General of WIPO;

(iii)   the European Community, from the expiration of three months after the deposit of its instrument of ratification or accession if such instrument has been deposited after the entry into force of this Treaty according to Article 20, or, three months after the entry into force of this Treaty if such instrument has been deposited before the entry into force of this Treaty;

(iv)   any other intergovernmental organization that is admitted to become party to this Treaty, from the expiration of three months after the deposit of its instrument of accession.

## Article 22

### No Reservations to the Treaty

No reservation to this Treaty shall be admitted.

COPYRIGHT TREATY

<h2 align="center">Article 23</h2>
<h3 align="center">Denunciation of the Treaty</h3>

This Treaty may be denounced by any Contracting Party by notification addressed to the Director General of WIPO. Any denunciation shall take effect one year from the date on which the Director General of WIPO received the notification.

<h2 align="center">Article 24</h2>
<h3 align="center">Languages of the Treaty</h3>

(1)   This Treaty is signed in a single original in English, Arabic, Chinese, French, Russian and Spanish languages, the versions in all these languages being equally authentic.

(2)   An official text in any language other than those referred to in paragraph (1) shall be established by the Director General of WIPO on the request of an interested party, after consultation with all the interested parties. For the purposes of this paragraph, "interested party" means any Member State of WIPO whose official language, or one of whose official languages, is involved and the European Community, and any other intergovernmental organization that may become party to this Treaty, if one of its official languages is involved.

<h2 align="center">Article 25</h2>
<h3 align="center">Depositary</h3>

The Director General of WIPO is the depositary of this Treaty.

<h2 align="center">AGREED STATEMENTS CONCERNING THE WIPO COPYRIGHT TREATY</h2>
<h3 align="center">Concerning Article 1(4)</h3>

The reproduction right, as set out in Article 9 of the Berne Convention, and the exceptions permitted thereunder, fully apply in the digital environment, in particular to the use of works in digital form. It is understood that the storage of a protected work in digital form in an electronic medium constitutes a reproduction within the meaning of Article 9 of the Berne Convention.

<h3 align="center">Concerning Article 3</h3>

It is understood that in applying Article 3 of this Treaty, the expression "country of the Union" in Articles 2 to 6 of the Berne Convention will be read as if it were a reference to a Contracting Party to this Treaty, in the application of those Berne Articles in respect of protection provided for in this Treaty. It is also understood that the expression "country outside the Union" in those Articles in the Berne Convention will, in the same circumstances, be read as if it were a reference to a country that is not a Contracting Party to this Treaty, and that "this Convention" in Articles 2(8), 2*bis*(2), 3, 4 and 5 of the Berne Convention will be read as if it were a reference to the Berne Convention and this Treaty. Finally, it is understood that a reference in Articles 3 to 6 of the Berne Convention to a "national of one of the countries of the Union" will, when these Articles are applied to this Treaty, mean, in regard to an intergovernmental organization that is a Contracting Party to this Treaty, a national of one of the countries that is member of that organization.

<h3 align="center">Concerning Article 4</h3>

The scope of protection for computer programs under Article 4 of this Treaty, read with Article 2, is consistent with Article 2 of the Berne Convention and on a par with the relevant provisions of the TRIPS Agreement.

<h3 align="center">Concerning Article 5</h3>

The scope of protection for compilations of data (databases) under Article 5 of this Treaty, read with Article 2, is consistent with Article 2 of the Berne Convention and on a par with the relevant provisions of the TRIPS Agreement.

### Concerning Articles 6 and 7

As used in these Articles, the expressions "copies" and "original and copies," being subject to the right of distribution and the right of rental under the said Articles, refer exclusively to fixed copies that can be put into circulation as tangible objects.

### Concerning Article 7

It is understood that the obligation under Article 7(1) does not require a Contracting Party to provide an exclusive right of commercial rental to authors who, under that Contracting Party's law, are not granted rights in respect of phonograms. It is understood that this obligation is consistent with Article 14(4) of the TRIPS Agreement.

### Concerning Article 8

It is understood that the mere provision of physical facilities for enabling or making a communication does not in itself amount to communication within the meaning of this Treaty or the Berne Convention. It is further understood that nothing in Article 8 precludes a Contracting Party from applying Article 11*bis*(2).

### Concerning Article 10

It is understood that the provisions of Article 10 permit Contracting Parties to carry forward and appropriately extend into the digital environment limitations and exceptions in their national laws which have been considered acceptable under the Berne Convention. Similarly, these provisions should be understood to permit Contracting Parties to devise new exceptions and limitations that are appropriate in the digital network environment.

It is also understood that Article 10(2) neither reduces nor extends the scope of applicability of the limitations and exceptions permitted by the Berne Convention.

### Concerning Article 12

It is understood that the reference to "infringement of any right covered by this Treaty or the Berne Convention" includes both exclusive rights and rights of remuneration.

It is further understood that Contracting Parties will not rely on this Article to devise or implement rights management systems that would have the effect of imposing formalities which are not permitted under the Berne Convention or this Treaty, prohibiting the free movement of goods or impeding the enjoyment of rights under this Treaty.

# APPENDIX J

---

# WORLD INTELLECTUAL PROPERTY ORGANIZATION PERFORMANCES AND PHONOGRAMS TREATY

(Adopted on December 20, 1996)

## Preamble

*The Contracting Parties,*

*Desiring* to develop and maintain the protection of the rights of performers and producers of phonograms in a manner as effective and uniform as possible,

*Recognizing* the need to introduce new international rules in order to provide adequate solutions to the questions raised by economic, social, cultural and technological developments,

*Recognizing* the profound impact of the development and convergence of information and communication technologies on the production and use of performances and phonograms,

*Recognizing* the need to maintain a balance between the rights of performers and producers of phonograms and the larger public interest, particularly education, research and access to information,

*Have agreed* as follows:

## CHAPTER I

### GENERAL PROVISIONS

### Article 1

### Relation to Other Conventions

(1)  Nothing in this Treaty shall derogate from existing obligations that Contracting Parties have to each other under the International Convention for the Protection of Performers, Producers of Phonograms and Broadcasting Organizations done in Rome, October 26, 1961 (hereinafter the "Rome Convention").

(2)  Protection granted under this Treaty shall leave intact and shall in no way affect the protection of copyright in literary and artistic works. Consequently, no provision of this Treaty may be interpreted as prejudicing such protection.

(3)  This Treaty shall not have any connection with, nor shall it prejudice any rights and obligations under, any other treaties.

### Article 2

### Definitions

For the purposes of this Treaty:

(a)  "performers" are actors, singers, musicians, dancers, and other persons who act, sing, deliver, declaim, play in, interpret, or otherwise perform literary or artistic works or expressions of folklore;

# PERFORMANCES AND PHONOGRAMS TREATY

(b)  "phonogram" means the fixation of the sounds of a performance or of other sounds, or of a representation of sounds, other than in the form of a fixation incorporated in a cinematographic or other audiovisual work;

(c)  "fixation" means the embodiment of sounds, or of the representations thereof, from which they can be perceived, reproduced or communicated through a device;

(d)  "producer of a phonogram" means the person, or the legal entity, who or which takes the initiative and has the responsibility for the first fixation of the sounds of a performance or other sounds, or the representations of sounds;

(e)  "publication" of a fixed performance or a phonogram means the offering of copies of the fixed performance or the phonogram to the public, with the consent of the rightholder, and provided that copies are offered to the public in reasonable quantity;

(f)  "broadcasting" means the transmission by wireless means for public reception of sounds or of images and sounds or of the representations thereof; such transmission by satellite is also "broadcasting"; transmission of encrypted signals is "broadcasting" where the means for decrypting are provided to the public by the broadcasting organization or with its consent;

(g)  "communication to the public" of a performance or a phonogram means the transmission to the public by any medium, otherwise than by broadcasting, of sounds of a performance or the sounds or the representations of sounds fixed in a phonogram. For the purposes of Article 15, "communication to the public" includes making the sounds or representations of sounds fixed in a phonogram audible to the public.

## Article 3

### Beneficiaries of Protection under this Treaty

(1)  Contracting Parties shall accord the protection provided under this Treaty to the performers and producers of phonograms who are nationals of other Contracting Parties.

(2)  The nationals of other Contracting Parties shall be understood to be those performers or producers of phonograms who would meet the criteria for eligibility for protection provided under the Rome Convention, were all the Contracting Parties to this Treaty Contracting States of that Convention. In respect of these criteria of eligibility, Contracting Parties shall apply the relevant definitions in Article 2 of this Treaty.

(3)  Any Contracting Party availing itself of the possibilities provided in Article 5(3) of the Rome Convention or, for the purposes of Article 5 of the same Convention, Article 17 thereof shall make a notification as foreseen in those provisions to the Director General of the World Intellectual Property Organization (WIPO).

## Article 4

### National Treatment

(1)  Each Contracting Party shall accord to nationals of other Contracting Parties, as defined in Article 3(2), the treatment it accords to its own nationals with regard to the exclusive rights specifically granted in this Treaty, and to the right to equitable remuneration provided for in Article 15 of this Treaty.

(2)  The obligation provided for in paragraph (1) does not apply to the extent that another Contracting Party makes use of the reservations permitted by Article 15(3) of this Treaty.

## CHAPTER II

## RIGHTS OF PERFORMERS

### Article 5

### Moral Rights of Performers

(1) Independently of a performer's economic rights, and even after the transfer of those rights, the performer shall, as regards his live aural performances or performances fixed in phonograms, have the right to claim to be identified as the performer of his performances, except where omission is dictated by the manner of the use of the performance, and to object to any distortion, mutilation or other modification of his performances that would be prejudicial to his reputation.

(2) The rights granted to a performer in accordance with paragraph (1) shall, after his death, be maintained, at least until the expiry of the economic rights, and shall be exercisable by the persons or institutions authorized by the legislation of the Contracting Party where protection is claimed. However, those Contracting Parties whose legislation, at the moment of their ratification of or accession to this Treaty, does not provide for protection after the death of the performer of all rights set out in the preceding paragraph may provide that some of these rights will, after his death, cease to be maintained.

(3) The means of redress for safeguarding the rights granted under this Article shall be governed by the legislation of the Contracting Party where protection is claimed.

### Article 6

### Economic Rights of Performers in their Unfixed Performances

Performers shall enjoy the exclusive right of authorizing, as regards their performances:

(i) the broadcasting and communication to the public of their unfixed performances except where the performance is already a broadcast performance; and

(ii) the fixation of their unfixed performances.

### Article 7

### Right of Reproduction

Performers shall enjoy the exclusive right of authorizing the direct or indirect reproduction of their performances fixed in phonograms, in any manner or form.

### Article 8

### Right of Distribution

(1) Performers shall enjoy the exclusive right of authorizing the making available to the public of the original and copies of their performances fixed in phonograms through sale or other transfer of ownership.

(2) Nothing in this Treaty shall affect the freedom of Contracting Parties to determine the conditions, if any, under which the exhaustion of the right in paragraph (1) applies after the first sale or other transfer of ownership of the original or a copy of the fixed performance with the authorization of the performer.

### Article 9

### Right of Rental

(1) Performers shall enjoy the exclusive right of authorizing the commercial rental to the public of the original and copies of their performances fixed in phonograms as determined in the national law of Contracting Parties, even after distribution of them by, or pursuant to, authorization by the performer.

(2)   Notwithstanding the provisions of paragraph (1), a Contracting Party that, on April 15, 1994, had and continues to have in force a system of equitable remuneration of performers for the rental of copies of their performances fixed in phonograms, may maintain that system provided that the commercial rental of phonograms is not giving rise to the material impairment of the exclusive right of reproduction of performers.

## Article 10

### Right of Making Available of Fixed Performances

Performers shall enjoy the exclusive right of authorizing the making available to the public of their performances fixed in phonograms, by wire or wireless means, in such a way that members of the public may access them from a place and at a time individually chosen by them.

## CHAPTER III

## RIGHTS OF PRODUCERS OF PHONOGRAMS

### Article 11

### Right of Reproduction

Producers of phonograms shall enjoy the exclusive right of authorizing the direct or indirect reproduction of their phonograms, in any manner or form.

### Article 12

### Right of Distribution

(1)   Producers of phonograms shall enjoy the exclusive right of authorizing the making available to the public of the original and copies of their phonograms through sale or other transfer of ownership.

(2)   Nothing in this Treaty shall affect the freedom of Contracting Parties to determine the conditions, if any, under which the exhaustion of the right in paragraph (1) applies after the first sale or other transfer of ownership of the original or a copy of the phonogram with the authorization of the producer of the phonogram.

### Article 13

### Right of Rental

(1)   Producers of phonograms shall enjoy the exclusive right of authorizing the commercial rental to the public of the original and copies of their phonograms, even after distribution of them by or pursuant to authorization by the producer.

(2)   Notwithstanding the provisions of paragraph (1), a Contracting Party that, on April 15, 1994, had and continues to have in force a system of equitable remuneration of producers of phonograms for the rental of copies of their phonograms, may maintain that system provided that the commercial rental of phonograms is not giving rise to the material impairment of the exclusive rights of reproduction of producers of phonograms.

### Article 14

### Right of Making Available of Phonograms

Producers of phonograms shall enjoy the exclusive right of authorizing the making available to the public of their phonograms, by wire or wireless means, in such a way that members of the public may access them from a place and at a time individually chosen by them.

## CHAPTER IV

## COMMON PROVISIONS

### Article 15

### Right to Remuneration for Broadcasting and Communication to the Public

(1)   Performers and producers of phonograms shall enjoy the right to a single equitable remuneration for the direct or indirect use of phonograms published for commercial purposes for broadcasting or for any communication to the public.

(2)   Contracting Parties may establish in their national legislation that the single equitable remuneration shall be claimed from the user by the performer or by the producer of a phonogram or by both. Contracting Parties may enact national legislation that, in the absence of an agreement between the performer and the producer of a phonogram, sets the terms according to which performers and producers of phonograms shall share the single equitable remuneration.

(3)   Any Contracting Party may in a notification deposited with the Director General of WIPO, declare that it will apply the provisions of paragraph (1) only in respect of certain uses, or that it will limit their application in some other way, or that it will not apply these provisions at all.

(4)   For the purposes of this Article, phonograms made available to the public by wire or wireless means in such a way that members of the public may access them from a place and at a time individually chosen by them shall be considered as if they had been published for commercial purposes.

### Article 16

### Limitations and Exceptions

(1)   Contracting Parties may, in their national legislation, provide for the same kinds of limitations or exceptions with regard to the protection of performers and producers of phonograms as they provide for, in their national legislation, in connection with the protection of copyright in literary and artistic works.

(2)   Contracting Parties shall confine any limitations of or exceptions to rights provided for in this Treaty to certain special cases which do not conflict with a normal exploitation of the performance or phonogram and do not unreasonably prejudice the legitimate interests of the performer or of the producer of the phonogram.

### Article 17

### Term of Protection

(1)   The term of protection to be granted to performers under this Treaty shall last, at least, until the end of a period of 50 years computed from the end of the year in which the performance was fixed in a phonogram.

(2)   The term of protection to be granted to producers of phonograms under this Treaty shall last, at least, until the end of a period of 50 years computed from the end of the year in which the phonogram was published, or failing such publication within 50 years from fixation of the phonogram, 50 years from the end of the year in which the fixation was made.

### Article 18

### Obligations concerning Technological Measures

Contracting Parties shall provide adequate legal protection and effective legal remedies against the circumvention of effective technological measures that are used by performers or producers of phonograms in connection with the exercise of their rights under this Treaty and that restrict acts, in respect of their performances or phonograms, which are not authorized by the performers or the producers of phonograms concerned or permitted by law.

## Article 19

### Obligations concerning Rights Management Information

(1)  Contracting Parties shall provide adequate and effective legal remedies against any person knowingly performing any of the following acts knowing, or with respect to civil remedies having reasonable grounds to know, that it will induce, enable, facilitate or conceal an infringement of any right covered by this Treaty:

(i)  to remove or alter any electronic rights management information without authority;

(ii)  to distribute, import for distribution, broadcast, communicate or make available to the public, without authority, performances, copies of fixed performances or phonograms knowing that electronic rights management information has been removed or altered without authority.

(2)  As used in this Article, "rights management information" means information which identifies the performer, the performance of the performer, the producer of the phonogram, the phonogram, the owner of any right in the performance or phonogram, or information about the terms and conditions of use of the performance or phonogram, and any numbers or codes that represent such information, when any of these items of information is attached to a copy of a fixed performance or a phonogram or appears in connection with the communication or making available of a fixed performance or a phonogram to the public.

## Article 20

### Formalities

The enjoyment and exercise of the rights provided for in this Treaty shall not be subject to any formality.

## Article 21

### Reservations

Subject to the provisions of Article 15(3), no reservations to this Treaty shall be permitted.

## Article 22

### Application in Time

(1)  Contracting Parties shall apply the provisions of Article 18 of the Berne Convention, *mutatis mutandis*, to the rights of performers and producers of phonograms provided for in this Treaty.

(2)  Notwithstanding paragraph (1), a Contracting Party may limit the application of Article 5 of this Treaty to performances which occurred after the entry into force of this Treaty for that Party.

## Article 23

### Provisions on Enforcement of Rights

(1)  Contracting Parties undertake to adopt, in accordance with their legal systems, the measures necessary to ensure the application of this Treaty.

(2)  Contracting Parties shall ensure that enforcement procedures are available under their law so as to permit effective action against any act of infringement of rights covered by this Treaty, including expeditious remedies to prevent infringements and remedies which constitute a deterrent to further infringements.

## CHAPTER V

## ADMINISTRATIVE AND FINAL CLAUSES

## Article 24

### Assembly

(1)(a)  The Contracting Parties shall have an Assembly.

(b)    Each Contracting Party shall be represented by one delegate who may be assisted by alternate delegates, advisors and experts.

(c)    The expenses of each delegation shall be borne by the Contracting Party that has appointed the delegation. The Assembly may ask WIPO to grant financial assistance to facilitate the participation of delegations of Contracting Parties that are regarded as developing countries in conformity with the established practice of the General Assembly of the United Nations or that are countries in transition to a market economy.

(2)(a)    The Assembly shall deal with matters concerning the maintenance and development of this Treaty and the application and operation of this Treaty.

(b)    The Assembly shall perform the function allocated to it under Article 26(2) in respect of the admission of certain intergovernmental organizations to become party to this Treaty.

(c)    The Assembly shall decide the convocation of any diplomatic conference for the revision of this Treaty and give the necessary instructions to the Director General of WIPO for the preparation of such diplomatic conference.

(3)(a)    Each Contracting Party that is a State shall have one vote and shall vote only in its own name.

(b)    Any Contracting Party that is an intergovernmental organization may participate in the vote, in place of its Member States, with a number of votes equal to the number of its Member States which are party to this Treaty. No such intergovernmental organization shall participate in the vote if any one of its Member States exercises its right to vote and vice versa.

(4)    The Assembly shall meet in ordinary session once every two years upon convocation by the Director General of WIPO.

(5)    The Assembly shall establish its own rules of procedure, including the convocation of extraordinary sessions, the requirements of a quorum and, subject to the provisions of this Treaty, the required majority for various kinds of decisions.

## Article 25

### International Bureau

The International Bureau of WIPO shall perform the administrative tasks concerning the Treaty.

## Article 26

### Eligibility for Becoming Party to the Treaty

(1)    Any Member State of WIPO may become party to this Treaty.

(2)    The Assembly may decide to admit any intergovernmental organization to become party to this Treaty which declares that it is competent in respect of, and has its own legislation binding on all its Member States on, matters covered by this Treaty and that it has been duly authorized, in accordance with its internal procedures, to become party to this Treaty.

(3)    The European Community, having made the declaration referred to in the preceding paragraph in the Diplomatic Conference that has adopted this Treaty, may become party to this Treaty.

## Article 27

### Rights and Obligations under the Treaty

Subject to any specific provisions to the contrary in this Treaty, each Contracting Party shall enjoy all of the rights and assume all of the obligations under this Treaty.

# PERFORMANCES AND PHONOGRAMS TREATY

## Article 28

### Signature of the Treaty

This Treaty shall be open for signature until December 31, 1997, by any Member State of WIPO and by the European Community.

## Article 29

### Entry into Force of the Treaty

This Treaty shall enter into force three months after 30 instruments of ratification or accession by States have been deposited with the Director General of WIPO.

## Article 30

### Effective Date of Becoming Party to the Treaty

This Treaty shall bind

    (i)   the 30 States referred to in Article 29, from the date on which this Treaty has entered into force;

    (ii)   each other State from the expiration of three months from the date on which the State has deposited its instrument with the Director General of WIPO;

    (iii)   the European Community, from the expiration of three months after the deposit of its instrument of ratification or accession if such instrument has been deposited after the entry into force of this Treaty according to Article 29, or, three months after the entry into force of this Treaty if such instrument has been deposited before the entry into force of this Treaty;

    (iv)   any other intergovernmental organization that is admitted to become party to this Treaty, from the expiration of three months after the deposit of its instrument of accession.

## Article 31

### Denunciation of the Treaty

This Treaty may be denounced by any Contracting Party by notification addressed to the Director General of WIPO. Any denunciation shall take effect one year from the date on which the Director General of WIPO received the notification.

## Article 32

### Languages of the Treaty

(1)   This Treaty is signed in a single original in English, Arabic, Chinese, French, Russian and Spanish languages, the versions in all these languages being equally authentic.

(2)   An official text in any language other than those referred to in paragraph (1) shall be established by the Director General of WIPO on the request of an interested party, after consultation with all the interested parties. For the purposes of this paragraph, "interested party" means any Member State of WIPO whose official language, or one of whose official languages, is involved and the European Community, and any other intergovernmental organization that may become party to this Treaty, if one of its official languages is involved.

## Article 33

### Depositary

The Director General of WIPO is the depositary of this Treaty.

## AGREED STATEMENTS CONCERNING THE WIPO PERFORMANCES AND PHONOGRAMS TREATY

### Concerning Article 1

It is understood that Article 1(2) clarifies the relationship between rights in phonograms under this Treaty and copyright in works embodied in the phonograms. In cases where authorization is needed from both the author of a work embodied in the phonogram and a performer or producer owning rights in the phonogram, the need for the authorization of the author does not cease to exist because the authorization of the performer or producer is also required, and vice versa.

It is further understood that nothing in Article 1(2) precludes a Contracting Party from providing exclusive rights to a performer or producer of phonograms beyond those required to be provided under this Treaty.

### Concerning Article 2(b)

It is understood that the definition of phonogram provided in Article 2(b) does not suggest that rights in the phonogram are in any way affected through their incorporation into a cinematographic or other audiovisual work.

### Concerning Articles 2(e), 8, 9, 12, and 13

As used in these Articles, the expressions "copies" and "original and copies," being subject to the right of distribution and the right of rental under the said Articles, refer exclusively to fixed copies that can be put into circulation as tangible objects.

### Concerning Article 3

It is understood that the reference in Articles 5(a) and 16(a)(iv) of the Rome Convention to "national of another Contracting State" will, when applied to this Treaty, mean, in regard to an intergovernmental organization that is a Contracting Party to this Treaty, a national of one of the countries that is a member of that organization.

### Concerning Article 3(2)

For the application of Article 3(2), it is understood that fixation means the finalization of the master tape ("bande-mère").

### Concerning Articles 7, 11 and 16

The reproduction right, as set out in Articles 7 and 11, and the exceptions permitted thereunder through Article 16, fully apply in the digital environment, in particular to the use of performances and phonograms in digital form. It is understood that the storage of a protected performance or phonogram in digital form in an electronic medium constitutes a reproduction within the meaning of these Articles.

### Concerning Article 15

It is understood that Article 15 does not represent a complete resolution of the level of rights of broadcasting and communication to the public that should be enjoyed by performers and phonogram producers in the digital age. Delegations were unable to achieve consensus on differing proposals for aspects of exclusivity to be provided in certain circumstances or for rights to be provided without the possibility of reservations, and have therefore left the issue to future resolution.

### Concerning Article 15

It is understood that Article 15 does not prevent the granting of the right conferred by this Article to performers of folklore and producers of phonograms recording folklore where such phonograms have not been published for commercial gain.

331

# PERFORMANCES AND PHONOGRAMS TREATY

## Concerning Article 16

The agreed statement concerning Article 10 (on Limitations and Exceptions) of the WIPO Copyright Treaty is applicable *mutatis mutandis* also to Article 16 (on Limitations and Exceptions) of the WIPO Performances and Phonograms Treaty.

## Concerning Article 19

The agreed statement concerning Article 12 (on Obligations concerning Rights Management Information) of the WIPO Copyright Treaty is applicable *mutatis mutandis* also to Article 19 (on Obligations concerning Rights Management Information) of the WIPO Performances and Phonograms Treaty.

# APPENDIX K

---

# WORLD INTELLECTUAL PROPERTY ORGANIZATION BEIJING TREATY ON AUDIOVISUAL PERFORMANCES

(Adopted on June 24, 2012)

(The United States has not yet ratified this treaty.)

## Preamble

*The Contracting Parties,*

*Desiring* to develop and maintain the protection of the rights of performers in their audiovisual performances in a manner as effective and uniform as possible,

*Recalling* the importance of the Development Agenda recommendations, adopted in 2007 by the General Assembly of the Convention Establishing the World Intellectual Property Organization (WIPO), which aim to ensure that development considerations form an integral part of the Organization's work,

*Recognizing* the need to introduce new international rules in order to provide adequate solutions to the questions raised by economic, social, cultural and technological developments,

*Recognizing* the profound impact of the development and convergence of information and communication technologies on the production and use of audiovisual performances,

*Recognizing* the need to maintain a balance between the rights of performers in their audiovisual performances and the larger public interest, particularly education, research and access to information,

*Recognizing* that the WIPO Performances and Phonograms Treaty (WPPT) done in Geneva on December 20, 1996, does not extend protection to performers in respect of their performances fixed in audiovisual fixations,

*Referring* to the Resolution concerning Audiovisual Performances adopted by the Diplomatic Conference on Certain Copyright and Neighboring Rights Questions on December 20, 1996,

*Have agreed as follows*:

## Article 1
### Relation to Other Conventions and Treaties

(1)   Nothing in this Treaty shall derogate from existing obligations that Contracting Parties have to each other under the WPPT or the International Convention for the Protection of Performers, Producers of Phonograms and Broadcasting Organizations done in Rome on October 26, 1961.

(2)   Protection granted under this Treaty shall leave intact and shall in no way affect the protection of copyright in literary and artistic works. Consequently, no provision of this Treaty may be interpreted as prejudicing such protection.

# AUDIOVISUAL PERFORMANCES TREATY

(3)   This Treaty shall not have any connection with treaties other than the WPPT, nor shall it prejudice any rights and obligations under any other treaties.

## Article 2

### Definitions

For the purposes of this Treaty:

(a)   "performers" are actors, singers, musicians, dancers, and other persons who act, sing, deliver, declaim, play in, interpret, or otherwise perform literary or artistic works or expressions of folklore;

(b)   "audiovisual fixation" means the embodiment of moving images, whether or not accompanied by sounds or by the representations thereof, from which they can be perceived, reproduced or communicated through a device;

(c)   "broadcasting" means the transmission by wireless means for public reception of sounds or of images or of images and sounds or of the representations thereof; such transmission by satellite is also "broadcasting"; transmission of encrypted signals is "broadcasting" where the means for decrypting are provided to the public by the broadcasting organization or with its consent;

(d)   "communication to the public" of a performance means the transmission to the public by any medium, otherwise than by broadcasting, of an unfixed performance, or of a performance fixed in an audiovisual fixation. For the purposes of Article 11, "communication to the public" includes making a performance fixed in an audiovisual fixation audible or visible or audible and visible to the public.

## Article 3

### Beneficiaries of Protection

(1)   Contracting Parties shall accord the protection granted under this Treaty to performers who are nationals of other Contracting Parties.

(2)   Performers who are not nationals of one of the Contracting Parties but who have their habitual residence in one of them shall, for the purposes of this Treaty, be assimilated to nationals of that Contracting Party.

## Article 4

### National Treatment

(1)   Each Contracting Party shall accord to nationals of other Contracting Parties the treatment it accords to its own nationals with regard to the exclusive rights specifically granted in this Treaty and the right to equitable remuneration provided for in Article 11 of this Treaty.

(2)   A Contracting Party shall be entitled to limit the extent and term of the protection accorded to nationals of another Contracting Party under paragraph (1), with respect to the rights granted in Article 11(1) and 11(2) of this Treaty, to those rights that its own nationals enjoy in that other Contracting Party.

(3)   The obligation provided for in paragraph (1) does not apply to a Contracting Party to the extent that another Contracting Party makes use of the reservations permitted by Article 11(3) of this Treaty, nor does it apply to a Contracting Party, to the extent that it has made such reservation.

## Article 5

### Moral Rights

(1)   Independently of a performer's economic rights, and even after the transfer of those rights, the performer shall, as regards his live performances or performances fixed in audiovisual fixations, have the right:

(i)   to claim to be identified as the performer of his performances, except where omission is dictated by the manner of the use of the performance; and

(ii)   to object to any distortion, mutilation or other modification of his performances that would be prejudicial to his reputation, taking due account of the nature of audiovisual fixations.

(2)   The rights granted to a performer in accordance with paragraph (1) shall, after his death, be maintained, at least until the expiry of the economic rights, and shall be exercisable by the persons or institutions authorized by the legislation of the Contracting Party where protection is claimed. However, those Contracting Parties whose legislation, at the moment of their ratification of or accession to this Treaty, does not provide for protection after the death of the performer of all rights set out in the preceding paragraph may provide that some of these rights will, after his death, cease to be maintained.

(3)   The means of redress for safeguarding the rights granted under this Article shall be governed by the legislation of the Contracting Party where protection is claimed.

## Article 6

### Economic Rights of Performers in their Unfixed Performances

Performers shall enjoy the exclusive right of authorizing, as regards their performances:

(i)   the broadcasting and communication to the public of their unfixed performances except where the performance is already a broadcast performance; and

(ii)   the fixation of their unfixed performances.

## Article 7

### Right of Reproduction

Performers shall enjoy the exclusive right of authorizing the direct or indirect reproduction of their performances fixed in audiovisual fixations, in any manner or form.

## Article 8

### Right of Distribution

(1)   Performers shall enjoy the exclusive right of authorizing the making available to the public of the original and copies of their performances fixed in audiovisual fixations through sale or other transfer of ownership.

(2)   Nothing in this Treaty shall affect the freedom of Contracting Parties to determine the conditions, if any, under which the exhaustion of the right in paragraph (1) applies after the first sale or other transfer of ownership of the original or a copy of the fixed performance with the authorization of the performer.

## Article 9

### Right of Rental

(1)   Performers shall enjoy the exclusive right of authorizing the commercial rental to the public of the original and copies of their performances fixed in audiovisual fixations as determined in the national law of Contracting Parties, even after distribution of them by, or pursuant to, authorization by the performer.

(2)   Contracting Parties are exempt from the obligation of paragraph (1) unless the commercial rental has led to widespread copying of such fixations materially impairing the exclusive right of reproduction of performers.

# AUDIOVISUAL PERFORMANCES TREATY

## Article 10

## Right of Making Available of Fixed Performances

Performers shall enjoy the exclusive right of authorizing the making available to the public of their performances fixed in audiovisual fixations, by wire or wireless means, in such a way that members of the public may access them from a place and at a time individually chosen by them.

## Article 11

## Right of Broadcasting and Communication to the Public

(1) Performers shall enjoy the exclusive right of authorizing the broadcasting and communication to the public of their performances fixed in audiovisual fixations.

(2) Contracting Parties may in a notification deposited with the Director General of WIPO declare that, instead of the right of authorization provided for in paragraph (1), they will establish a right to equitable remuneration for the direct or indirect use of performances fixed in audiovisual fixations for broadcasting or for communication to the public. Contracting Parties may also declare that they will set conditions in their legislation for the exercise of the right to equitable remuneration.

(3) Any Contracting Party may declare that it will apply the provisions of paragraphs (1) or (2) only in respect of certain uses, or that it will limit their application in some other way, or that it will not apply the provisions of paragraphs (1) and (2) at all.

## Article 12

## Transfer of Rights

(1) A Contracting Party may provide in its national law that once a performer has consented to fixation of his or her performance in an audiovisual fixation, the exclusive rights of authorization provided for in Articles 7 to 11 of this Treaty shall be owned or exercised by or transferred to the producer of such audiovisual fixation subject to any contract to the contrary between the performer and the producer of the audiovisual fixation as determined by the national law.

(2) A Contracting Party may require with respect to audiovisual fixations produced under its national law that such consent or contract be in writing and signed by both parties to the contract or by their duly authorized representatives.

(3) Independent of the transfer of exclusive rights described above, national laws or individual, collective or other agreements may provide the performer with the right to receive royalties or equitable remuneration for any use of the performance, as provided for under this Treaty including as regards Articles 10 and 11.

## Article 13

## Limitations and Exceptions

(1) Contracting Parties may, in their national legislation, provide for the same kinds of limitations or exceptions with regard to the protection of performers as they provide for, in their national legislation, in connection with the protection of copyright in literary and artistic works.

(2) Contracting Parties shall confine any limitations of or exceptions to rights provided for in this Treaty to certain special cases which do not conflict with a normal exploitation of the performance and do not unreasonably prejudice the legitimate interests of the performer.

## Article 14

## Term of Protection

The term of protection to be granted to performers under this Treaty shall last, at least, until the end of a period of 50 years computed from the end of the year in which the performance was fixed.

## Article 15

### Obligations concerning Technological Measures

Contracting Parties shall provide adequate legal protection and effective legal remedies against the circumvention of effective technological measures that are used by performers in connection with the exercise of their rights under this Treaty and that restrict acts, in respect of their performances, which are not authorized by the performers concerned or permitted by law.

## Article 16

### Obligations concerning Rights Management Information

(1)   Contracting Parties shall provide adequate and effective legal remedies against any person knowingly performing any of the following acts knowing, or with respect to civil remedies having reasonable grounds to know, that it will induce, enable, facilitate, or conceal an infringement of any right covered by this Treaty:

(i)   to remove or alter any electronic rights management information without authority;

(ii)   to distribute, import for distribution, broadcast, communicate or make available to the public, without authority, performances or copies of performances fixed in audiovisual fixations knowing that electronic rights management information has been removed or altered without authority.

(2)   As used in this Article, "rights management information" means information which identifies the performer, the performance of the performer, or the owner of any right in the performance, or information about the terms and conditions of use of the performance, and any numbers or codes that represent such information, when any of these items of information is attached to a performance fixed in an audiovisual fixation.

## Article 17

### Formalities

The enjoyment and exercise of the rights provided for in this Treaty shall not be subject to any formality.

## Article 18

### Reservations and Notifications

(1)   Subject to provisions of Article 11(3), no reservations to this Treaty shall be permitted.

(2)   Any notification under Article 11(2) or 19(2) may be made in instruments of ratification or accession, and the effective date of the notification shall be the same as the date of entry into force of this Treaty with respect to the Contracting Party having made the notification. Any such notification may also be made later, in which case the notification shall have effect three months after its receipt by the Director General of WIPO or at any later date indicated in the notification.

## Article 19

### Application in Time

(1)   Contracting Parties shall accord the protection granted under this Treaty to fixed performances that exist at the moment of the entry into force of this Treaty and to all performances that occur after the entry into force of this Treaty for each Contracting Party.

(2)   Notwithstanding the provisions of paragraph (1), a Contracting Party may declare in a notification deposited with the Director General of WIPO that it will not apply the provisions of Articles 7 to 11 of this Treaty, or any one or more of those, to fixed performances that existed at the moment of the entry into force of this Treaty for each Contracting Party. In respect of such Contracting Party, other Contracting Parties may limit the application of the said Articles to performances that occurred after the entry into force of this Treaty for that Contracting Party.

(3)   The protection provided for in this Treaty shall be without prejudice to any acts committed, agreements concluded or rights acquired before the entry into force of this Treaty for each Contracting Party.

(4)   Contracting Parties may in their legislation establish transitional provisions under which any person who, prior to the entry into force of this Treaty, engaged in lawful acts with respect to a performance, may undertake with respect to the same performance acts within the scope of the rights provided for in Articles 5 and 7 to 11 after the entry into force of this Treaty for the respective Contracting Parties.

## Article 20

### Provisions on Enforcement of Rights

(1)   Contracting Parties undertake to adopt, in accordance with their legal systems, the measures necessary to ensure the application of this Treaty.

(2)   Contracting Parties shall ensure that enforcement procedures are available under their law so as to permit effective action against any act of infringement of rights covered by this Treaty, including expeditious remedies to prevent infringements and remedies which constitute a deterrent to further infringements.

## Article 21

### Assembly

(1)(a)   The Contracting Parties shall have an Assembly.

(b)   Each Contracting Party shall be represented in the Assembly by one delegate who may be assisted by alternate delegates, advisors and experts.

(c)   The expenses of each delegation shall be borne by the Contracting Party that has appointed the delegation. The Assembly may ask WIPO to grant financial assistance to facilitate the participation of delegations of Contracting Parties that are regarded as developing countries in conformity with the established practice of the General Assembly of the United Nations or that are countries in transition to a market economy.

(2)(a)   The Assembly shall deal with matters concerning the maintenance and development of this Treaty and the application and operation of this Treaty.

(b)   The Assembly shall perform the function allocated to it under Article 23(2) in respect of the admission of certain intergovernmental organizations to become party to this Treaty.

(c)   The Assembly shall decide the convocation of any diplomatic conference for the revision of this Treaty and give the necessary instructions to the Director General of WIPO for the preparation of such diplomatic conference.

(3)(a)   Each Contracting Party that is a State shall have one vote and shall vote only in its own name.

(b)   Any Contracting Party that is an intergovernmental organization may participate in the vote, in place of its Member States, with a number of votes equal to the number of its Member States which are party to this Treaty. No such intergovernmental organization shall participate in the vote if any one of its Member States exercises its right to vote and vice versa.

(4)   The Assembly shall meet upon convocation by the Director General and, in the absence of exceptional circumstances, during the same period and at the same place as the General Assembly of WIPO.

(5)   The Assembly shall endeavor to take its decisions by consensus and shall establish its own rules of procedure, including the convocation of extraordinary sessions, the requirements of a quorum and, subject to the provisions of this Treaty, the required majority for various kinds of decisions.

## Article 22

### International Bureau

The International Bureau of WIPO shall perform the administrative tasks concerning the Treaty.

## Article 23

### Eligibility for Becoming Party to the Treaty

(1)   Any Member State of WIPO may become party to this Treaty.

(2)   The Assembly may decide to admit any intergovernmental organization to become party to this Treaty which declares that it is competent in respect of, and has its own legislation binding on all its Member States on, matters covered by this Treaty and that it has been duly authorized, in accordance with its internal procedures, to become party to this Treaty.

(3)   The European Union, having made the declaration referred to in the preceding paragraph in the Diplomatic Conference that has adopted this Treaty, may become party to this Treaty.

## Article 24

### Rights and Obligations under the Treaty

Subject to any specific provisions to the contrary in this Treaty, each Contracting Party shall enjoy all of the rights and assume all of the obligations under this Treaty.

## Article 25

### Signature of the Treaty

This Treaty shall be open for signature at the headquarters of WIPO by any eligible party for one year after its adoption.

## Article 26

### Entry into Force of the Treaty

This Treaty shall enter into force three months after 30 eligible parties referred to in Article 23 have deposited their instruments of ratification or accession.

## Article 27

### Effective Date of Becoming Party to the Treaty

This Treaty shall bind:

(i)   the 30 eligible parties referred to in Article 26, from the date on which this Treaty has entered into force;

(ii)   each other eligible party referred to in Article 23, from the expiration of three months from the date on which it has deposited its instrument of ratification or accession with the Director General of WIPO.

## Article 28

### Denunciation of the Treaty

This Treaty may be denounced by any Contracting Party by notification addressed to the Director General of WIPO. Any denunciation shall take effect one year from the date on which the Director General of WIPO received the notification.

## Article 29

### Languages of the Treaty

(1)   This Treaty is signed in a single original in English, Arabic, Chinese, French, Russian and Spanish languages, the versions in all these languages being equally authentic.

# AUDIOVISUAL PERFORMANCES TREATY

(2)   An official text in any language other than those referred to in paragraph (1) shall be established by the Director General of WIPO on the request of an interested party, after consultation with all the interested parties. For the purposes of this paragraph, "interested party" means any Member State of WIPO whose official language, or one of whose official languages, is involved and the European Union, and any other intergovernmental organization that may become party to this Treaty, if one of its official languages is involved.

### Article 30
### Depositary

The Director General of WIPO is the depositary of this Treaty.

## AGREED STATEMENTS CONCERNING THE BEIJING TREATY ON
## AUDIOVISUAL PERFORMANCES
### Concerning Article 1

It is understood that nothing in this Treaty affects any rights or obligations under the WIPO Performances and Phonograms Treaty (WPPT) or their interpretation and it is further understood that paragraph 3 does not create any obligations for a Contracting Party to this Treaty to ratify or accede to the WPPT or to comply with any of its provisions.

### Concerning Article 1(3)

It is understood that Contracting Parties who are members of the World Trade Organization (WTO) acknowledge all the principles and objectives of the Agreement on Trade-Related Aspects of Intellectual Property Rights (TRIPS Agreement) and understand that nothing in this Treaty affects the provisions of the TRIPS Agreement, including, but not limited to, the provisions relating to anti-competitive practices.

### Concerning Article 2(a)

It is understood that the definition of "performers" includes those who perform a literary or artistic work that is created or first fixed in the course of a performance.

### Concerning Article 2(b)

It is hereby confirmed that the definition of "audiovisual fixation" contained in Article 2(b) is without prejudice to Article 2(c) of the WPPT.

### Concerning Article 5

For the purposes of this Treaty and without prejudice to any other treaty, it is understood that, considering the nature of audiovisual fixations and their production and distribution, modifications of a performance that are made in the normal course of exploitation of the performance, such as editing, compression, dubbing, or formatting, in existing or new media or formats, and that are made in the course of a use authorized by the performer, would not in themselves amount to modifications within the meaning of Article 5(1)(ii). Rights under Article 5(1)(ii) are concerned only with changes that are objectively prejudicial to the performer's reputation in a substantial way. It is also understood that the mere use of new or changed technology or media, as such, does not amount to modification within the meaning of Article 5(1)(ii).

### Concerning Article 7

The reproduction right, as set out in Article 7, and the exceptions permitted thereunder through Article 13, fully apply in the digital environment, in particular to the use of performances in digital form. It is understood that the storage of a protected performance in digital form in an electronic medium constitutes a reproduction within the meaning of this Article.

340

### Concerning Articles 8 and 9

As used in these Articles, the expression "original and copies," being subject to the right of distribution and the right of rental under the said Articles, refers exclusively to fixed copies that can be put into circulation as tangible objects.

### Concerning Article 13

The Agreed statement concerning Article 10 (on Limitations and Exceptions) of the WIPO Copyright Treaty (WCT) is applicable *mutatis mutandis* also to Article 13 (on Limitations and Exceptions) of the Treaty.

### Concerning Article 15 as it relates to Article 13

It is understood that nothing in this Article prevents a Contracting Party from adopting effective and necessary measures to ensure that a beneficiary may enjoy limitations and exceptions provided in that Contracting Party's national law, in accordance with Article 13, where technological measures have been applied to an audiovisual performance and the beneficiary has legal access to that performance, in circumstances such as where appropriate and effective measures have not been taken by rights holders in relation to that performance to enable the beneficiary to enjoy the limitations and exceptions under that Contracting Party's national law. Without prejudice to the legal protection of an audiovisual work in which a performance is fixed, it is further understood that the obligations under Article 15 are not applicable to performances unprotected or no longer protected under the national law giving effect to this Treaty.

### Concerning Article 15

The expression "technological measures used by performers" should, as this is the case regarding the WPPT, be construed broadly, referring also to those acting on behalf of performers, including their representatives, licensees or assignees, including producers, service providers, and persons engaged in communication or broadcasting using performances on the basis of due authorization.

### Concerning Article 16

The Agreed statement concerning Article 12 (on Obligations concerning Rights Management Information) of the WCT is applicable *mutatis mutandis* also to Article 16 (on Obligations concerning Rights Management Information) of the Treaty.

# APPENDIX L

## SELECTED PROVISIONS OF THE FEDERAL TRADEMARK ACT

### § 1. (15 U.S.C.A. § 1051) Application for Registration; Verification

**(a) Application for Use of Trademark**

(1) The owner of a trademark used in commerce may request registration of its trademark on the principal register hereby established by paying the prescribed fee and filing in the Patent and Trademark Office an application and a verified statement, in such form as may be prescribed by the Director, and such number of specimens or facsimiles of the mark as used as may be required by the Director.

(2) The application shall include specification of the applicant's domicile and citizenship, the date of the applicant's first use of the mark, the date of the applicant's first use of the mark in commerce, the goods in connection with which the mark is used, and a drawing of the mark.

(3) The statement shall be verified by the applicant and specify that—

(A) the person making the verification believes that he or she, or the juristic person in whose behalf he or she makes the verification, to be the owner of the mark sought to be registered;

(B) to the best of the verifier's knowledge and belief, the facts recited in the application are accurate;

(C) the mark is in use in commerce; and

(D) to the best of the verifier's knowledge and belief, no other person has the right to use such mark in commerce either in the identical form thereof or in such near resemblance thereto as to be likely, when used on or in connection with the goods of such other person, to cause confusion, or to cause mistake, or to deceive, except that, in the case of every application claiming concurrent use, the applicant shall—

(i) state exceptions to the claim of exclusive use; and

(ii) shall specify, to the extent of the verifier's knowledge—

(I) any concurrent use by others;

(II) the goods on or in connection with which and the areas in which each concurrent use exists;

(III) the periods of each use; and

(IV) the goods and area for which the applicant desires registration.

(4) The applicant shall comply with such rules or regulations as may be prescribed by the Director. The Director shall promulgate rules prescribing the requirements for the application and for obtaining a filing date herein.

**(b) Application for Bona Fide Intention to Use Trademark**

(1) A person who has a bona fide intention, under circumstances showing the good faith of such person, to use a trademark in commerce may request registration of its trademark on the principal

register hereby established by paying the prescribed fee and filing in the Patent and Trademark Office an application and a verified statement, in such form as may be prescribed by the Director.

(2)    The application shall include specification of the applicant's domicile and citizenship, the goods in connection with which the applicant has a bona fide intention to use the mark, and a drawing of the mark.

(3)    The statement shall be verified by the applicant and specify—

(A)    that the person making the verification believes that he or she, or the juristic person in whose behalf he or she makes the verification, to be entitled to use the mark in commerce;

(B)    the applicant's bona fide intention to use the mark in commerce;

(C)    that, to the best of the verifier's knowledge and belief, the facts recited in the application are accurate; and

(D)    that, to the best of the verifier's knowledge and belief, no other person has the right to use such mark in commerce either in the identical form thereof or in such near resemblance thereto as to be likely, when used on or in connection with the goods of such other person, to cause confusion, or to cause mistake, or to deceive.

Except for applications filed pursuant to section 44, no mark shall be registered until the applicant has met the requirements of subsections (c) and (d) of this section.

(4)    The applicant shall comply with such rules or regulations as may be prescribed by the Director. The Director shall promulgate rules prescribing the requirements for the application and for obtaining a filing date herein.

**(c)  Amendment of Application Under Subsection (b) to Conform to Requirements of Subsection (a)**

At any time during examination of an application filed under subsection (b) of this section, an applicant who has made use of the mark in commerce may claim the benefits of such use for purposes of this chapter, by amending his or her application to bring it into conformity with the requirements of subsection (a) of this section.

**(d)  Verified Statement That Trademark Is Used in Commerce**

(1)    Within six months after the date on which the notice of allowance with respect to a mark is issued under section 1063(b)(2) of this title to an applicant under subsection (b) of this section, the applicant shall file in the Patent and Trademark Office, together with such number of specimens or facsimiles of the mark as used in commerce as may be required by the Director and payment of the prescribed fee, a verified statement that the mark is in use in commerce and specifying the date of the applicant's first use of the mark in commerce and those goods or services specified in the notice of allowance on or in connection with which the mark is used in commerce. Subject to examination and acceptance of the statement of use, the mark shall be registered in the Patent and Trademark Office, a certificate of registration shall be issued for those goods or services recited in the statement of use for which the mark is entitled to registration, and notice of registration shall be published in the Official Gazette of the Patent and Trademark Office. Such examination may include an examination of the factors set forth in subsections (a) through (e) of section 1052 of this title. The notice of registration shall specify the goods or services for which the mark is registered.

(2)    The Director shall extend, for one additional 6-month period, the time for filing the statement of use under paragraph (1), upon written request of the applicant before the expiration of the 6-month period provided in paragraph (1). In addition to an extension under the preceding sentence, the Director may, upon a showing of good cause by the applicant, further extend the time for filing the statement of use under paragraph (1) for periods aggregating not more than 24 months, pursuant to written request of the applicant made before the expiration of the last extension granted under this paragraph. Any request for an extension under this paragraph shall be accompanied by a verified statement that the applicant has a continued bona fide intention to use the mark in commerce

and specifying those goods or services identified in the notice of allowance on or in connection with which the applicant has a continued bona fide intention to use the mark in commerce. Any request for an extension under this paragraph shall be accompanied by payment of the prescribed fee. The Director shall issue regulations setting forth guidelines for determining what constitutes good cause for purposes of this paragraph.

(3) The Director shall notify any applicant who files a statement of use of the acceptance or refusal thereof and, if the statement of use is refused, the reasons for the refusal. An applicant may amend the statement of use.

(4) The failure to timely file a verified statement of use under paragraph (1) or an extension request under paragraph (2) shall result in abandonment of the application, unless it can be shown to the satisfaction of the Director that the delay in responding was unintentional, in which case the time for filing may be extended, but for a period not to exceed the period specified in paragraphs (1) and (2) for filing a statement of use.

**(e) Designation of Resident for Service of Process and Notices**

If the applicant is not domiciled in the United States the applicant may designate, by a document filed in the United States Patent and Trademark Office, the name and address of a person resident in the United States on whom may be served notices or process in proceedings affecting the mark. Such notices or process may be served upon the person so designated by leaving with that person or mailing to that person a copy thereof at the address specified in the last designation so filed. If the person so designated cannot be found at the address given in the last designation, or if the registrant does not designate by a document filed in the United States Patent and Trademark Office the name and address of a person resident in the United States on whom may be served notices or process in proceedings affecting the mark, such notices or process may be served on the Director.

**§ 2. (15 U.S.C.A. § 1052) Trademarks Registrable on Principal Register; Concurrent Registration**

No trademark by which the goods of the applicant may be distinguished from the goods of others shall be refused registration on the principal register on account of its nature unless it—

(a) Consists of or comprises immoral, deceptive, or scandalous matter; or matter which may disparage or falsely suggest a connection with persons, living or dead, institutions, beliefs, or national symbols, or bring them into contempt, or disrepute; or a geographical indication which, when used on or in connection with wines or spirits, identifies a place other than the origin of the goods and is first used on or in connection with wines or spirits by the applicant on or after one year after the date on which the WTO Agreement (as defined in section 2(9) of the Uruguay Round Agreements Act) enters into force with respect to the United States.

(b) Consists of or comprises the flag or coat of arms or other insignia of the United States, or of any State or municipality, or of any foreign nation, or any simulation thereof.

(c) Consists of or comprises a name, portrait, or signature identifying a particular living individual except by his written consent, or the name, signature, or portrait of a deceased President of the United States during the life of his widow, if any, except by the written consent of the widow.

(d) Consists of or comprises a mark which so resembles a mark registered in the Patent and Trademark Office, or a mark or trade name previously used in the United States by another and not abandoned, as to be likely, when used on or in connection with the goods of the applicant, to cause confusion, or to cause mistake, or to deceive: Provided, That if the Director determines that confusion, mistake, or deception is not likely to result from the continued use by more than one person of the same or similar marks under conditions and limitations as to the mode or place of use of the marks or the goods on or in connection with which such marks are used, concurrent registrations may be issued to such persons when they have become entitled to use such marks as a result of their concurrent lawful use in commerce prior to (1) the earliest of the filing dates of the applications pending or of any registration issued under this chapter; (2) July 5, 1947, in the case of registrations previously issued under the Act of March 3, 1881, or February 20, 1905, and continuing in full force and effect on that date; or (3) July 5, 1947, in the case of applications filed under the Act of February 20, 1905, and registered after July 5, 1947. Use prior to the filing date of any pending application or a registration shall not be required when the owner of such application or registration consents to the grant of a concurrent registration to the applicant. Concurrent registrations may also be issued by the Director when a court of competent jurisdiction has finally determined that more than one person is entitled to use the same or similar marks in commerce. In issuing concurrent registrations, the Director shall prescribe conditions and limitations as to the mode or place of use of the mark or the goods on or in connection with which such mark is registered to the respective persons.

(e)   Consists of a mark which (1) when used on or in connection with the goods of the applicant is merely descriptive or deceptively misdescriptive of them, (2) when used on or in connection with the goods of the applicant is primarily geographically descriptive of them, except as indications of regional origin may be registrable under section 1054 of this title, (3) when used on or in connection with the goods of the applicant is primarily geographically deceptively misdescriptive of them, (4) is primarily merely a surname, or (5) comprises any matter that, as a whole, is functional.

(f)   Except as expressly excluded in subsections (a), (b), (c), (d), (e)(3), and (e)(5) of this section, nothing in this chapter shall prevent the registration of a mark used by the applicant which has become distinctive of the applicant's goods in commerce. The Director may accept as prima facie evidence that the mark has become distinctive, as used on or in connection with the applicant's goods in commerce, proof of substantially exclusive and continuous use thereof as a mark by the applicant in commerce for the five years before the date on which the claim of distinctiveness is made. Nothing in this section shall prevent the registration of a mark which, when used on or in connection with the goods of the applicant, is primarily geographically deceptively misdescriptive of them, and which became distinctive of the applicant's goods in commerce before December 8, 1993.

A mark which would be likely to cause dilution by blurring or dilution by tarnishment under section 43(c), may be refused registration only pursuant to a proceeding brought under section 13. A registration for a mark which would be likely to cause dilution by blurring or dilution by tarnishment under section 43(c), may be canceled pursuant to a proceeding brought under either section 14 or section 24.

## § 3. (15 U.S.C.A. § 1053) Service Marks Registrable

Subject to the provisions relating to the registration of trademarks, so far as they are applicable, service marks shall be registrable, in the same manner and with the same effect as are trade-marks, and when registered they shall be entitled to the protection provided in this chapter in the case of trade-marks. Applications and procedure under this section shall conform as nearly as practicable to those prescribed for the registration of trade-marks.

## § 7. (15 U.S.C.A. § 1057) Certificates of Registration

### (a)  Issuance and Form

Certificates of registration of marks registered upon the principal register shall be issued in the name of the United States of America, under the seal of the United States Patent and Trademark Office, and shall be signed by the Director or have his signature placed thereon, and a record thereof shall be kept in the United States Patent and Trademark Office. The registration shall reproduce the mark, and state that the mark is registered on the principal register under this chapter, the date of the first use of the mark, the date of the first use of the mark in commerce, the particular goods or services for which it is registered, the number and date of the registration, the term thereof, the date on which the application for registration was received in the United States Patent and Trademark Office, and any conditions and limitations that may be imposed in the registration.

**(b) Certificate as Prima Facie Evidence**

A certificate of registration of a mark upon the principal register provided by this chapter shall be prima facie evidence of the validity of the registered mark and of the registration of the mark, of the owner's ownership of the mark, and of the owner's exclusive right to use the registered mark in commerce on or in connection with the goods or services specified in the certificate, subject to any conditions or limitations stated in the certificate.

**(c) Application to Register Mark Considered Constructive Use**

Contingent on the registration of a mark on the principal register provided by this chapter, the filing of the application to register such mark shall constitute constructive use of the mark, conferring a right of priority, nationwide in effect, on or in connection with the goods or services specified in the registration against any other person except for a person whose mark has not been abandoned and who, prior to such filing—

    (1)  has used the mark;

    (2)  has filed an application to register the mark which is pending or has resulted in registration of the mark; or

    (3)  has filed a foreign application to register the mark on the basis of which he or she has acquired a right of priority, and timely files an application under section 1126(d) of this title to register the mark which is pending or has resulted in registration of the mark.

**(d) Issuance to Assignee**

A certificate of registration of a mark may be issued to the assignee of the applicant, but the assignment must first be recorded in the United States Patent and Trademark Office. In case of change of ownership the Director shall, at the request of the owner and upon a proper showing and the payment of the prescribed fee, issue to such assignee a new certificate of registration of the said mark in the name of such assignee, and for the unexpired part of the original period.

**(e) Surrender, Cancellation, or Amendment by Registrant**

Upon application of the owner the Director may permit any registration to be surrendered for cancellation, and upon cancellation appropriate entry shall be made in the records of the United States Patent and Trademark Office. Upon application of the owner and payment of the prescribed fee, the Director for good cause may permit any registration to be amended or to be disclaimed in part: *Provided,* That the amendment or disclaimer does not alter materially the character of the mark. Appropriate entry shall be made in the records of the United States Patent and Trademark Office and upon the certificate of registration.

**(f) Copies of Patent and Trademark Office Records as Evidence**

Copies of any records, books, papers, or drawings belonging to the United States Patent and Trademark Office relating to marks, and copies of registrations, when authenticated by the seal of the United States Patent and Trademark Office and certified by the Director, or in his name by an employee of the Office duly designated by the Director, shall be evidence in all cases wherein the originals would be evidence; and any person making application therefor and paying the prescribed fee shall have such copies.

**(g) Correction of Patent and Trademark Office Mistake**

Whenever a material mistake in a registration, incurred through the fault of the United States Patent and Trademark Office, is clearly disclosed by the records of the Office a certificate stating the fact and nature of such mistake shall be issued without charge and recorded and a printed copy thereof shall be attached to each printed copy of the registration and such corrected registration shall thereafter have the same effect as if the same had been originally issued in such corrected form, or in the discretion of the Director a new certificate of registration may be issued without charge. All certificates of correction heretofore issued in accordance with the rules of the United States Patent and Trademark Office and the registrations to which they are attached shall have the same force and effect as if such certificates and their issue had been specifically authorized by statute.

### (h)  Correction of Applicant's Mistake

Whenever a mistake has been made in a registration and a showing has been made that such mistake occurred in good faith through the fault of the applicant, the Director is authorized to issue a certificate of correction or, in his discretion, a new certificate upon the payment of the prescribed fee: *Provided,* That the correction does not involve such changes in the registration as to require republication of the mark.

### § 8.  (15 U.S.C.A. § 1058) Duration, Affidavits and Fees

### (a)  Time Periods for Required Affidavits

Each registration shall remain in force for 10 years, except that the registration of any mark shall be canceled by the Director unless the owner of the registration files in the United States Patent and Trademark Office affidavits that meet the requirements of subsection (b), within the following time periods:

(1)   Within the 1-year period immediately preceding the expiration of 6 years following the date of registration under this Act or the date of the publication under section 12(c).

(2)   Within the 1-year period immediately preceding the expiration of 10 years following the date of registration, and each successive 10-year period following the date of registration.

(3)   The owner may file the affidavit required under this section within the 6-month grace period immediately following the expiration of the periods established in paragraphs (1) and (2), together with the fee described in subsection (b) and the additional grace period surcharge prescribed by the Director.

### (b)  Requirements for Affidavit

The affidavit referred to in subsection (a) shall—

(1)(A)   state that the mark is in use in commerce;

(B)   set forth the goods and services recited in the registration on or in connection with which the mark is in use in commerce;

(C)   be accompanied by such number of specimens or facsimiles showing current use of the mark in commerce as may be required by the Director; and

(D)   be accompanied by the fee prescribed by the Director; or

(2)(A)   set forth the goods and services recited in the registration on or in connection with which the mark is not in use in commerce;

(B)   include a showing that any nonuse is due to special circumstances which excuse such nonuse and is not due to any intention to abandon the mark; and

(C)   be accompanied by the fee prescribed by the Director.

### (c)  Deficient Affidavit

If any submission filed within the period set forth in subsection (a) is deficient, including that the affidavit was not filed in the name of the owner of the registration, the deficiency may be corrected after the statutory time period, within the time prescribed after notification of the deficiency. Such submission shall be accompanied by the additional deficiency surcharge prescribed by the Director.

**(d) Notice of Requirement**

Special notice of the requirement for such affidavit shall be attached to each certificate of registration and notice of publication under section 12(c).

**(e) Notification of Acceptance or Refusal**

The Director shall notify any owner who files any affidavit required by this section of the Director's acceptance or refusal thereof and, in the case of a refusal, the reasons therefor.

**(f) Designation of Resident for Service of Process and Notices**

If the owner is not domiciled in the United States, the owner may designate, by a document filed in the United States Patent and Trademark Office, the name and address of a person resident in the United States on whom may be served notices or process in proceedings affecting the mark. Such notices or process may be served upon the person so designated by leaving with that person or mailing to that person a copy thereof at the address specified in the last designation so filed. If the person so designated cannot be found at the last designated address, or if the owner does not designate by a document filed in the United States Patent and Trademark Office the name and address of a person resident in the United States on whom may be served notices or process in proceedings affecting the mark, such notices or process may be served on the Director.

## § 9. (15 U.S.C.A. § 1059) Renewal of Registration

(a) Subject to the provisions of section 8, each registration may be renewed for periods of 10 years at the end of each successive 10-year period following the date of registration upon payment of the prescribed fee and the filing of a written application, in such form as may be prescribed by the Director. Such application may be made at any time within 1 year before the end of each successive 10-year period for which the registration was issued or renewed, or it may be made within a grace period of 6 months after the end of each successive 10-year period, upon payment of a fee and surcharge prescribed therefor. If any application filed under this section is deficient, the deficiency may be corrected within the time prescribed after notification of the deficiency, upon payment of a surcharge prescribed therefor.

(b) If the Director refuses to renew the registration, the Director shall notify the registrant of the Director's refusal and the reasons therefor.

(c) If the registrant is not domiciled in the United States the registrant may designate, by a document filed in the United States Patent and Trademark Office, the name and address of a person resident in the United States on whom may be served notices or process in proceedings affecting the mark. Such notices or process may be served upon the person so designated by leaving with that person or mailing to that person a copy thereof at the address specified in the last designation so filed. If the person so designated cannot be found at the address given in the last designation, or if the registrant does not designate by a document filed in the United States Patent and Trademark Office the name and address of a person resident in the United States on whom may be served notices or process in proceedings affecting the mark, such notices or process may be served on the Director.

## § 13. (15 U.S.C.A. § 1063) Opposition to Registration

(a) Any person who believes that he would be damaged by the registration of a mark upon the principal register, including the registration of any mark which would be likely to cause dilution by blurring or dilution by tarnishment under section 1125(c) of this title, may, upon payment of the prescribed fee, file an opposition in the Patent and Trademark Office, stating the grounds therefor, within thirty days after the publication under subsection (a) of section 1062 of this title of the mark sought to be registered. Upon written request prior to the expiration of the thirty-day period, the time for filing opposition shall be extended for an additional thirty days, and further extensions of time for filing opposition may be granted by the Director for good cause when requested prior to the expiration of an extension. The Director shall notify the applicant of each extension of the time for filing opposition. An opposition may be amended under such conditions as may be prescribed by the Director.

(b)  Unless registration is successfully opposed—

(1)  a mark entitled to registration on the principal register based on an application filed under section 1051(a) or pursuant to section 1126 of this title shall be registered in the Patent and Trademark Office, a certificate of registration shall be issued, and notice of the registration shall be published in the Official Gazette of the Patent and Trademark Office; or

(2)  a notice of allowance shall be issued to the applicant if the applicant applied for registration under section 1051(b) of this title.

## § 14. (15 U.S.C.A. § 1064) Cancellation of Registration

A petition to cancel a registration of a mark, stating the grounds relied upon, may, upon payment of the prescribed fee, be filed as follows by any person who believes that he is or will be damaged, including as a result of a likelihood of dilution by blurring or dilution by tarnishment under section 43(c), by the registration of a mark on the principal register established by this chapter, or under the Act of March 3, 1881, or the Act of February 20, 1905:

(1)  Within five years from the date of the registration of the mark under this chapter.

(2)  Within five years from the date of publication under section 1062(c) of this title of a mark registered under the Act of March 3, 1881, or the Act of February 20, 1905.

(3)  At any time if the registered mark becomes the generic name for the goods or services, or a portion thereof, for which it is registered, or is functional, or has been abandoned, or its registration was obtained fraudulently or contrary to the provisions of section 1054 of this title or of subsection (a), (b), or (c) of section 1052 of this title for a registration under this chapter, or contrary to similar prohibitory provisions of such prior Acts for a registration under such Acts, or if the registered mark is being used by, or with the permission of, the registrant so as to misrepresent the source of the goods or services on or in connection with which the mark is used. If the registered mark becomes the generic name for less than all of the goods or services for which it is registered, a petition to cancel the registration for only those goods or services may be filed. A registered mark shall not be deemed to be the generic name of goods or services solely because such mark is also used as a name of or to identify a unique product or service. The primary significance of the registered mark to the relevant public rather than purchaser motivation shall be the test for determining whether the registered mark has become the generic name of goods or services on or in connection with which it has been used.

(4)  At any time if the mark is registered under the Act of March 3, 1881, or the Act of February 20, 1905, and has not been published under the provisions of subsection (c) of section 1062 of this title.

(5)  At any time in the case of a certification mark on the ground that the registrant (A) does not control, or is not able legitimately to exercise control over, the use of such mark, or (B) engages in the production or marketing of any goods or services to which the certification mark is applied, or (C) permits the use of the certification mark for purposes other than to certify, or (D) discriminately refuses to certify or to continue to certify the goods or services of any person who maintains the standards or conditions which such mark certifies:

*Provided,* That the Federal Trade Commission may apply to cancel on the grounds specified in paragraphs (3) and (5) of this section any mark registered on the principal register established by this chapter, and the prescribed fee shall not be required. Nothing in paragraph (5) shall be deemed to prohibit the registrant from using its certification mark in advertising or promoting recognition of the certification program or of the goods or services meeting the certification standards of the registrant. Such uses of the certification mark shall not be grounds for cancellation under paragraph (5), so long as the registrant does not itself produce, manufacture, or sell any of the certified goods or services to which its identical certification mark is applied.

## § 15. (15 U.S.C.A. § 1065) Incontestability of Right to Use Mark Under Certain Conditions

Except on a ground for which application to cancel may be filed at any time under paragraphs (3) and (5) of section 1064 of this title, and except to the extent, if any, to which the use of a mark registered on the principal register infringes a valid right acquired under the law of any State or Territory by use of a mark or trade name continuing from a date prior to the date of registration under this chapter of such registered mark, the right of the owner to use such registered mark in commerce for the goods or services on or in connection with which such registered mark has been in continuous use for five consecutive years subsequent to the date of such registration and is still in use in commerce, shall be incontestable: *Provided,* That—

(1)   there has been no final decision adverse to the owner's claim of ownership of such mark for such goods or services, or to the owner's right to register the same or to keep the same on the register; and

(2)   there is no proceeding involving said rights pending in the United States Patent and Trademark Office or in a court and not finally disposed of; and

(3)   an affidavit is filed with the Director within one year after the expiration of any such five-year period setting forth those goods or services stated in the registration on or in connection with which such mark has been in continuous use for such five consecutive years and is still in use in commerce, and other matters specified in paragraphs (1) and (2) of this section; and

(4)   no incontestable right shall be acquired in a mark which is the generic name for the goods or services or a portion thereof, for which it is registered.

Subject to the conditions above specified in this section, the incontestable right with reference to a mark registered under this chapter shall apply to a mark registered under the Act of March 3, 1881, or the Act of February 20, 1905, upon the filing of the required affidavit with the Director within one year after the expiration of any period of five consecutive years after the date of publication of a mark under the provisions of subsection (c) of section 1062 of this title.

The Director shall notify any registrant who files the above-prescribed affidavit of the filing thereof.

## § 22. (15 U.S.C.A. § 1072) Registration as Constructive Notice of Claim of Ownership

Registration of a mark on the principal register provided by this chapter or under the Act of March 3, 1881, or the Act of February 20, 1905, shall be constructive notice of the registrant's claim of ownership thereof.

## § 29. (15 U.S.C.A. § 1111) Notice of Registration; Display with Mark; Recovery of Profits and Damages in Infringement Suit

Notwithstanding the provisions of section 1072 of this title, a registrant of a mark registered in the Patent and Trademark Office, may give notice that his mark is registered by displaying with the mark the words "Registered in U.S. Patent and Trademark Office" or "Reg. U.S. Pat. & Tm. Off." or the letter R enclosed within a circle, thus ®; and in any suit for infringement under this chapter by such a registrant failing to give such notice of registration, no profits and no damages shall be recovered under the provisions of this chapter unless the defendant had actual notice of the registration.

## § 32. (15 U.S.C.A. § 1114) Remedies; Infringement; Innocent Infringement by Printers and Publishers

(1) Any person who shall, without the consent of the registrant—

(a) use in commerce any reproduction, counterfeit, copy, or colorable imitation of a registered mark in connection with the sale, offering for sale, distribution, or advertising of any goods or services on or in connection with which such use is likely to cause confusion, or to cause mistake, or to deceive; or

(b) reproduce, counterfeit, copy, or colorably imitate a registered mark and apply such reproduction, counterfeit, copy, or colorable imitation to labels, signs, prints, packages, wrappers, receptacles or advertisements intended to be used in commerce upon or in connection with the sale, offering for sale, distribution, or advertising of goods or services on or in connection with which such use is likely to cause confusion, or to cause mistake, or to deceive,

shall be liable in a civil action by the registrant for the remedies hereinafter provided. Under subsection (b) of this section, the registrant shall not be entitled to recover profits or damages unless the acts have been committed with knowledge that such imitation is intended to be used to cause confusion, or to cause mistake, or to deceive. As used in this paragraph, the term "any person" includes the United States, all agencies and instrumentalities thereof, and all individuals, firms, corporations, or other persons acting for the United States and with the authorization and consent of the United States, and any State, any instrumentality of a State, and any officer or employee of a State or instrumentality of a State acting in his or her official capacity. The United States, all agencies and instrumentalities thereof, and all individuals, firms, corporations, other persons acting for the United States and with the authorization and consent of the United States, and any State, and any such instrumentality, officer, or employee, shall be subject to the provisions of this Act in the same manner and to the same extent as any nongovernmental entity.

(2) Notwithstanding any other provision of this chapter, the remedies given to the owner of a right infringed under this chapter or to a person bringing an action under section 1125(a) or (d) of this title shall be limited as follows:

(A) Where an infringer or violator is engaged solely in the business of printing the mark or violating matter for others and establishes that he or she was an innocent infringer or innocent violator, the owner of the right infringed or person bringing the action under section 1125(a) of this title shall be entitled as against such infringer or violator only to an injunction against future printing.

(B) Where the infringement or violation complained of is contained in or is part of paid advertising matter in a newspaper, magazine, or other similar periodical or in an electronic communication as defined in section 2510(12) of Title 18, the remedies of the owner of the right infringed or person bringing the action under section 1125(a) of this title as against the publisher or distributor of such newspaper, magazine, or other similar periodical or electronic communication shall be limited to an injunction against the presentation of such advertising matter in future issues of such newspapers, magazines, or other similar periodicals or in future transmissions of such electronic communications. The limitations of this subparagraph shall apply only to innocent infringers and innocent violators.

(C) Injunctive relief shall not be available to the owner of the right infringed or person bringing the action under section 1125(a) of this title with respect to an issue of a newspaper, magazine, or other similar periodical or an electronic communication containing infringing matter or violating matter where restraining the dissemination of such infringing matter or violating matter in any particular issue of such periodical or in an electronic communication would delay the delivery of such issue or transmission of such electronic communication after the regular time for such delivery or transmission, and such delay would be due to the method by which publication and distribution of such periodical or transmission of such electronic communication is customarily conducted in accordance with sound business practice, and not due to any method or device adopted to evade this section or to prevent or delay the issuance of an injunction or restraining order with respect to such infringing matter or violating matter.

(D)(i)(I) A domain name registrar, a domain name registry, or other domain name registration authority that takes any action described under clause (ii) affecting a domain name shall not be liable for monetary relief or, except as provided in subclause (II), for injunctive relief, to any person for such action, regardless of whether the domain name is finally determined to infringe or dilute the mark.

(II) A domain name registrar, domain name registry, or other domain name registration authority described in subclause (I) may be subject to injunctive relief only if such registrar, registry, or other registration authority has—

(aa) not expeditiously deposited with a court, in which an action has been filed regarding the disposition of the domain name, documents sufficient for the court to establish the court's control and authority regarding the disposition of the registration and use of the domain name;

(bb) transferred, suspended, or otherwise modified the domain name during the pendency of the action, except upon order of the court; or

(cc) willfully failed to comply with any such court order.

(ii) An action referred to under clause (i)(I) is any action of refusing to register, removing from registration, transferring, temporarily disabling, or permanently canceling a domain name—

(I) in compliance with a court order under section 1125(d) of this title; or

(II) in the implementation of a reasonable policy by such registrar, registry, or authority prohibiting the registration of a domain name that is identical to, confusingly similar to, or dilutive of another's mark.

(iii) A domain name registrar, a domain name registry, or other domain name registration authority shall not be liable for damages under this section for the registration or maintenance of a domain name for another absent a showing of bad faith intent to profit from such registration or maintenance of the domain name.

(iv) If a registrar, registry, or other registration authority takes an action described under clause (ii) based on a knowing and material misrepresentation by any other person that a domain name is identical to, confusingly similar to, or dilutive of a mark, the person making the knowing and material misrepresentation shall be liable for any damages, including costs and attorney's fees, incurred by the domain name registrant as a result of such action. The court may also grant injunctive relief to the domain name registrant, including the reactivation of the domain name or the transfer of the domain name to the domain name registrant.

(v) A domain name registrant whose domain name has been suspended, disabled, or transferred under a policy described under clause (ii)(II) may, upon notice to the mark owner, file a civil action to establish that the registration or use of the domain name by such registrant is not unlawful under this chapter. The court may grant injunctive relief to the domain name registrant, including the reactivation of the domain name or transfer of the domain name to the domain name registrant.

(E) As used in this paragraph—

(i) the term "violator" means a person who violates section 1125(a) of this title; and

(ii) the term "violating matter" means matter that is the subject of a violation under section 1125(a) of this title.

(3)(A) Any person who engages in the conduct described in paragraph (11) of section 110 of title 17, United States Code, and who complies with the requirements set forth in that paragraph is not liable on account of such conduct for a violation of any right under this Act. This subparagraph does not preclude liability, nor shall it be construed to restrict the defenses or limitations on rights granted under this Act, of a person for conduct not described in paragraph (11) of section 110 of title 17, United States Code, even if that person also engages in conduct described in paragraph (11) of section 110 of such title.

(B) A manufacturer, licensee, or licensor of technology that enables the making of limited portions of audio or video content of a motion picture imperceptible as described in subparagraph (A) is not liable on account of such manufacture or license for a violation of any right under this Act, if such manufacturer, licensee, or licensor ensures that the technology provides a clear and conspicuous notice at the beginning of each performance that the performance of the motion picture is altered from the performance intended by the director or copyright holder of the motion picture. The limitations on liability in subparagraph (A) and this subparagraph shall not apply to a manufacturer, licensee, or licensor of technology that fails to comply with this paragraph.

(C) The requirement under subparagraph (B) to provide notice shall apply only with respect to technology manufactured after the end of the 180-day period beginning on the date of the enactment of the Family Movie Act of 2005.

(D) Any failure by a manufacturer, licensee, or licensor of technology to qualify for the exemption under subparagraphs (A) and (B) shall not be construed to create an inference that any such party that engages in conduct described in paragraph (11) of section 110 of title 17, United States Code, is liable for trademark infringement by reason of such conduct.

### § 33. (15 U.S.C.A. § 1115) Registration on Principal Register as Evidence of Exclusive Right to Use Mark; Defenses

#### (a) Evidentiary Value; Defenses

Any registration issued under the Act of March 3, 1881, or the Act of February 20, 1905, or of a mark registered on the principal register provided by this chapter and owned by a party to an action shall be admissible in evidence and shall be prima facie evidence of the validity of the registered mark and of the registration of the mark, of the registrant's ownership of the mark, and of the registrant's exclusive right to use the registered mark in commerce on or in connection with the goods or services specified in the registration subject to any conditions or limitations stated therein, but shall not preclude another person from proving any legal or equitable defense or defect including those set forth in subsection (b) of this section, which might have been asserted if such mark had not been registered.

#### (b) Incontestability; Defenses

To the extent that the right to use the registered mark has become incontestable under section 1065 of this title, the registration shall be conclusive evidence of the validity of the registered mark and of the registration of the mark, of the registrant's ownership of the mark, and of the registrant's exclusive right to use the registered mark in commerce. Such conclusive evidence shall relate to the exclusive right to use the mark on or in connection with the goods or services specified in the affidavit filed under the provisions of section 1065 of this title, or in the renewal application filed under the provisions of section 1059 of this title if the goods or services specified in the renewal are fewer in number, subject to any conditions or limitations in the registration or in such affidavit or renewal application. Such conclusive evidence of the right to use the registered mark shall be subject to proof of infringement as defined in section 1114 of this title, and shall be subject to the following defenses or defects:

    (1) That the registration or the incontestable right to use the mark was obtained fraudulently; or

    (2) That the mark has been abandoned by the registrant; or

(3) That the registered mark is being used by or with the permission of the registrant or a person in privity with the registrant, so as to misrepresent the source of the goods or services on or in connection with which the mark is used; or

(4) That the use of the name, term, or device charged to be an infringement is a use, otherwise than as a mark, of the party's individual name in his own business, or of the individual name of anyone in privity with such party, or of a term or device which is descriptive of and used fairly and in good faith only to describe the goods or services of such party, or their geographic origin; or

(5) That the mark whose use by a party is charged as an infringement was adopted without knowledge of the registrant's prior use and has been continuously used by such party or those in privity with him from a date prior to (A) the date of constructive use of the mark established pursuant to section 1057(c) of this title, (B) the registration of the mark under this chapter if the application for registration is filed before the effective date of the Trademark Law Revision Act of 1988, or (C) publication of the registered mark under subsection (c) of section 1062 of this title: *Provided, however,* That this defense or defect shall apply only for the area in which such continuous prior use is proved; or

(6) That the mark whose use is charged as an infringement was registered and used prior to the registration under this chapter or publication under subsection (c) of section 1062 of this title of the registered mark of the registrant, and not abandoned: *Provided, however,* That this defense or defect shall apply only for the area in which the mark was used prior to such registration or such publication of the registrant's mark; or

(7) That the mark has been or is being used to violate the antitrust laws of the United States; or

(8) That the mark is functional; or

(9) That equitable principles, including laches, estoppel, and acquiescence, are applicable.

## § 34. (15 U.S.C.A. § 1116) Injunctive Relief

### (a) Jurisdiction; Service

The several courts vested with jurisdiction of civil actions arising under this chapter shall have power to grant injunctions, according to the principles of equity and upon such terms as the court may deem reasonable, to prevent the violation of any right of the registrant of a mark registered in the Patent and Trademark Office or to prevent a violation under subsection (a), (c), or (d) of section 1125 of this title. Any such injunction may include a provision directing the defendant to file with the court and serve on the plaintiff within thirty days after the service on the defendant of such injunction, or such extended period as the court may direct, a report in writing under oath setting forth in detail the manner and form in which the defendant has complied with the injunction. Any such injunction granted upon hearing, after notice to the defendant, by any district court of the United States, may be served on the parties against whom such injunction is granted anywhere in the United States where they may be found, and shall be operative and may be enforced by proceedings to punish for contempt, or otherwise, by the court by which such injunction was granted, or by any other United States district court in whose jurisdiction the defendant may be found.

### (b) Transfer of Certified Copies of Court Papers

The said courts shall have jurisdiction to enforce said injunction, as provided in this chapter, as fully as if the injunction had been granted by the district court in which it is sought to be enforced. The clerk of the court or judge granting the injunction shall, when required to do so by the court before which application to enforce said injunction is made, transfer without delay to said court a certified copy of all papers on file in his office upon which said injunction was granted.

**(c)  Notice to Director**

It shall be the duty of the clerks of such courts within one month after the filing of any action, suit, or proceeding involving a mark registered under the provisions of this chapter to give notice thereof in writing to the Director setting forth in order so far as known the names and addresses of the litigants and the designating number or numbers of the registration or registrations upon which the action, suit, or proceeding has been brought, and in the event any other registration be subsequently included in the action, suit, or proceeding by amendment, answer, or other pleading, the clerk shall give like notice thereof to the Director, and within one month after the judgment is entered, appeal is taken, the clerk of the court shall give notice thereof to the Director, and it shall be the duty of the Director on receipt of such notice forthwith to endorse the same upon the file wrapper of the said registration or registrations and to incorporate the same as a part of the contents of said file wrapper.

**(d)  Civil Actions Arising Out of Use of Counterfeit Marks**

(1)(A)  In the case of a civil action arising under section 1114(1)(a) of this title or section 220506 of title 36, United States Code, with respect to a violation that consists of using a counterfeit mark in connection with the sale, offering for sale, or distribution of goods or services, the court may, upon ex parte application, grant an order under subsection (a) of this section pursuant to this subsection providing for the seizure of goods and counterfeit marks involved in such violation and the means of making such marks, and records documenting the manufacture, sale, or receipt of things involved in such violation.

(B)  As used in this subsection the term "counterfeit mark" means—

(i)  a counterfeit of a mark that is registered on the principal register in the United States Patent and Trademark Office for such goods or services sold, offered for sale, or distributed and that is in use, whether or not the person against whom relief is sought knew such mark was so registered; or

(ii)  a spurious designation that is identical with, or substantially indistinguishable from, a designation as to which the remedies of this Act are made available by reason of section 220506 of title 36, United States Code;

but such term does not include any mark or designation used on or in connection with goods or services of which the manufacture or producer was, at the time of the manufacture or production in question authorized to use the mark or designation for the type of goods or services so manufactured or produced, by the holder of the right to use such mark or designation.

(2)  The court shall not receive an application under this subsection unless the applicant has given such notice of the application as is reasonable under the circumstances to the United States attorney for the judicial district in which such order is sought. Such attorney may participate in the proceedings arising under such application if such proceedings may affect evidence of an offense against the United States. The court may deny such application if the court determines that the public interest in a potential prosecution so requires.

(3)  The application for an order under this subsection shall—

(A)  be based on an affidavit or the verified complaint establishing facts sufficient to support the findings of fact and conclusions of law required for such order; and

(B)  contain the additional information required by paragraph (5) of this subsection to be set forth in such order.

(4)  The court shall not grant such an application unless—

(A)  the person obtaining an order under this subsection provides the security determined adequate by the court for the payment of such damages as any person may be entitled to recover as a result of a wrongful seizure or wrongful attempted seizure under this subsection; and

(B)   the court finds that it clearly appears from specific facts that—

(i)   an order other than an ex parte seizure order is not adequate to achieve the purposes of section 1114 of this title;

(ii)   the applicant has not publicized the requested seizure;

(iii)   the applicant is likely to succeed in showing that the person against whom seizure would be ordered used a counterfeit mark in connection with the sale, offering for sale, or distribution of goods or services;

(iv)   an immediate and irreparable injury will occur if such seizure is not ordered;

(v)   the matter to be seized will be located at the place identified in the application;

(vi)   the harm to the applicant of denying the application outweighs the harm to the legitimate interests of the person against whom seizure would be ordered of granting the application; and

(vii)   the person against whom seizure would be ordered, or persons acting in concert with such person, would destroy, move, hide, or otherwise make such matter inaccessible to the court, if the applicant were to proceed on notice to such person.

(5)   An order under this subsection shall set forth—

(A)   the findings of fact and conclusions of law required for the order;

(B)   a particular description of the matter to be seized, and a description of each place at which such matter is to be seized;

(C)   the time period, which shall end not later than seven days after the date on which such order is issued, during which the seizure is to be made;

(D)   the amount of security required to be provided under this subsection; and

(E)   a date for the hearing required under paragraph (10) of this subsection.

(6)   The court shall take appropriate action to protect the person against whom an order under this subsection is directed from publicity, by or at the behest of the plaintiff, about such order and any seizure under such order.

(7)   Any materials seized under this subsection shall be taken into the custody of the court. For seizures made under this section, the court shall enter an appropriate protective order with respect to discovery and use of any records or information that has been seized. The protective order shall provide for appropriate procedures to ensure that confidential, private, proprietary, or privileged information contained in such records is not improperly disclosed or used.

(8)   An order under this subsection, together with the supporting documents, shall be sealed until the person against whom the order is directed has an opportunity to contest such order, except that any person against whom such order is issued shall have access to such order and supporting documents after the seizure has been carried out.

(9)   The court shall order that service of a copy of the order under this subsection shall be made by a Federal law enforcement officer (such as a United States marshal or an officer or agent of the United States Customs Service, Secret Service, Federal Bureau of Investigation, or Post Office) or may be made by a State or local law enforcement officer, who, upon making service, shall carry out the seizure under the order. The court shall issue orders, when appropriate, to protect the defendant from undue damage from the disclosure of trade secrets or other confidential information during the course of the seizure, including, when appropriate, orders restricting the access of the applicant (or any agent or employee of the applicant) to such secrets or information.

(10)(A) The court shall hold a hearing, unless waived by all the parties, on the date set by the court in the order of seizure. That date shall be not sooner than ten days after the order is issued and not later than fifteen days after the order is issued, unless the applicant for the order shows good cause for another date or unless the party against whom such order is directed consents to another date for such hearing. At such hearing the party obtaining the order shall have the burden to prove that the facts supporting findings of fact and conclusions of law necessary to support such order are still in effect. If that party fails to meet that burden, the seizure order shall be dissolved or modified appropriately.

(B)  In connection with a hearing under this paragraph, the court may make such orders modifying the time limits for discovery under the Rules of Civil Procedure as may be necessary to prevent the frustration of the purposes of such hearing.

(11)  A person who suffers damage by reason of a wrongful seizure under this subsection has a cause of action against the applicant for the order under which such seizure was made, and shall be entitled to recover such relief as may be appropriate, including damages for lost profits, cost of materials, loss of good will, and punitive damages in instances where the seizure was sought in bad faith, and, unless the court finds extenuating circumstances, to recover a reasonable attorney's fee. The court in its discretion may award prejudgment interest on relief recovered under this paragraph, at an annual interest rate established under section 6621(a)(2) of the Internal Revenue Code of 1986, commencing on the date of service of the claimant's pleading setting forth the claim under this paragraph and ending on the date such recovery is granted, or for such shorter time as the court deems appropriate.

## § 35. (15 U.S.C.A. § 1117) Recovery for Violation of Rights; Profits, Damages and Costs; Attorney Fees

(a)  When a violation of any right of the registrant of a mark registered in the Patent and Trademark Office, a violation under section 1125(a) or (d) of this title, or a willful violation under section 1125(c) of this title, shall have been established in any civil action arising under this chapter, the plaintiff shall be entitled, subject to the provisions of sections 1111 and 1114 of this title, and subject to the principles of equity, to recover (1) defendant's profits, (2) any damages sustained by the plaintiff, and (3) the costs of the action. The court shall assess such profits and damages or cause the same to be assessed under its direction. In assessing profits the plaintiff shall be required to prove defendant's sales only; defendant must prove all elements of cost or deduction claimed. In assessing damages the court may enter judgment, according to the circumstances of the case, for any sum above the amount found as actual damages, not exceeding three times such amount. If the court shall find that the amount of the recovery based on profits is either inadequate or excessive the court may in its discretion enter judgment for such sum as the court shall find to be just, according to the circumstances of the case. Such sum in either of the above circumstances shall constitute compensation and not a penalty. The court in exceptional cases may award reasonable attorney fees to the prevailing party.

(b)  In assessing damages under subsection (a) for any violation of section 32(1)(a) of this Act or section 220506 of title 36, United States Code, in a case involving use of a counterfeit mark or designation (as defined in section 34(d) of this Act), the court shall, unless the court finds extenuating circumstances, enter judgment for three times such profits or damages, whichever amount is greater, together with a reasonable attorney's fee, if the violation consists of—

(1)  intentionally using a mark or designation, knowing such mark or designation is a counterfeit mark (as defined in section 34(d) of this Act), in connection with the sale, offering for sale, or distribution of goods or services; or

(2)  providing goods or services necessary to the commission of a violation specified in paragraph (1), with the intent that the recipient of the goods or services would put the goods or services to use in committing the violation.

In such a case, the court may award prejudgment interest on such amount at an annual interest rate established under section 6621(a)(2) of the Internal Revenue Code of 1986, beginning on the date of the service of the claimant's pleadings setting forth the claim for such entry of judgment and ending on the date such entry is made, or for such shorter time as the court considers appropriate.

(c)   In a case involving the use of a counterfeit mark (as defined in section 1116(d) of this title) in connection with the sale, offering for sale, or distribution of goods or services, the plaintiff may elect, at any time before final judgment is rendered by the trial court, to recover, instead of actual damages and profits under subsection (a), an award of statutory damages for any such use in connection with the sale, offering for sale, or distribution of goods or services in the amount of—

(1)   not less than $1,000 or more than $200,000 per counterfeit mark per type of goods or services sold, offered for sale, or distributed, as the court considers just; or

(2)   if the court finds that the use of the counterfeit mark was willful, not more than $2,000,000 per counterfeit mark per type of goods or services sold, offered for sale, or distributed, as the court considers just.

(d)   In a case involving a violation of section 1125(d)(1) of this title, the plaintiff may elect, at any time before final judgment is rendered by the trial court, to recover, instead of actual damages and profits, an award of statutory damages in the amount of not less than $1,000 and not more than $100,000 per domain name, as the court considers just.

(e)   In the case of a violation referred to in this section, it shall be a rebuttable presumption that the violation is willful for purposes of determining relief if the violator, or a person acting in concert with the violator, knowingly provided or knowingly caused to be provided materially false contact information to a domain name registrar, domain name registry, or other domain name registration authority in registering, maintaining, or renewing a domain name used in connection with the violation. Nothing in this subsection limits what may be considered a willful violation under this section.

## § 40. (15 U.S.C.A. § 1122) Liability of States, Instrumentalities of States, and State Officials

### (a)  Waiver of Sovereign Immunity by the United States

The United States, all agencies and instrumentalities thereof, and all individuals, firms, corporations, other persons acting for the United States and with the authorization and consent of the United States, shall not be immune from suit in Federal or State court by any person, including any governmental or nongovernmental entity, for any violation under this chapter.

### (b)  Waiver of Sovereign Immunity by States

Any State, instrumentality of a State or any officer or employee of a State or instrumentality of a State acting in his or her official capacity, shall not be immune, under the eleventh amendment of the Constitution of the United States or under any other doctrine of sovereign immunity, from suit in Federal court by any person, including any governmental or nongovernmental entity for any violation under this chapter.

### (c)  Remedies

In a suit described in subsection (a) or (b) for a violation described therein, remedies (including remedies both at law and in equity) are available for the violation to the same extent as such remedies are available for such a violation in a suit against any person other than the United States or any agency or instrumentality thereof, or any individual, firm, corporation, or other person acting for the United States and with authorization and consent of the United States, or a State, instrumentality of a State, or officer or employee of a State or instrumentality of a State acting in his or her official capacity. Such remedies include injunctive relief under section 1116 of this title, actual damages, profits, costs and attorney's fees under section 1117 of this title, destruction of infringing articles under section 1118 of this title, the remedies provided for under sections 1114, 1119, 1120, 1124 and 1125 of this title, and for any other remedies provided under this chapter.

## § 43. (15 U.S.C.A. § 1125) False Designations of Origin, False Descriptions, and Dilution Forbidden

### (a) Civil Action

(1) Any person who, on or in connection with any goods or services, or any container for goods, uses in commerce any word, term, name, symbol, or device, or any combination thereof, or any false designation of origin, false or misleading description of fact, or false or misleading representation of fact, which—

(A) is likely to cause confusion, or to cause mistake, or to deceive as to the affiliation, connection, or association of such person with another person, or as to the origin, sponsorship, or approval of his or her goods, services, or commercial activities by another person, or

(B) in commercial advertising or promotion, misrepresents the nature, characteristics, qualities, or geographic origin of his or her or another person's goods, services, or commercial activities,

shall be liable in a civil action by any person who believes that he or she is or is likely to be damaged by such act.

(2) As used in this subsection, the term "any person" includes any State, instrumentality of a State or employee of a State or instrumentality of a State acting in his or her official capacity. Any State, and any such instrumentality, officer, or employee, shall be subject to the provisions of this Act in the same manner and to the same extent as any nongovernmental entity.

(3) In a civil action for trade dress infringement under this chapter for trade dress not registered on the principal register, the person who asserts trade dress protection has the burden of proving that the matter sought to be protected is not functional.

### (b) Importation

Any goods marked or labeled in contravention of the provisions of this section shall not be imported into the United States or admitted to entry at any customhouse of the United States. The owner, importer, or consignee of goods refused entry at any customhouse under this section may have any recourse by protest or appeal that is given under the customs revenue laws or may have the remedy given by this chapter in cases involving goods refused entry or seized.

### (c) Dilution by Blurring; Dilution by Tarnishment

(1) **Injunctive relief.** Subject to the principles of equity, the owner of a famous mark that is distinctive, inherently or through acquired distinctiveness, shall be entitled to an injunction against another person who, at any time after the owner's mark has become famous, commences use of a mark or trade name in commerce that is likely to cause dilution by blurring or dilution by tarnishment of the famous mark, regardless of the presence or absence of actual or likely confusion, of competition, or of actual economic injury.

(2) **Definitions.** (A) For purposes of paragraph (1), a mark is famous if it is widely recognized by the general consuming public of the United States as a designation of source of the goods or services of the mark's owner. In determining whether a mark possesses the requisite degree of recognition, the court may consider all relevant factors, including the following:

(i) The duration, extent, and geographic reach of advertising and publicity of the mark, whether advertised or publicized by the owner or third parties.

(ii) The amount, volume, and geographic extent of sales of goods or services offered under the mark.

(iii) The extent of actual recognition of the mark.

(iv) Whether the mark was registered under the Act of March 3, 1881, or the Act of February 20, 1905, or on the principal register.

(B)  For purposes of paragraph (1), "dilution by blurring" is association arising from the similarity between a mark or trade name and a famous mark that impairs the distinctiveness of the famous mark. In determining whether a mark or trade name is likely to cause dilution by blurring, the court may consider all relevant factors, including the following:

(i)   The degree of similarity between the mark or trade name and the famous mark.

(ii)  The degree of inherent or acquired distinctiveness of the famous mark.

(iii) The extent to which the owner of the famous mark is engaging in substantially exclusive use of the mark.

(iv)  The degree of recognition of the famous mark.

(v)   Whether the user of the mark or trade name intended to create an association with the famous mark.

(vi)  Any actual association between the mark or trade name and the famous mark.

(C)  For purposes of paragraph (1), "dilution by tarnishment" is association arising from the similarity between a mark or trade name and a famous mark that harms the reputation of the famous mark.

**(3)  Exclusions.** The following shall not be actionable as dilution by blurring or dilution by tarnishment under this subsection:

(A)  Any fair use, including a nominative or descriptive fair use, or facilitation of such fair use, of a famous mark by another person other than as a designation of source for the person's own goods or services, including use in connection with—

(i)   advertising or promotion that permits consumers to compare goods or services; or

(ii)  identifying and parodying, criticizing, or commenting upon the famous mark owner or the goods or services of the famous mark owner.

(B)  All forms of news reporting and news commentary.

(C)  Any noncommercial use of a mark.

**(4)  Burden of proof.** In a civil action for trade dress dilution under this Act for trade dress not registered on the principal register, the person who asserts trade dress protection has the burden of proving that—

(A)  the claimed trade dress, taken as a whole, is not functional and is famous; and

(B)  if the claimed trade dress includes any mark or marks registered on the principal register, the unregistered matter, taken as a whole, is famous separate and apart from any fame of such registered marks.

**(5)  Additional remedies.** In an action brought under this subsection, the owner of the famous mark shall be entitled to injunctive relief as set forth in section 34. The owner of the famous mark shall also be entitled to the remedies set forth in sections 35(a) and 36, subject to the discretion of the court and the principles of equity if—

(A)  the mark or trade name that is likely to cause dilution by blurring or dilution by tarnishment was first used in commerce by the person against whom the injunction is sought after the date of enactment of the Trademark Dilution Revision Act of 2006; and

(B)  in a claim arising under this subsection—

(i)   by reason of dilution by blurring, the person against whom the injunction is sought willfully intended to trade on the recognition of the famous mark; or

(ii)  by reason of dilution by tarnishment, the person against whom the injunction is sought willfully intended to harm the reputation of the famous mark.

**(6) Ownership of valid registration a complete bar to action.** The ownership by a person of a valid registration under the Act of March 3, 1881, or the Act of February 20, 1905, or on the principal register under this Act shall be a complete bar to an action against that person, with respect to that mark, that—

(A) is brought by another person under the common law or a statute of a State; and

(B)(i) seeks to prevent dilution by blurring or dilution by tarnishment; or

(ii) asserts any claim of actual or likely damage or harm to the distinctiveness or reputation of a mark, label, or form of advertisement.

**(7) Savings clause.** Nothing in this subsection shall be construed to impair, modify, or supersede the applicability of the patent laws of the United States.

**(d) Cyberpiracy Prevention**

(1)(A) A person shall be liable in a civil action by the owner of a mark, including a personal name which is protected as a mark under this section, if, without regard to the goods or services of the parties, that person

(i) has a bad faith intent to profit from that mark, including a personal name which is protected as a mark under this section; and

(ii) registers, traffics in, or uses a domain name that—

(I) in the case of a mark that is distinctive at the time of registration of the domain name, is identical or confusingly similar to that mark;

(II) in the case of a famous mark that is famous at the time of registration of the domain name, is identical or confusingly similar to or dilutive of that mark; or

(III) is a trademark, word, or name protected by reason of section 706 of Title 18 or section 220506 of Title 36.

(B)(i) In determining whether a person has a bad faith intent described under subparagraph (a), a court may consider factors such as, but not limited to

(I) the trademark or other intellectual property rights of the person, if any, in the domain name;

(II) the extent to which the domain name consists of the legal name of the person or a name that is otherwise commonly used to identify that person;

(III) the person's prior use, if any, of the domain name in connection with the bona fide offering of any goods or services;

(IV) the person's bona fide noncommercial or fair use of the mark in a site accessible under the domain name;

(V) the person's intent to divert consumers from the mark owner's online location to a site accessible under the domain name that could harm the goodwill represented by the mark, either for commercial gain or with the intent to tarnish or disparage the mark, by creating a likelihood of confusion as to the source, sponsorship, affiliation, or endorsement of the site;

(VI) the person's offer to transfer, sell, or otherwise assign the domain name to the mark owner or any third party for financial gain without having used, or having an intent to use, the domain name in the bona fide offering of any goods or services, or the person's prior conduct indicating a pattern of such conduct;

(VII) the person's provision of material and misleading false contact information when applying for the registration of the domain name, the person's intentional failure to maintain accurate contact information, or the person's prior conduct indicating a pattern of such conduct;

(VIII) the person's registration or acquisition of multiple domain names which the person knows are identical or confusingly similar to marks of others that are distinctive at the time of registration of such domain names, or dilutive of famous marks of others that are famous at the time of registration of such domain names, without regard to the goods or services of the parties; and

(IX) the extent to which the mark incorporated in the person's domain name registration is or is not distinctive and famous within the meaning of subsection (c) of this section.

(ii) Bad faith intent described under subparagraph (A) shall not be found in any case in which the court determines that the person believed and had reasonable grounds to believe that the use of the domain name was a fair use or otherwise lawful.

(C) In any civil action involving the registration, trafficking, or use of a domain name under this paragraph, a court may order the forfeiture or cancellation of the domain name or the transfer of the domain name to the owner of the mark.

(D) A person shall be liable for using a domain name under subparagraph (A) only if that person is the domain name registrant or that registrant's authorized licensee.

(E) As used in this paragraph, the term "traffics in" refers to transactions that include, but are not limited to, sales, purchases, loans, pledges, licenses, exchanges of currency, and any other transfer for consideration or receipt in exchange for consideration.

(2)(A) The owner of a mark may file an in rem civil action against a domain name in the judicial district in which the domain name registrar, domain name registry, or other domain name authority that registered or assigned the domain name is located if

(i) the domain name violates any right of the owner of a mark registered in the Patent and Trademark Office, or protected under subsection (a) or (c); and

(ii) the court finds that the owner—

(I) is not able to obtain in personam jurisdiction over a person who would have been a defendant in a civil action under paragraph (1); or

(II) through due diligence was not able to find a person who would have been a defendant in a civil action under paragraph (1) by—

(aa) sending a notice of the alleged violation and intent to proceed under this paragraph to the registrant of the domain name at the postal and e-mail address provided by the registrant to the registrar; and

(bb) publishing notice of the action as the court may direct promptly after filing the action.

(B) The actions under subparagraph (A)(ii) shall constitute service of process.

(C) In an in rem action under this paragraph, a domain name shall be deemed to have its situs in the judicial district in which

(i) the domain name registrar, registry, or other domain name authority that registered or assigned the domain name is located; or

(ii) documents sufficient to establish control and authority regarding the disposition of the registration and use of the domain name are deposited with the court.

(D)(i) The remedies in an in rem action under this paragraph shall be limited to a court order for the forfeiture or cancellation of the domain name or the transfer of the domain name to the owner of the mark. Upon receipt of written notification of a filed, stamped copy of a complaint filed by the owner of a mark in a United States district court under this paragraph, the domain name registrar, domain name registry, or other domain name authority shall

363

(I)   expeditiously deposit with the court documents sufficient to establish the court's control and authority regarding the disposition of the registration and use of the domain name to the court; and

(II)   not transfer, suspend, or otherwise modify the domain name during the pendency of the action, except upon order of the court.

(ii)   The domain name registrar or registry or other domain name authority shall not be liable for injunctive or monetary relief under this paragraph except in the case of bad faith or reckless disregard, which includes a willful failure to comply with any such court order.

(3)   The civil action established under paragraph (1) and the in rem action established under paragraph (2), and any remedy available under either such action, shall be in addition to any other civil action or remedy otherwise applicable.

(4)   The in rem jurisdiction established under paragraph (2) shall be in addition to any other jurisdiction that otherwise exists, whether in rem or in personam.

## § 45. (15 U.S.C.A. § 1127) Construction and Definitions; Intent of Chapter

In the construction of this chapter, unless the contrary is plainly apparent from the context—

The United States includes and embraces all territory which is under its jurisdiction and control.

The word "commerce" means all commerce which may lawfully be regulated by Congress.

The term "principal register" refers to the register provided for by sections 1051 to 1072 of this title, and the term "supplemental register" refers to the register provided for by sections 1091 to 1096 of this title.

The term "person" and any other word or term used to designate the applicant or other entitled to a benefit or privilege or rendered liable under the provisions of this chapter includes a juristic person as well as a natural person. The term "juristic person" includes a firm, corporation, union, association, or other organization capable of suing and being sued in a court of law.

The term "person" also includes the United States, any agency or instrumentality thereof, or any individual, firm, or corporation acting for the United States and with the authorization and consent of the United States. The United States, any agency or instrumentality thereof, and any individual, firm, or corporation acting for the United States and with the authorization and consent of the United States, shall be subject to the provisions of this chapter in the same manner and to the same extent as any nongovernmental entity.

The term "person" also includes any State, any instrumentality of a State, and any officer or employee of a State or instrumentality of a State acting in his or her official capacity. Any State, and any such instrumentality, officer, or employee, shall be subject to the provisions of this Act in the same manner and to the same extent as any nongovernmental entity.

The terms "applicant" and "registrant" embrace the legal representatives, predecessors, successors and assigns of such applicant or registrant.

The term "Director" means the Under Secretary of Commerce for Intellectual Property and Director of the United States Patent and Trademark Office.

The term "related company" means any person whose use of a mark is controlled by the owner of the mark with respect to the nature and quality of the goods or services on or in connection with which the mark is used.

The terms "trade name" and "commercial name" mean any name used by a person to identify his or her business or vocation.

The term "trademark" includes any word, name, symbol, or device, or any combination thereof—

(1)   used by a person, or

(2) which a person has a bona fide intention to use in commerce and applies to register on the principal register established by this chapter,

to identify and distinguish his or her goods, including a unique product, from those manufactured or sold by others and to indicate the source of the goods, even if that source is unknown.

The term "service mark" means any word, name, symbol, or device, or any combination thereof—

(1) used by a person, or

(2) which a person has a bona fide intention to use in commerce and applies to register on the principal register established by this chapter,

to identify and distinguish the services of one person, including a unique service, from the services of others and to indicate the source of the services, even if that source is unknown. Titles, character names, and other distinctive features of radio or television programs may be registered as service marks notwithstanding that they, or the programs, may advertise the goods of the sponsor.

The term "certification mark" means any word, name, symbol, or device, or any combination thereof—

(1) used by a person other than its owner, or

(2) which its owner has a bona fide intention to permit a person other than the owner to use in commerce and files an application to register on the principal register established by this chapter,

to certify regional or other origin, material, mode of manufacture, quality, accuracy, or other characteristics of such person's goods or services or that the work or labor on the goods or services was performed by members of a union or other organization.

The term "collective mark" means a trademark or service mark—

(1) used by the members of a cooperative, an association, or other collective group or organization, or

(2) which such cooperative, association, or other collective group or organization has a bona fide intention to use in commerce and applies to register on the principal register established by this chapter,

and includes marks indicating membership in a union, an association, or other organization.

The term "mark" includes any trademark, service mark, collective mark, or certification mark.

The term "use in commerce" means the bona fide use of a mark in the ordinary course of trade, and not made merely to reserve a right in a mark. For purposes of this chapter, a mark shall be deemed to be in use in commerce—

(1) on goods when—

(A) it is placed in any manner on the goods or their containers or the displays associated therewith or on the tags or labels affixed thereto, or if the nature of the goods makes such placement impracticable, then on documents associated with the goods or their sale, and

(B) the goods are sold or transported in commerce, and

(2) on services when it is used or displayed in the sale or advertising of services and the services are rendered in commerce, or the services are rendered in more than one State or in the United States and a foreign country and the person rendering the services is engaged in commerce in connection with the services.

A mark shall be deemed to be "abandoned" if either of the following occurs:

(1)   When its use has been discontinued with intent not to resume such use. Intent not to resume may be inferred from circumstances. Nonuse for 3 consecutive years shall be prima facie evidence of abandonment. "Use" of a mark means the bona fide use of such mark made in the ordinary course of trade, and not made merely to reserve a right in a mark.

(2)   When any course of conduct of the owner, including acts of omission as well as commission, causes the mark to become the generic name for the goods or services on or in connection with which it is used or otherwise to lose its significance as a mark. Purchaser motivation shall not be a test for determining abandonment under this paragraph.

The term "colorable imitation" includes any mark which so resembles a registered mark as to be likely to cause confusion or mistake or to deceive.

The term "registered mark" means a mark registered in the United States Patent and Trademark Office under this chapter or under the Act of March 3, 1881, or the Act of February 20, 1905, or the Act of March 19, 1920. The phrase "marks registered in the Patent and Trademark Office" means registered marks.

The term "Act of March 3, 1881", "Act of February 20, 1905", or "Act of March 19, 1920", means the respective Act as amended.

A "counterfeit" is a spurious mark which is identical with, or substantially indistinguishable from, a registered mark.

The term "domain name" means any alphanumeric designation which is registered with or assigned by any domain name registrar, domain name registry, or other domain name registration authority as part of an electronic address on the Internet.

The term "Internet" has the meaning given that term in section 230(f)(1) of the Communications Act of 1934 (47 U.S.C. 230(f)(1)).

Words used in the singular include the plural and vice versa.

The intent of this chapter is to regulate commerce within the control of Congress by making actionable the deceptive and misleading use of marks in such commerce; to protect registered marks used in such commerce from interference by State, or territorial legislation; to protect persons engaged in such commerce against unfair competition; to prevent fraud and deception in such commerce by the use of reproductions, copies, counterfeits, or colorable imitations of registered marks; and to provide rights and remedies stipulated by treaties and conventions respecting trademarks, trade names, and unfair competition entered into between the United States and foreign nations.

---

## 15 U.S.C.A. § 8131.   Cyberpiracy Protections for Individuals

### (1)  In General

#### (A)  Civil Liability

Any person who registers a domain name that consists of the name of another living person, or a name substantially and confusingly similar thereto, without that person's consent, with the specific intent to profit from such name by selling the domain name for financial gain to that person or any third party, shall be liable in a civil action by such person.

#### (B)  Exception

A person who in good faith registers a domain name consisting of the name of another living person, or a name substantially and confusingly similar thereto, shall not be liable under this paragraph if such name is used in, affiliated with, or related to a work of authorship protected under Title 17, including a work made for hire as defined in section 101 of Title 17, and if the person registering the domain name is the copyright owner or licensee of the work, the person intends to sell the domain name in conjunction with the lawful exploitation of the work, and such registration is not prohibited by a contract between the registrant and the named person. The exception under this subparagraph shall apply only to a civil action brought under paragraph (1) and shall in no manner limit the protections afforded under the Trademark Act of 1946 (15 U.S.C. 1051 et seq.) or other provision of Federal or State law.

**(2) Remedies**

In any civil action brought under paragraph (1), a court may award injunctive relief, including the forfeiture or cancellation of the domain name or the transfer of the domain name to the plaintiff. The court may also, in its discretion, award costs and attorneys fees to the prevailing party.

**(3) Definition**

In this section, the term "domain name" has the meaning given that term in section 45 of the Trademark Act of 1946 (15 U.S.C. 1127).

**(4) Effective Date**

This section shall apply to domain names registered on or after November 29, 1999.

# APPENDIX M

---

# SUPPLEMENTARY MATERIALS
# FOR THE TWELFTH EDITION

---

## PART 1

# COPYRIGHT

## CHAPTER 1

# THE BOUNDARIES OF
# COPYRIGHT

## 1. A FIRST LOOK AT COPYRIGHT

*Page 8.*      *Add to the end of footnote a:*

P. Samuelson, Evolving Conceptions of Copyright Subject-Matter, 78 U.Pitt.L.Rev. 17 (2016), offers criteria to consider in determining the copyrightability of subject matter not specifically enumerated in § 102.

*Page 10.*      *Add to the end of footnote d:*

C. Sprigman, Copyright and Creative Incentives: What We Know (And Don't), 55 Houston L.Rev. 451 (2017), concludes that copyright contributes to creative incentives in some contexts but not others and wonders whether we can better target copyright toward areas where it does the most good; A. Gilden, Copyright's Market Gibberish, 94 Wash.L.Rev. 1019 (2019), argues that copyright law forces creators to use market rhetoric in order to protect non-economic interests like reputation, psychological well-being, and privacy; S. Balganesh, Privative Copyright, 73 Vand.L.Rev. 1 (2020), examines the continuing role of copyright as an instrument of privacy protection.

*Page 12.*      *Add to the end of footnote e:*

R. Spoo, The Uncoordinated Public Domain, 35 Cardozo Arts & Ent.L.J. 107 (2016), laments the fact that many works are in the public domain in some countries but not others and suggests a treaty-based compulsory licensing scheme to facilitate use.

## 3. SEPARATING STATUTORY COPYRIGHT, COMMON LAW COPYRIGHT, AND THE PUBLIC DOMAIN

*Page 22.*      *Add to the end of Note (1):*

M. Trimble, U.S. State Copyright Laws: Challenge and Potential, 21 Stan.Tech.L.Rev. 66 (2017), examines the current role of state law in promoting innovation and creativity.

SUPPLEMENTARY MATERIALS

## 4. THE STATUTORY FORMALITIES

***Page 39.     Add to the end of the second paragraph in Note (1):***

The revised version of the Copyright Office's Circular 1, *Copyright Basics*, no longer suggests that copies of works first published with a copyright notice before March 1, 1989, but which are distributed after that date, might still require a copyright notice.

***Page 49.     Add to the end of footnote dd:***

Section 411(a) states that no civil action for copyright infringement shall be instituted until "registration of the copyright claim has been made." The question before the Supreme Court in Fourth Estate Public Benefit Corp. v. Wall-Street.com, LLC, 139 S.Ct. 881 (2019), was whether registration has been made "as soon as the claimant delivers the required application, copies of the work, and fee to the Copyright Office; or * * * only after the Copyright Office reviews and registers the copyright?" Although lamenting the fact that average processing times have increased from one to two weeks in the 1950s to seven months today, the Court was unanimous that "registration occurs, and a copyright claimant may commence an infringement suit, when the Copyright Office registers a copyright," Judge Ginsburg's opinion reminds us, however, that "a copyright owner can recover for infringement that occurred both before and after the registration."

***Page 50.     Add to the end of the carryover paragraph:***

The fee for online registration of a work by a single author that is not a work made for hire is now $45; other online registrations now cost $65. The fee for a paper filing is now $125.

***Page 50.     Add to the end of footnote ff:***

The reference to the Court of Appeals decision in Varsity Brands v. Star Athletica should state that timely registrations issued by the Copyright Office are entitled to so-called *Skidmore* deference when a defendant contests copyrightability in a subsequent infringement action. D. Burk, DNA Copyright in the Administrative State, 51 U.C. Davis L.Rev. 1297 (2018), examines the judicial deference given Copyright Office registration decisions.

***Page 50.     Add to the end of footnote gg:***

Legislation that would amend § 701 of the Copyright Act to make the Register of Copyrights a presidentially-appointed and Senate-confirmed position is pending in Congress. See Register of Copyrights Selection and Accountability Act of 2017, H.R. 1695, 115th Cong., 1st Sess. (2017).

# CHAPTER 2

# THE SUBJECT MATTER OF COPYRIGHT

## 1. ORIGINAL WORKS OF AUTHORSHIP

***Page 60.     Add to the beginning of footnote c:***

B. Beebe, *Bleistein*, The Problem of Aesthetic Progress, and the Making of American Copyright Law, 117 Colum.L.Rev. 319 (2017), analyzes the historical significance of the *Bleistein* case.

***Page 63.     Add to the end of the carryover paragraph:***

In Hall v. Swift, 125 U.S.P.Q.2d 1679 (C.D.Cal.2018), the plaintiff songwriters alleged that Taylor Swift had copied the phrase "Playas, they gonna play/And haters, they gonna hate" from the lyrics of their song in composing *Shake it Off*, which includes the phrases "players gonna play" and "haters gonna hate." The court said that short phrases are not generally protectable unless they are sufficiently creative. Here, the court held that the phrase was "too brief, unoriginal, and uncreative to warrant protection." The complaint was dismissed. However, the Ninth Circuit reversed and remanded, commenting that the complaint "plausibly alleged originality." Hall v.

Swift, 786 Fed.Appx. 711 (9th Cir.2019). In Kaseberg v. Conaco, LLC, 260 F.Supp.3d 1229 (S.D.Cal.2017), the court denied defendant comedian Conan O'Brien's motion for summary judgment in an infringement suit brought by a blogger who claimed that O'Brien used several of the plaintiff's jokes on his late-night television show. The court said that there was little doubt that jokes such as "The Washington Monument is ten inches shorter than previously thought. You know the winter has been cold when a monument suffers from shrinkage," merit copyright protection. In a deposition Conan O'Brien said, "Accusing a comedian of stealing a joke is the worst thing you can accuse them of, in my opinion, short of murder." The case was settled prior to trial.

### Page 64.　　Add to the end of Note (8):

In Rearden v. Walt Disney Co., 293 F.Supp.3d 963 (N.D.Cal.2018), the plaintiff owned a computer program that could transform film of an actor's face into output files that could be used to "retarget" the face onto another real or animated actor for use in motion pictures. The court held that the plaintiff could not claim ownership of the output files created when users employed the program to process film of actors for use in movies such as *Beauty and the Beast*.

### Page 64.　　Add to the end of Note (9):

The parties agreed to settle the monkey selfie case when the camera's owner agreed to donate 25 percent of future revenue from the photo to charitable organizations that protect crested macaques. Hagg, Who Owns a Monkey Selfie? Settlement Will Leave Him Smiling, N.Y. Times, Sept. 12, 2017. However, their joint motion to dismiss was denied by the Ninth Circuit, which had already heard oral arguments. In Naruto v. Slater, 888 F.3d 418 (9th Cir.2018), the court then held, "The Copyright Act does not expressly authorize animals to file copyright infringement suits under the statute. Therefore, based on this court's precedent in [Cetacean Cmty. v. Bush, 386 F.3d 1169 (9th Cir.2004)], Naruto lacks statutory standing to sue under the Copyright Act."

### Page 74.　　Add to the end of Note (1):

When two filmmakers sued to invalidate the copyright on the civil rights protest song "We Shall Overcome," the court held that changing the words "will" to "shall" and "down" to "deep," along with two small changes in the melody, were insufficient to qualify the song as a protectable derivative work based on an earlier public domain version of the work. We Shall Overcome Fd. v. Richmond Organization, Inc., 2017 WL 3981311 (S.D.N.Y.2017).

### Page 102.　　Add to the end of Note (6):

B. Frye, Against Creativity, 11 N.Y.U. J.L & Liberty 426 (2017), uses *Feist* to argue that copyright should focus on economic value rather than "creativity".

### Page 104.　　Add to the end of footnote k:

A 2018 follow-up study on the impact of the EU Database Directive by the European Commission concludes, "As in 2005, the *sui generis* right continues to have no proven impact on the production of databases, but a note of caution on this conclusion is needed, given the limited available evidence." European Commission, Evaluation of Directive 96/9/EC on the Legal Protection of Databases 19 (2018).

## 2.　THE LIMITS OF STATUTORY SUBJECT MATTER

### Page 155.　　Add to the end of footnote r:

Despite the Supreme Court's decision in Samsung Electronics v. Apple Inc., holding that damages for infringement of design patents could be limited to profits from the use of the infringing components rather than the entire infringing product, the jury on remand *increased* Apple's award for infringement of the design patents on its iPhone from $399 to $533 million.

# SUPPLEMENTARY MATERIALS

*Page 155.*    ***Add to the end of Note (1):***

In Automotive Body Parts Ass'n v. Ford Global Tech., LLC, 930 F.3d 1314 (C.A.F.C.2019), the court held that despite any consumer preference for replacement automobile body parts that restore the original appearance of the vehicle, that aesthetic appeal of the parts designs did not render the designs "functional" and thus ineligible for design patent protection.

*Page 170.*    ***Add to the end of Note (1):***

The *Star Athletica* case is analyzed in R. Denicola, Imaging Things: Copyright in Useful Articles After *Star Athletica v. Varsity Brands*, 79 U.Pitt.L.Rev. 635 (2018), which concludes that the Supreme Court's test ultimately turns on whether we still recognize the separated feature as designed to serve a utilitarian purpose, since it will then have an "intrinsic utilitarian function" and be barred from protection as a "useful article." R. Tushnet, Shoveling a Path After *Star Athletica*, 66 U.C.L.A. L.Rev. 1216 (2019), concludes that *Star Athletica* is unhelpful in dealing with three-dimensional designs. Noting that the plaintiff in *Star Athletica* had registered more than 200 two-dimensional uniform designs, L. Levi, The New Separability, 20 Vand.J.Ent. & Tech.L. 709 (2018), worries about the market foreclosure effects of multiple design registrations, although the actual copying requirement for copyright infringement would appear to make this less problematic than patent aggregations.

*Page 171.*    ***Add to the end of Note (3):***

In Silvertop Associates Inc. v. Kangaroo Mfg. Inc., 931 F.3d 215 (3d Cir.2019), the court held that although a banana costume was a useful article, the costume's "colors, lines, shape, and length" (apart from the cutout holes for the wearer's arms, legs, and face) were capable of independent existence as a sculptural work under the test in *Star Athletica*.

*Page 177.*    ***Add to the end of Note (2):***

P. Lee and M. Sunder, The Law of Look and Feel, 90 S.Cal.L.Rev. 529 (2017), takes a comprehensive look at design protection across all forms of intellectual property and concludes that protection may extend too far; J. Fromer and M. McKenna, Claiming Design, 167 U.Pa.L.Rev. 123 (2018), examines the problems associated with overlapping patent, trademark, and copyright protection for product designs.

*Page 179.*    ***Add to the end of Note (5):***

C. Holman, Charting the Contours of a Copyright Regime Optimized for Engineered Genetic Code, 69 Okla.L.Rev. 399 (2017), explores copyright protection for engineered genetic sequences.

*Page 187.*    ***Add to the end of the third full paragraph:***

B. Boyden, *Daly v. Palmer*, or the Melodramatic Origins of the Ordinary Observer, 68 Syr.L.Rev. 147 (2018), traces the ordinary observer standard for judging infringement to this 1868 case.

*Page 188.*    ***Add to the end of the carryover paragraph:***

The wildly popular videogame *Fortnite* has generated a rare spate of interest in copyright and choreography. Players of the online game can purchase "emotes"—dance moves that their game characters can perform. Several "celebrities" claim that developer Epic Games stole their signature dance moves. Alfonso Ribeiro, who played Carlton Banks on the television show *The Fresh Prince of Bel-Air,* claims that Epic stole his "Carlton" dance; Brooklyn rapper 2 Milly claims rights in his "Milly Rock" dance move; and the "Backpack Kid," who gained fame with his "Floss" dance, all filed suits against Epic Games, The suits were voluntarily dismissed by the plaintiffs in light of the Supreme Court's recent ruling that § 411's registration prerequisite was not satisfied by the mere filing of a registration application. However, although it will not preclude refiling the suits, the Copyright Office has now denied registration of the "Carlton" and "Milly Rock" dance moves, calling them simple routines of social dance steps that are ineligible for copyright as choreographic works.

*Page 196.     Add at the end of Note (4):*

# Georgia v. Public.Resource.Org, Inc.

Supreme Court of the United States, 2020.
140 S. Ct. 1498.

■ CHIEF JUSTICE ROBERTS delivered the opinion of the Court.

The Copyright Act grants potent, decades-long monopoly protection for "original works of authorship." 17 U. S. C. § 102(a). The question in this case is whether that protection extends to the annotations contained in Georgia's official annotated code.

We hold that it does not. Over a century ago, we recognized a limitation on copyright protection for certain government work product, rooted in the Copyright Act's "authorship" requirement. Under what has been dubbed the government edicts doctrine, officials empowered to speak with the force of law cannot be the authors of—and therefore cannot copyright—the works they create in the course of their official duties.

We have previously applied that doctrine to hold that non-binding, explanatory legal materials are not copyrightable when created by judges who possess the authority to make and interpret the law. See Banks v. Manchester, 128 U. S. 244 (1888). We now recognize that the same logic applies to non-binding, explanatory legal materials created by a legislative body vested with the authority to make law. Because Georgia's annotations are authored by an arm of the legislature in the course of its legislative duties, the government edicts doctrine puts them outside the reach of copyright protection.

I

A

The State of Georgia has one official code—the "Official Code of Georgia Annotated," or OCGA. The first page of each volume of the OCGA boasts the State's official seal and announces to readers that it is "Published Under Authority of the State."

The OCGA includes the text of every Georgia statute currently in force, as well as various non-binding supplementary materials. At issue in this case is a set of annotations that appear beneath each statutory provision. The annotations generally include summaries of judicial decisions applying a given provision, summaries of any pertinent opinions of the state attorney general, and a list of related law review articles and similar reference materials. In addition, the annotations often include editor's notes that provide information about the origins of the statutory text, such as whether it derives from a particular judicial decision or resembles an older provision that has been construed by Georgia courts. See, e.g., OCGA §§ 51–1–1, 53–4–2 (2019).

The OCGA is assembled by a state entity called the Code Revision Commission. In 1977, the Georgia Legislature established the Commission to recodify Georgia law for the first time in decades. The Commission was (and remains) tasked with consolidating disparate bills into a single Code for reenactment by the legislature and contracting with a third party to produce the annotations. A majority of the Commission's 15 members must be members of the Georgia Senate or House of Representatives. The Commission receives funding through appropriations "provided for the legislative branch of state government." OCGA § 28–9–2(c) (2018). And it is staffed by the Office of Legislative Counsel, which is obligated by statute to provide services "for the legislative branch of government." §§ 28–4–3(c)(4), 28–9–4. Under the Georgia Constitution, the Commission's role in compiling the statutory text and accompanying annotations falls "within the sphere of legislative authority." Harrison Co. v. Code Revision Comm'n, 244 Ga. 325, 330 (1979).

Each year, the Commission submits its proposed statutory text and accompanying annotations to the legislature for approval. The legislature then votes to do three things: (1) "enact[ ]" the "statutory portion of the codification of Georgia laws"; (2) "merge[ ]" the statutory portion "with [the] annotations"; and (3) "publish[ ]" the final merged product "by authority of the state" as "the 'Official Code of Georgia Annotated.' " OCGA § 1–1–1 (2019); see Code Revision Comm'n v. Public.Resource.Org, Inc., 906 F. 3d 1229, 1245, 1255 (CA11 2018); Tr. of Oral Arg. 8.

The annotations in the current OCGA were prepared in the first instance by Matthew Bender & Co., Inc., a division of the LexisNexis Group, pursuant to a work-for-hire agreement with the Commission. The agreement between Lexis and the Commission states that any copyright in the OCGA vests exclusively in "the State of Georgia, acting through the Commission." App. 567. Lexis and its army of researchers perform the lion's share of the work in drafting the annotations, but the Commission supervises that work and specifies what the annotations must include in exacting detail. See 906 F. 3d, at 1243–1244; App. 269–278, 286–427 (Commission specifications). Under the agreement, Lexis enjoys the exclusive right to publish, distribute, and sell the OCGA. In exchange, Lexis has agreed to limit the price it may charge for the OCGA and to make an unannotated version of the statutory text available to the public online for free. A hard copy of the complete OCGA currently retails for $412.00.

B

Public.Resource.Org (PRO) is a nonprofit organization that aims to facilitate public access to government records and legal materials. Without permission, PRO posted a digital version of the OCGA on various websites, where it could be downloaded by the public without charge. PRO also distributed copies of the OCGA to various organizations and Georgia officials.

In response, the Commission sent PRO several cease-and-desist letters asserting that PRO's actions constituted unlawful copyright infringement. When PRO refused to halt its distribution activities, the Commission sued PRO on behalf of the Georgia Legislature and the State of Georgia for copyright infringement. The Commission limited its assertion of copyright to the annotations described above; it did not claim copyright in the statutory text or numbering. PRO counterclaimed, seeking a declaratory judgment that the entire OCGA, including the annotations, fell in the public domain.

\* \* \*

II

We hold that the annotations in Georgia's Official Code are ineligible for copyright protection, though for reasons distinct from those relied on by the Court of Appeals. A careful examination of our government edicts precedents reveals a straightforward rule based on the identity of the author. Under the government edicts doctrine, judges—and, we now confirm, legislators—may not be considered the "authors" of the works they produce in the course of their official duties as judges and legislators. That rule applies regardless of whether a given material carries the force of law. And it applies to the annotations here because they are authored by an arm of the legislature in the course of its official duties.

## A

We begin with precedent. The government edicts doctrine traces back to a trio of cases decided in the 19th century. In this Court's first copyright case, Wheaton v. Peters, 8 Pet. 591 (1834), the Court's third Reporter of Decisions, Wheaton, sued the fourth, Peters, unsuccessfully asserting a copyright interest in the Justices' opinions. Id., at 617 (argument). In Wheaton's view, the opinions "must have belonged to some one" because "they were new, original," and much more "elaborate" than law or custom required. Id., at 615. Wheaton argued that the Justices were the authors and had assigned their ownership interests to him through a tacit "gift." Id., at 614. The Court unanimously rejected that argument, concluding that "no reporter has or can have any copyright in the written opinions delivered by this court" and that "the judges thereof cannot confer on any reporter any such right." Id., at 668 (opinion).

That conclusion apparently seemed too obvious to adorn with further explanation, but the Court provided one a half century later in Banks v. Manchester, 128 U. S. 244 (1888). That case concerned whether Wheaton's state-court counterpart, the official reporter of the Ohio Supreme Court, held a copyright in the judges' opinions and several non-binding explanatory materials prepared by the judges. Id., at 249–251. The Court concluded that he did not, explaining that "the judge who, in his judicial capacity, prepares the opinion or decision, the statement of the case and the syllabus or head note" cannot "be regarded as their author or their proprietor, in the sense of [the Copyright Act]." Id., at 253. Pursuant to "a judicial consensus" dating back to *Wheaton*, judges could not assert copyright in "whatever work they perform in their capacity as judges." *Banks*, 128 U. S, at 253 (emphasis in original). Rather, "[t]he whole work done by the judges constitutes the authentic exposition and interpretation of the law, which, binding every citizen, is free for publication to all." Ibid. (citing Nash v. Lathrop, 142 Mass. 29 (1886)).

In a companion case decided later that Term, Callaghan v. Myers, 128 U. S. 617 (1888), the Court identified an important limiting principle. As in *Wheaton* and *Banks*, the Court rejected the claim that an official reporter held a copyright interest in the judges' opinions. But, resolving an issue not addressed in *Wheaton* and *Banks*, the Court upheld the reporter's copyright interest in several explanatory materials that the reporter had created himself: headnotes, syllabi, tables of contents, and the like. *Callaghan*, 128 U. S., at 645, 647. Although these works mirrored the judge-made materials rejected in *Banks*, they came from an author who had no authority to speak with the force of law. Because the reporter was not a judge, he was free to "obtain[ ] a copyright" for the materials that were "the result of his [own] intellectual labor." 128 U. S., at 647.

These cases establish a straightforward rule: Because judges are vested with the authority to make and interpret the law, they cannot be the "author" of the works they prepare "in the discharge of their judicial duties." *Banks*, 128 U. S., at 253. This rule applies both to binding works (such as opinions) and to non-binding works (such as headnotes and syllabi). Ibid. It does not apply, however, to works created by government officials (or private parties) who lack the authority to make or interpret the law, such as court reporters. Compare ibid. with *Callaghan*, 128 U. S., at 647.

The animating principle behind this rule is that no one can own the law. "Every citizen is presumed to know the law," and "it needs no argument to show . . . that all should have free access" to its contents. *Nash,* 142 Mass. at 35 (cited by *Banks,* 128 U. S., at 253–254). Our cases give effect to that principle in the copyright context through construction of the statutory term "author." Id., at 253. Rather than attempting to catalog the materials that constitute "the law," the doctrine bars the officials responsible for creating the law from being considered the "author[s]" of "whatever work they perform in their capacity" as lawmakers. Ibid. (emphasis added). Because these officials are generally empowered to make and interpret law, their "whole work" is deemed part of the "authentic exposition and interpretation of the law" and must be "free for publication to all." Ibid.

If judges, acting as judges, cannot be "authors" because of their authority to make and interpret the law, it follows that legislators, acting as legislators, cannot be either. Courts have thus long understood the government edicts doctrine to apply to legislative materials. See, e.g., *Nash,* 142 Mass. at 35 (judicial opinions and statutes stand "on substantially the same footing" for purposes of the government edicts doctrine); Howell v. Miller, 91 F. 129, 130–131, 137–138 (CA6 1898) (Harlan, J., Circuit Justice, joined by then-Circuit Judge Taft) (analyzing statutes and supplementary materials under *Banks* and *Callaghan* and concluding that the materials were copyrightable because they were prepared by a private compiler).

Moreover, just as the doctrine applies to "whatever work [judges] perform in their capacity as judges," *Banks,* 128 U. S., at 253, it applies to whatever work legislators perform in their capacity as legislators. That of course includes final legislation, but it also includes explanatory and procedural materials legislators create in the discharge of their legislative duties. In the same way that judges cannot be the authors of their headnotes and syllabi, legislators cannot be the authors of (for example) their floor statements, committee reports, and proposed bills. These materials are part of the "whole work done by [legislators]," so they must be "free for publication to all." Ibid.

Under our precedents, therefore, copyright does not vest in works that are (1) created by judges and legislators (2) in the course of their judicial and legislative duties.

B

1

Applying that framework, Georgia's annotations are not copyrightable. The first step is to examine whether their purported author qualifies as a legislator.

As we have explained, the annotations were prepared in the first instance by a private company (Lexis) pursuant to a work-for-hire agreement with Georgia's Code Revision Commission. The Copyright Act therefore deems the Commission the sole "author" of the work. 17 U. S. C. § 201(b). Although Lexis expends considerable effort preparing the annotations, for purposes of copyright that labor redounds to the Commission as the statutory author. Georgia agrees that the author is the Commission. Brief for Petitioners 25.

The Commission is not identical to the Georgia Legislature, but functions as an arm of it for the purpose of producing the annotations. The Commission is created by the legislature, for the legislature, and consists largely of legislators. The Commission receives funding and staff designated by law for the legislative branch. Significantly, the annotations the Commission creates are approved by the legislature before being "merged" with the statutory text and published in the official code alongside that text at the legislature's direction. OCGA § 1–1–1; see 906 F. 3d, at 1245, 1255; Tr. of Oral Arg. 8.

If there were any doubt about the link between the Commission and the legislature, the Georgia Supreme Court has dispelled it by holding that, under the Georgia Constitution, "the work of the Commission; i.e., selecting a publisher and contracting for and supervising the codification of the laws enacted by the General Assembly, including court interpretations thereof, is within the sphere of legislative authority." *Harrison Co.*, 244 Ga., at 330 (emphasis added). * * *

2

The second step is to determine whether the Commission creates the annotations in the "discharge" of its legislative "duties." *Banks*, 128 U. S., at 253. It does. Although the annotations are not enacted into law through bicameralism and presentment, the Commission's preparation of the annotations is under Georgia law an act of "legislative authority," *Harrison Co.*, 244 Ga., at 330, and the annotations provide commentary and resources that the legislature has deemed relevant to understanding its laws. Georgia and Justice Ginsburg emphasize that the annotations do not purport to provide authoritative explanations of the law and largely summarize other materials, such as judicial decisions and law review articles. See post, at 1523–1524 (dissenting opinion). But that does not take them outside the exercise of legislative duty by the Commission and legislature. Just as we have held that the "statement of the case and the syllabus or head note" prepared by judges fall within the "work they perform in their capacity as judges," *Banks*, 128 U. S., at 253, so too annotations published by legislators alongside the statutory text fall within the work legislators perform in their capacity as legislators.

In light of the Commission's role as an adjunct to the legislature and the fact that the Commission authors the annotations in the course of its legislative responsibilities, the annotations in Georgia's Official Code fall within the government edicts doctrine and are not copyrightable.

III

* * *

* * * Georgia draws a negative inference from the fact that the Act excludes from copyright protection "work[s] prepared by an officer or employee of the United States Government as part of that person's official duties" and does not establish a similar rule for the States. § 101; see also § 105. But the bar on copyright protection for federal works sweeps much more broadly than the government edicts doctrine does. That bar applies to works created by all federal "officer[s] or employee[s]," without regard for the nature of their position or scope of their authority. Whatever policy reasons might justify the Federal Government's decision to forfeit copyright protection for its own proprietary works, that federal rule does not suggest an intent to displace the much narrower government edicts doctrine with respect to the States. That doctrine does not apply to non-lawmaking officials, leaving States free to assert copyright in the vast majority of expressive works they produce, such as those created by their universities, libraries, tourism offices, and so on.

* * *

377

## SUPPLEMENTARY MATERIALS

Georgia also appeals to the overall purpose of the Copyright Act to promote the creation and dissemination of creative works. Georgia submits that, without copyright protection, Georgia and many other States will be unable to induce private parties like Lexis to assist in preparing affordable annotated codes for widespread distribution. That appeal to copyright policy, however, is addressed to the wrong forum. As Georgia acknowledges, "[I]t is generally for Congress, not the courts, to decide how best to pursue the Copyright Clause's objectives." Eldred v. Ashcroft, 537 U. S. 186, 212 (2003). And that principle requires adherence to precedent when, as here, we have construed the statutory text and "tossed [the ball] into Congress's court, for acceptance or not as that branch elects." [Kimble v. Marvel Ent., LLC, 576 U.S. 446, 456 (2015).]

Turning to our government edicts precedents, Georgia insists that they can and should be read to focus exclusively on whether a particular work has "the force of law." Brief for Petitioners 32 (capitalization deleted). Justice Thomas appears to endorse the same view. See post, at 1515. But that framing has multiple flaws.

Most obviously, it cannot be squared with the reasoning or results of our cases—especially *Banks*. *Banks*, following *Wheaton* and the "judicial consensus" it inspired, denied copyright protection to judicial opinions without excepting concurrences and dissents that carry no legal force. 128 U. S., at 253 (emphasis deleted). As every judge learns the hard way, "comments in [a] dissenting opinion" about legal principles and precedents "are just that: comments in a dissenting opinion." Railroad Retirement Bd. v. Fritz, 449 U. S. 166, 177, n. 10 (1980). Yet such comments are covered by the government edicts doctrine because they come from an official with authority to make and interpret the law.

Indeed, *Banks* went even further and withheld copyright protection from headnotes and syllabi produced by judges. 128 U. S., at 253. Surely these supplementary materials do not have the force of law, yet they are covered by the doctrine. The simplest explanation is the one *Banks* provided: These non-binding works are not copyrightable because of who creates them—judges acting in their judicial capacity. See ibid.

The same goes for non-binding legislative materials produced by legislative bodies acting in a legislative capacity. There is a broad array of such works ranging from floor statements to proposed bills to committee reports. Under the logic of Georgia's "force of law" test, States would own such materials and could charge the public for access to them.

\* \* \*

Georgia minimizes the OCGA annotations as non-binding and non-authoritative, but that description undersells their practical significance. Imagine a Georgia citizen interested in learning his legal rights and duties. If he reads the economy-class version of the Georgia Code available online, he will see laws requiring political candidates to pay hefty qualification fees (with no indigency exception), criminalizing broad categories of consensual sexual conduct, and exempting certain key evidence in criminal trials from standard evidentiary limitations—with no hint that important aspects of those laws have been held unconstitutional by the Georgia Supreme Court. See OCGA §§ 21–2–131, 16–6–2, 16–6–18, 16–15–9 (available at www.legis.ga.gov). Meanwhile, first-class readers with access to the annotations will be assured that these laws are, in crucial respects, unenforceable relics that the legislature has not bothered to narrow or repeal. See §§ 21–2–131, 16–6–2, 16–6–18, 16–15–9 (available at https://store.lexisnexis.com/products/official-code-of-georgia-annotated-skuSKU6647 for $412.00).

378

If everything short of statutes and opinions were copyrightable, then States would be free to offer a whole range of premium legal works for those who can afford the extra benefit. A State could monetize its entire suite of legislative history. With today's digital tools, States might even launch a subscription or pay-per-law service.

There is no need to assume inventive or nefarious behavior for these concerns to become a reality. Unlike other forms of intellectual property, copyright protection is both instant and automatic. It vests as soon as a work is captured in a tangible form, triggering a panoply of exclusive rights that can last over a century. 17 U. S. C. §§ 102, 106, 302. If Georgia were correct, then unless a State took the affirmative step of transferring its copyrights to the public domain, all of its judges' and legislators' non-binding legal works would be copyrighted. And citizens, attorneys, nonprofits, and private research companies would have to cease all copying, distribution, and display of those works or risk severe and potentially criminal penalties. §§ 501–506. Some affected parties might be willing to roll the dice with a potential fair use defense. But that defense, designed to accommodate First Amendment concerns, is notoriously fact sensitive and often cannot be resolved without a trial. Cf. Harper & Row, Publishers, Inc. v. Nation Enterprises, 471 U. S. 539, 552, 560–561 (1985). The less bold among us would have to think twice before using official legal works that illuminate the law we are all presumed to know and understand.

Thankfully, there is a clear path forward that avoids these concerns—the one we are already on. Instead of examining whether given material carries "the force of law," we ask only whether the author of the work is a judge or a legislator. If so, then whatever work that judge or legislator produces in the course of his judicial or legislative duties is not copyrightable. That is the framework our precedents long ago established, and we adhere to those precedents today.

\* \* \*

For the foregoing reasons, we affirm the judgment of the Eleventh Circuit.

It is so ordered.

■ JUSTICE THOMAS, with whom JUSTICE ALITO joins, and with whom JUSTICE BREYER joins as to all but Part II-A and footnote 6, dissenting.

According to the majority, this Court's 19th-century "government edicts" precedents clearly stand for the proposition that "judges and legislators cannot serve as authors [for copyright purposes] when they produce works in their official capacity." Ante, at 1509. And, after straining to conclude that the Georgia Code Revision Commission (Commission) is an arm of the Georgia Legislature, ante, at 1508–1509, the majority concludes that Georgia cannot hold a copyright in the annotations that are included as part of the Official Code of Georgia Annotated (OCGA). This ruling will likely come as a shock to the 25 other jurisdictions—22 States, 2 Territories, and the District of Columbia—that rely on arrangements similar to Georgia's to produce annotated codes. See Brief for State of Arkansas et al. as Amici Curiae 15, and App. to id., at 1. Perhaps these jurisdictions all overlooked this Court's purportedly clear guidance. Or perhaps the widespread use of these arrangements indicates that today's decision extends the government edicts doctrine to a new context, rather than simply "confirm[ing]" what the precedents have always held. See ante, at 1505–1506. Because I believe we should "leave to Congress the task of deciding whether the Copyright Act needs an upgrade," American Broadcasting Cos. v. Aereo, Inc., 573 U. S. 431, 463 (2014) (Scalia, J., dissenting), I respectfully dissent.

## SUPPLEMENTARY MATERIALS

\* \* \*

These precedents establish that judicial opinions cannot be copyrighted. But they do not exclude from copyright protection notes that are prepared by an official court reporter and published together with the reported opinions. There is no apparent reason why the same logic would not apply to statutes and regulations. Thus, it must follow from our precedents that statutes and regulations cannot be copyrighted, but accompanying notes lacking legal force can be. See Howell v. Miller, 91 F. 129 (CA6 1898) (Harlan, J.) (explaining that, under *Banks* and *Callaghan*, annotations to Michigan statutes could be copyrighted).

\* \* \*

Allowing annotations to be copyrighted does not run afoul of any of these possible justifications for the government edicts doctrine. First, unlike judicial opinions and statutes, these annotations do not even purport to embody the will of the people because they are not law. The General Assembly of Georgia has made abundantly clear through a variety of provisions that the annotations do not create any binding obligations. OCGA § 1–1–7 states that "[a]ll historical citations, title and chapter analyses, and notes set out in this Code are given for the purpose of convenient reference and do not constitute part of the law." \* \* \*

\* \* \*

Second, unlike judges and legislators, the creators of annotations are incentivized by the copyright laws to produce a desirable product that will eventually earn them a profit. And though the Commission may require Lexis to follow strict guidelines, the independent synthesis, analysis, and creative drafting behind the annotations makes them analogous to other copyrightable materials. See Brief for Matthew Bender & Co., Inc., as Amicus Curiae 4–7.

Lastly, the annotations do not impede fair notice of the laws. As just stated, the annotations do not carry the binding force of law. They simply summarize independent sources of legal information and consolidate them in one place. Thus, OCGA annotations serve a similar function to other copyrighted research tools provided by private parties such as the American Law Reports and Westlaw, which also contain information of great "practical significance." Ante, at 1512. Compare, e.g., OCGA § 34–9–260 (annotation for Cho Carwash Property, L. L. C. v. Everett, 326 Ga. App. 6 (2014)) with Ga. Code Ann. § 34–9–260 (Westlaw's annotation for the same).

\* \* \*

For all these reasons, I would conclude that, as with the privately created annotations in *Callaghan*, Georgia's statutory annotations at issue in this case are copyrightable.

\* \* \*

In addition to its textual deficiencies, the majority's understanding of this Court's precedents fails to account for the critical differences between the role that judicial opinions play in expounding upon the law compared to that of statutes. The majority finds it meaningful, for instance, that Banks prohibited dissents and concurrences from being copyrighted, even though they carry no legal force. Ante, at 1511–1512. At an elementary level, it is true that the judgment is the only part of a judicial decision that has legal effect. But it blinks reality to ignore that every word of a judicial opinion—whether it is a majority, a concurrence, or a dissent—expounds upon the law in ways that do not map neatly on to the legislative function. Setting aside summary decisions, the reader of a judicial opinion will always gain critical insight into the reasoning underlying a judicial holding by reading all opinions in their entirety. Understanding the reasoning that animates the rule in turn provides pivotal insight into how the law will likely be applied in future judicial opinions.[6]

\* \* \*

\* \* \*

In addition to being flawed as a textual and precedential matter, the majority's rule will prove difficult to administer. According to one group of amici, nearly all jurisdictions with annotated codes use private contractors that "almost invariably prepare [annotations] under the supervision of legislative-branch or judicial-branch officials, including state legislators or state-court judges." Brief for State of Arkansas et al. as Amici Curiae 16–17. Under the majority's view, any one of these commissions or counsels could potentially be reclassified as an "adjunct to the legislature." Ante, at 1509. But the majority's test for ascertaining the true nature of these commissions raises far more questions than it answers.

\* \* \*

The majority's rule will leave in the lurch the many States, private parties, and legal researchers who relied on the previously bright-line rule. Perhaps, to the detriment of all, many States will stop producing annotated codes altogether. Were that to occur, the majority's fear of an "economy-class" version of the law will truly become a reality. See ante, at 1512–1513. As Georgia explains, its contract enables the OCGA to be sold at a fraction of the cost of competing annotated codes. For example, Georgia asserts that Lexis sold the OCGA for $404 in 2016, while West Publishing's competing annotated code sold for $2,570. Should state annotated codes disappear, those without the means to pay the competitor's significantly higher price tag will have a valuable research tool taken away from them. \* \* \*

■ JUSTICE GINSBURG, with whom JUSTICE BREYER joins, dissenting.

Beyond doubt, state laws are not copyrightable. Nor are other materials created by state legislators in the course of performing their lawmaking responsibilities, e.g., legislative committee reports, floor statements, unenacted bills. Ante, at 1517–1518. Not all that legislators do, however, is ineligible for copyright protection; the government edicts doctrine shields only "works that are (1) created by judges and legislators (2) in the course of their judicial and legislative duties." Ante, at 1508 (emphasis added). The core question this case presents, as I see it: Are the annotations in the Official Code of Georgia Annotated (OCGA) done in a legislative capacity? The answer, I am persuaded, should be no.

To explain why, I proceed from common ground. All agree that headnotes and syllabi for judicial opinions—both a kind of annotation—are copyrightable when created by a reporter of decisions, Callaghan v. Myers, 128 U. S. 617, 645–650 (1888), but are not copyrightable when created by judges, Banks v. Manchester, 128 U. S. 244, 253 (1888). That is so because "[t]he whole work done by . . . judges," ibid., including dissenting and concurring opinions,

---

[6]  For instance, this Court has not overruled Lemon v. Kurtzman, 403 U. S. 602 (1971), which pronounced a test for evaluating Establishment Clause claims. But a reader would do well to carefully scrutinize the various opinions in American Legion v. American Humanist Assn., 588 U. S. ___ (2019), to understand the markedly different way that this precedent functions in our current jurisprudence compared to when it was first decided. Moreover, sometimes a separate writing takes on canonical status, like Justice Jackson's concurrence regarding the executive power in Youngstown Sheet & Tube Co. v. Sawyer, 343 U. S. 579, 634–638 (1952) (opinion concurring in judgment and opinion of the Court); see also Katz v. United States, 389 U. S. 347, 360–361 (1967) (Harlan, J., concurring) (reasonable expectation of privacy Fourth Amendment test). Still other times, the reasoning in an opinion for less than a majority of the Court provides the explicit basis for a later majority's holding. See, e.g., McKinney v. Arizona, 589 U. S. ___, ___ (2020) (slip op., at 5) (discussing Ring v. Arizona, 536 U. S. 584, 612 (2002) (Scalia J., concurring)); \* \* \*

ranks as work performed in their judicial capacity. Judges do not outsource their writings to "arm[s]" or "adjunct[s]," cf. ante, at 1508, 1509, to be composed in their stead. Accordingly, the judicial opinion-drafting process in its entirety—including the drafting of headnotes and syllabi, in jurisdictions where that is done by judges—falls outside the reach of copyright protection.

One might ask: If a judge's annotations are not copyrightable, why are those created by legislators? The answer lies in the difference between the role of a judge and the role of a legislator. "[T]o the judiciary" we assign "the duty of interpreting and applying" the law, Massachusetts v. Mellon, 262 U. S. 447, 488 (1923), and sometimes making the applicable law, see Friendly, In Praise of Erie—and of the New Federal Common Law, 39 N. Y. U. L. Rev. 383 (1964). See also Marbury v. Madison, 1 Cranch 137, 177 (1803) ("It is emphatically the province and duty of the judicial department to say what the law is."). In contrast, the role of the legislature encompasses the process of "making laws"—not construing statutes after their enactment. *Mellon*, 262 U. S., at 488; see Patchak v. Zinke, 583 U. S. ___, ___ (2018) (plurality opinion) (slip op., at 5) ("[T]he legislative power is the power to make law."). The OCGA annotations, in my appraisal, do not rank as part of the Georgia Legislature's lawmaking process for three reasons.

First, the annotations are not created contemporaneously with the statutes to which they pertain; instead, the annotations comment on statutes already enacted. See, e.g., App. 268–269 (text of enacted laws are transmitted to the publisher for the addition of commentary); id., at 403–404 (publisher adds new case notes on a rolling basis as courts construe existing statutes).1 In short, annotating begins only after lawmaking ends. This sets the OCGA annotations apart from uncopyrightable legislative materials like committee reports, generated before a law's enactment, and tied tightly to the task of law-formulation.

Second, the OCGA annotations are descriptive rather than prescriptive. Instead of stating the legislature's perception of what a law conveys, the annotations summarize writings in which others express their views on a given statute. * * *

Third, and of prime importance, the OCGA annotations are "given for the purpose of convenient reference" by the public, § 1–1–7 (2019); they aim to inform the citizenry at large, they do not address, particularly, those seated in legislative chambers. Annotations are thus unlike, for example, surveys, work commissioned by a legislature to aid in determining whether existing law should be amended. * * *

Because summarizing judicial decisions and commentary bearing on enacted statutes, in contrast to, for example, drafting a committee report to accompany proposed legislation, is not done in a legislator's law-shaping capacity, I would hold the OCGA annotations copyrightable and therefore reverse the judgment of the Court of Appeals for the Eleventh Circuit.

## NOTE

Public.Resource.Org was also involved in another case that tested the ability of private organizations to use copyright to prevent the Internet distribution of their standards that had been incorporated into statutes and regulations. Avoiding the issue of whether privately-drafted standards incorporated into law can remain protected by copyright, the court limited its focus to the issue of fair use. Finding that the variations in the nature of the standards, as well as the differing nature of their incorporation, precluded a blanket determination of fair use, the court remanded for a standard by standard analysis. Amer. Soc'y for Testing and Materials v. Public.Resource.Org, Inc., 896 F.3d 437 (D.C. Cir.2018).

# CHAPTER 3

# SCOPE OF PROTECTION: INFRINGEMENT

## 1. IDEAS AND EXPRESSION IN WORKS OF FICTION

*Page 216.*     *Add to the end of Note (3):*

T. Reilly, Copyright and a Synergistic Society, 18 Minn.J.L., Sci. & Tech. 575 (2017), wholeheartedly defends copyright's focus on the individual creator.

## 2. MUSIC

*Page 224.*     *Add to the end of Note (3):*

Unicolors, Inc. v. Urban Outfitters, Inc., 853 F.3d 980 (9th Cir.2017), reaffirms in a fabric design case that copying can be inferred even absent evidence of access if the works are strikingly similar.

*Page 225.*     *Add to the end of the carryover paragraph:*

The Ninth Circuit affirmed the jury's verdict that Robin Thicke's hit *Blurred Lines* infringed the copyright in Marvin Gaye's song *Got To Give It Up,* despite a passionate argument by a dissenting judge that the result effectively extends copyright to a "musical style." Williams v. Gaye, 885 F.3d 1150 (9th Cir.2018). The Ninth Circuit soon faced another case testing the distinction between protectable musical expression and unoriginal musical fragments and style when the owner of a song released in 1967 claimed that Led Zeppelin's iconic 1971 song *Stairway to Heaven* was an infringement. The songs shared a similar chord sequence and descending baseline. (Although the suit was not filed until 2014, the Ninth Circuit pointed out that the Supreme Court's decision in Petrella v. Metro-Goldwyn-Mayer, Inc., 572 U.S. 663 (2014), held that laches is not a defense when the infringement is ongoing.) The court in Skidmore v. Led Zeppelin, 952 F.3d 1051 (9th Cir.2020) (en banc), first analyzed the boundaries of the copyrighted work. Since the distribution of a sound recording was not a publication of the musical work under the 1909 Act, federal copyright protection was based on the music's registration as an unpublished work. The statute required deposit of "one complete copy" of the unpublished work, and thus the plaintiff's copyright was limited to the material contained in the deposit copy. The trial court was therefore correct in refusing to allow the jury to hear recorded performances of the copyrighted work that contained additional embellishments. The court upheld a jury verdict that the works were not substantially similar. Along the way, the court said in a footnote that "the degree of overlap in original expression that is required for the similarity to be substantial is determined by the range of possible protectable expression. * * * More similarities are required to infringe if the range of protectable expression is narrow, because the similarities between the two works are likely to cover public domain or otherwise unprotectable elements." A week later, a district court applied *Skidmore* to vacate a jury verdict against Kate Perry and her song *Dark Horse,* which contained an 8-note ostinato allegedly similar to one in the plaintiff's work. The court in Gray v. Perry, 2020

WL 1275221 (C.D.Cal.2020), held that the musical phrase was not protectable expression. The plaintiff has appealed. J. Fishman, Music as a Matter of Law, 131 Harv.L.Rev. 1861 (2018), notes that although copyright's traditional focus on melody is substantively questionable, it does provide predictability for subsequent users. E. Lee, Fair Use Avoidance in Music Cases. 59 B.C.L.Rev. 1873 (2018), wonders why there are so few fair use precedents in non-parody music infringement cases; R. Ku, The First Amendment Implications of Copyright's Double Standard, 17 Va. Sports & Ent.L.J. 163 (2018), argues that copyright law unconstitutionally discriminates against "entertainment" works in applying doctrines like the idea/expression dichotomy and fair use.

### Page 233.    Add to the end of Note (2):

Moving beyond summary judgments in copyright infringement cases, defendants may sometimes gain even earlier relief through dismissal on the pleadings under rule 12(b)(6) if discovery would not strengthen the plaintiff's case. See, e.g., Tanksley v. Daniels, 902 F.3d 165 (3d Cir.2018): Rentmeester v. Nike, Inc., 883 F.3d 1111 (9th Cir.2018). O. Bracha, Not De Minimis: (Improper) Appropriation in Copyright, 68 Am.U.L.Rev. 139 (2018), emphasizes that the "improper appropriation" standard for liability entails more than mere non-de minimis copying; D. Gervais, Improper Appropriation, 23 Lewis and Clark L.Rev. 599 (2019), also laments that the standard is often understood in purely quantitative terms. C. Sprigman, The Filtration Problem in Copyright's "Substantial Similarity" Infringement Test, id. at 571, struggles to find procedures for jury trials that would better implement the idea/expression analysis.

## 3.  SUBSTANTIAL SIMILARITY IN VISUAL WORKS

### Page 250.    Add to the end of footnote i:

In 1984, photographer Jacobus Rentmeester took a famous photograph of University of North Carolina basketball player Michael Jordan. The setting for the photo was a grassy knoll on the campus where Rentmeester had installed a tall pole with a basketball hoop. He instructed Jordon to leap toward the basket with his legs spread wide in a ballet-like pose holding the basketball in one hand over his head. The photograph depicts Jordan silhouetted against the sky. Nike later had another outdoor photograph taken of Jordan that was obviously inspired by Rentmeester's and used it in advertising for Nike's Air Jordan shoes. Nike later used a solid black silhouette of Jordan's figure from its photo to create the iconic *Jumpman* logo that it has used in marketing billions of dollars of merchandise. In an infringement suit brought by Rentmeester, the court spoke at length about the originality of the pose and scene created by the plaintiff. However, it held that he could not copyright the balletic pose itself, but only the way it was expressed in his photograph. Although Nike's photo borrowed the general idea of the pose, it did not copy the details as expressed in the copyrighted work and thus there was no infringement as a matter of law. Rentmeester v. Nike, Inc., 883 F.3d 1111 (9th Cir.2018). T. Kogan, How Photographs Infringe, 19 Vand.J.Ent. & Tech.L. 353 (2017), analyzes liability for recreating and photographing a tableau that had been arranged and photographed by an earlier photographer; J. Silbey, Justifying Copyright in the Age of Digital Reproduction: The Case of Photographers, 9 U.C. Irvine L.Rev. 405 (2019), uses photography to test copyright's relationship to production.

## 4.  COPYRIGHT IN CHARACTERS

### Page 255.    Add to the end of Note (3):

In Daniels v. Walt Disney Co., 952 F.3d 1149 (9th Cir.2020), the plaintiff had created a set of five anthropomorphic characters representing various emotions that she pitched to Disney. Disney later made a movie entitled *Inside Out* that included five anthropomorphized emotions. The court said that "a character that lacks a core set of consistent and identifiable character traits and attributes is not protectable, because that character is not immediately recognizable as the same character whenever it appears." The physical appearances and traits across the various iterations of the plaintiff's characters were not sufficiently consistent for copyright protection.

*Page 273.    Add to the end of Note (3):*

Comedian Stephen Colbert played a conservative political commentator, also named Stephen Colbert, on a Comedy Central show called the *Colbert Report.* After Colbert left Comedy Central to host *The Late Show* on CBS, he reprised the character on his new show. Viacom, owner of Comedy Central, threatened to sue, alleging infringement of its copyrighted character. Colbert said that the character would never appear again. However, he later introduced the character's "identical twin cousin", also named Stephen Colbert. Does Viacom have a plausible claim of infringement?

# 6.  COMPUTER PROGRAMS

*Page 308.    Add to the end of the Note:*

On appeal, the Federal Circuit reversed and remanded, holding that Google's use of the Java code was not fair use as a matter of law. Oracle America, Inc. v. Google LLC, 886 F.3d 1179 (Fed.Cir.2018). The court said that Google's use was commercial and its verbatim copying was not transformative since it served the same function and purpose as the original work. The court also held that "there is no inherent right to copy in order to capitalize on the popularity of the copyrighted work or to meet the expectations of intended customers." The copying also had an adverse impact of the potential market for the copyrighted work since Google's use competed directly with Java in the mobile device market and affected potential markets that Oracle might enter or license in the future. The Supreme Court has granted a petition for certiorari. P. Samuelson and C. Asay, Saving Software's Fair Use Future, 31 Harv.J.L. & Tech. 539 (2018), worries that the refusal to recognize the fair use defense in *Oracle* will dangerously constrain innovation and competition in the software industry.

*Page 310.    Add to the end of Note (1):*

P. Samuelson, Functionality and Expression in Computer Programs: Refining the Tests for Software Copyright Infringement, 31 Berk.Tech.L.J. 1215 (2016), concludes that *Oracle* misapplied both § 102(b) and the merger doctrine resulting in an unjustified expansion of copyright protection; T. Armstrong, Symbols, Systems, and Software as Intellectual Property: Time for CONTU Part II?, 24 Mich.Telecomm. & Tech.L.Rev. 131 (2018), pushes for additional legislative guidance on the appropriate scope of protection for software, to be informed by a new advisory commission in the mold of the original CONTU.

# 7.  SOUND RECORDINGS

*Page 311.    Add to the end of the second paragraph of Section 7:*

Pre-1972 sound recordings finally obtained a form of federal protection in 2018. See the supplementary note for page 342, *infra.*

*Page 313.    Add to the end of the carryover paragraph:*

In a rare application of fair use to sampling, the Second Circuit in Estate of Smith v. Graham, 799 Fed.Appx. 36 (2d Cir.2020), held that a 35-second sample taken from a rap touting jazz that was used by hip-hop artists Drake and Jay-Z was a fair use. The defendants' seven-minute long work criticized the "jazz elitism" espoused in the original work. Another sampler also succeeded on a fair use defense in Oyewole v. Ora, 776 Fed.Appx. 42 (2d Cir.2019).

*Page 316.*    *Add to the end of Note (1):*

L. Mulraine, A Global Perspective on Digital Sampling, 52 Akron L.Rev. 697 (2019), supports a de minimis exception to sampling liability.

# 8. PERFORMANCE RIGHTS

*Page 334.*    *Add to the end of footnote t:*

Disney earned unwanted publicity when its licensing agent sent a demand for $250 to an elementary school P.T.A. that had shown Disney's *The Lion King* at a pizza and pajama fund-raiser that brought in $800. The movie DVD had been brought from home by one of the parents. (The licensing agent, Movie Licensing USA, said that some 25,000 schools nationwide have purchased licenses to show movies.) Hauser, School Screens "Lion King." Disney's Response? Pay Up., NY Times, Feb. 6, 2020, p. B3. The CEO of Disney eventually apologized and donated to the fundraiser.

*Page 336.*    *Add to the end of Note (6):*

The U.S. continues to report to the WTO that it will work with Congress and the EU to resolve the dispute over § 110(5).

*Page 336.*    *Add to the end of Note (9):*

The United States has ratified the Marrakesh Treaty, which promotes access to works by the visually impaired. Treaty obligations were implemented through amendments to §§ 121 and 122 of the Copyright Act.

*Page 340.*    *Add to the end of the carryover paragraph:*

After the Copyright Royalty Board raised the compulsory rates for sound recording performances by webcasters to 17 cents per one hundred streams for nonsubscription webcasters and 22 cents for subscription services, SoundExchange challenged the royalty rates in the D.C. Circuit. The rates were upheld in SoundExchange, Inc. v. Copyright Royalty Bd., 904 F.3d 41 (D.C. Cir.2018). Meanwhile, due to an increase in the Consumer Price Index, the Board in 2018 increased the rates from 17 to 18 cents for non-subscription webcasters and from 22 to 23 cents for subscription webcasters. In a separate proceeding, the Copyright Royalty Board substantially increased the statutory rate paid by Sirius XM for sound recording performances from 11 percent of gross revenue to 15.5 percent.

*Page 341.*    *Add to the end of footnote x:*

The Ninth Circuit in ABS Entertainment, Inc. v. CBS Corp., 900 F.3d 1113 (9th Cir.2018), held that remastered versions of pre-1972 sound recordings that differed from the originals solely by changes incident to the change in medium would not be protected by federal copyright. Thus, a claim under state law for unauthorized performance would not be preempted. The case was remanded for further fact-finding on the originality of the derivative recordings.

*Page 342.*    *Add to the end of Note (4):*

As the owners of pre-1972 sound recordings continued to push their performance right claims against digital services like Sirius Radio and Pandora under state law, the Supreme Court of Florida joined the New York Court of Appeals in holding that the state's common law did not recognize any exclusive right of public performance in pre-1972 sound recordings. Flo & Eddie, Inc. v. Sirius XM Radio, 229 So.3d 305 (Fla.2017). (The California Supreme Court declined to decide a similar question certified to it by the Ninth Circuit in light of the preemptive provisions of the newly enacted Music Modernization Act. See Flo & Eddie, Inc. v. Pandora Media, LLC, 789 Fed.Appx. 569 (9th Cir.2019).) In 2018, Congress finally stepped in with legislation adding a new § 1401 to the Copyright Act entitled, "Unauthorized Use of Pre-1972 Sound Recordings." The rights granted in § 1401 are not "copyrights," and thus the rules relating to matters like copyright notice and registration are not applicable. Under

§ 1401(a)(1), anyone who engages in "covered activity" with respect to a pre-1972 sound recording is subject to the same remedies as a copyright infringer. "Covered activity" is defined in § 1401(*l*)(1) as any activity that the owner of a copyright in a sound recording would have the exclusive right to do under the Copyright Act. Thus, the same rules on reproduction and digital performance that apply to copyrighted sound recordings now also apply to pre-1972 recordings. (Although the rules on registration are not applicable to pre-1972 sound recordings, § 1401(f)(5) requires a filing with the Copyright Office as a prerequisite to statutory damages and attorneys fees.) Protection under § 1401 lasts for 95 years from publication, but § 1401(a)(2) also adds to that duration a "further transition period" that varies with the age of the recordings. For pre-1923 recordings, protection will last until December 31, 2021; recordings published between 1923 and 1946 get 100 years of protection after publication; recordings published between 1947 and 1956 get 110 years of protection after publication. For all pre-1972 recordings first published after 1956, the transition period extends protection until 2067. Under the amended version of § 301(c), the rules on federal preemption now apply to state protection of pre-1972 sound recordings.

***Page 342.     Add to the end of footnote y:***

Licensing performance rights in music has become even more complicated. ASCAP, BMI, and SESAC have now been joined by a fourth collective named Global Music Rights whose library includes works by popular writers including Bruce Springsteen, the Eagles, and Pharrell Williams.

***Page 345.     Add to the end of footnote bb:***

Despite its 2016 announcement that it would not seek changes in the consent decrees that govern ASCAP and BMI, the Department of Justice is once again reviewing both decrees. The performing rights organizations support the review, but radio stations and small music users are opposed, emphasizing that ASCAP and BMI control over 90 per cent of the music licensing market. Congress too is skeptical. A provision in the recently-enacted music licensing bill requires the DOJ to notify Congress before acting to terminate the consent decrees.

# 9.  DISTRIBUTION, DISPLAY, AND DERIVATIVE RIGHTS

***Page 349.     Add to the end of the carryover paragraph:***

A plaintiff alleging infringement of its animal-shaped pillowcases failed in an attempt to hold Amazon liable for violating the exclusive distribution right in Milo & Gabby LLC v. Amazon.com, Inc., 693 Fed.Appx. 879 (Fed.Cir.2017). Although Amazon generated product pages on behalf of third-party sellers and in some instances provided shipping services, the court held that Amazon was not a "seller" or "distributor" since it did not itself transfer ownership of the products to purchasers.

***Page 355.     Add to the end of Note (4):***

ReDigi, the company that established an internet platform to enable resale of digital music files, was held liable for reproducing sound recordings owned by the plaintiff record companies in Capitol Records, LLC v. ReDigi Inc., 910 F.3d 649 (2d Cir.2018). ReDigi users downloaded the company's software, which could verify that a music file had been lawfully purchased and enabled the user to upload the file to ReDigi's server. The software then deleted the user's copy. (The software could not of course verify that the user did not have another copy of the music file on a different non-linked device.) Purchasers of the song could then download it from ReDigi. The court found that both the upload of the file to ReDigi and the download to the subsequent purchaser created reproductions of the original work. The copying was not a fair use since the copyrighted work was completely unchanged and the reproductions competed in the market with sales by the plaintiffs. The court declined to consider the lower court's alternative ground that

# SUPPLEMENTARY MATERIALS

ReDigi also violated the distribution right because it was not transferring the "particular" phonorecord that the user had purchased and thus could not invoke the first sale defense. In dicta, the Second Circuit quoted with apparent approval the proposition that the first sale doctrine would protect the sale and physical transfer of an iPod containing digital music files.

***Page 357.    Add to the end of Note (8):***

C. Newman, Vested Use-Privileges in Property and Copyright, 30 Harv.J.L. & Tech. 75 (2017), finds no inherent conflict between copyright—even the exclusive rights of distribution and display—and the traditional rights enjoyed by the owners of tangible property.

***Page 357.    Add to the end of Note (9):***

The company that markets the NBA 2K basketball simulation video games was sued by a company that owns exclusive licenses on tattoos that appear on the bodies of NBA stars such as LeBron James. Plaintiff claimed that the games violate its exclusive right of public display. Judge Swain in Solid Oak Sketches, LLC v. 2K Games, Inc., 2020 WL 1467394 (S.D.N.Y.2020), held that since the tattoos as they appeared in the games were less than one-tenth the size of the actual tattoos and were usually out of focus or obstructed because of the players' movements, the game tattoos were not substantially similar to the copyrighted works. The court also held that the players had implied non-exclusive licenses from the tattooists to use the tattoos as part of their likenesses D. Fagundes and A. Perzanowski, Clown Eggs, 94 Notre Dame L.Rev. 1313 (2019), uses the practice of clowns who memorialize their make-up using painted eggs to examine norm-based intellectual property protection; A. Adler and J. Fromer, Taking Intellectual Property Into Their Own Hands, 107 Cal.L.Rev. 145 (2019), examines what the authors see as a trend toward extra-legal self-help in dealing with appropriations of intellectual property.

***Page 374.    Add to the end of Note (3):***

D. Shipley, Derivative Works and Making Sense of the Maxim that "Others are Free to Copy the Original. They are not Free to Copy the Copy," 44 U. Dayton L.Rev. 231 (2019), examines a series of issues arising from the creation and copying of derivative works.

***Page 375.    Add to the end of Note (5):***

The Ninth Circuit in Disney Enters., Inc. v. VidAngel, Inc., 869 F.3d 848 (9th Cir.2017), upheld the preliminary injunction against VidAngel's movie-filtering service. VidAngel had decrypted movie DVDs and uploaded them onto its servers; customers could stream versions that were "filtered" according to their preferences. The court held that the defendant infringed the reproduction right when it copied the movies onto its servers. The Family Movie Act, codified in § 110(11), did not provide a defense since the filtered stream sent to customers was not "from an authorized copy of the motion picture" as required by the statute. A fair use defense also failed because the use was commercial and merely removing objectionable portions was not transformative. Plaintiffs were also likely to succeed on their DMCA circumvention claim. The movie studios eventually got a $62 million jury verdict and a permanent injunction.

# CHAPTER 4

# SCOPE OF PROTECTION: THE LIMITS OF LIABILITY

## 1. FAIR USE

*Page 404.* *Add to the end of Note (4):*

A surprise visit by President Trump to a wedding reception at the Trump National Golf Club generated a copyright suit involving a cellphone photo of Trump and the bride taken by a guest at the wedding. The photographer texted the photo to a friend, and it ultimately ended up on Instagram and then appeared on websites like CNN, the Washington Post, and Hearst's Esquire, which is supported by online advertisements. The photographer sued Hearst for infringement and won a summary judgment in Otto v. Hearst Comm., Inc., 345 F.Supp.3d 412 (S.D.N.Y.2018). Hearst's fair use defense was rejected. As to the purpose of the use, the court said, "It would be antithetical to the purposes of copyright protection to allow media companies to steal personal images and benefit from the fair use defense by simply inserting the photo in an article which only recites factual information—much of which can be gleaned from the photograph itself. * * * The Court does not believe that this is an 'extraordinary case' in which the need for news reporting should take precedence over copyright protections." As to the effect of the use, Judge Woods concluded that "[p]ublishing the Photograph without permission essentially destroys the primary market for its use." Another district court took a different tack when a professional photographer who posted a photo on her public Instagram account complained that a website had embedded her photo in a news story. Under Instagram's terms of use, users grant Instagram a non-exclusive, transferable license to posted content, and Instagram offers an application that allows others to share the posted content. Thus, the defendant, as a sublicensee, had the right to use the plaintiff's photograph. Her complaint was dismissed. Sinclair v. Ziff Davis, LLC, 2020 WL 1847841 (S.D.N.Y.2020).

*Page 406.* *Add to the end of Note (6):*

When the Federal Circuit applied Ninth Circuit law in Oracle America v. Google LLC, 886 F.3d 1179 (Fed.Cir.2018), to overturn the jury's verdict that Google's use of the Java code was fair use, the court offered these comments on the scope of appellate review of fair use: "[W]e conclude that whether the court applied the correct legal standard to the fair use inquiry is a question we review de novo, whether the findings relating to any relevant historical facts were correct are questions which we review with deference, and whether the use at issue is ultimately a fair use is something we also review de novo." On the role of a jury in fair use, the court said, "All jury findings relating to fair use other than its implied findings of historical fact must, under governing Supreme Court and Ninth Circuit law, be viewed as advisory only." The Supreme Court has granted a petition for certiorari. N. Snow, Who Decides Fair Use—Judge or Jury?, 94 Wash.L.Rev. 275 (2019), argues that the Federal Circuit in *Oracle* was wrong and that fair use is for the jury to decide.

*Page 413.* *Add to the end of Note (6):*

The Second Circuit has determined that the TVEyes news clipping service is not a fair use. Fox News Network, LLC v. TVEyes, Inc., 883 F.3d 169 (2d Cir.2018). TVEyes recorded all the broadcasts on over 1400 channels and created a text-searchable database that clients could use

# SUPPLEMENTARY MATERIALS

to find relevant clips. The client could then play a desired clip of up to ten minutes. The court held that the use was "at least somewhat transformative" since it allowed users to access material responsive to their interests. As to the amount used, the ten-minute clips likely provided users with all of the programming that they sought. "By providing Fox's content to TVEyes clients without payment to Fox TVEyes is in effect depriving Fox of licensing revenues from TVEyes or from similar entities. And Fox itself might wish to exploit the market for such a service rather than license it to others." After the Supreme Court declined to review the case, TVEyes agreed to a permanent injunction that bars it from including content from Fox News in its database.

*Page 417.*    *Add to the end of footnote g:*

Representatives of music copyright owners failed in their attempt to obtain relief under the Audio Home Recording Act, codified in Chapter 10 of the Copyright Act, against automobile makers whose cars included devices that could copy CDs for later playback. The D.C. Circuit in Alliance of Artists and Recording Cos. v. Denso Int'l America, Inc., 947 F.3d 849 (D.C. Cir.2020), held that the devices were not "digital audio recording device[s]" under the statute because their hard drives, which contained non-music related data and software in addition to the music files, were not "digital musical recording[s]."

*Page 434.*    *Add to the end of the first paragraph in Note (3):*

L. Heymann, Reasonable Appropriation and Reader Response, 9 U.C. Irvine L.Rev. 343 (2019), considers how to judge transformativeness from the perspective of a reasonable reader.

*Page 435.*    *Add to the end of Note (3):*

D. Shipley, A Transformative Use Taxonomy: Making Sense of the Transformative Use Standard, 63 Wayne L.Rev. 267 (2017), analyzes the evolution of the transformative use standard and its relationship to the exclusive right to prepare derivative works; J. Liu, An Empirical Study of Transformative Use in Copyright Law, 22 Stan.Tech.L.Rev. 163 (2019), examines the dominance and ambiguities of the transformative use element in fair use analysis.

*Page 436.*    *Add to the end of Note (7):*

C. Buccafusco, P. Heald, and W. Bu, Testing Tarnishment in Trademark and Copyright Law: The Effect of Pornographic Versions of Protected Marks and Works, 94 Wash.U.L.Rev. 341 (2016), uses experiments to cast doubt on the supposedly harmful effects of "tarnishing" uses of copyrighted works.

*Page 474.*    *Add to the end of Note (6):*

If the ultimate user has a license to make copies, the commercial copier is in a stronger position. In Great Minds v. Office Depot, 945 F.3d 1106 (9th Cir.2019), a non-profit educational organization had distributed materials under a Creative Commons license that allowed free reproduction for noncommercial use. School districts used Office Depot to make copies. The owner argued that Office Depot had infringed its copyrights by making commercial use not authorized by the license. The court held that the licensee could hire a third-party contractor like Office Depot to help implement the licensee's rights under the license.

*Page 487.*    *Add to the end of Note (1):*

The dispute between academic publishers like Cambridge University Press and Georgia State University made a second trip to the Eleventh Circuit. Following the initial remand, the lower court again held that only a few of the electronic course reserves were infringements. On appeal, the Eleventh Circuit once again held that the district court had improperly applied a mathematical formula in weighing the fair use factors rather than the "holistic review the Act demands." The case was remanded again. Cambridge Univ. Press v. Albert, 906 F.3d 1290 (11th Cir.2018). On its third try, the district court in a lengthy opinion once again held that most of the

390

excerpts were shielded by fair use. Cambridge Univ. Press v. Becker, 2020 WL 998763 (N.D.Ga.2020). Meanwhile, a jury in Texas awarded a small copyright owner $9.2 million in a suit against the state's largest school district for repeatedly reproducing and distributing the plaintiff's study guides in Houston high schools. Carpenter, Federal Jury: HISD Repeatedly Violated Copyright Laws, Owe Company $9.2M, Houston Chronicle, May 24, 2019.

**Page 491.** *Add to the end of the carryover paragraph:*

In a 2017 Discussion Document entitled *Section 108 of Title 17*, the Copyright Office offered a number of proposals to update the library exemptions in § 108 to accommodate digital copying. Some library groups fear that specific amendments to § 108 may actually restrict their rights by undermining their general fair use arguments.

## 2. CONTRIBUTORY AND VICARIOUS INFRINGERS

**Page 499.** *Add to the end of Note (1):*

When copyright owners sought to impose contributory liability on an Internet service provider in BMG Rights Management v. Cox Comm., Inc., 881 F.3d 293 (4th Cir.2018), the defendant challenged a jury instruction that permitted the imposition of contributory liability if the defendant "knew or should have known of such infringing activity." The Fourth Circuit responded that "[i]t is well-established that one mental state slightly less demanding than actual knowledge—willful blindness—can establish the requisite intent for contributory copyright infringement. This is so because the law recognizes willful blindness as equivalent to actual knowledge." However, "[t]he formulation 'should have known' reflects negligence and is therefore too low a standard." A retrial on remand was avoided by a subsequent settlement.

## 3. COPYRIGHT IN A DIGITAL AGE

**Page 511.** *Add to the end of the fourth paragraph:*

M. Chatterjee and J. Fromer, Minds, Machines, and the Law: The Case of Volition in Copyright Law, 119 Colum.L.Rev. 1887 (2019), offers a framework for analyzing when machine behavior might satisfy a volition requirement.

**Page 512.** *Add to the end of Note (1):*

In VHT, Inc. v. Zillow Group, Inc., 918 F.3d 723 (9th Cir.2019), the Ninth Circuit refused to hold the defendant real estate website directly liable for unauthorized photos uploaded by third parties. Quoting its decision in Perfect 10, Inc. v. Giganews, Inc., the court stated, "[T]o demonstrate volitional conduct, a party like VHT must provide some 'evidence showing [the alleged infringer] exercised control (other than by general operation of [its website]); selected any material for upload, download, transmission, or storage; or instigated any copying, storage, or distribution' of its photos." In another case, a foreign website owner who uploaded copyrighted content that could be streamed by users in the United States argued that volitional conduct is a requirement for direct infringement and such conduct is absent when it is the user who chooses the content and actuates the delivery system. The defense was unavailing. "Our court has yet to decide whether to read such a volitional conduct or proximate cause requirement into the Copyright Act, and we need not do so today. [Defendant's] conduct—'using its own equipment' to 'allow[ ] [users] to watch television programs, many of which are copyrighted,' by transmitting content upon a user's request, *Aereo*, 143 S.Ct. at 2506—constitutes infringement under *Aereo*'s binding authority, whatever the scope of any such requirement might otherwise be." Spanski Enter., Inc. v. Telewizja Polska, S.A. 883 F.3d 904 (D.C.Cir.2018).

## SUPPLEMENTARY MATERIALS

*Page 520.   Add to the end of the first paragraph in Note (1):*

The "server test" used in Perfect 10, Inc. v. Amazon.com, Inc. to protect Google from direct liability for infringement of the public display right when it linked to images stored on third-party servers was rejected in Goldman v. Breitbart News Network, LLC, 302 F.Supp.3d 585 (S.D.N.Y.2018). Various online news outlets and blogs embedded a tweet containing a photograph of New England Patriots quarterback Tom Brady in their news stories. The owner of the copyright in the photograph sued for infringement of the exclusive public display right. None of the defendants had copied and saved the photo onto their own servers; it was displayed through a link that retrieved the image from the Twitter servers where it was stored. Specifically disagreeing with *Perfect 10*, the court denied the defendants' motion for summary judgment, stating, "The plain language of the Copyright Act, the legislative history, and subsequent Supreme Court jurisprudence provide no basis for a rule the allows the physical location or possession of an image to determine who may or may not have 'displayed' a work within the meaning of the Copyright Act." The court held that the photograph had been displayed by the defendants. "[E]ach and every defendant itself took active steps to put a process in place that resulted in a transmission of the photos so that they could be visibly shown." The Second Circuit denied an interlocutory appeal. Most of the media defendants then settled with the photographer, who agreed to dismiss the entire lawsuit.

*Page 535.   Add to the end of Note (2):*

LiveJournal is a social media site that allows users to create thematic "communities" that upload and comment on content related to the theme. LiveJournal appoints unpaid "moderators" who review and then post material submitted by users. Plaintiff Mavrix Photographs sued, claiming that twenty of its copyrighted celebrity photographs had been posted on the LiveJournal site. Mavrix Photographs, LCC v. LiveJournal, Inc., 873 F.3d 1045 (9th Cir.2017). LiveJournal claimed protection under the safe harbor in § 512(c). The Ninth Circuit reversed the district court's summary judgment in favor of LiveJournal. The court said that the fact-finder could conclude that the moderators were agents of the defendant. "In that event, the fact finder must assess whether Mavrix's photographs were indeed stored at the direction of the users in light of the moderator's role in screening and posting the photographs." The Ninth Circuit later distinguished *Mavrix* in Ventura Content, LTD v. Motherless, Inc., 885 F.3d 597 (9th Cir.2018), where the owner of a website hosting pornography attempted to screen out child pornography, bestiality, and copyright infringement. "The moderators in *Mavrix* directed posting only if they thought the user-submitted material was 'new and exciting celebrity news.' [Defendant] and his contactor do not review whether the pornography submitted by users is 'new and exciting' or meets any other discretionary standards. The Motherless rule is 'anything legal stays.'" The *Mavrix* interpretation of "storage at the direction of a user" in § 512(c) is in contrast to the position taken by the Tenth Circuit in BWP Media USA, Inc. v. Clarity Digital Group, LLC, 820 F.3d 1175 (10th Cir.2016). There the defendant website had contracted with "examiners" to post material on its site. The copyright owner argued that the examiners were not "users" under the safe harbor provision. The court disagreed, stating in dicta that even if the examiners were employees or agents of the defendant, it would not be automatically excluded from the safe harbor. "[A] user is anyone who uses a website—no class of individuals is inherently excluded." The court also noted that "if the infringing content has merely gone through a screening or automated process, the ISP will generally benefit from the safe harbor's protection." As to whether the infringing material had been "stored at the direction" of a user, the court answered in the affirmative, arguing that although the defendant had encouraged the examiners to post material on general topics, it had not encouraged them to post infringing content.

*Page 536.    Add to the end of Note (3):*

The district court's decision barring Cox Communications, the nation's third largest Internet and cable provider, from the § 512 safe harbor because it failed to reasonably implement a termination policy for repeat infringers was affirmed in BMG Rights Management v. Cox Comms., Inc., 881 F.3d 293 (4th Cir.2018). Cox had adopted a 13-strike policy for termination and would often reinstate anyone whose account had been terminated. It had also automatically deleted millions of infringement notices sent by the plaintiffs' agent. Although that case was settled, it ramifications continue. When record labels and music publishers brought an infringement suit against Cox, the trial judge decided that Cox's behavior precluded any defense under the safe harbor provisions. The jury found Cox liable for willful contributory and vicarious infringement (despite Cox's flat fee subscription model). The Virginia jury awarded $1 billion in statutory damages for infringement of over 10,000 songs. Cox has moved for a new trial. Sony Music Ent. v. Cox Comm., No. 1:18–cv–950–LO–IDD (E.D. Va.). An argument by another ISP that its flat-fee subscription model precluded a finding of direct financial benefit from its customers' infringing use failed to win dismissal of a vicarious liability claim by record labels and music publishers in Warner Records Inc. v. Charter Comm., 2020 WL 1872387 (D. Col.2020).

*Page 537.    Add to the end of the carryover paragraph:*

S. McJohn and I. McJohn, Fair Use and Machine Learning, 12 Northeastern U.L.Rev. 99 (2020), explores whether fair use determinations are amenable to machine learning; D. Burk, Algorithmic Fair Use, 86 U.Chi.L.Rev. 283 (2019), worries that fair use protection could be narrowed by attempts to code for fair use in automated online policing mechanisms.

*Page 537.    Add to the end of Note (6):*

According to a 2016 report by Google entitled *How Google Fights Piracy*, 98 percent of copyright management on YouTube takes place through YouTube's automated Content ID system, with only 2 percent handled through DMCA takedown notices. The report also states that copyright owners choose to leave their content on YouTube in exchange for financial payments more than 95 percent of the time. M. Sag, Internet Safe Harbors and the Transformation of Copyright Law, 93 Notre Dame L.Rev. 499 (2017), worries about the displacement of traditional copyright rules by private agreements between copyright owners and large Internet platforms like YouTube. YouTube also has licensing agreements with major record labels and music performance licensing organizations like ASCAP and BMI, and by some estimates it is the world's most popular online destination for music. One study found that 55 percent of people who stream music use YouTube. Sisario, A Big Change Comes to Billboard's Album Chart: YouTube Streams, N.Y. Times, Dec. 13, 2019. Facebook too has deals with record labels and songwriters that allow users to include songs in the background of posted videos. A 2018 report commissioned by the Confederation of Societies of Authors and Composers concludes that because of the safe-harbor rules, user-upload sites like YouTube have an unfair advantage when they negotiate rates with copyright owners, leaving permission-based services such as Spotify and Apple Music at a competitive disadvantage.

*Page 538.    Add to the end of Note (9):*

Record companies, musicians groups, and Hollywood studios are continuing their push to rewrite the § 512 safe harbor, especially the notice and takedown rules. Content owners would prefer a "notice and staydown" scheme that would shift the burden to the websites to remove infringing material whenever it reappears after the owner has filed a takedown notice. The Senate Intellectual Property Subcommittee is holding hearings on a possible update of § 512, including the use of site-blocking technology. The European Union has adopted a Directive on Copyright in the Digital Single Market, updating earlier Directives that preceded the emergence of streaming and social media sites like YouTube and Twitter. Two provisions of the new Directive are particularly controversial. One requires that commercial news aggregation and media websites pay licensing fees to content originators for uses other than links or very short excerpts. Another dramatically alters the balance between rights-holders and websites that host content uploaded by users. The new Directive effectively makes content hosts liable for infringing material posted by users. In the absence of a license, the sites can avoid liability only by establishing that they made "best efforts" to obtain licenses from the owners, "best efforts" to prevent the unauthorized works from being made available on the site, responded expeditiously to take-down requests, and used "best efforts" to prevent future uploads of the removed content. Critics worry that the "filtering" that may be necessary to comply with these requirements will effectively censor users. In a 2020 report entitled *Section 512 of Title 17*, the Copyright Office noted that § 512 was largely supported by service providers but criticized by content owners. The study concludes that the system is tilted in favor of service providers and does not effectuate the balance intended by Congress. It questions whether the knowledge requirements as currently understood are too favorable to providers and wonders whether *Viacom*'s interpretation of "the right and ability to control" and *Lenz*'s view of the requirements for takedown notices are correct.

*Page 557.    Add to the end of Note (3):*

Music revenues in the U.S. from CDs, downloads, and streaming rose to $9.8 billion in 2018—still far below its peak in 1999. Streaming revenue now accounts for three-quarters of the total. Streaming service Spotify claims to have paid $10 billion in total music royalties. Sisario, Spotify Files to Go Public on the New York Stock Exchange, N.Y. Times, March 2, 2018. In another sign of the times, Apple is in the process of dismantling its iconic iTunes store as a separate entity. Roose, A Farewell for iTunes, N.Y. Times, June 3, 2019.

*Page 557.    Add to the end of the first full paragraph:*

In Signature Management Team, LLC v. Doe, 876 F.3d 831 (6th Cir.2017), the court held that although there is a presumption in favor of unmasking anonymous defendants after a judgment has been entered for the plaintiff, "[t]he court must engage in a fact-specific analysis that balances the extent to which unmasking would infringe on the exercise of Doe's First Amendment rights, against the strength of the presumption in favor of unmasking and the plaintiff's interest in unmasking Doe."

*Page 559.    Add to the end of Note (4):*

The International Federation of the Phonographic Industry website reports that as of 2018, 38 percent of global listeners still obtained some of their music through copyright infringement, using methods such as "stream ripping," downloading from cyber lockers, and peer-to-peer file sharing.

*Page 560.    Add to the end of Note (6):*

In a sign of the growing dominance of music streaming, superstar Taylor Swift agreed to return her music catalog to Spotify and other streaming services, ending the feud that had prompted her withdrawal from Spotify in 2014. Sisario, Taylor Swift Returns Her Music Catalog to Streaming Services, N.Y. Times, June 9, 2017. According to standard industry estimates, it takes 150 streams of every song on a ten-track album to equal the revenue from a single CD sale. Sisario, Stream New Album? Swift has Music Industry and Fans Guessing, N.Y. Times, Nov. 2017, p. B2.

***Page 561.    Add to the end of the first full paragraph:***

The Ninth Circuit in Cobbler Nevada, LLC v. Gonzales, 901 F.3d 1142 (9th Cir.2018), upheld the dismissal of direct and contributory copyright infringement claims premised solely on an allegation that the defendant was the registered owner of the IP address used to download a movie using the BitTorrent network. M. Sag and J. Haskell, Defense Against the Dark Arts of Copyright Trolling, 103 Iowa L.Rev. 571 (2018), suggests possible responses to the thousands of "John Doe" file-sharing suits filed by copyright owners seeking to monetize infringement litigation.

***Page 562.    Add to the end of Note (8):***

Piracy tracking firm Muso estimates that the seventh season of *Game of Thrones* was illegally downloaded or streamed more than a *billion* times.

***Page 562.    Add to the end of Note (9):***

Sales of e-books have flattened, possibly because of prices often higher than paperback editions, or simply because of digital fatigue by readers who spend all day in front of screens. Revenue from downloaded audiobooks, however, has tripled over the past five years as readers listen to works on smartphones and tablets. As with e-books, Amazon, through its Audible platform, is the dominant provider. It has begun buying audio rights directly from authors before they agree to terms with traditional book publishers. Alter, Listen Carefully, Book Lovers: Top Authors are Skipping Print, N.Y. Times, June 2, 2018, p. A1.

***Page 563.    Add to the end of Note (11):***

Yet another technological innovation is causing concern among copyright owners. Websites and apps now allow users to turn streamed content from services like Spotify or YouTube into permanent files that can be stored on smartphones and computers. Record companies claim that millions of tracks are copied every month using these stream-ripping services. Savage, Stream-Ripping is 'fastest growing' music piracy, BBC News, bbc.com/news/entertainment-arts-405 19137 (July 17, 2017).

***Page 567.    Add to the end of the carryover paragraph:***

The U.S. Copyright Office has released the Register's Report on *Section 1201 of Title 17* (2017). The Copyright Office did not propose changes to the basic framework of the anti-circumvention and anti-trafficking provisions embodied in § 1201. It recommended *against* a statutory exemption permitting circumvention for any lawful or noninfringing purpose. In connection with its triennial rulemaking on additional exemptions, the Copyright Office recommended a statutory amendment that would permit third-parties to assist in the exempted circumventions at the direction of the intended beneficiaries. It also announced that in future rulemaking proceedings it would permit petitioners seeking renewal of an exemption to rely on evidence submitted in prior proceedings. In October, 2018, the Librarian of Congress announced the latest set of triennial exemptions to the circumvention prohibition. Relying on the record from the previous rulemaking proceeding, the Librarian adopted the Copyright Office's recommendation to renew all of the existing exemptions. Among the new exemptions added in 2018 are an expansion of the cellphone unlocking exemption to include new as well as used devices, and an exemption to permit voice assistants like Alexa or Echo to run software from other sources. The most noteworthy addition is an exemption for software contained in a "smartphone or home appliance or home system, such as a refrigerator, thermostat, HVAC, or electrical system" for purposes of "diagnosis, maintenance, or repair." A. Perzanowski, The Limits of Copyright Office Expertise, 33 Berk.Tech.L.J. 733 (2018), argues that the Copyright Office's substantive rulemaking and policy recommendations outstrip the narrow scope of its expertise.

**Page 567.**     *Add to the end of last paragraph:*

The removal or alteration of "copyright management information" is actionable only if the defendant knew, or had reasonable grounds to know, "that it will induce, enable, facilitate, or conceal an infringement." The Ninth Circuit in Stevens v. CoreLogic, Inc., 893 F.3d 648 (9th Cir.2018), said that to satisfy that requirement, a plaintiff "must offer more than a bare assertion that 'when [copyright management information] metadata is removed, copyright infringement plaintiffs . . . lose an important method of identifying a photo as infringing.' Instead, the plaintiff must provide evidence from which one can infer that future infringement is likely, albeit not certain, to occur as a result of the removal or alteration of [copyright management information]." Emphasizing that a suit alleging a violation of § 1202 is not a suit for copyright infringement, the court in Diamondback Indus., Inc. v. Repeat Precision, LLC, 2019 WL 5842756 (N.D. Tex.2019), refused to dismiss a claim for removal of copyright management information despite the plaintiff's admitted lack of a copyright registration.

**Page 589.**     *Add to the end of the carryover paragraph:*

K. Garcia, Copyright Arbitrage, 107 Cal.L.Rev. 199 (2019), concludes that the increasing complexity of the Copyright Act makes judicial supervision of copyright law problematic and proposes increased delegation to administrative agencies.

# CHAPTER 5

# THE CALCULUS OF RIGHTS

## 1. DURATION AND TERMINATION OF TRANSFERS

**Page 604.**     *Add to the end of footnote c:*

E. Subotnik, Artistic Control After Death, 92 Wash.L.Rev. 253 (2017), proposes limits on the ability of authors to utilize state trust law to control the use of their works after death; A. Gilden, IP, R.I.P., 95 Wash.U.L.Rev. 639 (2017) attempts to understand and mediate the interests of the various stakeholders in a deceased author's cultural legacy.

**Page 606.**     *Add to the end of Note (2):*

For the first time in twenty years, works are once again entering the public domain as their copyrights reach the end of their extended 95-year term. Under § 305, copyrights run to the end of the calendar year, so on January 1, 2019, copyright expired on works first published in 1923. (Robert Frost's famed poem, *Stopping by Woods on a Snowy Evening*, was among them.) George Gershwin's *Rhapsody in Blue* and works by Eugene O'Neill and Agatha Christie went into the public domain on January 1, 2020. The process will continue on January 1 of every succeeding year. Any new copyright extension effort would likely face well-organized and well-funded opposition. K. Garcia, A Reconsideration of Copyright's Term, 71 Ala. L.Rev. 351 (2019), concludes that the short commercial life of most works does not justify the current duration of copyright.

*Page 608.    Add to the start of the Summary:*

Works first published before 1925 are now in the public domain.

*Page 610.    Add to the end of Note (1):*

The alternative termination window in § 203(a)(3) applicable to grants that cover "the right of publication of the work" was interpreted in Baldwin v. EMI Feist Catalog, Inc., 805 F.3d 18 (2d Cir.2015), to mean "first" publication. However, the Copyright Office has announced that it will not follow *Baldwin* and will instead interpret "publication" to mean "the date the work is published under the grant." 82 Fed.Reg. 45626 (Sept. 29, 2017). T. Evans, Statutory Heirs Apparent?: Reclaiming Copyright in the Age of Author-Controlled, Author-Benefiting Transfers, 119 W.Va.L.Rev. 297 (2016), suggests limiting the ability of statutory heirs under § 203 to terminate lifetime transfers by authors to non-profit organizations or author-controlled entities like trusts.

*Page 611.    Add to the end of Note (3):*

The termination right in § 304(d) that allows an author to recover the copyright for the twenty extra years added in 1998 by the Copyright Term Extension Act must be exercised within five years after the copyright reaches its 75th year. The right only applies to works whose § 304(c) 56th year termination window had already expired in 1998. All works for which that is true are now past the termination window in § 304(d).

*Page 616.    Add to the end of Note (8):*

Motion picture studios, like record companies,, are now facing the consequences of the § 203 termination right. In Horror Inc. v. Miller, 335 F.Supp.3d 273 (D.Conn.2018), the court held that the screenwriter for the horror movie classic *Friday the 13th* was not a studio employee and thus could exercise his termination right. The case is on appeal to the Second Circuit, where the studio is arguing that a writer's membership in the Writers Guild of America, which collectively bargains with the motion picture studies, makes screenwriters employees, thus preventing terminations. The work for hire argument will not help the studios fight off terminations by authors of the underlying stories and novels on which the movies are based. Because of the right to continue to utilize derivative works made during the term of the grant in § 203(b)(1), the studios' right to exploit the existing movies is not in jeopardy, but remakes, sequels, video games, and other new derivative works would require new licenses.

## 2. TRANSFERS OF INTERESTS: ASSIGNMENTS AND LICENSES

*Page 618.    Add to the end of footnote k:*

The court in Artifex Software, Inc. v. Hancom, Inc., 2017 WL 1477373 (N.D.Cal.2017), held that a plaintiff could pursue a breach of contract count in addition to a copyright infringement claim against a defendant who allegedly violated the terms of an open source software license. A contract claim could allow a plaintiff to challenge conduct that may be outside the geographic jurisdiction of U.S. copyright law.

## 3. CONTRACT INTERPRETATION WITH RESPECT TO NEW USES

***Page 636.    Add to the end of Note (2):***

The freelance writers who filed the class action suit against the New York Times and other major publishers in 2001 finally got their settlement checks in 2018. Peiser, Writers Receive $9 Million in 17-Year Copyright Battle, N.Y. Times, Apr. 30, 2018, p. B3.

## 4. DERIVATIVE WORKS AND UNDERLYING WORKS

***Page 642.    Add to the end of Note (2):***

The court in TCA Television Corp. v. McCollum, 839 F.3d 168 (2d Cir.2016), faced the question of whether a copyright renewal of a derivative work continued copyright protection for an underlying work incorporated into the derivative work. In the 1930s famed comedians Bud Abbott and Lou Costello created the classic comedy routine *Who's on First*. In 1940 they licensed the use of the routine in a motion picture. The motion picture company registered the copyright in the film, which it later renewed. In 1984, the movie company assigned its rights in the routine to the plaintiffs, who in 2015 sued the producers of the Broadway play *Hand to God*, which included parts of the routine. The Second Circuit ordered that the case be dismissed because the plaintiffs had failed to plead ownership of a valid copyright in the routine. The routine was a "freestanding" work that had been incorporated into the film, and as a "separate and independent" work, only the original creators could renew the copyright (which they had failed to do); it was not covered by the motion picture company's renewal of copyright for the movie.

## 5. WORK MADE FOR HIRE AND JOINT WORK

***Page 660.    Add to the end of Note (3):***

A group of musicians are seeking to use a class action to establish that sound recordings are not works for hire and are thus subject to § 203's termination right after 35 years. The suit alleges that record companies have routinely ignored termination notices filed by performers. The record companies have taken the position that their contracts specify work for hire status and that recordings are contributions to an album, which qualifies them as a contribution to a collective work under the statutory definition of work made for hire. Johansen v. Sony Music Corp., S.D.N.Y., No. 1:19–cv–1094 (2019).

***Page 660.    Add to the end of the first paragraph of Note (4):***

J. Hughes, Actors as Authors in American Copyright Law, 51 Conn.L.Rev. 1 (2019), examines Garcia v. Google and the issue of actors as authors of audiovisual works; J. Tehranian, Sex, Drones & Videotape: Rethinking Copyright's Authorship-Fixation Conflation in the Age of Performance, 68 Hastings L.J. 1319 (2017), questions strict adherence to the authorship as fixation approach in an effort to recognize greater rights in performers.

***Page 662.    Add to the end of Note (6):***

J. Sibley, Existential Copyright and Professional Photography, 95 Notre Dame L.Rev. 263 (2019), concludes on the basis of interviews with professional photographers that copyright's primary impact on the profession is its effect on contractual negotiations with clients.

*Page 668.    Add to the end of Note (4):*

L. Mulraine, Collision Course: State Community Property Laws and Termination Rights Under the Federal Copyright Act—Who Should Have the Right of Way?, 100 Marq.L.Rev. 1193 (2017), examines the intersection of termination rights and community property laws.

## 6.    INDUSTRIES AFFECTED BY COMPULSORY COPYRIGHT LICENSING

*Page 671.    Add to the end of footnote aa:*

In ABKCO Music, Inc. v. Sagan, 2018 WL 1746564 (S.D.N.Y.2018), the owners of 200 musical compositions sued the *Wolfgang's Vault* website for making unauthorized copies of the music in connection with its digital download and streaming service. The defendant owned a collection of audio and audiovisual recordings of live concert performances by famous artists such as The Rolling Stones, The Grateful Dead, Willie Nelson, Ray Charles, and Aretha Franklin, which it had obtained from the operators of concert venues. (The *Wall Street Journal* once described the recordings and associated artifacts as "the most important collection of rock memorabilia and recordings ever assembled." Smith, Pipe Dream: Music Stash Recalls When Rock was Young, Wall St.J., Dec. 13, 2005, p. B1.) The defendant claimed that it held valid compulsory licenses for the reproduction of the musical works under § 115. Citing *ABKCO Music v. Stellar Records*, the court held that the § 115 compulsory license does not cover the distribution of music in audiovisual works. As to the other recordings, the court noted that § 115(a)(1) states that the compulsory license does not cover the use of a musical work in the making of a phonorecord that duplicates an existing sound recording unless that existing recording was lawfully fixed and its owner consents to its use. Section 1101(a) forbids recording a live musical performance without the consent of the performers; since the defendant failed to establish the performers' consent to recording, the recordings had not been lawfully fixed and thus their use fell outside the scope of the compulsory license. However, finding that "the public's interest in access to these recordings counsels against the imposition of a permanent injunction," the court left the plaintiffs to pursue monetary relief for unpaid licensing fees.

*Page 671.    Delete the final sentence in the carryover paragraph.*

*Page 672.    Add to the end of Note (2):*

*Billboard* magazine estimates that major recording artists can receive anywhere from a 16 to 22 percent royalty rate on sales of sound recordings. As sales-based contract models are restructured to reflect the dominance of music streaming, artists are pushing for much higher royalty rates. Rys, BMG CEO "Cynical" About Streaming's Growth, Citing Artist Contracts, Billboard, Apr. 10, 2017.

*Page 673.    Replace the text of Note (4) with the following:*

Do streamed performances result in a "digital phonorecord delivery" that requires a license under § 115? The defining characteristic of a digital phonorecord delivery is the creation of "a specifically identifiable reproduction by or for any transmission recipient." § 115(e)(10). That subsection goes on to state, "A digital phonorecord delivery does not result from a real-time, noninteractive subscription transmission of a sound recording where no reproduction of the sound recording or the musical work embodied therein is made from the inception of the transmission through to its receipt by the transmission recipient in order to make the sound recording audible." The rule for *interactive* streaming is quite different. "An interactive stream is a digital phonorecord delivery." § 115(e)(13). Thus, interactive services like Spotify require not only performance licenses for both the musical works and sound recordings, but also licenses to reproduce the musical works that they stream. This requirement recognizes that interactive streaming is a substitute for purchases of digital downloads or physical copies of musical works. Obtaining individual reproduction licenses for all of those musical works was cumbersome, even with the existing compulsory licensing provisions in § 115. In 2018, Congress amended § 115 to create a compulsory blanket license for use by interactive digital services. § 115(d). A newly-created Mechanical Licensing Collective will maintain a database of music owners and distribute the proceeds of the licenses. The new compulsory blanket licenses will cover all reproductions inherent in the operation of an interactive streaming service. In 2019, the Copyright Royalty Board finalized an increase in the compulsory licensing rate payable by interactive streaming companies under § 115. The rate will rise from the previous rate of 10.5 percent of streaming revenue to 15.1 percent by 2022. Major interactive providers like Spotify and Amazon have appealed the increase to the D.C. Court of Appeals.

**Page 680.    Add to the end of footnote oo:**

After the Ninth Circuit denied a petition for a rehearing en banc of its decision that Internet television streaming services like FilmOn X are not entitled to utilize the compulsory license in § 111, FilmOn X settled its litigation in the Ninth, Seventh, and D.C. Circuits.

# CHAPTER 6

# JURISDICTION AND REMEDIES

## 1.   JURISDICTION OF FEDERAL AND STATE COURTS

**Page 683.    Add to the end of Note (6):**

The Copyright Alternative in Small-Claims Enforcement (Case) Act, (H.R. 2426 and S. 1273) has been overwhelmingly passed by the House of Representatives. The bill would create a Copyright Claims Board within the Copyright Office with jurisdiction to adjudicate infringement claims of $30,000 or less in damages. Defendants would have 60 days to opt out of any proceeding after receiving notice of a claim—a provision intended to insure that the system does not violate the right to a jury trial. Copyright owners argue that the system will provide an efficient and affordable means to enforce their rights. Songwriters and photographers are strong supporters. Opponents worry that the administrative system will encourage questionable claims, circumvent procedural safeguards, and stifle fair use and free speech. B. Depoorter, If You Build It, They Will Come: The Promises and Pitfalls of a Copyright Small Claims Process, 33 Berk.Tech.L.J. 711 (2018), discusses how to design a small claims adjudication system that would not encourage dubious or opportunistic infringement claims.

**Page 684.    Add to the end of Note (7):**

Declaring that "[w]hether an infringing performance that originates abroad but that ultimately reaches viewers in the United States can be actionable under the Copyright Act is a question of first impression in the federal appellate courts," the court in Spanski Enter., Inc. v. Telewizja Polska, S.A., 883 F.3d 904 (D.C.Cir.2018), answered "yes." Although the works were formatted and uploaded in Poland, the infringing performances occurred on computer screens in the United States.

*Page 684.* *Replace the Note on State Liability for Infringement with the following:*

## State and Federal Liability for Copyright Infringement

### Allen v. Cooper

Supreme Court of the United States, 2020.
140 S. Ct. 994.

■ JUSTICE KAGAN delivered the opinion of the Court.

In two basically identical statutes passed in the early 1990s, Congress sought to strip the States of their sovereign immunity from patent and copyright infringement suits. Not long after, this Court held in Florida Prepaid Postsecondary Ed. Expense Bd. v. College Savings Bank, 527 U.S. 627 (1999), that the patent statute lacked a valid constitutional basis. Today, we take up the copyright statute. We find that our decision in *Florida Prepaid* compels the same conclusion.

I

In 1717, the pirate Edward Teach, better known as Blackbeard, captured a French slave ship in the West Indies and renamed her *Queen Anne's Revenge*. The vessel became his flagship. Carrying some 40 cannons and 300 men, the *Revenge* took many prizes as she sailed around the Caribbean and up the North American coast. But her reign over those seas was short-lived. In 1718, the ship ran aground on a sandbar a mile off Beaufort, North Carolina. Blackbeard and most of his crew escaped without harm. Not so the *Revenge*. She sank beneath the waters, where she lay undisturbed for nearly 300 years.

In 1996, a marine salvage company named Intersal, Inc., discovered the shipwreck. Under federal and state law, the wreck belongs to North Carolina. See 102 Stat. 433, 43 U.S.C. § 2105(c); N.C. Gen. Stat. Ann. § 121–22 (2019). But the State contracted with Intersal to take charge of the recovery activities. Intersal in turn retained petitioner Frederick Allen, a local videographer, to document the operation. For over a decade, Allen created videos and photos of divers' efforts to salvage the *Revenge*'s guns, anchors, and other remains. He registered copyrights in all those works.

This suit arises from North Carolina's publication of some of Allen's videos and photos. Allen first protested in 2013 that the State was infringing his copyrights by uploading his work to its website without permission. To address that allegation, North Carolina agreed to a settlement paying Allen $15,000 and laying out the parties' respective rights to the materials. But Allen and the State soon found themselves embroiled in another dispute. Allen complained that North Carolina had impermissibly posted five of his videos online and used one of his photos in a newsletter. When the State declined to admit wrongdoing, Allen filed this action in Federal District Court. It charges the State with copyright infringement (call it a modern form of piracy) and seeks money damages.

North Carolina moved to dismiss the suit on the ground of sovereign immunity. It invoked the general rule that federal courts cannot hear suits brought by individuals against nonconsenting States. See State Defendants' Memorandum in No. 15–627 (EDNC), Doc. 50, p. 7. But Allen responded that an exception to the rule applied because Congress had abrogated the States' sovereign immunity from suits like his. See Plaintiffs' Response, Doc. 57, p. 7. The Copyright Remedy Clarification Act of 1990 (CRCA or Act) provides that a State

401

"shall not be immune, under the Eleventh Amendment [or] any other doctrine of sovereign immunity, from suit in Federal court" for copyright infringement. 17 U.S.C. § 511(a). * * *

## II

In our constitutional scheme, a federal court generally may not hear a suit brought by any person against a nonconsenting State. That bar is nowhere explicitly set out in the Constitution. The text of the Eleventh Amendment (the single most relevant provision) applies only if the plaintiff is not a citizen of the defendant State.[2] But this Court has long understood that Amendment to "stand not so much for what it says" as for the broader "presupposition of our constitutional structure which it confirms." Blatchford v. Native Village of Noatak, 501 U.S. 775, 779 (1991). * * *

No one here disputes that Congress used clear enough language to abrogate the States' immunity from copyright infringement suits. As described above, the CRCA provides that States "shall not be immune" from those actions in federal court. § 511(a); * * *

The contested question is whether Congress had authority to take that step. Allen maintains that it did, under either of two constitutional provisions. He first points to the clause in Article I empowering Congress to provide copyright protection. If that fails, he invokes Section 5 of the Fourteenth Amendment, which authorizes Congress to "enforce" the commands of the Due Process Clause. Neither contention can succeed. The slate on which we write today is anything but clean. *Florida Prepaid*, along with other precedent, forecloses each of Allen's arguments. * * *

## A

* * *

The problem for Allen is that this Court has already rejected his theory. The Intellectual Property Clause, as just noted, covers copyrights and patents alike. So it was the first place the *Florida Prepaid* Court looked when deciding whether the Patent Remedy Act validly stripped the States of immunity from infringement suits. In doing so, we acknowledged the reason for Congress to put "States on the same footing as private parties" in patent litigation. 527 U.S. at 647. It was, just as Allen says here, to ensure "uniform, surefire protection" of intellectual property. Reply Brief 10. That was a "proper Article I concern," we allowed. 527 U.S. at 648. But still, we said, Congress could not use its Article I power over patents to remove the States' immunity. We based that conclusion on Seminole Tribe v. Florida [517 U.S. 44 (1996)], decided three years earlier. There, the Court had held that "Article I cannot be used to circumvent" the limits sovereign immunity "place[s] upon federal jurisdiction." 517 U.S. at 73. That proscription ended the matter. Because Congress could not "abrogate state sovereign immunity [under] Article I," *Florida Prepaid* explained, the Intellectual Property Clause could not support the Patent Remedy Act. 527 U.S. at 636. And to extend the point to this case: if not the Patent Remedy Act, not its copyright equivalent either, and for the same reason. Here too, the power to "secur[e]" an intellectual property owner's "exclusive Right" under Article I stops when it runs into sovereign immunity. § 8, cl. 8.

---

[2] The Eleventh Amendment reads: "The Judicial Power of the United States shall not be construed to extend to any suit in law or equity, commenced or prosecuted against one of the United States by Citizens of another State, or by Citizens or Subjects of any Foreign State."

B

Section 5 of the Fourteenth Amendment, unlike almost all of Article I, can authorize Congress to strip the States of immunity. The Fourteenth Amendment "fundamentally altered the balance of state and federal power" that the original Constitution and the Eleventh Amendment struck. *Seminole Tribe*, 517 U.S. at 594. Its first section imposes prohibitions on the States, including (as relevant here) that none may "deprive any person of life, liberty, or property, without due process of law." Section 5 then gives Congress the "power to enforce, by appropriate legislation," those limitations on the States' authority. That power, the Court has long held, may enable Congress to abrogate the States' immunity and thus subject them to suit in federal court. See Fitzpatrick v. Bitzer, 427 U.S. 445, 456 (1976).

For an abrogation statute to be "appropriate" under Section 5, it must be tailored to "remedy or prevent" conduct infringing the Fourteenth Amendment's substantive prohibitions. City of Boerne v. Flores, 521 U.S. 507, 519 (1997). * * * That means a congressional abrogation is valid under Section 5 only if it sufficiently connects to conduct courts have held Section 1 to proscribe. * * *

All this raises the question: When does the Fourteenth Amendment care about copyright infringement? Sometimes, no doubt. Copyrights are a form of property. See Fox Film Corp. v. Doyal, 286 U.S. 123, 128 (1932). And the Fourteenth Amendment bars the States from "depriv[ing]" a person of property "without due process of law." But even if sometimes, by no means always. Under our precedent, a merely negligent act does not "deprive" a person of property. See Daniels v. Williams, 474 U.S. 327, 328 (1986). So an infringement must be intentional, or at least reckless, to come within the reach of the Due Process Clause. See id., at 334, n. 3 (reserving whether reckless conduct suffices). And more: A State cannot violate that Clause unless it fails to offer an adequate remedy for an infringement, because such a remedy itself satisfies the demand of "due process." See Hudson v. Palmer, 468 U.S. 517, 533 (1984). That means within the broader world of state copyright infringement is a smaller one where the Due Process Clause comes into play.

Because the same is true of patent infringement, *Florida Prepaid* again serves as the critical precedent. That decision defined the scope of unconstitutional infringement in line with the caselaw cited above—as intentional conduct for which there is no adequate state remedy. See 527 U.S. at 642–643, 645. It then searched for evidence of that sort of infringement in the legislative record of the Patent Remedy Act. And it determined that the statute's abrogation of immunity—again, the equivalent of the CRCA's—was out of all proportion to what it found. That analysis is the starting point of our inquiry here. And indeed, it must be the ending point too unless the evidence of unconstitutional infringement is materially different for copyrights than patents. * * *

Could, then, this case come out differently? Given the identical scope of the CRCA and Patent Remedy Act, that could happen only if the former law responded to materially stronger evidence of infringement, especially of the unconstitutional kind. Allen points to a significant disparity in how Congress created a record for the two statutes. See Brief for Petitioners 7–10, 47–50. Before enacting the CRCA, Congress asked the then-Register of Copyrights, Ralph Oman, to submit a report about the effects of the Eleventh Amendment on copyright enforcement. * * *

* * * Despite undertaking an exhaustive search, Oman came up with only a dozen possible examples of state infringement. He listed seven court cases brought against States

403

(with another two dismissed on the merits) and five anecdotes taken from public comments (but not further corroborated). See Oman Report, at 7–9, 90–97. In testifying about the report, Oman acknowledged that state infringement is "not widespread" and "the States are not going to get involved in wholesale violation of the copyright laws." Hearings on H. R. 1131 before the Subcommittee on Courts, Intellectual Property, and the Administration of Justice, 101st Cong., 1st Sess., 53 (1989) (House Hearings). * * *

* * * Likewise, the legislative record contains no information about the availability of state-law remedies for copyright infringement (such as contract or unjust enrichment suits)—even though they might themselves satisfy due process. Those deficiencies in the record match the ones *Florida Prepaid* emphasized. See 527 U.S. at 643–645. Here no less than there, they signal an absence of constitutional harm.

Under *Florida Prepaid*, the CRCA thus must fail our "congruence and proportionality" test. *Boerne*, 521 U.S. at 520. As just shown, the evidence of Fourteenth Amendment injury supporting the CRCA and the Patent Remedy Act is equivalent—for both, that is, exceedingly slight. And the scope of the two statutes is identical—extending to every infringement case against a State. It follows that the balance the laws strike between constitutional wrong and statutory remedy is correspondingly askew. In this case, as in *Florida Prepaid,* the law's "indiscriminate scope" is "out of proportion" to any due process problem. 527 U.S. at 646–647; see supra, at 1005–1006. In this case, as in that one, the statute aims to "provide a uniform remedy" for statutory infringement, rather than to redress or prevent unconstitutional conduct. 527 U.S. at 647; see supra, at 1005–1006. And so in this case, as in that one, the law is invalid under Section 5.

That conclusion, however, need not prevent Congress from passing a valid copyright abrogation law in the future. In doing so, Congress would presumably approach the issue differently than when it passed the CRCA. At that time, the Court had not yet decided *Seminole Tribe*, so Congress probably thought that Article I could support its all-out abrogation of immunity. See supra, at 1002. And to the extent it relied on Section 5, Congress acted before this Court created the "congruence and proportionality" test. See supra, at 1004. For that reason, Congress likely did not appreciate the importance of linking the scope of its abrogation to the redress or prevention of unconstitutional injuries—and of creating a legislative record to back up that connection. But going forward, Congress will know those rules. And under them, if it detects violations of due process, then it may enact a proportionate response. That kind of tailored statute can effectively stop States from behaving as copyright pirates. Even while respecting constitutional limits, it can bring digital Blackbeards to justice.

### III

*Florida Prepaid* all but prewrote our decision today. That precedent made clear that Article I's Intellectual Property Clause could not provide the basis for an abrogation of sovereign immunity. And it held that Section 5 of the Fourteenth Amendment could not support an abrogation on a legislative record like the one here. For both those reasons, we affirm the judgment below.

It is so ordered.

■ JUSTICE THOMAS, concurring in part and concurring in the judgment.
* * *

Finally, I believe the question whether copyrights are property within the original meaning of the Fourteenth Amendment's Due Process Clause remains open. The Court relies on Fox Film Corp. v. Doyal, 286 U.S. 123 (1932), to conclude that "[c]opyrights are a form of property." Ante, at 1004. But *Fox Film Corp.* addressed "property" in the context of state tax laws, not the Due Process Clause. 286 U.S. at 128. And although we stated in *Florida Prepaid* that patents are "property" for due process purposes, we did not analyze the Fourteenth Amendment's text, and neither of the cases we cited involved due process. * * * Because the parties agree that petitioners' copyrights are property, and because the Fourteenth Amendment does not authorize this statute's abrogation of state sovereign immunity either way, we need not resolve this open question today. I would, however, be willing to consider the matter in an appropriate case. * * *

■ JUSTICE BREYER, with whom JUSTICE GINSBURG joins, concurring in the judgment.

[Justice Breyer reiterated his position that the Court had erred in *Seminole Tribe* when it held that Congress could not invoke its power under Article I to abrogate state immunity.] But recognizing that my longstanding view has not carried the day, and that the Court's decision in *Florida Prepaid* controls this case, I concur in the judgment.

## NOTES AND QUESTIONS

**(1)**  How likely is it that Congress will take up Justice Kagan's invitation to try again? Note that although it has been more than two decades since the Court in *Florida Prepaid* invalidated the attempt to abrogate state immunity for patent infringement, there has been no congressional response. However, citing *Allen,* two members of the Senate Judiciary Committee have asked the Copyright Office and the U.S. Patent and Trademark Office to conduct a study on the extent to which intellectual property owners are being injured by infringements committed by state governments.

**(2)**  Despite the immunity of states from monetary liability for copyright infringement, state officials with a sufficient connection to the infringement presumably still remain subject to suit for injunctive relief to stop a continuing infringement under the rule in Ex Parte Young, 209 U.S. 123 (1908). See, e.g., National Ass'n of Bds. of Pharmacy v. Bd. of Regents of Univ. Sys. of Ga., 633 F.3d 1297 (11th Cir.2011).

**(3)**  Relief under state law for copyright infringements by state entities is problematic. In Univ. of Houston Sys. v. Jim Olive Photography, 580 S.W.3d 360 (Tex.Ct.App.2019), the court held that a state university's infringement of the plaintiff's photograph did not constitute a "taking" under the state or federal constitution because the state's use merely cost the plaintiff a licensing fee; it did not deprive him of his copyright.

**(4)**  Note that the *federal* government has waived its own sovereign immunity for patent and copyright infringement in 28 U.S.C. § 1498. The remedy for copyright infringement, however, is limited to an action by the copyright owner "for the recovery of his reasonable and entire compensation as damages for such infringement, including the minimum statutory damages as set forth in section 504(c) of title 17, United States Code." Thus, a plaintiff cannot enjoin an infringement by the federal government.

### Page 687.    *Add to the end of footnote c:*

When the U.S. Postal Service accidentally used a photograph of plaintiff's replica of the Statue of Liberty on a postage stamp (and sold almost 5 billion of the stamps), the Court of Federal Claims used the fair market value of a license as the measure of damages against the United States under 28 U.S.C. § 1498(b). Although the Postal Service said that it never pays more than $5,000 for a stamp design, the court held that the government could not use that arbitrary figure to limit liability. It ultimately awarded $3.5 million. Davidson v. United States, 138 Fed.Cl. 159 (2018).

## SUPPLEMENTARY MATERIALS

## 2. STANDING TO SUE

**Page 687.    Add to the end of footnote d:**

The Second Circuit agreed with Righthaven v. Hoehn, holding, "The plain language of the Act does not authorize infringement actions by mere assignees of the bare right to sue—entities that do not hold and indeed never held any section 106 exclusive right in the allegedly infringed-upon work." John Wiley & Sons, Inc. v. DRK Photo, 882 F.3d 394 (2d Cir.2018).

**Page 690.    Add to the end of Note (5):**

Disney sells movies in Combo Packs containing Blu-ray and DVD discs along with a code for a digital download. Redbox bought the packages and separately sold the download codes. Disney claimed that Redbox was guilty of contributory infringement because users had been authorized to use the download code only if they also owned the physical discs. Redbox argued that Disney was engaged in copyright misuse. Disney countered that there was no misuse because it was not seeking to protect non-copyrighted products. The court held that there was nevertheless copyright misuse because Disney was using the copyright in the digital content to restrict transfer of the physical discs, which undermined the owners' rights under the first sale doctrine in § 109(a). Disney Enter., Inc. v. Redbox Automated Retail, LLC, 2018 WL 1942139 (C.D.Cal.2018). Disney quickly revised its licensing terms, limiting use of the digital download codes to recipients or family members who had obtained the codes as part of a Combo Pack. The court then granted Disney a preliminary injunction. 336 F.Supp.3d 1146 (C.D.Cal.2018). Redbox later agreed to a permanent injunction that prohibits it from selling Disney download codes.

## 3. THE BATTERY OF REMEDIES

**Page 696.    Add to the end of Note (1):**

The Fifth Circuit in Southern Credentialing Support Serv., LLC v. Hammond Surgical Hosp., LLC, 946 F.3d 780 (5th Cir.2020), held that the bar on statutory damages created by § 412 applies even if a defendant who has commenced an infringement prior to registration violates a different exclusive right after the registration. The court declined to decide whether the bar would apply if there was a substantial time gap between the pre-registration and post registration infringements.

**Page 697.    Add to the end of Note (2):**

The court in FameFlynet, Inc. v. Shoshanna Collection, LLC, 282 F.Supp.3d 618 (S.D.N.Y.2017), recited the following factors as relevant to the amount of statutory damages: "(1) the infringer's state of mind; (2) the expenses saved, and profits earned, by the infringer; (3) the revenue lost by the copyright holder; (4) the deterrent effect on the infringer and third parties; (5) the infringer's cooperating in providing evidence concerning the value of the infringing material; and (6) the conduct and attitude of the parties." According to the Ninth Circuit, "willfulness" for purposes of statutory damages means that the defendant was "actually aware of the infringing activity" or the actions "were the result of reckless disregard for, or willful blindness to" the plaintiff's rights. VHT, Inc. v. Zillow Group, Inc., 918 F.3d 723 (9th Cir.2019). T. Evans, User "Safer Harbor" from Statutory Damages: Remixing the DOC's IP Task Force White Paper, 54 San Diego L.Rev. 79 (2017), advocates more lenient statutory damage rules to protect accidental infringers.

***Page 697.     Add to the end of footnote g:***

Sullivan v. Flora, Inc., 936 F.3d 562 (7th Cir.2019), surveys the caselaw on what constitutes "one work" for purposes of statutory damages. Disagreeing with Bryant v. Media Rights Prods., the Seventh Circuit held that the issue was whether the related works have value only as a composite whole, or whether each has standalone value. M. Kaminski and G. Rub, Copyright's Framing Problem, 64 UCLA L.Rev. 1102 (2017), examines the policy issues affecting how courts define the "work" for purposes of various copyright doctrines when it consists of a combination of smaller constituents.

***Page 697.     Add to the end of Note (3):***

B. Depoorter, Copyright Enforcement in the Digital Age: When the Remedy is the Wrong, 66 U.C.L.A. L.Rev. 400 (2019), bemoans the bargaining leverage the possibility of "willful" statutory damages gives to copyright owners.

***Page 700.     Add to the end of Note (2);***

The Third Circuit in TD Bank N.A. v. Hill, 928 F.3d 259 (3d Cir.2019), undertook a thorough analysis of the factors that govern the award of permanent injunctions in copyright cases. The court vacated a permanent injunction, holding that the prospect of continuing infringement is not itself sufficient to establish irreparable harm. Here, the plaintiff did not sell or use the infringed work and had no intention of doing so. The public interest in access to expressive works also weighed against an injunction, especially where the copyright holder pursued an injunction to suppress unwelcome speech.

***Page 702.     Add to the end of the first paragraph:***

The "full costs" that a court may award under § 505 are limited to the six categories of costs specified in the general federal cost statute, 28 U.S.C. §§ 1821, 1920. Rimini Street, Inc. v. Oracle USA, Inc., 139 S.Ct. 873 (2019).

# PART 2

# UNFAIR COMPETITION AND OTHER DOCTRINES BEYOND COPYRIGHT

## CHAPTER 7

# THE ROOTS OF UNFAIR COMPETITION

### 3. PREEMPTION

*Page 764.    Add to the end of the first full paragraph:*

Claims for conversion, embezzlement, larceny, and violation of the Virginia Computer Crimes Act raised against a defendant who had copied computer data were all held to be preempted under § 301 in OpenRisk, LLC v. MicroStrategy Services Corp., 876 F.3d 518 (4th Cir.2017). According to the court, none of the elements required by the various state causes of action made them qualitatively different from copyright infringement.

*Page 766.    Add to the end of Note (5):*

The Fifth and Tenth Circuits recently reached different conclusions on the preemption of state misappropriation claims. In Motion Medical Techs., L.L.C. v. Thermotek, Inc., 875 F.3d 765 (5th Cir.2017), the court held that a claim for misappropriation under Texas law against a defendant who copied emails, website data, product codes, administrative filings, and billing reports was preempted. The material was within the subject matter of copyright regardless of whether it was actually protectable under the Copyright Act, and the Texas cause of action for misappropriation was not qualitatively different from federal copyright infringement. However, in SCO Group, Inc. v. International Business Machines Corp., 879 F.3d 1062 (10th Cir.2018), the Tenth Circuit, applying New York law, held that a misappropriation claim against a copier of computer code survived. The court concluded that the New York misappropriation cause of action included an element of "bad faith" such as fraud, deception, or abuse of a fiduciary or confidential relationship and was thus not equivalent to a copyright infringement claim.

*Page 777.    Add to the end of Note (1):*

The continuing importance of a constitutional preemption analysis that reaches beyond the limits of § 301 is emphasized in G. Rub, A Less-Formalistic Copyright Preemption, 24 J.Intell.Prop.L. 327 (2017).

*Page 779.    Add to the end of Note (3):*

G. Rub, Copyright Survives: Rethinking the Copyright-Contract Conflict, 103 Va.L.Rev. 1141 (2017), finds that contracts have not significantly affected the general contours of copyright protection.

# CHAPTER 8

# APPLICATIONS OF UNFAIR COMPETITION

## 2. SOUND RECORDINGS

*Pages 803–04.    Replace the text on pp. 803–04 with the following:*

State record piracy statutes like the one applied in Goldstein v. California penalized the duplication of sound recordings. *Goldstein* dealt with recordings that were made before sound recordings were given federal protection in 1972; the Supreme Court said Congress had left those recordings subject to state control. For post-1972 recordings, the preemptive provisions in § 301 apply. As part of the grant of federal protection to pre-1972 in 2018, § 301(c) was amended to make state protection for pre-1972 recordings subject to the general preemption rules in § 301.

## 3. TITLES

*Page 825.    Add to the end of Note (3):*

Record label Empire Distribution brought a trademark infringement claim against Fox in connection with a television show entitled *Empire* about a fictional music label called Empire Enterprises. The Ninth Circuit in Twentieth Century Fox Television v. Empire Distribution, Inc., 875 F.3d 1192 (9th Cir.2017), invoked the special protection for titles of expressive works adopted in Rogers v. Grimaldi, which holds that a title does not violate the Lanham Act "unless the title has no artistic relevance to the underlying work whatsoever, or if it has some artistic relevance, unless the title explicitly misleads as to the source or content of the work." The court said that the title was used for artistically relevant reasons since the show was set in New York, the Empire State, and was about a music and entertainment empire. The title was not explicitly misleading since the show contained no overt or explicit references to Empire Distribution.

## 4. CHARACTERS

*Page 848.    Add to the end of footnote m:*

Unsurprisingly, Disney remains the world's number one character licensor, with themed products generating over $56 billion in retail sales during 2016. Barnes, Aaaand, Action (Figure), N.Y. Times, May 23, 2017, p. B1. M. Sunder, Intellectual Property in Experience, 117 Mich.L.Rev. 197 (2018), explores the limits of an owner's merchandising rights in the context of fan activities.

# CHAPTER 9

# MORAL RIGHTS AND PUBLICITY RIGHTS

## 1. PROTECTION OF "MORAL RIGHTS"

***Page 858.*** ***Add to the end of footnote b:***

The Ninth Circuit in Fahmy v. Jay-Z, 891 F.3d 823 (9th Cir.2018), reaffirmed the principle that the rule of "national treatment" under Berne does not require the United States to recognize the moral rights that foreign nationals may enjoy under their domestic law.

***Page 867.*** ***Add to the end of footnote c:***

A Copyright Office report entitled *Authors, Attribution, and Integrity: Examining Moral Rights in the United States* (2019), suggests that Congress may wish to amend § 43(a) to specifically include false representations regarding authorship of communicative works.

***Page 870.*** ***Add to the end of Note (7):***

The Copyright Office in *Authors, Attribution, and Integrity: Examining Moral Rights in the United States* (2019), concludes that a claim for falsely attributing a work to an author is still actionable under § 43(a). P. Goold, The Lost Tort of Moral Rights Invasion, 51 Akron L.Rev. 1093 (2017), examines the rise of state law moral rights protection in the mid-20th century, and its subsequent stagnation.

***Page 880.*** ***Add to the end of footnote g:***

After author Harper Lee granted a license for a stage production of *To Kill a Mockingbird*, lawsuits were required to settle a complaint by her estate that the play's portrayal of Atticus Finch, the lawyer who defends a black defendant accused of raping a white girl, strayed too far from his depiction in the novel. Paulson and Alter, Broadway "Mockingbird" Survives Court Challenge Over Script, N.Y. Times, May 11, 2018, p. C4.

***Page 882.*** ***Add to the end of the first full paragraph:***

The Copyright Office's *Authors, Attribution, and Integrity: Examining Moral Rights in the United States* (2019), recommends an amendment to the definition of "works of visual art" that would keep advertising or promotional material directed at a cause or viewpoint within the scope VARA. The report also recommends an expansion of the test for "recognized stature" to include the opinion of the relevant community for the particular art medium.

***Page 883.*** ***Add to the end of the carryover paragraph:***

In 1989, following a series of stock market reverses, a *Charging Bull* sculpture symbolizing optimism was placed in a city park near the New York Stock Exchange. In 2017, in commemoration of International Women's Day, a statue of *Fearless Girl*, with hands on her hips, was placed facing *Charging Bull*. The sculptor who created the bull sent cease and desist letters to the city and the financial company that sponsored *Fearless Girl*, claiming that the positioning of the new sculpture violated his right to preserve the integrity of his work under the Visual Artists Rights Act by changing its optimistic message into "a negative force and threat." Does the creator of *Charging Bull* have a plausible claim under VARA? He also claimed that the placement of *Fearless Girl* resulted in the creation of an unauthorized derivative work in violation of his copyright in *Charging Bull*. 93 Pat., Tm. & Copyr.J. (BNA) 3649 (2017). A. Bridy, Fearless Girl Meets Charging Bull: Copyright and the Regulation of

Intertextuality, 9 U.Cal. Irvine L.Rev. 293 (2019), compares U.S. and European approaches to the issues raised by the confrontation between *Fearless Girl* and *Charging Bull*.

**Page 884.     *Add to the end of the carryover paragraph:***

Following a trial on the merits, the defendant owner of the 5Pointz building was held liable for violating the graffiti artists' rights under the Visual Artists Rights Act. Cohen v. G&M Realty L.P., 320 F.Supp.3d 421 (E.D.N.Y.2018). There was testimony that many of the works could have been removed from the walls of the building before its destruction, but the owner failed to provide the artists with notice of the intention to destroy the works that would have provided a defense to their claims under § 113(d)(2). Thus, the artists could assert their right under § 106A(a)(3)(B) to prevent destruction of works of "recognized stature." The court found that 45 of the works had achieved that status, and the defendant was liable for their destruction. The court determined that the defendant had acted willfully and awarded maximum statutory damages of $150,000 per work, for a total of $6,750,000. The Second Circuit affirmed, noting "[w]e see in VARA nothing that excludes temporary artwork from attaining recognized stature," citing the emergence of "street art" as a major category of contemporary art. The court held that the property owner's intentional decision to destroy the works without waiting for three months as required under § 113(d)(2) justified the trial court's conclusion that the violation had been willful, thus permitting the award of maximum statutory damages. Castillo v. G&M Realty L.P., 950 F.3d 155 (2d Cir.2020). The 5Pointz saga and its implications for the protection of moral rights are examined in R. Chused, Moral Rights: The Anti-Rebellion Graffiti Heritage of 5Pointz, 41 Colum.J.L. & Arts 583 (2018).

**Page 889.     *Add to the end of Note (3):***

B. Frye, Equitable Resale Royalties, 24 J.Intell.Prop.L. 237 (2017), concludes that an efficient resale royalty system should distribute the proceeds more broadly to less successful artists.

**Page 890.     *Add to the end of Note (4):***

The Ninth Circuit in Close v. Sotheby's, Inc., 894 F.3d 1061 (9th Cir.2018), affirmed the lower court's conclusion that the California Resale Royalty Act is preempted under § 301 because it creates rights that are equivalent to the federal distribution right as limited by the first sale doctrine. "[A]t root, both concern the distribution of copies of artwork and define artists' right (or lack thereof) to payment on downstream sales of those copies." D. Shipley, Droit de Suite, Copyright's First Sale Doctrine and Preemption of State Law, 39 Hastings Comm. & Ent.L.J. 1 (2017), agrees with the conclusion that the California Resale Royalty Act is preempted because it frustrates the purposes of copyright's first sale doctrine.

## 2.  PUBLICITY AND PRIVACY

**Page 895.     *Add to the end of Note (4)(d):***

Lohan v. Take-Two Interactive Software, Inc., 97 N.E.3d 389 (N.Y.2018), involved a suit by actress Lindsay Lohan against the maker of the *Grand Theft Auto* video game. She claimed that a character in the game was a look-a-like and violated her rights under the New York privacy statute. The New York Court of Appeals agreed that an avatar in a video game could constitute a "portrait" under the New York law, but affirmed a dismissal of the complaint because here the character was not reasonably identifiable as the plaintiff.

# SUPPLEMENTARY MATERIALS

***Page 905.***     ***Add to the end of footnote q:***

M. LaFrance, Choice of Law and the Right of Publicity: Rethinking the Domicile Rule, 37 Cardozo Arts & Ent.L.Rev. 1 (2019), is critical of the widespread reliance on the law of the decedent's domicile in determining post-mortem publicity rights.

***Page 906.***     ***Add to the end of Note (4):***

M Bartholomew, The Political Economy of Celebrity Rights, 38 Whittier L.Rev. 1 (2018), offers explanations for the gradual expansion of the right of publicity.

***Page 907.***     ***Add to the end of footnote r:***

Famed opera star Maria Callas, deceased since 1977, is yet another performer who has been resurrected in the form of a hologram for a "live" performance. She shared the program with Roy Orbison, dead since 1988. Tommassini, What Maria Callas's Hologram Tells Us, N.Y. Times, Jan. 16, 2018, p. C1. The business of creating holographic performances is critically examined in Binelli, Dead Runners, N.Y. Times, Jan. 12, 2020, p. MM20. A project recently announced by a Hollywood studio takes things to another level. After negotiating for permission from his heirs, Magic City Films is producing a Vietnam War-era film called *Finding Jack* with iconic actor James Dean in a leading role. Dean died in 1955 at the age of 24. Holson, A C.G.I. James Dean? Some in Hollywood See "An Awful Precedent", N.Y. Times, Nov. 7, 2019).

***Page 925.***     ***Add to the end of the second paragraph:***

The Seventh Circuit in Daniels v. FanDuel, Inc., 884 F.3d 672 (7th Cir.2018), was more cautious than the Eighth Circuit in C.B.C. Distrib. v. Major League Baseball, which held that a game website's first amendment right to use information on player performances superseded the players' publicity claims. The Seventh Circuit instead certified the question of whether the use of players' names and statistics violates Indiana's right of publicity statute to the Indiana Supreme Court, withholding judgment on the constitutional issue. In Daniels v. FanDuel, Inc., 109 N.E.3d 390 (Ind.2018), the Supreme Court of Indiana responded by declaring that the use of the players' names, pictures, and statistics in a fantasy football contest fell within the Indiana right of publicity statute's exception for "material that has newsworthy value" and hence did not violate the players' rights.

***Page 926.***     ***Add to the end of Note (1):***

The suit by former NFL players for the unauthorized use of their identities by Electronic Arts in its "historic team" version of the *Madden NFL* video game was settled before trial following the remand by the Ninth Circuit. California became the first state to pass legislation mandating that college athletes be permitted to exploit their publicity rights—a position that conflicts with NCAA eligibility rules. Other states are enacting similar statues, and Congress has also threatened to act. The NCAA is in the process of revising its regulations. Witz, N.C.A.A. Outlines Plan to Let Athletes Make Endorsement Deals, N.Y. Times, Apr. 29, 2020.

***Page 929.***     ***Add to the end of Note (4):***

A California appellate court ordered the dismissal of actress Olivia de Havilland's statutory and common law right of publicity claims lodged against the producers of a television miniseries about her relationship with movie stars Bette Davis and Joan Crawford. The use of her identity was protected by the first amendment. De Havilland v. FX Network, LLC, 230 Cal.Rptr.3d 625 (Cal.App.2018).

## CHAPTER 10

# COMPENSATION FOR "IDEAS"

*Page 941.    Add to the end of Note (3):*

Defendant ABC won a summary judgment on an implied-in-fact contract claim brought by a plaintiff who had submitted a script in 1977 that he alleged had been used in the creation of the ABC television series *LOST*. ABC argued independent creation. "Evidence of access and substantial similarities may indeed raise an inference of use," but here that inference was dispelled by "clear, positive, and uncontradicted" evidence that ABC independently created *LOST*. Spinner v. American Broadcasting Cos., Inc., 155 Cal.Rptr.3d 32 (Cal.App.2013).

*Page 946.    Add at the beginning of Note (1):*

The *Desny* implied-in-fact contract claim upheld in Montz v. Pilgrim Films & Television was summarized by the Ninth Circuit in Jordan-Benal v. Universal City Studios, Inc., 859 F.3d 1184 (9th Cir.2017): "To state a claim for breach of an implied-in-fact contract based on the submission of a screenplay, a plaintiff must allege that: (1) he submitted the screenplay for sale to the defendants; (2) he conditioned the use of the screenplay on payment; (3) the defendants knew or should have known of the condition; (4) the defendants voluntarily accepted the screenplay; (5) the defendants actually used the screenplay; and (6) the screenplay had value."

# PART 3

# INTERNATIONAL COPYRIGHT

## CHAPTER 11

# U.S. INTERNATIONAL COPYRIGHT RELATIONS

## 1.  THE POSITION BEFORE 1891

*Page 957.    Add to the end of the first paragraph:*

R. Spoo, Courtesy Paratexts: Informal Publishing Norms and the Copyright Vacuum in Nineteenth-Century America, 69 Stan.L.Rev. 637 (2017), describes how American publishers created a makeshift copyright regime to regulate competition over unprotected foreign works, including payments to foreign authors and recognition of informal exclusive U.S. publishing rights.

SUPPLEMENTARY MATERIALS

## 2. FROM THE CHACE ACT TO THE 1976 COPYRIGHT ACT

*Page 959.    Add to the end of the first full paragraph:*

J. Rothchild, How the United States Stopped Being a Pirate Nation and Learned to Love International Copyright, 39 Pace L.Rev. 361 (2018), recounts the nineteenth century efforts to extend U.S. copyright protection to foreign authors.

## 4. THE BERNE CONVENTION, TRIPS, AND BEYOND

*Page 972.    Add to the end of Note (5):*

The United States insisted on strong intellectual property protection in the newly-negotiated United States-Mexico-Canada Trade Agreement (USMCA), which replaced the North American Free Trade Agreement (NAFTA). The agreement calls for a copyright duration of life-plus-seventy years, which will force Canada to extend its duration by twenty years. It also includes requirements for safe-harbor protections for internet service providers along the lines of § 512, which will require changes in Mexican law. United States copyright law does not require any revisions to comply with the agreement.

*Page 972.    Replace Note (6) with the following:*

According to the International Intellectual Property Alliance's *Copyright Industries in the U.S. Economy: The 2018 Report*, the core copyright industries (primarily music, movies, television, print, software, and video games) contributed $1.3 *trillion* to the U.S. economy in 2017, employing nearly 5.7 million workers. Foreign sales exceeded $191 billion.

# TABLE OF CASES

The principal cases are in bold type.

# TABLE OF CASES